THE
unofficial GUIDE
ᵀᴼLas Vegas

2019

COME CHECK US OUT!

Supplement your valuable guidebook with tips, news, and deals by visiting our websites:

theunofficialguides.com
touringplans.com

Also, while there, sign up for The Unofficial Guides newsletter for even more travel tips and special offers.

Join the conversation on social media:

 @theUGSeries

 theUnofficialGuides

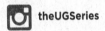 theUGSeries

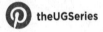 theUGSeries

#theUGseries

Other Unofficial Guides

The Disneyland Story: The Unofficial Guide to the Evolution of Walt Disney's Dream

Universal vs. Disney: The Unofficial Guide to American Theme Parks' Greatest Rivalry

The Unofficial Guide to Disney Cruise Line

The Unofficial Guide to Disneyland

The Unofficial Guide to Mall of America

The Unofficial Guide to Universal Orlando

The Unofficial Guide to Walt Disney World

The Unofficial Guide to Walt Disney World with Kids

The Unofficial Guide to Washington, D.C.

MAPS *and* ILLUSTRATIONS

ACKNOWLEDGMENTS

THE PEOPLE OF LAS VEGAS love their city and spare no effort to assist a writer trying to dig beneath the facade of flashing neon. It is important to them to communicate that Las Vegas is a city with depth, diversity, and substance. "Don't just write about our casinos," they demand. "Take the time to get to know us."

We made every effort to do just that, enabled each step of the way by some of the most sincere and energetic folks a writer could hope to encounter. Thanks to gambling pro **Anthony Curtis** for his tips on the best places to play. **Xania V. Woodman** and **Mark Adams** handled the nightlife scene, and **Camille Cannon** learned to pole-dance on our behalf. Restaurant critic **Al Mancini** ate his way through dozens of new restaurants to update our dining chapter.

Jim McDonald of the Las Vegas Police Department shared his experiences and offered valuable suggestions for staying out of trouble. **Larry Olmsted** evaluated Las Vegas golf courses, **Chris McBeath** created our spa chapter, and forest ranger **Debbie Savage** assisted us in developing material on wilderness recreation. Thanks also to **Seth Kubersky,** who reviewed shows and attractions.

Much gratitude to Steve Jones, Annie Long, Molly Merkle, Holly Cross, Darcie Vance, Emily Beaumont, and Meghan Brawley, the pros who turned all this effort into a book.

INTRODUCTION

◧ ON *a* PLANE *to* LAS VEGAS

I NEVER WANTED TO GO TO LAS VEGAS. I'm not much of a gambler and have always thought of Las Vegas as a city dedicated to separating folks from their money. As it happens, however, I have some involvement with industries that hold conventions and trade shows there. For some years I was able to persuade others to go in my place. Eventually, of course, it came my turn to go, and I found myself aboard a Delta jumbo jet on my first trip to Las Vegas.

Listening to the banter of those around me, I became aware that my fellow passengers were divided into two distinct camps. Some obviously thought themselves on a nonstop flight to paradise and could not have been happier. Too excited to remain seated, they cavorted up and down the aisles, clapping one another on the back. The other passengers, by contrast, groused and grumbled, lamenting their bad luck and cursing those who had made a trip to such a place necessary.

To my surprise, I thoroughly enjoyed Las Vegas. I had a great time without gambling and have been back many times with never a bad experience. The people are friendly, the food is good, the hotels are among the nicest in the country, it's an easy town to find your way around, and there is plenty to do (24 hours a day, if you are so inclined).

It's hard to say why so many folks have such strong feelings about Las Vegas (even those who have never been there). Among our research team, we had people willing to put their kids in boarding school for a chance to go, while others begged off to have root-canal surgery or prune their begonias. A third group wanted to go very badly but maintained the pretense of total indifference, reminding me of people who own five TVs yet profess never to watch television. They clearly had not mustered the courage to come out of the closet.

What I discovered during my first and subsequent visits is that the nongambling public doesn't know very much about Las Vegas. Many people cannot see beyond the gambling, cannot see that there could possibly be anything of value in Las Vegas for nongamblers or those only marginally interested in gambling.

When you ask these people to describe their ideal vacation, they wax eloquent about lazy days relaxing in the sun, playing golf, enjoying the luxury of resort hotels, eating in fine restaurants, sightseeing, shopping, and going to the theater. Outdoor types speak no less enthusiastically about fishing, boating, hiking, and, in winter, skiing. As it happens, Las Vegas offers all of this. Gambling is just the tip of the iceberg in Las Vegas, but it's all many people can see.

Las Vegas is, of course, about gambling, but there's so much more. Vegas has sunny, mild weather two-thirds of the year, some of the finest hotels and restaurants in the world, the most diversified celebrity and production-show entertainment to be found, unique shopping, internationally renowned golf courses, and numerous attractions. For the outdoor enthusiast, Red Rock Canyon National Conservation Area, Lake Mead National Recreation Area, and Toiyabe National Forest offer some of the most beautiful wilderness resources in North America.

This guide is designed for those who *want* to go to Las Vegas but also for those who *have* to go to Las Vegas. If you are a recreational gambler and/or an enthusiastic vacationer, we will show you ways to have more fun, make the most of your time, and spend less money. If you are one of the skeptics, unwilling companions of gamblers, business travelers, or people who think they would rather be someplace else, we will help you discover the seven-eighths of the Las Vegas iceberg that is hidden.

—*Bob Sehlinger*

SOMETHING OLD, SOMETHING NEW, SOMETHING IMAGINARY, SOMETHING TRUE

IT'S COMMON FOR FRIENDS TO ASK where to get a taste of "old Las Vegas." Unfortunately, old Las Vegas exists primarily as an artifact. Today's Sin City doesn't comport with its historic reputation. Though the myth of old Las Vegas persistently lingers on in the minds of most visitors, it differs starkly from reality.

Though a few old gourmet rooms, showrooms, and lounges have survived, the Las Vegas of loss-leader buffets, cut-rate hotel rooms, cheap drinks, and cramped, smoky casinos is long gone. More remarkably, gone also is the hotel's dependence on gambling as its main revenue source. Luxury guest rooms, expensive entertainment, meals for two topping $250, world-class spas, and immense open casinos that are tourist attractions unto themselves are the new normal. Today, for many hotels, nongaming revenue sources make up 60% and more of total income.

At present, all but roughly a dozen Strip hotels target the luxury market. Middle market properties have mostly been brought to luxury standards by new owners, or demolished. Every place is now a "boutique" hotel—never mind some properties have hundreds of rooms.

When we began covering Las Vegas, the casinos were predominantly independent. Each had a distinct identity free of the corporate veneer that blankets Las Vegas today. Personality, or the lack thereof, was defining. As with cakes at a church fund-raiser, what was on the inside was what mattered. Now it's the icing that attracts attention, or, expressed differently, the icon in the front yard: Statue of Liberty, pyramid, volcano, Eiffel Tower, canal with gondolas . . . you choose. Inside, the product is largely the same. Four casino corporations now run most of Las Vegas. On the Strip it's worse. Two companies—Caesars Entertainment (CET) and MGM Resorts International (MRI)—own every Strip casino except the Tropicana, Venetian, Palazzo, Stratosphere, Cosmopolitan, TI, SLS, Casino Royale, and the Wynn Resorts—17 out of 27 casinos. Standards for restaurants, hotel rooms, entertainment, theme, and just about everything else offer all the predictability of an upscale chain hotel. The maverick casinos and their rough-and-tumble owners are all but gone, and with them the gritty, boom-or-bust soul of this gambling town. Making a clichéd joke a fulfilled prophecy—Las Vegas has in fact become Disneyland..

Dining has seen the same transformation. Hotel restaurants formerly covered a whole range of price points. At present, however, midrange eateries are scarce, with few options available between famous-chef, expense-account restaurants and the hotel coffee shop. Buffets, once bargain central, now cost upward of $40 for the better ones. Nightclubs and lounges, likewise, have become prohibitively pricey and increasingly exclusive. Ditto for entertainment, with many shows selling tickets at $100 and up according to the *Las Vegas Advisor*. Vegas for visitors has become a have/have-not town.

You can still find bargains, but you have to work harder and dig deeper, and that's assuming you know where to look. We'll point you in the right direction, but Las Vegas for the budget conscious will be ever more a challenge.

unofficial **TIP**
A few high-quality afternoon productions offer a bargain alternative to the mortgage-the-farm-priced shows playing the major showrooms.

A bright spot is all the condos and timeshares built in the past 10 years. Most don't have casinos, but splendid accommodations can be had for amazingly good rates through Vacation Rentals by Owner (VRBO) and resort rental management agencies. Home-share and rental powerhouse Airbnb.com offers more than 300 choices in the Las Vegas Valley. The vacation rentals compete directly with hotels for heads-in-beds and have had some moderating effect on hotel rates.

During low and shoulder seasons, a number of hotels not only discount rooms but also throw in free show tickets and other sweeteners. The Mirage promoted $85-per-night rooms packaged with a $40 dining credit and admission for four to its Secret Garden attraction. To find deals coupled with sweeteners check your favorite search engine for "name of hotel and promotions"—for example, "Caesars Palace and promotions." Also check lvahotels.com.

So coming full circle, if you'd like a taste of the old Las Vegas, a few vestiges remain. Live the myth while you can. Tomorrow, or soon after, it will largely be gone. While you can, walk Glitter Gulch, linger over a steak at Top of Binion's Steakhouse, or treat yourself to the duck flambé anise at Hugo's Cellar at the Four Queens. Make no mistake, this is not slumming; each example represents the best of Las Vegas in both a current and historical sense. And if you wait too long? Well, enjoy the new Las Vegas: systematically planned, highly polished, absolutely regimented, and totally plastic.

Though we loved the sultry, wide-open, sinful feel of the old Vegas, we can't argue that corporate Las Vegas has built an Oz that no maverick dreamer could have envisioned. Whether the old Las Vegas or the new Las Vegas is better, we'll leave you to judge.

LETTERS, COMMENTS, AND QUESTIONS FROM READERS

WE EXPECT TO LEARN FROM OUR MISTAKES, as well as from the input of our readers, and to improve with each edition. Many of those who use the Unofficial Guides write to us to ask questions, make comments, or share their own discoveries and lessons learned in Las Vegas. We appreciate all such input, both positive and critical, and encourage our readers to continue writing. Readers' comments and observations are frequently incorporated in revised editions of the Unofficial Guides and contribute immeasurably to their improvement.

How to Write the Author

Bob Sehlinger
The Unofficial Guide to Las Vegas
2204 First Ave. S., Suite 102
Birmingham, AL 35233
unofficialguides@menasharidge.com

If you write us, rest assured that we won't release your name and address to any mailing-list companies, direct-mail advertisers, or other third parties. Unless you tell us otherwise, we'll assume that you're OK with being quoted in the Unofficial Guides. Be sure to put your return address on both your letter and the envelope; the two sometimes get separated. If you email us, tell us where you're from. And please remember, our work often takes us out of the office for long periods of time, so forgive us if our response is delayed.

Reader Survey

At the back of this guide, you will find a short questionnaire that you can use to express opinions concerning your Las Vegas visit. Clip the questionnaire along the dotted line and mail it to the above address.

HOW INFORMATION IS ORGANIZED: BY SUBJECT AND BY GEOGRAPHIC AREAS

TO GIVE YOU FAST ACCESS to information about the *best* of Las Vegas, we've organized material in several formats.

HOTELS Because most people visiting Las Vegas stay in one hotel for the duration of their trip, we summarize our coverage of hotels in charts, maps, ratings, and rankings that allow you to quickly focus your decision-making process. In our hotel profiles on pages 80–145, we concentrate our coverage on the specific variables that differentiate one hotel from another: location, size, room quality, services, amenities, and cost. Accommodations are compared by rankings on pages 149–151, and the hotels' vital information is provided in the chart on pages 155–170.

RESTAURANTS We give you a lot of detail when it comes to restaurants. Because you will probably eat a dozen or more restaurant meals during your stay, and because not even you can predict what kind of fare you might be in the mood for on, say, Saturday night, we provide detailed profiles of the very best restaurants Las Vegas has to offer.

ENTERTAINMENT AND NIGHTLIFE Visitors frequently try several different shows or clubs during their stay. Because shows and nightspots, like restaurants, are usually selected spontaneously after arriving in Las Vegas, we believe detailed descriptions are warranted. All continuously running stage shows and celebrity showrooms are profiled and reviewed in the entertainment chapter of this guide. The best nightspots in Las Vegas are profiled alphabetically under nightlife in the same chapter.

GEOGRAPHIC AREAS Though it's easy to find your way around in Las Vegas, you may not have a car or the inclination to venture far from your hotel. To help you locate the best restaurants, shows, nightspots, and attractions convenient to where you are staying, we have divided the city into geographic areas:

• South Strip and Environs	• West of Strip	• East of Strip
• Mid-Strip and Environs	• Downtown Las Vegas	
• North Strip and Environs	• Southeast Las Vegas–Henderson	

All profiles of hotels, restaurants, and nightspots include area names. For example, if you are staying at the Flamingo and are interested in Italian restaurants within walking distance, scanning the restaurant profiles for restaurants in the Mid-Strip area will provide you with the most convenient choices.

COMFORT ZONES For each hotel-casino we have created a profile that describes the casino's patrons and gives you some sense of how it might feel to spend time there. The purpose of the comfort-zone section is to help you find the hotel-casino at which you will feel most welcome and at home. These comfort-zone descriptions begin on page 78 in Part 1, Accommodations and Casinos.

LAS VEGAS: *An Overview*

GATHERING INFORMATION

LAS VEGAS HAS THE BEST selection of complimentary visitor guides of any American tourist destination we know. Available at the front desk or concierge table at almost every hotel, the guides provide a wealth of useful information on gaming, gambling lessons, shows, lounge entertainment, sports, buffets, meal deals, tours and sightseeing, transportation, shopping, and special events. Additionally, most of the guides contain coupons for discounts on dining, shows, attractions, and tours.

Recommended publications include **Las Vegas Magazine** (lasvegas magazine.com), affiliated with the *Las Vegas Sun* newspaper; **Vegas2 Go;** and **Where Magazine of Las Vegas** (wheremagazine.com). All have much of the same information discussed above, plus feature articles. The best magazine for keeping abreast of nightlife, concerts, and happenings is **Las Vegas Weekly** (lasvegasweekly.com). Although all of the freebie Las Vegas visitor magazines contain valuable information, they are rah-rah rags, and their primary objective is to promote. So don't expect any critical reviews of shows, restaurants, attractions, or anything else for that matter.

The **Las Vegas Advisor** is a 12-page monthly newsletter containing some of the most useful consumer information available on gaming, dining, and entertainment, as well as deals on rooms, drinks, shows, and meals. With no advertising or promotional content, the newsletter serves its readers with objective, prescriptive, no-nonsense advice, presented with a sense of humor. The *Advisor* also operates a dynamite website at lvahotels.com. At a subscription rate of $50 a year (or $37 a year for an online membership), the *Advisor* is the best investment you can make if you plan to spend four or more days in Las Vegas each year. If you are a one-time visitor but wish to avail yourself of all this wisdom, single copies of the *Las Vegas Advisor* can be purchased for $5 at the *Las Vegas Advisor* website with the other subscription options or at the Gamblers Book Club inside the Gambler's General Store at 800 South Main St. Downtown (☎ 702-382-7555 or 800-522-1777; gamblersbookclub.com). For additional information:

Las Vegas Advisor/Huntington Press
3665 S. Procyon Ave.
Las Vegas, NV 89103
☎ 702-252-0655 or 800-244-2224; lvahotels.com

Las Vegas and the Internet

The explosive growth of Las Vegas is not only physical but also virtual. Following are the best places to go on the web to launch yourself into Las Vegas cyberspace.

The site of the *Las Vegas Advisor,* **lvahotels.com,** is a great source of information on recent and future developments, hotels, dining,

Las Vegas Strip Area

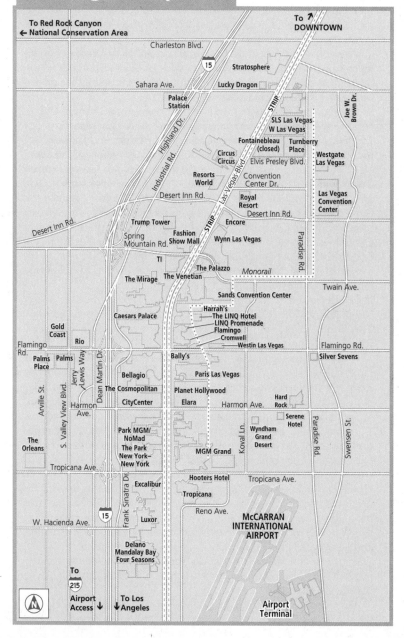

To Red Rock Canyon
← National Conservation Area

To ↗
DOWNTOWN

Charleston Blvd.

15

Stratosphere

Sahara Ave.

Lucky Dragon

Palace
Station

Highland Dr.

Industrial Rd.

STRIP

SLS Las Vegas
W Las Vegas

Fontainebleau
(closed)

Turnberry
Place

Circus
Circus

Elvis Presley Blvd.

Westgate
Las Vegas

Joe W. Brown Dr.

Resorts
World

Convention
Center Dr.

Desert Inn Rd.

Las Vegas Blvd.

Royal
Resort

Las Vegas
Convention
Center

Desert Inn Rd.

STRIP

Desert Inn Rd.

Trump Tower

Encore

Spring
Mountain Rd.

Fashion
Show Mall

Wynn Las Vegas

Paradise Rd.

TI

The Palazzo

Monorail

The Mirage

The Venetian

Twain Ave.

Sands Convention Center

Caesars Palace

Harrah's
The LINQ Hotel
LINQ Promenade
Flamingo
Cromwell
Westin Las Vegas

Gold
Coast

Rio

Flamingo Rd.

Flamingo
Rd.

Palms
Place

Palms

Silver Sevens

Jerry Lewis Way

Bally's

Dean Martin Dr.

Arville St.

S. Valley View Blvd.

Bellagio

Paris Las Vegas

The Cosmopolitan

Planet Hollywood

Harmon
Ave.

CityCenter

Elara

Harmon Ave.

Hard
Rock

The
Orleans

Park MGM/
NoMad

Serene
Hotel

Koval Ln.

Wyndham
Grand
Desert

Paradise Rd.

Swensen St.

The Park
New York–
New York

MGM Grand

Tropicana Ave.

Hooters Hotel

Tropicana Ave.

Frank Sinatra Dr.

Excalibur

Tropicana

Reno Ave.

15

Luxor

McCARRAN
INTERNATIONAL
AIRPORT

W. Hacienda Ave.

Delano
Mandalay Bay
Four Seasons

To
215

N

Airport
Access ↓

To Los
↓ Angeles

Airport
Terminal

entertainment, and gambling. The site features everything you need to plan your trip, as well as informative blogs and podcasts. It also has a function for finding hotel deals (located in the column on the left side of the home page). You can sort the results by price. A forum with user questions, maps, and other visitor information is also available.

The official website of the **Las Vegas Convention and Visitors Authority** is **lasvegas.com.** This site has hundreds of links to hotels, casinos, the airport, and area transportation, plus information on the convention center, sightseeing, and dining.

Another big Las Vegas travel website, with an excellent listing of hotels and their dining and entertainment options, is **vegas.com.** Try *Las Vegas Weekly*'s **lasvegasweekly.com** for nightlife. Another good site for entertainment info is *Las Vegas Magazine*'s **lasvegasmagazine.com.**

The most active Las Vegas message board/forum is **lasvegasadvisor.com/forum.** Divided into two forums, one for members/subscribers and one that anyone can access, the *Las Vegas Advisor* forums offer posts on a vast array of Vegas and gambling topics. The forum open to nonmembers has an aptly named Vegas Free-For-All category. Just about anything you'd want to know is in the Vegas Free-For-All forum . . . somewhere. At last count there were almost 18,000 topics in the forum, so finding the nugget of information you need can be challenging. The members-only forum, conversely, is nicely organized, allowing a direct route to the topic of your choice. Another message board/forum that we like is Vegas Message Board (**vegasmessageboard.com**). This forum is free, but you must register to post. It's nicely organized, with 25 self-explanatory categories.

The best sites for finding discounts on hotels are **lvahotels.com,** the most reliable source for the best rates (see pages 63–65), and **kayak.com,** which allows you to compare room rates offered by a wide range of discounters. Another contender is **hotels.boxed.com,** with good deals but a limited selection. Boxed also sells a range of nontravel products.

Hotels make deals available to select markets and populations through the use of discount codes. For example, a deal targeted to San Diego, California, will be publicized in that area and a special code will be provided to obtain the discount when booking a reservation. However, for most codes, anyone who has the code can use it, even if they are not in the area or market being targeted. Good resources for finding these codes are Smarter Vegas at **smartervegas.com,** where promotional codes for the city's best hotels are routinely available, and Las Vegas Hotel Promotions at **vegas-hotels-online.com.**

Find promotional tickets for Las Vegas shows, including celebrity headliners, at **vegas.com/shows.** Note that not all tickets offered on the site are discounted.

Discounts on rental cars are available at **mousesavers.com.** Though the site is dedicated to saving money at Walt Disney World and Disneyland, the rental car discounts listed can be used anywhere.

Las Vegas Weather and Dress Chart

MONTH	POOLS (O = OPEN)
JANUARY Average daytime temp. 57° F | Average evening temp. 32° F *Recommended attire:* Coats and jackets are a must.	–
FEBRUARY Average daytime temp. 50° F | Average evening temp. 37° F *Recommended attire:* Dress warmly—jackets and sweaters.	–
MARCH Average daytime temp. 69° F | Average evening temp. 42° F *Recommended attire:* Sweaters for days but a jacket at night.	O
APRIL Average daytime temp. 78° F | Average evening temp. 50° F *Recommended attire:* Still cool at night—bring a jacket.	O
MAY Average daytime temp. 88° F | Average evening temp. 50° F *Recommended attire:* Sweater for evening, but days are warm.	O
JUNE Average daytime temp. 99° F | Average evening temp. 68° F *Recommended attire:* Days are hot; evenings are moderate.	O
JULY Average daytime temp. 105° F | Average evening temp. 75° F *Recommended attire:* Bathing suits.	O
AUGUST Average daytime temp. 102° F | Average evening temp. 73° F *Recommended attire:* Dress for the heat—spend time at a pool!	O
SEPTEMBER Average daytime temp. 95° F | Average evening temp. 65° F *Recommended attire:* Days warm, sweater for evening.	O
OCTOBER Average daytime temp. 81° F | Average evening temp. 53° F *Recommended attire:* Bring a jacket or sweater for evening.	O
NOVEMBER Average daytime temp. 67° F | Average evening temp. 40° F *Recommended attire:* Sweaters and jackets for days, but coats at night.	–
DECEMBER Average daytime temp. 58° F | Average evening temp. 34° F *Recommended attire:* Coats and jackets are a must—dress warmly.	–

WHEN TO GO TO LAS VEGAS

THE BEST TIME TO GO TO LAS VEGAS is in the spring or fall, when the weather is pleasant. If you plan to spend most of your time indoors, it doesn't matter what time of year you choose. If you intend to golf, play tennis, run, hike, bike, or boat, try to go in March, April, early May, October, November, or early December. Spring and winter can be exceedingly windy. Once, on an April kayak trip down the Black Canyon of the Colorado, 22-mph winds actually blew us upstream!

Because spring and fall are the nicest times of year, they are also the most popular. The best time for special deals is December (after the National Finals Rodeo in early December and excluding the week between Christmas and New Year's), January, and the summer months.

Weather in December, January, and February can vary incredibly. While high winds, cold, rain, and snow are not unheard of, chances are better that temperatures will be mild and the sun will shine. Though the weather is less dependable than in spring or fall, winter months are gener-

unofficial **TIP**
The winter months in Las Vegas provide an unbeatable combination of good value and choice of activities.

ally well suited to outdoor activities. We talked to people who in late February water-skied on Lake Mead in the morning and snow-skied in the afternoon at Lee Canyon. From mid-May through mid-September, however, the heat is blistering. During these months, it's best to follow the example of the gambler or the lizard—stay indoors or under a rock.

Crowd Avoidance

In general, weekends are busier than weekdays. The exceptions are holidays and when large conventions or special events are held. Most Las Vegas hotels have a lower guest-room rate for weekdays than for weekends. Las Vegas hosts huge conventions and special events (rodeos, prize fights) that tie up hotels, restaurants, transportation, showrooms, and traffic for a week at a time. Likewise, major sporting events, such as the Super Bowl, the World Series, and the NBA championship, fill every hotel in town on weekends. If you prefer to schedule your visit at a time when things are less frantic, we provide a calendar that lists the larger citywide conventions and regularly scheduled events to help you avoid the crowds.

unofficial **TIP**
For a stress-free arrival at the airport, good availability of rental cars, and a quick hotel check-in, try to arrive Monday afternoon through Thursday morning (Tuesday and Wednesday are best).

Because conventions of more than 12,000 attendees can cause problems for the lone vacationer, the list of conventions and special events below will help you plan your vacation dates. Included are the convention date, the number of people expected to attend, and the convention location. For a complete list of conventions scheduled

CONVENTIONS AND SPECIAL EVENTS CALENDAR

DATES	CONVENTION/EVENT	ATTENDANCE	LOCATION
2018			
Oct 2–3	InsureTech Connect	6,000	MGM Grand
Oct 7–10	ABC Kids Expo	7,000	LVCC
Oct 8–10	National Assoc. of Convenience Stores, Inc. Expo	30,000	LVCC
Oct 9–11	G2E: Global Gaming Expo	26,000	Sands Expo Ctr.
Oct 11–14	American International Motorcycle Expo	25,000	Mandalay Bay
Oct 16–18	IMEX America	12,000	Sands Expo Ctr.
Oct 18–20	Specialty Graphics National Convention	23,000	LVCC
Oct 19–21	Live Design International	14,000	LVCC
Oct 30–Nov 1	International Fastener Expo	5,500	Mandalay Bay
Oct 30–Nov 2	Automotive Aftermarket Industry Week	160,000	LVCC
Oct 31–Nov 2	International Pool/Spa/Patio Expo	10,000	Mandalay Bay
Nov 6–10	SupplySide West Expo Trade Show & Conference	14,700	Mandalay Bay
Nov 14–16	National Marijuana Business Conference	10,000	LVCC/Westgate
Nov 14–17	Diving Equipment & Marketing Assoc. Show	10,000	LVCC/Westgate
Nov 15–17	Mecum Collector Car Auctions	15,000	LVCC/Westgate
Nov 23–25	Motor Trend International Auto Show	17,000	LVCC
Nov 24–25	SnowJam Ski & Snowboard Show	5,000	LVCC
Dec 4–6	64th International Respiratory Convention & Expo	5,000	Mandalay Bay
Dec 5–6	National Groundwater Association Expo	4,500	LVCC/Westgate

CONVENTIONS AND SPECIAL EVENTS CALENDAR

DATES	CONVENTION/EVENT	ATTENDANCE	LOCATION
2019			
Jan 8–11	Consumer Technology Association—CES 2019	175,000	LVCC/Westgate
Jan 22–25	International Surface Event	25,000	Mandalay Bay
Jan 22–25	Shooting, Hunting, & Outdoor Trade Show	61,000	Sands Expo/Venetian
Jan 22–24	Sports Licensing & Tailgate Show	4,000	LVCC/Westgate
Jan 22–25	World of Concrete	60,000	LVCC/Westgate
Jan 27–31	Winter Las Vegas Market	50,000	World Market Center
Feb 6–12	American Bar Association Mid-Year Conference	4,000	Caesars Palace
Feb 19–21	International Builders Show	60,000	LVCC
Feb 19–21	Kitchen and Bath Industry Show	33,000	LVCC/Westgate
Mar 5–7	International Pizza Expo	12,000	LVCC/Westgate
Mar 6–7	International Wireless Communications Expo	12,000	LVCC/Westgate
Mar 12–16	American Academy of Orthopaedic Surgeons Anual Meeting	33,500	Venetian
Mar 17–20	ASD Winter Market Week	46,000	LVCC/Westgate
Mar 26–27	Nightclub and Bar Show	39,000	LVCC/Westgate
Mar 27–28	Digital Signage Expo	6,000	Westgate
Apr 1–4	National Association of Theatre Owners CinemaCon	5,000	Caesars Palace
Apr 8–11	National Association of Broadcasters Convention	103,000	LVCC/Westgate
Apr 23–26	International Sign Expo	19,500	Mandalay Bay
Apr 26–28	LVL UP Technology & Gaming Expo	13,000	LVCC/Westgate
May 6–9	ServiceNow Inc.	22,000	Venetian
May 7–9	National Hardware Show	37,000	LVCC/Westgate
May 7–9	Waste Expo	12,500	LVCC/Westgate
May 20–22	RECon	37,000	LVCC/Westgate
May 31–June 4	Las Vegas Antique Jewelry & Watch Show	7,500	LVCC/Paris LV
June 3–5	Design Automation Conference	8,000	LVCC
June 6–8	American Institute of Architects Conference	15,000	LVCC/Wynn
June 11–13	World Tea Expo	7,500	LVCC/Westgate
June 15–17	IECSC International Beauty Show	25,000	LVCC
June 23–25	Society for Human Resource Management Conference & Expo	18,000	LVCC/Westgate
July 17–20	Assoc. of Woodworking & Furnishing Suppliers Fair	18,500	LVCC/Westgate
July 28–31	ASD Summer Market Week	44,000	LVCC/Westgate
July 28–Aug 1	Summer Las Vegas Market	50,000	World Market Center
Sep 8–11	International Baking Industry Expo	22,000	LVCC/Westgate
Sep 10–12	IMEX America	10,000	Sands Expo/Venetian
Sep 11–14	Las Vegas Souvenir & Resort Gift Show	6,000	Westgate
Sep 13–14	Mr. Olympia	45,000	Orleans
Sep 14–17	National Electrical Contractors Convention	5,500	Mandalay Bay
Sep 18–29	Building Industry Consulting Service Conference	4,500	Mandalay Bay
Sep 19–21	International Vision Expo West	23,000	Sands Expo/Venetian
Sep 23–25	Packaging Machinery Manufacturers Institute Expo	45,000	LVCC/Westgate

during your visit, go to vegasmeansbusiness.com and click on "Convention Calendar." You can enter dates and get a full list or narrow it with different keywords or search terms. Although there are usually 6–12 conventions being staged in Las Vegas at any given time, the effect of any convention or trade show on hotels, shows, and restaurants is negligible citywide for conventions of 10,000 or fewer, except at the host hotel or convention venue. Note that four or five concurrent conventions averaging 4,000 attendees each can impact tourism to the same extent as one large convention.

A larger Las Vegas hotel can handle small conventions without a hiccup. However, if you stay somewhere that's hosting a convention, avoid arriving or departing on the same day as the attendees.

ARRIVING *and* GETTING ORIENTED

IF YOU DRIVE, you will have to travel through the desert to reach Las Vegas. Make sure your car is in good shape. Check your spare tire and toss a couple of gallons of water in the trunk, just in case. Once en route, pay attention to your fuel and temperature gauges. Virtually all commercial air traffic into Las Vegas uses McCarran International Airport. At McCarran, a well-designed facility with good, clear signs, you will have no problem finding your way from the gate to the baggage-claim area, though it is often a long walk. Fast baggage handling is not the airport's strongest suit, so you might have to wait a long time on your luggage.

If you do not intend to rent a car, getting from the airport to your hotel is no problem. You have several options.

SHUTTLE SERVICES Three companies provide service at McCarran: **Bell Trans** (airportshuttlelasvegas.com), **Showtime Tours** (showtimetourslv.com), and **SuperShuttle** (shuttlelasvegas.com). Cost is about $7.50–$15 one-way and $13–$18 round-trip. Sedans and limousines cost about $70–$150 one-way. The shuttle service counters are in the hall just outside the baggage-claim area in Terminal 1. At Terminal 3, shuttles are located outside on Level Zero.

TAXIS For taxis, the fare is the same no matter how many passengers are traveling (maximum five). Cabs charge a $3.50 trip fee with $0.23 per ¹⁄₁₂ mile thereafter. If a taxi ride originates at McCarran International Airport, an additional airport surcharge of $2 per trip is added. Cab fare to Strip locations is $17–$32 one-way, plus tip. One-way taxi fares to Downtown run about $37–$44. For more accurate point-to-point cab fare estimates see taxi-calculator.com. Fares are regulated and should not vary from company to company. Note that some cabs in southern Nevada do not accept credit cards. If you plan to take a taxi from the airport, it's a good idea to check out the best route on googlemaps.com. Some cab drivers will take a circuitous route to bump up fares. Be mindful, however, that traffic in Las Vegas is horrendous and that a route that seems circuitous may take less time than a more direct route. The most common "long-haul" route used to pad fares is traveling to Strip hotels or Downtown via the airport tunnel to I-215 and I-15. Cabs are available at the curb on the east side of baggage claim.

TAXI OPERATORS

- Ace Cab Co. ☎ 702-736-8383
- Nellis Cab Co. ☎ 702-248-1111
- ANLV ☎ 702-643-1041
- Union ☎ 702-736-8444
- Henderson Taxi ☎ 702-384-2322
- Western Cab ☎ 702-736-8000
- Yellow Checker and Star Transportation ☎ 702-873-2000

RIDE-SHARING SERVICES **Lyft** (lyft.com), **Uber** (uber.com), and similar services use ordinary people and their cars as an informal taxi service. Customers use a mobile app to find drivers in their area and to estimate the length and cost of the ride. Both Uber and Lyft can save you money versus a regular cab. On a recent trip from Downtown to the Strip, for example, Uber charged us $10.60, while the return taxi ride along the same route, in the same traffic, was $18.40. Plus, with Uber no tip is required. In periods of peak demand, however, Uber uses what it calls "surge rates," which can be much more expensive than a cab. Uber alerts you on the app that surge rates are in effect and tells you exactly what the cost per mile will be. If it's more than you are ready to pay, simply decline, and no car will be dispatched.

The process for using Uber and Lyft at the airport is the same. Once you've collected your bags, open the app and select your terminal.

Terminals 1 and 3: From baggage claim, take the elevator near door #2 up to Level 2. Cross the pedestrian bridge on Level 2 to the Terminal 1 Parking Garage. The ride-share pickup is located on Level 2M of the parking garage.

At Strip hotels, Uber and Lyft pickups are generally routed to secondary valet areas rather than at the property's main entrance.

Additional information concerning ground transportation is available at the McCarran website (mccarran.com) and at the Nevada Taxi Cab Authority's website (taxi.nv.gov).

EXITING THE AIRPORT If you rent a car, you will need to catch the courtesy shuttle to the new consolidated McCarran Rent-A-Car Center located about 2 miles from the airport. The shuttle boards at the middle curb of the authorized vehicle lanes just outside terminal doors 10 and 11 on the ground level. The individual car-rental companies no longer operate shuttles of any kind, so all car-rental customers use the same shuttle. For a detailed discussion of rental cars, see pages 14–20.

If someone is picking you up, go to ground level on the opposite side of the baggage-claim building (away from the main terminal) to the baggage-claim and arrivals curb. If your ride wants to park and meet you, hook up on the ground level of the baggage-claim building where the escalators descend from the main terminal.

There are two ways to exit the airport by car. You can depart via the old route, Swenson Street, which runs north–south roughly paralleling the Strip, or you can hop on the I-215 spur. Dipping south from the airport, I-215 connects with I-15. The tunnel and I-215 will often deliver you to a point of huge congestion and delays where I-215 intersects I-15. As a general rule, exiting the airport on Swenson and then turning left (west) on the closest east–west street to your destination is the best bet for all Strip hotels. Swenson is also a better route if you're going to the Las Vegas Convention Center, to the University of Nevada, Las Vegas (UNLV), or to hotels on or east of the Strip.

unofficial **TIP**
Any use of cell phones while driving is now against the law in Las Vegas. Keep your phone in your pocket and avoid big fines.

CONVENIENCE CHART To give you an idea of your hotel's convenience to popular destinations such as the Strip, Downtown, the Las Vegas Convention Center, UNLV, and the airport, we provide a section on getting around in the next chapter. It includes a "convenience chart" that lists estimated times by foot or cab from each hotel to the destinations outlined on pages 42–44. In the same section are tips for avoiding traffic congestion and for commuting between the Strip and Downtown.

RENTAL CARS

ALL OF THE RENTAL-CAR COMPANIES previously located at the airport terminal, plus a few off-site companies, have moved to the huge McCarran Rent-A-Car Center situated 2 miles south of the airport. The airport provides large buses departing approximately every 5 minutes for the 7-to-12-minute commute to the facility. On arriving at the Rent-A-Car Center, you'll find all of the rental-car companies listed in the chart below on the ground floor.

RENTAL-CAR AGENCIES AT THE McCARRAN RENT-A-CAR CENTER		
ADVANTAGE/US RENT A CAR	800-777-9377	us-rentacar.com
ALAMO	800-462-5266	alamo.com
AVIS	800-331-1212	avis.com
BUDGET	800-922-2899	budget.com
DOLLAR	800-800-4000	dollar.com
ENTERPRISE	800-736-8222	enterprise.com
HERTZ	800-654-3131	hertz.com
NATIONAL CAR RENTAL	800-227-7368	nationalcar.com
PAYLESS CAR RENTAL	800-729-5377	paylesscarrental.com
THRIFTY	800-367-2277	thrifty.com

When the rental-car companies were located at the airport, rental customers arrived at the rental counters in a relatively steady stream.

At the off-airport location, however, rental customers arrive by the busload, inundating the rental counters. Now, the only way to avoid a substantial wait to be processed is to join the special-customer clubs of the respective rental-car companies. These clubs (or programs) allow you to bypass the regular queue and to receive preferential processing. Just visit the website of the company of your choice and you'll see instructions for signing up. You don't have to rent cars often to join. Sign up about four weeks before you make a rental reservation so you'll have your membership number when you're ready to reserve.

Because the Rent-A-Car Center shuttles run more often than buses provided by the rental-car companies under the old system, it doesn't take any longer than before to commute to the center or to get back to the airport once you've returned your car. En route to the Rent-A-Car Center, sit near a door so that you can be one of the first to disembark. If you're traveling with others, let them attend to the luggage while you sprint to the rental counter. This will ensure that you'll be ahead of your fellow bus passengers. To avoid a free-for-all of passengers trying to retrieve their bags from the onboard storage racks, most bus drivers prefer to handle luggage loading and unloading. It's about order and safety, not tips, so just go with it. Generally, after all riders have disembarked, the driver will unload the luggage via the rear doors.

All of the rental cars are under one roof. Upon completion of your paperwork you'll be directed to a specified area of the garage to pick up your car. Having picked up your car, chances are about 95% that you'll find yourself disoriented in a part of Las Vegas you've never laid eyes on. Follow the instructions below to reach your final destination.

After you pick up your rental car, you'll exit the Rent-A-Car Center onto Gilespie Street, where you'll find signs directing you to the Strip as well as to I-15 and I-215. Unfortunately, if you follow the signs, you'll end up in a traffic jam of the first order (welcome to Las Vegas!), owing to an inadequate number of right-turn lanes and a multitude of traffic signals. The exit from the Rent-A-Car Center onto Gilespie Street forces you to turn right (south), but to avoid the traffic jams you really want to be heading in the opposite direction (north) on Gilespie. From the Rent-A-Car Center exit, this can be accomplished by working your way immediately across the southbound lanes on Gilespie to a left-turn lane and then making a U-turn. Alternatively, you can go another block or so south and then turn around less hurriedly. Once you're headed northbound on Gilespie do the following:

TO REACH THE LAS VEGAS CONVENTION CENTER, UNLV, AND HOTELS ON THE EAST SIDE OF THE STRIP, head north on Gilespie Street and turn right onto George Crockett Road. Follow signs to the airport via the Airport Connector. You'll pass through a tunnel under the runways and pop out on Swenson Street just before the intersection with Tropicana. Use the maps in this guide to reach your final destination from there.

TO REACH DOWNTOWN AND HOTELS ON THE WEST SIDE OF THE STRIP VIA I-15, head north from the Rent-A-Car Center on Gilespie, cross the

Rental-Car Return and Pickup

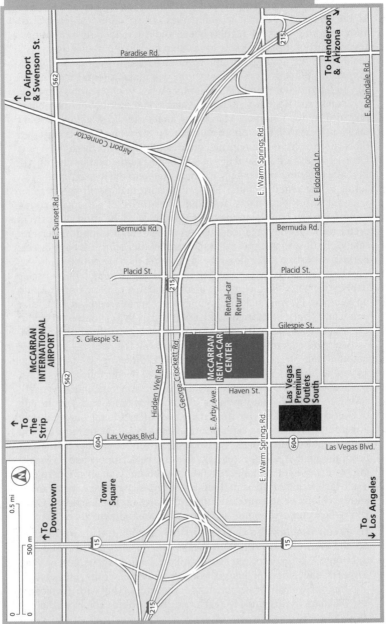

bridge over I-215, and turn left on Hidden Well Road. Follow Hidden Well Road to I-15 (northbound only). Use the maps in this guide to navigate to your final destination from there.

Note: Project Neon is a multiyear, ongoing widening of I-15 between Sahara Avenue and the US 95/I-515 interchange downtown. The project also includes new and redesigned ramps. During rush hours you may be better off traveling downtown on surface streets. From the rental car facility, head back to the airport and go through the tunnel, emerging on Swenson Street. Continue straight on Swenson. After crossing E. Desert Inn Road, Swenson becomes Joe W. Brown, which intersects Sahara Avenue. Turn left on Sahara, staying in the far right lane. From there, turn right (north) on S. Las Vegas Boulevard to downtown.

TO ACCESS I-215 NORTHWEST TOWARD RED ROCK CANYON AND SUMMERLIN, go north on Gilespie, cross the bridge over I-215, and turn left on Hidden Well Road. Follow Hidden Well Road to the I-215 westbound ramp.

The following directions do not require going north on Gilespie:

TO ACCESS I-215 SOUTHEAST TOWARD HENDERSON, GREEN VALLEY, AND LAKE LAS VEGAS, turn right on Gilespie from the Rent-A-Car Center and turn left at the first traffic signal onto Warm Springs Road. Follow Warm Springs Road west to the intersection of I-215.

TO ACCESS LAS VEGAS BOULEVARD SOUTH OF THE I-15/I-215 INTER-CHANGE, stay in the far-right lane on exiting the Rent-A-Car Center and turn right on Warm Springs Road. Warm Springs Road intersects Las Vegas Boulevard South.

TO ACCESS I-15 SOUTHBOUND TOWARD LAUGHLIN AND LOS ANGELES, turn right on Gilespie from the Rent-A-Car Center and then right on Warm Springs Road. After two blocks, turn south on Las Vegas Boulevard South, then right on Blue Diamond Road. Follow the signs to I-15.

Fortunately, returning your rental car is much easier and there is little opportunity to become embroiled in a serious traffic jam near the Rent-A-Car Center. The same cannot be said, however, of I-15 and I-215, especially during rush hours. If you are coming from the east side of the Strip, take Paradise Road to the airport and follow the well-marked signs to the rental-car return. Likewise, as you come toward the airport on I-15 and I-215, follow the rental-car-return signs.

Rental cars are comparatively cheap in Las Vegas, but taxes and fees are not. Here's what you can expect to pay:

Airport Access Fee	10.5%
Customer Facility Charge	14.7%
Rental Tax	13%
State Tax	9%
Vehicle License Fee	5.9%
Total	53.1%

The base rate for a rental from Dollar in 2018 was $203.55. Mandatory taxes and fees added another $108.92 for a total of $312.47.

You can avoid the customer facility charge and the airport access fee by renting at a nonairport location, such as your hotel. However, it's not unusual for agencies to bump up the base rate at such locations.

In the dollar-and-cents department, prices fluctuate so much from week to week that it's anyone's guess who will offer the best deal during your visit. Usually the best deals are on the company's website, but expedia.com, carrentals.com, and kayak.com are often worth checking, especially if you're visiting during a particularly busy time, such as during a citywide convention. On rental company websites, counterintuitively, you can often get a better deal if you don't indicate that you're a member of AAA, AARP, and the like. After you get your quote, see if you can improve the deal by trying again, entering your organization or age information.

Be aware that Las Vegas is a feast-or-famine city when it comes to rental-car availability. On many weekends, or when a citywide convention is in town, it may be impossible to get a rental car unless you reserved way in advance. If, on the other hand, you come to town when business is slow, the rental agencies will practically give you a car. We have been able to rent from the most expensive companies for as little as $22 a day under these circumstances. If you are visiting during a slow time, reserve a car in advance to cover yourself, and then, on arrival, ask each rental company to quote you its best price. If you can beat the price on your reserved car, go for it.

One of the best places for rental-car deals is mousesavers.com, a site dedicated to finding deals at Disneyland and Walt Disney World. Some of the rental-car discounts are for Orlando and Southern California only, but many others apply anywhere in the United States. You can also do an online search for promo codes. If you want to rent from Avis, for example, enter "Avis Promo Codes" or "Avis Coupon Codes."

Another way to score a deal on a rental car is to bid on priceline .com. We've used Priceline to get cars at less than $20 per day. Understand, however, that if your bid is accepted, the entire rental cost will be nonrefundably charged to your credit card. In other words, no backing out for any reason. Before placing your bid, check our conventions and special events calendar on pages 10–11. If there's a big convention in town, demand will be high and a lowball bid might not work.

When you (or your travel agent) call to reserve a rental car, ask for the smallest, least expensive car in the company's inventory, even if you ultimately intend to rent a larger vehicle. It's possible that you will be upgraded without charge when you arrive. If not, rental agencies frequently offer on-site upgrade incentives that beat any deals you can make in advance. Always compare daily and weekly rates.

If you decline insurance coverage on the rental car because of protection provided by your credit card, be aware that the coverage provided by the credit card is secondary to your regular auto insurance policy.

In most situations the credit-card coverage only reimburses you the deductible on your regular policy. Happily, most car insurance covers rental cars as well as your personal vehicle. If you're not sure about your coverage, contact your insurance agent. Also be aware that some car-rental contracts require that you drive the car only in Nevada. If you, like many tourists, visit Hoover Dam or trek out to the Grand Canyon, you will cross into Arizona. Another item to check in advance, if applicable, is whether your rental agency charges for additional drivers.

When you rent your car, make sure you understand the implications of bringing it back empty of fuel. Some companies will charge as much as $9 per gallon if they have to fill the tank on return. At one agency, we returned a car with between a third and a half-tank of gas remaining and were charged the same as if we had coasted in with a completely empty tank. Also, beware of signs at the car-rental counters reading GAS TODAY—$3 PER GALLON or some such. That usually applies to the price of the gas already in the car when you rent it, not the price per gallon of a fill-up should you return the car empty. The price per gallon for a fill-up on return will be somewhere in the fine print of your rental contract.

Another rental-car problem we encountered involved a pinhead-size chip on the windshield. Understanding the fine print of rental car contracts, and because we always decline the insurance offered by the agencies, we inspect our cars thoroughly for any damage before accepting the car and leaving the lot. In this instance, as always, we inspected the car thoroughly and did not notice any windshield flaws. When we returned the car after three days, we were requested to remain at the counter to complete an "accident report."

*un*official **TIP**
Before you leave the lot, inspect your rental car with care, examining every inch, and have the rental agency record anything you find.

Insisting that we were unaware of any damage, we requested that the car be retrieved for our inspection. Still unable to find the alleged damage, we asked the counter agent to identify it for us. The agent who was responsible for the accident report then had to scrutinize the windshield before she could find the mark, even though she knew its exact location from the employee who checked the car in. The conclusion to be drawn here is that if you decline coverage, the rental agency may hold you responsible for even the tiniest damage—damage so slight that you may never notice it. Check your car out well before you leave. This will not inhibit them from charging you for damage sustained while the car is in your possession, but at least you will have the peace of mind of knowing that they are not putting one over on you.

The cavernous Rent-A-Car Center is not well lighted, making a thorough inspection of your rental car difficult. If necessary, move it to a better illuminated part of the garage before exiting. If you cannot locate a brighter place, use the flashlight feature on your smartphone. Speaking of smartphones, take pictures of any damage you uncover. Note that damage on recently washed cars that are still partially wet is especially hard to spot.

Some rental companies will charge you for "loss of use" if you have an accident that takes the car out of use. Because some car insurance policies do not pay loss-of-use charges, check your coverage with your insurance agent before you rent.

MEGABUS, GREYHOUND, AND FLIXBUS

IF YOU'RE COMING FROM SOUTHERN CALIFORNIA, consider **Megabus.** A round-trip on the Wi-Fi–equipped modern buses runs about $30, less than most round-trip cab rides to and from the airport. There are four buses a day departing from Union Station's Patsaouras Transit Plaza Bay and terminating at the RTC South Strip Transfer Terminal. The trip takes 5–6 hours. Visit us.megabus.com for schedules and additional information.

Greyhound runs express buses from southern California to Las Vegas. Five or six express buses run each day, making a pit stop in either Barstow or San Bernardino. Travel time is about 5–6 hours, including the stop. Round-trip prices range from $52 to $268 (for a fully refundable ticket).

A new bus service, **FlixBus,** offers service to and from Las Vegas and a number of California, Nevada, and Arizona cities. The service is marketed to individuals who normally travel to Las Vegas in their own car. FlixBus, which already operates in Europe, points out that on the bus you can work, relax, or sleep while you travel. Vegas-bound buses make stops at the Strip and Downtown. Launched in 2018, FlixBus uses six regional bus partners: Arrow Stage Lines, American Explorer Motorcoach, Gray Line Arizona, Pacific Coachways, Transportation Charter Services, and USA Coach Services. All buses have free Wi-Fi, "onboard entertainment," and power outlets and USB ports for every seat. In 2018, FlixBus offered cut-rate, market-entry pricing for its routes. For more information, visit flixbus.com or call ☎ 855-626-8585.

RECREATIONAL AND MEDICAL MARIJUANA

ON JULY 1, 2017, Nevada became the fifth state to legalize recreational marijuana. Adults 21 and over with a valid ID may purchase up to one ounce of marijuana to smoke or one-eighth ounce of edibles or concentrates from licensed retail outlets, for the most part those that have been participating in the Nevada medical marijuana program (see below). In addition to Nevada residents, out-of-state visitors are also eligible to make purchases. Recreational marijuana remains illegal to consume in public, including the Strip, hotels, and casino floors. Violators can be fined $600.

Nevada is also one of 24 states where medical marijuana is legal. Retail locations have proliferated in Las Vegas because medical marijuana is now available to non–Nevada residents who meet several qualifiers. Thanks to the new local reciprocity law, you can present your valid out-of-state medical marijuana license, along with a prescription from your doctor. You must also show a government-issued proof-of-identity document that includes your age and will be required to sign an affidavit confirming that you are 21 or older. Cannabis is sold in several manifestations, including loose varieties, vapes, pre-roll, oils, capsules, tinctures, cosmetics and other derma products, snacks, and beverages. Everything sold in legal pot clinics is lab tested for THC and CBD quotient, and glossy catalogs detail the effects of different strains. Most locations take cash only or a debit card; several have ATMs on site. Four dispensaries are convenient to Downtown and the Strip: **Essence** (2307 Las Vegas Blvd. S., ☎ 702-978-7591, essencevegas.com); **The Grove** (4647 S. Swenson, ☎ 702-463-5777, thegrovenv.com); **Inyo** (2520 S. Maryland Pkwy. #2, ☎ 702-707-8888, inyolasvegas.com); and **Releaf** (2244 Paradise Road, ☎ 702-209-2400, lasvegasreleaf. com). While some dispensaries advertise delivery service, new laws could restrict deliveries to the address on registration cards.

Recreational marijuana, though legal in Nevada, is illegal on airport property. For those who have some left over from their stay, McCarran Airport has installed "amnesty boxes"—green metal containers (bolted to the concrete no less), where you can off-load the weed. They are located in a dozen places outside the terminals and at the rental-car center.

In the terminals, if you're caught with pot at a TSA security checkpoint, the local police will be summoned. If the amount is less than the one-ounce limit for possession, no charges will be pressed, but the experience will be very unpleasant, and you might miss your flight. If the amount is over the limit, you can be arrested and charged with felony possession. While searching for weed is not a TSA priority, the rules are pretty clear if they bump into some. Also, consider that if you manage to get it to your destination airport, there may be security personnel with dogs working the baggage-claim area.

LAS VEGAS CUSTOMS AND PROTOCOL

IN A TOWN WHERE THE MOST BIZARRE behavior imaginable is routinely tolerated, it is ironic that so many visitors obsess over what constitutes proper protocol. This mentality stems mainly from the myriad customs peculiar to gaming and the *perceived* glamour of the city itself. First-timers attach a great deal of importance to "fitting in." What makes this task difficult, at least in part, is that half of the people with whom they are trying to fit in are first-timers too.

The only hard rules for being accepted Downtown or on the Strip are to have a shirt on your back, shoes on your feet, some manner of clothing below the waist, and a little money in your pocket. Concerning the latter, there is no maximum. The operational minimum is bus fare back to wherever you came from.

This notwithstanding, there are some basic areas in which Las Vegas first-timers tend to feel especially insecure.

GAMBLING The various oddities of gaming protocol are described in this book under the casino games in Part 3, Gambling (pages 299–333). Despite appearances, however, gambling is very informal. While it is intelligent not to play a game when/if you do not know how, it is unwarranted to abstain because you are uncertain of the protocol. What little protocol exists (things like holding your cards above the table and keeping your hands away from your bet once play has begun) has evolved to protect the house and honest players from cheats. Dealers (a generic term for those who conduct table games) are not under orders to be unfriendly, silent, or rigid. Observe a game that interests you before you sit down. Assure yourself that the dealer is personable and polite. Never play in a casino where the staff is surly or cold; life's too short.

However, there are a few faux pas that will raise the hackles of the house or fellow gamblers. In craps, for example, bouncing the dice off the table and onto the floor is looked upon with disapprobation. When the dice are passed to you, you don't have to roll. If you're overly anxious, just opt out and pass the dice to the person next to you. In blackjack, playing stupidly does not actually alter the fate of your tablemates, but they think it does. If you double down on a pair of fours, more cards will be dealt to your two hands than if you had followed basic strategy and hit. Those playing to your left tend to think that some of the cards dealt to you should have been theirs. It's a dumb reason to get mad, but it happens more often than you'd think. Slot players are very proprietary about their machines. Make absolutely sure that a machine is free before you start playing.

EATING IN FANCY RESTAURANTS Many are meat-and-potatoes places with fancy names, so there is no real reason to be intimidated. Others are designer, pay-big-bucks restaurants with famous chefs. In either case, service is friendly. Men will feel more comfortable in sport coats, but ties are rarely worn. Women turn up in everything from slacks and blouses to evening wear. When you sit down, a whole platoon of waiters will attend you. Do not remove your napkin from the table; only the waiters are allowed to place napkins in the laps of patrons. After the ceremonial placement of the napkin, the senior waiter will speak. When he concludes, you may order cocktails, consider the menu, sip your water, or engage in conversation. If your waiters seem stuffy or aloof, ask them to grind peppercorns or grate Parmesan cheese on something. This will usually loosen them up.

There will be enough utensils on the table to perform a triple bypass. These items are considered expendable; use a different utensil for each dish and surrender it to the waiter along with the empty plate at the end of each course.

A frequent challenge in fancy restaurants is deciphering the menu. Asian restaurants love whimsical names such as "Happy Family" (apparently a dish that's quite content lounging in the wok) and "Delicious Surprise" (from the open-your-mouth-and-close-your-eyes department). Just as common is the euphemistically stated menu. For example, "Succulent free-range chicken simmered in its own juices with a medley of farm-fresh vegetables." Translation: chicken stew. Worst of all are French and Italian eateries that, for the sake of authenticity

(?), offer their menus in the native tongue with little or no translation. C'mon already, we can't afford to bring a translator, and no, even if it originated in Bologna, Bolognese sauce isn't made from baloney.

TIPPING Because about a third of the resident population of Las Vegas are service providers in the tourist industry, there is no scarcity of people to tip. From the day you arrive until the day you depart, you will be interacting with porters, cabbies, valet-parking attendants, bellhops, waiters, maître d's, dealers, bartenders, housekeepers, and others.

Tipping is an issue that makes some travelers very uncomfortable. How much? When? To whom? Not leaving a tip when one is customary makes you feel inexperienced. Not knowing how much to tip makes you feel vulnerable and out of control. Is the tip you normally leave at home appropriate in Las Vegas?

The most important thing to bear in mind is that a tip is not automatic, nor is it an obligation. A tip is a reward for good service. The suggestions in the "Tipping Guidelines" chart on page 24 are based on traditional practices in Las Vegas.

WALKING THE MEAN STREETS On exiting your Strip hotel you may be greeted by Spongebob Square Pants, Mickey Mouse, Donald Duck, and a veritable menagerie of less-famous characters, as well as musicians, jugglers, spray paint artists, and magicians. These are mostly locals in costume who, for a set amount or tip, will pose for a photo. Some of the costumed photo-op bunch are wonderfully amusing; others are not so much, including a minority who are simply pesky. Considering all of the above, the choice to interact is yours.

With cameras all over the place, aggressive panhandling is unusual on the Strip and Downtown. Most begging for money locate themselves on public property, such as pedestrian bridges, where they sit with a sign describing their need. Give if you're inclined or walk on. Annoying but harmless are so-called slappers, who endeavor to hand you some printed advertisement or leaflet ("slapping" comes from the habit of smacking the handouts together to attract your attention). Though some distribute coupons for discounted drinks or shows, most are trying to drum up business for private dancers and escort services.

Finally, we advise you *not* to buy bottled water from street vendors either on the Strip or Downtown. The bottles are not sealed, and it's open to speculation where the water came from. If you want to beat minibar or hotel shop prices, go to a convenience store.

PARKING

PARKING HAS ALWAYS been free in Las Vegas—until now, that is. In 2015, MGM Resorts International (MRI) instituted paid valet and self-parking for most of its properties under the dubious guise of enhancing a guest's experience. There was a huge blowback, of course, but they persevered, and true to form Caesars Entertainment casinos, the Cosmopolitan, and Wynn properties followed suit in 2016 with no doubt more on the way. (See "Valet Parking" under "Tipping Guidelines"

TIPPING GUIDELINES

PORTERS A dollar a bag

CAB DRIVERS A lot depends on service and courtesy. For good service tip $5 or 15%–20% of the total fare. If you are asking the cabbie to take you only a block or two, the fare will be small, but your tip should be large ($5) to make up for his wait in line and to partially compensate him for missing a better-paying fare. Add an extra dollar for a lot of luggage handling.

RIDE-SHARE DRIVERS Both Uber and Lyft include an in-app tipping feature that allows you to add a tip to your overall charge. If you're compelled to tip, the suggested amount is 10%–20%.

VALET PARKING Many hotels and casinos now charge a fixed fee for valet parking. Fees are currently $12–$30 (depending how long your car is parked) but will probably go higher. This development has led drivers to use valet parking in nearby hotels and shopping venues that don't charge and walk to their intended destination. As you might imagine, the result was these venues charging fees in self-defense. If you are fortunate enough to use valet service where you're not charged a set fee, follow these tipping suggestions: Two dollars is correct if the valet is courteous and demonstrates some hustle. A dollar will do if the service is just OK. Only pay when you take your car out, not when you leave it. Because valet attendants pool their tips, both of the individuals who assist you (coming and going) will be taken care of. If the valet service is jammed, hand over $20 to the person who takes your claim ticket and tell him you'd like the car brought up right away. You'll be moved to the head of the line.

BELLMEN When a bellhop greets you at your car with a rolling cart and handles all of your bags, $5 is about right. The more luggage you carry yourself, of course, the less you should tip. Sometimes bellhops who handle only a small bag or two will put on a real performance when showing you your room. We had a bellhop in one hotel walk into our room, crank up the air-conditioner, turn on the TV, open the blinds, flick on the lights, flush the commode, and test the water pressure in the tub. Give us a break. We tipped the same as if he had simply opened the door and put our luggage in the room.

WAITERS Whether in a coffee shop, a gourmet room, or ordering from room service, the standard gratuity for acceptable service is 15%–20% of the total tab, before sales tax. At a self-serve buffet or brunch, it is customary to leave 5%–10% for the folks who bring your drinks and bus your dishes.

COCKTAIL WAITERS AND BARTENDERS Tip by the round. For two people, $1 a round; for more than two people, $2 a round. For a large group, use your judgment: Is everyone drinking beer or is the order long and complicated? In casinos where drinks are sometimes on the house, it is considered good form to tip the server $1 per round.

DEALERS AND SLOT ATTENDANTS If you are winning, it is a nice gesture to tip the dealer or place a small bet for him. How much depends on your winnings and on your level of play. With slot attendants, tip when they perform a specific service or you hit a jackpot. In general, unless other services are also rendered, it is not customary to tip change makers or cashiers.

KENO RUNNERS Tip if you have a winner or if the runner provides exceptional service. How much to tip will vary with your winnings and level of play.

SHOWROOM MAÎTRE D'S, CAPTAINS, AND SERVERS There is more to this than you might expect. If you are planning to take in a show, see our suggestions for tipping in Part 2, Entertainment and Nightlife on pages 190–192.

HOTEL MAIDS On checking out, leave $3–$5 for each day you stayed (more if you're really messy), providing the service was good.

on page 24.) Downtown it's just as bad, if not worse. We still use the Binion's garage, but to get your ticket validated you have to spend some money. It doesn't have to be much (we usually buy a Coke at the bar). Both on the Strip and Downtown, being a hotel guest or a players club member reduces or eliminates the parking charge.

FENDER BENDERS

CURRENTLY, LAS VEGAS METRO POLICE will respond to non-injury traffic accidents, but it's at the discretion of the drivers involved. If any involved driver believes that police assistance is warranted—for example, if the other driver involved is uncooperative—he can dial 311 to report a non-injury accident and wait for police to respond to the scene. If you have such an accident, and especially if you choose not to call the police, we advise you to take photographs, exchange insurance information, obtain contact info from witnesses, and, if the other driver is agreeable, write a short summary of what happened that both of you sign. If the other driver demurs, write a summary anyway while the facts are fresh in your mind. All of the above information may be helpful to your insurance company.

For the record, Nevada is not a no-fault state, thus liability has to be assigned. Also, auto insurance is mandated in Nevada, but because there are so many out-of-state drivers, you should confirm that your policy has uninsured and under-insured motorist coverage. Finally, the Nevada Division of Insurance has posted tips on its website at doi.nv.gov. Click on "News & Notices" at the top, then click "Press Releases," and scroll way, way down to find the release titled "Nevada Division of Insurance Offers Auto Accident Tips to Las Vegas Drivers."

BRINGING YOUR PET TO LAS VEGAS

FOR THE MOST PART *pet* in Las Vegas means a dog. Various restrictions apply, including weight limitations. Major hotels that welcome pets include **Trump International, Westin Las Vegas, Four Seasons, Delano,** and **Alexis Park Hotel.** The best pet programs can be found at the Caesars Entertainment properties: **Bally's, Caesars Palace, Flamingo, The Cromwell, Harrah's, The LINQ Hotel & Casino, Paris, Planet Hollywood,** and **Rio.** These hotels have set aside specific floors and public areas that are designated as pet-friendly sections. There are on-property pathways and relief areas, as well as grooming, pet sitters and pet walkers, and a directory of on-call veterinarians. Leashed canine guests must check in with their owners and weigh less than 50 pounds. A maximum of two dogs are permitted per room. An amenity package for pooches includes special dishes for food and water, doggie snacks, and comfy sleeping mats. Depending on the hotel, the rate is $25–$100 plus tax per night. Pet stays can be booked at caesars.com or ☎ 800-427-7247.

A list of all Las Vegas hotels that welcome pets can be found at officialpethotels.com and dogfriendly.com.

LAS VEGAS *as a*
FAMILY DESTINATION

LAS VEGAS IS PREDOMINANTLY an adult tourist destination. Casinos are very particular about who's occupying their beds, and the least preferred customers of all are families with children. Children can't gamble, they annoy adults who come to Las Vegas to avoid kids, and they reduce or make impossible the time their parents spend in the casino.

However, if you don't object to being persona non grata, Las Vegas is a great place for a family vacation. Food and lodging are a good value for the dollar, and there are an extraordinary number of things that the entire family can enjoy together. If you take your kids to Las Vegas *and forget gambling,* Las Vegas compares favorably with every family tourist destination in the United States. The rub, of course, is that gambling in Las Vegas is pretty hard to ignore.

Persons under age 21 are not allowed to gamble, nor are they allowed to hang around while *you* gamble. If you are gambling, your children have to be somewhere else. On the Strip and Downtown, the choices are limited. After a short time, you will discover that the current options for your children's recreation and amusement are as follows:

1. You can simply allow your children to hang out. Given this alternative, the kids will swim a little, watch some TV, eat as much as their (or your) funds allow, throw water balloons out of any hotel window that has not been hermetically sealed, and cruise up and down the Strip (or Fremont Street) on foot, ducking in and out of souvenir stores and casino lobbies.

2. If your children are a mature age 10 or older, you can turn them loose at the Adventuredome at Circus Circus. The kids, however, will probably cut bait and go cruising after about an hour or two.

3. You can hire a babysitter to come to your hotel room and tend your children. This works out pretty much like option 1, without the water balloons and the cruising.

4. You can abandon the casino (or whatever else you had in mind) and "do things" with your kids. Swimming and eating (as always) will figure prominently into the plan, as will excursions to places that have engaged the children's curiosity. You can bet that your kids will want to go to the Adventuredome at Circus Circus. The white tigers, dolphins, and exploding volcano at the Mirage; The Forum Shops; and the Stratosphere Tower are big hits with kids. New York–New York features a roller coaster. If you have two children and do a fraction of all this stuff in one day, you will spend $80–$250 for the four of you, not counting meals and transportation.

   If you have a car, however, there are lots of great, inexpensive places to go—enough to keep you busy for days. We recommend Red Rock Canyon and Hoover Dam, for sure. On the way to Hoover Dam, you can stop for a tour of the Ethel M. Chocolate Factory (see page 450 for details).

   A great day excursion (during the spring and fall) is a guided raft trip through the Black Canyon on the Colorado River. This can easily be combined with a visit to Hoover Dam. Trips to the Valley of Fire State Park (driving, biking, hiking) are also recommended during the spring and fall.

Around Las Vegas there are a number of real museums and museums-tourist attractions. The Discovery Children's Museum (adjacent to the Smith Center Downtown) is worthwhile, affordable, and a big favorite with kids age 14 and younger. While you are in the neighborhood, try the Natural History Museum almost directly across the street.

5. You can pay someone else to take your kids on excursions. Some in-room sitters (bonded and from reputable agencies) will take your kids around if you foot the bill. For recommendations, check with the concierge or front desk of your hotel. An organization called **Nannies & Housekeepers U.S.A.** (☎ 702-451-0021; nahusa.com) offers 24/7 in-room babysitting and puts their sitters through a lengthy and rigorous screening; they are the exclusive babysitting agency for many Las Vegas hotels, including Wynn Las Vegas, Wynn Encore, and MGM Grand. If your kids are over age 12, you can send them on one of the guided tours advertised by the various local visitor magazines.

Hotels that Solicit Family Business

Now that Excalibur is out of the family trade, Circus Circus stands alone as the only casino that welcomes children. Circus Circus actively seeks the family market with carnival game midways. A great setup for the casinos, the midways turn a nice profit while innocuously introducing the youngsters to games of chance. In addition, Circus Circus operates the Adventuredome theme park and offers free circus acts each evening, starring top-notch talent, including aerialists (flying trapeze artists).

Parents traveling with children are grudgingly accepted at all of the larger hotels, though certain hotels are better equipped to deal with children than others. If your children are water puppies, Mandalay Bay, Venetian, M Resort, Planet Hollywood, Flamingo, Monte Carlo, MGM Grand, Mirage, Aria, Rio, Tropicana, Caesars Palace, Wynn Las Vegas, Wynn Encore, Bellagio, Red Rock Resort, Green Valley Ranch, and TI have the best pools in town. Westgate Las Vegas, SLS, and Hard Rock Hotel, among others, also have excellent swimming facilities.

If your kids are older and into sports, the MGM Grand, Caesars Palace, Westgate Las Vegas, and Bally's offer the most variety.

For childcare and special programs, The Orleans, Red Rock Resort, Boulder Station, Texas Station, Sunset Station, Santa Fe Station, and Green Valley Ranch provide childcare facilities.

Our favorite hotel for a family vacation is **Green Valley Ranch Resort,** a Station casino and resort about 15 minutes southeast of the Strip. Its location is convenient to Lake Mead, Hoover Dam, the Black Canyon of the Colorado, and Red Rock Canyon, for starters. It has great swimming areas, good restaurants, and lovely guest rooms. And when you want to sneak into the casino or have an adults-only meal, there is a Kids Quest childcare center. Best of all, Green Valley Ranch is isolated. There's no place nearby where your kids can get into trouble (right!).

PART ONE

ACCOMMODATIONS *and* CASINOS

WHERE *to* STAY: *Basic Choices*

LAS VEGAS HAS AN ASTOUNDING INVENTORY of about 150,000 hotel rooms. (Washington, DC, by way of contrast, has 31,000.) Occupancy rates exceed 93% on weekends and average 87.7% for the whole week, compared with a national average of 65.6%. During the Great Recession, a large number of unsold time-shares and condos were added to the city hotel inventory; for the most part these remain, along with a nearly equal number of units available for rent through their owners. **Airbnb** (airbnb.com) is also active in Las Vegas, offering accommodations in private homes. If being near (as opposed to right on) the Strip works for you, there are some great bargains to be had.

THE LAS VEGAS STRIP AND DOWNTOWN

FROM A VISITOR'S PERSPECTIVE, Las Vegas is more or less a small town that's fairly easy to navigate. Most major hotels and casinos are in two areas: **Downtown** or close to the **Strip** (**Las Vegas Boulevard**).

While the Downtown hotels and casinos are generally older and smaller than those on the Strip, a number of large and elegant hotels are located here as well. What mainly differentiates Downtown is the incredible concentration of casinos and hotels in a relatively small area. Along **Fremont Street,** Downtown's main thoroughfare, the casinos present a continuous, dazzling galaxy of neon and twinkling lights for more than four city blocks. Known as "Glitter Gulch," these dozen-plus gambling emporiums stand cheek-by-jowl in colorful profusion in an area barely larger than a parking lot at a good-sized shopping mall.

The Downtown casinos are a wildly varied lot, combining extravagant luxury and sophistication with rowdy Wild West–boomtown decadence. Though not directly comparable, Downtown Las Vegas has the feel of New Orleans's Bourbon Street: alluring, exotic, wicked, and, above all, diverse. Here, cowboy, businessperson, showgirl, and retiree alike mix easily. And, like Bourbon Street, it's all accessible on foot.

If Downtown is the French Quarter of Las Vegas, then the Strip is Plantation Row. Here, huge resort hotel–casinos sprawl like estates along a 4-mile section of Las Vegas Boulevard South. Each property is a destination unto itself, with accommodations, gambling, restaurants, pools, spas, landscaped grounds, and even golf courses.

Although the Strip is technically a specific segment of Las Vegas Boulevard South, the larger surrounding area is usually included when discussing hotels, casinos, restaurants, and attractions. East and parallel to the Strip is **Paradise Road,** where the Las Vegas Convention Center and several hotels are located. Also included in the Strip area are hotels and casinos on streets intersecting Las Vegas Boulevard, as well as properties to the immediate west of the Strip (on the far side of I-15).

CHOOSING A HOTEL

THE VARIABLES THAT FIGURE MOST prominently in choosing a hotel are price, location, your itinerary, and your quality requirements. A vast selection of lodging is available, with myriad combinations of price and value. Given this, your main criteria for selecting a hotel should be (1) its location and (2) your itinerary.

The Strip Versus Downtown for Leisure Travelers

Though some excellent hotels are located elsewhere around town, the choice for most vacation travelers is whether to stay Downtown or on (or near) the Strip. Downtown offers a good choice of hotels, restaurants, and gambling but only a limited choice of entertainment and fewer amenities such as swimming pools and spas.

If you have a car, the Strip is 8–15 minutes from Downtown on I-15; if you don't, public transportation from Downtown to the Strip is affordable and as efficient as traffic allows. If you stay on the Strip, you're more likely to need a car or other transportation: hotels here are spread over a much wider area than hotels Downtown.

On the Strip, one has a sense of space, with many of the hotels constructed on a grand scale. Entertainment is varied and extensive, and recreational offerings rival those of the world's leading resorts.

Downtown is a multicultural, multilingual melting pot with an adventurous, raw, robust feel: an endless blur of action, movement, and light. Diversity and history combine to lend vitality and excitement to this older part of Las Vegas, an essence more tangible and real than the plastic, fantastic themes of many large Strip establishments.

Though both areas run the gamut when it comes to visitors, Downtown has an earthy, working-person ambience: truckers, ranchers, welders, secretaries. In contrast, high rollers, suburbanites, millennials, and business travelers tend to predominate on the Strip.

Downtown: Phoenix Rising

For years, Downtown casinos watched from the sidelines as Strip hotels turned into veritable tourist attractions. There was nothing Downtown to rival the exploding volcano at the Mirage, the theme park at Circus Circus, the pirate battle at Treasure Island (TI), or the view from the Stratosphere Tower. As gambling revenue dwindled and more customers defected to the Strip, Downtown casino owners finally got serious about mounting a counterattack.

That counterattack, the **Fremont Street Experience,** was launched at the end of 1995. Its basic purpose was to transform Downtown into an ongoing event, a continuous party. Fremont Street through the heart of Glitter Gulch was forever closed to vehicular traffic and turned into a park, with terraces, outdoor stage concerts, and landscaping. Transformative events on the ground aside, the main draw of the Fremont Street Experience is, literally, up in the air. Four blocks of Fremont are covered by a 1,400-foot-long, 90-foot-high "space frame"—an enormous, vaulted geodesic matrix that totally canopies Fremont Street. In addition to providing nominal shade, the space frame serves as the stage for a nighttime attraction: set into the inner surface of the space frame are 12.5 million LEDs, which come to life in a multisensory, computer-driven show. The LEDs are augmented by 40 speakers on each block, booming symphonic sound in syncopation with the lights. By creating an aesthetically pleasing environment, Las Vegas–style, the project united all of the casinos in a sort of diverse gambling mall.

Much of Las Vegas's economic and tourist growth has centered on Fremont Street. While politicos have forged ahead with various redevelopment projects throughout the Las Vegas Valley, the most dynamic development is the collective renaissance of hotels in the vicinity of the Fremont Street Experience. Confident of the positive direction in which the area is heading, several aging properties in Downtown's casino corridor have completed extensive revitalizations: The **Plaza** was thoroughly renovated; the **Golden Nugget** added the Rush Tower, with 500 rooms; Fitzgeralds was renamed **The D Las Vegas** and received an exterior face-lift and interior makeover; the **El Cortez** has been updated and added a wing of 64 Cabana Suites; the **Golden Gate** constructed a five-story tower with 100 rooms; and the Lady Luck became the **Downtown Grand Hotel & Casino.** The total number of guest rooms completed is approximately 2,800 in eight properties. Much of these interior–exterior remodels maintain a nostalgic Vegas vibe, but though it continues to glitter, Fremont Street is no longer a gulch.

But in spite of all this, we at the *Unofficial Guide* are appalled by the city's general lack of commitment to improving Downtown's infrastructure, particularly the traffic situation. The market, in terms of aggregate number of gamblers, is undeniably located out on the Strip. To lure this market Downtown is to fight only half the battle—the other half is to make it easy for all those folks on the Strip to get Downtown.

Shut-eye in Sin City: A Caveat About Noise

Both Downtown and on the Strip, street entertainment of various ilks can pose problems for people trying to sleep. On the Strip it's traffic and erupting volcanoes, while Downtown it's a couple of outdoor concert stages plus the soundtrack of the Fremont Street Experience. The noise situation is more problematic Downtown because the hotels are not as tall and many guest room windows lack adequate soundproofing. The stage at the western end of Fremont in particular hosts rock bands that literally rattle the windows of the Plaza, Golden Gate, and to a lesser extent the Golden Nugget. If you stay at one of these hotels and plan to be in the sack before 1 a.m., request a room in the back of the house.

Visiting Las Vegas on Business

If you're going to Las Vegas for a trade show or convention, you will want to lodge as close as possible to the meeting site (ideally within easy walking distance) or, alternatively, near a monorail station. Many Strip hotel-casinos—including the Flamingo, The Venetian, Wynn Las Vegas, Paris, Bellagio, Mandalay Bay, Planet Hollywood, Westgate Las Vegas, Aria, Encore, MGM Grand, TI, Tropicana, Mirage, Caesars Palace, Harrah's, and Bally's—host meetings from 100 to upward of 5,000 attendees, offer lodging for citywide shows and conventions held at the Las Vegas Convention Center and the Sands Expo and Convention Center, and have good track records with business travelers. Our maps will help you figure out which properties are near your meeting site.

Because most large meetings and trade shows are headquartered at the convention center or on the Strip, lodging on the Strip is more convenient than staying Downtown. Citywide conventions often provide shuttle service from the major hotels to the Las Vegas Convention Center, and, of course, cabs, Uber, Lyft, and the monorail are available too. Las Vegas traffic is a mess, however, particularly in the late afternoon.

LARGE HOTEL-CASINOS VERSUS SMALL HOTELS AND MOTELS

LODGING PROPERTIES IN LAS VEGAS range from tiny motels with a dozen rooms to colossal hotel-casino complexes of 5,000 rooms. Determining which size is better for you depends on how you plan to spend your time in Las Vegas.

If your itinerary calls for a car and a lot of coming and going, the big hotels can be a big pain—it can take upwards of 15 minutes to get from your room to your car if you use on-site self-parking. We heard from a young couple staying at the Westgate Las Vegas who left their room 40 minutes before they were to see a show at the Mirage. After trooping to their van in the hotel's remote parking lot, the couple discovered they had forgotten their show tickets. By the time the husband ran back to their room to fetch the tickets and returned to the van, only 5 minutes remained to drive to the Mirage, park, and hustle to the showroom. They ended up missing the first 15 minutes of the performance.

Valet parking is easy to access, with most valet services located just a short walk from the guest elevators—but whether it saves you any time depends on when you retrieve your car. We've waited more than 40 minutes to get our car in the morning, when many guests are checking out or leaving for the day. Valets are also inundated after show performances.

With the advent of hotels and casinos charging set fees for valet parking, it can be an expensive proposition. Over and above the set fee, of course, a tip is still expected.

If you plan to use your car frequently and don't want to deal with the hassles of faraway lots, huge garages, and parking fees/valet tips, choose a small hotel or motel that provides quick and convenient access to your car.

Peace and quiet can also be reasons for choosing a smaller hotel. Many Vegas visitors object to passing through a casino whenever they go to or leave their room. Staying at a smaller property without a casino or a large nongaming property (like the Renaissance Las Vegas) affords an escape from flashing lights and the never-ending noise of slot machines.

The ease of checking in and out of a smaller property has its own appeal. When we visited the registration lobby of one of the larger hotels on a Friday afternoon, it reminded us of JFK Airport during a winter storm. Guests were stacked dozens deep in the check-in lines. Others, having abandoned any hope of registering in the near future, slept curled up around their luggage or sat reading on the floor. The lobby was awash in suitcases, hanging bags, and people milling about. Though hotel size and check-in efficiency are not always inversely related, the sight of a registration lobby fitted out like the queuing area of Disneyland's Jungle Cruise should be enough to make a sane person think twice. To alleviate this issue, Caesars Entertainment properties have installed self check-in kiosks at their Strip hotels (Caesars Palace, Planet Hollywood, Paris, Bally's, Flamingo, and Harrah's), as well as the nearby Rio. They will look familiar if you've used an automated airline boarding pass dispenser; simply scan your driver's license or passport and the oversize ATM will pull up your reservation. You may be given the opportunity to upgrade on the spot, and your room key cards will either be printed for you, or you'll receive electronic notification to return when your room is ready. Travelers can trim their check-in time even further by starting the process online in advance of their arrival if they book through caesars.com or Caesars Play by Total Rewards mobile app. You can't slip these machines a folded bill in hopes of getting a better room, but the lack of human touch will seem worthwhile when you aren't wasting an hour waiting for a desk clerk.

What's more, bigger doesn't necessarily mean better when it comes to room quality—in Las Vegas, you'll find both luxurious and threadbare rooms in properties of every size. On the other hand, larger hotels usually ensure a superior range of amenities in addition to 24/7 gambling and dining, entertainment, and shopping: spas, fitness centers, concierge services, dry cleaning, and the like.

If you spill a Cosmo on your khakis, however, think twice before ponying up for your hotel's laundry service—you'll pay by the piece, which is to say through the nose. Instead, take advantage of a local wash-and-fold service. We like **Wizard of Suds** (4275 Arville St., ☎ 702-873-1453, laundromatinlasvegas.com), where the courteous staff will tend to your dirties for cheap. At $1.49 per pound (10-pound minimum), with quick turnaround if you drop off before noon, it can't be beat.

If you plan to tour mostly on foot, you're attending a convention, or you're a night owl who wants to immerse yourself in the Vegas experience, a large hotel in a good location has advantages. In addition to having the aforementioned amenities close at hand, you can find something fun to do at any hour. Many showrooms offer late-night shows, and quite a few hotels (Sam's Town, Suncoast, Gold Coast, The Orleans, South Point, Red Rock, Texas Station, Sunset Station, and Santa Fe Station) have late-night bowling. **Brooklyn Bowl** at the LINQ, the only bowling complex on the Strip, is open nightly, 5 p.m.–1 or 2 a.m. (3545 Las Vegas Blvd. S., ☎ 702 862-2695, brooklynbowl.com/las-vegas).

WHAT'S *in an* ADDRESS?

DOWNTOWN

THE HEART OF THE DOWNTOWN casino area is "Glitter Gulch," or Fremont Street between Fourth Street (on the east) and Main Street (on the west). Hotel-casinos situated along this four-block stretch include the **Plaza Hotel, Golden Gate, Binion's Gambling Hall, Golden Nugget, Fremont, Four Queens,** and **The D Las Vegas.** Parallel to Fremont and one block north is Ogden Avenue, where the **California** and **Downtown Grand** are located; **Main Street Station** is on the corner of Main Street and Ogden.

All Downtown hotel-casinos are centrally positioned and convenient to the action with the exception of the **El Cortez,** which sits three blocks to the east. While there is a tremendous difference in quality and price among the Downtown properties, the locations of all the hotels are excellent. When you stay Downtown, everything is within a 5-minute walk. By comparison, on the Strip it takes longer to walk from the entrance of Caesars Palace to the entrance of the Mirage, next door, than to cover the whole four blocks of the casino center Downtown.

*un*official **TIP**
Be aware that even in the Mandalay Bay–Stratosphere stretch of the Strip, some sections are more desirable than others.

THE STRIP

WHILE LOCATION ISN'T a major concern when you're choosing a hotel Downtown, it is of paramount importance when you're selecting a hotel on the Strip.

We once received a flier from a casino proclaiming that it was "right on the Strip." The assertion was supported with a photo showing the casino's marquee and those of several other casinos in a neat row with their neon ablaze. If you're not familiar with Las Vegas, however, you'd probably never guess that the photo was taken with a lens that eliminated all sense of distance. While the advertised casino appeared to be next door to the other casinos in the picture, in reality it was almost a mile away.

A common variation on the same pitch is "Stay Right on the Las Vegas Strip at Half the Price!" Again, this is deceptive: unless you live here, what you probably don't know is that the Strip—Las Vegas Boulevard South—starts southwest of the airport and runs all the way Downtown, a distance of about 7 miles. Aside from the South Point Hotel, several miles south of the airport, only the 4-mile section between Mandalay Bay and the Stratosphere composes what visitors think of as the Strip. South of Mandalay Bay are the airport boundary, some small motels, discount shopping, and desert; north of the Stratosphere en route to Downtown, the Strip is sprinkled with wedding chapels, fast-food joints, and more small motels.

The Best Locations on the Strip

Mandalay Bay anchors the south end of the Strip, and at the other end are the **Stratosphere** and the **SLS/W Hotel.** In between are distinct clusters of hotels and casinos.

STRIP CLUSTER 1: THE CLUSTER OF THE GIANTS At the intersection of the Strip and Tropicana Avenue are five of the world's largest hotels. The **MGM Grand Hotel** is the third-largest hotel in the world. Diagonally across the intersection from the MGM Grand is the **Excalibur,** the twelfth-largest hotel in the world. The other two corners of the intersection are occupied by **New York–New York** and the **Tropicana.** Nearby to the south are the **Luxor** (ninth largest) and **Mandalay Bay,** the **Four Seasons,** and the **Delano** (collectively eighth largest). To the north is the **Park MGM/NoMad** on the Strip. **Hooters** is situated on Tropicana Avenue across from the MGM Grand. From the intersection of the Strip and Tropicana Avenue, it's a half-mile walk south to **Mandalay Bay.**

Including all the hotels from Mandalay Bay to the Park MGM/NoMad, Strip Cluster 1 challenges the status, at least in terms of appeal and diversity, of Strip Cluster 3 at the heart of the Strip. Progress always has its dark side, however: in this case, it's the phenomenal increase of traffic and congestion on East Tropicana Avenue as it nears the Strip.

STRIP CLUSTER 2 At Harmon Avenue and the Strip is MRI's **CityCenter,** a mammoth three-hotel lodging, dining, shopping, entertainment, and gaming complex with approximately 6,000 rooms and suites—it's truly a city within a city. Positioned at the northeast corner of CityCenter is the indie **Cosmopolitan**—a bi-towered, 3,027-suite glittering high-rise with full casino, 18 restaurants, three pools, a showroom, and much more. Situated across the Strip from CityCenter and The Cosmo is **Planet Hollywood,** a hip hotel that targets younger Vegas visitors with its shows, nightlife, and restaurants. **Elara,** a Hilton Grand Vacation Club property, rubs shoulders with Planet Hollywood. Planet Hollywood is also attached to the **Miracle Mile Shops.** Collectively, CityCenter, The Cosmopolitan, Elara, and Planet Hollywood compose the most exciting and avant-garde combination on the Strip.

Hotel Clusters

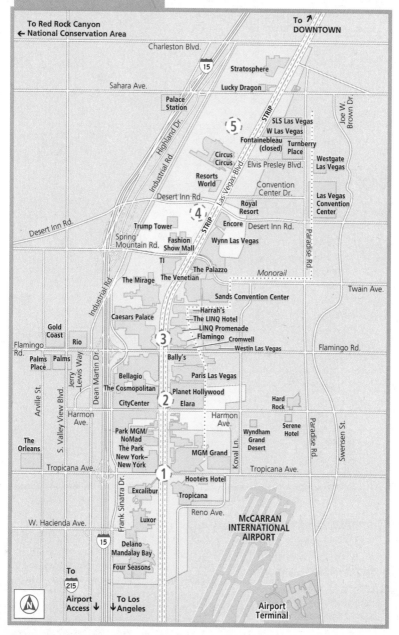

To Red Rock Canyon
← National Conservation Area

To ↗
DOWNTOWN

Charleston Blvd.

15

Stratosphere

Sahara Ave.

Lucky Dragon

Palace
Station

STRIP

5

SLS Las Vegas

W Las Vegas

Fontainebleau
(closed)

Turnberry
Place

Highland Dr.

Circus
Circus

Elvis Presley Blvd.

Westgate
Las Vegas

Industrial Rd.

Resorts
World

Convention
Center Dr.

Desert Inn Rd.

Las Vegas
Convention
Center

Royal
Resort

4

STRIP

Desert Inn Rd.

Trump Tower

Encore

Desert Inn Rd.

Spring
Mountain Rd.

Fashion
Show Mall

Wynn Las Vegas

Las Vegas Blvd.

TI

The Palazzo

Monorail

The Mirage

The Venetian

Twain Ave.

Industrial Rd.

Sands Convention Center

Caesars Palace

Harrah's

The LINQ Hotel

LINQ Promenade

Gold
Coast

Rio

3

Flamingo

Cromwell

Westin Las Vegas

Paradise Rd.

Flamingo Rd.

Flamingo
Rd.

Bally's

Palms
Place

Palms

Jerry

Lewis Way

Dean Martin Dr.

Paris Las Vegas

Bellagio

Arville St.

S. Valley View Blvd.

The Cosmopolitan

Planet Hollywood

2

CityCenter

Elara

Hard
Rock

Harmon
Ave.

Harmon
Ave.

The
Orleans

Park MGM/
NoMad

The Park

New York–
New York

Wyndham
Grand
Desert

Serene
Hotel

Koval Ln.

Paradise Rd.

Swensen St.

MGM Grand

Tropicana Ave.

Frank Sinatra Dr.

1

Tropicana Ave.

Hooters Hotel

Excalibur

Tropicana

Reno Ave.

McCARRAN
INTERNATIONAL
AIRPORT

W. Hacienda Ave.

Luxor

15

Delano

Mandalay Bay

Four Seasons

To
215

Airport
Access ↓

To Los
↓Angeles

Airport
Terminal

Downtown Accommodations

■ **ACCOMMODATIONS**

1. Binion's Gambling Hall
   (Only casino open)
2. California
3. The D
4. Downtown Grand
5. El Cortez
6. El Cortez Cabana Suites
7. Four Queens
8. Fremont
9. Golden Gate
10. Golden Nugget
11. Main Street Station
12. Plaza

STRIP CLUSTER 3: THE GRAND CLUSTER From Flamingo Road to Spring Mountain Road (also called Sands Avenue and, farther east, Twain Avenue) is the greatest numerical concentration of major hotels and casinos on the Strip. At Flamingo Road and Las Vegas Boulevard are

unofficial **TIP**
If you wish to stay on the Strip and prefer to walk wherever you go, Cluster 3 is the best location.

Bally's, Caesars Palace, The Cromwell, Paris, and **Bellagio.** East on Flamingo Road is the **Westin Las Vegas.** Toward town on the Strip are the **Flamingo, O'Shea's, LINQ Hotel & Casino, Mirage, Harrah's, Casino Royale, The Venetian/Palazzo,** and **TI.** Also in this cluster are the posh **Forum**

South Strip Accommodations

■ ACCOMMODATIONS

1. Courtyard by Marriott Las Vegas South
2. Days Inn at Wild Wild West
3. Delano at Mandalay Bay
4. Excalibur
5. Fairfield Inn & Suites Las Vegas South
6. Four Seasons at Mandalay Bay
7. Hampton Inn Tropicana
8. Hilton Garden Inn Las Vegas Strip South
9. Holiday Inn Express
10. Hooters Casino Hotel
11. Luxor
12. M Resort
13. Mandalay Bay
14. Manor Suites
15. MGM Grand
16. New York–New York
17. Orleans
18. Park MGM/NoMad
19. Residence Inn by Marriott Las Vegas South
20. Signature at MGM Grand
21. Silverton
22. South Point
23. Tropicana

Shops and **Grand Canal Shoppes.** A leisure traveler could stay a week in this section (without ever getting in a car or cab) and not run out of interesting sights, restaurants, or entertainment. On the downside, traffic congestion in this cluster is the worst in the city.

STRIP CLUSTER 4 Another nice section of the Strip is from Spring Mountain Road up to **Wynn Encore** and **Wynn Las Vegas.** This cluster, pretty much in the center of the Strip, will also include **Resorts World Las Vegas,** across the Strip from the Wynn resorts. The 3,000-room, Chinese-themed property has not announced a projected opening date. Once open, it will adversely impact Strip traffic between Spring Mountain Road and Convention Center Drive. For the moment, however, visitors

Mid-Strip Accommodations

■ ACCOMMODATIONS

1. Bally's
2. Bellagio
3. Caesars Palace
4. Casino Royale
5. CityCenter
6. The Cosmopolitan
7. The Cromwell
8. Elara
9. Flamingo
10. Gold Coast
11. Harrah's
12. LINQ Hotel & Casino
13. Mirage
14. The Palazzo
15. Palms
16. Paris
17. Planet Hollywood
18. Rio
19. TI
20. The Venetian
21. Westin Las Vegas
22. Wynn Encore
23. Wynn Las Vegas

who prefer a major hotel on the Strip but want to avoid daily traffic snarls couldn't ask for a more convenient location. Though the Wynns are about a quarter mile from the nearest casino cluster in either direction, they are within a 10-minute walk of **Fashion Show Mall,** offering some of the most diverse upscale shopping in the United States. There are also some very good restaurants here, both in the hotels and in the mall. This cluster is a 4-minute cab ride (or a 20-minute walk) from the convention center.

STRIP CLUSTER 5 The next cluster up the Strip is between Convention Center Drive and a bit beyond Sahara Avenue. Arrayed along a stretch slightly more than a half mile long is **Circus Circus** with its Adventure-dome theme park. At the intersection of Las Vegas Boulevard and Sahara Avenue is the **SLS/W Hotel,** on the site of the old Sahara. About a third of a mile north from the SLS/W is the **Stratosphere.** Though fairly isolated if you intend to walk, these hotels provide convenient access to the Strip, the convention center, and Downtown by car or on the monorail.

North Strip Accommodations

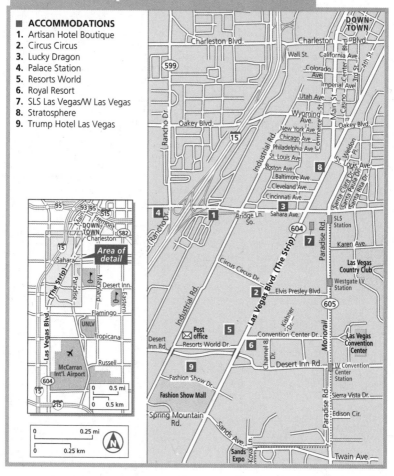

- **■ ACCOMMODATIONS**
1. Artisan Hotel Boutique
2. Circus Circus
3. Lucky Dragon
4. Palace Station
5. Resorts World
6. Royal Resort
7. SLS Las Vegas/W Las Vegas
8. Stratosphere
9. Trump Hotel Las Vegas

JUST OFF THE STRIP

IF YOU HAVE A CAR and being right on the Strip isn't a requirement, there are some excellent hotel-casinos on Paradise Road and to the east and west of the Strip on intersecting roads. Offering exceptional value are the **Rio, Palms,** and **Gold Coast** on Flamingo Road; **Palace Station** and **Lucky Dragon** (currently in Chapter 11) on Sahara Avenue; and **The Orleans** on Tropicana Avenue. All are less than a half mile west of the Strip and are situated at access ramps to I-15, 5–10 minutes from Downtown. To the east of the Strip are the **Hard Rock, Serene, Wyndham Grand Desert,** and **Alexis Park** on Harmon Avenue; the **Tuscany, Silver Sevens,** and **Platinum** on Flamingo Road; and the **Westgate Las Vegas** on Paradise Road, among others.

East of Strip Accommodations

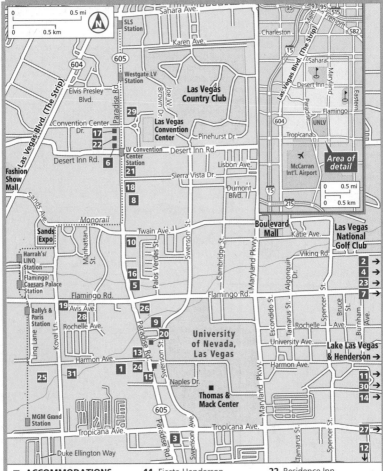

■ ACCOMMODATIONS

1. Alexis Park Resort
   and Villas
2. Arizona Charlie's Boulder
3. Best Western McCarran Inn
4. Boulder Station
5. Candlewood Suites
6. Courtyard by Marriott
7. Eastside Cannery
8. Embassy Suites Convention
   Center
9. Embassy Suites in Las Vegas
10. Fairfield Inn Las Vegas
    Airport

11. Fiesta Henderson
12. Green Valley Ranch
13. Hard Rock Hotel
14. Hilton at Lake Las Vegas
15. Hyatt Place
16. La Quinta Las Vegas
    Airport
17. Las Vegas Marriott
18. Mardi Gras Hotel
    and Casino
19. Platinum Hotel
20. Red Roof Inn
21. Renaissance Las Vegas

22. Residence Inn
    by Marriott LVCC
23. Sam's Town
24. Serene
25. Signature at
    MGM Grande
26. Silver Sevens
27. Sunset Station
28. Tuscany
29. Westgate Las Vegas
30. Westin Lake Las Vegas
31. Wyndham Grand Desert

BOULDER HIGHWAY, GREEN VALLEY, SUMMERLIN, AND NORTH LAS VEGAS

TWENTY MINUTES FROM THE STRIP in North Las Vegas are **Texas Station, Fiesta Rancho,** the **Cannery, Aliante Casino + Hotel,** and, on the edge of civilization, **Santa Fe Station.** All have good restaurants, comfortable guest rooms, and lively, upbeat themes. Hotel-casinos on Boulder Highway southeast of town include **Boulder Station, Sam's Town, Eastside Cannery,** and **Arizona Charlie's Boulder.** Also to the southeast are **Sunset Station, Fiesta Henderson,** and **Green Valley Ranch Resort and Spa.** West of town is the posh **JW Marriott Las Vegas and Rampart Casino,** with two upscale hotels and the Tournament Players Club (TPC) at the Canyons Golf Course. Nearby are the **Suncoast** and the unique **Red Rock Resort.** Also northwest of the Strip is **Arizona Charlie's Decatur.**

GETTING AROUND:
Location and Convenience

LAS VEGAS LODGING CONVENIENCE CHART

THE CHART ON PAGES 42–44 will give you a feel for how convenient specific hotels and motels are to common Las Vegas destinations. Both walking and car-commuting times are figured on the conservative side. You should be able to do a little better than the times indicated, particularly by car, unless you're traveling during rush hour or attempting to navigate the Strip on a weekend evening.

Monorail times listed include loading and unloading as well as the actual commuting times. The Strip monorail stations are located at the far rear of the host casinos, so, for example, the walk from the Strip entrance of the MGM Grand to the station is about 7–10 minutes. The MGM Grand station is the closest station to the Excalibur on the west side of the Strip. From your guest room at the Excalibur, it will take about 25–30 minutes to walk to the MGM Grand station. In our experience, because of the walking required to reach the nearest monorail station from casinos on the Strip's west side, you might want to consider a cab or Uber/Lyft if you're in a hurry. Always check traffic conditions before you hop in a cab—if the Strip is gridlocked (very common), head for the monorail. (*Note:* In this discussion and in the chart on pages 42–44, *cab* encompasses both taxis and ride-sharing services.)

Commuting to Downtown from the Strip

Commuting to Downtown from the Strip is not too bad on I-15 during non–rush hours. From the Strip, you can get on or off I-15 at Tropicana Avenue, Flamingo Road, Spring Mountain Road, or Sahara Avenue. Once on I-15 heading north, stay in the right lane and follow the signs for Downtown and US 95 South. Exiting onto Casino Center Boulevard

Continued on page 44

COMMUTING TIMES IN MINUTES

FROM	TO LAS VEGAS STRIP	TO CONVENTION CENTER	TO DOWNTOWN	TO McCARRAN AIRPORT	TO UNLV THOMAS & MACK CENTER
Alexis Park Resort	5/cab	8/cab	15/cab	5/cab	6/cab
Aliante Casino + Hotel	35/cab	40/cab	25/cab	47/cab	49/cab
Arizona Charlie's Boulder	12/cab	18/cab	12/cab	20/cab	22/cab
Arizona Charlie's Decatur	19/cab	18/cab	12/cab	21/cab	20/cab
Artisan Hotel Boutique	5/walk	5/cab	14/cab	14/cab	14/cab
Atrium Suites	4/cab	6/cab	15/cab	6/cab	6/cab
Bally's	on Strip	8/mono	15/cab	7/cab	7/cab
Bellagio	on Strip	14/cab	15/cab	11/cab	12/cab
Best Western McCarran Inn	6/cab	9/cab	15/cab	4/cab	7/cab
Binion's Gambling Hall	14/cab	15/cab	Downtown	19/cab	19/cab
Boulder Station	19/cab	18/cab	12/cab	21/cab	20/cab
Caesars Palace	on Strip	12/cab	12/cab	10/cab	10/cab
California	13/cab	15/cab	Downtown	19/cab	19/cab
Candlewood Suites	5/cab	6/cab	15/cab	6/cab	6/cab
Cannery	23/cab	26/cab	20/cab	30/cab	30/cab
Casino Royale	on Strip	7/mono	14/cab	10/cab	10/cab
Circus Circus	on Strip	5/cab	13/cab	14/cab	13/cab
CityCenter Hotels	on Strip	12/cab	14/cab	15/cab	11/cab
The Cosmopolitan	on Strip	12/cab	14/cab	15/cab	11/cab
Courtyard Las Vegas South	4/cab	14/cab	15/cab	8/cab	12/cab
Courtyard Paradise Road	4/cab	5/walk	15/cab	9/cab	8/cab
The Cromwell	on Strip	7/mono	15/cab	8/cab	9/cab
The D Las Vegas	14/cab	15/cab	Downtown	17/cab	17/cab
Days Inn at Wild Wild West	3/cab	13/cab	14/cab	8/cab	11/cab
Delano Las Vegas	on Strip	14/cab	15/cab	7/cab	13/cab
Downtown Grand	14/cab	15/cab	4/walk	18/cab	17/cab
Eastside Cannery	20/cab	25/cab	30/cab	19/cab	18/cab
El Cortez	11/cab	15/cab	6/walk	16/cab	17/cab
El Cortez Cabana Suites	11/cab	15/cab	7/walk	16/cab	17/cab
Elara	on Strip	8/cab	15/cab	7/cab	8/cab
Ellis Island	4/cab	6/cab	14/cab	8/cab	8/cab
Embassy Suites Convention Ctr.	6/cab	10/walk	15/cab	9/cab	7/cab
Embassy Suites in Las Vegas	4/cab	6/cab	15/cab	6/cab	6/cab
Excalibur	on Strip	13/cab	14/cab	7/cab	8/cab
Fairfield Inn Las Vegas Airport	5/cab	5/cab	15/cab	9/cab	8/cab
Fairfield Inn and Suites Las Vegas South	4/cab	14/walk	15/cab	8/cab	12/cab
Fiesta Henderson	18/cab	17/cab	19/cab	17/cab	15/cab
Fiesta Rancho	18/cab	18/cab	10/cab	22/cab	22/cab
Flamingo	on Strip	7/mono	13/cab	8/cab	8/cab

Note: By *cab* we mean transportation by taxi, Uber, Lyft, and private automobile.
Mono stands for monorail.

COMMUTING TIMES IN MINUTES (continued)

FROM	TO LAS VEGAS STRIP	TO CONVENTION CENTER	TO DOWNTOWN	TO McCARRAN AIRPORT	TO UNLV THOMAS & MACK CENTER
Four Queens	15/cab	15/cab	Downtown	19/cab	17/cab
Four Seasons	on Strip	14/cab	15/cab	7/cab	13/cab
Fremont	15/cab	15/cab	Downtown	19/cab	17/cab
Gold Coast	4/cab	13/cab	14/cab	10/cab	10/cab
Golden Nugget	14/cab	15/cab	Downtown	18/cab	19/cab
Green Valley Ranch Resort and Spa	15/cab	18/cab	16/cab	15/cab	14/cab
Hampton Inn Tropicana	10/walk	6/cab	9/cab	10/cab	6/cab
Hard Rock Hotel	4/cab	6/cab	15/cab	6/cab	6/cab
Harrah's	on Strip	5/mono	15/cab	10/cab	10/cab
Hilton Garden Inn	13/cab	23/cab	26/cab	14/cab	21/cab
Hilton Lake Las Vegas	45/cab	49/cab	43/cab	37/cab	46/cab
Holiday Inn Express	4/cab	14/cab	15/cab	8/cab	12/cab
Hooters	5/walk	11/mono	15/cab	6/cab	8/cab
Hyatt Place	4/cab	7/walk	15/cab	10/cab	9/cab
JW Marriott Las Vegas	18/cab	21/cab	15/cab	23/cab	24/cab
La Quinta Las Vegas Airport	5/cab	6/cab	15/cab	6/cab	6/cab
Las Vegas Marriott Suites	14/cab	5/walk	15/cab	10/cab	9/cab
LINQ Hotel & Casino	on Strip	5/mono	15/cab	10/cab	10/cab
Lucky Dragon*	4/walk	7/cab	9/cab	14/cab	15/cab
Luxor	on Strip	13/cab	15/cab	8/cab	10/cab
M Resort	20/cab	27/cab	30/cab	22/cab	27/cab
Main Street Station	14/cab	15/cab	Downtown	19/cab	19/cab
Mandalay Bay	on Strip	14/cab	16/cab	7/cab	13/cab
Manor Suites	10/cab	17/cab	20/cab	12/cab	17/cab
Mardi Gras Hotel and Casino	6/cab	10/walk	15/cab	9/cab	7/cab
MGM Grand	on Strip	11/mono	15/cab	9/cab	9/cab
Mirage	on Strip	6/mono	15/cab	11/cab	10/cab
New York-New York	on Strip	11/mono	15/cab	11/cab	12/cab
The Orleans	4/cab	15/cab	14/cab	11/cab	11/cab
Palace Station	4/cab	10/cab	10/cab	14/cab	15/cab
The Palazzo	on Strip	6/mono	14/cab	8/cab	8/cab
Palms	5/cab	13/cab	14/cab	10/cab	10/cab
Paris	on Strip	9/mono	15/cab	8/cab	8/cab
Park MGM/NoMad	on Strip	12/cab	15/cab	11/cab	12/cab
Planet Hollywood	on Strip	8/cab	15/cab	7/cab	8/cab
Platinum Hotel	8/walk	5/cab	17/cab	7/cab	7/cab
Plaza Hotel	14/cab	15/cab	Downtown	19/cab	18/cab
Ramada Las Vegas	5/cab	5/cab	14/cab	8/cab	10/cab
Red Rock Resort	18/cab	21/cab	15/cab	23/cab	24/cab

* Currently in Chapter 11 bankruptcy

COMMUTING TIMES IN MINUTES (continued)

FROM	TO LAS VEGAS STRIP	TO CONVENTION CENTER	TO DOWNTOWN	TO McCARRAN AIRPORT	TO UNLV THOMAS & MACK CENTER
Red Rock Resort	18/cab	21/cab	15/cab	23/cab	24/cab
Red Roof Inn	4/cab	5/cab	15/cab	10/cab	9/cab
Renaissance Las Vegas	5/cab	10/walk	14/cab	9/cab	8/cab
Residence Inn Convention Ctr.	4/cab	6/cab	15/cab	12/cab	12/cab
Residence Inn Las Vegas South	4/cab	14/cab	15/cab	8/cab	12/cab
Resorts World Las Vegas	on Strip	6/cab	9/cab	14/cab	16/cab
Rio	5/cab	14/cab	13/cab	10/cab	10/cab
Royal Resort	3/walk	5/cab	14/cab	13/cab	11/cab
Sam's Town	20/cab	25/cab	20/cab	18/cab	17/cab
Santa Fe Station	27/cab	30/cab	23/cab	33/cab	36/cab
Serene	4/cab	6/cab	15/cab	6/cab	6/cab
Silver Sevens	5/cab	6/cab	15/cab	6/cab	6/cab
Silverton	10/cab	17/cab	20/cab	12/cab	17/cab
SLS Las Vegas/W Las Vegas	on Strip	6/mono	13/cab	13/cab	11/cab
South Point	16/cab	23/cab	26/cab	18/cab	23/cab
Stratosphere	3/cab	7/cab	9/cab	14/cab	14/cab
Suncoast	18/cab	21/cab	15/cab	23/cab	24/cab
Sunset Station	18/cab	17/cab	18/cab	16/cab	15/cab
Texas Station	17/cab	16/cab	13/cab	22/cab	22/cab
TI	on Strip	8/cab	14/cab	11/cab	10/cab
Tropicana	on Strip	11/mono	15/cab	6/cab	9/cab
Tru by Hilton	10/cab	15/cab	22/cab	5/cab	10/cab
Trump Hotel Las Vegas	10/walk	10/cab	11/cab	13/cab	11/cab
Tuscany	5/cab	5/cab	14/cab	8/cab	10/cab
The Venetian	on Strip	6/cab	14/cab	8/cab	8/cab
Westgate Las Vegas	5/mono	5/walk	13/cab	10/cab	8/cab
Westin Lake Las Vegas	45/cab	49/cab	43/cab	37/cab	46/cab
Westin Las Vegas	4/walk	11/mono	15/cab	7/cab	7/cab
Wyndham Grand Desert	10/walk	8/cab	12/cab	7/cab	5/cab
Wynn Encore	on Strip	8/cab	13/cab	10/cab	9/cab
Wynn Las Vegas	on Strip	8/cab	13/cab	10/cab	9/cab

Continued from page 41

will put you in the middle of Downtown, with several large parking garages conveniently at hand. Driving time to Downtown varies from about 16 minutes from the south end of the Strip (I-15 via Tropicana Avenue) to about 6 minutes from the north end (I-15 via Sahara Avenue). I-15, however, is totally overwhelmed during rush hour from 7 to 9 a.m. and 3:30 to 7 p.m. During these hours, you're better off using surface streets.

A major highway construction development, Project Neon, has closed access ramps to northbound US 95 and caused lane closures on the Casino Center exit from southbound US 95. This has rerouted drivers seeking to access I-15 south to the Martin Luther King Boulevard exit off Charleston Boulevard, wreaking havoc during the afternoon rush hour. Road work is projected to last until the summer of 2019 but will probably last longer. An 81-foot-tall, high-occupancy vehicle flyover bridge from southbound US 95 to southbound I-15 and a widening of a 3.7-mile stretch of I-15 between Sahara Avenue and the Downtown intersection of I-15, US 95, US 93, and I-515, known as the Spaghetti Bowl, are key elements of the project. Other work includes the creation of a diamond interchange at I-15 and Charleston Boulevard.

If Project Neon has I-15 North snarled up, your best bet may be to commute via surface streets. If your hotel is on the east side of the Strip, go east, turning left (north) onto Swenson Street. Continue straight on Swenson. Crossing East Desert Inn Road, Swenson becomes Joe W. Brown, which intersects Sahara Avenue. Turn left onto Sahara, staying in the far-right lane. From there, turn right (north) onto Las Vegas Boulevard South to Downtown. If you are staying on the west side of the Strip, take Industrial Road (which runs behind the west Strip hotels), turning right on West Wyoming Road. After several blocks turn left onto Las Vegas Boulevard South and proceed Downtown.

There are 10 or more apps designed to alert you to traffic problems and to find alternative routes. For a good list of apps with commentary on each, see apppicker.com/applists/23756/the-best-iphone-apps-for-traffic-information.

Commuting to the Strip from Downtown

If you're heading to the Strip from Downtown, you can pick up US 95 North (and then I-15 South) by going north on either Fourth Street or Las Vegas Boulevard. Driving time from Downtown to the Strip takes 10–20 minutes, depending on your destination. Once again, be mindful of the road construction described above. If I-15 is gridlocked, take Las Vegas Boulevard South to the Strip.

Free Connections

Traffic on the Strip is so awful that the hotels, both individually and in groups, have created alternatives for getting around, as follows:

1. On the west side, a shuttle tram serves the Excalibur, Luxor, Mandalay Bay, Four Seasons, and the Delano.
2. Coast Casinos operates a shuttle connecting the Gold Coast, The Orleans, and the LINQ.
3. M Resort provides shuttle service to and from the airport and Tropicana.
4. A tram connects the Spa Tower of the Bellagio to the Park MGM/NoMad with an intermediate stop at Crystals shopping complex at CityCenter.
5. A tram connects TI and the Mirage, though the hike to the tram takes more time than to commute back and forth on the Strip.
6. The Palms has shuttle service to Caesars Palace and the Forum Shops from 11 a.m. to 6 p.m.

7. Rampart Casino runs a shuttle to and from Fashion Show Mall.

8. Red Rock Resort provides shuttles to and from the airport and to Fashion Show Mall.

9. Sam's Town provides shuttles to the Strip and Downtown.

10. The Silverton provides shuttles to the airport and Aria.

LAS VEGAS MONORAIL

THE LAS VEGAS MONORAIL runs the 4-mile route between the MGM Grand and the SLS Las Vegas. The route parallels the Strip between Tropicana and Sands Avenues and then cuts east to the Las Vegas Convention Center and Westgate Las Vegas before continuing to the last stop at the SLS/W Hotel. Trains run about every 10 minutes between 7 a.m. and midnight on Monday, until 2 a.m. Tuesday–Thursday, and until 3 a.m. on weekends. Riding from one end of the line to the other takes about 15 minutes and includes seven stops. The fare for a one-way ride is $5; a better deal is a one-day fare (24 hours from first use) at $14 or a three-day unlimited fare for $30. Check lvmonorail.com for special rates. The monorail is a godsend to convention and trade-show attendees commuting from Strip hotels to the Las Vegas Convention Center and the Sands Exposition Center.

unofficial **TIP**
Because monorail stations are located at the extreme rear of the casinos served, you're better off walking to your destination if you're traveling less than a mile.

COMMONLY USED PUBLIC-TRANSPORTATION ROUTES				
	ROUND-TRIP FROM/TO	**HOURS OF OPERATION**	**FREQUENCY OF SERVICE**	**FARE**
MONORAIL	MGM Grand/SLS and W Hotel	Mon., 7 a.m.–midnight; Tues.–Th., 7 a.m.-2 a.m.; (3 a.m. weekends)	Every 5 minutes	$5
RTC DEUCE LINE	South Strip Transfer Terminals/Downtown Transportation Center	24/7	Every 12 minutes	$3

BUSES

THE REGIONAL TRANSPORTATION COMMISSION of Southern Nevada (**RTC**) provides reliable bus service at reasonable rates. Although one-way fares along the Strip are $6 for the double-decker Deuce, one-way fares in residential areas are just $3. An all-day pass for the Strip costs $8, and an all-day pass for residential areas is $5. The pass is good for 24 hours from the time of purchase. Exact fare is required; children ages 5 and under ride free. RTC buses are equipped with wheelchair lifts and bicycle racks, both provided free. Disabled persons who are certified in their home state for door-to-door service should call ☎ 702-676-1834 or 702-228-4800 for reservations; those not certified in their home state are ineligible for door-to-door service in Las Vegas. For general route and fare information or to request a schedule through the mail, call ☎ 702-228-7433 or visit rtcsnv.com/transit.

THE LIGHTS OF LAS VEGAS: TRAFFIC ON THE STRIP

DURING THE PAST DECADE, Las Vegas has experienced exponential growth—growth that, unfortunately, hasn't been matched by the development of necessary infrastructure. Imagine a town designed for about 300,000 people being inundated by a million or so refugees (all with cars), and you have a sense of what's happening here.

The Strip, where a huge percentage of the local population works and where more than 80% of tourists and business travelers stay, has become a clogged artery in the heart of the city. The heaviest traffic on the Strip is between Tropicana Avenue and Spring Mountain Road, in the heart of the Strip. Throughout the day and night, local traffic combines with gawking tourists, shoppers, and cruising teenagers to create a 3-mile-long, bumper-to-bumper bottleneck.

"The lights of Las Vegas" used to refer to the marquees of the casinos. Today, however, it means the long, multifunctional traffic lights found at most every intersection on the Strip. These lights, which flash a different signal for every possible turn and direction, combine with an ever-increasing number of vehicles to ensure that nobody goes anywhere. The worst snarls occur at the intersection of the Strip and Flamingo Road; trying to cross the Strip on perpendicular east-to-west-running roads is also exceedingly difficult.

Desert Inn Road, which tunnels under the Strip, is the fastest way to get from one side to the other. Unfortunately, if you're heading west, Desert Inn Road is hard to access on the east side of the Strip, especially from Paradise Road. To use the tunnel from the east side, turn west on Desert Inn Road from Swenson Street.

Strip traffic is the Achilles heel of Las Vegas development and growth. While the city and the hospitality industry dance around the issue, traffic gets worse and worse. Some 48,000 hotel rooms were added along the Strip during the 1990s, about 30,000 more have come online since 2000, and another 10,000 or more are planned or under way.

The monorail, while a great alternative to driving, has not noticeably relieved gridlock; plus, stations are positioned so far to the rear of the casinos that walking is faster than taking the train for distances up to one mile. In another effort, I-15 between Downtown and the I-215 junction to the south has been widened and the interchanges improved. Again, while welcome, that project has done little to alleviate traffic, and another major road work project, not to be completed until 2019, is causing mayhem on I-15 and at the Spaghetti Bowl intersection Downtown. Interestingly, the only initiative that has worked is the construction of elevated pedestrian bridges over the major Strip intersections. In addition to improving safety, the bridges remove pedestrians from the street, leaving the battlefield to vehicles.

Coping with Las Vegas Traffic

Even more challenging than beating the casinos in Las Vegas is beating the traffic. As it stands, visitors have few good alternatives for getting around, and there are lots of places you'll want to avoid.

NORTH–SOUTH ROADS TO KNOW

Las Vegas Boulevard South Connects the Strip to Downtown Las Vegas. Avoid between Tropicana Avenue and Spring Mountain Road.

I-15 Avoid between the I-15/I-215 interchange and Downtown.

Swenson Street/Joe W. Brown Drive Best north–south alternative on the east side of the Strip. Runs from the airport to East Sahara Avenue.

Paradise Road Tends to clog between the Las Vegas Convention Center and Twain Avenue. Good north–south alternative south of Twain. Leads directly to the airport.

Koval Lane Avoid between Twain and Tropicana Avenues 3–8:30 p.m.

Dean Martin Drive Best north–south alternative on the west side of the Strip.

Frank Sinatra Drive Parallels I-15 and the Strip and offers easy access to some hotels on the west side of the Strip.

South Main Street Low-traffic alternative for commuting Downtown from the Strip. Intersects Las Vegas Boulevard South at East St. Louis Avenue near the Stratosphere.

We at the *Unofficial Guide* feel the impact directly when we conduct our research in Las Vegas. Where once we required about 5–20 minutes to go from one Strip hotel to another by car, we now allocate over an hour. If our destination is a mile or less away, we just walk.

When you plan your Vegas visit, it's essential to get a handle on how much moving around will be necessary. The most stress-free trip is one where you can walk anywhere you need to go. Choose a hotel near the restaurants, shows, and attractions you wish to experience. If you're attending a convention or trade show, stay at a hotel within easy walking distance of the convention center, at one of the hotels on the east side of the Strip connected to the Las Vegas Monorail, or at a hotel such as Wynn Las Vegas or Wynn Encore that provides a free shuttle service.

If you're thinking you can lodge on the west side of the Strip and walk across the street to catch the monorail, think again. The average time to walk from the main elevator bank of a west-side Strip hotel to an east-side monorail station is 30 minutes or more. It takes a comparable amount of time to walk from an east-side hotel that doesn't have a monorail station to one that does.

If you're like us and need to use a car, you're probably better off at one of the hotels on the west side of the Strip or, alternatively, one of the off-Strip properties (more about those later). Either way, you'll need to study a map of Las Vegas and familiarize yourself with the road network surrounding the Strip (see our map on page 51).

If your visit centers around the Strip, here are the key roads to avoid and roads that will make getting around easier:

LAS VEGAS BOULEVARD SOUTH (THE STRIP) The worst traffic on the Strip occurs from Tropicana Avenue north to Spring Mountain Road (Twain Avenue). Avoid this stretch whenever possible. North of Spring Mountain, traffic on Las Vegas Boulevard South flows pretty smoothly all the way to Downtown except for where it crosses Sahara Avenue.

EAST-WEST ROADS TO KNOW

Sahara Avenue Usually congested at the intersection with the Strip. Otherwise fine.

Desert Inn Road Tunnels under the Strip. Best road for commuting to the west side from the east side and vice versa.

Twain Avenue/Spring Mountain Road Crosses the Strip at one of the more efficient intersections.

Harmon Avenue Currently T-intersects the Strip and doglegs into CityCenter and then crosses over I-15 to the west side.

Flamingo Road Extremely congested westbound at the intersection with the Strip. **Avoid.**

Tropicana Avenue Flows well except westbound at the intersection with the Strip.

I-215 Westbound, avoid the I-15 North exit.

I-15 The main north–south freeway, I-15 stays jammed from the I-215 interchange south of Las Vegas to the US 95 interchange near Downtown. Avoid this section between 7 and 10 a.m. and from 2:45 until 7:15 p.m. Even during nonrush periods, traffic moves at a crawl, but at least it moves. Between 8:30 p.m. and 6:30 a.m. is the least congested period of the day. If you use I-15 during daylight hours, your best bet is to stay in the right lanes so you can bail at the next exit if necessary.

SOUTH DEAN MARTIN DRIVE AND FRANK SINATRA DRIVE The best alternate north–south route on the west side of the strip is South Dean Martin Drive, which becomes Industrial Road after it passes under the interstate highway to the east side of I-15 at West Twain Avenue. Dean Martin Drive/Industrial Road closely parallels the Strip and I-15 and is the best choice for accessing Circus Circus, Adventuredome, Trump Las Vegas, Fashion Show Mall, CityCenter and The Cosmopolitan (via Jerry Lewis Way and West Harmon Avenue), and Excalibur, Luxor, and Mandalay Bay (including Four Seasons and the Delano) via Aldebaran Avenue and West Hacienda Avenue.

You can likewise easily access TI and the Mirage by taking Mel Torme Way east from Industrial Road, and Caesars Palace and the Forum Shops by taking Frank Sinatra Drive off Industrial Road to Jay Sarno Way.

Dean Martin Drive/Industrial Road is also the best way to access east–west streets, including Sahara Avenue, Spring Mountain Road, Flamingo Road, and Tropicana Avenue. An easy route Downtown is Industrial Road north turning east (right) on Wyoming Road and then north again on South Main Street or Las Vegas Boulevard South.

Frank Sinatra Drive can be accessed from I-15 northbound, West Russell Road, and Industrial Road. Running north–south directly behind hotels situated on the west side of the Strip, it provides easy access to self-parking at Mandalay Bay/Delano, Luxor, Excalibur, Park MGM/NoMad, Caesars, and Fashion Show Mall. It does *not* provide public access to New York–New York, CityCenter, The Shops at Crystals, The Cosmopolitan, or Bellagio. Frank Sinatra Drive is a main thoroughfare for Strip hotel employees to access employee parking lots and becomes very congested between 7:30–9:30 a.m. and 2:30–5:30 p.m., when hotel shift changes occur.

SWENSON STREET On the east side of the Strip, the traffic situation is more complex. Although a half mile or more from the Strip, Swenson Street is the most free-flowing north–south traffic artery east of the Strip. Swenson runs from I-215 and the airport all the way north to East Sahara Avenue; the name changes to Joe W. Brown Drive after crossing Desert Inn Road. If you're driving north, you can take Swenson/Joe W. Brown for its full length. Going south, you'll be diverted to Paradise Road, a block to the west, as Swenson becomes one-way northbound between the airport and Harmon Avenue and Paradise Road becomes one-way southbound from Harmon to the airport.

KOVAL LANE Slightly to the west and running parallel to Swenson Street and Paradise Road, Koval Lane was once great for dodging Strip traffic. Now it's gridlocked except during nonrush periods. This is unfortunate, as Koval links roads providing rear access to parking at the MGM Grand, Flamingo, LINQ Hotel & Casino, Harrah's, and The Venetian.

Smaller streets joining Koval to the garages remain largely free of congestion, but on Koval you're likely to get stuck on the section from Tropicana Avenue north to Twain Avenue. Afternoons from 3 to about 8:30 p.m., Koval is especially bad. During this period, your best bet for reaching the valet or self-parking areas of the hotels mentioned above is to access Harmon Avenue westbound from Swenson or Paradise, cross Koval, and then turn right on Linq Lane. Coming out of the garages onto Linq will frequently land you in some congestion at the Linq–Harmon intersection, but suffering three cycles of the traffic signal is about as bad as it gets. Finally, adding to the congestion, the LINQ entertainment and shopping complex has its own parking lot accessible from Koval between Flamingo and Twain.

THE TUNNEL An extension of Paradise Road tunnels under the airport runways and connects to I-215 and beyond to the rental-car return center. The approach to the tunnel gets really jammed between 2:45 and 6:30 p.m., so if you're returning a rental car during those hours, give yourself extra time. An alternative, particularly if you're coming from west of the Strip, is to take Dean Martin Drive to Warm Springs Road. Turn east (left) on Warm Springs, cross I-15, and proceed four big blocks to Gilespie Street. Go left at Gilespie to the rental car center. If you're coming west from Green Valley or Henderson on I-215, taking the tunnel northbound to Swenson Street is a better way to reach Strip destinations than continuing to I-15 northbound.

Other Considerations

Coming and going at Strip hotels is a pain in the patootie, with traffic congestion, as previously discussed, being the main culprit. It's a lamentable fact that the Strip, or, more properly, Las Vegas Boulevard South,

Best Routes to Avoid Traffic Congestion

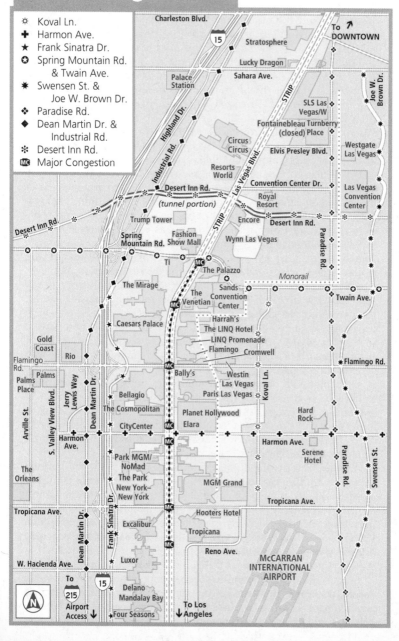

- ☼ Koval Ln.
- ✚ Harmon Ave.
- ★ Frank Sinatra Dr.
- ✪ Spring Mountain Rd. & Twain Ave.
- ✳ Swensen St. & Joe W. Brown Dr.
- ❖ Paradise Rd.
- ◆ Dean Martin Dr. & Industrial Rd.
- ✳ Desert Inn Rd.
- Ⓜ Major Congestion

Charleston Blvd.

15

Stratosphere

To ↗ DOWNTOWN

Lucky Dragon

Palace Station

Sahara Ave.

SLS Las Vegas/W

Joe W. Brown Dr.

Highland Dr.

STRIP

Fontainebleau Turnberry (closed) Place

Circus Circus

Elvis Presley Blvd.

Westgate Las Vegas

Resorts World

Las Vegas Blvd.

Convention Center Dr.

Industrial Rd.

Desert Inn Rd.

(tunnel portion)

Royal Resort

Las Vegas Convention Center

Desert Inn Rd.

Trump Tower

STRIP

Encore

Desert Inn Rd.

Spring Mountain Rd.

Fashion Show Mall

Wynn Las Vegas

Paradise Rd.

TI

Ⓜ

The Palazzo

Monorail

Twain Ave.

The Mirage

Sands Convention Center

The Venetian

Ⓜ

Caesars Palace

Harrah's

The LINQ Hotel

LINQ Promenade

Flamingo Cromwell

Gold Coast

Rio

Flamingo Rd.

Palms

Ⓜ

Bally's

Westin Las Vegas

Koval Ln.

Flamingo Rd.

Palms Place

Jerry Lewis Way

Dean Martin Dr.

Paris Las Vegas

Arville St.

S. Valley View Blvd.

Bellagio

The Cosmopolitan

Planet Hollywood Elara

Hard Rock

Harmon Ave.

CityCenter

Ⓜ

Harmon Ave.

Serene Hotel

The Orleans

Park MGM/ NoMad

The Park New York– New York

MGM Grand

Paradise Rd.

Swensen St.

Tropicana Ave.

Frank Sinatra Dr.

Ⓜ

Hooters Hotel

Tropicana Ave.

Dean Martin Dr.

Excalibur

Tropicana

Reno Ave.

W. Hacienda Ave.

Ⓜ

Luxor

McCARRAN INTERNATIONAL AIRPORT

N

To **215** Airport Access ↓

15

Delano Mandalay Bay

Four Seasons

To Los ↓ Angeles

stays in a perpetual state of gridlock. This is especially true of the 2 miles between Tropicana and Spring Mountain Road, with the balled-up epicenter right in the middle at the intersection of the Strip and Flamingo Road. If your hotel is anywhere along this stretch, exploring Las Vegas beyond walking distance is only slightly less troublesome than losing your luggage. Most visitors staying in the affected area simply choose to stay put, missing much of what Las Vegas has to offer.

From this part of the Strip, escaping the gaming ghetto in your rental ride is not easily accomplished. In and out is easier at hotels on the west side of the Strip, owing to the network of side streets previously described. The east side of the Strip is not as blessed. Here, from your hotel's rear or side exit, you have to navigate a maze of tiny roads from which you can make your way to Flamingo Road or north–south Koval Lane, which has its own gridlock issues. Linq Lane makes things less complicated but still not easy.

If you plan to tour the Las Vegas area by car, your best bet is to avoid this part of the Strip altogether, but if you feel you must be in the middle of the action, coming and going is easier from hotels on the west side. For each side of the Strip, the goal is to exit the property to its rear or side rather than getting on Las Vegas Boulevard South.

Other factors make coming and going challenging. One is the complexity of hotel self-parking garages: if Stanley had been trying to locate Dr. Livingstone in self-parking at The Venetian, he never would have found him. Most parking structures are multistory affairs arranged in a labyrinth of crisscrossing lanes and confusing ramps. Upon entering the garage, you'll notice dozens of exit signs. Upon departing, when you need them, you won't see any. Some properties, such as the MGM Grand, are so large that you exit the garage into a spaghetti tangle of interior roads from which you must find your way to some thoroughfare you've actually heard of.

Other points of confusion are legion. For example, when self-parking at The Cromwell, on the corner of the Strip and Flamingo Road, you are somehow shunted into the garage at the Flamingo. Here's a tip: to locate your car when you're ready to depart, drop pebbles after parking to mark your route into the casino. Alternatively, hope the rental company can find the car when you can't.

Another factor is the distance from your room to the self-parking garage or lot. Believe us, it can be quite a hike, sometimes taking as much as 15–20 minutes of winding through shops and the casino to reach self-parking. Hotels where you really hope you didn't leave something necessary in your room include the **MGM Grand, Excalibur, Vdara, Caesars Palace, Bally's, Planet Hollywood, Cromwell, Rio, Venetian, Palazzo, Westgate, and Mandalay Bay,** as well as, to a lesser extent, the **Mirage, TI, SLS/W Hotel, Circus Circus,** and **Park MGM/NoMad.**

Easy access to self-parking can be found at the **Cosmopolitan, Wynn, Encore, Tropicana,** and **Bellagio** (though here you must enter and exit via the Strip). In all cases, the location of your room in a particular hotel can add or subtract 10 minutes or more.

Many non-Strip hotels make good jumping-off points for exploration. You can't beat **Green Valley Ranch,** southeast of the Strip, if Lake Mead, the Colorado River, or Hoover Dam is on your agenda. Green Valley Ranch (greenvalleyranch.sclv.com) is only a 10-minute drive from the Strip but feels like a different world. **Red Rock Resort** (redrock.sclv.com), with eye-popping views of Red Rock Canyon and the Las Vegas valley, is primo for bikers, climbers, hikers, golfers, and road trippers who want to enjoy the unique features of the high-desert canyon land. Not far away and less pricey is the **Suncoast** (suncoast casino.com), surrounded by golf courses and sporting floor-to-(almost)-ceiling windows with superb vistas of the mountains. Also on the west side and plopped in a golfer's Eden is the **Rampart Casino at The Resort at Summerlin** (theresortatsummerlin.com). Though golf is king, Summerlin is also home to a burgeoning lineup of great restaurants and is known as a top Las Vegas shopping destination. At the intersection of Blue Diamond Road and I-15 is the **Silverton** (silverton casino.com), providing ideal access to Cottonwood Valley for mountain biking and hiking, several attractions, and, a bit to the north, Red Rock Canyon National Conservation Area. As a kicker, the Silverton has a Bass Pro Shop with enough dead animals decorating the store to fill an ark. It's great selfie territory.

Parking

VALET PARKING All Strip hotels offer both valet and self-parking. The majority of hotels on the Strip now charge a set fee for valet parking (see the chart on page 56). Some fees cover the whole day and others a specific duration, for example four hours. It's an outright money grab that most hotels are latching onto. And, yes, you're still expected to tip. In most instances hotel guests and players club members get a discounted rate.

Many hotels provide valet service at both the front and rear entrances. As a general rule, the hotel's main entrance will be busier than the rear entrance. The problem with main-entrance valet service is that you will probably exit onto the traffic of the Strip. With rear-entrance valet, you usually have the option to exit onto a side street. Though most valet services are pretty efficient, they do get swamped from time to time, such as when a show or concert has just concluded or in the morning when folks are checking out.

SELF-PARKING With the exceptions of the Bellagio and New York–New York, self-parking is easier at the hotels on the west side of the Strip. At any parking garage, don't park until you've found the garage entrance to the casino or the elevators leading to it. This can be tricky because some elevators deliver you to a walkway or sidewalk on the ground level quite removed from the casino. Staying oriented in such large garages is challenging, but what you want to do is park as close as possible to the most direct entrance to the hotel or casino. There are always elevators, so it doesn't really matter on which level you park, as long as you're near the casino entrance or the elevators that descend to

SELF-PARKING, East Strip

HOTELS ON THE EAST SIDE OF THE STRIP *(north–south)*

WYNN ENCORE Use self-parking garage off the Strip. You can access the hotel elevators, casino, and showrooms from self-parking faster than by using the valet service.

WYNN LAS VEGAS Use self-parking garage off the Strip for the reasons above.

THE VENETIAN/PALAZZO Very confusing self-parking garage. There is rear access from Koval Lane and front access from the Strip. Both are subject to congestion. Park at Wynn Las Vegas or Fashion Show Mall and walk to The Venetian, or use valet parking.

HARRAH'S Straightforward garage. To access it, drive west on Harmon Avenue, then right on Linq Lane and left on Winnick Avenue.

THE LINQ Somewhat confusing but linear. To access it, drive west on Harmon Avenue, then right on Linq Lane and left on Winnick Avenue.

FLAMINGO Confusing garage layout. Park at Harrah's and walk to the Flamingo.

THE CROMWELL Self-parking garage off Flamingo Road. Hard to access because traffic waiting for the light at Flamingo and the Strip blocks the entrance.

BALLY'S Drive east on Harmon Avenue and then left on Linq Lane to the garage.

PARIS Drive east on Harmon Avenue and then left on Linq Lane to the garage.

PLANET HOLLYWOOD Very confusing garage accessible from Harmon Avenue. After parking you must walk through the Miracle Mile Shops to reach the hotel.

MGM GRAND Parking is accessible via Tropicana Avenue westbound or off Koval Lane. Very difficult to exit onto Koval Lane. To exit go north on Linq Lane out of the garage and take the first left (west) to the Strip.

TROPICANA Go west on Tropicana Avenue, then left on Koval Lane and right on Reno Avenue. Large outdoor parking lot plus parking garage. Easy access by foot to Excalibur, MGM Grand, and New York–New York.

it. Our experience is that close-in parking spots are most readily available on the second to highest level. If a garage has five levels, for example, you're more likely to find available close-in spots on level four than on the other levels. Some of the garages are huge, so always jot down the level and row where you've parked. We should note that all of the hotels listed in the self-parking chart above have Strip parking and valet entrances *except* Park MGM/NoMad, New York–New York, MGM Grand, Bally's, and The Cromwell. The objective of this chart is to help you avoid Strip traffic by accessing the hotels (where possible) from other streets.

SELF-PARKING DOWNTOWN We always park at **Binion's** garage on Casino Center Drive, between Stewart and Ogden Avenues. It's centrally located and rarely crowded. You have to play or buy something (a Coke, for example) to have your ticket punched at Binion's cashier's cage.

YOU KNEW IT WAS COMING Irrespective of how hated resort fees are, hotels bludgeon us with them anyway. The latest ancillary charge: paid parking. In 2017, MRI resorts, Caesars Entertainment hotels, the Cosmopolitan, and others began charging for self- and valet parking (tip extra). There are different rates for hotel guests, loyalty-program members, and nonresident guests. As usual, the stated rationale is to "enhance the guest experience." The outcry has been immediate and

SELF-PARKING, West Strip

HOTELS ON THE WEST SIDE OF THE STRIP (north-south)

CIRCUS CIRCUS Large outdoor lot and garages accessible from Industrial Road.

FASHION SHOW MALL Garage near the Strip is an excellent place to park if you're going to Wynn Las Vegas, The Palazzo, The Venetian, or TI. Enter from Spring Mountain Road or West Fashion Show Drive. Work your way to the southeast corner of the garage near the Neiman Marcus valet entrance. Along the wall that borders the Strip, look for a green, grassy area and stairs leading up to the Strip.

TI Very straightforward garage—among the most convenient on the Strip. Best access is via Spring Mountain Road.

MIRAGE Access also off Spring Mountain Road. A little convoluted, but just follow the signs.

FORUM SHOPS From Industrial Road, go south on Frank Sinatra Drive and then turn left on Jay Sarno Way.

CAESARS PALACE From Industrial Road, go south on Frank Sinatra Drive and then turn left on Jay Sarno Way.

BELLAGIO The only way to access the Bellagio is via the Strip. Valet service is good here, though. Just don't get caught when half the audience from Cirque du Soleil's "O" suddenly appears at the valet claim desk.

CITYCENTER AND THE COSMOPOLITAN From Dean Martin Drive, turn west on Jerry Lewis Way, then left on West Harmon. Don't be surprised if they rename this section of West Harmon CityCenter Drive or some such.

PARK MGM Take Frank Sinatra Drive to Park Avenue.

EXCALIBUR Excalibur has some of the most distant, far-flung parking of any hotel in Las Vegas. The closest parking is off East Reno Avenue or in the south end of the parking garage at Luxor Drive and East Reno. Luxor Drive is accessible via Dean Martin Drive, then west on Aldebaran Avenue, then right (east) on West Hacienda Avenue (West Mandalay Bay Drive), and finally left on Luxor Drive.

LUXOR This is one of our favorite parking garages. Park on the top level. Take Dean Martin Drive, then go west on Aldebaran Avenue, then right (east) on West Hacienda Avenue (West Mandalay Bay Drive), and finally left on Luxor Drive.

MANDALAY BAY Take Dean Martin Drive, then go west on Aldebaran Avenue, then right (east) on West Hacienda Avenue (West Mandalay Bay Drive), and finally right on Luxor Drive.

deafening, but so far, has fallen on deaf ears. See our chart on the following page for a listing of parking fees for Strip hotels.

Free self-parking can still be found on the Strip, and valet parking is also free at the following properties except for a tip: Casino Royale, The Palazzo, SLS, Stratosphere, TI, Tropicana, Trump Tower, and The Venetian. A good way to beat parking fees is to park at a nearby shopping venue with free valet parking and walk to your final destination. These include Crystals, Fashion Show Mall (also free parking in surface lots and garage), and Miracle Mile Shops.

Free parking within easy walking distance of the Strip is available at Hooters, Royal Resort, and Westin Las Vegas. Free parking is also available at the following properties, which are more distant to the Strip but also provide free shuttle service to the Strip: Gold Coast, JW Marriott (Rampart Casino), M Resort, The Orleans, Sam's Town, and Silverton. The Rio offers free parking but no shuttle.

PARKING FEES FOR STRIP HOTELS

ARIA Self-parking: $9 for 1-2 hours; $15 for 2-4 hours; $18 for 4-24 hours. Valet parking: $21 for up to 2 hours; $24 for 2-4 hours; $30 for 4-24 hours.

BALLY'S Self-parking: $9 for 1-4 hours; $12 for 4-24 hours; $12 per day after the first 24 hours. Valet parking: $15 for up to 4 hours; $20 for 4-24 hours; $20 per day after the first 24 hours.

BELLAGIO Self-parking: $9 for 1-2 hours; $15 for 2-4 hours; $18 for 4-24 hours. Valet parking: $21 for up to 2 hours; $24 for 2-4 hours; $30 for 4-24 hours.

CAESARS PALACE Self-parking: $12 for 1-4 hours; $15 for 4-24 hours; $15 per day after the first 24 hours. Valet parking: $18 for up to 4 hours; $23 for 4-24 hours; $23 per day after the first 24 hours.

CIRCUS CIRCUS Self-parking: The only MGM Resorts' hotel-casino that doesn't charge for self-parking. Valet parking: $10 for up to 4 hours; $15 for 4-24 hours.

COSMOPOLITAN Self-parking: $7 for 1-4 hours; $10 for 4-24 hours; $10 per day after the first 24 hours. Valet parking: $13 for up to 4 hours; $18 for 4-24 hours; $18 per day after the first 24 hours.

THE CROMWELL Self-parking: $9 for 1-4 hours; $12 for 4-24 hours; $12 per day after the first 24 hours. Valet parking: $15 for up to 4 hours; $20 for 4-24 hours; $20 per day after the first 24 hours.

DELANO Self-parking: $9 for 1-2 hours; $12 for 2-4 hours; $15 for 4-24 hours. Valet parking: $16 for up to 2 hours; $18 for 2-4 hours; $24 for 4-24 hours.

EXCALIBUR Self-parking: $6 for 1-2 hours; $8 for 2-4 hours; $10 for 4-24 hours. Valet parking: $12 for up to 2 hours; $14 for 2-4 hours; $16 for 4-24 hours.

FLAMINGO Self-parking: $9 for 1-4 hours; $12 for 4-24 hours; $12 per day after the first 24 hours. Valet parking: $15 for up to 4 hours; $20 for 4-24 hours; $20 per day after the first 24 hours.

HARRAH'S Self-parking: $9 for 1-4 hours; $12 for 4-24 hours; $12 per day after the first 24 hours. Valet parking: $15 for up to 4 hours; $20 for 4-24 hours; $20 per day after the first 24 hours.

LINQ Self-parking: $9 for 1-4 hours; $12 for 4-24 hours; $12 per day after the first 24 hours. Valet parking: $15 for up to 4 hours; $20 for 4-24 hours; $20 per day after the first 24 hours.

LUXOR Self-parking: $6 for 1-2 hours; $8 for 2-4 hours; $10 for 4-24 hours. Valet parking: $12 for up to 2 hours; $14 for 2-4 hours; $16 for 4-24 hours.

MANDALAY BAY Self-parking: $9 for 1-2 hours; $12 for 2-4 hours; $15 for 4-24 hours. Valet parking: $16 for up to 2 hours; $18 for 2-4 hours; $24 for 4-24 hours.

MGM GRAND Self-parking: $9 for 1-2 hours; $12 for 2-4 hours; $15 for 4-24 hours. Valet parking: $16 for up to 2 hours; $18 for 2-4 hours; $24 for 4-24 hours.

MIRAGE Self-parking: $9 for 1-2 hours; $12 for 2-4 hours; $15 for 4-24 hours. Valet parking: $16 for up to 2 hours; $18 for 2-4 hours; $24 for 4-24 hours.

NEW YORK-NEW YORK Self-parking: $9 for 1-2 hours; $12 for 2-4 hours; $15 for 4-24 hours. Valet parking: $16 for up to 2 hours; $18 for 2-4 hours; $24 for 4-24 hours.

NOBU Valet parking: $13 for up to 4 hours; $18 for 4-24 hours.

PARIS Self-parking: $9 for 1-4 hours; $12 for 4-24 hours; $12 per day after the first 24 hours. Valet parking: $15 for up to 4 hours; $20 for 4-24 hours; $20 per day after the first 24 hours.

PARK MGM/NOMAD Self-parking: $9 for 1-2 hours; $12 for 2-4 hours; $15 for 4-24 hours. Valet parking: $16 for up to 2 hours; $18 for 2-4 hours; $24 for 4-24 hours.

PLANET HOLLYWOOD Self-parking is free. Valet parking: $13 for up to 4 hours; $18 for 4-24 hours; $18 per day after the first 24 hours.

VDARA Self-parking at Aria: $9 for 1-2 hours; $15 for 2-4 hours; $18 for 4-24 hours. Valet parking: $21 for up to 2 hours; $24 for 2-4 hours; $30 for 4-24 hours.

WYNN AND ENCORE Self-parking: $7 for first 2 hours; $12 for 2-4 hours; $15 for up to 24 hours. Valet parking: $13 for up to 4 hours; $18 for up to 24 hours. Self-parking free for hotel guests.

ROOM RESERVATIONS:
Getting a Good Room,
Getting a Good Deal

FOR DECADES, LAS VEGAS had the highest hotel room–occupancy rates in the United States, averaging 93% on weekends and 85.2% during the week. Except for hotels that cater to the luxury market, the addition of a glut of new rooms to the city's room inventory has created a buyer's market. Some of the newly available rooms come from condo projects that were originally intended to be residences.

THE WACKY WORLD OF
LAS VEGAS HOTEL RESERVATIONS

THOUGH THERE ARE ALMOST 150,000 hotel rooms in Las Vegas, getting one is not always a simple proposition. In the large hotel-casinos, there are often five or more separate departments that have responsibility for room allocation and sales. Of the total number of rooms in any given hotel, a number are at the disposal of the casino; some are administered by central reservations or the front desk; some are allocated to independent wholesalers for group and individual travel packages; others are blocked for special events (fights, Super Bowl weekend, and the like); and still others are at the disposal of the sales and marketing department for meetings, conventions, wedding parties, and other special groups. Hotels that are part of a large chain (Holiday Inn and such) have some additional rooms administered by their national reservations systems.

At most hotels, department heads meet regularly to review all the room allocations. If rooms blocked for a special event—say, a golf tournament—aren't selling, some of those rooms will be redistributed to other departments. Since special events and large conventions are scheduled far in advance, the decision-makers have significant lead time. In most hotels, a major reallocation of rooms takes place 40–50 days before the dates for which the rooms are blocked, with minor reallocations made right up to the event in question.

If a reservations representative informs you that no rooms are available for the dates you've requested, it doesn't mean the hotel is sold out but, rather, that central reservations has no more rooms remaining in its allocation. That doesn't necessarily mean that all the rooms have been reserved by guests, however—some rooms may be reserved for high rollers or persons doing business with the hotel's sales department, while others will be in the hands of tour wholesalers or blocked for conventions. The good news: such rooms not committed to by a certain date are reallocated, so a second call to central reservations may get you the room that was unavailable when you called two weeks earlier.

THE INTERNET REVOLUTION

PURCHASING TRAVEL ON THE INTERNET has revolutionized the way both consumers and hotels do business. For you, it makes shopping for a hotel and finding good deals much easier. For the hotel, it makes possible a system of room-inventory management often referred to as dynamic pricing or "nudging." Here's how it works: Many months in advance, hotels establish rates for each day of the coming year. In developing their rate calendar, they take into consideration all of the variables that affect occupancy in their hotel as well as in Las Vegas in general. They consider weekend versus weekday demand; additional demand stimulated by holidays, major conventions, trade shows, and sporting events; and the effect of the four seasons of the year on occupancy.

After rates for each date are determined, the rates are entered into the hotel's reservation system. Then hotel management sits back to see what happens. If the bookings for a particular date are in accord with management's expectations, no rate change is necessary. If demand is greater than management's forecast for a given date, they might raise the rate to take advantage of higher-than-expected bookings. If demand eases off, the hotel can revert back to the original rate.

If demand is less than expected, the hotel will begin nudging—that is, incrementally decreasing the rate for the day or days in question until booking volume increases to the desired level. Though this sort of rate manipulation has been an integral part of room inventory management for decades, the internet has made it possible to rethink and alter room rates almost at will. A hotel can theoretically adjust rates hourly on its own website. Major internet travel sellers (also called online travel agencies, or OTAs) such as Travelocity, Hotels.com, and Expedia, among others, are fast and agile and quite capable of getting a special deal (that is, a lower rate) in front of travel purchasers almost instantaneously. For the hotel, this means they can manage their inventory on almost a weekly or daily basis, nudging toward full occupancy by adjusting their rates according to demand.

Of course, the hotels don't depend entirely on the internet. Lower rates and various special deals are also communicated by email to preferred travel agents and sometimes directly to consumers (especially players-club members) by email, print ads, or direct-mail promotions.

GETTING THE BEST DEAL ON A ROOM

COMPARED TO HOTEL RATES in other destinations, lodging in Las Vegas is so relatively inexpensive that the following cost-cutting strategies may seem gratuitous. Yes, there are $500-per-night rooms, but if you are accustomed to paying $130 a night for a hotel room, you can afford 80% or more of the hotels in town. You may not be inclined to wade through all the options listed below to save $20 or $30 a night. If, on the other hand, you would like to obtain top value for your dollar, read on.

	ROOM RATES AND PACKAGES	SOLD OR ADMINISTERED BY
1.	Gambler's rate	Casino or hotel
2.	December, January, and summer specials	Hotel room reservations or marketing department
3.	Internet discounts	Internet travel vendors
4.	Wholesaler packages	Independent wholesalers
5.	Tour-operator packages	Tour operators
6.	Reservation-service discounts	Independent wholesalers and consolidators
7.	Corporate rate	Hotel room reservations
8.	Hotel standard-room rate	Hotel room reservations
9.	Convention rate	Convention sponsor

Sorting Out the Sellers and the Options

To book a room in a particular hotel for any given date, there are so many different in-house departments as well as outside tour operators and wholesalers selling rooms, that it's almost impossible to find out who is offering the best deal. This is not because the various deals are so hard to compare but because it is so difficult to identify all the sellers.

The chart above lists the types of rates and packages available, ranked from the best to the worst value. The room-rate ranking is subject to some interpretation: A gambler's rate may, at first glance, seem to be the least expensive option, next to a free room. If, however, the amount of money a guest is obligated to wager (and potentially lose) is factored in, the gambler's rate might be by far the most expensive.

Complimentary and Discounted Rooms for Gamblers

Most Las Vegas visitors are at least peripherally aware that casinos provide complimentary or greatly discounted rooms to gamblers. It is not unusual, therefore, for a business traveler, a low-stakes gambler, or a non-gambling tourist to attempt to take advantage of these deals. What they quickly discover is that the casino has very definite expectations of any guest whose stay is wholly or partially subsidized by the house. If you want a gambler's discount on a room, they will ask what game(s) you intend to play, the amount of your average bet, how many hours a day you usually gamble, where (at which casinos) you have played before, and how much gambling money you will have available on this trip. They may also request that you make an application for credit or provide personal information about your occupation, income, and bank account.

If you somehow bluff your way into a comp or discounted room, you can bet that your gambling will be closely monitored after you arrive. If you fail to give the casino an acceptable amount of action, expect to be charged the nondiscounted room rate when you check out.

Even for those who expect to do a fair amount of gambling, a comp or discounted room can be a mixed blessing. By accepting the casino's hospitality, you incur a certain obligation (the more they give you, the bigger the obligation). You will be expected to do most (if not all) of your gambling in the casino where you are staying, and you will also be expected to play a certain number of hours each day. If this was your intention all along, great. On the other hand, if you thought you would like to try several casinos or take a day and run over to Hoover Dam, you may be painting yourself into a corner.

Taking Advantage of Special Deals

When you call, always ask the reservationist if the hotel has any package deals or specials. If you plan to gamble, be sure to ask about gaming specials. If you do not anticipate gambling enough to qualify for a gambling package, ask about other types of deals. On the internet, always check the hotel's website. It's also helpful to Google the name of the hotel and the word *promotion*. This sometimes turns up deals on dining and entertainment as well as room rates.

Hotels generally offer their best deals to gamblers, so the smart thing is to get yourself categorized as a gambler on their snail-mail and email lists by enrolling in the casinos' players clubs (loyalty programs). In the past, you had to sign up in person at the casino, but now you can join the clubs of the casinos listed in the chart below online. Unfortunately, for those not listed, you still have to join in person. You're under no obligation to bet a nickel, but you'll rack in all the good deal notifications nonetheless.

PLAYERS CLUBS THAT ACCEPT ONLINE REGISTRATION
• Aria • Bally's • Bellagio • Boulder Station • Caesars Palace • California
• The Cosmopolitan • The Cromwell • Downtown Grand • Ellis Island
• Excalibur • Fiesta Rancho • Fiesta Henderson • Flamingo
• Fremont • Gold Coast • Golden Gate • Green Valley Ranch
• Hard Rock • Harrah's • LINQ Hotel & Casino • Luxor • Main Street Station
• Mandalay Bay • MGM Grand • Mirage • New York–New York
• The Orleans • Palace Station • Palazzo • Palms • Paris • Park MGM
• Planet Hollywood • Plaza • Rampart • Red Rock Resort • Rio
• Sam's Town • Silverton • SLS • South Point • Suncoast
• Sunset Station • Texas Station • Venetian • Westgate LV

Being a member of a hotel's players club can also come in handy when rooms are scarce. Once, trying to book a room, we were told the hotel was sold out. When we mentioned that we had a players card, the reservationist miraculously found us a room. If you are a players-club member, it is often better to phone the club-member services desk instead of the hotel-reservations desk.

If you don't see a hotel that you're interested in listed in the chart, check its website for a "sign our guestbook" feature or some equivalent. This, at a minimum, will get you on the hotel's email list to receive news and offers of various kinds.

As far as rooms go, it's rare in our experience to find a deal on the hotel's website that's better than the ones they quote you on the phone. A reservationist on the phone knows she has a good prospect on the line and will work with you within the limits of her authority. On the web there's no give or negotiation: it's a take-it-or-leave-it deal.

Finally, many hotels really haven't learned how to merchandise rooms through their website.

Having shopped the hotel for deals, start checking out Las Vegas vacation or weekend packages advertised in your local newspaper (digital or print version), and compare what you find with packages offered in the Sunday edition of the *Los Angeles Times* or on its website.

Timing Is Everything

Timing is everything when booking a room in Las Vegas. If a particular hotel has only a few rooms to sell for a specific date, it will often, as we discussed earlier, bounce up the rate for those rooms as high as it thinks the market will bear. Conversely, if the hotel has many rooms available for a certain date, it will lower the rate accordingly. The practice remains operative all year, although the likelihood of hotels having a lot of rooms available is obviously greater during off-peak periods. As an example, we checked rates at an upscale nongaming hotel during two weeks in October. Depending on the specific dates, the rate for the suite in question ranged from $80 (a steal) to $255 (significantly overpriced) per night.

Which day of the week you check in can also save or cost you some money. At some hotels a standard room runs 20% less if you check in on a Monday through Thursday (even though you may stay through the weekend). If you check into the same room on a weekend, your rate will be higher and may not change if you keep your room into the following week. A more common practice is for the hotel to charge a lower rate during the week and a higher rate on the weekend.

NO ROOM AT THE INN (FOR REAL) More frequently than you would imagine, Las Vegas hotels overbook their rooms. This happens when guests do not check out on time, when important casino customers arrive on short notice, and when the various departments handling room allocations get their signals crossed. When this occurs, guests who arrive holding reservations are told that their reservations have been canceled.

To protect yourself, always guarantee your first night with a major credit card (even if you do not plan to arrive late) and insist on a written confirmation of your reservation. When you arrive and check in, have your written confirmation handy.

Precautions notwithstanding, the hotel still might have canceled your reservation. When a hotel is overbooked, it will take care of its serious gambling customers first, its prospective gambling customers (leisure travelers) second, and business travelers last. If you are told that you have no room, demand that the hotel honor your reservation by finding you a room or by securing you a room at another hotel of comparable or better quality at the same rate. Should the desk clerk balk at doing this, demand to see the reservations manager. If the reservations manager stonewalls, go to the hotel's general manager. Whatever you do, don't leave until the issue has been resolved to your satisfaction.

Hotels understand their obligation to honor a confirmed reservation, but they often fail to take responsibility unless you hold their feet to the fire. We have seen convention-goers, stunned by the news that they have no room, simply turn around and walk out. Wrong. The hotel owns the problem, not you. You should not have to shop for another room.

HOW TO GET THE BEST DEAL ON THE INTERNET

THE INTERNET, UNMATCHED in terms of efficient and timely distribution of information, has become the primary resource for travelers seeking to shop for and book their own flights, hotels, rental cars, entertainment, and travel packages. It's by far the best direct-to-consumer distribution channel in history.

Before the internet, travel companies depended on travel agents or direct contact with customers via telephone. Transaction costs were high because the producers were obligated to pay commissions and fund labor-intensive in-house reservations departments.

With the advent of the internet, inexpensive e-commerce transactions became possible. Airlines and rental-car companies were able to effectively cut travel agents out of the sales process and move most of their booking activity to their own websites. Hotels followed suit with their own websites but also continued to sell to wholesalers and through travel agents.

It didn't take long before independent websites appeared that sold travel products from a wide assortment of suppliers, often at deep discounts. These sites, called *online travel agents,* or OTAs, include such familiar names as **Travelocity, Orbitz, Priceline, Expedia, Hotels .com,** and **Hotwire** and attract huge numbers of customers.

In the beginning, hotels paid the OTAs about the same commission as they paid travel agents, but then the OTAs began applying the thumbscrews, transitioning hotels from a simple commission model to what's called a merchant model. Under this model, hotels provide an OTA with a deeply discounted room rate, which the OTA then marks up and sells. The difference between the marked-up price and the discounted rate provided by the hotel is the OTA's gross profit.

The merchant model, originally devised for wholesalers and tour operators, has been around since long before the internet. Wholesalers and tour operators, then and now, must commit to a certain volume of business, commit to guaranteed room allotments, pay deposits, and bundle the discounted rates with other travel services so that the actual hotel rate remains hidden within the bundle. The merchant model costs the hotel 2 to 2.5 times the normal travel agent commission, considered justifiable because the wholesalers and tour operators also promote the hotel though brochures, trade shows, print ads, and events.

OTAs, in contrast, demand the equivalent of a wholesale commission and higher but are not subject to any of the requirements imposed on wholesalers and tour operators. The OTAs don't have to commit to a specified volume of sales or keep discounted rates opaque. Hotels give up 20%–50% of gross profit and are rewarded by having their rock-bottom rates plastered all over the internet with corresponding damage to their image and brand. The cost of a direct multiday booking on the hotel's own website is $10–$12, including website hosting, marketing costs, website analytics, and management fees. This is several times cheaper than the same booking through an OTA.

By way of example, an OTA might demand a 30% discount off the hotel's best available published rate. So if the hotel is offering rooms at $100, the rate to the OTA would be $70 ($100 less 30% = $70). The OTA then marks up the rate and posts it on its site. The OTA might sell the room for $100, the same rate advertised on the hotel's site, or it might undercut the hotel by offering the room for $95 or less. When the OTA sells the room it pays the hotel $70 and pockets whatever the mark-up is. As you can see, the hotel makes $100 if it sells the room itself but only $70 for the same room if it's sold by an OTA. For the hotel, doing business with OTAs is very expensive.

In the hotel industry, occupancy rates are important, but simply getting people in beds doesn't guarantee a profitable operation. A more critical metric is revenue per available room, or RevPAR. For a hotel full of guests who booked through an OTA, RevPAR will be 20%–50% lower than a full house of guests who booked the hotel directly (either via the hotel's website or by phone).

It's no wonder, then, that hotels and OTAs have a love–hate relationship. Likewise, it's perfectly understandable that it's a priority for hotels to increase direct bookings through their website and minimize OTA bookings. Current economic conditions, coupled in Las Vegas with a glut of rooms exceeding demand, makes this strategy difficult.

The problem is that the better-known OTAs draw a lot more website traffic than the hotel's (or even the hotel chain's) website. So the challenge for the hotel becomes how to shift room shoppers away from the OTAs and channel them to the hotel's website.

The Silver Bullet

For years we've been looking for a fast, easy way to help you find the best hotel rates in Las Vegas. Search engines such as **kayak.com** are helpful. They search large numbers of OTAs to determine which OTA has the best price for a particular hotel on a given night. Problem is, the rates that come up might not approximate the lowest obtainable, and in any event are subject to vagaries in demand the shopper might not be aware of, such as conventions and sporting events.

Enter the *Las Vegas Advisor,* the newsletter and gambling book publisher that has been providing subscribers with no-nonsense consumer information and tips on Las Vegas for years. Their publications are candid, straightforward, and pull no punches. Simply put, they can be trusted to put their readers first (also a primary objective of the *Unofficial Guides*).

Like the *Las Vegas Advisor* newsletter, its **lvahotels.com** website is the most objective source of information on Las Vegas available on the internet and is the preferred site for frequent Las Vegas visitors, especially gamblers. Assessing the needs of its readership and the needs of hotels, the *Advisor* developed an elegant win-win solution that would secure its readers the best room rates and at the same time provide hoteliers a powerful incentive to offer the best possible rates.

Here's how it works. Participating hotels provide the *Advisor* with truly exceptional deals on rooms and other services, which the *Advisor* lists on its website. Each deal has a code number. When you click on a specific deal you're routed to the hotel's website for additional information and booking. The hotel pays the *Advisor* a small commission for sending the booking its way, but only a fraction of what it would sacrifice in gross profit if the room were sold through an OTA.

The hotel's incentive for giving the *Advisor* the best deals available are as follows:

1. Bookings are made directly with the hotel, thus increasing both occupancy and RevPAR.

2. The *Advisor* website is a high-traffic site, visited exclusively (unlike OTA sites) by persons specifically interested in Las Vegas.

3. The *Advisor* has a longstanding record of objective consumer reporting and analysis, so the hotel knows its deals will be regarded as legitimate and trustworthy.

4. A large percentage of the *Advisor*'s visitors and readers are gamblers, the most desirable customer for any hotel with a casino.

5. The *Advisor* program is what's called a "disintermediary" model, a fancy name for cutting out the middlemen (intermediaries) in the channels of distribution.

To check out the deals, go to lvahotels.com. On the home page click "LVA Hotel Deals," down a little bit on the left side of the page. All of the hotels offering special rates will appear. You'll notice that a number of the deals listed include extras, such as resort credit, meals, entertainment, or other sweeteners, in addition to the room. If you find a special that sounds good, an additional click will link to the hotel's website for more information and booking.

At the insistence of the hotels, some of the best discounts are not listed on the website but can be accessed by signing up for the LVA Gold Membership. This costs nothing and can be accomplished quickly online without divulging any sensitive personal information. Special deals not available on the website are emailed to LVA Gold Members weekly. What's going on here is some legal and semantic hair-splitting. If a deal is listed on the *Advisor* site, it's regarded as "published" or public. Hotels have some restrictions concerning published deals. On the other hand, if deals are offered to a certain population that has requested information, in this case LVA Gold Member subscribers, then the hotel has more latitude in regard to what it can offer.

Tests

In multiday tests of the LVA program, we found that it does indeed offer incredible deals on hotel rates but that the participating hotels control the availability of those deals (and change them at their discretion, sometimes without notifying the *Advisor*). Such control is to be expected, given that the hotels are trying to boost RevPAR for days or periods of low occupancy. Consequently, being flexible concerning your proposed dates, and especially being willing to plan your stay to incorporate some weeknights (i.e., Sunday through Thursday), vastly improves your chances of getting the best deal. Searching for available dates will require some work on your part—work that you may judge well worth the effort to save $40 or $50 per night, but perhaps not so much to save only $10 or $15 a night over the best OTA rates. Sometimes, if you don't find the quoted promotional rate for the days you want, there are other deals for the same hotel on the LVA site, perhaps $10 to $20 more than the deal you wanted but still much better than OTA rates.

Many participating hotels offer availability calendars when you click through to their sites, so you can determine pretty quickly when the deal you're interested in is available. Four or five months can be viewed in just a couple of seconds. Hotel sites that don't have availability calendars, however, are irritating. On these you have to keep entering different specific dates in hopes of finding the rate listed on the *Advisor*'s site. For a dozen hotels, we had to search weekday rates three to four months out before finding the quoted rate listed on the *Advisor*'s site. If a visitor plugs away entering date after date (like we did) and finally gets to the middle of summer before he finds the advertised rate, he'll think, "Big deal, everybody knows there are great deals in the dead of summer." There's nothing deceptive or dishonest here, but it makes you put in a lot of effort only to come away unsuccessful in the end.

Since LVA launched the hotel-deals program it has made a lot of refinements, and recent tests have garnered better rates with less effort. As the program matures, we hope that hotel sites that don't have availability calendars will add them, if for no other reason than to stay competitive.

There's evidently demand for a number of hotels with which the *Advisor* has no direct business relationship. These include Downtown hotels and some Strip and near-Strip hotels, such as Hard Rock, Westgate Las Vegas, and The Orleans. The *Advisor* is currently engaged in bringing these properties into its hotel direct program, but in the meantime it makes them available through bestofvegas.com. Because this site is itself an OTA, you probably won't score as deep a discount for the hotels booked through it. If you want to book one of these hotels, check the bestof vegas.com rate and then phone the hotel directly and ask them for their lowest rate. Or, if you want to be more direct, quote the bestofvegas. com rate and ask if they can beat it or offer room upgrades or other goodies to sweeten the deal.

The LVA site works best for four- and five-star properties, though sometimes three-star hotels throw dining, shows, and room upgrades into the mix to create a really great value. As is often asked, "How much time do you spend in your room anyway?"

HOTEL-SPONSORED PACKAGES

IN ADDITION TO SELLING rooms through internet retailers, tour operators, consolidators, and wholesalers, most hotels periodically offer exceptional deals of their own. Sometimes the packages are specialized, as with golf packages, or are offered only at certain times of the year.

unofficial **TIP**
Regarding hotel specials, hotel reservationists do not usually inform you of existing specials or offer them to you. In other words, **you have to ask.**

Promotion of hotel specials tends to be limited to the hotel's primary markets, which for most properties is Southern California, Arizona, Utah, Colorado, Hawaii, Texas, and the Midwest. If you live in other parts of the country, you can take advantage of the packages but probably won't see them advertised in your local newspaper.

Some hotel packages are unbelievable deals. Once, for instance, a hotel offered three nights' free lodging, no strings attached, to any adult from Texas. On certain dates in November, December, and January, the Flamingo offered a deal that included a room for two or more nights at $35 per night (tax inclusive), with two drinks and a show thrown in for good measure. In July 2018, 35 hotels offered rates less than $40. Look for the hotel specials in Southern California newspapers, check the promotion code sites previously listed, or just call the hotel and ask.

HOW TO EVALUATE A TRAVEL PACKAGE

HUNDREDS OF LAS VEGAS PACKAGE TRIPS and vacations are offered to the public each year. Almost all include round-trip transportation to Las Vegas and lodging. Sometimes a package will include room tax, transportation from the airport, a rental car, shows, meals, welcome parties, and/or souvenirs.

Las Vegas packages are among the best travel values available, and for good reason. Las Vegas competes head-to-head with Atlantic City for eastern travelers and with Reno, Lake Tahoe, Laughlin, and other Nevada destinations for western visitors; within Las Vegas, Downtown competes with the Strip, and individual hotels go one-on-one to improve their share of the market. In addition to the fierce competition for the destination traveler, the extraordinary profitability of gambling also works on the consumer's behalf to keep Las Vegas travel economical. For a large number of hotels, amazing values in dining and lodging are used to lure visitors to the casino.

Packages should be a win–win proposition for both the buyer and the seller. The buyer (or travel agent) has to make only one phone call and deal with a single salesperson to set up the whole trip. The seller, likewise, has to deal with the buyer just once, eliminating the need for separate sales, confirmations, and billings. In addition to streamlining selling, processing, and administration, some packagers also buy airfares in bulk on contract like a broker playing the commodities market. Buying or guaranteeing a large number of airfares in advance allows the packager to buy them at a significant savings from posted fares.

The same practice also applies to hotel rooms. Because selling packages is an efficient way of doing business and the packager can often buy individual components (airfare, lodging) in bulk at a discount, savings in operating expenses realized by the seller are sometimes passed on to the buyer. So the package is not only convenient but an exceptional value. In any event, this is the way it's *supposed* to work.

In practice, the seller occasionally realizes all of the economies and passes none of the savings along to the buyer. In some instances, packages are loaded with extras that cost the packager next to nothing but run the retail price sky-high. While this is not as common with Las Vegas packages as those to other destinations, it occurs frequently enough to warrant some comparison shopping.

When considering a package, choose one that includes features you are sure to use. Second, if cost is of greater concern than convenience, call or check online to see what the package would cost if you booked its individual components (airfare, lodging, rental car) on your own. If the package price is less than the à la carte cost, the package is a good deal. Even if the costs are about the same, the package is probably still worth it for the convenience.

AN EXAMPLE Bob's friends Carl and Peggy were grad students looking for an affordable package to Las Vegas in September. Delta Vacations had a bare-bones package that included a room at the Mirage, round-trip airfare, and all taxes but not resort fees for $1,456 ($728 per person). For their flight, the couple chose basic economy to keep costs down and a run-of-the-house room (the hotel decides what kind of room to assign).

They then checked components of the package priced individually. The same flight on Delta was $350 per person or $700 total. Checking Southwest, they found flights at the same times of day for $392 per person. Calling the Mirage, a run-of-the-house room for five nights would cost $1,008 with taxes. Because the Southwest flights were more expensive, they decided to fly Delta.

Putting it all in a spreadsheet, it looked like this:

OPTION A: Delta Vacation package for 2	$1,456
OPTION B: Booking their own air and lodging	
Lodging, including tax	$1,008
Airfare on Delta for 2	$700
TOTAL	**$1,708**

In this case, the package would save them $252 ($1,708 – $1,456). Be aware that it doesn't always work out this way. We analyze dozens of packages each year, and there are as many bad deals as good deals. The point is, always do your homework.

HOTEL RESORT FEES

FREQUENT TRAVELERS are all too well acquainted with added fees and surcharges, some hidden and some stated up front. Many such fees were initiated during the depth of the last recession to make up for lost volume. Sales are back up, however, and the original rationale for the ancillary charges is hardly defensible, but once the hand is in the cookie jar it is loathe to withdraw.

Airline à la carte fees are despised but tolerated because they are industry wide (read inescapable) with one or two exceptions, most notably Southwest Airlines. Though Southwest doesn't charge for the first two bags of checked luggage, it continues to expand fees for a variety of boarding and seating options. At least with Southwest, however, you can always opt out. (For a comparative chart of airline fees, see airfarewatchdog.com, using the pull-down menu under "Airlines.")

Like airlines, hotel development is capital intensive in the extreme, and the major players are willing to risk antagonizing guests to boost the bottom line. As Ted Mandigo, a hotel consultant, put it, "There's a lot of institutional ownership of properties, and they're very aggressive about the return on their investment. They've watched the airlines nickel and dime people for features and extra services, and the hotel industry has adopted that as an approach."

In the hotel business this "approach" consists of adding so-called resort fees to room rates. If you're searching for a Las Vegas hotel on the internet and you're using one or more of the various search engines, the alternatives that come up will often not include or mention resort fees. Thus, a room that seems like a good deal at $100 a night is conspicuously less so if you tack on a $25 per day resort fee, plus, if you have a car, valet and self-parking fees. Worse, the resort fee is often the tip of the iceberg, meaning that you're likely to incur other charges for other services, most of which have historically been included in the price of the room.

Resort fees usually run $10–$45 per day plus tax, with $32 and up being the norm at upscale hotels and $15–$25 the norm for midrange properties. Features and services included in resort fees are all over the map. A common package consists of in-room internet, local and toll-free phone calls, fitness center access, and complimentary printing of boarding passes. Depending on the hotel, other possible perks and services might include a daily newspaper, valet parking, tennis court access, in-room safes, in-room coffeemakers, two bottles of water daily, incoming and sometimes outgoing faxes (usually with page-count limitations), internet in the public areas, notary public services, shuttle services, and various discounts and deals for on-site restaurants, shows, shops, and attractions. Sometimes, to the consternation of guests, even pool access is listed as a feature. The resort fee covers a set package, so there's no cherry picking the features and services you want. Because most guests don't use all the features, and because many features cost the hotel little or nothing, most of the fee flows to the hotel's bottom line.

Fortunately, hotels don't march in lockstep like the airlines, and many differentiate their product by charging nominal resort fees or not charging resort fees at all. Resort fees are less prevalent at Downtown hotels. By contrast, all MGM Resorts International hotels levy resort fees (Aria, Vdara, Mandarin Oriental, Mirage, MGM Grand, Bellagio, New York–New York, Park MGM, Excalibur, Luxor, Mandalay Bay, and Circus Circus), as do all Caesars Entertainment properties (Caesars Palace, Bally's, LINQ Hotel & Casino, Harrah's, Flamingo, Paris, The Cromwell, Rio, and Planet Hollywood). A frequently updated list of resort fees and what they include can be found at lasvegasadvisor .com/resort-fee-hotels and lasvegasdirect.com, but these, as of press time, are the remaining hotels that do *not* charge resort fees: California, Casino Royale Best Western Plus, Elara (at Planet Hollywood),

Four Queens, Fremont, Main Street Station, Royal Resort, and Wyndham Grand Desert.

If you find a hotel with a low or no resort fee, you may not be quite out of the woods. Take internet service, for example. Bandwidth available almost always supports basic office tasks and checking email but will prove inadequate if you want to Skype or stream movies. Some hotels that are wired to do all of the above are implementing a tiered-service plan, where basic service, slower but adequate for web surfing and email, is included in the room rate or resort fee package. On the other hand, if you have multiple bandwidth-hogging devices or want to Skype or stream movies over a high-speed connection, an additional fee is charged. Note that older hotels are less likely to provide stellar internet service because they are extremely expensive to retrofit. When it's done, the hotel often charges premium prices for sub-par access. Also be aware that even in modern hotels, there may not be an internet server on every floor. When you check in, ask for a floor with an internet server. Finally, the majority of midrange and budget hotels do not charge for internet access, or alternatively roll it into the room rate—it's one of the ways they differentiate their product.

If there's no resort fee, things usually in the resort fee package, such as fitness-center access, printing boarding passes, and receiving faxes, might be billed separately on an à la carte basis. Even so, at least you're using what you pay for.

There are several fees that you'll be seeing more often. The majority of resorts are charging for parking, and we expect more will follow suit. Several hotels are beginning to charge for baggage storage, as when you check out but store your luggage with the bell desk until you're ready to go to the airport. Another trend, which will make you reconsider using the minibar, is a restocking fee for items consumed. In addition to the $5 Diet Coke, already expensive enough, you'll be charged an extra $2.95–$5 per item for restocking. Also look for early-departure penalties and more draconian cancellation policies. Concerning the latter, it's happening. If you're not in the habit of reading the cancellation policy of your reservation, now's a good time to start.

THE HOTEL CREDIT CARD SCAM

IN A VERY CONVINCING SCAM that's metastasizing all over the country, a guest receives a phone call in his room. The caller addresses him by name and may know the names of others in the same room. Usually, apologetically, the caller purports to be calling from the front desk and tells you there has been a system failure and that she needs the credit card number of the card that was used at check-in in order to expedite your checkout. In some versions the scam is very elaborate, with the caller offering her employee number, putting her "manager" on the line, offering a discount on your bill for the inconvenience, offering to hang up so you can dial zero to verify the legitimacy of the call, or, in lieu of providing her your card info, inviting you to come to the front desk and handle the matter in person. All bluff. The calls are often made in the middle of the night when you're sleepy and don't have your thinking cap on, and when you're naturally reluctant to get dressed and hoof down to the front desk.

Here's what you need to know: (1) A hotel won't ask you to provide sensitive information on the phone and (2) a hotel won't call you in the middle of the night. At this juncture, the authorities don't know how the scammers are matching guest room phone numbers with the names of the occupants. If any version of this happens to you, hang up and phone hotel security.

OTHER HOTEL SCAMS

MANY SCAMMERS PUT UP PAGES online that look polished and official and may even include logos of well-known hotel brands. They'll happily sell you a room, paid for in advance with your credit card, and email you credible-looking confirmation documents. The problem is, they never contact the hotel to make the booking. In a variation, they do make the booking but fail to pay the hotel, leaving you to pay when you arrive. Online sellers such as Priceline and Expedia are pretty safe but are plagued by foreign pop-ups from scammers. To be safe, never click a pop-up that routes you to a third-party website regardless of how good the deal sounds. Some pop-ups list spurious phone numbers (often staffed by scammers posing as reservationists) and legit-looking URLs— say, **qualityinn.hotelreservations.net.** Fake websites have become such a problem, in fact, that real hotel sites are often labeled "Official Site."

 For **BUSINESS TRAVELERS**

CONVENTION RATES: HOW THE SYSTEM WORKS

BUSINESS TRAVELERS, particularly those attending trade shows or conventions, are almost always charged more for their rooms than leisure travelers. For big meetings, called citywide conventions, huge numbers of rooms are blocked in hotels all over town. These rooms are reserved for visitors attending the meeting in question and are usually requested and coordinated by the meeting's sponsoring organization in cooperation with the Las Vegas Convention and Visitors Authority.

Individual hotels negotiate a nightly rate with the convention sponsor, who then frequently sells the rooms through a central reservations system of its own. Because the hotels would rather have gamblers or leisure travelers than people attending conventions (who usually have limited time to gamble), the negotiated price tends to be high, often $10–$50 per night above the going rate.

Meeting sponsors, of course, blame convention rates on the hotels. Meanwhile, the hotels maintain a stoic silence, not wishing to alienate meeting organizers.

To be fair, convention sponsors should be given some credit simply for having their meeting in Las Vegas. Even considering the inflated convention rates, meeting attendees will pay 15%–40% less in Las Vegas for comparable lodging than in other major convention cities. As for the rest, well, let's take a look.

Sam Walton taught the average American that if you buy a large quantity of something, you should be able to obtain a better price (per item) than if you buy just one or two of it. If someone can buy a single hotel room for $90, why then must a convention sponsor, negotiating for 900 rooms for five nights in the same hotel (4,500 room nights in hotel jargon), settle for a rate of $110 per night?

Many Las Vegas hotels take a hard-line negotiating position with meeting sponsors because (1) every room occupied by a convention-goer is one less room available for gamblers and (2) they figure that most business travelers are on expense accounts.

In addition, timing is a critical factor in negotiating room rates. Hotels don't want business travelers occupying rooms on weekends or during the more popular times of the year. Convention sponsors who want to schedule a meeting during high season (when hotels fill their rooms no matter what) can expect to pay premium rates. In addition, and regardless of the time of year, many hotels routinely charge stiff prices to convention-goers as a sort of insurance against lost opportunity. "What if we block our rooms for a trade show one year in advance," a sales manager asked, "and then a championship prizefight is announced for that week?"

A spokesman for the Las Vegas Convention and Visitors Authority says that higher room rates for conventioneers are not unreasonable given a hotel's commitment to the sponsor to hold rooms in reserve. But reserved rooms, or room blocks, fragment a hotel's inventory of available rooms, and often make it harder, not easier, to get a room in a particular hotel. The bottom line is that convention-goers pay a premium price for the benefit of having rooms reserved for their meeting—rooms that would be cheaper, and often easier to reserve, if the sponsor had not reserved them in the first place. For a major citywide convention, it is not unusual for attendees to collectively pay in excess of $1 million for the peace of mind of having rooms reserved.

Whether room-blocking is really necessary is an interesting question. The Las Vegas Convention and Visitors Authority works with convention sponsors to ensure that there is never more than one citywide meeting in town at a time and to make sure that sponsors do not schedule their conventions at a time when Las Vegas hotels are otherwise normally sold out (National Finals Rodeo week, Super Bowl weekend, New Year's, and so on). Unfortunately for meeting planners, some major events (prizefights, tennis matches) are occasionally scheduled in Las Vegas on short notice. If a meeting planner does not block rooms and a big fight is announced for the week the meeting is in town, the attendees may be unable to find a room. This is such a nightmare to convention sponsors that they cave in to high convention rates rather than risk not having rooms. The actual likelihood of a major event being scheduled at the same time as a large convention is small, though the specter of this worst-case scenario is a powerful weapon in the bargaining arsenal of the hotels.

Working Through the Maze

If you attempt to bypass the sponsoring organization and go directly through the hotel, the hotel will either refer you to the convention's central reservations number or quote you the same high price. Even if you do not identify yourself as a convention-goer, the hotel will figure it out by the dates you request. In most instances, even if you lie and insist that you are not attending the convention in question, the hotel will make you pay the higher rate or claim to be sold out.

By way of example, we tried to get reservations at Bally's for a major trade show in the spring that draws about 30,000 attendees. The show runs six days plus one day for setting up, or seven days total, Saturday through Friday. Though this example involves Bally's, we encountered the same scenario at every hotel we called.

When we phoned reservations at Bally's and gave them our dates, they immediately asked if we would be attending a convention or trade show. When we answered in the affirmative, they gave us the official sponsor's central reservations phone number in New York. We called the sponsor and learned that a single room at Bally's (one person in one room) booked through them would cost $130 per night, including room tax. The same room (we found from other sources) booked directly through Bally's would cost $98 with tax included.

We called Bally's back and asked for the same dates, this time disavowing any association with the trade show, and were rebuffed. Obviously skeptical of our story, the hotel informed us that they were sold out for the days we requested. Unconvinced that the hotel was fully booked, we had two different members of our research team call. One attempted to make reservations from Wednesday of the preceding week through Tuesday of the trade show week, while our second caller requested a room from Wednesday of the trade show week through the following Tuesday. These respective sets of dates, we reasoned, would differ sufficiently from the show dates to convince Bally's that we were not conventioneers. In each case we were able to make reservations for the dates desired at the $98-per-night rate.

It should be stressed that a hotel treats the convention's sponsoring organization much like a wholesaler who reserves rooms in a block for a negotiated price. What the convention, in turn, charges its attendees is out of the hotel's control. Once a hotel and convention sponsor come to terms, the hotel either refers all inquiries about reservations to the sponsor or accepts bookings at whatever nightly rate the sponsor determines. Since hotels do not want to get in the way of their convention sponsors (who are very powerful customers) or, alternatively, have convention attendees buying up rooms intended for other, nonconvention customers, reservations departments carefully screen room requests during convention periods.

Strategies for Beating Convention Rates

1. CHECK THE INTERNET Unlike packagers and wholesalers, internet sellers serve as a communications nexus and can often point you to a hotel you had not considered that still has rooms available, or to a property that has some last-minute rooms because of cancellations. Try the aforementioned lvahotels.com, kayak.com, or one of the promotion-code sites. If you link to the hotel's website through a deal on lvahotels.com, you'll most likely be classified as a gambler.

2. BUY A PACKAGE FROM A TOUR OPERATOR OR A WHOLESALER This tactic makes it unnecessary to deal with the convention's central reservations office or with an individual hotel's reservations department. Many packages allow you to buy extra days at a special discounted room rate if the package dates do not coincide perfectly with your meeting dates.

If you are able to beat the convention rate by booking a package or through the internet, don't blow your cover when you check in. If you walk up to the registration desk in a business suit and a convention ID badge, the hotel will void your package and charge you the full convention rate. If you are supposed to be a tourist, act like one, particularly when you check in and check out.

3. FIND A HOTEL THAT DOES NOT PARTICIPATE IN THE CONVENTION ROOM BLOCKS Many of the Downtown, North Las Vegas, and Boulder Highway hotels, as well as a few of the Strip hotels, do not make rooms available in blocks for conventions. If you wish to avoid convention rates, obtain a list of your convention's "official" hotels from the sponsoring organization and match it against the hotels listed in this guide. Any hotel listed in this book that does not appear on the list supplied by the meeting sponsors is not participating in blocking rooms for your convention. This means you can deal with the nonparticipating hotels directly and should be able to get their regular rates.

STRIP-AREA HOTELS THAT RARELY PARTICIPATE IN ROOM BLOCKS		
• Four Seasons	• Artisan (west of Strip)	• The Cromwell
DOWNTOWN HOTELS THAT SELDOM PARTICIPATE IN ROOM BLOCKS		
• California	• El Cortez	• The D Las Vegas
• Four Queens	• Fremont	• Golden Gate

Most citywide trade shows and conventions are held at the Las Vegas Convention Center. If you stay at any of the nonparticipating hotels, you will have to commute to the convention center by shuttle, cab, monorail, or car.

4. RESERVE LATE Thirty to sixty days prior to the opening of a convention or show, the front-desk room-reservations staff in a given hotel will take over the management of rooms reserved for the meeting from the hotel's sales and marketing department. "Room Res," in conjunction with the general manager, is responsible for making sure that the hotel is running at peak capacity for the dates of the show. The general manager has the authority to lower the room rate from the price negotiated with the sponsor. If rooms are not being booked for the convention in accordance with the hotel's expectations, the general manager will often return a number of reserved rooms to general inventory for sale to the public.

A convention-goer who books at the last minute might obtain a lower rate than an attendee who booked early through the sponsor's central-housing service. Practically speaking, however, be aware that the farther from the convention center or headquarters a hotel is, the better your chances of finding a discounted room at the last minute.

Room Blocks from a Different Perspective

Room blocks are high-volume business for hotels. Convention sponsors leveraging this volume can often obtain deal sweeteners such as catered events, hospitality suites, entertainment, and a whole range of other services and extras that make the convention experience richer and more enjoyable for attendees. If you book your room outside the room block, it could compromise the sponsoring organization's negotiating position for subsequent conventions. Also, organizations that cannot fill a sufficient percentage of their contracted room blocks often must pay attrition damages. This is especially true for conventions that contract a room block only in the convention headquarters hotel. The takeaway here is that you can help the sponsoring organization enhance the quality of the meeting by supporting the room block.

THE LAS VEGAS CONVENTION CENTER

THE LAS VEGAS CONVENTION CENTER (**LVCC**) is the largest single-level convention and trade show facility in the United States and recently acquired the coveted World Trade Center site designation. Last year Las Vegas hosted 55 of the largest trade shows and conventions, more than the next two destinations combined. Annually, the city hosts more than 22,000 meetings, generating $6.3 billion to the local economy and supporting 54,800 jobs.

The 3.2-million-square-foot LVCC, which includes more than 2 million square feet of exhibition space, is divided into two main buildings: the **South Hall** and the older **North Hall.** A pedestrian bridge over Desert Inn Road connects the two. In addition to the exhibit areas, the center has a lobby and public areas, a kitchen that can cater a banquet for 12,000 people, and 144 meeting rooms seating 20–7,500 delegates. Serving as headquarters for shows and conventions drawing as many as 150,000 attendees, the convention center is on Paradise Road, one very long block off the Strip and 3 miles from the airport.

For both exhibitors and attendees, the Las Vegas Convention Center is an excellent site for a meeting or trade show. Large and small exhibitors can locate and access their exhibit sites with a minimum of effort. Numerous loading docks and huge bay doors make loading and unloading quick and simple for large displays arriving by truck.

Smaller displays transported in vans and cars are unloaded on the north side of the main hall and can be carried or wheeled directly to the exhibit area without climbing stairs or using elevators. The exhibit areas and meeting rooms are well marked and easy to find.

The two major restaurants in the Convention Center are **Luckys** in the Grand Lobby and **Aces** in the South Hall. Throughout the complex are 18 permanent concessions with fast-food choices in sidewalk settings: a deli; two Starbucks; fresh soups, sandwiches, and salads; Mexican; Asian; pasta and pizza; and burgers, hot dogs, and barbecue. Free Wi-Fi is available in all lobbies and in the two large restaurants. Especially helpful to business travelers is **Speed Check Advance,** the on-site baggage handler that checks luggage for five airlines from 3 to 12 hours before departure and delivers to McCarran Airport prior to flight time. Ideally, you and your gear will arrive together. Two on-site business centers provide a menu of services. The large **Visitor Information Center** sits next to the escalators at the base of the north pedestrian bridge across Paradise Road. A concierge desk handles show tickets and tours inside the main entrance. State-of-the-art internet, data, and telephone products are available throughout the complex. The LVCC is easily navigable with a profusion of locator maps and data screens.

The Convention Authority's new transportation center is under construction on the west side of Paradise Road on the former site of the Riviera Hotel. Having erased a glamorous piece of 1950s history that was the Strip's first high-rise resort, the expansion will upgrade and enhance the transportation component at the Convention Center as it is transformed into the Las Vegas Global Business District. The 26-acre blue-chip piece of real estate will include additional exhibit space and meeting rooms, a trade center, food services, parking, and a designated loading area for buses and taxis, long needed at the super-busy facility. A huge convenience for meeting attendees will be vehicle and pedestrian access from Las Vegas Boulevard South to the new site. An elevated walkway over Paradise Road will direct convention attendees to the main complex. The project is scheduled to be completed in 2021.

For more information, call ☎ 702-892-0711 or browse lvcva.com.

Lodging within Walking Distance of the Las Vegas Convention Center

Although participants in citywide conventions lodge all over town, a few hotels are within easy walking distance of the LVCC. Next door, and closest, is the huge **Westgate Las Vegas.** The Westgate routinely serves as headquarters for meetings and shows in the convention center and provides, if needed, an additional 220,000 square feet of exhibit, ballroom, banquet, special event, and meeting-room space. Many smaller conventions conduct all their meetings, including exhibits, at the Westgate. The walk from the lobby of the Westgate to the LVCC is about 5 minutes for most people.

HOTELS WITHIN A 20-MINUTE WALK OF THE CONVENTION CENTER		
CIRCUS CIRCUS	3,770 rooms	18-minute walk
COURTYARD (MARRIOTT)	149 rooms	6-minute walk
HILTON GRAND VACATIONS LVCC	419 suites	17-minute walk
HYATT PLACE	202 suites	7-minute walk
LAS VEGAS MARRIOTT CONVENTION CENTER	278 suites	9-minute walk
MARDI GRAS HOTEL AND CASINO	314 suites	12-minute walk
RENAISSANCE LAS VEGAS (MARRIOTT)	548 rooms	5-minute walk
RESIDENCE INN (MARRIOTT)	192 suites	10-minute walk
ROYAL RESORT	191 rooms	15-minute walk
WESTGATE LAS VEGAS	2,956 rooms	5-minute walk

Marriott offers 1,466 rooms with a range of price points among five properties in proximity to the LVCC. Across the street on Paradise Road is **SpringHill Suites.** A half block west on Convention Center Drive is the **Las Vegas Marriott,** with 278 guest rooms. Adjacent to the convention center on the south is the upscale **Renaissance Las Vegas,** with 548 rooms, and directly across from the LVCC on Paradise Road are two economy properties, the **Residence Inn** and **Courtyard by Marriott.**

The **Royal Resort** is an inexpensive property a long block west on Convention Center Drive. **Embassy Suites** is farther away—three blocks south on Paradise Road—but is closer to restaurants.

Cabs and Shuttles to the Convention Center

Large citywide conventions often provide complimentary bus service from major hotels to the convention center. If you're staying at a smaller hotel and wish to use the shuttle bus, walk to the nearest large hotel on the shuttle route. Though cabs are plentiful and efficient in Las Vegas, they are sometimes in short supply at convention or trade show opening and closing times. Ride-sharing services such as Uber and Lyft help make up the shortfall but may charge "surge rates" (see page 13) in peak demand times that are much more expensive than cab fares.

Public transportation—**RTC** buses—is also available from the larger hotels (see pages 45–46). Exact fare is required.

Your best bet is to stay within walking distance of the convention center. If that's not possible, you'll probably want to rent a car rather than depend on cabs, ride-sharing services, and shuttles.

Monorail to the Convention Center

If you're staying at a hotel in the section of the Strip between Tropicana and Sands (Spring Mountain Road) Avenues or at SLS or the Stratosphere, the best way to commute to the convention center is via the monorail. It's a no-brainer for guests in hotels on the east side of the Strip. For convention-goers who are lodging on the west side of the Strip, it's often a long walk to the nearest station. If traffic on the Strip isn't snarled, west-siders may want to take a cab or use a ride-sharing service. Most

Distance from the Convention Center

hotels on the west side of the Strip have rear or side entrances that allow cabbies to choose an alternate route if the Strip is gridlocked.

Lunch Alternatives for Convention and Trade-Show Attendees

The convention center's food service provides a better-than-average lunch and snack selection. As at most convention centers, however, prices are high. Outside of the convention center, but within walking distance, are the buffet and coffee shop at the Westgate and restaurants at the Renaissance Las Vegas. The better restaurants at the Westgate are not open for lunch.

The restaurants mentioned above provide decent food and fast service but are bustling eateries not particularly conducive to a quiet business lunch. At 3900 Paradise Road, however, **Park Center** (only 3 minutes from the convention center by cab and a little less than a mile by foot) offers several quiet, high-quality ethnic restaurants, including

Moroccan, Brazilian, and Asian cuisines. Also located in the shopping center is a sub shop and an American steakhouse.

Café 325, in the Las Vegas Marriott on Convention Center Drive, is open 6:30 a.m.–10:30 p.m. for casual dining, as is **ENVY Steakhouse** in the Renaissance next door to the center's South Hall. **The Barrymore** in the Royal Resort is also a good choice. At the intersection of Las Vegas Boulevard South and Convention Center Drive are **Denny's, Kimchi Korean BBQ,** and the **Peppermill,** long a local favorite.

Parking at the Las Vegas Convention Center

In all, there are 5,200 parking spaces for cars in nine color-coded parking lots at the LVCC. The most convenient parking is in the Silver Lots right in front of the main entrance. The largest and third-most convenient parking is in the Gold Lots across Paradise Road north of Convention Center Drive. On the east side of the convention center are the Blue, Orange, Red, and Green Lots. The Blue Lot, tucked into the northeast corner of the property, is second only to the Silver Lots in convenience but is used exclusively by convention-center employees. The Orange Lot on the southeast side is likewise convenient, but it is largely reserved for tractor-trailer parking during large trade shows. The Red Lot is adjacent to the South Hall and is a good choice if the South Hall is where you'll spend most of your time. Finally, the Green Lot is the most remote of all, though more acceptable if your primary business is in the South Hall.

Though access to the exhibit floor varies from meeting to meeting, attendees are often required to enter through the convention center's main entrance off Paradise Road. If not parked in the Gold or Silver lots, convention-goers must hike around the complex to reach the front door (a 7- to 12-minute walk). For other meetings, attendees with proper credentials (those with registration badges) are permitted to enter the exhibit halls by one of several doors along the sides of the convention center halls. As a rule, getting out is not as hard as getting in, and attendees are usually permitted to exit through the side doors.

COMFORT ZONES:
Matching Guests with Hotels

WE REMEMBER A GOOD FRIEND, a 32-year-old single woman, who, in search of a little romance, decided to take a Caribbean cruise. Thinking that one cruise was pretty much like any other, she signed up for a cruise without doing much shopping around. She ended up on a boat full of retired couples who played bingo or bridge every evening and were usually in the sack by 10:30 p.m. Our friend mistakenly assumed, as have many others, that cruises are homogeneous products. In fact, nothing could be further from the truth. Each cruise provides a tailored experience to a specific and narrowly defined market. If our friend had done her homework, she could have booked passage on a boat full of young single people and danced and romanced into the night.

In Las Vegas, it is likewise easy to assume that all the hotels and casinos are fairly similar. True, they all have guest rooms, restaurants, and the same mix of games in the casino, but each property molds its offerings to appeal to a well-defined audience. This concerted effort to please a specific population of guests creates what we call a "comfort zone." If you are among the group a hotel strives to please, you will feel comfortable and at home and will have much in common with the other guests. However, if you fail to determine the comfort zone before you go, you may end up like our friend—on the wrong boat.

Visitors come to Las Vegas to vacation and play or to attend a meeting or convention. While these reasons for coming to Las Vegas are not mutually exclusive, there is a marked difference between a recreational visitor and a business traveler. The vacationer is likely to be older (45 years and up), retired, and from the Midwest, Southern California, Arizona, Colorado, Texas, or Hawaii. The business traveler is younger on average and comes from just about anywhere. Individual hotels and casinos pay close attention to these differences and customize their atmosphere, dining, and entertainment to satisfy a specific type of traveler.

The California Hotel, Downtown, for example, targets Hawaiians and maintains a food store and restaurants that supply their clientele with snacks and dishes from the islands. On the Boulder Highway, Sam's Town is geared toward cowboys and retired travelers. Entertainment at Sam's Town consists of bowling and country-western dancing. Circus Circus on the Strip attracts the RV crowd (with its own RV park) but also offers large, low-priced rooms, buffets, free circus acts, and an amusement park to lure families. The Cosmopolitan, Palms, Planet Hollywood, and the Hard Rock Hotel target a hip, younger audience, while the Westgate and The Venetian, both next door to the convention centers, go the extra mile to make business travelers feel at home.

Some hotels are posh and exclusive, while others are more spartan and intended to appeal to younger or more frugal visitors. Each property, however, from its lounge entertainment to its guest-room decor or the dishes served in its restaurants, is packaged with a certain type of guest in mind.

Because Las Vegas is basically a very informal town, you will not feel as out of place as our friend did on her cruise if you happen to end up in the wrong hotel. At any given property, there is a fairly broad range of clientele. There always will be hotels where you experience a greater comfort level than at others, however. In a place as different as Las Vegas, that added comfort can sometimes mean a lot.

DEMOCRACY IN THE CASINOS

WHILE LAS VEGAS HOTELS AND CASINOS continue to be characterized as appealing to "high rollers" or "grinds," the distinction has become increasingly blurred. High rollers (or whales), of course, are wealthy visitors who come to gamble in earnest, while grinds are less affluent folks who grudgingly bet their money a nickel or quarter at a time. For many years, the slot machine was symbolic of the grinds. Unable to join the action of the high-stakes table games, these gamblers would sit for hours pumping the arms of the slots. More recently, however, the slots are the symbol of casino profitability, contributing anywhere from 40% to 100% to a given casino's gambling revenues.

The popularity of the slot machine, video poker, and other single-player games among gamblers of all types has democratized the casino. The casinos recognize that the silver-haired lady at the quarter slots is an extremely valuable customer and that it is good business to forgo the impression of exclusivity in order to make her comfortable. In Las Vegas there are casinos that maintain the illusion of catering to an upper-crust clientele while quietly practicing an egalitarianism that belies any such pretense. By virtue of its economic clout, the slot machine has broadened the comfort zone of the stuffiest casinos and made Las Vegas a friendlier, more pleasant place.

THE FEEL OF THE PLACE

LAS VEGAS'S HOTEL-CASINOS have distinct personalities. While all casinos contain slot machines, craps tables, and roulette wheels, the feel of each particular place is unique, a product of the combined characteristics of management, patrons, and design. This feel, or personality, determines a hotel-casino's comfort zone, the ambience that makes one guest feel totally at home while another runs for the exit.

HOW TO AVOID READING THE HOTEL-CASINO DESCRIPTIONS If you don't care how a place "feels" but just want to know whether it has room service and tennis courts, or when checkout time is, you can skip to the alphabetical Hotel Information Chart at the end of this chapter.

HOTELS *with* CASINOS

Aliante Casino + Hotel (aliantegaming.com)

THE CLASSY ALIANTE CASINO + HOTEL in North Las Vegas is the only high-rise within a 9-mile radius. The tower stands boldly against the nearby Sheep Mountain range in the northwest Las Vegas Valley. This desert chic metro-resort borders the master-planned development of Aliante (meaning "to soar"), about 20 minutes north of Downtown Las Vegas via I-15, and is adjacent to the intersection of the North 215 Expressway and Aliante Parkway. Given the suburban location and distance from tourist attractions and facilities, a car is a must. The customer base is predominantly vacationers visiting family and friends, motor-sports enthusiasts, business travelers, and locals.

Designed to merge with the stark beauty of the surrounding desert, Aliante Casino + Hotel blends the region's neutral color palette and natural materials. The 40-acre complex includes a 202-room hotel; casino with smoke-free poker area, 170-seat sports book with individual screens, 40 table games, and more than 2,000 slot and video-poker machines; five restaurants and a food court; showroom; fitness center and spa; 16-screen Regal IMAX Theater; and 14,000-square-foot conference center.

ETA, a trendy lounge, features DJ entertainment and dancing. On weekends, eclectic headliner concerts at moderate prices invigorate the Access Showroom.

Food seekers can choose from several brand names at the eateries that ring the casino. The hotel's flagship dining experience, complete with a lovely outdoor patio, is MRKT (pronounced Market) Sea & Land. Try The Salted Lime for margaritas and Mexican fare, or check out Bistro 57 for European-inspired dishes. The Medley Buffet offers Tex-Mex, American, barbecue, Asian, and Italian cooking stations; a salad board; and freshly made hand-packed ice cream at the dessert bar.

The nine-story tower houses tasteful rooms of approximately 400 square feet. Sustaining the rich beige-and-chocolate color scheme throughout the guest rooms are creamy marble, tan granite, and dark woods, again emphasizing organic textures. About 60% percent of the accommodations are configured with showers only, so if you prefer a tub, be sure to request one. All rooms include flat-panel TVs, minibars, and iPod docking stations and are wired for high-speed internet. Eastward-facing rooms have a sweeping view of the Sheep Mountains and the southeast Las Vegas skyline. To the west, rooms look toward Mount Charleston and the Spring Mountains. Despite the expansive panoramas, the views are somewhat bleak—definitely not the desert at its best. The expressway's proximity notwithstanding, the tower is silent and tranquil.

Situated off the lobby, the spacious first-floor pool oasis is shaded by tall palms. A fitness center overlooks the pool. Just across the street is Aliante Golf Club. Joggers can enjoy a run in nearby Aliante Discovery Nature Park.

Although Aliante is somewhat remote, it is not isolated by any means and is a good-choice getaway for guests seeking style, value, and sophistication in a contemporary urban desert retreat.

Arizona Charlie's Boulder and Decatur
(arizonacharlies.com)

PATRONIZED MAINLY BY LOCALS, Arizona Charlie's is the working person's casino with a southwestern ranch flavor. Everything is informal. And it's busy. There is an energy, a three-ring circus feel—lots of slots, some table games, a sports book, several restaurant options, and a lounge. The hotel rooms are passable, but the real reason to patronize Arizona Charlie's is the video poker—they're among the best machines in town, and considering what town you're in, this means they're among the best machines anywhere. The original Arizona Charlie's is on Decatur, west of the Strip. The newer Arizona Charlie's Boulder is on the Boulder Highway.

Bally's (caesars.com/ballys-las-vegas)

BALLY'S BILLS ITSELF AS "the classic Las Vegas experience." Targeted to the gamer of any age, the emphasis is clear when you step inside the main entrance from under the broad, sky-lit porte cochere. On your right, a football-field-long casino stretches beyond you. The casino is immense, open, and elegantly modern—sophisticated in a formal, understated way, like a tuxedo. Active without being claustrophobic, and classy without being stiff, Bally's captures the style of modern European casinos without sacrificing American informality. On the left of the same great room is the registration desk, and a coffee bar and newsstand are conveniently located directly in the lobby area. Originally themed for Hollywood, now Bally's doesn't bear much of a specific visual motif. This is not a shortcoming. Bally's simply carries itself with a certain forthrightness, with a kind of class that says "We are confident to be who we are—timeless Las Vegas."

Both the Jubilee (South) Tower and Resort (North) Tower rooms have been fully renovated and are more spacious than the norm at 450 square feet. These rooms dazzle with signature shades of chile red, white, and brown, creating an upbeat and contemporary look. All rooms have plenty of lighting and feature flat-panel TVs and Wi-Fi, and many have wet bars and refrigerators. Updated marble bathrooms feature walk-in showers (but no tubs), with a make-up counter beside the bathroom. One-bedroom suites have king-size beds and a whirlpool spa. To enjoy this layout you should be very comfortable with your traveling partner, as most of the bathroom is exposed to the sleeping area.

Bally's is blessed with exceptional restaurants and one of the better buffets in Las Vegas. Dining options are BLT Steak, SEA: The Thai Experience, Tequila Taqueria, Buca di Beppo, Nosh, Nathan's, and LavAzza. Nightlife venues include Evening Call, Indigo Lounge (fashionable attire required), and Sully's Bar.

Among other diversions, Bally's offers *Real Bodies,* an anatomy exhibit featuring actual human bodies and organs, and on the lighter side, Twilight Zone Mini Golf. Tubular bowling is also offered at the minigolf.

Although quite spread out, Bally's is easy to navigate. Amenities include a 13,000-square-foot health club and spa. Bally's was one of the first hotels to create an extensive retail arcade, located in the basement level but easily accessible from the casino and conference center. There's also a small parking lot nearby and a bank of entry doors so shoppers can easily access the shops and bypass the casino. Among the Bally's Avenue vendors are home decor, clothing, bling, and a food court.

The spacious acreage in front of the Strip entrance to Bally's is now occupied by the Grand Bazaar Shops Las Vegas, an eclectic mix of approximately 120 shops, including retail, fast food, full-serve dining, and watering holes. The complex is divided along three west-to-east pedestrian walkways that all lead to the Bally's entrance.

For those who drive, the guest parking is all valet out front. There is limited self-parking in the back, but it is mainly for oversize vehicles. The hot tip is to park at Bally's sister property, Paris Las Vegas (the hotels are internally connected). Demonstrating legitimate concern about the traffic congestion on the Strip, Bally's joined with the MGM Grand in constructing a monorail that was the first link in the Las Vegas Monorail line. Subsequently, the monorail was extended north along the Strip, with a loop over to the Las Vegas Convention Center. Bally's also offers a free shuttle every 30 minutes to take you to Rio and Harrah's (both Caesars Entertainment properties).

Bally's caters to meetings and conventions and is one of the few hotels where you will not feel out of place in a business suit. Guests are frequently under age 40 here and come from all over, but particularly Southern California, Chicago, and elsewhere in the Midwest. Bally's also has a loyal Spanish-speaking clientele.

Bellagio (bellagio.com)

WITH ITS MAIN ENTRANCE OFF THE STRIP just south of Flamingo Road, the Bellagio is inspired by an Italian village overlooking Lake Como in the sub-Alpine north of Italy. The facade of the Bellagio will remind you somewhat of the themed architecture Steve Wynn employed at TI, only this time it's provincial

Italian instead of Caribbean. The Bellagio village is arrayed along the west and north sides of a man-made lake, where dancing fountains provide allure and spectacle, albeit more dignified than the Mirage's exploding volcano.

Rising behind the village facade in a gentle curve is the 3,933-room hotel, complete with a casino, restaurants, a shopping complex, a spa, and a pool. A 33-story Spa Tower has 819 hotel rooms and 109 suites. Bundled with the tower are a restaurant, four shops, and additional convention space. Imported marble is featured throughout, even in the guest rooms and suites, as are original art, traditionally styled furnishings, and European antiques. Guest rooms and meeting rooms also feature large picture windows affording views of lushly landscaped grounds and formal gardens.

The 2,568 guest rooms in the original Bellagio Tower feature jewel-toned color palettes derived from the property's extensive gardens, floral pageants, and fountains. Inspired by the hotel's renowned horticultural exhibits, botanical photographs line the walls, and there is enough lighting to illuminate a Cirque du Soleil performance. Most welcome is the laptop-size safe and iHome docking station in the nightstand. Each room features a minibar and high-speed internet.

Surprisingly, the Italian village theme of Bellagio's lakefront facade is largely abandoned in the hotel's interior. Though a masterpiece of integrated colors, textures, and sight lines, the interior design reflects no strong sense of theme. In two steps, passing indoors, you go from a provincial village on a very human scale to a monumentally grand interior with proportions reminiscent of national libraries. The vast spaces are exceedingly tasteful and unquestionably sophisticated, yet they fail to evoke the fun, whimsy, and curiosity so intrinsic to the Mirage and TI.

Perhaps because Las Vegas has conditioned us to a plastic, carnival sort of stimulation, entering the Bellagio is like stepping from the midway into the basilica. The surroundings impress but do not engage our emotions—except, of course, for the art, and that is exactly the point. Seen as a rich, neutral backdrop for the extraordinary works of art displayed throughout Bellagio, the lapse of thematic continuity is understandable. No theme could compete, and none should.

The art is everywhere, even on the ceiling of the registration lobby, where a vibrant, colorful blown-glass piece by Dale Chihuly hangs. Wonderful works are showcased in the Bellagio's restaurants. Original Picassos, for example, are on exhibit in the restaurant of the same name. The Bellagio Gallery of Fine Art is touted as Las Vegas's premier art gallery.

Architecturally, Bellagio's most creative and interesting spaces are found in its signature conservatory and botanical gardens and in its restaurants. As you walk into the main entrance the primary garden is straight ahead. The opulent and oversize displays change seasonally according to the theatrical floral whimsies of the supremely accomplished botanical staff.

If you spend time at the Bellagio, visit each of the restaurants for a moment, if only to take in their stunning design. Many of Bellagio's restaurants, including a Las Vegas branch of Le Cirque, feature panoramic views. Some offer both indoor and outdoor dining experiences. Spago, Wolfgang Puck's flagship restaurant, moved from the Forum Shops to Bellagio in 2018. The restaurant features an open-air patio with prime views of the Bellagio's fountains. Spago's bar, boasting brass fixtures, smoked-oak wood floors, as well as leather chairs and couches, is home to a plush wine bar. In addition to the restaurants, Bellagio serves one of Las Vegas's best—and not unexpectedly one of the city's most expensive—buffets. With the exception of the buffet and coffee shop, Bellagio's restaurants require reservations, preferably made a month to six weeks before you leave home.

The Bellagio's showroom hosts a production of the justly acclaimed Cirque du Soleil. Though terribly expensive, the show is one of Cirque's most challenging productions yet, featuring a one-of-a-kind set that transforms seamlessly from hard surface to water. Like Bellagio itself, the Cirque production *"O"* (from the pronunciation of the French word *eau,* meaning "water") lacks the essential humor and humanness of Cirque's *Mystère* at TI but is nonetheless one of the hottest Cirque tickets in town.

Retailers in the shopping venue include Chanel, Tiffany, Prada, and Giorgio Armani. Bellagio's purported target market includes high rollers and discriminating business travelers who often eschew gaming properties.

If you stay at Bellagio, you will find the same basic informality typical of the rest of the Strip, and, surprisingly, you will encounter in the hotel more people like you than super-rich. Expressed more directly, Bellagio is a friendly place to stay and gamble and not at all pretentious.

Binion's (binions.com)

BINION'S IS ONE OF THE ANCHORS of Glitter Gulch. The casino is large and active, with row upon row of slots clanking noisily under a suffocatingly low ceiling. The table games are less congested, occupying an extended vertical space canopied by mirrors. With an Old West theme executed in the obligatory reds and lavenders, Binion's is dark, but not dark enough to slow the enthusiasm of the locals and "real gamblers" who hang out there. One of the city's top spots for poker and craps, Binion's is famous for not having any maximum bet limitations. You can bet $1 million on a single roll of the dice if you wish.

Twenty or so stories up is the Top of Binion's Steakhouse restaurant and lounge, offering a great view of the city. The recession hit Downtown Las Vegas harder than the Strip. One of the casualties was the hotel at Binion's, which closed and was mothballed in 2010. Prospects for its reopening appear slim.

Boulder Station (boulderstation.com)

SITUATED ON BOULDER HIGHWAY an easy 10 minutes from Downtown Las Vegas and 10 miles from McCarran Airport, Boulder Station is one of the smaller of the 11 Station Casinos properties but boasts the largest gaming area. It is the fraternal twin of Station Casinos' matriarch Palace Station, with its concert schedule and appetizing affordable menus in multiple restaurants and bars.

All 300 guest rooms in the 15-floor tower emit a fresh, contemporary appeal with a bold color scheme of scarlet, coffee, and black. Safes are available at the front desk. Room service is available 6 a.m.–9 p.m.

The low-ceilinged casino zigzags through several wings and boasts the newest animated slots with 2,900 machines, 34 table games, E-Z baccarat, Texas Hold 'Em, three-card poker, a bewildering variety of Asian card games, keno, bingo, a poker room, and a superior 33-screen race and sports book. Meal options abound with a diversity of fast-food choices (Burger King, Subway, Winchell's, Slices Pizzeria, Starbucks), along with The Broiler Steakhouse, the stylish Pasta Cucina, Guadalajara, 24-hour Grand Café, Viva Salsa, and the multitudinous Feast Buffet. Generous portions are the hallmark of Boulder Station's food service. A variegated show series leans toward 1970s and '80s rock and blues, country-western acts, and current jazz artists in the 600-seat Railhead Lounge.

The rear of the property houses a video arcade and an 11-screen movie theater alongside an indoor kids' playground. The pool and fitness center are adequate but minuscule. Along with valet parking and a rear garage, there are acres of free parking on all sides, a testament to the casino's popularity with locals. Boulder Station is convenient for guests who prefer the east side of Las Vegas or who wish to be near the Lake Mead National Recreation Area.

Caesars Palace (caesarspalace.com)

MORE THAN 50 YEARS OLD, Caesars Palace was the first of the themed hotels and casinos to fully realize its potential, and it is among the foremost at staying fresh through constant updating and remodeling. The perennial classic that reinvents itself, Caesars is a must-see, even if you don't stay there.

An exercise in whimsical fantasy and excess, Caesars' Roman theme has been executed with astounding artistry and attention to detail. Everywhere fine mosaics, handsome statuary, mythological references, and famous sculptures delight the eye and mind. Creating an atmosphere of informality in surroundings too pretentious to believe is hard to pull off, but that is exactly what Caesars Palace has done.

If Caesars was on a small scale, it would be exquisite kitsch, but it's on a grand scale that elevates you into some kind of time machine, where the bustling commerce of ancient Rome lives again. Gambling at Caesars does feel a little like pitching horseshoes in the Supreme Court, but, incredibly, it works. Everywhere the vaulted ceilings, classic statuary, and graceful arches easily accommodate the legions (pun intended) of slots, activity of the pits, shopping, dining, and lolling about in opulent pools surrounded by towering gardens.

Caesars Palace provides three spacious and luxurious casinos, including a poker room with celebrity events, many excellent restaurants and cafés, beautiful landscaping, and top celebrity entertainment. For all of the guests who inhabit its 3,348 superb rooms, Caesars has all of the services and amenities of a world-class resort.

The pool area is arguably the most stately in Las Vegas. Framed by hotel towers, the complex offers six different pools, all in the Roman motif, including the 10,000-square-foot pool of the Temple, which is capped by a rotunda and decorated with marble and mosaics. For lusty sinews there's the Neptune pool with 5,000 square feet for lap swimmers; for European-style (aka topless) bathers, the Venus pool is neatly tucked away within an evergreen enclave. All pools have cabanas available for rent.

Caesars is constantly renovating and reinventing its hotel towers. Guests can choose from an amazing array of rooms and suites in six towers: Julius, Forum, Palace, Octavius, Augustus, and the Nobu Hotel (formerly Caesars' Centurion Tower; see details on pages 86–87). The oldest tower, Julius, had its guest rooms renovated in 2017, bringing it up to par with the other, newer towers, and the Palace Tower, the resort's largest tower, completed its renovation in 2018.

Note that the Octavius Tower adjoins the Augustus Tower to form the southernmost section of the property. The towers have their own entrance off Flamingo with valet but no self-parking. The entrance leads to a small registration lobby that allows Octavius and Augustus guests to bypass Caesars' busy main front desk.

Some say the spa is Caesars' best-kept secret. With the Roman penchant for water joys, it's logical that Caesars would have a full line of luxurious treatments and settings for men and women. Situated on the second floor of the Augustus Tower, the spa has 51 therapy rooms; signature Roman baths with hot, cold, and tepid pools; and sculpted stone chaise longues submerged in heated pools and designed as pre-massage relaxers.

Caesars is on a roll with its nightlife scene. Omnia features an ultralounge, main room with dance floor, and a rooftop garden. Cleopatra's Barge, a decades-old dance club on a free-floating boat, continues to rock on. Nearby is Spanish Steps, a DJ-powered lounge, and Vista Cocktail Lounge is an excellent spot for pre- or post-show cocktails.

For the less nocturnal, there are two shopping venues. At the Appian Way (look for the *David*) you can purchase apparel, gifts, art, and jewelry, including Caesars logo items. The extensive Forum Shops is an entirely different kind of experience, giving Caesars Palace the distinction of offering one of the most unusual themed shopping complexes in the United States, with 160 merchants and 12 restaurants and specialty food shops. Ambling through its gently cobblestoned "streets," replete with slightly sloping gutters, the sightseer and shopper alike can be delighted and charmed by full-scale fountains featuring Neptune and Bacchus and building facades topped by second-story "residences," all set against the background of a sweeping Italian sky at sunset. At every turn, you find the perfect blend of old-world commerce and cutting-edge merchandise.

Featured restaurants include Rao's, a clone of Frank Pelligrino's fabled Italian eatery in New York; Beijing Noodle No. 9; Atlantic City legend Old Homestead Steakhouse; Mesa Grill; Nobu by chef Nobu Matsuhisa; and Mr. Chow. The star in the lineup is Restaurant Guy Savoy, overlooking the Roman Plaza. Headed by Parisian restaurateur Guy Savoy, the restaurant offers one of the most singular dining experiences in town. For casual dining, there's Gordon Ramsay Pub & Grill; Cafe Americano; and Forum Food Court. In 2018, Gordon Ramsay's Hell's Kitchen opened in front of the property along the Strip, along with Giada De Laurentiis's second restaurant, Pronto, in the spot that housed Payard Patisserie. The Bacchanal Buffet features many made-to-order specialties and is located in a large sun-drenched room overlooking the Garden of the Gods pool complex; it's a welcome balm in counterpoint to the constant clamor of the gaming floor.

Originally designed for high rollers, from the beginning Caesars opened its arms to the world, marketing far and wide. Enjoyed by a broad range of clientele from the East, the Midwest, and Southern California, it's also popular with Asian and Hispanic visitors. Of course, it also hosts meetings and caters to business travelers in its conference center. No matter what the motivation for a visit, each guest—supported by a staff of 6,000—no doubt feels like Caesar.

NOBU HOTEL AT CAESARS PALACE (nobucaesarspalace.com) Ever the vanguard, Caesars has remodeled its Centurion Tower into a luxury Japanese hotel that melds with the resort's Roman Empire theme. The interior of the tower has been transformed into a stylish boutique hotel managed by high-end international brand Nobu Hospitality and is designated Nobu Hotel Las Vegas. Tapping into the global vision of Chef Nobu Matsuhisa, the 181 tranquil guest rooms feature natural materials, a low L-shaped leather sofa, fine white linens, a refrigerator stocked with

Asian snacks and spirits, silk robes and slippers, and other amenities reflecting time-honored Japanese hospitality and service. Enhancing the muted cream, black, and gray rooms are expressionist and classic ethnic art and calligraphy created specifically for each unit. Bathrooms refine the design of a traditional Japanese bathhouse. Standard rooms have small closets and no desks nor bathtubs. Completing the tradition is a red DO NOT DISTURB tassel.

Situated off the Appian Way retail mall, the minimalist Nobu lobby is managed by Japanese-speaking staff and concierges. A ritual tea service welcomes guests, who are then escorted through a Zen garden and up in the artistic wood-paneled elevator to their accommodations for personalized in-room iPad registration. At the tower's base is the large yet intimate 327-seat Nobu Restaurant and Lounge, featuring private booths, a sushi bar, and teppanyaki tables. On-site Nobu chefs also provide 24-hour room service with both Western and distinctly Asian selections. Expect a truly all-Nipponese experience.

California (thecal.com)

A FRIENDLY ALOHA SPIRIT REIGNS at Downtown's California Hotel. Despite its West Coast name, the property provides a taste of Hawaii, Las Vegas style. From the floral-shirted staff, tropical decor, and Island cuisine to the steel guitar music in the background, except for the casino, the Cal could be beachfront in Honolulu. With the sports book upstairs, the full casino covers two levels and includes a variety of Asian games of chance.

Dining options at the Cal include the famed Redwood Steakhouse (formerly the Redwood Bar and Grill), which, unfortunately, no longer serves the off-menu porterhouse steak special; California Noodle House, serving a variety of Asian dishes; the 24-hour Market Street Cafe; and Aloha Specialties for Island fare. The luau-inspired Holo Holo bar and the Cal Sports Lounge, combining the race and sports book with a visually dynamic lounge, are the places to kick back and grab a drink.

Recently refreshed guest rooms have a subdued tropical color palette and are furnished with a flat-panel TV and a refrigerator. In-room Wi-Fi is available as part of the resort fee. A no-frills 40-by-20-foot pool sits rooftop.

The mezzanine Bridge Arcade off the sports book features Hawaiian-flavored retail shops and eateries. Along the crossover to sister property Main Street Station is the Golden Arm Wall of Fame, honoring players who successfully held the dice and rolled craps for longer than an hour. Two blocks north of the Fremont Street Experience, this Boyd Gaming property is practically the Las Vegas headquarters for the sizeable Hawaiian and Filipino market.

Cannery and Eastside Cannery (cannerycasino.com)

FOUR MILES NORTH OF DOWNTOWN on Craig Road, the Cannery opened in January 2003 and expanded in 2004 with the usual locals' formula: big casino, small hotel. The theme has nothing to do with Steinbeck or fish, though the industrial, 1940s-style structure of corrugated metal and steel beams would be right at home on Cannery Row. Instead, produce, specifically vegetables and fruit, take center stage with murals and paintings of colossal berries, apples, and veggies.

The roomy, uncluttered casino is roughly circular, surrounding an elevated lounge. Restaurants, including a Mexican eatery, the Waverly steakhouse, an Italian restaurant, a fast-food court, and a respectable buffet, are arrayed around the periphery. For entertainment, there's a 16-screen movie theater and The Club for concerts.

Guest rooms are smallish, with oak-finish furniture and brightly colored soft goods. Views from guest-room windows are about as uninspiring as it gets.

Eastside Cannery opened in 2009 on Boulder Highway near Sam's Town. A copy of the original Cannery in many ways, Eastside offers clearly superior guest rooms with floor-to-ceiling windows in its sleek hotel tower. The restaurant lineup includes Carve Steakhouse; Snaps, a 24-hour café; and a deli. In addition to the usual table games and the locals' favorite slots, Eastside offers bingo and an active poker room. The Eastside Events Center is a venue large enough for concerts and boxing matches, while the more intimate Marilyn's Lounge showcases top Las Vegas lounge acts. Like the Cannery, Eastside targets locals, but the upscale rooms, club scene, restaurants, poker room, and lounge entertainment make it a good play for visitors as well.

Casino Royale (casinoroyalehotel.com)

ANY SIMILARITY BETWEEN THIS CASINO ROYALE and the James Bond playground of the same name is strictly coincidental. The Las Vegas version is a lively place ready to show you a good time with low-limit games, penny slots, reasonable room rates, and inexpensive dining options within and nearby. The low-rise Casino Royale inhabits a zillion-dollar location nestled between The Venetian and Harrah's hotel towers and directly across Las Vegas Boulevard from the Mirage and TI. The casino is chaotic, noisy, and congested, with seven double doorways spaced along 170 feet of Strip frontage. The unpretentious main entrance is obscured by limitless pedestrians, and if you're rolling luggage, it's an effort to reach the tiny front desk, which is situated behind racks of sale clothing, giving the impression that you're entering a bargain basement.

Now a Best Western Plus, all 152 rooms on four floors were recently remodeled. Entry into each hallway is by key-card access only. On-site dining options include an Outback Steakhouse, a 24/7 White Castle, a 24/7 Denny's, and a food court at the rear of the gaming area. Next door are Chipotle, Panda Express, and McDonald's.

The small kidney-shaped pool is surrounded on three sides by monumental buildings, so tanning is relegated to mornings, but the area is marginally cooler in the shade during summer afternoons. Fortunately, libations are available. Parking is located at the rear of the hotel. If you can't find center-Strip lodging at the mega-hotels, this property is a convenient and value-priced substitute.

Circus Circus (circuscircus.com)

CIRCUS CIRCUS IS VERY LIKELY the only hotel on the Strip that has an escalator from within the casino to a McDonald's, and that tells you pretty much what you need to know. Although most hotels do not cater to families with young children, Circus Circus is a notable exception. For parents who must bring their children, it's a good alternative and a bargain to boot.

With so many swarming, milling, and mewing short people, the lobby can sometimes remind you of a day-care center. The main casino has a second level called the Midway with good reason, as it features the simple kinds of games found at a state fair venue (wham a spring-loaded chicken into a moving pot and win a prize sort of thing). At the core of the Midway is a small grandstand featuring very competent regular circus acts, also primarily for children. Additional circus acts have been added to the daily show schedule of aerialists and acrobatic artists above the casino floor, with a new show every 45 minutes between 11:30 a.m. and midnight daily. These are Cirque du Soleil–quality performers who prefer day jobs and the flexibility of rotating schedules. The entire casino affair is obviously designed as an easy hand-off platform for such directives as, "Here, honey, you take the kids for 45 minutes while I go play the quarter slots."

In 1993, Circus Circus launched what is now the Adventuredome, formerly Grand Slam Canyon, a desert canyon–themed amusement park totally enclosed in a giant pink dome. Here guests can enjoy two roller coasters, spinner rides, and more. A detailed description of Adventuredome can be found in Part Five on pages 423–424. Maps and signs throughout the facility indicate the "Green Zone," where children are allowed (because the law against children lingering in the gaming areas is very strictly enforced in Las Vegas). Children can walk through the casino if they must, but the general atmosphere does not encourage this practice.

Perhaps because of price, in addition to families, Circus Circus also attracts some seniors and novice gamblers who don't mind dodging strollers and jacked-up kids in this ADD paradise. The labyrinthine casino has low ceilings and is frenetic, loud, and always busy, but sometimes, in contrast to the main public spaces, it can seem like an oasis of sanity. Nickel slots abound, as do table games. The circus theme, both colorful and wholesome, is extended to every conceivable detail of the hotel's physical space and operation. However, most of the garish circus theme decor that once defined guest rooms at Circus Circus has happily given way to more restful, mature colors and appointments.

About 3,000 guest rooms are distributed among three towers: the original Casino Tower with 15 floors over the gaming area, the Skyrise Tower with 29 floors and its own parking garage along the north edge, and the West Tower of 35 levels above the lobby and closest to valet parking and the two immense southside parking garages. The ample rooms in each tower have been remodeled and happily have lost their flashy pink carnival flair. The neon colors have been diffused to mellow beige and ochre tones with swatches of avocado, claret, or blue; the new color palette provides a sensation of sanity and a getaway from the frenzy in the public areas below. Flat-panel TVs and cherry furniture lend a contemporary feel, and all rooms have Wi-Fi and internet access. Connecting rooms are available in all towers.

Offset from the central hotel complex and across Circus Circus Drive is the five-wing, low-rise Manor Motor Lodge. The 700-plus rooms here have also been refreshed. The complex includes two pools with a snack bar, kids' playground, and a separate garage, as well as parking lots beside the individual lodges. Access to the motor lodge from hotel central is via the Promenade Level overpass, which connects with an enclosed moving sidewalk along Circus Circus Drive. The Promenade houses the Adventuredome, several restaurants, and shops selling bling and rhinestone-studded everything.

Adjacent the Manor is a KOA Campground with 170 big-rig sites, a private pool, a hot tub and sauna, a playground, a launderette, pet runs, and a convenience store. RV-less visitors can rent an RV on-site. Drivers should avoid the difficult west exit on busy Industrial Drive, the Strip alternative for locals during rush hours.

Circus Circus has a very good steakhouse (one of the only escapes from the circus theme); a huge, inexpensive buffet; and a monorail shuttle that connects the property's two main buildings. And, to give credit for great innovation, Circus Circus was the first casino to set aside a nonsmoking gaming area. A hotel tower, as well as a shopping and restaurant arcade, adjoin Adventuredome. The arcade restaurants provide Circus Circus with much-needed alternatives to the steakhouse and the buffet. For parents with children, Circus Circus is a great alternative, but for happily child-free others, it might feel more like a zoo.

CITYCENTER

A DESTINATION WITHIN A DESTINATION, CityCenter is truly dazzling. From glass towers reflecting sunlight by day to a skyline of crystalline pillars aglow at night, the 67-acre hotel, residence, and shopping complex between the Park MGM and Bellagio Resorts transcends anything in Las Vegas or elsewhere.

The zillion-dollar metroplex is comprised of Aria, a 61-story, 4,004-room casino resort; Vdara and Mandarin Oriental (soon to be rebranded as a Waldorf Astoria), two nongaming hotels and residences; Veer, the dual-tower residential condominium; Crystals entertainment and retail district; plus interior and exterior space featuring a $40 million curated public fine-art program. Prominently fronting a quarter mile on the Las Vegas Strip, the first impression of CityCenter is visually vertical and geometric. Reminiscent of Dorothy's awestruck reaction to the Emerald City, you will be overwhelmed by the glass-covered facades of the hotel spires and the roof of Crystals. Each is distinguished by a signature hue. Facing the complex and looking left to right, the towers are the silver-blue Mandarin Oriental, white-hot Aria, lemon-tinted Veer, and slate-black Vdara. In front is the multiangled clear roof of Crystals.

For this city within a city, the elevated promenade begins at the Strip and draws visitors into the innovative development. The campus is configured with pedestrian passageways through an informal outdoor-indoor contemporary art museum. More than 15 extraordinary paintings, sculptures, and large-scale works in a variety of postmodern styles created by world-class artists are displayed. Maya Lin, Claes Oldenburg and Coosje van Bruggen, Henry Moore, Richard Long, Jenny Holzer, and Nancy Rubins are represented. Set aside at least 90 minutes for a self-conducted tour. Brochures describing the bold and eclectic collection are available on site, and small plaques detail each work. It's a must-see for art lovers!

There are only two auto entrances into the development from the Strip and one from Dean Martin Drive via Jerry Lewis Way and West Harmon Avenue. The north entrance into CityCenter is a west turn onto Harmon Avenue from the stoplight on Las Vegas Boulevard South or straight on Harmon crossing Las Vegas Boulevard. It traverses the entire north side and exits 1.5 miles to the west after crossing over the busy I-15 freeway. Midway through CityCenter on Harmon Avenue is an elevated circular drive with signage directing vehicles to Vdara and the north entrance of Aria. A second street south of Harmon Avenue is named CityCenter Place, which also has a stoplight on the Strip. That west turn will put you onto CityCenter Place, which is short and becomes a semicircle passing Veer Towers, Crystals, Aria's main entrance, and then returning to the Strip. The Mandarin Oriental is accessed by a left turn immediately after turning onto CityCenter Place.

Valet parking and pickup is available at both entrances to Aria, the Vdara, and at Mandarin Oriental. Valet parking for Veer and Crystals is located in the subterranean parking garage. The self-parking garage is convenient to the Mandarin Oriental and Aria by foot and to Crystals and Vdara via the tram. The garage itself is less confusing than most, with elevators to the hotels and tram station situated at the northeast corner of each level. On each level about 20% of available spaces are marked "no parking," presumably to accommodate modest pillars that intrude into the parking space. Practically speaking, however, most cars sedan size and smaller could fit very nicely in the verboten spaces.

CityCenter has its own tram gliding between the Bellagio and Park MGM resorts with an intermediate stop at Crystals. The Bellagio station serves Vdara; the Crystals station serves Aria, Veer, and Crystals; and the Park MGM station serves the Mandarin Oriental and Aria.

For pedestrians, the Strip sidewalk is elevated from CityCenter Place to Harmon Avenue. There is also an elevated sidewalk on the latter into the complex, but only along the north side. On CityCenter Place, the walkway gradually inclines 20 feet until it reaches Aria. There is no exterior walkway diagonally across the complex, but the tram will ferry walkers. So immense is the complex, there is an on-site fire station and power plant.

Aria Resort and Casino at CityCenter (aria.com)

THE SHOWPIECE OF CITYCENTER is the ultramodern Aria Resort and Casino, midpoint in the 67-acre complex. Just as Aria ascends to placement in the Las Vegas skyline, the name derives from an elaborate melody for a single voice rising musically. The 61-story imposing and graceful curved-glass hotel includes 4,004 rooms, nine bars and lounges, 16 restaurants, a spa and salon, a shopping arcade, an esports studio, a pool deck, a sizable conference center, subterranean parking, and the only casino within the CityCenter development.

The 150,000-square-foot casino is well configured with natural light streaming through walls of angled windows. Along the edge, private salons house high-end table games and slots, while various zones divide the extensive casino floor into more intimate sections.

Guest rooms and suites are richly appointed with customized furniture and accents of mocha, taupe, and sienna. Average room size is 520 square feet. These rooms are a techie's delight, with one user-friendly remote controlling the temperature, drapes, lights, music, TV, wake-up calls, and other guest services. Laptops, cameras, and game consoles can be connected to the LCD high-def TV. This TV can also be programmed to wake guests through controlled lights, drapes, and music. Safes are large enough to secure a laptop and other valuables. As a result of the hotel's unusual squares-on-curves architectural design, every room has front and corner views through floor-to-ceiling windows. Twice-daily housekeeping and turndown service complete the room amenities.

International cuisines satisfying every palate abound with restaurants from casual cafés and bistros to steakhouses and gourmet dining. Asian cuisine includes Blossom for classic Chinese, Lemongrass for modern Thai, barMASA for nouvelle Japanese, and Tetsu, featuring teppan dining within barMASA. Presenting European cuisine are Spain's Julian Serrano tapas lounge, Jean-Georges Steakhouse for steak and seafood, Michael Mina's Bardot Brasserie for Parisian brasserie fare, and Aria Patisserie. Not to be outdone, American cuisine is well represented by Shawn McLain's Sage and Five50 Pizza Bar, Herringbone, Aria Café, and The Buffet. Try Javier's for authentic Mexican cuisine. Several themed bars and lounges keep the venues buzzing.

At Liquid, the vast 215,000-square-foot elevated pool complex that can accommodate up to 1,500 guests, there are three oval pools, the secluded adult (topless) pool, fountains, and several hot tubs set in a tropical forest of palm, acacia, and pine trees. Fifty cabanas are interspersed among the water features and abundant foliage. Breeze Café provides all-day refreshments.

In addition to a complete menu of international beauty treatments, the 80,000-square-foot, two-level Spa at Aria includes a full-service beauty salon and barbershop, redwood saunas, eucalyptus steam rooms, a salt room, heated stone beds, fitness and group exercise studios, a co-ed balcony pool, meditation rooms, and a tanning area. Spa treatments are available poolside at Liquid.

Aria is a benchmark of sustainable environmental programs. Through contemporary design, water-and-energy conservation measures, use of natural and recycled materials, indoor air filtering, on-site generated power, and extensive use of natural light, CityCenter has earned seven coveted Leadership in Energy and Environmental Design (LEED) Gold certifications.

Four artists in CityCenter's $40 million public art program are displayed at Aria. At the lower north valet exit on Harmon Circle, Jenny Holzer has created *Vegas,* an elongated LED sign stretching 266 feet and incorporating scrolling text to entertain guests. Three elegant stainless steel columns by sculptor Tony Cragg welcome visitors into the self-parking lobby atrium. At the mezzanine level, suspended over the Promenade, floats Antony Gormley's *Feeling Material XXVIII,* an 8-foot spiral steel bar conveying the human body and visually suggesting stillness centered in a field of energy. The reception area houses celebrated artist Maya Lin's signature work, *Silver River.* Suspended above the front desk is the 84-foot shimmering interpretation of the Colorado River cast entirely in reclaimed silver.

Aria offers an unbeatable blend of visionary architecture, cutting-edge technology, impressive dining, distinguished personalized service, high-adrenalin entertainment, lush surroundings, and environmentally conscious design.

Mandarin Oriental/Waldorf Astoria at CityCenter
(mandarinoriental.com and waldorfastoria3.hilton.com)

THE MANDARIN ORIENTAL AT CITYCENTER was sold in 2018 and will be rebranded as a Waldorf Astoria. Because no timetable for the changeover was available at press time, we will continue to refer to the hotel as the Mandarin Oriental in the following profile and throughout this edition.

With a prime Strip-front placement, the 47-story Mandarin Oriental is the first hotel on the left when entering CityCenter via CityCenter Place. Exuding a refined Asian flavor reminiscent of its corporate origins, the 392-room nongaming boutique hotel provides Eastern hospitality in a Western setting. Half hotel and half condominium, the lower floors are transient accommodations, and the upper half are residences. In the tower's center is the spectacular 23rd-level sky lobby.

After entering the streetside porte cochere, the elevator whisks guests up to check-in on the 23rd floor. This midtower placement of lobby, bars, and restaurants is distinctive, and the skyline view from the Mandarin Bar is one of the best in Las Vegas. Twist by Pierre Gagnaire specializes in modern French preparations. The intimate Tea Lounge serves traditional high tea along with a mix of exotic and herbal beverages. MOzen Bistro offers international and pan-Asian fare alongside a theater kitchen near the third-floor, glass-walled conference center.

Merging Asian decor and Western design, the 850-square-foot deluxe rooms have a contemporary look and Eastern zest with dark woods, vibrant red accents, and stylized Oriental patterns. All rooms have walk-in closets and valet privacy closets for room deliveries. Catering to business travelers, accommodations include spacious desks, internet access, and plug-and-play capabilities with room-control technologies managing the entertainment center, drapes, and lights from one component. Bathrooms highlight the skyline view through an exterior window and feature a separate freestanding tub and shower. Another window with a retractable curtain separates the bathroom from the bedroom. Flat-panel TVs are embedded in the mirrors with double sinks underneath.

Swimmers will be keen on the two narrow lap pools on the eighth-level pool deck. Between them is a small center island shaped like a fan—the hotel's logo. White lounges and private cabanas line the perimeter surrounding the pools, two hot tubs, and a plunge. The outdoor poolside café serves light meals and snacks. A wind wall shields guests from gusts. The soothing bilevel 27,000-square-foot Spa at Mandarin Oriental is located near the pool on the seventh and eighth floors. A business center and small conference facility assist business travelers. Cell-phone and laptop rentals are available, as are secretarial services.

The works of two Japanese artists are prominently displayed within the hotel. The entrance showcases Masatoshi Izumi's *Cactus Life—Living with Earth,* a minutely carved 16-foot basalt lava sculpture honoring balance in nature. The lobby features three glazed ceramic monoliths by Jun Kaneko. These three rotund pieces of the *Untitled Dango Series* typify their Japanese name "dumpling." Inside the Tea Lounge, Jack Goldstein's fiery 8-by-8-foot acrylic *Untitled (Volcano)* brings vigor to the quiet setting. In the courtyard near the hotel's entrance is poised *Typewriter Eraser, Scale X.* This celebrated work by Dutch pop artists Claes Oldenburg and Coosje van Bruggen is a 4-ton, 19-foot fiberglass-and-stainless-steel rendering of a huge red-and-blue typewriter eraser. The connecting walkway area is also a great spot to view two murals by Richard Long, which are visible through the lobby windows of Veer Towers across the street.

Parking and valet service are available at the porte cochere and also beneath the hotel. When entering from the Strip onto CityCenter Place, the left turn to the Mandarin Oriental is in the center of the road and a short distance in. Some parking is also available in the garage south of the hotel with entry from the Park MGM access road. Directly in front of the Mandarin Oriental on the Las Vegas Strip is a pharmacy and souvenir gift shop.

The hotel appeals to globetrotters familiar with the extensive Mandarin Oriental name, business travelers, and tourists wishing to experience the Mandarin's well-deserved reputation for refined Eastern hospitality. With the exception of the occasionally busy sky lobby, the Mandarin Oriental Las Vegas is serene and zenlike.

Vdara Hotel at CityCenter (vdara.com)

VDARA WAS THE FIRST of the three hotels at CityCenter to debut. Rising 57 floors into rarified air, the stylish all-suite nonsmoking, nongaming hotel and spa is situated in the northwest quadrant of CityCenter between Aria and Bellagio. Vdara is connected to its sister property, the Bellagio Spa Tower, by an enclosed elevated walkway. Bordering the hotel on the west side is a small park with benches. Just east of the entrance is Karim Rashid's *Seven Continents of the World* sculpture with connecting silver spheres representing the fusion of cultures among land masses. The name *Vdara* was conceived to convey a sense of international sophistication.

An art-infused property, Vdara's main entrance at Harmon Circle is dominated by *Big Edge,* Nancy Rubins's cantilevered 50-by-80-foot work of art incorporating more than 200 colorful aluminum canoes, rowboats, and other small aquatic vessels fused together to create a bouquet of boats in a desert harborage. The abstract Expressionist *Damascus Gate Variation I,* an 8-by-32-foot fluorescent resin work of linked semicircles by Frank Stella, overlooks the reception desk. Two vertical stacked die-cut paper tapestries cascade on the east and west walls of the concierge lobby near the elevator bank. Titled *Day for Night, Night for Day* by Peter Wegner, together they parallel sunrise and sunset with appropriate solar and lunar colors reflecting the transition. To reflect the space, Wegner has added an original celestial light fixture suspended between the two pieces. On loan from the Bellagio, *Lucky Dream,* an 8.5-by-14-foot collage of found objects by Robert Rauschenberg, is in the lobby.

The three overlapping, crescent-shaped jet black and silver towers afford wondrous views of Las Vegas and the surrounding mountains. Corner rooms present the most panoramic sight lines. All guest rooms have heat-reflective horizontal windows. Imparting a residential feel, the expansive and tony 575-plus-square-foot suites feature king or double-queen bedrooms and a pull-out queen sofa in the living room. Large bathrooms, some with windows, continue the hotel's spa theme with large soaking tubs and separate showers. Many accommodations provide a washer-dryer unit. For guests choosing to dine in, all suites are furnished with a refrigerator, stocked minibar, microwave, cook-top stove, and dishwasher. There is 24-hour room service, a food-stocking service, and an on-site mini-mart for provisions. About 1,150 of the hotel's 1,495 suites are for nightly rental; the balance are residential condominiums.

A focal point is Espa spa at levels two and three. This peaceful wood-paneled, 16,000-square-foot spa offers men's and women's salons; three relaxation lounges; eucalyptus steam, sauna, and heated plunge; holistic health treatments; a work-out room; a spa retail store; and a champagne-and-smoothie bar with vegan and vegetarian snacks. Personal trainers and fitness classes are available to guests willing to temporarily suspend relaxation. Market Café Vdara, open 6 a.m. to midnight, is the only on-site restaurant. Other restaurants listed on Vdara's website are in Aria or elsewhere in CityCenter.

On the second level above the porte cochere is the landscaped Sky Pool, with swimming and dipping options of varying sizes and depths. Among the cabanas is a semisecluded plunge. Sky Lounge on the pool deck serves specialty cocktails, tapas, and appetizers. Loungers gazing skyward have a stunning view of the surrounding urban cityscape.

Parking is valet only at the main entrance. The business center and 10,000-square-foot conference area are near the front desk.

Vdara is a smallish hotel by Las Vegas standards, yet the level of service is high. The staff has an uncanny ability to remember the names of all guests. Vdara has an air of quiet seclusion, a hideaway in the midst of a busy urban center. The resort is ideal for those who favor a more restful and exclusive Las Vegas experience yet desire proximity to CityCenter and access to its nearby action and energy.

The Cosmopolitan of Las Vegas
(cosmopolitanlasvegas.com)

GLITTERING IS THE WORD best ascribed to this unthemed, design-driven high-end super-resort. The property exudes energy and an offbeat hipness, making it truly an indie hotel. Positioned at the northeast corner of the CityCenter complex, the dual-tower hotel offers a full casino, 14 restaurants, three pools, a showroom, a nightclub, a spa, a retail arcade, two fitness centers, tennis courts, three floors of meeting space, and subterranean parking. Situated on 8.7 acres, this footprint makes the layout overwhelmingly vertical with plenty of escalators and elevators: ride more, walk less. Pedestrian overpasses along CityCenter lead into the second level, three entrances provide access from the Strip, and there are large foyers at the East and West Towers from the West Harmon Avenue approach.

The literal and figurative centerpiece of the property, and its premier attraction, is the soaring 65-foot showcase chandelier of opulent transparent crystal drapes suspended from the fourth floor. Comprised of 2 million octagon-shaped crystal beads, these translucent panels enclose three cocktail lounges on three levels. Enjoy a beverage as walls of sparkling curtains shimmer around you.

Epitomizing an affluent lifestyle, the distinctive Terrace Studios, configured as 620-square-foot suites, are spacious and handsomely appointed. Each includes a den with sofa, easy chairs, and a desk separated by a low divider and a small kitchen. The latest technology allows guests to book reservations for the spa, restaurants, and shows and preset music, lights, heat, and air-conditioning. For a few dollars more, the slightly larger City Studios are similarly configured and decorated. Most rooms have sliding glass doors opening onto private open-air terraces with wicker loveseats and footstools, allowing guests to enjoy views of the Bellagio's lake and gardens, the towers of CityCenter, the Strip's skyline, or the Las Vegas cityscape. Smoking is allowed on the terraces. The Cosmo is spending more than $100 million to upgrade all of its 3,027 rooms. If you do the math, that's about $33,000 per room.

Countless glistening reflective surfaces of clear and colored glass, metal, marble, tile, crystals, bulbs, and mirrors invigorate the curved 110,000-square-foot casino. Overhead is a rampage of visually voluptuous designer lighting that delineates the slot, table games, roulette, and high-limit sections. Sheer fabrics divide gaming sectors but do not minimize the size of the casino. Along the periphery are the 1950s vintage Vesper lounge adjacent to the lobby, Henry's Scottish-themed restaurant and bar at the north entrance, and the street-level Bond Bar. Because of horizontal space constraints, the race and sports book is not adjacent to the casino but located on the second floor. The Chelsea Showroom, booking top-flight, nontraditional rock, R&B, and rap acts, is in the fourth-floor convention area.

Three distinct rooftop pools grace the property. Largest is the fourth-floor Boulevard Pool on the east side, which overlooks the Strip and has an infinity pool, heated pool, Jacuzzis, and a play area with Ping-Pong, volleyball, croquet, a pool table, and more. The Overlook is a six-level sunning and shading terrace with lounges, daybeds, and tables with umbrellas. A stage provides entertainment, including summer concerts and movies. The Overlook Bar and Grill serves alfresco small plates and blue-plate specials. The Marquee Club Day Pool on the south side has four levels of lounges, tables, and umbrellas along with three-story cabana lofts. In the evening it is an extension of the nightclub. The 14th floor's permanently sunlit southern exposure houses the curving Bamboo Pool, with stationary in-pool mattresses, cabanas dotting the perimeter, and a bar.

The posh four-level Marquee nightclub is divided into three sections: the small Boom Box features high-tech audio and visual; the quiet (really!) Library looks like an English club with dark woods, deep leather chairs and divans, pool tables, and shelves of books about Las Vegas; and the three-stage main club opens onto the private area of the Boulevard Pool.

All restaurants make their Las Vegas debut at the Cosmo, and many are clustered on the third floor: José Andrés's Jaleo tapas bar; Scarpetta, offering seasonal Italian cuisine; high-end STK chop house with on-site DJ; Estiatorio Milos, with fresh Mediterranean fish and crustaceans flown in daily; Rose. Rabbit. Lie., combining upscale dining and creative cocktails; Beauty & Essex, with small plates and classic cocktails; Blue Ribbon, from award-winning chefs and restaurateurs Bruce and Eric Bromberg; Zuma for modern Japanese cuisine; and Red Plate for Chinese fare. Framed menus are mounted at all host counters. A second-level space that used to be the sports book is now called Block 16 Urban Eatery and Bar. The five restaurants in the collection are Hattie B's Hot Chicken; District: Donuts. Sliders. Brew. from New Orleans; Lardo and Pok Pok Wing from Portland; and Tekka Bar: Handroll & Sake, which originated in Las Vegas. New on the bar scene is Ghost Donkey, a tequila and mescal cocktail bar from New York City. They join Va Bene Café, Holsteins for burgers, Eggslut, Momofuku, and China Poblano with noodle and tacos to eat in or take out.

The high-end, second-floor cavalcade of shops features retailers who have no brick-and-mortar stores elsewhere in Las Vegas. Tucked away in the convention area is the Wicked Spoon buffet. For a great photo opportunity, check out the giant spike heels along the corridor.

The serene Sahra ("desert") Spa & Hammam offers holistic treatments in a 30,000-square-foot Turkish- and Moroccan-themed facility designed with native desert materials. The Violet Salon provides hair, nail, and other beauty services.

Each tower has its own fitness center. The larger 5,250-square-foot, 14th-floor gym in the West Tower overlooks the tennis courts and at the far end features a boxing studio with regulation ring for sparring. The smaller 14th-floor, 2,087-square-foot East Tower gym is open 24 hours. Both facilities provide every conceivable model of exercise machine on the market. Outdoor Pilates and yoga classes or individual instruction can be scheduled.

In the lobby, too few counters and only four kiosks for automated check-in mean significant waits. To compensate, a staff of floaters with iPads monitors the area to assist guests. Concierges are stationed throughout the main floor, including the casino, to provide more accessibility and service to guests.

In keeping with their neighbor CityCenter's commitment to public art, The Cosmopolitan takes it to a new level: the entire property is a gallery of nontraditional art forms. At P3 art studio, visitors can observe on-site artists at work. Cutting-edge creativity prevails in new mediums: from the commissioned garage graffiti to abstract wall murals, LED displays, the four-sided electronic rooftop marquee with revolving artwork, and faux cigarette machines dispensing diminutive original pieces of jewelry, prints, ceramics, and paintings.

Vehicle entry into the hotel's expansive porte cochere is on West Harmon Avenue, the north entrance into CityCenter. Drivers need to pay attention because at the entry several lanes quickly converge into separate driveways for valet, guest registration, and ramps leading down to the underground garage's five floors. Glass elevators at both ends whisk guests to the casino and restaurant-retail levels. Avoid the north exit, which leads to a small alley that allows right turns only, crossing the busy sidewalk on the Strip. Day and night, the wait to turn is interminable as pedestrians stroll by.

The target guest market for the Cosmo is millennials, sophisticated urban dwellers, and travelers with a taste for the offbeat. The Cosmopolitan is fun and mildly unconventional. While the resort is a serious contender for the Las Vegas visitor, the refreshing impression imparted by the hotel is that it does not take itself too seriously and exudes a sense of fun.

The Cromwell (thecromwell.com)

THIS CORNERSTONE PROPERTY, at the lively Flamingo center-Strip inter-section, is an upscale gentrification by Caesars Entertainment of the workaday Bill's Gamblin' Hall & Saloon (née Barbary Coast). The aristocratic new name implies noblesse and style; the glamorous space is the manifestation of all things vibrant.

Standard rooms in the 188-room high-end boutique hotel are Parisian-infused, with hardwood floors, dark wood, and vintage leather furnishings. Custom photographs adorn the walls, and one panel is lined with ornate violet Regency wallpaper. Rooms are equipped with flat-panel TVs and Wi-Fi. All units have two minibars: one with traditional drinks and snacks, and a beauty bar provisioned with cosmetics and toiletries. The black-and-white mosaic tiled showers (no tubs) recall a turn-of-the-century *salle de bain,* complete with whimsical French-English idioms scrawled inside. Windows, uncommon in Las Vegas hotel bathrooms, are part of the scenario here. A complimentary morning coffee cart and late-afternoon iced teas, lemonades, and flavored waters are placed along the hallways on each floor. Many rooms on the north side face the Flamingo hotel tower just a few feet away and have limited light and sight lines. Other rooms on the north side look across a covered gap in the Cromwell at a wall. Worse, the covered top of the gap leaves these rooms in perpetual depressing shade with the overall effect of looking into a tunnel. Ask for a room on the south side of the resort. Lower floors could be noisy because the south side fronts hectic Flamingo Road, a major east-west artery crossing the city. High up on the west (Strip) or south sides should provide a quieter experience.

Most of the property's second floor is dedicated to Food Network chef Giada De Laurentiis's GIADA restaurant. An exhibition kitchen, antipasto bar, and alfresco dining with a panoramic view are attractive features of the eatery, which specializes in fresh pastas and California-style Italian cuisine. Lobby bars include the Interlude Lounge and the clubby library-inspired Bound, which also serves barrista-style early-riser coffee and pastries. The property's zenith is the three-level, 65,000-square-foot rooftop Drai's Beachclub Nightclub and outdoor pool complex overlooking the Strip and encompassed by the nocturnal blaze of thousands of lights from surrounding hotel towers. To describe this rarified setting as gorgeous is an understatement. The two palm-lined day pools are surrounded with bungalows, cabanas, and daybeds that easily transition into the post-sunset nightlife DJ experience. Downstairs, the celebrated Drai's After Hours club (open 1–8 a.m.) has returned to the original black-and-gold basement site where it all began back in 1997.

Given the intimate nature of the property, the casino is cozy as well; 440 slots join 66 table games and a secluded high-limit gaming salon on the entry level. A recent addition is a sports book featuring advanced technology and superb picture quality. Starring roles go to the 32-foot-long by 9-foot-tall LED video wall and a 9-foot-by-5-foot LED odds wall. Guest-centric touches include a complimentary happy hour on weekends 5–6 p.m.

Parking has always been a problem at this location with access and egress possible only from Flamingo Road in the block before its intersection with the Strip. This block is notorious for bumper-to-bumper traffic backing up from the intersection. The Cromwell, therefore, is not a great choice if you plan a lot of coming and going in your car. Taxis, of course, face the same problem. If you need a cab, your best bet is to catch one at the Flamingo Resort next door. If you must drive to the Cromwell, heed the following information.

The hotel's porte cochere is on the north side of Flamingo Road and reachable from the westbound lanes only. Two adjacent covered driveways lead taxis and private automobiles from Flamingo Road onto the property. Signage indicates both taxi and valet lanes. A third sign points to the far right lane directing drivers to the nearby self-parking garage that is shared with the Flamingo. In addition to the two Flamingo Road entries, vehicles heading to the hotel from northbound Las Vegas Boulevard can take a quick right turn after the stoplight at Flamingo Road onto a pedestrian-packed access street that bisects the real estate belonging to the Cromwell and Flamingo hotels. Directional signs indicate the main entrance and valet parking areas of each property—the Flamingo is to the left and the Cromwell to the right.

There is one exit to Flamingo Road from the Cromwell porte cochere, but that egress is a challenge because traffic is dense and relentless at all hours. It is possible to head in just one direction—west to the intersection at the Strip. No U-turns! The previously mentioned access street between the two hotels is an easier exit heading east (right) under the elevated monorail tracks to Linq Lane. A right turn at the stoplight at Linq Lane takes drivers one short block to Flamingo Road, where a traffic signal permits turns of choice. Allow extra time to navigate these maneuvers.

To be clear, there is no on-site self-parking at the Cromwell; the garage is shared with the neighboring Flamingo hotel. To reach self-parking, take the designated right lane exiting the covered driveways, turn right on the access street, and make a third right turn into the multilevel parking garage. When departing the garage, make a right turn to reach Linq Lane. The walk from the shared garage back to the lobby is an obstacle course, although the garage does provide stairways on the Cromwell (west) side. The services of Lewis and Clark plus a compass would be helpful here. For all of this convenience you're charged a mere $12 a day.

The D Las Vegas (thed.com)

THE D LAS VEGAS HOTEL-CASINO is the second metamorphosis of the original Sundance Hotel built in 1979, which at 34 floors was once the tallest building in Nevada. The property was reincarnated as Fitzgeralds Casino & Hotel, and after two decades has now been rebranded as the dynamic D Las Vegas. Shedding its Irish theme and leaving shamrocks in the dust of renovation, the hotel is moving forward with a fresh look and lively demeanor paralleling the resurgence of Fremont Street. It is no coincidence that the "D" moniker symbolizes Downtown.

The most obvious cosmetic changes occur on the facade and inside the two-level casino. The first floor is lined with cutting-edge slots and video games, a sports book, and table games hosted by high-energy dancing dealers. Longbar, Las Vegas's most lengthy bar at 100 feet, hugs the west wall, displaying 15 giant flat-panel TVs and 36 video games atop the extended counter. Rotating acts provide live music day and night. The second level houses the keno lounge and an authentic 1950s-era gaming experience, including vintage coin-fed one-armed bandits, a green-felt jungle, and other retro gambling devices. Even the background music, highlighting the fabled Rat Pack members, enhances the time capsule. On Fremont Street, the outdoor D Bar concocts specialty and frozen cocktails created by agile bartenders who juggle careening bottles as part of the show. A one-way escalator shuttles guests to the casino's second floor.

The hotel's 629 value-priced rooms have been updated with contemporary taupe and persimmon hues. Restaurants on the second floor include Andiamo Steakhouse, D Grill, and a murder mystery dinner show. An afternoon comedy club shares space later in the corner showroom with *Defending the Caveman*. The upstairs Vue Bar balcony is a great spot to watch zipliners zoom past. The registration area, valet parking, and the parking garage are on the south side of the hotel with the entrance on Carson Street.

Borrowing a phrase from composer Cole Porter, the new look is D-lightful . . . it's D-limit . . . it's D-lovely.

Days Inn at Wild Wild West (daysinn.com/lasvegas)

JUST WEST OF THE STRIP, at Exit 37 off I-15 at Tropicana Avenue, Wild Wild West is a small, 260-room hotel and casino that is convenient to the Strip, Downtown, and the airport. Its guest rooms are cheerful and comfortable. For east-facing rooms, however, there is a lot of road noise from I-15. The casino offers mostly slots and video poker, with a few table games and a sports book thrown in to keep up appearances. There is a lounge, a pool and Jacuzzi, and in case you're packing a pig, a barbecue pit. The adjacent Wild Wild West Truck Plaza offers more than 15 acres of paved and lighted parking, security patrol, and easy access from I-15. Also available are diesel and unleaded fuel, a truck wash, convenience store, and weigh station. Wild Wild West markets to locals and truckers.

Delano (delanolasvegas.com)

WITHIN THE MANDALAY BAY resort complex, Delano Las Vegas is a stand-alone, 46-floor tower that was originally known as THEhotel. Now a sister property to Morgans Hotel Group's Delano in Miami's South Beach, the Las Vegas concept debuts a cool white aseptic vogue. The Garden Lobby provides a luxurious and serene interior landscape with boulders stacked front and center, translucent drapery columns, an aerial rock sculpture, and warm woods and beige flooring bringing Nevada's Mojave Desert indoors. An expansive mosaic of the Grand Canyon is inlaid on the marble floor and surrounded by patterned tiles resembling drifting sands. Serving sandwiches, pastries, artisanal teas, and more, 3940 Coffee and Tea features comfy seating and a fireplace and does double duty serving cocktails later in the day. It's a quiet place to gear up or wind down. Across the foyer, the Franklin lounge offers contemporary sounds and small plates throughout the evening.

The 1,100 all-suite accommodations are 725-750 square feet each and elicit a midcentury-modern look with white bedding, tufted white headboards, and sheer drapes. A white love seat, white desk with chair, media center with flat-panel TV, refrigerator, and wet bar complete the accoutrements. The only accents in the all-ivory surroundings are the beige carpet and a chocolate leather side chair. A conversation piece is the ice bucket modeled after 32nd President Franklin Delano Roosevelt's hat box. Along with a large spa-style bath, each unit includes a powder room just inside the tiled entry.

On-site restaurants are chef Alain Ducasse's spectacular Rivea on the 46th floor, serving French and Italian cuisine, and Della's Kitchen, a farm-to-urban kitchen concept near registration on the main level. The BATHHOUSE Spa is open daily and includes a smallish gym, salon, saunas, and steam rooms. The target market at the Delano is Gen Xers and upscale travelers familiar with the Morgans brand.

Downtown Grand (downtowngrand.com)

IN LAS VEGAS, the past has a way of colliding with the future. This is particularly true Downtown. The original 1946 structure that housed the vintage Lady Luck hotel-casino for 35 years has morphed into the Downtown Grand hotel-casino. This bold industrial-chic property sits at the center of the Downtown 3rd redevelopment complex at 3rd Street and Ogden Avenue, one block north of the Fremont Street Experience. A combination of rustic and urban rawness novel in local casino design, the entirely rebuilt property resembles an early-20th-century factory, using the shell of the Lady Luck and its original catwalks, exposed trusses, ducts, and old brick walls, which can be seen in the public areas. These elements provide a hip yet nostalgic look.

The hotel's five-lane main entrance and porte cochere encompass the entire block of 4th Street between Ogden and Stewart Avenues, while the lobby is mid-casino and spills out onto 3rd Street. The property includes the 17-floor East and the 25-floor West Towers bisected by 3rd Street and connected by an elevated transparent pedestrian walkway. An escalator zips up three levels to where elevators then transport hotel guests to accommodations in either tower. The 650-room inventory features an eclectic combination of modern furniture and clean retro design. The handsome guest rooms are predominantly beige and brown with splashes of chartreuse or cobalt. About 20% of the rooms have a subtle Chinese motif and color scheme and feature electric teapots and an assortment of Chinese teas.

For on-site dining, visit Freedom Beat, located off the casino floor, for highly eclectic American cusisine. The Downtown Grand also claims several restaurants across from the casino on N. Third Street. Sidebar, primarily a drinking establishment, also offers appetizers and four main course selections.

The casino offers 700 slots, baccarat, an assortment of 30 tables, including a pit of Asian games, a race and sports book, and a poker room. An early adopter of esports (electronic sports, competitive video gaming), the Grand has a dedicated esports lounge on the casino floor and was the first American casino to take bets on competitive video gaming.

Citrus Grand Pool Deck, the 40,000-square-foot, south-facing, third-level pool area, can accommodate up to 1,200 people for sun worship and soirees and features a restaurant, a fire pit, cabanas, chaises, umbrella tables, and an alfresco gaming area. Adjacent to the pool complex is the fitness center and spa. Valet parking is available, and free self-parking is in the hotel's garage on Ogden Avenue.

Downtown 3rd, the privatized 3rd Street area between Ogden and Stewart Avenues, is a cutting-edge hub of indoor-outdoor bars and restaurants managed by the Downtown Grand. Among the food and beverage establishments on the street are Hogs & Heifers Saloon, Pizza Rock, and Triple George Grill. The north end is anchored by the National Museum of Organized Crime and Law Enforcement and flanked by a farmers' market that entices with fresh produce and homemade specialty food products every Friday, 9 a.m.–2 p.m.

It must be said that the Downtown Grand is pretty boring, with little entertainment or much of anything going on in the evening. It depends instead on the preexisting bars and restaurants arrayed along 3rd Street and the action on Fremont Street, two blocks away.

El Cortez (elcortezhotelcasino.com)

THE STORIED EL CORTEZ IS THE NEXUS of the funky Fremont East enter-tainment district in the rejuvenated Downtown. Immediately east of the five-block Fremont Experience, the 72-plus-year-old hotel at Sixth and Fremont has under-gone a transformation and added an annex of 64 glitzy cabana suites to the exist-ing tower, bringing total room inventory to 364. The hotel-casino, one of the most historic in Las Vegas, was owned by the infamous Bugsy Siegel in the mid-1940s. The property retains the original façade, a wing of sleeping rooms, and a section of the casino built in 1941 and is listed on the National Register of Historic Places. The casino also operates under Las Vegas's oldest gaming license, issued in 1941.

In the hotel's main tower, guest rooms were renovated in 2018 and sport a Spanish colonial look contrasting with modern accents and art. Exposed wood beams, carved four-poster beds, and accent rugs on wood floors give off a hacienda vibe, while Vegas-inspired art decorates the walls. Located directly above the casino and reached by a stairway are the hotel's original accommodations, with queen beds and decorated in a modified island motif.

In a freestanding building across Ogden Avenue are the stylish black-and-white Art Deco Cabana Suites. The all-king rooms feature glass furniture, black carpet, metal lamps, mirrors, and shiny patterned wallpaper. A black bench, white faux leather headboard, white linens, and lime green walls complete the look. All accom-modations are equipped with a flat-panel TV, Wi-Fi, and iPod dock. The Cabana Suites maintain a separate check-in with a small lobby. A business center and gym are also located in this wing.

Tucked away in the rambling and comfortable casino are several cozy slot nooks; included in the slot inventory are 245 coin machines, long gone from most casinos. Along with its famous poker room, blackjack, roulette, craps, keno, and a sports book are also available. The friendly, 24-hour Siegel's 1941 coffee shop and Naked City Pizza are the hotel's dining options. A holdover from the old days is meal service alongside the gaming tables for uninterrupted casino play. A lobby bar and lounge are opposite check-in, and two more bars are interspersed along the slot floor. A gift shop and vintage barber shop are also nearby.

The handsome brick porte cochere and valet entrance are on South 6th Street. Free parking in the low-ceilinged garage is accessed from South 7th Street—lower antennas and watch luggage racks! With the front desk at the west entrance, the valet side is far more convenient.

Ellis Island Casino and Brewery (ellisislandcasino.com)

ELLIS ISLAND, ON KOVAL LANE near Harmon Avenue just minutes from the Strip, is the most modest casino imaginable, but it's a treasure for those in the know. Its $12 complete New York Strip–steak dinner has been among the best meal deals in town for years (you have to join the players club to get the bargain price). Wash it down with a craft beer from the on-site microbrewery. The casino is joined at the hip to the equally modest Ellis Island Hotel (formerly a Super 8).

Excalibur (excalibur.com)

THE EXCALIBUR IS A HOTEL IN TRANSITION, attempting to chunk its family business for a more adult, middle-income market. Although it's difficult to transform a medieval-themed casino the size of an airplane hanger, Excalibur has succeeded to a remarkable degree. The hotel lobby and casino are now tasteful, with dark woods and stylish lighting fixtures. Gone are the cheap plastic look rendered in a Walmart color palette and the ridiculous faux Knights of the Round Table artifacts. There are still vestiges of Ozzie and Harriet's decorating touch, but the Excalibur no longer assaults the senses like it did in the good olde days.

The guest rooms likewise have received a makeover—the medieval theme has been mercilessly exorcised and replaced by surprisingly luxurious rooms replete with plush bedding, dark-wood furnishings, and contemporary baths. Though the windows are not huge, the views are great.

Excalibur's restaurants and shops are on the top floor of three levels. On the lower floor is a midway-type games arcade and the showroom, where jousting tournaments are featured. Other entertainment offerings include a male strip show and a Bee Gees tribute show. The cavernous middle level contains the casino.

The Excalibur is (for the moment) the twelfth-largest hotel in the world and the seventh largest in Las Vegas, and it certainly features the world's largest hotel parking lot (so far removed from the entrance that trams are dispatched to haul in patrons). If you can get past the parking-lot commute and the fact that most guest rooms have showers only (no tubs), and you do not object to joining the masses, there is good value at the Excalibur. The food is good and economically priced, as is the entertainment. The staff is friendly and accommodating, and you won't go deaf or blind, or become claustrophobic, in the casino. A high-energy nightclub, several pools, a spa, and a workout facility round out Excalibur's product mix. If you need a change of pace, a covered walkway connects the Excalibur with the Luxor next door, pedestrian bridges provide direct access to New York–New York and the Tropicana, and an overhead train runs to Luxor and Mandalay Bay.

Fiesta Henderson (fiestahendersonlasvegas.com)

FIESTA HENDERSON'S PARENT COMPANY, Station Casinos, has stripped this property of its stuffed monkeys and lions (it was formerly The Reserve) and made it southwestern-Mexican in flavor. Located southeast of Las Vegas at the intersection of I-515 and West Lake Mead Drive, Fiesta Henderson offers a 37,000-square-foot casino, a 12-screen movie theater, three restaurants, a buffet, a food court, and three bars. The quiet and romantic Fuego Restaurant is one of our favorite places for prime rib. As is the case with all Station Casinos, the Fiesta Henderson caters primarily to locals.

Fiesta Rancho (fiestarancholasvegas.com)

THE FIESTA RANCHO WAS THE FIRST of two casinos to be situated at the intersection of Rancho Drive and Lake Mead Boulevard in North Las Vegas (the other is Texas Station). With 100 guest rooms and a video-poker-packed, 40,000-square-foot casino (including the Spin City annex), the Fiesta features an Old Mexico theme. Entertainment includes a lounge, a nightclub, and a $40 million ice arena. Restaurants specializing in southwestern food are the Fiesta's major draw. An excellent buffet features a mesquite grill. A food court and a Denny's round out the dining options. There is a basic outdoor swimming pool and, perhaps equally enticing on a hot day, a tequila bar (20 different margaritas—*iolé!*). The Fiesta depends primarily on local clientele.

Flamingo (caesars.com/flamingo-las-vegas)

ONE OF THE EARLIEST RESORTS on the Las Vegas Strip, the Flamingo opened in 1946 at the south end of old Highway 91, the empty dirt road heading out of town to Los Angeles. Named after gangster Bugsy Siegel's leggy girlfriend's long limbs, which he likened to those of the slinky bird, the Flamingo has down-played its hot pink signature shade and upgraded most of its 3,626 guest rooms while rebranding the four-tower complex. A more masculine look forgoes the tropical theme and reinvigorates the almost 70-year-old property, but not to worry—the pink isn't gone completely, it's just less pervasive, so the decor is less flashy.

Guest rooms now feature macho colors of ebony, charcoal, and crimson juxtaposed with gray walls. Pink is understated with a small faux fur coverlet, a humorous touch atop the white bed linens. In homage to its historic past, the Flamingo has added a photo of the original hotel in each room, along with abstract prints.

The main casino's race and sports book, keno lounge, and high-limit area have been remodeled as well. A large food court houses Johnny Rockets, Pan Asian, Bonnano's NY Pizza, and LA Subs. The Paradise Garden Buffet is just off the casino. Adding to the restaurant repertoire are Center Cut Steakhouse and Carlos 'n Charlie's Mexican cantina and pool-view patio.

Along the north side of the property, joining Jimmy Buffett's energetic Margaritaville restaurant, is the Strip-side Margaritaville-branded casino and deck equipped with 220 themed slots, 22 table games, and youthful dealers in tropical attire high-fiving players when they hit 21. This perch for Parrotheads and fun-seekers sports chandeliers shaped like lime slices, beachlike flooring, a 20-foot model of the world's largest margarita, and a retail outlet anchored by the 5 O'Clock Somewhere bar.

The gated Beach Club pool and waterslide playground is small for the size of the property; however, the adjacent 15 acres of lush gardens and palms incorporate a wildlife sanctuary that is a habitat for a flock of flamingos, a passel of penguins, and an exotic bird aviary. Turtles, koi, ducks, and swans paddle this Xanadu's ponds and streams. The dense landscape, waterfall, and gazebo provide a rain forest backdrop for photos and weddings.

The hotel's entertainment lineup includes *X Burlesque,* singing siblings Donny and Marie Osmond, *Legends in Concert,* and *Piff the Magic Dragon.* The property lacks a nightclub, but with the nonstop party at Margaritaville, it is not missed.

Additional amenities include a spa and fitness center and golf privileges at two Caesars Entertainment courses. The Flamingo is the southern gateway to the LINQ entertainment district. Small dogs are welcome.

Four Queens (fourqueens.com)

SITUATED IN THE HEART OF DOWNTOWN, Four Queens offers good food, respectable hotel rooms, and a cheery casino. Joining its neighbor, the Golden Nugget, as a member of the "All Right to Be Bright Club," the Four Queens casino was among the first to abandon the standard brothel red in favor of a glistening, light decor offset by a tropical-print carpet. The result, as at the Golden Nugget, is a gaming area that feels fun, upbeat, and clean. Loyal Four Queens hotel guests tend to be middle-aged or older and come from Southern California, Texas, Hawaii, and the Midwest. The Four Queens also caters to the motor-coach-tour market. In the casino there is a mix of all ages and backgrounds. Locals love Hugo's Cellar restaurant, a Las Vegas landmark and one of the last vintage Las Vegas gourmet rooms.

Four Seasons (fourseasons.com/lasvegas)

THE AAA FIVE-DIAMOND FOUR SEASONS was the first hotel-within-a-hotel in Las Vegas. The concept of a high-end boutique hotel within a larger gaming property took flight at the millennium's turn back in 1999. The successful result has influenced other fusions, but it happened here first. The sophisticated Four Seasons inventory of 424 guest rooms is allocated to the 35th–39th levels of Mandalay Bay Resort's towers. Rooms reflect an Art Deco influence, with a cool black, white, and silver color scheme. Floor-to-ceiling windows afford abundant views of the Strip, McCarran Airport's three runways, or the extensive Vegas Valley.

The Verandah restaurant specializes in seasonal regional Italian cuisine. Guests can savor alfresco dining day or night, and a formal tea service is presented weekdays 3–4 p.m. Open nightly is the esteemed Charlie Palmer Steak. PRESS, the indoor-outdoor lobby bar, offers a barista experience, libations, and small plates. A 24-hour business center serves a diverse clientele of international visitors.

The palm-lined pool features a pool bar, hot tub, kids' pool, and playground. Access is from the elevator lobby by the spa and fitness center. The Four Seasons' private pool area is separate from Mandalay Bay's Beach; however, Four Seasons guests are welcome at the multihydrous complex.

The Four Seasons' porte cochere is to the left of Mandalay Bay's entrance on Las Vegas Boulevard South, but guests can access the hotel from Mandalay Bay's casino through a designated door and an elegant marble-floored hallway leading into the Four Seasons lobby. We recommend using valet parking; self-parking is inconvenient and a long trek from the distant Mandalay Bay parking garage or convention area. This tranquil nongaming hotel caters to the luxury market and guests seeking anonymity.

Fremont (fremontcasino.com)

THE FREMONT IS ONE OF THE LANDMARKS of Downtown Las Vegas. Acquired by the Boyd family in 1985, the Fremont offers good food, budget lodging, and a robust casino. Several years ago they redecorated and considerably brightened the casino, which is noisy and crowded. The table games are roomily accommodated beneath a high ceiling ringed in neon, while the slots are crammed together along narrow aisles like turkeys on their way to market. Locals love the Fremont, as do Asians, Hawaiians, and the inevitable Southern Californians. The Fremont, like all Boyd properties, is friendly, informal, and comfortable.

Gold Coast (goldcoastcasino.com)

SITUATED A HALF MILE WEST of the strip on Flamingo Boulevard, the lively Gold Coast feels right in the middle of the Strip's bustling action. The property recently remodeled all 711 sleeping rooms with a soothing cream, taupe, and gray color scheme, creating a serene environment away from the casino's buzz. Wi-Fi and internet access are available for a low fee.

The genial and rambling casino offers generous gaming odds, along with afternoon and evening lounge acts. Restaurants include T.G.I. Friday's, the Cornerstone steakhouse, Ping Pang Pong for Chinese, the Noodle Exchange, Ports of Call buffet, Red Zone sports bar, Java Vegas, and Subway. Bowlers will love the 70-lane, cutting-edge bowling complex above the casino; the complex also houses a video arcade and Nevada's largest bingo hall, seating 720 players. There's a low-rise covered parking garage in front of the hotel, but for easier check-in, the larger east garage and valet service have better access to the reception area.

The Gold Coast is a popular gathering spot for locals and a member of the respected Boyd Gaming Group, long known for great deals and low rates. The hotel specializes in competitively priced NASCAR and National Finals Rodeo packages.

Golden Gate (goldengatecasino.com)

THE OLDEST HOTEL IN LAS VEGAS, the Golden Gate is a vintage property with an even more vintage casino. Retaining its historical flavor, the casino has been updated and enlarged, and a five-story wing has been added at the south end. While the main pedestrian entrance remains on the Fremont Street Experience, the south side now sports a porte cochere facing Carson Street. The remodeled registration area with period furniture and memorabilia adjoins that entry lobby. Most of the interior is little changed since the hotel opened in 1906 as the Hotel Nevada at 1 Fremont St., across from the train depot. New patterned ceiling tile, freshly painted red and brown walls, and natural stonework are evocative of the way it was. Pillars, dark woods, chandeliers, carved glass, and mirrors in the low-ceilinged gaming area create the illusion that you're gambling during the Roaring Twenties. The flapper-costumed Dancing Dealers add nightly fun to this ambience.

The aura at today's Golden Gate is old is new again. The original guest rooms in the older building are beyond compact, and none of the 106 rooms are similar in size and configuration, reminiscent of a time before building codes and uniformity. Rooms are decorated in black, white, and red. Queens and double-doubles are available. Bathrooms are tiny with stall showers, and the floors retain their centenary black-and-white tile. The new 500-square-foot tower rooms repeat the signature tobacco and brick shades in the casino. All rooms have been upgraded and offer Wi-Fi and iHome docking stations. Bathrooms are larger but again feature showers only.

As the Hotel Nevada, the Golden Gate was assigned Las Vegas's first telephone number, "1," and proudly displays the town's first telephone, along with old ledgers, registers, and other historical documents from the era. In the 1930s, the hotel was inanely called the "Sal Sagev" ("Las Vegas" in reverse), but it was rechristened the Golden Gate in 1951, when new owners from San Francisco took over. The same family has owned the property ever since.

The Golden Gate closed its only restaurant and stopped offering its famous shrimp cocktail. Management asserts that the shrimp cocktail will be revived when a new restaurant comes on line. OneBar, the casino's permanent outside bar on Fremont Street, features bar-top dancers, frozen drinks, beer, and Flair bartenders whose cocktail-creation skills are showstoppers. A bandstand provides live music nightly. The hotel appeals to the budget-minded, Gen X–ers interested in a historic property, and old-timers reliving Las Vegas's very early days.

Golden Nugget (goldennugget.com/lasvegas)

THE UNDISPUTED FLAGSHIP of the Downtown hotels and one of the most meticulously maintained and managed properties in Las Vegas, the Golden Nugget is smack in the middle of Glitter Gulch. The hotel offers well-appointed guest rooms, a showroom, lounge entertainment, excellent restaurants, a large pool, a first-rate spa, a shopping arcade, a workout room, two on-site Starbucks, and a chapel and wedding planner. The casino is clean and breezy, with white enameled walls and white lights. The feel here is definitely upscale, though comfortable and informal.

The Golden Nugget recently underwent a $200 million renovation and expansion, the first since 1973 for the perpetual AAA Four-Diamond Award winner. At the heart of the improved Golden Nugget are a 500-room hotel tower and the renovated 600-seat showroom. Other elements of the makeover include a covered porte cochere, a VIP lounge, Vic and Anthony's steakhouse, and Lillie's Asian Cuisine, specializing in Cantonese and Szechuan fare. Plus, the spa and fitness center have been modernized and expanded. The most intriguing touch is the reconfiguration of the swimming complex to surround a 30-foot-deep shark aquarium (more on that below). Overlooking the aquarium is a revamped buffet, and integrated into the shark tank and pool is Grotto, a trattoria-style Italian restaurant.

The Golden Nugget's 25-floor smoke-free Rush Tower brings Strip-scene energy to Downtown's premium property. Located on the west side of the hotel's footprint, where First Street right-angles Carson Avenue, the tower has a separate porte cochere with valet parking. The 500 Rush rooms are 20% larger than the rest of the hotel's inventory, with a marginally higher rate. Boasting a brown, orange, and gold palette with cream down comforters and linens and a dark leather sectional and ottoman, the rooms resemble an upscale condo and impart a southwestern zen flavor. The sizable bathrooms feature parquet floors, oversize tub–glass shower combos, and double raised sinks. King rooms make up 95% of the tower's inventory.

Snaking through the Rush lobby is a dazzling white, umber, and yellow crystal chandelier, which coils above the registration counter. The area includes two restaurants: Red Sushi and Chart House, housing a 75-gallon coral-reef fish tank surrounded by turquoise walls and floors. Upstairs is Troy Liquor Bar nightclub, with a splendid outdoor patio overlooking the Fremont Street Experience. Entertainers such as Tanya Tucker, Charlie Daniels, Pure Prairie League, and Gary Lewis and the Playboys log short gigs in the showroom.

The three-level Tank aquatorium was voted among the "Top Ten Extreme Pools" by the Travel Channel. The focal point is a 30-foot-deep, 200,000-gallon carnivorous fish aquarium, which sharks call home. A three-story yellow tube shoots thrill seekers down an elongated chute that becomes clear acrylic straight through the shark habitat . . . all the better to see you with, my dear. H2O offers drinks and snacks near a fire pit with comfortable seating. Blackjack is available at shaded gaming tables. The circular second level includes seven private cabanas; the third level features the Hideout, with a bar and lounge, warm-water infinity pool, and six more cabanas.

In the lobby near the hotel's display of authentic golden nuggets, you can purchase gold from an untraditional ATM Machine. GOLD-to-go dispenses 24-karat-gold bars in seven weight choices from 1 gram to 250 grams. With spot pricing, the cost can fluctuate every 10 minutes depending on the gold market. Gold coins and Golden Nugget souvenir pieces are also available. Each is presented in a gift box. Cash only!

Though the Golden Nugget has always been Downtown's prestige address, the Rush Tower and top-to-bottom makeover catapulted it into the rarefied atmosphere of the premiere Strip resorts. More, the Golden Nugget's renovation and expansion helped trigger the metamorphosis of all of Downtown Las Vegas.

Green Valley Ranch Resort, Spa, and Casino
(greenvalleyranchresort.com)

IF YOU LIKE PAMPERING AND FRESH AIR with your gambling and dining, you'll love Green Valley Ranch. This indulgent Mediterranean Mission–style retreat, perched on a hill overlooking the distant Strip and the mountains, is in an upscale residential area about 15 minutes southeast of the Strip at the intersection of Green Valley Parkway and the I-215 Beltway. The property offers a 490-room hotel, a casino with 55 table games and more than 2,650 slot and video-poker machines, eight restaurants (including a buffet), a spa, and a 10-screen cinema complex. Like all Station Casinos, Green Valley Ranch provides locals with high-pay slots, good dining, an excellent players' club, and high-quality lounge entertainment.

Unlike most Station Casinos, however, Green Valley Ranch is very upscale. The restaurants are trendy, featuring some of Las Vegas's best-known chefs. Watering holes include the elegant Drop Bar, the Lobby Bar, and Sip. The hotel and its enfolding guest rooms are truly luxurious. Many of the guest rooms feature great views of the pool and spa areas and/or the desert and Strip beyond.

The 8-acre pool complex is lovely, more reminiscent of a country club than a Las Vegas hotel. Features include vanishing-edge pools near the spa and a large, centrally located swimming pool with a sandy beach at one end, perfect for the kids. There is also a small grassy playground.

Dining options abound. Hank's is a plush, masculine chop house and martini bar. The Feast Buffet is one of Las Vegas's best. Pizza Rock, Turf Grill, Tides Seafood and Sushi Bar, Borracha Mexican Cantina, Bottiglia for "rustic" Italian fare, a café, and a food court complete the culinary collage.

The 30,000-square-foot spa is a real star. The curving path from the hotel proper to the relaxation center is lined by a small vineyard offset by red roses. In addition to a wonderful array of treatments, the soothing architectural aesthetics at Green Valley do their part in providing a higher-quality experience. For example, on the treadmills you can meditate on the Zen sculpture arising from the three-lane lap pool or contemplate the Spring Mountains. The steam room has an outdoor view. Pilates and yoga classes are held in a perfect wood, glass, and mirrored high-ceilinged studio.

Located within easy striking distance of Lake Mead, Hoover Dam, the Black Canyon of the Colorado, and Red Rock Canyon, Green Valley Ranch offers a super option for families, the outdoor-oriented traveler, and for those who believe in the healing powers of being pampered.

Hard Rock Hotel (hardrockhotel.com)

IN 2018, VIRGIN HOTELS acquired the Hard Rock Hotel and plans to rebrand the property in the fall of 2019 following renovation of guest rooms, restaurants, and public spaces. The reflagged hotel will feature divided guest rooms, where a sliding door separates the sleeping section from the bath and vanity. The hotel's lounges and restaurants will include a Commons Club, a restaurant during the day and a nightclub after hours.

Until then, Hard Rock Hotel and Casino, living up to its name, honestly rocks around the clock. The hotel is fun, comfortable, and informal. Powerful music elevates the energy level with a constant percussive din.

The 18-floor Paradise Tower, the larger of HRH's two towers, has 490 tribal tattoo rock-and-roll decadent rooms with all the high-tech bells and whistles. Bathrooms are spacious but offer showers only. This tower is convenient to the conference area. Request a poolside room for a voyeur's view overlooking the tropical gardens.

The all-suite HRH Tower, with a higher level of service, appeals to an older, more affluent demographic. The tower's subdued lobby provides guests with a private registration area. A KISS photo-montage tapestry, a gigantic hologram of Jimi Hendrix, and Michael Jackson's $50,000 sequined white glove grace the lobby's black walls.

Guest rooms have a clean, contemporary look in muted beige, white, and black with parquet floors at the entry. A glass wall divides the bedroom and bath, with an optional curtain. Every room features a wet bar and photos and lithographs of iconic rock stars. A detached wall with back-to-back wide-screen TVs divides the sitting area and bedroom. Guests will want to rock out to the in-room Sound Matters Sound Bar jukebox, with 2,000 songs available at a touch. Choose a genre, artist, or decade and download songs to your own iPod.

A recent 40,000-square-foot casino extension where The Joint (Las Vegas's first rock venue) used to be features an international pit offering pai gow, baccarat, mini- and midi-baccarat, slots, and a high-limit room. Both casinos exhibit museum-quality rock memorabilia. The upsized Joint showroom seats 4,000 and features top rock artists. While the sound system is state-of-the-art, the floor-seating configuration is not inclined, so sight lines are poor from the middle and rear of the showroom.

The 25,000-square-foot Reliquary Water Sanctuary & Spa creates a luxurious experience in spartan surroundings. Although there are detached areas for men and women, the high-decibel bathhouse and lounge are coed. Treatment rooms include an area for couples massage with a tub and four-person party rooms with treatment beds and TVs for bachelor and bachelorette groups. There's also a small fitness center with an adjoining hair salon. Another well-equipped fitness center with a steam room and Jacuzzi is located downstairs.

The extensive Beach Club pool complex is notorious for its televised anything-goes Rehab parties. Five pools are divided into two sections, with the walled Rehab zone imposing a cover charge on afternoons when a TV crew is filming. An elevated infinity pool adjoins the Skybar and Restaurant and overlooks the shallow dish pool. The complex features island-themed evening concerts. Avoid the Rehab side on summertime Sundays if you're seeking solitude and the sounds of silence.

The 14,000-square-foot Vanity Nightclub is adorned with antique mirrors, crystals, pearl light fixtures, diamond patterns, and shiny copper walls pierced with metallic gold threads. Above the dance floor is the centerpiece $1 million cyclone chandelier, composed of 20,000 LED lights that can produce a Technicolor image, text, or movies. Unlike other clubs, Vanity boasts open seating. A fire pit dominates the casual outdoor patio overlooking the Beach Club.

Along the casino perimeter and in the shopping arcade are restaurants Nobu, Pink Taco, MB Steak, Fú Asian Kitchen, Oyster Bar, Culinary Dropout (an ultrahip gastropub), Goose Island Pub, Mr. Lucky's diner, Pizza Forte, and Fuel Café. Boutiques include Affliction (trendwear), Hart & Huntington Tattoo Co., and John Varvatos (men's clothing with a bandstand and musical instruments so shoppers can jam or be jammed).

Situated 0.75 mile east of the Strip, the Hard Rock's Paradise Road at Harmon Avenue location eliminates many of the traffic hassles confronting Strip visitors and gives guests excellent access to the airport, Las Vegas Convention Center, and major freeways I-15, I-215, and I-95. HRH caters to all ages but targets the hip and wannabes primarily from Southern California, the Midwest, Canada, and Asia. Lots of satisfaction here, but it's not for the faint of heart or hard of hearing. If you're a rock fan from any era, this is rock-and-roll heaven if you don't mind the constant, ear-numbing wall of sound.

Harrah's (harrahslasvegas.com)

A LAS VEGAS STAPLE, jazzy Harrah's occupies the middle of the Strip's most prestigious block and is within easy walking distance of Bally's, the Flamingo, the

Mirage, Caesars Palace, Paris, Bellagio, The Venetian, and TI. Unpretentious and upbeat, Harrah's offers 2,652 guest rooms, as well as a beautiful showroom, a comedy club, above-average restaurants, a buffet alongside the casino, a dance club, a pool, an exercise room, and a spa. A property-wide guest room renovation began with a rethink of the 600-room, 72-suite Valley Tower, now featuring sleek modern decor, hardwood floors, and area rugs.

Harrah's theme celebrating carnival and Mardi Gras is evident in the two giant gold-leaf court jesters hefting a 10-ton, 22-foot-diameter globe that first welcome you on either side of the main hotel entrance, and a gold-swirled ceiling above the registration area continues the theme. The casino is decorated with brightly colored confetti-patterned carpet, ceiling murals, and fiber-optic lighting. Although the theme treatment is bright, it has a somewhat tired feeling, rather like a Mardi Gras dawn.

The L-shaped casino of 87,000 square feet is loud beyond average. It can be entered directly from the Strip alongside an open-air lounge with talented bartenders and a stage that hosts mostly rock music. This covered amphitheater adds to the raucous, let-loose feeling of Harrah's, but it might interrupt the sleep of some guests.

Though it is hard to imagine anyone not feeling comfortable at Harrah's, its clientele tends to be older visitors from the Midwest and Southern California, as well as business and convention travelers.

Other enticements include a large but otherwise unremarkable swimming area where you get sound bleed from the outdoor stage, a cozy upscale steakhouse with a view of the Strip, and an outdoor plaza with fountains. With its "Let the good times roll" spirit, Harrah's is a blend of modern and vintage Las Vegas.

Hilton Lake Las Vegas (hilton.com)

ORIGINALLY A RITZ-CARLTON, then the Ravella for a short stint, this non-gaming, 349-room Lake Las Vegas resort is now owned by Hilton. Within tranquil surroundings, the 15-acre lakefront property is approximately 22 miles from McCarran Airport and 25 miles from the Las Vegas Strip.

The rectangular lobby is furnished in gleaming dark woods and rich area rugs over tile and wood floors and divided into three sections: a business networking lounge with handsome library tables and complimentary Wi-Fi hookups, a center social lounge, and the Firenze Bar serving cocktails and light dinners. Cocktails are served on the outdoor terrace overlooking the formal Florentine garden and fire pit, the marina, and the lake. Downstairs, Café Medici is open for breakfast and lunch.

Situated on eight floors, the 486-square-foot guest rooms are serenely decorated in a pale Mediterranean palette. Marble bathrooms are large with a two-sink vanity, weight scale (ouch!), and separate tub and shower.

Stretching across the west lip of the lake is the three-story 375-foot Ponte Vecchio Bridge. Sailboats and kayaks glide underneath the bridge. This wing of the hotel houses guest rooms facing east toward the lake or west toward the stark desert hillsides. An additional parking lot lies at the north end of the span.

The peaceful 30,000-square-foot two-story spa is a separate building across from the hotel's circular drive and sits atop a sandy beach and waterfall with handsome heated pool adjacent at water's edge. A fitness center, salon services, a variety of European massages, and 24 holistic treatment rooms are available. The facility includes a private garden proffering outdoor yoga classes, exercise sessions, and a meditation area. A restful terrace overlooks the pool, gardens, and the lagoon. For guests relishing the outdoors, hiking and biking trails hug the lake, and paddle boats, canoes, and kayaks are available for rental.

Valet parking is accessible and convenient. The parking garage near the southside meeting rooms is a distant stroll from the lobby and elevators. A wedding chapel, wedding planner, and florist are also on site. The business center is in the conference area.

Nearby Casino MonteLago offers 275 slot machines and electronic table games. Golf is available at the nearby Southshore Golf Club, the first Jack Nicklaus Signature Course in Nevada. The hotel can arrange airport transfers, but most guests prefer to rent a car for flexibility. Pets are accepted.

Hooters Casino Hotel (hooterscasinohotel.com)

LET'S GET ONE THING SETTLED at the beginning. If you like Hooters—the chain of restaurants featuring hot wings and other pub grub served by waitresses in tight T-shirts and short shorts—then you'll love the Hooters Casino Hotel. If you don't like Hooters restaurants, you won't much care for this place either, as the Hooters "mystique" is omnipresent. However, if you're not constitutionally averse to the brand, you might be surprised at how well the restaurateurs transformed the darkly dank San Remo into this bright, happening, and admittedly fun place.

The casino floor looks remarkably like a Hooters restaurant, with the same light blonde wood, cheerful lighting, and simple orange accents. A large Hooters-like square bar greets you at the front door. At the gaming tables, dealers are often attired in full Hooters livery. In addition to a pleasant lounge and coffee shop, there's an actual Hooters restaurant inside as well, and it draws huge lines of eager diners at peak times. A Steak 'n Shake rounds out the dining options. A decent-size pool dominates the back of the hotel, complete with waterfall, pool bar, and stage for live music. Guest rooms have abandoned the original Hooter orange motif in favor of restful shades of gray and dark furniture. The reasonable room rates, utter lack of pretension or attitude, and party-hearty atmosphere draw a mix of middle-aged patrons and college kids, with a few families thrown in for good measure. Although Hooters has been a breakout hit, it was sold in 2015 to a New York–based investment firm for $70 million. A new name is on the horizon, but the Hooters restaurant will remain.

JW Marriott Las Vegas/Rampart Casino
(jwlasvegasresort.com; rampartcasino.com)

THE JW MARRIOTT LAS VEGAS was the first of several upscale properties to offer a Scottsdale–Palm Beach resort experience as an alternative to the madness of the Strip. Situated west of town near Red Rock Canyon, the property consists of two southwestern-style hotels built around the Tournament Players Club (TPC) golf course. The classy, circular Rampart Casino (named after the road on which it is located) is operated by an independent contractor and targets the local market. The JW Marriott operates primarily as a meeting venue with a secondary emphasis on golf and the resort's exceptional spa.

Standard hotel rooms are huge at 560 square feet. In many rooms, French doors open onto a balustrade overlooking the pools and gardens (11 acres of palms and pines tower over the winding pools, waterfalls, and walkways), or better yet, the mountains to the west, a stirring alternative to the usual neon. Baths feature a whirlpool tub, separate shower, bathrobes, and telephone.

Fine dining includes the Hawthorne Grill, a steakhouse, and Spiedini for Italian. The buffet here is one of the better spreads in town. Although the lounges offer live entertainment, there is no showroom. A high-tech race and sports book with adjoining bar and lounge were added to the product mix in 2018. The JW Marriott is pricey but perfect for those who come to enjoy the beauty and recreational resources of the mountains and valleys west of Las Vegas. Only minutes away are world-class hiking, rock climbing, mountain biking, and road biking.

The LINQ Hotel & Casino (caesars.com/thelinq)

CAESARS WORLD HAS YET AGAIN rebranded and re-energized the former Imperial Palace. This incarnation is the LINQ Hotel & Casino, capitalizing on the nearby LINQ entertainment district.

During the property's brief stint as The Quad, interior renovations were completed that eliminated the tired Asian motif and introduced a contemporary look to the public spaces, including the front desk and lobby, retail arcade, and fifth-floor restaurant area. The expanded casino is now awash in designer shades of red, taupe, and black. A new spa and pool deck complete the package.

Guest rooms and suites have been renovated and are now urban-chic, with modern furnishings, floor-to-ceiling windows, high-tech gadgets, and Wi-Fi. Some rooms can accommodate up to five guests with a colorful configuration that includes two queen beds plus a twin-size bunk loft.

The front entrance has been relocated to the north side of the complex and can be accessed by driving through the parking garage via Koval Road on the east side of the property, or through the Harrah's tunnel off Las Vegas Boulevard South. A covered pedestrian walkway to The LINQ entertainment district commences at Harrah's Carnival Food Court and passes through The LINQ Hotel. There are also two reconfigured entries from the Strip.

Current entertainment offerings include Mat Franco's *Magic Reinvented Nightly.*

Guy Fieri, UNLV hometown grad and Emmy Award–winning chef, launched his first local restaurant, Guy Fieri's Vegas Kitchen & Bar, at the LINQ Hotel. Also included in the dining inventory are Chayo Mexican Kitchen and Hash House A Go Go. Many more dining, drinking, and entertainment choices are adjacent at The LINQ entertainment district, including the popular Brooklyn Bowl, featuring 32 bowling lanes, a huge music venue, and the Blue Ribbon restaurant.

Lucky Dragon (luckydragonlv.com)

THE LUCKY DRAGON opened in 2017, during the the flamboyant year of the rooster, which is characterized by meticulousness, optimism, and profitable joint ventures, all auspicious for gaming, per the Chinese zodiac. The hotel's name itself reflects the zodiac's primary symbol for good luck and power. Unfortunately, however, it didn't take very long before the Lucky Dragon's luck ran out. On January 4, 2018, the casino, the spa, and almost all restaurants closed. That left the hotel and the gift shop to struggle along while owners sought a buyer for the property. As of this writing, no prospective buyer has come forward, and some investors and creditors are advocating abandoning the property. Assuming the hotel remains open, the following will give you a sense of the place.

This Asian-themed property is a tribute to feng shui: crimson and gold decor, interior spatial innovations, and stunning red glass exteriors. A slender nine-story needle with 204 rooms and suites on six levels, this hotel is a blend of Far East gaming and culture meeting the New West. The white rooms are appointed with contemporary low-rise furnishings, red garnishes, framed silk paintings, and traditional Chinese calligraphy wall art. Signage is printed in both Chinese and English.

Luxor (luxor.com)

THE LUXOR IS ON THE STRIP, south of Tropicana Avenue next to the Excalibur. Representing Mandalay Resort Group's (now MRI's) first serious effort to attract a more upscale, less family-oriented clientele, the Luxor is among the more tasteful of Las Vegas's themed hotels. Though originally not believed to be on a par with TI and the MGM Grand, the Luxor may be the most distinguished graduate of the much-publicized hotel class of 1993. While the MGM Grand is larger and TI originally more ostentatious, the Luxor demonstrates an unmatched creativity and architectural appeal.

Rising 30 stories, the Luxor is a huge pyramid with guest rooms situated around the outside perimeter from base to apex. Guest-room hallways circumscribe a hollow core containing the world's largest atrium. Inside the atrium, inclinators rise at a 39-degree angle from the pyramid's corners to access the guest floors. While the perspective from inside the pyramid is stunning, it is easy to get disoriented. Stories about hotel guests wandering around in search of their rooms are legend. After reviewing many complaints from readers, we seriously recommend carrying a small pocket compass.

The Luxor's main entrance is from the Strip via a massive sphinx. From the sphinx, guests are diverted into small entryways designed to resemble the interior passages of an actual pyramid. From these tunnels, guests emerge into the dramatic openness of the Luxor's towering atrium. Rising imposingly within the atrium is an exotic cityscape. The Luxor has succumbed to the let's-nuke-our-theme contagion and has driven the Egyptians back to Egypt.

Proceeding straight ahead at ground level from the main entrance brings you into the open and attractive 120,000-square-foot casino. One level below the casino and the main entrance is the Luxor's main showroom. Entertainment includes Blue Man Group; *Fantasy,* a topless revue; Cirque's *Criss Angel MINDFREAK Live!,* a magic-themed production show; and comedy headliner, Carrot Top. One floor above entry level, on a mezzanine of sorts, is an array of structures that reach high into the atrium. These dramatic buildings and facades transform the atrium, which is home to two exhibits. *Bodies . . . The Exhibition* is an extraordinary and riveting introduction to human anatomy through authentic, preserved human bodies. It takes you stepwise through every part of the human body, explaining its many systems. The other exhibit is *Titanic: The Artifact Exhibition,* which takes guests on a chronological odyssey from the design and building of the ocean liner to life on board to its sinking. In a bid to attract millennials, Luxor closed its nightclub to make way for an esports arena with a competition stage, LED video wall, daily gaming stations, and a television-quality production studio.

Flanking the pyramid are two hotel towers that are part of an expansion, which also includes a health spa and fitness center and additional meeting and conference space. Guest rooms are some of the warmest and most visually appealing in Las Vegas. In all, the Luxor offers 4,450 guest rooms.

Restaurants include a sports bar, Public House, Tender Steaks and Seafood, Rice and Company (specializing in Asian cuisines), T&T (Tacos and Tequila), and a food court. The Luxor's large, attractive pool complex, surrounded by private cabanas, desperately needs some additional plants and trees. Paid self-parking is not as much a problem at the Luxor as at most large properties. Valet parking is quick and efficient but expensive. The Luxor is within a 5- to 12-minute walk of the Excalibur, the Tropicana, and the MGM Grand. A moving walkway connects the Luxor to the Excalibur and an overhead "cable liner" (a monorail propelled by a cable à la San Francisco cable cars) connects it with Mandalay Bay.

M Resort (themresort.com)

M RESORT, SITUATED AT Las Vegas Boulevard South and Saint Rose Parkway, about 10 miles from Mandalay Bay, is the most upscale resort south of the Strip. The *M* of M Resort could easily stand for "mirage," given how it rises all by itself, shimmering in the desert. That letter, however, is actually from the family name Marnell, in honor of founder and CEO Anthony Marnell III. Active in Las Vegas hospitality and gaming for decades, the Marnells previously built and operated the Rio, establishing a reputation for style and innovation. The Marnells have always produced a high-quality experience geared to the local population. With a refreshing lack of spectacle and abundance of modern elegance, M Resort is specifically located to serve the affluent residential developments in the south Las Vegas Valley.

The well-configured casino with spacious aisles groups similar slots together with ample playing room. Blackjack, pai gow, mini-baccarat, roulette, and craps are arranged in small groups of eight tables. Dealers are assigned to the same table for an entire month, so players partial to a lucky dealer can return to his table. The race and sports book is intimate, seating just 50 people, but absolutely cutting-edge.

The 110,000-square-foot Villagio Del Sole and Entertainment Piazza is expansive. Bamboo and palm trees line the left side of the marble entry staircase where running water tumbles over large marble cubes along the steps. Private cabanas line the perimeter of the grounds, and two hot tubs are positioned at each rear corner along with a fire pit and tall metal torches. Tucked away on the west side is the Daydream pool for adults. The infinity pool is divided along the center by a walkway scattered with orange daybeds. An outdoor stage at the north end of the pool features concerts regularly. During normal operations, with just 390 rooms at the M, the 2.3-acre pool area is seldom congested.

Dining options include the Studio B buffet, which includes unlimited beer and wine for dinner and adds special seafood dishes to the usual lineup on weekends. With the exception of the Studio B buffet and Vig Deli, the restaurants have terraces and outdoor dining to take advantage of the breathtaking view of Las Vegas, enhanced by the hotel's elevation (400 feet higher than the Strip). To better control the quality and price point of meat offerings, the resort maintains a butcher shop on the premises, with fresh beef, pork, and lamb flown in from its own Montana ranch. Fine-dining options include Anthony's, specializing in prime steak, seafood, and an oyster bar, and Marinelli's for regional Italian cuisine and homemade pastas. Rounding out the dining mix are Jayde Fuzion, for sushi and Asian specialties, and Burgers and Brews, an all-adult venue after 4 p.m.

Lounges are stylish and feature some of the best free entertainment anywhere. Check out the Ravello lounge for high-energy music that includes all the classics of rock, pop, and jazz as well as modern favorites. If you crave a taste of the grape or the fruit of the barley, M has you covered. 32º Draft offers 96 different beers on tap, while at Hostile Grape, a chic and cozy wine cellar, you can sample 160 different wines by the glass. Vintages from all the great wine-producing areas of the world are represented. Oh yeah, cola and soft-drink fans have their oasis, too, with a free soft-drink dispenser just off the casino, a first in any casino.

Guest rooms feature floor-to-ceiling windows with electric drapes, Bose radios, iPod docking stations, and flat-panel TVs, as well as bathroom TVs embedded in the mirrors. Standard rooms are large at 420 square feet, and views can be either of the Nevada desert landscape to the south or the Strip to the north, overlooking the pool. The luxury bath has a glass wall that faces the center of the room and the window.

Though it feels remote, M Resort is only a 10- to 12-minute drive on I-15 from the heart of the Strip. One caution, however: Do not miss the Saint Rose Parkway exit when you're driving southbound. It's 23 miles to the next exit. Parking is still free at the M, but you will pay a $25-per-day resort fee.

Main Street Station (mainstreetcasino.com)

SITUATED ON MAIN STREET between Ogden and Stewart Avenues in Downtown Las Vegas, Main Street Station originally opened in 1992 as a paid-admission nighttime entertainment complex with a casino on the side. Owned and managed by an Orlando, Florida, entrepreneur with no casino experience, it took Main Street Station less than a year to go belly-up. The property was acquired several years later by Boyd Gaming, which used Main Street Station's hotel to accommodate overflow guests from the California across the street. In 1997, the Boyds reopened the casino, restaurants, and shops, and added a brewpub.

The casino is one of the most unusual in town (thanks largely to the concept of the original owner). With the feel of a turn-of-the-20th-century gentlemen's club and enough antiques, original art, and oddities to furnish a museum, Main Street Station is a must-see. With its refurbished guest rooms, brewpub, good buffet, and unusual casino, it is both interesting and fun, adding some welcome diversity to the Downtown hospitality mix. Main Street Station is connected to the California Hotel across the street by an overhead corridor.

Mandalay Bay (mandalaybay.com)

MANDALAY BAY OPENED on March 2, 1999, on the site of the old Hacienda, which was imploded on New Year's Day 1998. It completes the Mandalay Bay "Miracle Mile," which stretches along the Strip south from the Bellagio and includes CityCenter, Park MGM/NoMad, New York–New York, the Excalibur, Luxor, and finally Mandalay Bay. A cable liner connects Excalibur, Luxor, and Mandalay Bay every 15 minutes, 24 hours a day (it stops at Luxor on the northbound leg only).

Mandalay Bay, with 4,756 rooms (including the on-site Four Seasons Hotel and the Delano), is a megaresort in the true sense of the overworked word. Within the sprawling complex are the 43-story, three-wing tower; a 12,000-seat arena; a 1,600-seat theater; an 1,800-seat House of Blues concert venue; two dozen restaurants; an 11-acre water park; three large lounges; and the second-largest convention facility in Las Vegas. Mandalay Bay had Las Vegas's first hotel-within-a-hotel on the property: the 424-room Four Seasons. The whole schmear cost a cool billion plus. Adjoining the main casino is a second on-site hotel, the Delano, with 1,120 suites. Both the Four Seasons and the Delano are profiled in this section under their own names.

But that's not the half of it because Mandalay Bay isn't your standard megaresort. It's clear that the planners and designers set out to take a few risks and appeal to a young, hip, fun-seeking market—as opposed to Bellagio, which targets a more refined, sophisticated, older clientele. All the different ideas jammed into Mandalay Bay might not always add up to a cohesive whole, but so many parts of the sum are unique that you can't help being intrigued.

The signature spectacle is the four-story wine tower at Manhattan celebrity chef Charlie Palmer's restaurant, Aureole. This nearly 50-foot-tall glass-and-stainless-steel structure stores about 10,000 bottles of wine. Lovely, athletic women dressed all in black manipulate the motorized cable, one on each of the four sides, that raises them up to retrieve a selected bottle and lowers them back down to deliver it.

Red Square Russian restaurant has a one-of-a-kind refrigerated walk-in showcase, open to the public, that stores 200 different varieties of vodka at 15°F. Drinks are served on a long bar top that has a thick strip of ice running its length. The House of Blues restaurant and entertainment complex serves food (Southern-style and Creole-Cajun) and has the world's largest collection of Deep South folk art, as well as a strange dark bar with a crucifix theme. House of Blues also puts on a Sunday gospel brunch and holds rock and pop concerts in its 1,800-seat theater. Beef eaters are well served with two upscale chop houses, Michael Mina's STRIPSTEAK and Charlie Palmer Steak at Four Seasons. Other restaurants include Wolfgang Puck's Lupo (serving Italian fare), Fleur by Hubert Keller (serving globally inspired small plates), Rick Moonen's RM Seafood, Border Grill (serving Mexican cuisine), Kumi (with modern Japanese cuisine), a noodle room, a coffee shop, an adequate but somewhat disappointing buffet, and ice-cream and coffee counters.

In the nightlife department, Eyecandy Sound Lounge & Bar, a sprawling DJ dance venue, makes clubbing hassle-free, while Light nightclub lures guests with its stable of resident DJs. If you need to cool your jets, try minus5° Ice Bar.

A main attraction at Mandalay Bay is Shark Reef, a 90,000-square-foot aquarium exhibit with a walk-through acrylic tunnel. The aquarium is home to about 2,000 marine species, including Nile crocodiles, moray eels, stingrays, and, of course, sharks.

The 11-acre Mandalay Bay Beach has a lazy river, a placid pool, a beachfront café and bar, and a wedding chapel. The centerpiece, however, is a huge wave pool. The surf can be cranked up from 1 to 6 feet.

Speaking of acreage, the casino is typically monumental, with plenty of elbow-room between machines and tables. The race and sports book boasts one of the largest screens in town, which is only right because the book is so big the screen must be seen from long distances. The 80-seat (each one an oversize, velour-covered easy chair) lounge and the large poker room are connected.

Mandalay Bay is the second-largest meeting and convention venue in Las Vegas and has its own entrance separate from the main entrance to the hotels and casino. It's located near the Shark Reef attraction and is a great place to be picked up by Lyft or Uber.

The Shoppes at Mandalay Place, in the pedestrian passage that connects Mandalay Bay with the Luxor, features boutiques and restaurants.

MGM Grand (mgmgrand.com)

MGM GRAND CLAIMS THE DISTINCTION of having Vegas's largest casino. Within the 112-acre complex, there is a 16,800-seat special-events arena, 380,000 square feet of convention space, 171,500 square feet of casino space, and a multi-level paid parking facility. There's also a small casino outside the lobby of the

Mansion, MGM's ultra-upscale whale digs. Finally, a 6.6-acre pool-and-spa complex took over a chunk of the long-defunct amusement park along with the dedicated convention center.

The MGM Grand is on the northeast corner of Tropicana Avenue and the Strip. The Strip entrance passes beneath a 45-foot-tall MGM Lion atop a 25-foot pedestal, all surrounded by three immense digital displays. The lion entrance leads to a domed rotunda with table games, and from there to the MGM Grand's four larger casinos. All casinos are roomy and plush, with high ceilings and a comfortable feeling of openness.

A second entrance, with a porte cochere 15 lanes wide, serves vehicular traffic from Tropicana Avenue. For all practical purposes, this is the main entrance to the MGM Grand, permitting you to go directly to the hotel lobby and its 53 check-in windows without lugging your belongings through the casinos. Just beyond the registration area is the elevator core, with 35 elevators servicing 30 guest floors.

Beyond the elevator core, a wide passageway leads toward five of the MGM Grand's many restaurants. The MGM Grand's supernova restaurant is Joël Robuchon, which serves a French culinary feast of the highest quality and greatest exclusivity. Other fine-dining stars in the hotel's galaxy include L'Atelier de Joël Robuchon, serving more fine French cuisine via counter service (dishes are prepared in front of you); Tom Colicchio's Craftsteak, offering beef and seafood; Hecho en Vegas, a Mexican restaurant; Fiamma, an Italian trattoria; Morimoto, a Japanese restaurant; Emeril's New Orleans Fish House, offering Creole-Cajun dishes; Hakkasan, specializing in modern Cantonese; and Wolfgang Puck Bar & Grill and Crush for fancy American cuisine. Less formal are Michael Mina Pub 1842, Tap Sports Bar, and the Avenue Café. MGM Grand's buffet adjoins the casinos between the porte cochere and lion entrances. For fast food there is a food court.

There are two showrooms at the MGM Grand. The 740-seat Hollywood Theater features headliners, and the larger *KÀ* Theatre is home to Cirque du Soleil's *KÀ*. The Brad Garrett comedy club has moved downstairs between the parking garage and an underground retail passageway. JABBAWOCKEEZ, a dance production, completes the lineup. Hakkasan, MGM Grand's premiere nightspot, features celebrity DJs, high-tech lighting, and three levels of activity with a variety of areas and atmospheres. Entertainment is also offered in the casino's four lounges. In addition, the MGM Grand's special-events arena can accommodate boxing, tournament tennis, rodeo, and basketball, as well as major exhibitions.

Amenities at the MGM Grand, not unexpectedly, are among the best in Las Vegas. The swimming complex is huge—23,000 square feet of pool area, with five interconnected pools graced with bridges, fountains, and waterfalls. Other highlights of the complex include an artificial stream to float in, a poolside bar, and luxury cabanas. Adjoining the swimming area is a complete health club and spa. For those to whom recreation means pumping quarters into a machine, there is an electronic games arcade supplemented by a "games-of-skill" midway. A recent addition is Level Up, an interactive, tech-savvy, skill-based adult playground. Also at MGM Grand, but with its entrance on Koval Lane, is Topgolf, a tiered driving range and entertainment complex (see page 425). In the transportation department, the MGM Grand is the southern terminus of the Las Vegas Monorail.

The lion logo remains, but the Hollywood theme predicated by the hotel's name is gone with the wind, and in its place are a sleek 21st-century vogue and the latest in-room technology. Remember that the MGM Grand is the third-largest hotel in the world, so be prepared for a hike from the elevator banks to your accommodations. Request a higher floor where the views are spectacular.

A rare enclave of peace and privacy, MGM Grand's Signature condo-hotel towers are a 5- to 7-minute walk east of the main casino. Conspicuous by its absence is on-site gambling. For more details on the Signature, see page 144.

Mirage (mirage.com)

THE MIRAGE HAS HAD AN IMPACT on the Las Vegas tourist industry that will be felt for years to come. By challenging all the old rules and setting new standards for design, ambience, and entertainment, the Mirage precipitated the development of a class of super-hotels in Las Vegas, redefining the thematic appeal and hospitality standard of hotel-casinos.

Exciting and compelling without being whimsical or silly, the Mirage has demonstrated that the public will respond enthusiastically to a well-executed concept. Blending the stateliness of marble with the exotic luxury of tropical greenery and the straightforward lines of polished bamboo, the Mirage has created a spectacular environment that artfully integrates casino, showroom, shopping, restaurants, and lounges. Both lavish and colorful, inviting and awe-inspiring, the Mirage has avoided cliché. Not designed to replicate a famous palace or be the hotel version of Goofy Golf, the Mirage makes an original statement.

An atrium rain forest serves as a central hub from which guests can proceed to all areas of the hotel and casino. Behind the hotel's front desk, a 60-foot-long aquarium contains small and colorful tropical fish. Outside, instead of blinking neon, the Mirage has a 55-foot-tall erupting volcano that disrupts traffic on the Strip every hour on the hour (7–9 p.m.). There is also a live dolphin exhibit and a modern showroom that is among the most well designed and technologically advanced in Las Vegas.

For fine dining, the Mirage boasts OTORO Robata Grill & Sushi and Tom Colicchio's Heritage Steak, a chop, seafood, and lobster house. For more casual fare, try LVB Burgers, Carnegie Deli, or California Pizza Kitchen. For bulk eaters, there is an excellent and affordable buffet. *LOVE,* a Cirque du Soleil production based on the music of the Beatles, plays in one of two showrooms. Amenities include a swimming and sunning complex with waterfalls, inlets, and an interconnected series of lagoons; a shopping arcade; and a spa with exercise equipment. The casino is huge and magnificently appointed, yet informal, with its tropical motif and piped-in Jimmy Buffett music. Guest rooms at the Mirage are among the nicest in town.

With its indoor jungle and traffic-snarling volcano, the Mirage remains one of Clark County's top tourist attractions. Whether by foot, bus, cab, or bicycle, every Las Vegas visitor makes at least one pilgrimage. The Mirage has become the Strip's melting pot and hosts the most incredible variety of humanity imaginable.

New York–New York (newyorknewyork.com)

WHEN IT OPENED IN 1997, this architecturally imaginative hotel-casino set a new standard for the realization of Las Vegas megaresort themes. It's a small joint by megaresort standards ("only" around 2,000 rooms), but the triumph is in the details. Guest rooms are in a series of distinct towers reminiscent of a mini–Big Apple skyline, including the Empire State, Chrysler, and Seagram Buildings. Though the buildings are connected, each offers a different decor and ambience.

A half-size Statue of Liberty and a replica of Grand Central Station lead visitors to one entrance, while the Brooklyn Bridge leads to another. The interior of the property is broken into themed areas such as Greenwich Village, Wall Street, and Times Square. The casino, one of the most visually interesting in Las Vegas, looks like an elaborate movie set. Table games and slots are sandwiched between shops, restaurants, and a jumble of street facades.

The street scenes are well executed, conveying both a sense of urban style and tough grittiness. New York–New York sacrificed much of its visual impact, however, by not putting in an imitation sky. At Sunset Station, by contrast, the Spanish architecture is augmented significantly by vaulted ceilings, realistically lighted and painted with clouds. This sort of finishing touch could have done wonders for New York–New York.

Like its namesake, New York–New York is congested to the extreme, awash day and night with curious sightseers. There are so many people just wandering around gawking that there's little room left for hotel guests and folks who actually came to gamble. Because aisles and indoor paths are far too narrow to accommodate the crowds, New York–New York succumbs periodically to a sort of pedestrian gridlock.

Manhattan rules, however, do not apply at New York–New York: it's OK here to make eye contact and decidedly rude to shove people out of the way to get where you want to go. If you find yourself longing for the thrill of a New York cab ride, go hop on the roller coaster. New York–New York's coaster isn't the only one on the Strip, but it's the only one where you can stand on the street and hear the riders scream.

The showroom features Cirque du Soleil's *Zumanity*. Lounges include a dueling-pianos bar, a high-energy dance club, and a Coyote Ugly bar. Based on the movie of the same name, the bar features a platoon of dancing female bartenders with enough attitude to stop a real New Yorker dead in his tracks.

Guest rooms at New York–New York have been renovated and upgraded. However, the swimming area and health and fitness center are just average. Full-service restaurants are a little better than average, though Gallagher's Steakhouse, a real Big Apple import, can hold its own with any beef place, in or out of Las Vegas. Nine Fine Irishmen is a pub serving up live Irish music nightly, along with excellent pub fare that proves the Irish cuisine has come a long way. There is no buffet. Counter-service fast food is quite interesting, if not altogether authentic New York. Pedestrian bridges connect New York–New York to the MGM Grand and Excalibur.

The Orleans (orleanscasino.com)

THE ORLEANS IS JUST WEST OF I-15 on Tropicana Avenue. Marketed primarily to locals, The Orleans has a New Orleans–bayou theme executed in a hulking cavern of a building. The casino is festive with bright carpets, high ceilings, a two-story replication of a French Quarter street flanking the table games, and a couple of nifty bars. The Orleans has a celebrity showroom that attracts great talent. For fine dining there's Prime Rib Loft. The buffet, which serves Creole-Cajun dishes, is good but can't quite match Louisiana standards. Casual choices include Big Al's Oyster Bar and Bailiwick. Upstairs, over the slots and buffet area, is a 70-lane bowling complex. The Orleans Arena is a 9,000-seat facility. Two hotel towers with a total of 1,886 large guest rooms, an 18-screen movie complex, a games arcade, and a child-care center complete the package.

Palace Station (palacestation.com)

THE FIRST OF THE RAILROAD-THEMED Station Casinos, Palace Station is abandoning its decades-old persona for "midcentury modern design." We're not sure what that is exactly, or what century is being referenced, but the makeover is shaking up everything. The renovation includes a new casino floor and bingo room, a resort-style pool, new exterior and additional parking, two new restaurants, an updated buffet and food court, and two new bars.

Located 4 minutes off the strip on West Sahara Avenue, Palace Station is a local favorite that also attracts tourists. With great lounge acts, a first-rate buffet, an oyster bar, dependable restaurants that continuously offer amazing specials, a tower of renovated guest rooms, good prices, and a location that permits access to both Downtown and the Strip in less than 10 minutes, Palace Station is a standard setter for locals' casinos. The casino is large and busy with a heavy emphasis on slots (which are supposedly loose—that is, having a high rate of payoff). It's also a great venue for Bingo, with a 350-seat, state-of-the-art room.

Palace Station, redesign notwithstanding, has not changed its name. Finally, it is one of the few hotels to offer free shuttles to the airport and the Strip.

Palms (palms.com)

THE PALMS HAS BEEN REENERGIZED with contemporary nightlife spaces and culinary spots, an expanded pool complex, a reconfigured casino, and upgraded guest rooms. The resort where trendy and affluent Gen X and Y guests partied 12 years ago has matured, and so have the guests, with all transitioning to a more upscale experience.

Guest rooms in the Ivory and Fantasy Towers are cutting-edge with purple and cream velvet and splashes of bright turquoise or red. White linens are topped by violet bolsters, and above the headboards are arresting murals that combine palm leaves and eyes that follow you around the room. Wide windows offer Strip or mountain views.

Though the casino is roomy, at 95,000 square feet, it's the Palms' nightlife mix that sets the hotel apart. Atop the 55-story Fantasy Tower are the open-air Apex Social Club and The View, a nightclub and lounge, respectively, with panoramic views of the entire Las Vegas Valley. On the casino floor are Camden Cocktail Lounge and Tonic, and off the lobby you'll find the Rojo Lounge. A show lounge, a 14-screen cinema, and Pearl—a very cool concert venue—complete the entertainment mix.

The restaurant lineup, equally impressive, leads off with with Scotch 80 Prime, specializing in dry-aged beef washed down with rare and vintage Scotch whiskies, and Vetri Cucina from Philadelphia, serving upscale Italian. Less formal is Mabel's BBQ, a Cleveland import. Other options include Send Noodles for Chinese, an excellent buffet at A.Y.C.E., and Lucky Penny, a 24/7 coffee shop.

One of the more interesting additions is the bar, called Unknown, from British art provocateur Damien Hirst. The most arresting piece of art is a segmented shark, preserved in glass-and-steel tanks of formaldehyde and mounted atop the white marble bar. Yikes!

The Palms is too far from the Strip for most guests to feel comfortable walking. For those with a car, however, the coming and going is easy, and the hotel location on West Flamingo Road facilitates accessing Strip casinos via alternate routes rather than joining the gridlock on Las Vegas Boulevard.

Recently acquired by Red Rock Resorts (Station Casinos), the Palms joins their lineup of prestigious and well-managed properties, which includes Green Valley Ranch, Red Rock Resort, and seven Station Casinos.

Paris (parislasvegas.com)

ON THE STRIP NEXT TO BALLY'S and across from Bellagio, Paris trots out a French-Parisian theme in much the same way New York–New York caricatures the Big Apple. Paris has its own 50-story Eiffel Tower (with a restaurant halfway up) and an Arc de Triomphe. Thrown in for good measure are the Champs-Élysées, Parc Monceau, and the Palais Garnier.

Like New York–New York, Paris presents its iconography in a whimsical way. The casino sits in a parklike setting roughly arrayed around the base of the Eiffel Tower, three legs of which protrude through the roof of the casino. The video-poker schedules are lackluster, but the casino offers all of the usual table games.

Flanking the tower and branching off from the casino are dining and shopping venues designed to re-create Parisian and rural *petit village* street scenes. Though spacious, the casino and other public areas at Paris are exceedingly busy, bombarding the senses with color, sound, and activity. While at The Venetian you have the sense of entering a grand space, at Paris the feeling is more of envelopment.

The hotel towers, with almost 3,000 guest rooms, rise in an L shape framing the Eiffel Tower. Rooms are quite nice and rank along with the dining as one of Paris's best features. Rooms on the Strip side are endowed with a view of the octagon-shaped pool and the giant reproduced tower itself.

The pool complex is on the roof. The facility is spacious but rather plain and under-developed in comparison with the rest of the property. A spa and health club connect both to the pool area and the hotel.

The flagship Eiffel Tower Restaurant is situated 11 stories above the Strip in the, of course, Eiffel Tower. Several other restaurants, closer to the ground, and including the buffet, also feature French cuisine. Options include Gordon Ramsay Steak; Mon Ami Gabi, serving French bistro fare on an outdoor terrace overlooking the Strip; Martorano's Italian Restaurant; and Le Café Île St. Louis, a sidewalk café serving classic French and American cuisine 24/7. There's also a Budweiser-sponsored Beer Park on an elevated terrace, offering a huge selection of draft beers, pool tables, and a fine view of the Bellagio fountains, as well as Hexx candy shop, roasting cacao in-house for handmade gourmet chocolates that start at $4 for a 1.05-ounce bar.

In the entertainment department, Paris features *Inferno,* which mixes illusions with fire stunts, and hypnotist Anthony Cools. You'll find two shopping venues. The Paris-Bally's Promenade offers French jewelry, women's accessories, an art gallery of French and French-inspired work, and more. Le Boulevard houses boutiques, a gourmet food shop, and a newsstand, among other shops. And, of course, if you don't mind a little waiting, you can take an elevator to the top of the Eiffel Tower for a knockout view of the Strip.

Paris and its next-door neighbor, Bally's, share a monorail station, making both hotels a very convenient choice if you're attending a convention at the Las Vegas Convention Center.

Park MGM *(formerly Monte Carlo)* and NoMad Hotel
(parkmgm.com)

A NAME CHANGE and complete reimagining will introduce the former Monte Carlo as the Park MGM. Named after the adjoining 8-acre Park entertainment district, the result is a re-themed high-end resort of 2,700 rooms, plus a boutique hotel of 290 suites and rooms on levels 30–32 under the insouciant NoMad brand. All elements and references to the Monte Carlo have been removed, with the transformation costing about $550 million.

Guest rooms have been renovated in red or green color schemes, with dark wood headboards and bright white bedding. Of the color choices, the green rooms are the more restful. Eclectic wall art is framed and arrayed in number on almost every wall. Standard in each room is a bench seat in front of the window, a round table, and a leather chair. The 290 guest rooms on the upper floors will be rebranded as the NoMad Las Vegas, a hotel-within-a-hotel. That project will be completed by the end of 2018.

The Park MGM lobby resides under a spreading tree sculpture by Brazilian artist Henrique Oliveira, that, pardon our PR language, is one of a kind and simply stunning. Behind the front desk is *Dreamscape III, VI,* a hypnotic multimedia piece by Shahram Karimi and Shoja Azari that incorporates movement in a nature panorama. The lobby and public areas are of human scale and have a boutique hotel vibe. The swimming complex, with three separate pools, an oversize spa, and various bars and lounges, is likewise arranged in smaller, more intimate spaces.

Arguably, the large rectangular casino is the least changed, retaining the Monte Carlo's sparkling chandeliers, intricate crown molding, and stained glass ceiling. New, however, is the Moneyline Sports Book & Bar, a nonsmoking complex centered around a rectangular bar with more than two dozen TV screens positioned overhead. The dark woods, booths, and brass accents impart a masculine clubby feel. Limited-menu, counter-service dining is also featured.

Restaurants include the south of France–inspired Primrose, with a cozy adjacent library-like Parlor Room, as well as a terrace overlooking the pool, and Bavette's Steakhouse and Bar, which specializes in dry-aged bone-in cuts and seafood towers. A speakeasy-style lounge at the back of the restaurant offers a full menu and restful seclusion.

Entertainment begins with the Park Theater, one of the first transformative elements to come on line. Essentially a plush space showcasing celebrity headliner and one-of-a-kind productions, the theater is home to extended engagements with Lady Gaga, Bruno Mars, Cher, and Ricky Martin, among others. Next door to the Park MGM is the T-Mobile Arena, hosting all manner of productions and events, including Las Vegas Knights NFL hockey games.

Planet Hollywood (caesars.com/planet-hollywood)

PLANET HOLLYWOOD IS THE LATEST AND BEST incarnation of the Aladdin. The Aladdin opened in 1963 as the Tally Ho but was renamed the King's Crown in 1964. In 1966, the King's Crown was purchased by Milton Prell, who gave the property a $3 million face-lift with an Arabian Nights theme and dubbed it the Aladdin. For the next 30 years, the Aladdin changed ownership many times, which resulted in an eclectic, constantly shifting identity.

While the Aladdin was choking on its own mixed metaphors, the real estate it occupied became increasingly valuable. In the late 1990s, the Aladdin was once more acquired and promptly blown up to make way for a brand-new Aladdin, where the exotic Arabian Nights theme could realize its full potential and where there was room for a Middle Eastern bazaar–themed mall to compete with Caesars' Forum Shops and The Venetian's Grand Canal Shoppes. Though the vision of the new Aladdin was executed with flair and imagination, it failed to attract enough patrons to offset the considerable debt. After passing into receivership, the Aladdin was sold in 2003 to Planet Hollywood and Starwood Hotels, and then again in 2010 to Caesars Entertainment.

From the beginning, Planet Hollywood, or PH as it bills itself now, was committed to throwing the exhausted Arabian Nights under the bus in favor of a youthful, upscale, Hollywood look. Clubby and masculine with dark woods and rich textiles, the PH is drop-dead gorgeous. Carpet patterns and stone works capture the feel and beauty of a desert canyon and integrate them into a whole that is both sophisticated and relaxing. Dozens of casinos awe and overwhelm the senses, but only a handful are artful and soothing.

Placement of the hotel lobby separates quite distinctly the bustle of guests and baggage from the casino, eliminating the flow of almost all transitory traffic in the casino. The casino floor, at almost three acres, offers the usual slots and table games but feels more exclusive. In fact, the whole casino has the ambience of sequestered high-roller gaming areas in other hotels. As for theme, there are some strictly Hollywood touches, but in the public areas it's quite understated.

In a move to market to millennials, PH has introduced the first high-tech, fully skill-based casino games in Nevada. The future of such games is in the hands of the Nevada Gaming Control Board, which authorized the beta test. Results were promising, players' total unfamiliarity with the games notwithstanding.

Guest rooms have a cool, contemporary vibe; include coffeemakers and mini-fridges; and offer either Strip or fountain views. Additional accommodations are available in Elara, a nongaming, all-suite timeshare property positioned over the Miracle Mile shopping mall. For additional information on Elara, see page 142.

Planet Hollywood's three showrooms, the 7,000-seat Zappos Theater plus two additional showrooms in the adjoining Miracle Mile Shops, make PH one of the most happening entertainment venues in Las Vegas. The shopping venue has undergone a multimillion-dollar makeover, which converted the original Middle Eastern Bazaar design to a more contemporary look. PH also has a rooftop pool and a Spa by Mandara.

Retained from the Aladdin is the Spice Market Buffet. Fine-dining options include Gordon Ramsay Burger; KOI, serving Japanese-California fusion fare; and a clone of New York City's Strip House restaurant. A host of more casual restaurants, including Yolö's for Mexican and P.F. Chang's, round out the options.

Self-parking at Planet Hollywood is very confusing, and you must troop through the Miracle Mile Shops to reach the hotel or casino. If you are a hotel guest, definitely plan on using lobby entrance paid valet parking. If you're going to hit the shops, paid self-parking is fine.

PH targets an under-50 market from the southwestern United States and is also active in the European, Asian, and Latin American markets.

Plaza (plazahotelcasino.com)

THE VALUE-PRICED PLAZA has the distinction of being the only hotel in Las Vegas with its own railroad station, though passenger trains no longer run on this stretch of track. Occupying the historic site of the 16.5-acre Union Pacific train depot, the iconic Plaza Hotel and Casino at 1 Main Street presides at the west entrance to the Fremont Street Experience. The property has been completely renovated, including its two towers with 22 floors, casino, and public spaces. With tower elevators nearby, the front desk and lobby are just steps from the

10,000-light porte cochere. The lively adjacent lounge beckons with happy-hour drink specials and an eclectic mix of live entertainment. Located just off the casino is a 5,000-square-foot event space with two stages and 18 big-screen televisions.

The sleek remodeled rooms, some of the largest Downtown, boast a sitting area and portable refrigerators. Every room is adorned with an imposing 1970s black-and-white photo of the original Union Plaza. Views from both towers sweep above Downtown and suburban Las Vegas.

The casino features 820 of the latest and greatest video poker machines and slots, a full pit of popular casino games, William Hill Race and Sports Book, as well as a private pit where groups can gamble and party together. Bingo, now a rarity in most Downtown casinos, is also available.

Casual restaurants are the Hash House A Go-Go and Pop Up Pizza. Adjoining the lobby are a video arcade, a sundries shop, and a food court. On the third floor, and named after Las Vegas's popular former mob lawyer and mayor Oscar Goodman, the signature Oscar's Steakhouse is well positioned under the glass dome with an unparalleled sight line down Glitter Gulch and its neon canopy. Entertainment includes rotating afternoon lounge acts and short-run production and game shows in the showroom.

Real Results, a fitness studio and gym known for its group training classes, has a 5,000-square-foot gym at the Plaza and offers group and individual classes. The expansive fifth-floor Sports Deck features Downtown's only tennis and pickleball courts, a pool with chaises and cabanas, plus a hot tub and cocktail bar. Use of the parking garage at the property's south entrance is included in the hotel resort fee. Customers are drive-ins from surrounding states, the Midwest, and Texas, as well as Hawaiians.

Red Rock Casino Resort Spa (redrock.sclv.com)

CONTINUING THE UPSCALE EVOLUTION begun with Green Valley Ranch Resort and Spa, Station Casinos (now Red Rock Resorts) created a very similar and even tonier property in the Red Rock Casino Resort Spa. Set about 10 miles west of the Strip on Charleston Boulevard and isolated from any other property of similar stature, Red Rock attempts to make itself a destination worth the trip. It's an impressive place, with a low, curving, monolithic roofline meant to echo the desert landscape and slopes of nearby Red Rock Canyon. Inside, stone, wood, and glass predominate; again, forms and colors are often meant to echo the surrounding geography. The overall impression is reminiscent of an accessible, upscale desert spa hotel, as opposed to the more glitzy palaces on the Strip. The casino's arrangement is similar to that of Green Valley Ranch—wide alleys between banks of slots and rings of table games—and the two casinos even share some of the same restaurants. Several of the restaurants open onto the pool area, which, while not staggeringly huge, is quite elegant. Tiers of outdoor lounges and patios overlook smaller wading pools and rentable cabanas, plus the inevitable pool bar. As you proceed farther through the casino, the feel gets more and more "local"; the entrance on the far end is in fact specifically geared to locals, with close parking on the outside and local-friendly assortments of games right inside the door. This is also where you find the attached movie theater and Kids Quest children's complex, making it convenient to drop off the offspring en route to the casino.

Red Rock Resort takes advantage of its location by offering a number of outdoor adventure programs, including guided rock climbing, hiking, kayaking, and mountain biking outings, among others. The spa at Red Rock Resort can hold its own with any on the Strip in variety of treatments and amenities offered.

Rooms and suites are extremely mod in appearance and in amenities, mixing chocolate browns and other earth tones with high-tech gadgetry and high-end appointments. Best of all, however, are the guest-room views. West-facing rooms look out onto Red Rock Canyon, while east-facing rooms peer down the valley to the Strip.

Dining at Red Rock Resort is predominantly casual, except for T-Bones Chophouse. Other options include Yard House, Lucille's Bar-B-Que, a top-notch buffet, a café, and quick eats. In the entertainment department, Rocks Lounge is the place for wee-hour dancing, while Onyx Bar and Lucky Bar provide stunning settings for a drink. For the sedentary there's a 16-screen cinema, and for the more active a 72-lane bowling complex.

Finally, a navigation note: Although Red Rock Resort is located at the West Charleston Boulevard exit off I-215, it's faster to commute to the Strip and Downtown on West Charleston. It's usually about a 25-minute trip.

Rio (riolasvegas.com)

THE RIO IS ONE OF LAS VEGAS'S great treasures. Vibrantly decorated in a Latin American carnival theme, the Rio offers resort luxury at local prices. The guest rooms (all plush one-room suites) offer exceptional views and can be had for the price of a regular room at many other Las Vegas hotels. The combination of view, luxury, and price makes the Rio a great choice for couples on romantic getaways or honeymoons. On Flamingo Road, 3 minutes west of the Strip, the Rio also allows easy access to Downtown via I-15.

The Rio's dining scene is headed by VooDoo Steak & Lounge, Guy Fieri's El Burro Borracho, All-American Bar and Grille, and Royal India Bistro. Rounding out the Rio's restaurant lineup are KJ Dim Sum & Seafood, the Wine Cellar & Tasting Room, Hash House A Go Go, Pho Da Nang Vietnamese Kitchen, and Smashburger. The Rio's buffet is perennially near the top of everyone's hit parade. Carnival World Buffet offers 300 dishes from a dozen cuisines prepared fresh daily.

With five showrooms and a high-energy stage show in the casino, the Rio's entertainment mix is one of the most varied and extensive in Las Vegas. Long-running shows include the *Penn & Teller* comedy-magic show and the *Chippendales* beefcake revue. Nightspots include the rooftop VooDoo Lounge, one of the city's most dynamic and enduring clubs, and Flirt Lounge, where guys can flirt with women warmed up by a just-concluded *Chippendales* show. Factoring in the extensive Masquerade Village shopping arcade, a workout room, and an elaborate swimming area, the Rio offers exceptional quality in every respect. Festive and bright without being tacky or overdone, the casino is so large that it's easy to get disoriented.

If it's thrills you're seeking, check out the Rio's high-intensity thrill ride, VooDoo ZipLine. This 70-second zip ride packs a big adrenaline punch. If you prefer to keep your feet on the ground, try KISS Monster Mini Golf. For details, see Part 5, page 427.

The Rio has completed a rework of its 2,520 all-suite inventory. The carnival decor no longer encroaches on the guest rooms, which have introduced the current fewer-frills look, but there is still plenty of space to samba and drink caipirinhas. Each standard suite is an airy 600 square feet with a defined parlor. Flashes of pomegranate on pillows and other vivid touches accent the ivory-and-cocoa duvet and dark furniture. For additional sleeping space in the king rooms, the couch expands into a double bed. The Pet Stay program welcomes small dogs for a per-night charge.

The Rio staff ranks high in terms of hospitality, warmth, and an eagerness to please. The Rio is one of the few casinos to successfully target both locals and out-of-towners, particularly Southern Californians.

Royal Resort (royalhotelvegas.com)

A REVIVAL OF THE FORMER and very tired Royal Las Vegas, the refashioned Royal Resort is a boutique inn with 191 rooms. At 99 Convention Center Drive, the Royal is well positioned on the corridor between the Strip and the Las Vegas Convention Center.

The lobby, with its original white marble floors, now resembles an art gallery and exhibits a gilt pool table, Haight-Ashbury washed piano, Foosball and shuffle board games, photographs and mixed media, and a collection of shoe art Imelda Marcos would appreciate. The somber lobby bar borders on Gothic, with its dark counters, tables, and stools. Guest rooms are modest but comfortable and have balconies.

The upscale Barrymore is the property's only restaurant and offers an updated take on vintage 1960s menu selections. Nearby are a heated outdoor patio and comfortable inside bar with a welcoming ambience.

The pool area features four bright cabanas and an elevated spa with three waterfalls. The business center hides two computer stations and displays an IBM Selectric typewriter in keeping with the hotel's quirky look. Acres of free parking at the rear of the property provide easy drive-in access. Occasionally the lot becomes an outdoor art and music festival. This niche hotel speaks to trendy indies, millenniums, and those wanting to get their mojo back. It's a kick to visit this off-beat property that has generated lots of buzz.

Sam's Town (samstownlv.com)

ABOUT 20 MINUTES EAST of the strip on Boulder Highway, Sam's Town is a long, rambling set of connected buildings with an Old West mining-town motif. In addition to the hotel and casino, there is an 18-screen cinema, a bowling complex, a very good buffet, one of Las Vegas's better Mexican eateries, a steakhouse, a barbecue joint, a T.G.I. Friday's, a café, and two RV parks. Roxy's lounge is popular with both locals and visitors and features an eclectic mix of live music and dancing. Sam's Town Live is the Boulder Strip's first real concert venue.

Other pluses include a free-form pool, a sand volleyball court, and a spa. Joining the "let's be an attraction" movement, Sam's Town offers an atrium featuring plants, trees, footpaths, waterfalls, and even a "mountain." A waterfall in the atrium is the site of a free but very well-done fountains-and-light show (keep your eye on the robotic wolf). Frequent customers, besides the locals, include seniors and cowboys.

Santa Fe Station (santafestationlasvegas.com)

SANTA FE STATION is about 20 minutes northwest of Las Vegas, just off US 95. Like Sam's Town, the Rio, and the Suncoast, Santa Fe Station targets both locals and tourists. Bright and airy, with a warm southwestern decor, Santa Fe Station is one of the more livable hotel-casinos in Las Vegas.

Santa Fe Station offers a spacious casino with a poker room and sports book. Restaurants include the upscale Charcoal Room steakhouse, as well as a Mexican restaurant and Station Casino's signature Feast buffet. The Chrome showroom features an eclectic mix of country and rock headliners, and there is also entertainment in the lounge. In addition to a pool, there is a bowling complex and a movie theater. Guest rooms, also decorated in a southwestern style, are nice and a good value.

Silver Sevens (silversevenscasino.com)

AFFINITY GAMING, which acquired Terrible's from the locally prominent Herbst Family, renamed the property to capitalize on gaming's lucky number 7 and Nevada's reputation as the Silver State. The result is the Silver Sevens Hotel & Casino, still a no-frills property offering exceptional rates and value for the budget-minded traveler. A renovation of the 326 low-rise and tower rooms has imparted a cool aura and created a tranquil space away from the hotel's busy public areas.

The iconic Terrible's cowboy mascot has been donated to Downtown's expanding Neon Museum, and the hotel's current look is classy vintage Vegas. The casino has been reconfigured, and players can choose from 21, craps, roulette, slots, video games, and a sports book. On the upper level a buffet, 24-hour café, and expanded bingo parlor can be accessed by an escalator. Doubling as hotel check-in and cashier's cage, the guest services desk sits at the far end of the casino. Unless the ventilation system was on the blink the days we visited, Silver Sevens is the smokiest casino in Las Vegas. The well-trimmed grounds and pool area offer a quiet oasis. Just outside the casino and convenient to the tower rooms is the rear parking garage, and there's easy access to acres of parking in front of the hotel. Silver Sevens, located at the intersection of East Flamingo and Paradise Roads, is less than a mile from the Strip and 2 miles from the airport. Complimentary shuttle service to McCarran Airport runs 4 a.m.–9 p.m. Guests are an equal mix of Canadian and Asian tourists and locals.

Silverton (silvertoncasino.com)

SOUTHWEST OF LAS VEGAS at the Blue Diamond Road exit off I-15, Silverton opened in 1994 as Boomtown, with a nicely executed Old West mining-town theme. The casino has since removed or replaced much of the mining paraphernalia, however. The Silverton just might be the best-kept secret in Las Vegas. Its luxurious guest rooms feature dark hardwood furniture, leather couches, pillow-top mattresses, and tile bathrooms. Thick drapes and good soundproofing insulate the rooms from highway noise. At rack rates of about $120, Silverton hotel rooms are among the best values.

As concerns dining, the Twin Creeks Steakhouse can hold its own with any chophouse in town, and the 24-hour Sundance Grill, aside from serving excellent food, is a gorgeous room, reminiscent in decor of the celebrity chef restaurants on the Strip. On the quirky side is the Shady Grove Lounge, with a 1967 Airstream trailer and a couple of bowling lanes worked into the theme. There's also a Mexican restaurant and an excellent buffet. And good lounge entertainment is a Silverton's tradition.

The large casino is designed around $5 million worth of freshwater and saltwater aquariums. And speaking of fish, an adjacent retail development includes a 165,000-square-foot Bass Pro Shops Outdoor World megastore with indoor archery, a putting range, a driving range, and a stuffed specimen of every mammal on Earth. There's probably more dead stuff in the Bass Pro Shops than in many cemeteries. Even if you're not outdoorsy, this veritable natural history museum is worth a visit. Reminiscent of the expansion that added the Bass Pro Shop, the Silverton is developing Silverton Village, an open-air shopping center with a 150-room Hyatt Place hotel.

Just 10 minutes from the Strip, Silverton is in a great position to snag Southern Californians. It also targets the RV crowd with a large, full-service RV park across the street.

SLS Las Vegas (slslasvegas.com)

PREVIOUSLY THE LEGENDARY SAHARA HOTEL and once the bastion of the Rat Pack, Louis Prima, and Keely Smith and friends, the property has been transformed into the sleek SLS Las Vegas, bringing new vitality and a So-Cal beat to the dormant North Strip neighborhood. Of the original hotel's DNA, three towers have been completely renovated, while the layout of the '50s-era low-rise core buildings has been brought up to standard. Perimeter palm trees suggest a West Coast skyline, while the crisp white and glass façades exude a sophisticated Sunset Strip motif and house a maze of restaurants, lounges, bars, and nightclubs. Clubbers will want to immediately don their drinking shoes. Adding to the mix are the redesigned reception area, casino, and conference center. The original pool complex has been modernized, and a second rooftop pool has been installed above the casino.

The inventory of 1,327 streamlined guest rooms is spread throughout three historic towers: the World Tower comprises high-tech-driven standard hotel rooms aimed toward business travelers, while the Story Tower, with in-room bar/vanity combos, is the party tower adjacent to the main pool. The stylish, minimalist rooms, many with balconies, are predominantly white with splashes of muted rose or bright saffron on black plaid or brown swirl-patterned carpet. A white sofa is strategically placed at the end of the king beds. Desks, side tables, and lamps are chrome. Reminiscent of the days when Strip hotel rooms were sizable, these accommodations are airier than expected, but the bathrooms are snug. The LUX suite tower has joined Starwood Resorts' trendy W brand, linking hotel guests with Starwood's Preferred Guest loyalty program. The W tower has its own lobby, spa, pool deck, and bar exclusively for its guests. W guest rooms are classified as "Wonderful," "Fabulous," and "Spectacular," and look like they were designed by a hip Marie Antoinette.

The restaurants also have an LA vibe and include Bazaar Meat by chef José Andrés, Katsuya by master sushi chef Katsuya Uechi, and Cleo for Mediterranean cuisine. More casual dining options include Northside Café & Chinese Kitchen, 800 Degrees Neapolitan Pizzeria, and Perq coffee. Positioned along the hotel's Strip frontage is an indoor-outdoor patio housing Umami Burger, Monkey Bar, an alfresco beer garden, and the sports book. The nightclub duo is celeb-centric Sayers Club and The Foundry. Several boutiques offer men's and women's fashions, jewelry, sundries, beachwear, and beauty products. The Away Spa and Fitness Center offers herbal wraps, massages, beauty treatments, and other rehab services.

Depending on how you look at it, the SLS is the first or last stop on the monorail line. Now closer to the hotel's Paradise Road entrance, the boarding station has been moved from its original position across the vast eastside parking lot. The abundant 2,500-space parking garage is best entered from Paradise Road. Despite its glitz, the resort offers affordable rates. Its target market is young, trendy Southern Californians.

South Point (southpointcasino.com)

ACQUIRED BY MICHAEL GAUGHAN, the South Point sits almost alone in a huge desert plot off the south end of Las Vegas Boulevard, well away from the Strip. Rising up with nothing of comparable size anywhere nearby, South Point looks gigantic. This isn't just a trick of perspective, as South Point contains 2,163 large guest rooms, an 80,000-square-foot casino, two lounges, an enormous bingo auditorium, and a unique equestrian center. The latter, touted as one of the better indoor horse facilities in the country, includes a 4,600-seat arena and 1,200 climate-controlled horse stalls. The equestrian center hosts a number of prestigious equestrian events each year. For those without a horse, there's a 64-lane bowling complex, a 500-seat showroom that doubles as a dance club, a spa and fitness center, and a manicured swimming pool complex. Restaurants include Michael's Gourmet Room, a longtime Las Vegas culinary standard setter; the Silverado Steakhouse; an Italian bistro; an oyster bar; Primarily Prime Rib; Baja Miguel's Mexican; and a better-than-average buffet.

The decor of public spaces is ostensibly inspired by design accents from Southern California and the Pacific Coast, but the overriding visual theme is lots and lots and lots of yellow—deep golds to light wheats to every other shade in the crayon box. It's attractive and soothing, though not particularly memorable or interesting. Locals and regional guests are much beloved, and the roomy casino floor is a vast, open rectangle designed for their enjoyment. You only need walk along the walls to find the restaurants and lounges; the bowling lanes and bingo hall are up an escalator. The guest rooms are quite large and have Serta Perfect Sleeper mattresses.

Stratosphere (stratospherehotel.com)

KNOWN PRIMARILY FOR its high-altitude thrill rides at the top of the "tallest (1,149 feet) free-standing observation tower in the United States," the Stratosphere decanted money into its guest rooms and casino and emerges crisp, bright, and a more significant player in the mid-priced competition for tourists. The main entrance is now directly on the Strip, and an impressive porte cochere replaces the original side-street entry. The hotel has 909 Stratosphere Select-grade accommodations, which cost $10–$20 more than a standard room. And the standard rooms are worthy, with a comfortable color scheme of cream-and-taupe bedding accented with cherry furniture. The upgrade to the Select level is the standard room with more attention to decor.

The 80,000-square-foot casino meanders, the result of consecutive additions to the property. Spectral cove lighting along the ceiling changes hues throughout the hours and is engaging to watch. You'll find the standard mix of table games and slots. Along the perimeter are Starbucks, the C (circular) Bar, and Sin City Hops. The sports book telecasts daily sports events and horse racing on large-screen TVs.

The huge eighth-floor pool deck faces south and west for plenty of sun. Blue lounges and chartreuse umbrellas provide color and cover alongside two free-form pools and several white cabanas. There's a store for pool necessities, and bikini-clad Blackjack dealers provide eye candy during the summer months. For great food, a well-kept secret is the pool's Café Bar at Level 8, offering unique sandwiches at attractive prices. The mojito and margarita menu entices as well. A 24-hour fitness center is outfitted with weights and exercise machines and is free to hotel guests. The Roni Josef Salon and Spa provides beauty treatments and massages. Both are in the second-floor Tower Shops arcade. Restaurants include the Top of the World, Crafted Buffet, 24-hour Roxy's 50s Diner, Nunzio's Pizzeria, and Fellini's for Italian.

The property's crown jewel is the four-floor Observation Deck at levels 106 through 109, offering unsurpassed *National Geographic*–quality views of Las Vegas, the surrounding desert, mountains, and beyond. Level 106 boasts the rotating haute cuisine

Top of the World restaurant, open for lunch and dinner. The Level 107 Lounge, Las Vegas's highest bar, is the focal point of the 107th floor. Level 108 features the indoor observation deck and Air Bar nightclub. The outdoor observation deck and entrance to three thrill rides are on Level 109. The most recent attraction, Sky Jump, is a controlled free fall from the 108th floor. For details on these thrill rides, see pages 427–429.

The vast parking garage is on the west side of the property. At the bottom of the garage, escalators whisk guests into the casino, where the friendly information staff provides spot-on assistance. Clients are primarily regional drive- and fly-ins and adrenaline junkies seeking an airborne rush.

Suncoast (suncoastcasino.com)

LIKE MOST OF THE COAST CASINOS, Suncoast is designed to attract locals. Located west of Las Vegas in Summerlin near some of the area's best golf courses, Suncoast offers high-return slots and video poker, a surprisingly good (for a locals joint) fitness center, 64 lanes of bowling, and a 16-screen movie complex. In the food department, the clubby SC Prime Steakhouse tops the roster. There's also a decent buffet, as well as restaurants serving Italian and Chinese. The casino is open and uncrowded, rendered in a southwestern-Mission style. A 500-seat showroom and a pool round out the offerings. For its size (427 rooms and an 80,000-square-foot casino), Suncoast offers a pretty amazing array of attractions and amenities. Perhaps Suncoast's most extraordinary yet unheralded feature is the breathtaking view of the mountains to the west as seen through floor-to-ceiling windows in every guest room. And, speaking of mountains, the Suncoast is a perfect location for anyone interested in hiking, rock climbing, mountain biking, or road biking in the nearby canyons and valleys.

Sunset Station (sunsetstation.com)

SUNSET STATION, the fourth Station Casino (after Palace, Boulder, and Texas), is just off I-215 in the far southeast Las Vegas Valley, about a 20-minute drive from the Strip. The 21-story tower presides over a residential neighborhood; with 457 rooms, Sunset is large for a locals' casino. It's also one of the classiest, most highly themed, and architecturally realized of the Station Casinos, decorated to replicate a Spanish village. The casino's centerpiece, the Gaudí Bar, reflects the eccentric vision of Barcelona architect Antoni Gaudí.

Station's formula of good food, lounge entertainment, childcare, and extra touches prevails. It boasts a steakhouse, Italian and Mexican restaurants, the Feast Buffet, an oyster bar, a 24-hour coffee shop, and fast food galore. There's also a Kids Quest childcare center, the 500-seat Club Madrid lounge, a 13-screen cinema, and a $26 million bowling center—the largest in Las Vegas. Extras include a pool and plaza area featuring two sand volleyball courts, a badminton court, and a 5,000-seat amphitheater.

Texas Station (texasstation.com)

ALSO OWNED BY STATION CASINOS, Texas Station has a single-story full-service casino with 91,000 square feet of gaming space, decorated with black carpet sporting cowboy designs such as gold, boots, ropes, revolvers, covered wagons, and such. The atmosphere is contemporary Western, a subtle blend of Texas ranch culture and Spanish architecture. This property offers full-service restaurants serving steak and American cuisine, a good buffet, an oyster bar, plenty of fast-food options, three bars, a dance hall, a 60-lane bowling center, child-care facilities, and an 18-screen movie theater.

TI (Treasure Island)

(treasureisland.com)

ONE OF THREE MEGACASINO RESORTS that opened during the fall of 1993, Treasure Island is now the hipper TI. On the southwest corner of the Strip at Spring Mountain Road next door to the Mirage, TI is Caribbean in style. Management thought the original buccaneer theme was juvenile and Disneyesque, and further believed it was responsible for luring thousands of unwanted families with children to the resort. So down came all the pirate hats, sabers, skulls, and crossbones of the joint's decor. The current adult version is fine but a little dull by comparison. TI has also scrapped its most iconic attraction, the pirates versus sirens battle, replacing it with, of all things, a CVS pharmacy.

The casino continues the neutered Caribbean theme, with carved panels and whitewashed, beamed ceilings over black carpet punctuated with fuchsia, sapphire blue, and emerald green. The overall impression is one of tropical comfort: exciting but easy on the eye and spirit. In addition to the usual slots and table games, a comfortable sports book is provided.

The main interior passageway leads to a shopping arcade, restaurants, and the buffet. Dining selections include Pho, serving Vietnamese fare; Pizzeria Francesco's; Phil's Italian Steak House; Gilley's BBQ; and Señor Frog's, a sort of honky tonk serving Mexican cuisine. TI amenities include a beautifully landscaped swimming area and a luxurious, well-equipped health club and spa.

TI is home to Cirque du Soleil's extraordinary *Mystère*, which is performed in a custom-designed 1,629-seat theater. Nightlife options include Señor Frog's and a Gilley's Saloon, complete with a mechanical bull. In the space facing center Strip above the CVS pharmacy is Marvel Avengers S.T.A.T.I.O.N. (see page 429), an interactive exhibit featuring Marvel comic book and robot superheroes.

Guest rooms at TI are situated in a Y-shaped, coral-colored tower. Decorated in soft, earth-toned colors, the rooms provide a restful retreat from the bustling casino. Additionally, the rooms feature large windows affording a good view of the Strip (on the east side) or of the mountains and sunset. The balconies that are visible in photos of TI are strictly decorative and cannot be accessed from the guest rooms. Self-parking is easier at TI than at most Strip hotels. Valet parking is fast and efficient. An elevated tram connects TI to the Mirage next door.

Tropicana (troplv.com)

THE SOUTHERNMOST HOTEL on the east side of Las Vegas Boulevard South, the Tropicana is well located at the busy intersection of Tropicana Avenue and the Strip across from the MGM Grand, New York–New York, and the Excalibur. Once the "Tiffany of the Strip," the completely renovated Tropicana has been reinvented with a South Beach theme. Vibrant tropical colors and music, natural light, and equatorial fibers and florals percolate throughout the property. The upgrades have created a fun-in-the-sun laid-back lifestyle in the midprice market. With the deconstruction of an entire wing and a phalanx of rooms enlarged as lofts, inventory has decreased to a cozy 1,658 rooms, almost placing the Trop in Las Vegas's boutique class of properties.

Oversize standard guest rooms feature jungle red-and-white spreads, a desk console, and a russet-cushioned daybed. Instead of drapes, plantation shutters cover the windows, and even more unusual—the windows open! Coffeemakers and refrigerators are available on request for a small fee.

The reconfigured oblong casino offers 21 tables, midi and mini-baccarat, roulette, and craps. Overhead remains the hotel's original Art Nouveau Tiffany stained glass ceiling. A poker room, slots, video poker, and the high-limit area dominate the casino's sidelines. The large sports book and pub near the front desk have been updated and conveniently have an outside entrance. The rotunda has become a party pit gaming area next to the Ambhar Lounge.

The Sky Beach Club provides luxuriant pool gardens, some of the most famous in Las Vegas, with 4.2 acres of mature palms and lawn embracing two pools, waterfalls, a lagoon cave, and two heated Jacuzzis—all surrounded by white chaises. An outdoor café-bar features swim-up blackjack, sand volleyball, champagne beds, lounges, cabanas, misters, bottle service with hors d'oeuvres, outdoor concerts, and a private island at pool center.

The three-level Mandara Spa overlooks the lush pool from the south side, with each floor specializing in a specific fitness and spa component: exercise room, an aesthetician salon and barber shop, and massage treatment rooms.

For dining, on the main floor you'll find Savor the Buffet, which overlooks the pool. Close by is the South Beach food court. On the second floor are the spare and elegant Oakville Steakhouse and Carla Pellegrino's Bacio, a delightful upscale trattoria. Robert Irvine's Public House and Red Lotus Asian Kitchen, offering a sort of greatest-hits version of dishes from Thailand, Japan, Korea, China, and Vietnam, round out the Trop's dining options.

In the Convention Pavilion are the wedding chapel, business center, and a second Starbucks. Entertainment options include the Laugh Factory comedy club and the Tropicana Lounge with free (for now) live music.

Tuscany (tuscanylv.com)

THE TUSCANY'S LODGING footprint is 15 three-story buildings spread over several acres with an abundance of drive-up parking. Mature landscaping of tall shade trees and extensive grass is vigilantly maintained, and the complex feels like a large residential compound. Off the lobby near the fireplace are Tuscany Gardens Italian restaurant and the Piazza lounge, which features nightly live music or a DJ and dancing. Caffé Bottega displays luscious pastries, sandwiches, and drinks. Pub 365, a gastropub, is a hot spot for beer lovers and features a rotating collection of 365 different beers. Although connected by a passageway, the lobby and the casino are separate wings. Marilyn's Café with a take-out counter is in the casino, along with the games typical of a full casino—but all are downsized.

An all-suite property, the Tuscany's midsize studio suites feature a neutral look with a brown-and-cream color scheme. Walls display stereotypical watercolor prints of Italian villages. TVs sit on a bureau against the window, creating a glare if you're watching during the daytime. Tiny kitchens include a round table with two chairs, a wet bar, a small refrigerator, and a coffeemaker; microwaves can be requested. Bathrooms are serviceable with a separate tub and shower and one sink.

Amenities include two fenced pools (one a lap pool) and a fitness center with coin laundry. Wi-Fi is free in the public areas, but there is a charge for in-room internet.

THE VENETIAN AND THE PALAZZO

The Venetian (venetian.com)

THESE TWO SEPARATE AND DISTINCT sister properties, owned by Las Vegas Sands Inc., rise side by side on the Strip at Sands Boulevard and together sustain an inventory of 7,100 rooms.

The Venetian draws its theme from the plazas, architecture, and canals of Venice, Italy, and follows the example of New York–New York, Mandalay Bay, Luxor, and Paris Las Vegas in bringing the icons of world travel to Las Vegas. Visiting The Venetian is like taking a trip back to the artistic, architectural, and commercial center of the world in the 16th century. You cross a 585,000-gallon canal on the steep-pitched Rialto Bridge, shadowed by the Campanile Bell Tower, to enter the Doge's Palace. Inside, reproductions of famous frescoes, framed by 24-karat-gold molding, adorn the 65-foot domed ceiling at the casino entrance. The geometric design of the flat-marble lobby floor provides an M. C. Escher–like optical illusion that gives the sensation of climbing stairs—a unique touch. Behind the front desk is a large illustrated map of the island city, complete with buildings, landmarks, gondolas, and ships. Characters in period costumes from the 12th to 17th centuries roam the public areas, singing opera, performing mime, and jesting.

The Venetian casino has been completely reconfigured, resulting in a whole new look. At 116,000 square feet, the casino is larger than that of most Strip competitors. When the Palazzo casino came online, the overall resort topped out at more than 200,000 square feet of casino. The Venetian casino is styled to resemble a Venetian palace with architecture and decor representative of the city's Renaissance era. Period frescoes on recessed ceilings over the table games depict Italian villas and palaces. The huge and ornate casino offers 139 table games and 1,700 slot and video-poker machines. The perimeter of the casino houses a fast-food court, along with French, Italian, and southwestern restaurants, and one of the fanciest coffee shops in town.

Upstairs are the Grand Canal Shoppes, with more than 60 stores, mostly small boutiques. The Escher-like floor design continues throughout the shopping venue, with different colors and shapes providing variations on the theme. The centerpiece of the mall is the quarter-mile Grand Canal itself, enclosed by brick walls and wrought-iron fencing and cobbled with small change. Gondolas ply the waterway, steered and powered by gondoliers who serenade their passengers. Passing beneath arched bridges, the canal ends at a colossal reproduction of St. Mark's Square. Like The Forum Shops, the Grand Canal Shoppes are arranged beneath a vaulted ceiling painted and lighted to simulate the sky. The Venetian adjoins its sister property, The Palazzo, via a shopping mall that connects the Grand Canal Shoppes to The Shoppes at The Palazzo, which offer an additional 49 stores and six restaurants.

The Venetian's restaurants, most designed by well-known chefs, provide a range of dining environments and culinary choices. Thomas Keller's Bouchon and Lorena Garcia's Chica are some of the culinary powerhouses represented. TAO Asian Bistro and legendary nightclub is the top grossing restaurant in the United States.

An all-suite hotel, The Venetian offers guest accommodations averaging 700 square feet and divided into sleeping and adjoining sunken living areas. The living-room areas provide adequate space for meetings or entertaining. Every suite has been recently upgraded to meet the Palazzo criteria and shares its similar subdued earth-toned palette, with pops of colorful peach creating a classy urban Apennine look. The property is LEED Gold Certified.

The five-acre swimming complex and spa area are situated on the rooftop over the shopping venue and are well insulated from the bustle of the Strip. You'll find two standard pools, one lounge pool, and a hot tub. One of the largest of its kind in the country, the ultra-upscale bilevel Canyon Ranch Spa offers fitness equipment and classes, therapies, and sauna and steam rooms, as well as a 40-foot indoor rock-climbing wall, medical center, beauty salon, and café.

The Venetian targets the convention market with its mix of high-end business lodging, power restaurants, unique shopping, and proximity to Sands Expo and Convention Center. The Venetian certainly welcomes tourists and gamblers, who come mostly on the weekend, but the other five days are largely monopolized by the tradeshow crowds.

The Palazzo (palazzo.com)

IT'S A TESTAMENT to The Palazzo's designers to see tourists who've already walked past replica pyramids, New York City skyscrapers, and million-dollar fountain displays still whip out their cell-phone cameras the first time they see The Palazzo's lobby. Much more pedestrian-friendly than the neighboring (and similarly ultraluxe) Wynn or the down-the-Strip Bellagio, The Palazzo is arguably the best combination of shopping, dining, and lodging in Las Vegas.

Opened in December 2007, The Palazzo is connected to The Venetian by walkways and the Grand Canal waterway. Like The Venetian, The Palazzo employs in its public spaces such architectural touches as arched passageways, Doric columns, fountains, and painted ceilings in neutral beige, yellow, and brown hues. Even with a three-story lobby, however, The Palazzo's decor is more subtle than that of The Venetian. That subtlety extends to The Palazzo's 105,000-square-foot casino, where the tables and slots seem to have slightly more walking room between them than at, say, the Bellagio. The net effect is a quieter, more relaxed feel. Depending on your preference (and your luck), you might consider this either a welcome relief or boring beyond words.

The Palazzo's restaurants cover everything from Italian to Peruvian, including two steakhouses associated with celebrity chefs: Wolfgang Puck's CUT and Eric Bauer's Morel's French Steakhouse and Bistro. Asian cuisine is also well represented with Noodle Asia, Hong Kong Café, and Sushisamba. If you're in the mood for Italian, Lavo is the fancy place, and Grimaldi's Pizzeria is the café. In-room dining has an equally wide variety of choices and isn't as expensive as one might think, given the setting.

Shopping options abound at The Shoppes at The Palazzo, with 49 upscale stores, including Barneys New York, Michael Kors, and Christian Louboutin. Slightly more affordable options are available at The Venetian's Grand Canal Shoppes, which connect to The Palazzo's stores.

A Canyon Ranch Spa provides everything from massages, facials, and a full health club to simple haircuts. While reservations for all-day treatments are recommended, we didn't have any trouble getting a walk-in hair appointment on 15 minutes' notice during one of the busier times of the year.

The Palazzo's 3,066 rooms are all suites. Rooms come in 720-, 940-, or 1,280-square-foot configurations. All have sunken living rooms and two flat-panel TVs; most have a single king bed, but some 940-square-foot rooms also have two queen beds. Bathrooms are spacious, and showers boast multiple massage heads with enough water pressure to work out the knots in your spine after a long day hunched over the slots; it's one of the best showers we've had in any hotel in the United States.

Similar to concierge floors is the Prestige lounge and business center section of the Palazzo tower. For $100 more per night, guests receive a daily newspaper; internet connectivity; access to the Azure luxury pool complex and Canyon Ranch Spa; Continental breakfast; all-day teas, coffees, desserts, and fruit; and a nightly cocktail and hors d'oeuvres reception. The 23rd-floor lounge (open 7 a.m.–9 p.m.) also provides champagne check-in, meeting space and work counters, and other business services.

Service at The Palazzo is excellent: the staff is prompt and easy to find. When we asked for directions, more often than not an employee would walk us to our destination rather than describe how to get there.

Westgate Las Vegas (westgateresorts.com)

WESTGATE RESORTS HAS TAKEN OVER the hotel-casino that was briefly the LVH—Las Vegas Hotel & Casino—and for many years the fabled Las Vegas Hilton. The self-contained 64-acre resort is a decidedly by-the-book classic 1970s property. Room inventory is unchanged at 2,956 rooms; it is still one of the largest convention facilities in town; and it maintains the world's largest race and sports book and 74,000-square-foot casino, along with 10 restaurants, 4 lounges and bars, and headline entertainment.

Westgate Las Vegas has the advantage of being adjacent to the Las Vegas Convention Center. What it lacks in convenient access to the Strip (a 10- to 12-minute walk or 5-minute monorail ride away), it makes up for in one-stop partying for the conventioneer who can go to sessions via a hall connecting the hotel and convention center. Consequently, this hotel does more meeting, trade-show, and convention business than any other hotel in town. Operating under the valid assumption that many of its guests may never leave the hotel during their Las Vegas stay (except to go to the convention center), Westgate is an oasis of self-sufficiency. It boasts a huge pool, an exercise room, a shopping arcade, a buffet, and a coffee shop. It is also next door to a golf course.

Architecture is vintage high-rise—bland, smooth, and unmemorable, but not unpleasant. All guest rooms have crisp white and sunny decor with comfortable work space and seating. In 2018, Westgate's freestanding outdoor sign, already the world's largest at 28 stories tall, was souped-up. Now the sign's state-of-the-art LED video displays cover a combined 15,000 square feet, with 16mm LED display areas of nearly 5,600,000 pixels.

Westgate has a decent buffet and some good fine-dining options with enough ethnic and culinary variety to keep most guests happy. The main showroom hosts big-name headliners, while the intimate Westgate Cabaret hosts musical acts and small production shows.

Westgate is the most convenient place to stay in town if you are attending a trade show or convention at the Las Vegas Convention Center. If, however, you are in Las Vegas for pleasure, staying there is like being in exile. To go anywhere, you will need a cab, a car, or the monorail with a station right at the hotel. If you park in one of the property's far-flung, self-parking lots, it will take you as long as 15 minutes to reach your car from your room.

Westin Lake Las Vegas (westinlakelasvegas.com)

THEMED AFTER THE MYTHIC 1942 film *Casablanca,* the 493-room Westin resort is perfect for an exotic desert getaway, with a spectacular backdrop at the east end of Lake Las Vegas and a view of Lake Mead in the near distance. The property envelops you with its sultry Moroccan vibe, invoking images of minarets, magic carpets, caravans, and camels from the moment you enter the lobby. A quick glimpse at the expanse of two lakes through floor-to-ceiling windows verifies that you have reached a 21st-century oasis.

The main entry, beyond the tree-lined circular drive and fountain guarded by sculptured desert tortoises, is positioned at the fourth level of the property. Guest rooms extend along Levels 1–7 in two wings. The large and comfortable Berber-influenced accommodations reaffirm the desert-inspired decor with dark wood furniture, an unusual red bureau, hammered metal-framed mirrors, leather chair and ottoman, white linens, and wall art depicting Arabic cityscapes. Room service is available 24/7. Accommodations offer a view of Lake Las Vegas or the resort grounds and surrounding mountains—the lakeside rooms are definitely worth the slightly higher rate.

The heart of the property is the tri-level Arabesque indoor lounge connected to the outdoor patio. Inside, the seating and appointments reflect the Saharan motif. Sam's piano bar ("Play it again") is tucked inside.

The palm-shaded lower patio includes an infinity pool, waterfall, two fireplaces, and several conversation areas overlooking a lagoon and sandy beach where kayaks and paddle boats are available for aquatic excursions. Jogging and biking trails are also nearby. A dock in the Andalucian Gardens tethers small watercraft.

Dining choices include Rick's Café, Marrakesh Express deli, Marssa Steak & Sushi, the Arabesque Lounge, and a poolside bar and grill.

A business center and gift and resort wear shops adjoin the conference area, while the fitness center and spa are situated downstairs from the patio. A wedding planner and chapel are also on site. Although there was gaming in the film's Rick's Café, this restyled version of Casablanca is without a casino. The hotel can arrange airport pick-up, but given the sequestered location, a car would ease transportation.

WYNN RESORTS

Wynn Las Vegas (wynnlasvegas.com)

IN 2018, HOTEL VISIONARY STEVE WYNN resigned amid allegations of sexual misconduct, but he left an endurable imprint on Wynn Las Vegas and Wynn Encore, not to mention the entire city of Las Vegas. With each property he developed on the Las Vegas Strip, Wynn's vision for the ultimate megaresort-casino became more sophisticated. Wynn Las Vegas opened in May 2005 and did so without exploding volcanoes, jets of water undulating to Frank Sinatra tunes, or pirate-versus-siren skirmishes. The handsome swoosh of the sunlit-copper glass facade stands in stark contrast to the immediate, raucous fun of traditional Las Vegas hotel-casinos. Up close, the building positively looms, and there's no attraction, no show, no kitsch visible to the passerby from any vantage point. That is the point. This mega–hotel-casino wasn't designed to lure visitors in from the sidewalk. Instead, it is internally focused, stylish, and mysterious. It's grown-up, and it's for grown-ups in the best sense of the word.

Wynn Las Vegas is all about exclusivity. The resort was ostensibly designed to bring to mind the exclusive boutique hotels of New York City, but with 2,716 rooms, 200,000 square feet of meeting space, a 111,000-square-foot casino, 76,000 square feet of shopping, an art gallery, and 22 places to have a meal or whet your whistle, that's one hell of a boutique. The trick, and it's done well, is to create intimate spaces within the larger whole.

But don't think that the exclusivity means that tourists and visitors aren't welcome at Wynn Las Vegas. Just the opposite. We found the staff to be one of the most courteous and helpful of any major resort on the Strip. The cocktail servers make frequent passes on the casino floor, the front desk and concierge are pleased to answer questions, and the security staff monitoring who goes where is kind and not in the least condescending.

One of the most remarkable aspects of this resort is that entering visitors aren't immediately shunted through a brain-rattling casino cavern, as is typical in most hotel-casinos. This adds to the impression that WLV is a resort first and a casino second. From both the main entrance, off the Strip, and the south entrance, off Sands Avenue, visitors are welcomed with a spacious, verdant atrium lobby. The ceiling is a high, domed skylight above an elaborate indoor garden where balls of flowers dangle like oversize Christmas ornaments from the branches of trees overhead. In addition to these two main entrances, the South Tower entrance, reserved for guests staying in the Tower, shares a drive with the south entrance.

In the casino proper, to the left of the lobby, ceilings are raised over aisles and walkways and lowered over the gaming tables, instead of the other way around, as is common in many casino designs. We at the *Unofficial Guide* have lamented for years the suffocating atmosphere in most casinos and are pleased as punch to find a casino that provides gamblers with natural light and room to breathe. Another gaming amenity at WLV is a poolside casino (guests only), where you can work on your tan while you empty your wallet. Of course, there is the usual run of slots and gaming tables in the casino area, a 26-table poker room, a fully renovated sports book, baccarat, and so on.

The resort is loaded with exclusive brands and nowhere-else-in-Vegas shopping, most positioned along the Esplanade, which begins across the main entrance lobby from the casino. Boutiques include Chanel, Louis Vuitton, Cartier, and many others. Then there are the shops exclusive to WLV: Wynn & Company Watches and the Wynn Collection. By all means check out the shopping on the Esplanade, but be aware that there aren't any retailers here you're likely to find in the mall at home. If you're prepared to drop $500 (and up) for a pair of fabulous heels, this is your place. If you need an extra pair of khakis or flip-flops, head across the street to the Fashion Show Mall.

There are many upscale options for a drink or a meal at WLV, all under the guidance of VP of Culinary Operations David Snyder. Both Wynn Las Vegas and sister resort Wynn Encore have their share of celebrity chefs. At Wynn, however, the chefs do more than lend their name to the restaurant—they actually prepare your meal. Steve Wynn insists that his chefs take full responsibility, and that includes being present. Standouts include Tableau for American fare, Costa di Mare for Mediterranean seafood and shell-fish (AAA Four-Diamond winner), SW Steakhouse, Wing Lei for French-influenced Shanghai specialties, La Cave for small plates, and Lakeside Seafood for nouvelle American cuisine (and a spectacular view overlooking the Lake of Dreams).

"Water features" are an integral part of creating intimate spaces at Wynn Las Vegas. The five different water features are keyed to various viewing areas such as registration, nightclubs, and restaurants. Probably the ultimate WLV water feature is *Le Rêve*. Under the creative direction of Franco Dragone, creator of Cirque du Soleil's watery *"O,"* *Le Rêve* is an aquatic Cirque-style show performed in the round. On the Wynn Las Vegas website, this warning is issued: "You will get wet in rows A through C of every section. In row A you may get soaked."

If *Le Rêve* inspires you to get wet, wade into the dog bone–shaped swimming pool, the long stretch of which will give lap swimmers just about 100 yards for stroking. The water is kept at a constant 82°F, and the landscaping surrounding you will delight and soothe when you come up for air. There is a complete spa, and the gym has Cybex equipment with plenty of amenities, such as one of the best free-weight training areas we've seen.

Aim high, if you can, in your choice of rooms, for the elevators are speedy, gentle, and quiet. Your reward will be an exhilarating view of the Strip or the mountains through your room's floor-to-ceiling window wall. All guest rooms have a sunny and soothing residential aura. Deluxe tower accommodations are 640 square feet, and the warm schematic includes colors near the top of the rainbow—lemon and tawny yellows, butterscotch, and cream with rust accents. Attention to detail, a Wynn given, is prevalent in each room. The Signature Dream Beds were specially designed for the hotel.

A big plus here is the self-parking garage, which is closer to the guest elevators than valet parking. There's not a large hotel in Las Vegas that matches it for convenience.

Wynn Encore (wynnlasvegas.com)

WYNN LAUNCHED CONSTRUCTION on a second hotel on the first anniversary of Wynn Las Vegas. This 2,034-suite hotel, called Wynn Encore, is similar in size and design to the original hotel. More than an expansion of Wynn Las Vegas, Encore is a full-scale resort with a 74,000-square-foot casino, an elaborate pool complex, five fine-dining venues, a half-dozen lounges and bars (including a hot and très-chic nightclub), a showroom, an upscale shopping venue, and, of course, a spa and fitness center. Standard accommodations at Encore are 700-square-foot suites with separate sleeping and sitting areas. According to Steve Wynn, the casino is modeled on the Wynn Macau casino.

The signature components of Encore's environment are the color red, flowers, natural sunlight, and butterflies. The rich, vibrant reds signify luck—appropriate for a gaming establishment—and the whimsical, beautiful, and colorful butterflies denote evolution and change. The flowers, predominantly red roses and red chrysanthemums, are effusive throughout.

The Oriental influence at Encore is apparent from the moment you arrive at the hotel's dual porte cocheres, where two bronze sculptures greet arrivals. The Foo Dogs are replicas of large canines that historically guarded Asian palaces and temples by thwarting evil spirits. One dog sitting over a ball representing earth symbolizes power, and the other straddling a baby is the symbol of good fortune. Guests are invited to rub the paws of each dog.

The entire hotel feels open and airy. A deluge of sunlight flows though vaulted translucent ceilings and vertical windows at the main entrance atrium, as well as in the casino, conference center, shopping area, and nooks overlooking the pool. Those same windows transmit radiant moonlight as well. Affecting the light are lustrous white-and-beige marble floors and walls, which reflect the glow.

Restaurants include Sinatra, serving classical Italian cuisine; Wazuzu, featuring pan-Asian preparations; Andrea's, for Asian fusion; and Jardin, a casual alfresco venue. All Encore restaurants offer a sophisticated and visually exciting environment.

The largest water features are the two oval plunges immediately outside the casino. The pools impart a St. Tropez vibe with white cabanas, lily pods (reclining cushions surrounding umbrellas), and in-pool daybeds. The Resort pool is bordered by a formal garden of slender amphora vases, flowering plants, palms, and magnolia trees. The European pool's island bar encourages guests to dip their feet while enjoying cocktails. Several blackjack tables are positioned poolside. Adjacent to XS nightclub, this lounge area merges with the nightclub's festive and sultry environment after dark.

Unlike many casinos that are an enormous spread of tables and slots, the Encore gaming floor is sectioned by columns and drapery to suggest intimacy and privacy. In addition to the standard casino games, Encore offers both pai gow and pai gow tiles. Roulette slots are included among the 1,600 slot and video-poker machines. For gaming comfort, there are low- and high-rise blackjack tables. Recently, Encore premiered its new race and sports book, featuring three betting stations and 21 TVs with screens ranging from 60 to 120 inches.

The second floor of the 61,000-square-foot Spa and Salon at Encore combines marble, flowing water, sunlight, and huge windows to provide an opulent indoor-outdoor feeling while you are beautified and pampered. The wow factor occurs at the entry to the 51 treatment rooms housed along two dimly lit extended passages featuring water silently sliding down cylindrical urns. At the far end is an inscrutable Buddha. A well-equipped fitness center adjoins the spa.

The Esplanade shopping arcade is well placed and leads to not only the Encore Theater but also completes a seamless transition from Encore into the Wynn Las Vegas casino. At the southwest end of the Esplanade is the Le Rêve Theater at Wynn Las Vegas. At the northeast end of the Esplanade is the XS nightclub. Between these entertainment and nightlife venues are 27,000 square feet of shopping bliss.

Encore nightlife centers around XS (as in "excess"), a plush lounge arranged around lighted pools in a design that emulates the curves of the female body. Because XS is contiguous with Encore's outdoor pool, there is limited complimentary seating at the pool's lounge tables. If you're fortunate enough to score a complimentary seat, maybe you can make up for it by ordering an Ono—a champagne–cognac mix that sells for $10,000 and is served with XS-logo silver cufflinks for men or a black-pearl pendant necklace for women.

Guest rooms at Encore offer lovely views of the Strip or Downtown through floor-to-ceiling, wall-to-wall windows with electric-powered drapes and sheers. The sleeping area is separated from the living area by a three-foot partition crowned by a high-definition TV on a swivel base. Seating in the living room is oriented to enjoying the vistas, with no furniture of any kind blocking the windows. Baths offer a separate tub and shower, as well as a private toilet with a locking door. Room lighting is high-tech with multiple control panels. With a lot of head-scratching you can figure it out on your own, but we recommend having someone from the bell staff or housekeeping give you a lesson. Signature suites are located at the west end of the hotel tower and have their own private reception area and elevators. Views are superior there (though not by much), and the suites are a bit wider than the standard suites.

Wynn Encore and Wynn Las Vegas each have a self-parking garage. The Wynn LV parking garage, between the Encore and Wynn LV resorts and entered from the Strip, is more convenient for those heading toward the Encore casino, Esplanade arcade, XS nightclub, and the Encore and Wynn LV showrooms. A subtle door in the northeast corner on the garage's second level provides an almost-covert entry into the Esplanade. The larger Encore parking garage is on the property's east side and is accessed from the Strip and an extended drive on the north side of the property. That entry is handier to the front desk, conference area, spa, and hotel elevators. Like the Wynn LV garage, an LED sign at each level indicates the number of spots still available.

Coming and going is easy at Encore. The main entrance is on the Strip, but in a section that's rarely congested. You can exit Encore onto the Strip in either direction or onto eastbound Desert Inn Road. Both Wynn LV and Encore provide complimentary shuttle service to the Las Vegas Convention Center and the Convention Center monorail station.

NAVIGATING *the* LAND *of the* GIANTS

GRAND HOTELS OF LAS VEGAS are celebrated on television, in film, and in countless advertisements. These are the prestige properties in a town that counts more hotel rooms than any other city in the world. Located along the center and southern end of the Strip, these mammoths beckon with their glamour and luxury. Specifically we're talking about:

• Aria	• Bellagio	• Caesars Palace	• Cosmopolitan
• Luxor	• Mandalay Bay/Four Seasons/Delano		• MGM Grand
• Mirage	• NY–NY	• Paris Las Vegas	• Park MGM/NoMad
• Planet Hollywood	• TI	• Venetian/Palazzo	• Wynn Resorts

But can so many hotels actually mean less choice? From a certain perspective, the answer is yes. The Strip, you see, is suffering a paroxysm of homogeneity. After you've chosen your preferred icon (Statue of Liberty, Eiffel Tower, pyramid, gondolas, volcano, and so on), you've done the heavy lifting. Aside from theme, or lack thereof, the hotels are pretty much the same. First, they're all so large that walking to the self-parking garage is like taking a hike. Second, there are high-quality guest rooms in all of the properties. This is a far cry from previous decades, say, when only a handful of hotels offered rooms comparable to what you'd find at a garden-variety Hyatt or Marriott. Third, all of the megahotels are distinguished by designer restaurants, each with its big-name chef, that are too expensive for the average guest to afford. Ditto for most of the showrooms.

So let's say you're a person of average means and you want to stay in one of the new, glitzy super-hotels. Location is not important to you as long as it's on the Strip. How do you choose? If you have a clear preference for gondolas over trapeze acts, or sphinx over lions, simply select the hotel with the theme that fires your fantasies. If, however, you're pretty much indifferent when it comes to the various themes, make your selection on the basis of price. Using the internet, your travel agent, and the resources provided in this guide, find the colossus that offers the best deal. Stay there and venture out on foot to check out all the other hotels. Believe us, once you're ensconced, having the Empire State Building outside your window instead of a statue of Caesar won't make any difference.

As it happens, there are also a number of livable but more moderately priced hotels mixed in among the giants, specifically:

• Bally's	• Casino Royale	• Excalibur	• Flamingo
• Harrah's	• LINQ Hotel & Casino	• Tropicana	

Some of these hotels were the prestige addresses of the Strip before the building boom of the past two decades. They are still great places, however, and properties where you can afford to eat in the restaurants and enjoy a show. Best of all, they are located right in the heart of the action. It's cool, of course, to come home and say that you stayed at Wynn Las Vegas, but you could camp at the Excalibur for a week for what a Wynn Las Vegas weekend would cost.

BUSINESS HOTELS

MOST BUSINESS TRAVELERS stay in hotels with casinos or in all-suite hotels. There are two nongaming hotels, however, that merit special mention.

Renaissance Las Vegas Hotel (renaissancelasvegas.com)

NEXT TO THE LAS VEGAS CONVENTION CENTER sits the Renaissance Las Vegas, a haven of tranquility amid the buzz and traffic surrounding the vast meeting complex next door. This 15-floor property on Paradise Road is a 548-room, nonsmoking, nongaming sanctuary. The oversize guest rooms have restful sage, apricot, and beige accents with cherry furniture. Well suited for business travelers, accommodations include a lounge chair with ottoman, an ergonomic chair and rectangular work desk, a coffeemaker, dual-line phone, internet access, and complimentary newspaper. Bathrooms feature glass showers, separate tubs, marble floors, and granite counters. Guests with platinum and gold membership status can access the Club Lounge (on the 15th floor), which provides complimentary breakfast and evening cocktails and appetizers, a boarding-pass station, and concierge service.

Through the main lobby, the large center courtyard has windows on three sides. A cozy outdoor area includes tables, lounges, daybeds, and circle beds. Patio heaters warm the space on cool evenings. Food and beverage service is available. A small heated swimming pool and detached whirlpool are at the opposite end of the courtyard. The area is protected on all sides by the hotel's high walls—a welcome feature on Las Vegas's perennially windy days.

Award-winning ENVY Steakhouse, with a unique red marble floor, is open daily. There is also a glass-enclosed Wine Room, with more than 400 vintages and seating for 20. An abbreviated menu is available in the adjoining bar.

Amenities include a business center, 24-hour in-room dining, a health club, an activities concierge, valet parking, a coffee café, and a sundries shop. The property is close to the monorail stop at the convention center but is four lengthy blocks to the Strip—better to cab it.

Westin Las Vegas (westinvegas.com)

TALK ABOUT PHOENIX RISING. Westin acquired the old Maxim hotel, a place where business travelers reluctantly stayed when they couldn't get into Bally's, and transformed it into a high-end boutique hotel that now caters to business travelers. The guest rooms, though small, are exceptionally nice. There is ample meeting space for small meetings and conventions. If you travel with Fido, he's welcome at the Westin (they even supply a special dog bed), though you will have to pay a $35 cleaning fee and a $150 pet deposit. Travelers with some downtime can enjoy the pool, full-service spa, and fitness center. As for dining, the Westin offers Jake & Eli, serving whisky and steak, and a Starbucks. Situated about a block from the heart of the Strip, the Westin is within easy walking distance of dozens of shows and hundreds of restaurants. If you have a car, the Westin has ample parking and is easy to enter and exit.

 # SUITE HOTELS

SUITES

THE TERM *SUITE* IN LAS VEGAS covers a broad range of accommodations. The vast majority of suites are studio suites consisting of a larger-than-average room with a conversation area (couch, chair, and coffee table) and a refrigerator added to the usual inventory of basic furnishings. In a one-bedroom suite, the conversation area is normally in a second room separate from the sleeping area. One-bedroom suites are not necessarily larger than studio suites in terms of square footage but are more versatile. Studio and one-bedroom suites are often available in Las Vegas for about the same rate as a standard hotel room.

Larger hotels, with or without casinos, usually offer roomier, more luxurious multiroom suites. Floor plans and rates for these premium suites can usually be obtained on the hotel's website.

There are some suite hotels that do not have casinos. Patronized primarily by business travelers and nongamblers, these properties offer a quiet alternative to the glitz and frenetic pace of the hotel-casinos. Because there is no gambling to subsidize operations, however, suites at properties without casinos are usually (but not always) more expensive than suites at hotels with casinos.

While most hotels with casinos offer suites, only the Rio, The Cosmopolitan, Tuscany, Signature at MGM Grand, Vdara at CityCenter, Delano Las Vegas, Wynn Encore, and The Venetian/Palazzo are all-suite properties. The basic studio suite is a plush, one-room affair with a wet bar and a sitting area but no kitchen facilities. The Rio sometimes makes its suites available at $49 per night and is one of the best lodging values in town. In addition, Signature and Tuscany are by far the easiest to get in and out of if you have a car.

Many thousands of condos and time-shares, some stand-alone nongaming properties and others associated with established casinos, were being developed when the bottom fell out of the economy. The majority of these condos were pre-sold and under contract but for obvious reasons never closed. Now developers are trying to stay afloat by making these units available to the general public. If you check the travel search engine kayak.com or lvahotels.com, a number of these properties will pop up, usually at extremely attractive rates. As a corollary, developers dumping condos and timeshares into the city's room inventory has put downward pressure on hotel rates across the board.

■ SUITE HOTELS *without* CASINOS

Alexis Park Resort (alexispark.com)

THIS 495-SUITE NONGAMING PROPERTY was one of the first in Las Vegas to create this concept in the 1980s. Situated on 16 acres, the 19 buildings house a variety of suites ranging in size from bedroom-parlor combos to large bilevel lofts. The standard junior suite is one room with a king or double-double beds sharing space with a hide-a-bed love seat, two side chairs, and a desk. A corner wet bar with granite counters encloses a refrigerator, coffeemaker, and storage cabinets. Microwaves are available on request. In the larger one-bedroom suites, a Jacuzzi tub and glass-enclosed shower are alongside the king-size bed. There is a separate large living room with easy chairs and a sofa, more kitchen space, and a small powder room. Architectural prints line the walls. Ice machines are nearby. The property features three medium-size fenced pools and mature lawns and landscaping. Buildings are freshly painted, but the passageways underneath stairwells are underlit and all walkways are in need of resurfacing. The exterior of the complex appears fatigued. Along with a comedy club, the lobby includes an internet station, poolside Alexis Gardens restaurant, and Pegasus lounge. Other amenities include a hair salon, business center, and a small fitness center with limited equipment. Room service is available, and pets are accepted.

Elara (hilton.com)

IF YOUR IDEA OF NIRVANA is a luxury hotel atop a cosmopolitan shopping center, the Elara is a good choice. The hotel is positioned over the Miracle Mile shopping arcade and is an upscale satellite of the Planet Hollywood Resort & Casino. Accessible from East Harmon Avenue, the 52-story all-suite red-and-blue tower offers several suite combinations to a maximum of four bedrooms with a parlor. The top five floors are residential condos, and the lower 47 are vacation-ownership hotel suites. All units feature high-tech components along with fully equipped granite and stainless-steel kitchens. Next to the king bed in the spacious sleeping room is a zebra-striped chaise and mirrored whirlpool tub. There are four flat-panel TVs throughout. A spectacular rectangular pool, framed by tall palms, faces south for all-day rays and no sun blockage by vertical buildings. Other amenities include room service, a business center, a gift shop, a gym, Starbucks, and 24-hour concierge service. Elara is about a five-minute stroll through the mall's south wing to reach the hotel's nucleus. This is a plus and a minus for guests: The plus is nongaming serenity with immediate access to eclectic shopping, and the minus is the significant distance to all Planet Hollywood venues. Guests preferring to stay towerside can sample the 15 culinary offerings within the Miracle Mile. The property offers front-door valet parking, but self-parking is only available in the Miracle Mile garage.

Hyatt Place Las Vegas (lasvegas.place.hyatt.com)

AT PARADISE ROAD AND HARMON AVENUE, Hyatt Place Las Vegas offers contemporary one-room suites at good prices. In addition to a small fitness center, an outdoor pool, and a few small meeting rooms, Hyatt Place serves a complimentary Continental breakfast. By taxi, Hyatt Place is about 4 minutes from the Strip and 5 minutes from the Las Vegas Convention Center.

Mardi Gras Hotel and Casino (mardigrasinn.com)

THE MARDI GRAS OFFERS SPARTAN SUITES at good rates. Quiet, with a well-manicured courtyard and a pool, the Mardi Gras is only a short walk from the Las Vegas Convention Center. There is a coffee shop on the property, and a number of good restaurants are less than half a mile away. Though a sign in front of the property advertises a casino, there is only a small collection of slot machines.

Platinum Hotel (theplatinumhotel.com)

THIS TRICOLOR, 17-STORY TOWER is one mega block from the famed Four Corners intersection of the Strip. An intimate all-suite, casino-less retreat, it's a non-Vegas hotel in the middle of Las Vegas. This property is a sleeper. The lobby looks and feels like a high-end high-rise. The Platinum's standard one-bedroom, the 910-square-foot Solitaire Suite, is huge in comparison to similar accommodations elsewhere. At the entry is a fully equipped kitchen. All bathrooms boast large Jacuzzi tubs, double sinks, and a separate glass shower. The celadon-and-tan bedrooms easily handle two double-queens or one king plus an easy chair or loveseat. In the parlor are a queen sofa sleeper, side chair, coffee table, desk, and Bose radio. High-speed wireless internet access and overnight laundry are available. Both the bedroom and parlor are furnished with flat-panel TVs. The even larger 1,150-square-foot Princess Suite contains the aforementioned accoutrements plus a washer and dryer and fireplaces in the bedroom and living room. All units feature balconies. West-facing rooms oversee the center Strip area, while east-facing rooms reveal suburban Las Vegas and Sunrise Mountain. Extended stays are welcome. Amenities include a year-round, heated indoor-outdoor pool; Kil@watt restaurant (open for breakfast and lunch); WELL Spa; and a fitness center.

Residence Inn (residenceinn.com)

ACROSS FROM THE LAS VEGAS CONVENTION CENTER, the Residence Inn by Marriott offers comfortable one- and two-bedroom suites with full kitchens. Patronized primarily by business travelers on extended stays, the Residence Inn provides a more homelike atmosphere than most other suite properties. While there is no restaurant at the hotel, there is an excellent selection within a half-mile radius. Amenities include a pool, hot tubs, and a coin laundry. A second Residence Inn is about a mile away at the Hughes Center.

Serene (serenevegas.com)

THIS ALL-SUITE BOUTIQUE HOTEL sits directly across from the Hard Rock Hotel and Casino. Formerly the St. Tropez and Rumor, the remodeled property is swathed in black, silver, and white with plum and metal accents, creating a crisp mid-century techno vibe. Like its boisterous neighbor, the hotel is geared toward a youthful market. The 149 suites feature charcoal walls and dark gray carpet with cream bedding and plum accents. Most accommodations feature an elevated triangular hot tub alongside the bed. The living room includes a love seat, coffee table, and a side chair. All rooms have garden-view patios or balconies. The pool complex offers cabanas and daybeds and a plush lawn for hammocks and chaises. With the property's circular configuration, self-parking is limited, but free valet parking is available. Because the property has no gym, Serene has a reciprocal agreement with the Hard Rock, so guests are invited to use the fitness facilities across the street.

The Signature at MGM Grand (signaturemgmgrand.com)

LOCATED A 5- TO 7-MINUTE WALK east of MGM's main casino, the Signature condo-hotel towers provide a welcome respite from the frantic action of Las Vegas, yet still offer proximity to the bustle and endless amenities and entertainment options at MGM Grand. Suite accommodations feature floor-to-ceiling windows, full kitchens, flat-panel TVs, Jacuzzi tubs, and high-speed internet connections. Signature's suites are not especially large but are beautifully appointed, and many units have private balconies. Each tower has its own pool, 24-hour concierge service, lounge, deli, fitness center, business center, and a private entrance with valet parking. The private entrance on Harmon Avenue makes for easy coming and going if you have a car. And it's only a 5-minute walk to the MGM Grand monorail station.

SpringHill Suites Las Vegas Convention Center (marriott.com)

WITH AN OUTDOOR POOL AND HOT TUB, a fitness center, a full-service restaurant, and room service, SpringHill Suites offers the amenities you would expect from a Marriott. And the small building and easy access to parking make the property easy to navigate. Suites are tastefully decorated, though not as plush as some Marriott properties. SpringHill Suites is directly across from the convention center, with a monorail station adjacent, and two blocks from the Strip.

Trump International Hotel Las Vegas (trumplasvegashotel.com)

TRUMP LAS VEGAS is a nongaming all-suite hotel located on Fashion Show Drive about 600 yards west of the Strip. It's a hotel, not a tourist attraction, offering studios and one-, two-, and three-bedroom suites. Its 64-story tower is situated to provide good views in every direction through floor-to-ceiling windows. While there is no showroom or nightclub, there is gourmet dining at the DJT (Donald J. Trump) restaurant, libations at the H2(eau) lounge, an adequate pool, and an excellent spa and fitness center. When we inspected Trump Las Vegas we were immediately struck by the quiet of the place. From the lobby to the restaurants to the guest suites, it was restful and relaxing. The suites provide all the connectivity a business traveler could want, as well as full kitchens in the one- to three-bedroom units. Furnishings are Scandinavian contemporary, mixing dark and blond wood tones and restful pastel soft goods. Though it's a 10-minute walk to the Strip, Trump is directly across Fashion Show Drive from the Fashion Show Mall, Las Vegas's largest shopping venue. The Las Vegas Convention Center is about 10 minutes away by cab, and the Sands Convention Center is about 10 minutes distant by foot.

Wyndham Grand Desert (wyndhamgranddesert.com)

A TIMESHARE PROPERTY, THE WYNDHAM GRAND DESERT offers large one- and two-bedroom suites with fully equipped kitchens, washers and dryers, dining rooms, and plenty of closet and storage space. Living rooms feature a pull-out sofa and flat-panel TV. The main complex with lobby, restaurants, spa, and two fitness centers surrounds an expansive pool area that's nicely manicured but short on shade. There is no casino. A separate, freestanding hotel tower is located next door to the west. Internet access is free but spotty on floors lacking internet servers. The Grand Desert can be accessed from both Harmon Avenue and Koval Lane, making coming and going easy. Parking is all at ground level. Though a timeshare, you are not required to suffer a sales presentation, but you can easily arrange one if you're interested. South-facing guest rooms overlook the airport but are out of range of airport noise. Bargain rates are frequently available on VRBO.com

HOTELS *with* BALCONIES

LAS VEGAS IS A GREAT PLACE TO HAVE FUN and, for some, a great place to get married. Evidently, it's also a favorite place for splashy suicides. Consequently, very few Las Vegas hotels have balconies. Likewise, bugs are a problem—those tiny critters can fly a lot higher than you might think. Following is a list of the hotels with at least some balconies. At Hooters, Royal Resort, and the Trop, you have to request a balcony room:

• Cosmopolitan	• Hooters	• Platinum	• Royal Resort
• Signature at MGM Grand	• Staybridge Suites	• Tropicana Garden Rooms	

LAS VEGAS MOTELS

BECAUSE THEY MUST COMPETE with the huge hotel-casinos, many Las Vegas motels offer great rates or provide special amenities, such as a complimentary breakfast. Like the resorts, motels often have a very specific clientele. La Quinta Inn, for instance, caters to government employees, while the Hampton Inn Las Vegas North on Craig Road primarily serves folks visiting Nellis Air Force Base.

For the most part, national motel chains are well represented in Las Vegas. We have included enough chain and independent motels in the following ratings-and-rankings section to give you a sense of how these properties compare with hotel-casinos and all-suite hotels. Because chain hotels are known entities to most travelers, no descriptions are provided beyond the room-quality ratings. After all, a Comfort Inn in Las Vegas is pretty much like a Comfort Inn in Louisville, and we are all aware by now that Motel 6 leaves the light on for you.

LAS VEGAS HOSTELS

LAS VEGAS HAS THREE HOSTELS: **Hostel Cat,** on Las Vegas Boulevard halfway between the Strip and Fremont Street; **Sin City Hostel,** right next door; and the **Las Vegas Hostel,** located downtown on Fremont at 14th Street. Las Vegas Hostel is easily the most attractive of the three, with 38 shared and private rooms, all with new furniture, mattresses, and bedding, along with en suite bathrooms. It also features a modest pool, a communal kitchen, and complimentary breakfast. Hostel patrons are young and mostly international, visiting from Australia, Europe, and Central and South America. Accommodations begin at $20 per night. Staff-led activities might include pub crawls, movie nights, and pool parties. See lasvegashostel.net/en_US or call ☎ 702-385-1150.

RV CAMPING *in* LAS VEGAS

SOME CASINOS, including Main Street Station, Circus Circus, Sam's Town, and Arizona Charlie's (Boulder), operate RV campgrounds with full facilities. There are also quite a few KOA or independent campgrounds. Of these, we prefer **Las Vegas RV Resort** (lasvegasrvresort.com, ☎ 866-846-5432), one of the largest in town with 390 sites. Limited to adults, this palm tree–lined RV complex is located two blocks north of Sam's Town on Boulder Highway at 3890 S. Nellis Blvd. The 18-acre resort offers full hook-ups for pull-thrus and multiple slide-outs. Standard, deluxe, and premium sites are available. Each site includes a picnic table. Amenities include a heated pool and hot tub, a clubhouse with lounge seating and big-screen TV, two Laundromats, multiple shower and restroom facilities, free Wi-Fi, and two pet runs. A small fitness facility is open daily, 8 a.m.–11 p.m. Propane deliveries can be preordered. Daily, weekly, or monthly rentals are available.

ACCOMMODATIONS:
Rated and Ranked

WHAT'S IN A ROOM?

EXCEPT FOR CLEANLINESS, state of repair, and decor, most travelers do not pay much attention to hotel rooms. There is, of course, a discernible standard of quality and luxury that differentiates Motel 6 from Holiday Inn, Holiday Inn from Marriott, and so on. In general, however, most hotel guests fail to appreciate that some rooms are better engineered than other rooms. Contrary to what you might suppose, designing a hotel room is (or should be) a lot more complex than picking a bedspread to match the carpet and drapes. Making the room usable to its occupants is an art, a planning discipline that combines both form and function.

Decor and taste are important, certainly. No one wants to spend several days in a room where the furnishings are dated, garish, or even ugly. But beyond the decor, there are variables that determine how "livable" a hotel room is. In Las Vegas, for example, we have seen some beautifully appointed rooms that are simply not well designed for human habitation. The next time you stay in a hotel, pay attention to the details and design elements of your room. Even more than decor, these are the things that will make you feel comfortable and at home.

ROOM RATINGS

TO SEPARATE PROPERTIES according to the relative quality, tastefulness, state of repair, cleanliness, and size of their standard rooms, we have grouped them into classifications denoted by stars. Star ratings in this guide apply to Las Vegas properties only and do not necessarily correspond to ratings awarded by Forbes, AAA, or other travel critics.

Star ratings apply to *room quality only* and describe the property's standard accommodations. For almost all hotels and motels, a "standard accommodation" is a hotel room with either one king bed or two queen beds. In an all-suite property, the standard accommodation is either a studio or one-bedroom suite. Also, in addition to standard accommodations, many hotels offer luxury rooms and special suites, which are not rated in this guide. Star ratings for rooms are assigned without regard to location or whether a property has a casino, restaurant(s), recreational facilities, entertainment, or other extras.

In addition to stars, we also employ a numerical rating system. Our rating scale is 0–100, with 100 as the best possible rating and zero (0) as the worst. Numerical ratings are presented to show the difference we perceive between one property and another. Rooms at the Suncoast, Stratosphere, and The Orleans, for instance, are all rated as ★★★½ (three-and-a-half stars). In the supplemental numerical ratings, the Suncoast and the Stratosphere are rated 82 and 79, respectively, while The Orleans is rated 75. This means that within the three-and-a-half-star category, the Suncoast and the Stratosphere are comparable, and both have somewhat nicer rooms than The Orleans.

HOW THE HOTELS COMPARE

ON PAGES 149–151 is a comparison of hotel rooms in town. In some instances, a one- or two-room suite can be had for the same price or less than that of a hotel room.

If you have used an earlier edition of this guide, you will notice that many of the ratings and rankings have changed. These changes are occasioned by such positive developments as guest-room renovation, improved maintenance, and improved housekeeping. Failure to properly maintain guest rooms and poor housekeeping affect the ratings negatively. Finally, some ratings change as a result of enlarging our sample size. Because we cannot check every room in a hotel, we inspect a number of randomly chosen rooms. The more rooms we inspect in a particular hotel, the more representative our sample is of the property as a whole.

The guest rooms in many Las Vegas hotels can vary widely in quality. In most hotels the better rooms are situated in high-rise structures known locally as "towers." More modest accommodations, called "garden rooms," are routinely found in one- and two-story outbuildings. It is important to understand that not all rooms in a particular hotel are the same. When you make inquiries or reservations, always define the type of room you are talking about.

Finally, before you begin to shop for a hotel, take a hard look at this letter we received from a couple in Hot Springs, Arkansas:

> We canceled our room reservations to follow the advice in your book [and reserved a hotel room highly ranked by the Unofficial Guide]. We wanted inexpensive, but clean and cheerful. We got inexpensive, but [also] dirty, grim, and depressing. I really felt disappointed in your advice and the room. It was the pits. That was the one real piece of information I needed from your book! The room spoiled the holiday for me aside from our touring.

Needless to say, this letter was as unsettling to us as the bad room was to our reader. Our integrity as travel journalists, after all, is based on the quality of the information we provide to our readers. Even with the best of intentions and the most conscientious research, however, we cannot inspect every room in every hotel. What we do, in statistical terms, is take a sample: we check out several rooms selected at random in each hotel and base our ratings and rankings on those rooms. The inspections are conducted anonymously and without the knowledge of the management. Although it would be unusual, it is certainly possible that the rooms we randomly inspect are not representative of the majority of rooms at a particular hotel. Another possibility is that the rooms we inspect in a given hotel are representative but that by bad luck a reader is assigned a room that is inferior. When we rechecked the hotel our reader disliked, we discovered that our rating was correctly representative, but that he and his wife had unfortunately been assigned to one of a small number of threadbare rooms scheduled for renovation.

The key to avoiding disappointment is to snoop around in advance. We recommend that you check out the hotel's website before you book. Be forewarned, however, that some hotel chains use the same guest room photo for all hotels in the chain; a specific guest room may not resemble the website photos. When you or your travel agent call, ask how old the property is and when your guest room was last renovated. If you arrive and are assigned a room inferior to that which you had been led to expect, demand to be moved to another room consistent with your expectations.

Cost estimates are based on the hotel's published rack rates for standard rooms, averaged between weekday and weekend prices.

Continued on page 152

HOW THE HOTELS COMPARE

HOTEL	OVERALL RATING	ROOM RATING	COST ($=$50)	LOCATION
DELANO *(all suites)*	★★★★★	96	$$$$$+	South Strip
WYNN ENCORE	★★★★★	96	$$$$$+	Mid-Strip
WYNN LAS VEGAS	★★★★★	96	$$$$-	Mid-Strip
ARIA AT CITYCENTER	★★★★½	95	$$$$+	Mid-Strip
BELLAGIO	★★★★½	95	$$$$$-	Mid-Strip
CAESARS PALACE	★★★★½	95	$$$$	Mid-Strip
COSMOPOLITAN	★★★★½	95	$$$$$+	Mid-Strip
FOUR SEASONS AT MANDALAY BAY	★★★★½	95	$$$$$	South Strip
PALMS	★★★★½	95	$$$$	West of Strip
THE PALAZZO *(all suites)*	★★★★½	95	$$$$$	Mid-Strip
TRUMP INTERNATIONAL HOTEL LAS VEGAS *(all suites)*	★★★★½	95	$$$+	West of Strip
VDARA AT CITYCENTER	★★★★½	95	$$$$-	Mid-Strip
MANDARIN ORIENTAL/WALDORF ASTORIA AT CITYCENTER	★★★★½	94	$$$$$$-	Mid-Strip
NOBU HOTEL	★★★★½	94	$$$$$+	Mid-Strip
SIGNATURE AT MGM GRAND *(all suites)*	★★★★½	94	$$$$-	East of Strip
THE VENETIAN	★★★★½	94	$$$$$	Mid-Strip
ELARA	★★★★½	93	$$$$$-	Mid-Strip
MANDALAY BAY	★★★★½	92	$$$$$-	South Strip
PARIS	★★★★½	91	$$$$+	Mid-Strip
PARK MGM	★★★★½	91	$$$+	Mid-Strip
RED ROCK RESORT	★★★★½	91	$$$$$$-	Summerlin
M RESORT	★★★★½	90	$$$+	South of Las Vegas
MGM GRAND	★★★★½	90	$$$$$-	South Strip
MIRAGE	★★★★½	90	$$$$-	Mid-Strip
RENAISSANCE LAS VEGAS	★★★★½	90	$$+	East of Strip
HARD ROCK HOTEL	★★★★	89	$$$+	East of Strip
TROPICANA	★★★★	89	$$$+	South Strip
ALIANTE HOTEL + CASINO	★★★★	88	$$$-	North Las Vegas
FLAMINGO	★★★★	88	$$$+	Mid-Strip
HILTON LAKE LAS VEGAS	★★★★	88	$$$$-	Henderson
JW MARRIOTT LAS VEGAS	★★★★	88	$$$$-	Summerlin
PLATINUM HOTEL	★★★★	88	$$$+	East of Strip
SILVERTON	★★★★	88	$$+	South of Las Vegas
WESTIN LAKE LAS VEGAS	★★★★	88	$$$$	Henderson
WYNDHAM GRAND DESERT	★★★★	88	$$$$$$-	East of Strip
EMBASSY SUITES CONVENTION CENTER	★★★★	87	$$+	East of Strip
GREEN VALLEY RANCH RESORT AND SPA	★★★★	87	$$$$$$	Henderson

HOW THE HOTELS COMPARE (continued)

HOTEL	OVERALL RATING	ROOM RATING	COST ($=$50)	LOCATION
LUXOR	★★★★	87	$$+	South Strip
PLANET HOLLYWOOD	★★★★	87	$$$$	Mid-Strip
EMBASSY SUITES IN LAS VEGAS	★★★★	86	$$$-	East of Strip
RIO	★★★★	86	$$$	Mid-Strip
BALLY'S	★★★★	85	$$$+	Mid-Strip
GOLDEN NUGGET (Rush Tower)	★★★★	85	$$$$	Downtown
LUCKY DRAGON	★★★★	85	$$	North Strip
NEW YORK–NEW YORK	★★★★	85	$$$$-	South Strip
THE CROMWELL	★★★★	85	$$$$$$-	Mid-Strip
LAS VEGAS MARRIOTT	★★★★	84	$$$-	East of Strip
PALACE STATION	★★★★	84	$$$-	West of Strip
TI (Treasure Island)	★★★★	84	$$$+	Mid-Strip
EASTSIDE CANNERY	★★★★	83	$$-	Boulder Highway
HARRAH'S	★★★★	83	$$$+	Mid-Strip
RESIDENCE INN BY MARRIOTT LAS VEGAS CONVENTION CENTER	★★★★	83	$$$$$+	East of Strip
RESIDENCE INN BY MARRIOTT LAS VEGAS SOUTH	★★★★	83	$$$-	West of Strip
SLS	★★★★	83	$$+	North Strip
SUNSET STATION	★★★★	83	$$$-	Henderson
W LAS VEGAS	★★★★	83	$$$$+	North Strip
GOLD COAST	★★★½	82	$$+	West of Strip
SUNCOAST	★★★½	82	$$	Summerlin
CIRCUS CIRCUS (TOWER ROOMS)	★★★½	81	$$+	North Strip
EXCALIBUR	★★★½	81	$$+	South Strip
SOUTH POINT	★★★½	81	$$$-	South of Las Vegas
THE LINQ HOTEL & CASINO	★★★½	81	$$$$	Mid-Strip
SERENE	★★★½	80	$$+	East of Strip
TUSCANY	★★★½	80	$$$+	East of Strip
WESTGATE LAS VEGAS	★★★½	80	$$+	East of Strip
WESTIN LAS VEGAS	★★★½	80	$$$$-	East of Strip
CANDLEWOOD SUITES	★★★½	79	$$+	East of Strip
COURTYARD BY MARRIOTT LV CONVENTION CENTER	★★★½	79	$$$-	East of Strip
EL CORTEZ CABANA SUITES	★★★½	79	$$$	Downtown
HOOTERS CASINO HOTEL	★★★½	79	$$	South Strip
PLAZA	★★★½	79	$$$-	Downtown
SAM'S TOWN	★★★½	79	$$+	Boulder Highway
STRATOSPHERE	★★★½	79	$$+	North Strip
THE D LAS VEGAS	★★★½	79	$$$-	Downtown

HOW THE HOTELS COMPARE (continued)

HOTEL	OVERALL RATING	ROOM RATING	COST ($=$50)	LOCATION
ALEXIS PARK RESORT	★★★½	78	$$+	East of Strip
ARTISAN HOTEL BOUTIQUE	★★★½	78	$$$-	North Strip
GOLDEN NUGGET	★★★½	78	$$$$-	Downtown
BOULDER STATION	★★★½	76	$$-	Boulder Highway
DOWNTOWN GRAND	★★★½	76	$$$-	Downtown
SILVER SEVENS	★★★½	76	$+	East of Strip
COURTYARD BY MARRIOTT LAS VEGAS SOUTH	★★★½	75	$$+	South Strip
FAIRFIELD INN & SUITES LAS VEGAS SOUTH	★★★½	75	$$-	South Strip
GOLDEN GATE	★★★½	75	$$-	Downtown
MAIN STREET STATION	★★★½	75	$$$-	Downtown
THE ORLEANS	★★★½	75	$$+	South Strip
ARIZONA CHARLIE'S BOULDER	★★★	74	$+	Boulder Highway
FIESTA HENDERSON	★★★	74	$$-	Henderson
MARDI GRAS HOTEL AND CASINO	★★★	73	$+	East of Strip
SANTA FE STATION	★★★	73	$$-	Rancho Drive
EL CORTEZ	★★★	72	$$$-	Downtown
FAIRFIELD INN LAS VEGAS CONVENTION CENTER	★★★	72	$$$-	East of Strip
HAMPTON INN TROPICANA	★★★	72	$$$	South Strip
HILTON GARDEN INN LAS VEGAS STRIP SOUTH	★★★	72	$$$	South of Las Vegas
HYATT PLACE	★★★	72	$$$$-	East of Strip
BEST WESTERN MCCARRAN INN	★★★	71	$$+	East of Strip
HOLIDAY INN EXPRESS	★★★	71	$$$-	West of Strip
CIRCUS CIRCUS (manor rooms)	★★★	70	$$	North Strip
FOUR QUEENS	★★★	70	$$$-	Downtown
FREMONT	★★★	70	$$+	Downtown
ROYAL RESORT	★★★	70	$+	North Strip
TEXAS STATION	★★★	70	$$-	Rancho Drive Area
LA QUINTA LAS VEGAS AIRPORT NORTH	★★★	69	$$$-	East of Strip
DAYS INN AT WILD WILD WEST	★★★	68	$	South Strip
RED ROOF INN	★★★	68	$$-	East of Strip
CALIFORNIA	★★★	67	$$$+	Downtown
MANOR SUITES	★★★	67	$$-	South of Las Vegas
ARIZONA CHARLIE'S DECATUR	★★★	66	$+	West Las Vegas
CANNERY	★★½	64	$$$-	North Las Vegas
CASINO ROYALE	★★½	64	$$$$-	Mid-Strip
FIESTA RANCHO	★★½	62	$$	Rancho Drive

Continued from page 148

Rack rates are in a continual state of flux, so with a little effort you should be able to significantly beat the rates listed. Each "$" represents $50. Thus a cost symbol of "$$$" means a room (or suite) at that hotel will cost about $150 a night.

THE TOP 30 BEST DEALS IN LAS VEGAS

IN ADDITION TO LISTING the nicest rooms in town, we also reorder the list to rank the best combinations of quality and value in a room. Again, rankings are made without consideration of location or the availability of restaurants, recreation, entertainment, and/or amenities.

A reader recently complained to us that he had booked one of our top-ranked rooms in terms of value and had been very disappointed in the room. We noticed that the room the reader occupied had a quality rating of ★★½. We would remind you that the value ratings are intended to give you some sense of value received for dollars spent. A ★★½ room at $30 may have the same value rating as a ★★★★ room at $85, but that does not mean the rooms will be of comparable quality. Regardless of whether it's a good deal or not, a ★★½ room is still a ★★½ room. Listed on the facing page are the best room buys for the money, regardless of location or star classification, based on average rack rates.

WHEN ONLY THE BEST WILL DO

THE TROUBLE WITH PROFILES is that details and distinctions are sacrificed in the interest of brevity and information accessibility. For example, while dozens of properties are listed as having swimming pools, we've made no qualitative discriminations. In the alphabetized profiles, a pool is a pool.

In actuality, of course, though most pools are quite basic and ordinary, some (Wynn Las Vegas, Wynn Encore, Mirage, Tropicana, Flamingo, Park MGM, MGM Grand, Planet Hollywood, Mandalay Bay, Bellagio, Caesars Palace, M Resort, The Venetian, JW Marriott Las Vegas, Aria at CityCenter, and the Rio) are pretty spectacular. To distinguish the exceptional from the average in a number of categories, we provide a best-of list below.

MOST VISUALLY INTERESTING HOTELS		
1. The Venetian	**9.**	Red Rock Resort
2. Caesars Palace	**10.**	Mirage
3. Wynn Las Vegas/Wynn Encore	**11.**	New York–New York
4. Bellagio	**12.**	Paris Las Vegas
5. Aria at CityCenter	**13.**	M Resort
6. Main Street Station	**14.**	Rio
7. Mandalay Bay	**15.**	The Cosmopolitan
8. Luxor	**16.**	Planet Hollywood

Continued on page 154

THE TOP 30 BEST DEALS

	HOTEL	STAR RATING	RATING	ROOM COST	LOCATION
1.	SILVER SEVENS	★★★½	76	$+	East of Strip
2.	DAYS INN AT WILD WILD WEST	★★★	68	$	South Strip
3.	EASTSIDE CANNERY	★★★★	83	$$−	Boulder Highway
4.	ARIZONA CHARLIE'S BOULDER	★★★	74	$+	Boulder Highway
5.	RENAISSANCE LAS VEGAS	★★★★½	90	$$+	East of Strip
6.	EMBASSY SUITES CONVENTION CENTER	★★★★	87	$$+	East of Strip
7.	LUXOR	★★★★	87	$$+	South Strip
8.	MARDI GRAS HOTEL AND CASINO	★★★	73	$+	East of Strip
9.	BOULDER STATION	★★★½	76	$$−	Boulder Highway
10.	ROYAL RESORT	★★★	70	$+	North Strip
11.	ARIZONA CHARLIE'S DECATUR	★★★	66	$+	West Las Vegas
12.	GOLDEN GATE	★★★½	75	$$−	Downtown
13.	SILVERTON	★★★★	88	$$+	South of Las Vegas
14.	FAIRFIELD INN & SUITES LAS VEGAS SOUTH	★★★½	75	$$−	South Strip
15.	HOOTERS CASINO HOTEL	★★★½	79	$$	South Strip
16.	SUNCOAST	★★★½	82	$$	Summerlin
17.	SLS	★★★★	83	$$+	North Strip
18.	WESTGATE LAS VEGAS	★★★½	80	$$+	East of Strip
19.	PARK MGM	★★★★½	91	$$$+	Mid-Strip
20.	SAM'S TOWN	★★★½	79	$$+	Boulder Highway
21.	ALIANTE HOTEL + CASINO	★★★★	88	$$$−	North Las Vegas
22.	PALACE STATION	★★★★	84	$$$−	West of Strip
23.	TRUMP INTERNATIONAL HOTEL LAS VEGAS (all suites)	★★★★½	95	$$$+	West of Strip
24.	SERENE	★★★½	80	$$+	East of Strip
25.	MANOR SUITES	★★★	67	$$−	South of Las Vegas
26.	EMBASSY SUITES IN LAS VEGAS	★★★★	86	$$$−	East of Strip
27.	EXCALIBUR	★★★½	81	$$+	South Strip
28.	GOLD COAST	★★★½	82	$$+	West of Strip
29.	WYNN LAS VEGAS	★★★★★	96	$$$$−	Mid-Strip
30.	STRATOSPHERE	★★★½	79	$$+	North Strip

BEST FOR SHOPPING ON-SITE OR WITHIN AN 8-MINUTE WALK

1. Caesars Palace
2. The Venetian
3. Mirage
4. Wynn Las Vegas/Wynn Encore
5. TI
6. Planet Hollywood
7. CityCenter
8. Trump International Hotel Las Vegas
9. The Cosmopolitan

BEST BUFFETS

1. Caesars Bacchanal Buffet
2. The Cosmopolitan Wicked Spoon Buffet
3. Aria Buffet
4. Bellagio Buffet
5. Wynn Buffet
6. Mirage Cravings
7. Paris's Le Village Buffet
8. Feast GVR/Feast Texas Station
9. M Resort Studio B Buffet
10. Treasure Island Buffet

BEST DINING (Expense No Issue)

1. The Cosmopolitan
2. Wynn Las Vegas/Wynn Encore
3. The Venetian/Palazzo
4. CityCenter
5. Bellagio
6. Caesars Palace
7. MGM Grand
8. Mandalay Bay
9. Mirage
10. Paris

BEST DINING (For Great Value)

1. The Orleans
2. Suncoast
3. California
4. Main Street Station
5. Gold Coast
6. Palace Station
7. South Point
8. Fiesta Rancho
9. Boulder Station
10. Sam's Town

BEST SUNDAY BRUNCHES

- **Aria:** Bardot Brasserie and Herringbone • **Bally's:** Sterling Brunch
- **Forum Shops:** Border Brunch • **House of Blues at Mandalay Bay:** Gospel Brunch
- **Venetian:** Chica • **Wynn Las Vegas:** Buffet at Wynn

BEST FOR BOWLING

- Gold Coast • The Orleans • Red Rock Resort • Sam's Town
- Sante Fe Station • South Point • Sunset Station • Texas Station

BEST SPAS

- Bellagio • Caesars Palace • CityCenter: Aria, Mandarin Oriental, Vdara • The Cosmopolitan
- Green Valley Ranch Resort and Spa • Mandalay Bay/Delano/Four Seasons • MGM Grand
- Mirage • Park MGM • The Palazzo • Paris Las Vegas • Red Rock Resort • TI
- Trump Hotel Las Vegas • The Venetian • Wynn Encore • Wynn Las Vegas

BEST FOR GOLF

- Aliante Casino + Hotel • Hilton Lake Las Vegas • JW Marriott Las Vegas • Suncoast
- Westgate Las Vegas

BEST FOR TENNIS

- Bally's • Westgate LV

Hotel Information Chart

Alexis Park Resort
★★★½
375 E. Harmon Ave.
Las Vegas, NV 89169
☎ 702-796-3300
FAX 702-796-4334
TOLL-FREE 800-582-2228
alexispark.com

RACK RATE	$$+
ROOM QUALITY	78
LOCATION	East of Strip
NO. OF ROOMS	495
CHECKOUT TIME	11
NONSMOKING	•
CONCIERGE	•
CONVENTION FACIL.	•
MEETING ROOMS	•
VALET PARKING	—
RV PARK	Limited
ROOM SERVICE	•
FREE BREAKFAST	—
FINE DINING/TYPES	Continental
COFFEE SHOP	•
24-HOUR CAFE	—
BUFFET	Breakfast
CASINO	—
LOUNGE	•
SHOWROOM	—
GIFTS/DRUGS/NEWS	•
POOL	•
EXERCISE ROOM	•

Aliante Casino + Hotel ★★★★
7300 Aliante Pkwy.
North Las Vegas, NV 89084
☎ 702-692-7777
TOLL-FREE 877-477-7627
aliantecasinohotel.com

RACK RATE	$$$–
ROOM QUALITY	88
LOCATION	North Las Vegas
NO. OF ROOMS	202
CHECKOUT TIME	Noon
NONSMOKING	•
CONCIERGE	•
CONVENTION FACIL.	•
MEETING ROOMS	•
VALET PARKING	•
RV PARK	—
ROOM SERVICE	•
FREE BREAKFAST	—
FINE DINING/TYPES	Steak, seafood, Italian, Mexican
COFFEE SHOP	•
24-HOUR CAFE	•
BUFFET	•
CASINO	•
LOUNGE	•
SHOWROOM	•
GIFTS/DRUGS/NEWS	•
POOL	•
EXERCISE ROOM	•

Aria at CityCenter ★★★★½
3730 Las Vegas Blvd. S.
Las Vegas, NV 89109
☎ 702-590-7111
FAX 702-590-7112
TOLL-FREE 866-359-7757
aria.com

RACK RATE	$$$$+
ROOM QUALITY	95
LOCATION	Mid-Strip
NO. OF ROOMS	4,004
CHECKOUT TIME	11
NONSMOKING	•
CONCIERGE	•
CONVENTION FACIL.	•
MEETING ROOMS	•
VALET PARKING	•
RV PARK	•
ROOM SERVICE	•
FREE BREAKFAST	—
FINE DINING/TYPES	Steak, Spanish, Thai, Mexican, American
COFFEE SHOP	•
24-HOUR CAFE	•
BUFFET	•
CASINO	•
LOUNGE	•
SHOWROOM	•
GIFTS/DRUGS/NEWS	•
POOL	•
EXERCISE ROOM	Health spa

Arizona Charlie's Boulder
★★★
4575 Boulder Hwy.
Las Vegas, NV 89121
☎ 702-951-9000
FAX 702-951-1046
TOLL-FREE 888-236-9066
arizonacharliesboulder.com

RACK RATE	$+
ROOM QUALITY	74
LOCATION	Boulder Hwy.
NO. OF ROOMS	301
CHECKOUT TIME	11
NONSMOKING	•
CONCIERGE	—
CONVENTION FACIL.	•
MEETING ROOMS	•
VALET PARKING	—
RV PARK	•
ROOM SERVICE	—
FREE BREAKFAST	—
FINE DINING/TYPES	American, steak
COFFEE SHOP	•
24-HOUR CAFE	•
BUFFET	•
CASINO	•
LOUNGE	•
SHOWROOM	Live music
GIFTS/DRUGS/NEWS	•
POOL	•
EXERCISE ROOM	—

Arizona Charlie's Decatur ★★★
740 S. Decatur Blvd.
Las Vegas, NV 89107
☎ 702-258-5111
FAX 702-258-5192
TOLL-FREE 888-236-8645
arizonacharliesdecatur.com

RACK RATE	$+
ROOM QUALITY	66
LOCATION	West Las Vegas
NO. OF ROOMS	258
CHECKOUT TIME	11
NONSMOKING	•
CONCIERGE	—
CONVENTION FACIL.	•
MEETING ROOMS	•
VALET PARKING	•
RV PARK	—
ROOM SERVICE	—
FREE BREAKFAST	—
FINE DINING/TYPES	American, steak
COFFEE SHOP	•
24-HOUR CAFE	•
BUFFET	•
CASINO	•
LOUNGE	•
SHOWROOM	Local bands
GIFTS/DRUGS/NEWS	•
POOL	•
EXERCISE ROOM	—

Artisan Hotel Boutique ★★★½
1501 W. Sahara Ave.
Las Vegas, NV 89102
☎ 702-214-4000
FAX 702-733-1571
TOLL-FREE 800-554-4092
artisanhotel.com

RACK RATE	$$$–
ROOM QUALITY	78
LOCATION	North Strip
NO. OF ROOMS	63
CHECKOUT TIME	11
NONSMOKING	•
CONCIERGE	•
CONVENTION FACIL.	—
MEETING ROOMS	•
VALET PARKING	•
RV PARK	—
ROOM SERVICE	—
FREE BREAKFAST	—
FINE DINING/TYPES	Tapas
COFFEE SHOP	—
24-HOUR CAFE	—
BUFFET	—
CASINO	—
LOUNGE	•
SHOWROOM	—
GIFTS/DRUGS/NEWS	—
POOL	•
EXERCISE ROOM	•

HOTEL INFORMATION CHART *(continued)*

Bally's ★★★★
3645 Las Vegas Blvd. S.
Las Vegas, NV 89109
☎ 702-739-4111
FAX 702-967-4405
TOLL-FREE 800-634-3434
ballyslasvegas.com

RACK RATE	$$$+
ROOM QUALITY	85
LOCATION	Mid-Strip
NO. OF ROOMS	2,814
CHECKOUT TIME	11
NONSMOKING	Floors
CONCIERGE	•
CONVENTION FACIL.	•
MEETING ROOMS	•
VALET PARKING	•
RV PARK	—
ROOM SERVICE	•
FREE BREAKFAST	—
FINE DINING/TYPES	Steak, seafood, Italian, Mexican
COFFEE SHOP	•
24-HOUR CAFE	•
BUFFET	•
CASINO	•
LOUNGE	•
SHOWROOM	Production show, headliners
GIFTS/DRUGS/NEWS	•
POOL	•
EXERCISE ROOM	Health spa/tennis

Bellagio ★★★★½
3600 Las Vegas Blvd. S.
Las Vegas, NV 89109
☎ 702-693-7444
FAX 702-693-8585
TOLL-FREE 888-987-6667
bellagio.com

RACK RATE	$$$$$−
ROOM QUALITY	95
LOCATION	Mid-Strip
NO. OF ROOMS	3,933
CHECKOUT TIME	11
NONSMOKING	•
CONCIERGE	•
CONVENTION FACIL.	•
MEETING ROOMS	•
VALET PARKING	•
RV PARK	—
ROOM SERVICE	•
FREE BREAKFAST	—
FINE DINING/TYPES	Italian, Japanese, American, French, Mediterranean
COFFEE SHOP	•
24-HOUR CAFE	•
BUFFET	•
CASINO	•
LOUNGE	•
SHOWROOM	Production show
GIFTS/DRUGS/NEWS	•
POOL	•
EXERCISE ROOM	Health spa

Boulder Station ★★★½
4111 Boulder Hwy.
Las Vegas, NV 89121
☎ 702-432-7777
FAX 702-432-7730
TOLL-FREE 800-683-7777
boulderstation.com

RACK RATE	$$−
ROOM QUALITY	76
LOCATION	Boulder Hwy.
NO. OF ROOMS	300
CHECKOUT TIME	Noon
NONSMOKING	•
CONCIERGE	•
CONVENTION FACIL.	•
MEETING ROOMS	•
VALET PARKING	•
RV PARK	—
ROOM SERVICE	•
FREE BREAKFAST	—
FINE DINING/TYPES	Steak, seafood, Italian, Mexican
COFFEE SHOP	•
24-HOUR CAFE	•
BUFFET	•
CASINO	•
LOUNGE	•
SHOWROOM	Live music
GIFTS/DRUGS/NEWS	•
POOL	•
EXERCISE ROOM	•

Casino Royale ★★½
3411 Las Vegas Blvd. S.
Las Vegas, NV 89109
☎ 702-737-3500
FAX 702-650-4743
TOLL-FREE 800-854-7666
casinoroyalehotel.com

RACK RATE	$$$$−
ROOM QUALITY	64
LOCATION	Mid-Strip
NO. OF ROOMS	152
CHECKOUT TIME	11
NONSMOKING	•
CONCIERGE	•
CONVENTION FACIL.	—
MEETING ROOMS	—
VALET PARKING	—
RV PARK	—
ROOM SERVICE	—
FREE BREAKFAST	—
FINE DINING/TYPES	American, steak, pizza
COFFEE SHOP	•
24-HOUR CAFE	•
BUFFET	•
CASINO	•
LOUNGE	•
SHOWROOM	—
GIFTS/DRUGS/NEWS	•
POOL	•
EXERCISE ROOM	—

Circus Circus ★★★½/★★★*
2880 Las Vegas Blvd. S.
Las Vegas, NV 89109
☎ 702-734-0410
FAX 702-734-2268
TOLL-FREE 800-634-3450
circuscircus.com

RACK RATE	$$+/$$
ROOM QUALITY	81/70*
LOCATION	North Strip
NO. OF ROOMS	3,773
CHECKOUT TIME	11
NONSMOKING	Floors
CONCIERGE	—
CONVENTION FACIL.	•
MEETING ROOMS	•
VALET PARKING	•
RV PARK	•
ROOM SERVICE	•
FREE BREAKFAST	—
FINE DINING/TYPES	Steak, Italian, Mexican
COFFEE SHOP	•
24-HOUR CAFE	•
BUFFET	•
CASINO	•
LOUNGE	•
SHOWROOM	Circus acts, theme park
GIFTS/DRUGS/NEWS	•
POOL	•
EXERCISE ROOM	•

tower rooms/manor rooms

The Cosmopolitan ★★★★½
3708 Las Vegas Blvd. S.
Las Vegas NV 89109
☎ 702-698-7000
FAX 702-698-7007
TOLL-FREE 877-551-7778
cosmopolitanlasvegas.com

RACK RATE	$$$$$+
ROOM QUALITY	95
LOCATION	Mid-Strip
NO. OF ROOMS	3,027
CHECKOUT TIME	11
NONSMOKING	•
CONCIERGE	•
CONVENTION FACIL.	•
MEETING ROOMS	•
VALET PARKING	•
RV PARK	—
ROOM SERVICE	•
FREE BREAKFAST	—
FINE DINING/TYPES	American, Italian, Mediterranean, French, Asian
COFFEE SHOP	•
24-HOUR CAFE	•
BUFFET	•
CASINO	•
LOUNGE	•
SHOWROOM	•
GIFTS/DRUGS/NEWS	•
POOL	•
EXERCISE ROOM	Health spa/tennis

Caesars Palace ★★★★½
3570 Las Vegas Blvd. S.
Las Vegas, NV 89109
☎ 702-731-7110
FAX 702-866-1700
TOLL-FREE 800-634-6661
caesarspalace.com

RACK RATE	$$$$
ROOM QUALITY	95
LOCATION	Mid-Strip
NO. OF ROOMS	4,000
CHECKOUT TIME	11
NONSMOKING	Floors
CONCIERGE	•
CONVENTION FACIL.	•
MEETING ROOMS	•
VALET PARKING	•
RV PARK	—
ROOM SERVICE	•
FREE BREAKFAST	—
FINE DINING/TYPES	Chinese, French, Japanese, Italian, steak, American
COFFEE SHOP	•
24-HOUR CAFE	•
BUFFET	•
CASINO	•
LOUNGE	•
SHOWROOM	Celebrity headliners
GIFTS/DRUGS/NEWS	•
POOL	•
EXERCISE ROOM	Health spa

California ★★★
12 E. Ogden Ave.
Las Vegas, NV 89101
☎ 702-385-1222
FAX 702-388-2670
TOLL-FREE 800-634-6505
thecal.com

RACK RATE	$$$+
ROOM QUALITY	67
LOCATION	Downtown
NO. OF ROOMS	781
CHECKOUT TIME	Noon
NONSMOKING	•
CONCIERGE	—
CONVENTION FACIL.	—
MEETING ROOMS	•
VALET PARKING	•
RV PARK	—
ROOM SERVICE	•
FREE BREAKFAST	—
FINE DINING/TYPES	Pasta, seafood, steak, Hawaiian
COFFEE SHOP	•
24-HOUR CAFE	•
BUFFET	•
CASINO	•
LOUNGE	•
SHOWROOM	—
GIFTS/DRUGS/NEWS	•
POOL	•
EXERCISE ROOM	—

Cannery ★★½
2121 E. Craig Rd.
Las Vegas, NV 89030
☎ 702-507-5700
FAX 702-507-5750
TOLL-FREE 866-999-4899
cannerycasinos.com

RACK RATE	$$$–
ROOM QUALITY	64
LOCATION	North Las Vegas
NO. OF ROOMS	201
CHECKOUT TIME	Noon
NONSMOKING	•
CONCIERGE	—
CONVENTION FACIL.	—
MEETING ROOMS	•
VALET PARKING	•
RV PARK	—
ROOM SERVICE	—
FREE BREAKFAST	—
FINE DINING/TYPES	American, Italian, Mexican, steak
COFFEE SHOP	•
24-HOUR CAFE	•
BUFFET	•
CASINO	•
LOUNGE	•
SHOWROOM	Live music
GIFTS/DRUGS/NEWS	•
POOL	•
EXERCISE ROOM	—

Courtyard by Marriott Las Vegas Convention Center ★★★½
3275 Paradise Rd.
Las Vegas, NV 89169
☎ 702-791-3600
FAX 702-796-7981
TOLL-FREE 888-236-2427
marriott.com

RACK RATE	$$$$–
ROOM QUALITY	79
LOCATION	East of Strip
NO. OF ROOMS	149
CHECKOUT TIME	Noon
NONSMOKING	•
CONCIERGE	•
CONVENTION FACIL.	—
MEETING ROOMS	•
VALET PARKING	—
RV PARK	—
ROOM SERVICE	—
FREE BREAKFAST	—
FINE DINING/TYPES	American
COFFEE SHOP	—
24-HOUR CAFE	—
BUFFET	• (Breakfast only)
CASINO	—
LOUNGE	•
SHOWROOM	—
GIFTS/DRUGS/NEWS	—
POOL	•
EXERCISE ROOM	•

Courtyard by Marriott Las Vegas South ★★★½
5845 Dean Martin Dr.
Las Vegas, NV 89118
☎ 702-895-7519
FAX 702-895-7568
TOLL-FREE 800-321-2211
marriott.com

RACK RATE	$$+
ROOM QUALITY	75
LOCATION	South Strip
NO. OF ROOMS	146
CHECKOUT TIME	Noon
NONSMOKING	•
CONCIERGE	—
CONVENTION FACIL.	—
MEETING ROOMS	•
VALET PARKING	—
RV PARK	—
ROOM SERVICE	—
FREE BREAKFAST	—
FINE DINING/TYPES	American
COFFEE SHOP	—
24-HOUR CAFE	—
BUFFET	• (Breakfast only)
CASINO	—
LOUNGE	•
SHOWROOM	—
GIFTS/DRUGS/NEWS	—
POOL	•
EXERCISE ROOM	•

The Cromwell ★★★★
3595 Las Vegas Blvd. S.
Las Vegas, NV 89109
☎ 702-777-3777
TOLL-FREE 844-426-2766
caesars.com/cromwell

RACK RATE	$$$$$$–
ROOM QUALITY	85
LOCATION	Mid-Strip
NO. OF ROOMS	188
CHECKOUT TIME	11
NONSMOKING	•
CONCIERGE	•
CONVENTION FACIL.	—
MEETING ROOMS	•
VALET PARKING	•
RV PARK	—
ROOM SERVICE	•
FREE BREAKFAST	—
FINE DINING/TYPES	Italian
COFFEE SHOP	•
24-HOUR CAFE	•
BUFFET	—
CASINO	•
LOUNGE	•
SHOWROOM	•
GIFTS/DRUGS/NEWS	•
POOL	•
EXERCISE ROOM	Health spa

HOTEL INFORMATION CHART *(continued)*

The D Las Vegas ★★★½
301 Fremont St.
Las Vegas, NV 89101
☎ 702-388-2400
FAX 702-388-2181
TOLL-FREE 800-274-5825
thed.com

RACK RATE	$$$-
ROOM QUALITY	81
LOCATION	Downtown
NO. OF ROOMS	629
CHECKOUT TIME	Noon
NONSMOKING	Floors
CONCIERGE	•
CONVENTION FACIL.	—
MEETING ROOMS	•
VALET PARKING	•
RV PARK	—
ROOM SERVICE	•
FREE BREAKFAST	—
FINE DINING/TYPES	Steak, American
COFFEE SHOP	•
24-HOUR CAFE	•
BUFFET	—
CASINO	•
LOUNGE	•
SHOWROOM	•
GIFTS/DRUGS/NEWS	•
POOL	•
EXERCISE ROOM	•

Delano ★★★★★
3940 Las Vegas Blvd. S.
Las Vegas, NV 89119
☎ 702-632-7777
FAX 702-632-7888
TOLL-FREE 877-632-5400
delanolasvegas.com

RACK RATE	$$$$$+
ROOM QUALITY	96
LOCATION	South Strip
NO. OF ROOMS	1,110
CHECKOUT TIME	11
NONSMOKING	•
CONCIERGE	•
CONVENTION FACIL.	•
MEETING ROOMS	•
VALET PARKING	•
ROOM SERVICE	•
FREE BREAKFAST	—
FINE DINING/TYPES	American, French, Italian
COFFEE SHOP	•
24-HOUR CAFE	Nearby
BUFFET	Nearby
CASINO	Nearby
LOUNGE	•
SHOWROOM	Production show, live music
GIFTS/DRUGS/NEWS	•
POOL	•
EXERCISE ROOM	Health spa

Downtown Grand ★★★½
206 N. 3rd St.
Las Vegas, NV 89101
☎ 702-719-5100
TOLL-FREE 855-384-7263
downtowngrand.com

RACK RATE	$$$-
ROOM QUALITY	76
LOCATION	Downtown
NO. OF ROOMS	650
CHECKOUT TIME	11
NONSMOKING	•
CONCIERGE	•
CONVENTION FACIL.	—
MEETING ROOMS	•
VALET PARKING	•
RV PARK	—
ROOM SERVICE	—
FREE BREAKFAST	—
FINE DINING/TYPES	American, Italian
COFFEE SHOP	—
24-HOUR CAFE	—
BUFFET	—
CASINO	•
LOUNGE	•
SHOWROOM	—
GIFTS/DRUGS/NEWS	—
POOL	•
EXERCISE ROOM	•

El Cortez Cabana Suites ★★★½
651 E. Ogden Ave.
Las Vegas, NV 89101
☎ 702-385-5200
FAX 702-474-3726
TOLL-FREE 800-634-6703
elcortezhotelcasino.com

RACK RATE	$$$
ROOM QUALITY	79
LOCATION	Downtown
NO. OF ROOMS	64
CHECKOUT TIME	Noon
NONSMOKING	•
CONCIERGE	—
CONVENTION FACIL.	—
MEETING ROOMS	—
VALET PARKING	• (at El Cortez)
RV PARK	—
ROOM SERVICE	•
FREE BREAKFAST	—
FINE DINING/TYPES	—
COFFEE SHOP	—
24-HOUR CAFE	—
BUFFET	—
CASINO	—
LOUNGE	•
SHOWROOM	—
GIFTS/DRUGS/NEWS	—
POOL	—
EXERCISE ROOM	•

Embassy Suites Convention Center ★★★★
3600 S. Paradise Rd.
Las Vegas, NV 89169
☎ 702-893-8000
FAX 702-893-0378
TOLL-FREE 800-362-2779
hilton.com

RACK RATE	$$+
ROOM QUALITY	87
LOCATION	East of Strip
NO. OF ROOMS	286
CHECKOUT TIME	11
NONSMOKING	•
CONCIERGE	•
CONVENTION FACIL.	•
MEETING ROOMS	•
VALET PARKING	—
RV PARK	—
ROOM SERVICE	•
FREE BREAKFAST	•
FINE DINING/TYPES	American
COFFEE SHOP	—
24-HOUR CAFE	—
BUFFET	—
CASINO	—
LOUNGE	•
SHOWROOM	—
GIFTS/DRUGS/NEWS	•
POOL	•
EXERCISE ROOM	•

Embassy Suites in Las Vegas ★★★★
4315 Swenson St.
Las Vegas, NV 89119
☎ 702-795-2800
FAX 702-795-1520
TOLL-FREE 800-362-2779
hilton.com

RACK RATE	$$$-
ROOM QUALITY	86
LOCATION	East of Strip
NO. OF ROOMS	220
CHECKOUT TIME	11
NONSMOKING	•
CONCIERGE	•
CONVENTION FACIL.	—
MEETING ROOMS	•
VALET PARKING	•
RV PARK	—
ROOM SERVICE	—
FREE BREAKFAST	•
FINE DINING/TYPES	American
COFFEE SHOP	—
24-HOUR CAFE	—
BUFFET	—
CASINO	—
LOUNGE	—
SHOWROOM	—
GIFTS/DRUGS/NEWS	•
POOL	•
EXERCISE ROOM	•

Eastside Cannery ★★★★
5255 Boulder Hwy.
Las Vegas, NV 89122
☎ 702-856-5300
eastsidecannery.com

RACK RATE	$$-
ROOM QUALITY	83
LOCATION	Boulder Hwy.
NO. OF ROOMS	300
CHECKOUT TIME	Noon
NONSMOKING	•
CONCIERGE	—
CONVENTION FACIL.	•
MEETING ROOMS	•
VALET PARKING	•
RV PARK	—
ROOM SERVICE	•
FREE BREAKFAST	—
FINE DINING/TYPES	Steak, American, Asian
COFFEE SHOP	•
24-HOUR CAFE	•
BUFFET	•
CASINO	•
LOUNGE	•
SHOWROOM	•
GIFTS/DRUGS/NEWS	•
POOL	•
EXERCISE ROOM	—

Elara ★★★★½
80 E. Harmon Ave.
Las Vegas, NV 89109
☎ 702-669-6700
FAX 702-669-6948
TOLL-FREE 800-445-8667
hilton.com

RACK RATE	$$$$$-
ROOM QUALITY	93
LOCATION	Mid-Strip
NO. OF ROOMS	1,201
CHECKOUT TIME	10
NONSMOKING	•
CONCIERGE	•
CONVENTION FACIL.	—
MEETING ROOMS	—
VALET PARKING	•
RV PARK	—
ROOM SERVICE	•
FREE BREAKFAST	—
FINE DINING/TYPES	—
COFFEE SHOP	•
24-HOUR CAFE	—
BUFFET	—
CASINO	—
LOUNGE	—
SHOWROOM	—
GIFTS/DRUGS/NEWS	•
POOL	•
EXERCISE ROOM	•

El Cortez ★★★
600 E. Fremont St.
Las Vegas, NV 89101
☎ 702-385-5200
FAX 702-474-3726
TOLL-FREE 800-634-6703
elcortezhotelcasino.com

RACK RATE	$$$-
ROOM QUALITY	72
LOCATION	Downtown
NO. OF ROOMS	363
CHECKOUT TIME	Noon
NONSMOKING	•
CONCIERGE	—
CONVENTION FACIL.	•
MEETING ROOMS	•
VALET PARKING	•
RV PARK	—
ROOM SERVICE	—
FREE BREAKFAST	—
FINE DINING/TYPES	Steak, Pizza
COFFEE SHOP	—
24-HOUR CAFE	•
BUFFET	—
CASINO	•
LOUNGE	•
SHOWROOM	—
GIFTS/DRUGS/NEWS	•
POOL	—
EXERCISE ROOM	—

Excalibur ★★★½
3850 Las Vegas Blvd. S.
Las Vegas, NV 89109
☎ 702-597-7777
FAX 702-597-7009
TOLL-FREE 800-937-7777
excalibur.com

RACK RATE	$$+
ROOM QUALITY	81
LOCATION	South Strip
NO. OF ROOMS	3,991
CHECKOUT TIME	11
NONSMOKING	Floors
CONCIERGE	—
CONVENTION FACIL.	•
MEETING ROOMS	•
VALET PARKING	•
RV PARK	—
ROOM SERVICE	•
FREE BREAKFAST	—
FINE DINING/TYPES	Mexican, steak, Italian, American
COFFEE SHOP	•
24-HOUR CAFE	•
BUFFET	•
CASINO	•
LOUNGE	•
SHOWROOM	Production show, Tournament of Kings
GIFTS/DRUGS/NEWS	•
POOL	•
EXERCISE ROOM	•

Fiesta Henderson ★★★
777 W. Lake Mead Pkwy.
Henderson, NV 89015
☎ 702-558-7000
FAX 702-567-7373
TOLL-FREE 888-899-7770
fiestahendersonlasvegas.com

RACK RATE	$$-
ROOM QUALITY	74
LOCATION	Henderson
NO. OF ROOMS	224
CHECKOUT TIME	Noon
NONSMOKING	Floors
CONCIERGE	—
CONVENTION FACIL.	—
MEETING ROOMS	•
VALET PARKING	•
RV PARK	—
ROOM SERVICE	—
FREE BREAKFAST	—
FINE DINING/TYPES	Steak, seafood, Mexican
COFFEE SHOP	•
24-HOUR CAFE	•
BUFFET	•
CASINO	•
LOUNGE	•
SHOWROOM	Live music
GIFTS/DRUGS/NEWS	•
POOL	•
EXERCISE ROOM	—

Fiesta Rancho ★★½
2400 N. Rancho Dr.
Las Vegas, NV 89130
☎ 702-631-7000
FAX 702-638-3605
TOLL-FREE 888-899-7770
fiestarancho.sclv.com

RACK RATE	$$
ROOM QUALITY	62
LOCATION	Rancho Drive
NO. OF ROOMS	100
CHECKOUT TIME	Noon
NONSMOKING	•
CONCIERGE	—
CONVENTION FACIL.	•
MEETING ROOMS	•
VALET PARKING	•
RV PARK	—
ROOM SERVICE	—
FREE BREAKFAST	—
FINE DINING/TYPES	Mexican, Italian, steak, American
COFFEE SHOP	•
24-HOUR CAFE	•
BUFFET	•
CASINO	•
LOUNGE	•
SHOWROOM	—
GIFTS/DRUGS/NEWS	•
POOL	•
EXERCISE ROOM	—

HOTEL INFORMATION CHART (continued)

Flamingo ★★★★
3555 Las Vegas Blvd. S.
Las Vegas, NV 89109
☎ 702-733-3111
FAX 702-733-3285
TOLL-FREE 855-270-6517
flamingolasvegas.com

RACK RATE	$$$+
ROOM QUALITY	88
LOCATION	Mid-Strip
NO. OF ROOMS	3,626
CHECKOUT TIME	11
NONSMOKING	Floors
CONCIERGE	—
CONVENTION FACIL.	•
MEETING ROOMS	•
VALET PARKING	•
RV PARK	—
ROOM SERVICE	•
FREE BREAKFAST	—
FINE DINING/TYPES	Steak, Mexican, Japanese
COFFEE SHOP	•
24-HOUR CAFE	•
BUFFET	•
CASINO	•
LOUNGE	•
SHOWROOM	Production show, comedy, headliners
GIFTS/DRUGS/NEWS	•
POOL	•
EXERCISE ROOM	Health spa/tennis

Four Queens ★★★
202 Fremont St.
Las Vegas, NV 89101
☎ 702-385-4011
FAX 702-387-5160
TOLL-FREE 800-634-6045
fourqueens.com

RACK RATE	$$$-
ROOM QUALITY	70
LOCATION	Downtown
NO. OF ROOMS	690
CHECKOUT TIME	Noon
NONSMOKING	Floors
CONCIERGE	—
CONVENTION FACIL.	—
MEETING ROOMS	•
VALET PARKING	•
RV PARK	—
ROOM SERVICE	•
FREE BREAKFAST	—
FINE DINING/TYPES	American
COFFEE SHOP	•
24-HOUR CAFE	•
BUFFET	•
CASINO	•
LOUNGE	•
SHOWROOM	•
GIFTS/DRUGS/NEWS	•
POOL	•
EXERCISE ROOM	—

Four Seasons at Mandalay Bay ★★★★½
3960 Las Vegas Blvd. S.
Las Vegas, NV 89119
☎ 702-632-5000
FAX 702-632-5195
TOLL-FREE 877-632-5000
fourseasons.com/lasvegas

RACK RATE	$$$$$
ROOM QUALITY	95
LOCATION	South Strip
NO. OF ROOMS	424
CHECKOUT TIME	Noon
NONSMOKING	•
CONCIERGE	•
CONVENTION FACIL.	•
MEETING ROOMS	•
VALET PARKING	•
RV PARK	—
ROOM SERVICE	•
FREE BREAKFAST	—
FINE DINING/TYPES	American, steak, seafood, Italian, French, Japanese
COFFEE SHOP	—
24-HOUR CAFE	—
BUFFET	—
CASINO	—
LOUNGE	—
SHOWROOM	—
GIFTS/DRUGS/NEWS	•
POOL	•
EXERCISE ROOM	Health spa

Golden Nugget ★★★★/★★★½
129 E. Fremont St.
Las Vegas, NV 89101
☎ 702-385-7111
FAX 702-387-4422
TOLL-FREE 800-634-3454
goldennugget.com

RACK RATE	$$$$/$$$$-
ROOM QUALITY	85/78
LOCATION	Downtown
NO. OF ROOMS	2,838
CHECKOUT TIME	11
NONSMOKING	Floors
CONCIERGE	•
CONVENTION FACIL.	•
MEETING ROOMS	•
VALET PARKING	•
RV PARK	—
ROOM SERVICE	•
FREE BREAKFAST	—
FINE DINING/TYPES	Italian, Asian, steak, seafood, sushi
COFFEE SHOP	•
24-HOUR CAFE	•
BUFFET	•
CASINO	•
LOUNGE	•
SHOWROOM	Headliners
GIFTS/DRUGS/NEWS	•
POOL	•
EXERCISE ROOM	•

Green Valley Ranch Resort and Spa ★★★★
2300 Paseo Verde Pkwy.
Henderson, NV 89052
☎ 702-617-7777
FAX 702-617-7778
TOLL-FREE 866-782-9487
greenvalleyranchresort.com

RACK RATE	$$$$$$
ROOM QUALITY	87
LOCATION	Henderson
NO. OF ROOMS	495
CHECKOUT TIME	Noon
NONSMOKING	•
CONCIERGE	•
CONVENTION FACIL.	•
MEETING ROOMS	•
VALET PARKING	•
RV PARK	—
ROOM SERVICE	•
FREE BREAKFAST	—
FINE DINING/TYPES	Italian, steak, seafood, Asian
COFFEE SHOP	•
24-HOUR CAFE	•
BUFFET	•
CASINO	•
LOUNGE	•
SHOWROOM	Headliners
GIFTS/DRUGS/NEWS	•
POOL	•
EXERCISE ROOM	•

Hard Rock Hotel ★★★★
4455 Paradise Rd.
Las Vegas, NV 89109
☎ 702-693-5000
FAX 702-693-5021
TOLL-FREE 800-473-7625
hardrockhotel.com

RACK RATE	$$$+
ROOM QUALITY	89
LOCATION	East of Strip
NO. OF ROOMS	1,504
CHECKOUT TIME	11
NONSMOKING	Floors
CONCIERGE	•
CONVENTION FACIL.	•
MEETING ROOMS	•
VALET PARKING	•
RV PARK	—
ROOM SERVICE	•
FREE BREAKFAST	—
FINE DINING/TYPES	Steak, seafood, Mexican, Asian, pub
COFFEE SHOP	•
24-HOUR CAFE	•
BUFFET	—
CASINO	•
LOUNGE	•
SHOWROOM	Live music
GIFTS/DRUGS/NEWS	•
POOL	•
EXERCISE ROOM	Health spa

Fremont ★★★
200 E. Fremont St.
Las Vegas, NV 89101
☎ 702-385-3232
FAX 702-385-6270
TOLL-FREE 800-634-6182
fremontcasino.com

RACK RATE	$$+
ROOM QUALITY	70
LOCATION	Downtown
NO. OF ROOMS	477
CHECKOUT TIME	Noon
NONSMOKING	•
CONCIERGE	—
CONVENTION FACIL.	•
MEETING ROOMS	•
VALET PARKING	•
RV PARK	—
ROOM SERVICE	—
FREE BREAKFAST	—
FINE DINING/TYPES	Ribs, Chinese, American, steak, seafood
COFFEE SHOP	•
24-HOUR CAFE	—
BUFFET	•
CASINO	•
LOUNGE	•
SHOWROOM	—
GIFTS/DRUGS/NEWS	•
POOL	—
EXERCISE ROOM	—

Gold Coast ★★★½
4000 W. Flamingo Rd.
Las Vegas, NV 89103
☎ 702-367-7111
FAX 702-367-8575
TOLL-FREE 800-331-5334
goldcoastcasino.com

RACK RATE	$$+
ROOM QUALITY	82
LOCATION	Mid-Strip
NO. OF ROOMS	712
CHECKOUT TIME	Noon
NONSMOKING	Floors
CONCIERGE	—
CONVENTION FACIL.	•
MEETING ROOMS	•
VALET PARKING	•
RV PARK	—
ROOM SERVICE	—
FREE BREAKFAST	—
FINE DINING/TYPES	Steak, Chinese, American
COFFEE SHOP	•
24-HOUR CAFE	—
BUFFET	•
CASINO	•
LOUNGE	•
SHOWROOM	Dancing
GIFTS/DRUGS/NEWS	•
POOL	•
EXERCISE ROOM	•

Golden Gate ★★★½
1 Fremont St.
Las Vegas, NV 89101
☎ 702-385-1906
TOLL-FREE 800-426-1906
goldengatecasino.com

RACK RATE	$$-
ROOM QUALITY	75
LOCATION	Downtown
NO. OF ROOMS	106
CHECKOUT TIME	Noon
NONSMOKING	•
CONCIERGE	—
CONVENTION FACIL.	—
MEETING ROOMS	—
VALET PARKING	—
RV PARK	—
ROOM SERVICE	—
FREE BREAKFAST	—
FINE DINING/TYPES	—
COFFEE SHOP	•
24-HOUR CAFE	•
BUFFET	•
CASINO	•
LOUNGE	—
SHOWROOM	—
GIFTS/DRUGS/NEWS	•
POOL	—
EXERCISE ROOM	—

Harrah's ★★★★
3475 Las Vegas Blvd. S.
Las Vegas, NV 89109
☎ 702-369-5000
FAX 702-369-6014
TOLL-FREE 800-214-9110
caesars.com/harrahs-las-vegas

RACK RATE	$$$+
ROOM QUALITY	83
LOCATION	Mid-Strip
NO. OF ROOMS	2,652
CHECKOUT TIME	11
NONSMOKING	•
CONCIERGE	•
CONVENTION FACIL.	•
MEETING ROOMS	•
VALET PARKING	•
RV PARK	—
ROOM SERVICE	•
FREE BREAKFAST	—
FINE DINING/TYPES	Steak, seafood, Italian, Asian
COFFEE SHOP	•
24-HOUR CAFE	•
BUFFET	•
CASINO	•
LOUNGE	•
SHOWROOM	Production show, comedy show, magic show
GIFTS/DRUGS/NEWS	•
POOL	•
EXERCISE ROOM	Health spa

Hooters Casino Hotel ★★★½
115 E. Tropicana Ave.
Las Vegas, NV 89109
☎ 702-739-9000
FAX 702-736-1120
TOLL-FREE 866-584-6687
hooterscasinohotel.com

RACK RATE	$$
ROOM QUALITY	79
LOCATION	South Strip
NO. OF ROOMS	689
CHECKOUT TIME	11
NONSMOKING	Floors
CONCIERGE	•
CONVENTION FACIL.	•
MEETING ROOMS	•
VALET PARKING	•
RV PARK	—
ROOM SERVICE	•
FREE BREAKFAST	—
FINE DINING/TYPES	American, steak, seafood, wings
COFFEE SHOP	•
24-HOUR CAFE	•
BUFFET	•
CASINO	•
LOUNGE	•
SHOWROOM	•
GIFTS/DRUGS/NEWS	•
POOL	•
EXERCISE ROOM	•

Hyatt Place ★★★
4520 Paradise Rd.
Las Vegas, NV 89169
☎ 702-369-3366
FAX 702-369-0009
TOLL-FREE 888-492-8847
lasvegas.place.hyatt.com

RACK RATE	$$$$-
ROOM QUALITY	72
LOCATION	East of Strip
NO. OF ROOMS	202
CHECKOUT TIME	Noon
NONSMOKING	•
CONCIERGE	—
CONVENTION FACIL.	—
MEETING ROOMS	•
VALET PARKING	—
RV PARK	—
ROOM SERVICE	—
FREE BREAKFAST	•
FINE DINING/TYPES	American
COFFEE SHOP	—
24-HOUR CAFE	—
BUFFET	—
CASINO	—
LOUNGE	—
SHOWROOM	—
GIFTS/DRUGS/NEWS	—
POOL	•
EXERCISE ROOM	•

HOTEL INFORMATION CHART (continued)

	JW Marriott Las Vegas ★★★★	Las Vegas Marriott ★★★★	The LINQ Hotel & Casino ★★★½
	221 N. Rampart Blvd.	325 Convention Center Dr.	3535 Las Vegas Blvd. S.
	Las Vegas, NV 89145	Las Vegas, NV 89109	Las Vegas, NV 89109
	☎ 702-869-7777	☎ 702-650-2000	☎ 702-731-3311
	FAX 702-869-7339	FAX 702-650-9466	FAX 702-731-3063
	TOLL-FREE 877-869-8777	TOLL-FREE 800-236-2427	TOLL-FREE 800-351-7400
	marriott.com	marriott.com	caesars.com/thelinq
RACK RATE	$$$$–	$$$–	$$$$
ROOM QUALITY	88	84	81
LOCATION	Summerlin	East of Strip	Mid-Strip
NO. OF ROOMS	548	278	2,700
CHECKOUT TIME	Noon	Noon	11
NONSMOKING	•	•	•
CONCIERGE	•	—	•
CONVENTION FACIL.	•	•	•
MEETING ROOMS	•	•	•
VALET PARKING	•	•	•
RV PARK	—	—	—
ROOM SERVICE	•	•	•
FREE BREAKFAST	—	—	—
FINE DINING/TYPES	American, Irish, Italian, Japanese	American	American, Mexican
COFFEE SHOP	•	—	•
24-HOUR CAFE	•	—	—
BUFFET	•	—	—
CASINO	•	—	•
LOUNGE	•	—	•
SHOWROOM	•	—	•
GIFTS/DRUGS/NEWS	•	•	•
POOL	•	•	•
EXERCISE ROOM	Health spa	•	Health spa

	Main Street Station ★★★½	Mandalay Bay ★★★★½	Mandarin Oriental/Waldorf Astoria at CityCenter ★★★★½
	200 N. Main St.	3950 Las Vegas Blvd. S.	3752 Las Vegas Blvd. S.
	Las Vegas, NV 89101	Las Vegas, NV 89119	Las Vegas, NV 89109
	☎ 702-387-1896	☎ 702-632-7777	☎ 702-590-8888
	FAX 702-386-4421	FAX 702-632-7234	FAX 702-590-8880
	TOLL-FREE 800-713-8933	TOLL-FREE 877-632-7800	TOLL-FREE 888-881-9578
	mainstreetcasino.com	mandalaybay.com	mandarinoriental.com/lasvegas
RACK RATE	$$$–	$$$$$–	$$$$$$–
ROOM QUALITY	75	92	94
LOCATION	Downtown	South Strip	Mid-Strip
NO. OF ROOMS	407	3,209	392
CHECKOUT TIME	Noon	11	11
NONSMOKING	•	Floors	•
CONCIERGE	•	•	•
CONVENTION FACIL.	•	•	•
MEETING ROOMS	•	•	•
VALET PARKING	•	•	•
RV PARK	•	—	—
ROOM SERVICE	—	•	•
FREE BREAKFAST	—	—	—
FINE DINING/TYPES	Brewery	Japanese, French, Italian, Mexican	Asian, French
COFFEE SHOP	•	•	•
24-HOUR CAFE	—	•	—
BUFFET	•	•	—
CASINO	•	•	Adjacent
LOUNGE	—	•	•
SHOWROOM	•	Headliners, live music, sports	—
GIFTS/DRUGS/NEWS	•	•	Adjacent
POOL	•	•	•
EXERCISE ROOM	—	Health spa	Health spa

* Lucky Dragon ★★★★
300 W. Sahara Ave.
Las Vegas, NV 89102
☎ 702-889-8018
FAX 702-868-1322
luckydragonlv.com

RACK RATE	$$
ROOM QUALITY	85
LOCATION	North Strip
NO. OF ROOMS	203
CHECKOUT TIME	11
NONSMOKING	•
CONCIERGE	—
CONVENTION FACIL.	•
MEETING ROOMS	•
VALET PARKING	—
RV PARK	—
ROOM SERVICE	—
FREE BREAKFAST	—
FINE DINING/TYPES	—
COFFEE SHOP	—
24-HOUR CAFE	—
BUFFET	—
CASINO	—
LOUNGE	—
SHOWROOM	—
GIFTS/DRUGS/NEWS	•
POOL	•
EXERCISE ROOM	—

** currently in Chapter 11 bankruptcy
(casino, restaurants, and spa closed)*

Luxor ★★★★
3900 Las Vegas Blvd. S.
Las Vegas, NV 89119
☎ 702-262-4444
FAX 702-262-4405
TOLL-FREE 877-386-4658
luxor.com

RACK RATE	$$+
ROOM QUALITY	87
LOCATION	South Strip
NO. OF ROOMS	4,450
CHECKOUT TIME	11
NONSMOKING	•
CONCIERGE	•
CONVENTION FACIL.	•
MEETING ROOMS	•
VALET PARKING	•
RV PARK	—
ROOM SERVICE	•
FREE BREAKFAST	—
FINE DINING/TYPES	American, seafood, steak, Asian, Mexican
COFFEE SHOP	•
24-HOUR CAFE	•
BUFFET	•
CASINO	•
LOUNGE	•
SHOWROOM	Production show
GIFTS/DRUGS/NEWS	•
POOL	•
EXERCISE ROOM	Health spa

M Resort ★★★★½
12300 Las Vegas Blvd. S.
Henderson, NV 89044
☎ 702-797-1000
TOLL-FREE 877-673-7678
themresort.com

RACK RATE	$$$+
ROOM QUALITY	90
LOCATION	Henderson
NO. OF ROOMS	390
CHECKOUT TIME	11
NONSMOKING	•
CONCIERGE	•
CONVENTION FACIL.	•
MEETING ROOMS	•
VALET PARKING	•
RV PARK	—
ROOM SERVICE	•
FREE BREAKFAST	—
FINE DINING/TYPES	Steak, Italian, American, Asian
COFFEE SHOP	•
24-HOUR CAFE	•
BUFFET	•
CASINO	•
LOUNGE	•
SHOWROOM	•
GIFTS/DRUGS/NEWS	•
POOL	•
EXERCISE ROOM	Health spa

Mardi Gras Hotel and Casino ★★★
3500 Paradise Rd.
Las Vegas, NV 89169
☎ 702-731-2020
FAX 702-731-4005
TOLL-FREE 800-634-6501
mardigrasinn.com

RACK RATE	$+
ROOM QUALITY	73
LOCATION	East of Strip
NO. OF ROOMS	314
CHECKOUT TIME	11
NONSMOKING	•
CONCIERGE	—
CONVENTION FACIL.	—
MEETING ROOMS	•
VALET PARKING	—
RV PARK	—
ROOM SERVICE	•
FREE BREAKFAST	—
FINE DINING/TYPES	American
COFFEE SHOP	—
24-HOUR CAFE	—
BUFFET	—
CASINO	Slots only
LOUNGE	•
SHOWROOM	—
GIFTS/DRUGS/NEWS	—
POOL	•
EXERCISE ROOM	—

MGM Grand ★★★★½
3799 Las Vegas Blvd. S.
Las Vegas, NV 89109
☎ 702-891-1111
FAX 702-891-3036
TOLL-FREE 877-880-0880
mgmgrand.com

RACK RATE	$$$$$–
ROOM QUALITY	90
LOCATION	South Strip
NO. OF ROOMS	5,044
CHECKOUT TIME	11
NONSMOKING	Floors
CONCIERGE	•
CONVENTION FACIL.	•
MEETING ROOMS	•
VALET PARKING	•
RV PARK	—
ROOM SERVICE	•
FREE BREAKFAST	—
FINE DINING/TYPES	Steak, seafood, Cajun, Italian, Chinese, French
COFFEE SHOP	•
24-HOUR CAFE	•
BUFFET	•
CASINO	•
LOUNGE	•
SHOWROOM	Production show, visiting headliners
GIFTS/DRUGS/NEWS	•
POOL	•
EXERCISE ROOM	Health spa/tennis

Mirage ★★★★½
3400 Las Vegas Blvd. S.
Las Vegas, NV 89109
☎ 702-791-7111
FAX 702-792-7632
TOLL-FREE 800-627-6667
mirage.com

RACK RATE	$$$$–
ROOM QUALITY	90
LOCATION	Mid-Strip
NO. OF ROOMS	3,044
CHECKOUT TIME	11
NONSMOKING	Floors
CONCIERGE	•
CONVENTION FACIL.	•
MEETING ROOMS	•
VALET PARKING	•
RV PARK	—
ROOM SERVICE	•
FREE BREAKFAST	—
FINE DINING/TYPES	Asian, seafood, Italian, American
COFFEE SHOP	•
24-HOUR CAFE	•
BUFFET	•
CASINO	•
LOUNGE	•
SHOWROOM	Production show, headliner
GIFTS/DRUGS/NEWS	•
POOL	•
EXERCISE ROOM	Health spa

HOTEL INFORMATION CHART *(continued)*

New York–New York ★★★★
3790 Las Vegas Blvd. S.
Las Vegas, NV 89109
☎ 702-740-6969
FAX 702-740-6700
TOLL-FREE 866-815-4365
newyorknewyork.com

RACK RATE	$$$$–
ROOM QUALITY	85
LOCATION	South Strip
NO. OF ROOMS	2,024
CHECKOUT TIME	11
NONSMOKING	Floors
CONCIERGE	•
CONVENTION FACIL.	•
MEETING ROOMS	•
VALET PARKING	•
RV PARK	—
ROOM SERVICE	•
FREE BREAKFAST	—
FINE DINING/TYPES	Steak, Chinese, Italian, Mexican, Irish, deli
COFFEE SHOP	•
24-HOUR CAFE	•
BUFFET	• (Breakfast only)
CASINO	•
LOUNGE	•
SHOWROOM	Production show, comedy
GIFTS/DRUGS/NEWS	•
POOL	•
EXERCISE ROOM	Health spa

Nobu Hotel ★★★★½
3570 Las Vegas Blvd. S.
Las Vegas, NV 89109
☎ 702-785-6677
TOLL-FREE 800-634-6661
nobucaesarspalace.com

RACK RATE	$$$$$+
ROOM QUALITY	94
LOCATION	Mid-Strip
NO. OF ROOMS	181
CHECKOUT TIME	11
NONSMOKING	•
CONCIERGE	•
CONVENTION FACIL.	At Caesars
MEETING ROOMS	At Caesars
VALET PARKING	•
RV PARK	—
ROOM SERVICE	•
FREE BREAKFAST	—
FINE DINING/TYPES	Japanese
COFFEE SHOP	At Caesars
24-HOUR CAFE	At Caesars
BUFFET	At Caesars
CASINO	At Caesars
LOUNGE	•
SHOWROOM	At Caesars
GIFTS/DRUGS/NEWS	•
POOL	•
EXERCISE ROOM	Health spa

The Orleans ★★★½
4500 W. Tropicana Ave.
Las Vegas, NV 89103
☎ 702-365-7111
FAX 702-365-7500
TOLL-FREE 800-675-3267
orleanscasino.com

RACK RATE	$$+
ROOM QUALITY	75
LOCATION	South Strip
NO. OF ROOMS	1,885
CHECKOUT TIME	Noon
NONSMOKING	•
CONCIERGE	•
CONVENTION FACIL.	•
MEETING ROOMS	•
VALET PARKING	•
RV PARK	—
ROOM SERVICE	•
FREE BREAKFAST	—
FINE DINING/TYPES	Steak, Cajun, seafood, Asian, Mexican
COFFEE SHOP	•
24-HOUR CAFE	•
BUFFET	•
CASINO	•
LOUNGE	Pub
SHOWROOM	Headliners, sports events
GIFTS/DRUGS/NEWS	•
POOL	•
EXERCISE ROOM	Health spa

Paris ★★★★½
3655 Las Vegas Blvd. S.
Las Vegas, NV 89109
☎ 702-946-7000
FAX 702-946-4405
TOLL-FREE 877-796-2096
parislasvegas.com

RACK RATE	$$$$+
ROOM QUALITY	91
LOCATION	Mid-Strip
NO. OF ROOMS	2,916
CHECKOUT TIME	11
NONSMOKING	Floors
CONCIERGE	•
CONVENTION FACIL.	•
MEETING ROOMS	•
VALET PARKING	•
RV PARK	—
ROOM SERVICE	•
FREE BREAKFAST	—
FINE DINING/TYPES	French, Italian, steak
COFFEE SHOP	•
24-HOUR CAFE	•
BUFFET	•
CASINO	•
LOUNGE	•
SHOWROOM	Dancing
GIFTS/DRUGS/NEWS	•
POOL	•
EXERCISE ROOM	Health spa/tennis

Park MGM ★★★★½
3770 Las Vegas Blvd. S.
Las Vegas, NV 89109
☎ 702-730-7777
FAX 702-730-7200
TOLL-FREE 800-311-8999
montecarlo.com

RACK RATE	$$$+
ROOM QUALITY	91
LOCATION	South Strip
NO. OF ROOMS	3,000
CHECKOUT TIME	11
NONSMOKING	Floors
CONCIERGE	•
CONVENTION FACIL.	•
MEETING ROOMS	•
VALET PARKING	•
RV PARK	—
ROOM SERVICE	•
FREE BREAKFAST	—
FINE DINING/TYPES	Steak, Asian, Mexican, Italian, American
COFFEE SHOP	•
24-HOUR CAFE	•
BUFFET	•
CASINO	•
LOUNGE	•
SHOWROOM	•
GIFTS/DRUGS/NEWS	•
POOL	•
EXERCISE ROOM	Health spa

Planet Hollywood ★★★★
3667 Las Vegas Blvd. S.
Las Vegas, NV 89109
☎ 702-736-7114
FAX 702-785-5558
TOLL-FREE 877-333-9474
planethollywoodresort.com

RACK RATE	$$$$
ROOM QUALITY	87
LOCATION	Mid-Strip
NO. OF ROOMS	2,567
CHECKOUT TIME	11
NONSMOKING	•
CONCIERGE	•
CONVENTION FACIL.	•
MEETING ROOMS	•
VALET PARKING	•
RV PARK	—
ROOM SERVICE	•
FREE BREAKFAST	—
FINE DINING/TYPES	Asian, steak, Mexican, burgers
COFFEE SHOP	•
24-HOUR CAFE	•
BUFFET	•
CASINO	•
LOUNGE	•
SHOWROOM	Headliners
GIFTS/DRUGS/NEWS	•
POOL	•
EXERCISE ROOM	Health spa

Palace Station
★★★½
2411 W. Sahara Ave.
Las Vegas, NV 89102
☎ 702-367-2411
FAX 702-367-2478
TOLL-FREE 800-678-2846
palacestation.com

RACK RATE	$$$–
ROOM QUALITY	84
LOCATION	North Strip
NO. OF ROOMS	576
CHECKOUT TIME	Noon
NONSMOKING	Floors
CONCIERGE	•
CONVENTION FACIL.	•
MEETING ROOMS	•
VALET PARKING	•
RV PARK	—
ROOM SERVICE	•
FREE BREAKFAST	—
FINE DINING/TYPES	Seafood, steak, Chinese, Mexican, American
COFFEE SHOP	•
24-HOUR CAFE	•
BUFFET	•
CASINO	•
LOUNGE	•
SHOWROOM	Comedy, music
GIFTS/DRUGS/NEWS	•
POOL	•
EXERCISE ROOM	•

The Palazzo ★★★★½
3325 Las Vegas Blvd. S.
Las Vegas, NV 89109
☎ 702-607-7777
FAX 702-414-1100
TOLL-FREE 866-263-3001
palazzo.com

RACK RATE	$$$$$
ROOM QUALITY	95
LOCATION	Mid-Strip
NO. OF ROOMS	3,064
CHECKOUT TIME	11
NONSMOKING	•
CONCIERGE	•
CONVENTION FACIL.	•
MEETING ROOMS	•
VALET PARKING	•
RV PARK	—
ROOM SERVICE	•
FREE BREAKFAST	—
FINE DINING/TYPES	Steak, Italian, Asian, French, Mexican
COFFEE SHOP	•
24-HOUR CAFE	•
BUFFET	—
CASINO	•
LOUNGE	•
SHOWROOM	Production show
GIFTS/DRUGS/NEWS	•
POOL	•
EXERCISE ROOM	Health spa

Palms ★★★★½
4321 W. Flamingo Rd.
Las Vegas, NV 89103
☎ 702-942-7777
FAX 702-942-6999
TOLL-FREE 866-942-7777
palms.com

RACK RATE	$$$$
ROOM QUALITY	95
LOCATION	Mid-Strip
NO. OF ROOMS	1,303
CHECKOUT TIME	11
NONSMOKING	Floors
CONCIERGE	•
CONVENTION FACIL.	•
MEETING ROOMS	•
VALET PARKING	•
RV PARK	—
ROOM SERVICE	•
FREE BREAKFAST	—
FINE DINING/TYPES	French, steak, Italian
COFFEE SHOP	•
24-HOUR CAFE	•
BUFFET	•
CASINO	•
LOUNGE	•
SHOWROOM	Headliners
GIFTS/DRUGS/NEWS	•
POOL	•
EXERCISE ROOM	Health spa

Platinum Hotel ★★★★
211 E. Flamingo Rd.
Las Vegas, NV 89169
☎ 702-365-5000
FAX 702-636-2500
TOLL-FREE 877-211-9211
theplatinumhotel.com

RACK RATE	$$$+
ROOM QUALITY	88
LOCATION	East of Strip
NO. OF ROOMS	255
CHECKOUT TIME	11
NONSMOKING	•
CONCIERGE	•
CONVENTION FACIL.	•
MEETING ROOMS	•
VALET PARKING	•
RV PARK	—
ROOM SERVICE	•
FREE BREAKFAST	—
FINE DINING/TYPES	American
COFFEE SHOP	•
24-HOUR CAFE	—
BUFFET	—
CASINO	—
LOUNGE	•
SHOWROOM	—
GIFTS/DRUGS/NEWS	•
POOL	•
EXERCISE ROOM	•

Plaza ★★★
1 Main St.
Las Vegas, NV 89101
☎ 702-386-2110
FAX 702-382-8281
TOLL-FREE 800-634-6575
plazahotelcasino.com

RACK RATE	$$$–
ROOM QUALITY	79
LOCATION	Downtown
NO. OF ROOMS	1,372
CHECKOUT TIME	11
NONSMOKING	Floors
CONCIERGE	•
CONVENTION FACIL.	•
MEETING ROOMS	•
VALET PARKING	•
RV PARK	—
ROOM SERVICE	•
FREE BREAKFAST	—
FINE DINING/TYPES	American, Continental
COFFEE SHOP	•
24-HOUR CAFE	•
BUFFET	•
CASINO	•
LOUNGE	•
SHOWROOM	Production show, comedy
GIFTS/DRUGS/NEWS	•
POOL	• (Rooftop)
EXERCISE ROOM	•

Red Rock Resort ★★★★½
11011 W. Charleston Blvd.
Las Vegas, NV 89135
☎ 702-797-7777
FAX 702-797-7745
TOLL-FREE 866-767-7773
redrocklasvegas.com

RACK RATE	$$$$$$–
ROOM QUALITY	91
LOCATION	Summerlin
NO. OF ROOMS	816
CHECKOUT TIME	11
NONSMOKING	Floors
CONCIERGE	•
CONVENTION FACIL.	•
MEETING ROOMS	•
VALET PARKING	•
RV PARK	—
ROOM SERVICE	•
FREE BREAKFAST	—
FINE DINING/TYPES	American, steak, Italian
COFFEE SHOP	•
24-HOUR CAFE	•
BUFFET	•
CASINO	•
LOUNGE	•
SHOWROOM	Piano bar, live entertainment
GIFTS/DRUGS/NEWS	•
POOL	•
EXERCISE ROOM	Health spa

HOTEL INFORMATION CHART (continued)

Renaissance Las Vegas
★★★★½
3400 Paradise Rd.
Las Vegas, NV 89169
☎ 702-784-5700
FAX 702-735-3130
TOLL-FREE 800-750-0980
renaissancelasvegas.com

RACK RATE	$$+
ROOM QUALITY	90
LOCATION	East of Strip
NO. OF ROOMS	548
CHECKOUT TIME	Noon
NONSMOKING	Floors
CONCIERGE	•
CONVENTION FACIL.	•
MEETING ROOMS	•
VALET PARKING	•
RV PARK	—
ROOM SERVICE	•
FREE BREAKFAST	—
FINE DINING/TYPES	Steak, American
COFFEE SHOP	•
24-HOUR CAFE	—
BUFFET	—
CASINO	—
LOUNGE	•
SHOWROOM	—
GIFTS/DRUGS/NEWS	•
POOL	•
EXERCISE ROOM	•

Residence Inn by Marriott Las Vegas Convention Center ★★★★
3225 Paradise Rd.
Las Vegas, NV 89109
☎ 702-796-9300
FAX 702-796-9562
TOLL-FREE 800-677-8328
marriott.com

RACK RATE	$$$$$+
ROOM QUALITY	83
LOCATION	East of Strip
NO. OF ROOMS	192
CHECKOUT TIME	Noon
NONSMOKING	Floors
CONCIERGE	—
CONVENTION FACIL.	—
MEETING ROOMS	•
VALET PARKING	—
RV PARK	—
ROOM SERVICE	—
FREE BREAKFAST	•
FINE DINING/TYPES	—
COFFEE SHOP	—
24-HOUR CAFE	—
BUFFET	—
CASINO	—
LOUNGE	—
SHOWROOM	—
GIFTS/DRUGS/NEWS	—
POOL	•
EXERCISE ROOM	•

Residence Inn by Marriott Las Vegas South ★★★★
5875 Dean Martin Dr.
Las Vegas, NV 89118
☎ 702-795-7378
FAX 702-795-3288
TOLL-FREE 800-677-8328
marriott.com

RACK RATE	$$$-
ROOM QUALITY	83
LOCATION	South Strip
NO. OF ROOMS	160
CHECKOUT TIME	Noon
NONSMOKING	•
CONCIERGE	—
CONVENTION FACIL.	—
MEETING ROOMS	—
VALET PARKING	—
RV PARK	—
ROOM SERVICE	—
FREE BREAKFAST	•
FINE DINING/TYPES	—
COFFEE SHOP	—
24-HOUR CAFE	—
BUFFET	—
CASINO	—
LOUNGE	—
SHOWROOM	—
GIFTS/DRUGS/NEWS	•
POOL	•
EXERCISE ROOM	•

Santa Fe Station ★★★
4949 N. Rancho Dr.
Las Vegas, NV 89130
☎ 702-658-4900
FAX 702-658-4919
TOLL-FREE 866-767-7771
santafestationlasvegas.com

RACK RATE	$$-
ROOM QUALITY	73
LOCATION	Rancho Drive
NO. OF ROOMS	200
CHECKOUT TIME	Noon
NONSMOKING	•
CONCIERGE	—
CONVENTION FACIL.	•
MEETING ROOMS	•
VALET PARKING	•
RV PARK	—
ROOM SERVICE	—
FREE BREAKFAST	—
FINE DINING/TYPES	Mexican, steak, seafood, American
COFFEE SHOP	•
24-HOUR CAFE	•
BUFFET	•
CASINO	•
LOUNGE	•
SHOWROOM	•
GIFTS/DRUGS/NEWS	•
POOL	•
EXERCISE ROOM	•

Serene ★★★½
455 East Harmon Ave.
Las Vegas, NV 89169
☎ 702-369-2281
FAX 702-369-1150
serenevegas.com

RACK RATE	$$+
ROOM QUALITY	80
LOCATION	East of Strip
NO. OF ROOMS	149
CHECKOUT TIME	11
NONSMOKING	•
CONCIERGE	—
CONVENTION FACIL.	—
MEETING ROOMS	•
VALET PARKING	•
RV PARK	—
ROOM SERVICE	—
FREE BREAKFAST	•
FINE DINING/TYPES	—
COFFEE SHOP	—
24-HOUR CAFE	—
BUFFET	—
CASINO	—
LOUNGE	—
SHOWROOM	—
GIFTS/DRUGS/NEWS	•
POOL	•
EXERCISE ROOM	—

Signature at MGM Grand ★★★★★
145 E. Harmon Ave.
Las Vegas, NV 89109
☎ 702-797-6000
FAX 702-797-6150
TOLL-FREE 877-727-0007
signaturemgmgrand.com

RACK RATE	$$$$-
ROOM QUALITY	96
LOCATION	East of Strip
NO. OF ROOMS	1,728
CHECKOUT TIME	11
NONSMOKING	•
CONCIERGE	•
CONVENTION FACIL.	—
MEETING ROOMS	•
VALET PARKING	•
RV PARK	—
ROOM SERVICE	•
FREE BREAKFAST	—
FINE DINING/TYPES	Steak, seafood, Cajun, Italian, Chinese, French
COFFEE SHOP	•
24-HOUR CAFE	•
BUFFET	—
CASINO	•
LOUNGE	•
SHOWROOM	—
GIFTS/DRUGS/NEWS	•
POOL	•
EXERCISE ROOM	•

Rio ★★★★
3700 W. Flamingo Rd.
Las Vegas, NV 89103
☎ 702-252-7777
FAX 702-967-3890
TOLL-FREE 800-752-9746
riolasvegas.com

RACK RATE	$$$
ROOM QUALITY	86
LOCATION	Mid-Strip
NO. OF ROOMS	2,522
CHECKOUT TIME	11
NONSMOKING	Floors
CONCIERGE	•
CONVENTION FACIL.	•
MEETING ROOMS	•
VALET PARKING	•
RV PARK	—
ROOM SERVICE	•
FREE BREAKFAST	—
FINE DINING/TYPES	Mexican, Chinese, Indian, seafood, steak
COFFEE SHOP	•
24-HOUR CAFE	•
BUFFET	•
CASINO	•
LOUNGE	•
SHOWROOM	Live entertainment, headliners
GIFTS/DRUGS/NEWS	•
POOL	•
EXERCISE ROOM	Health spa

Royal Resort ★★★
99 Convention Center Dr.
Las Vegas, NV 89109
☎ 702-735-6117
FAX 702-735-2546
TOLL-FREE 800-634-6118
royalhotelvegas.com

RACK RATE	$+
ROOM QUALITY	70
LOCATION	North Strip
NO. OF ROOMS	191
CHECKOUT TIME	11
NONSMOKING	Floors
CONCIERGE	•
CONVENTION FACIL.	—
MEETING ROOMS	—
VALET PARKING	—
RV PARK	—
ROOM SERVICE	—
FREE BREAKFAST	—
FINE DINING/TYPES	American
COFFEE SHOP	—
24-HOUR CAFE	—
BUFFET	—
CASINO	—
LOUNGE	—
SHOWROOM	•
GIFTS/DRUGS/NEWS	—
POOL	•
EXERCISE ROOM	•

Sam's Town ★★★½
5111 Boulder Hwy.
Las Vegas, NV 89122
☎ 702-456-7777
FAX 702-454-8014
TOLL-FREE 800-897-8696
samstownlv.com

RACK RATE	$$+
ROOM QUALITY	79
LOCATION	Boulder Highway
NO. OF ROOMS	645
CHECKOUT TIME	Noon
NONSMOKING	•
CONCIERGE	•
CONVENTION FACIL.	—
MEETING ROOMS	•
VALET PARKING	•
RV PARK	•
ROOM SERVICE	•
FREE BREAKFAST	—
FINE DINING/TYPES	Steak, American
COFFEE SHOP	•
24-HOUR CAFE	•
BUFFET	•
CASINO	•
LOUNGE	•
SHOWROOM	•
GIFTS/DRUGS/NEWS	•
POOL	•
EXERCISE ROOM	—

Silver Sevens ★★★½
4100 S. Paradise Rd.
Las Vegas, NV 89109
☎ 702-733-7000
FAX 702-791-2423
TOLL-FREE 800-640-9777
silversevenscasino.com

RACK RATE	$+
ROOM QUALITY	76
LOCATION	East of Strip
NO. OF ROOMS	326
CHECKOUT TIME	11
NONSMOKING	•
CONCIERGE	•
CONVENTION FACIL.	—
MEETING ROOMS	•
VALET PARKING	•
RV PARK	—
ROOM SERVICE	•
FREE BREAKFAST	—
FINE DINING/TYPES	American, Chinese, Mexican
COFFEE SHOP	•
24-HOUR CAFE	•
BUFFET	•
CASINO	•
LOUNGE	•
SHOWROOM	—
GIFTS/DRUGS/NEWS	•
POOL	•
EXERCISE ROOM	•

Silverton ★★★★
3333 Blue Diamond Rd.
Las Vegas, NV 89139
☎ 702-263-7777
FAX 702-893-7405
TOLL-FREE 866-122-4608
silvertoncasino.com

RACK RATE	$$+
ROOM QUALITY	88
LOCATION	South of Las Vegas
NO. OF ROOMS	300
CHECKOUT TIME	Noon
NONSMOKING	Floors
CONCIERGE	—
CONVENTION FACIL.	—
MEETING ROOMS	•
VALET PARKING	•
RV PARK	—
ROOM SERVICE	•
FREE BREAKFAST	—
FINE DINING/TYPES	Seafood, steak, Mexican
COFFEE SHOP	•
24-HOUR CAFE	•
BUFFET	•
CASINO	•
LOUNGE	•
SHOWROOM	•
GIFTS/DRUGS/NEWS	•
POOL	•
EXERCISE ROOM	—

SLS ★★★★
2535 Las Vegas Blvd. S.
Las Vegas, NV 89109
☎ 855-761-7757
slslasvegas.com

RACK RATE	$$+
ROOM QUALITY	83
LOCATION	North Strip
NO. OF ROOMS	1,327
CHECKOUT TIME	Noon
NONSMOKING	•
CONCIERGE	•
CONVENTION FACIL.	—
MEETING ROOMS	•
VALET PARKING	•
RV PARK	—
ROOM SERVICE	•
FREE BREAKFAST	—
FINE DINING/TYPES	Eclectic, Asian, Mediterranean
COFFEE SHOP	•
24-HOUR CAFE	•
BUFFET	—
CASINO	•
LOUNGE	•
SHOWROOM	•
GIFTS/DRUGS/NEWS	•
POOL	•
EXERCISE ROOM	Health spa

HOTEL INFORMATION CHART *(continued)*

	South Point ★★★½	Stratosphere ★★★½	Suncoast ★★★½
	9777 Las Vegas Blvd. S.	2000 Las Vegas Blvd. S.	9090 Alta Dr.
	Las Vegas, NV 89123	Las Vegas, NV 89104	Las Vegas, NV 89145
	☎ 702-796-7111	☎ 702-380-7777	☎ 702-636-7111
	FAX 702-797-8041	FAX 702-380-7732	FAX 702-636-7288
	TOLL-FREE 866-796-7111	TOLL-FREE 800-998-6937	TOLL-FREE 877-677-7111
	southpointcasino.com	stratospherehotel.com	suncoastcasino.com
RACK RATE	$$$–	$$+	$$
ROOM QUALITY	81	79	82
LOCATION	South of Las Vegas	North Strip	Summerlin
NO. OF ROOMS	2,163	2,429	420
CHECKOUT TIME	Noon	11	Noon
NONSMOKING	•	Floors	
CONCIERGE	—	•	—
CONVENTION FACIL.	•	•	•
MEETING ROOMS	•	•	•
VALET PARKING	•	•	•
RV PARK	—	Oversize parking	
ROOM SERVICE	•	•	•
FREE BREAKFAST	—	—	•
FINE DINING/TYPES	Italian, seafood, Asian, steak, Mexican	Seafood, steak, Italian, American	Italian, Chinese, American, seafood, Mexican
COFFEE SHOP		•	•
24-HOUR CAFE	•	•	•
BUFFET	•	•	•
CASINO	•	•	•
LOUNGE	•	•	•
SHOWROOM	Live music	Production show	Headliners
GIFTS/DRUGS/NEWS	•	•	•
POOL	•	•	•
EXERCISE ROOM	•	Health spa	•

	Tropicana ★★★★	Trump International Hotel Las Vegas ★★★★½	Tuscany ★★★½
	3801 Las Vegas Blvd. S.	2000 Fashion Show Dr.	255 E. Flamingo Rd.
	Las Vegas, NV 89109	Las Vegas, NV 89109	Las Vegas, NV 89169
	☎ 702-739-2222	☎ 702-982-0000	☎ 702-893-8933
	FAX 702-739-3648	FAX 702-476-8450	FAX 702-947-5994
	TOLL-FREE 888-826-8767	TOLL-FREE 866-939-8786	TOLL-FREE 877-887-2261
	troplv.com	trumplasvegashotel.com	tuscanylv.com
RACK RATE	$$$+	$$$+	$$$+
ROOM QUALITY	89	95	80
LOCATION	South Strip	North Strip	East of Strip
NO. OF ROOMS	1,658	1,282	716
CHECKOUT TIME	11	11	11
NONSMOKING	Floors	•	Floors
CONCIERGE	•	•	•
CONVENTION FACIL.	•	—	•
MEETING ROOMS	•	•	•
VALET PARKING	•	•	•
RV PARK	—	—	—
ROOM SERVICE	•	•	•
FREE BREAKFAST	—	—	•
FINE DINING/TYPES	Steak, American, Italian	American, Mediterranean	Italian, American
COFFEE SHOP	•		•
24-HOUR CAFE	•	24-hour in-suite dining	•
BUFFET	•	—	—
CASINO	•	—	•
LOUNGE	•	—	•
SHOWROOM	Production show, comedy club, magic	—	—
GIFTS/DRUGS/NEWS	•	•	•
POOL	•	•	•
EXERCISE ROOM	Health spa	Health spa	•

Sunset Station ★★★★
1301 Sunset Rd.
Henderson, NV 89014
☎ 702-547-7777
FAX 702-547-7744
TOLL-FREE 800-678-2846
sunsetstation.com

RACK RATE	$$$–
ROOM QUALITY	83
LOCATION	Henderson
NO. OF ROOMS	457
CHECKOUT TIME	11
NONSMOKING	Floors
CONCIERGE	—
CONVENTION FACIL.	—
MEETING ROOMS	•
VALET PARKING	•
RV PARK	—
ROOM SERVICE	•
FREE BREAKFAST	—
FINE DINING/TYPES	American, Italian, steak, seafood, Mexican
COFFEE SHOP	•
24-HOUR CAFE	•
BUFFET	•
CASINO	•
LOUNGE	•
SHOWROOM	Concerts
GIFTS/DRUGS/NEWS	•
POOL	•
EXERCISE ROOM	•

Texas Station ★★★
2101 Texas Star Ln.
Las Vegas, NV 89030
☎ 702-631-1000
FAX 702-631-8120
TOLL-FREE 800-654-8888
texasstation.com

RACK RATE	$$–
ROOM QUALITY	70
LOCATION	Rancho Drive Area
NO. OF ROOMS	200
CHECKOUT TIME	11
NONSMOKING	Floors
CONCIERGE	—
CONVENTION FACIL.	•
MEETING ROOMS	•
VALET PARKING	•
RV PARK	—
ROOM SERVICE	—
FREE BREAKFAST	—
FINE DINING/TYPES	Seafood, steak, oyster bar
COFFEE SHOP	•
24-HOUR CAFE	•
BUFFET	•
CASINO	•
LOUNGE	•
SHOWROOM	•
GIFTS/DRUGS/NEWS	•
POOL	•
EXERCISE ROOM	—

TI (Treasure Island) ★★★★
3300 Las Vegas Blvd. S.
Las Vegas, NV 89109
☎ 702-894-7111
FAX 702-894-7414
TOLL-FREE 800-288-7206
treasureisland.com

RACK RATE	$$$+
ROOM QUALITY	84
LOCATION	Mid-Strip
NO. OF ROOMS	2,885
CHECKOUT TIME	11
NONSMOKING	Floors
CONCIERGE	—
CONVENTION FACIL.	•
MEETING ROOMS	•
VALET PARKING	•
RV PARK	—
ROOM SERVICE	•
FREE BREAKFAST	—
FINE DINING/TYPES	Italian, seafood, American
COFFEE SHOP	•
24-HOUR CAFE	•
BUFFET	•
CASINO	•
LOUNGE	•
SHOWROOM	Production show
GIFTS/DRUGS/NEWS	•
POOL	•
EXERCISE ROOM	Health spa

Vdara at CityCenter ★★★★½
2600 W. Harmon Ave.
Las Vegas, NV 89109
☎ 702-590-2111
FAX 702-590-2112
TOLL-FREE 866-745-7767
vdara.com

RACK RATE	$$$$–
ROOM QUALITY	95
LOCATION	Mid-Strip
NO. OF ROOMS	1,450
CHECKOUT TIME	11
NONSMOKING	•
CONCIERGE	•
CONVENTION FACIL.	•
MEETING ROOMS	•
VALET PARKING	•
RV PARK	—
ROOM SERVICE	•
FREE BREAKFAST	—
FINE DINING/TYPES	—
COFFEE SHOP	•
24-HOUR CAFE	—
BUFFET	—
CASINO	Adjacent at Aria
LOUNGE	•
SHOWROOM	—
GIFTS/DRUGS/NEWS	—
POOL	•
EXERCISE ROOM	Health spa

The Venetian ★★★★½
3355 Las Vegas Blvd. S.
Las Vegas, NV 89109
☎ 702-414-1000
FAX 702-414-1100
TOLL-FREE 866-659-9643
venetian.com

RACK RATE	$$$$$
ROOM QUALITY	94
LOCATION	Mid-Strip
NO. OF ROOMS	3,015
CHECKOUT TIME	11
NONSMOKING	Floors
CONCIERGE	•
CONVENTION FACIL.	•
MEETING ROOMS	•
VALET PARKING	•
RV PARK	—
ROOM SERVICE	•
FREE BREAKFAST	—
FINE DINING/TYPES	Italian, French, Asian, American, Mexican
COFFEE SHOP	•
24-HOUR CAFE	•
BUFFET	—
CASINO	•
LOUNGE	•
SHOWROOM	Headliners, production show
GIFTS/DRUGS/NEWS	•
POOL	•
EXERCISE ROOM	Health spa

W Las Vegas ★★★★
2535 Las Vegas Blvd. S
Las Vegas, NV 89109
☎ 702-761-8700
FAX 702-761-8709
TOLL-FREE 877-822-0000
wlasvegas.com

RACK RATE	$$$$+
ROOM QUALITY	83
LOCATION	North Strip
NO. OF ROOMS	289
CHECKOUT TIME	Noon
NONSMOKING	•
CONCIERGE	•
CONVENTION FACIL.	•
MEETING ROOMS	•
VALET PARKING	•
RV PARK	—
ROOM SERVICE	•
FREE BREAKFAST	—
FINE DINING/TYPES	Eclectic, Asian, Mediterranean, steak
COFFEE SHOP	•
24-HOUR CAFE	•
BUFFET	—
CASINO	•
LOUNGE	•
SHOWROOM	—
GIFTS/DRUGS/NEWS	•
POOL	•
EXERCISE ROOM	Health spa

Hotel Information Chart *(continued)*

Westgate Las Vegas ★★★½
3000 Paradise Rd.
Las Vegas, NV 89109
☎ 702-732-5111
FAX 702-732-5805
TOLL-FREE 888-732-7117
westgateresorts.com

RACK RATE	$$+
ROOM QUALITY	80
LOCATION	East of Strip
NO. OF ROOMS	2,952
CHECKOUT TIME	11
NONSMOKING	•
CONCIERGE	•
CONVENTION FACIL.	At adjoining SLS
MEETING ROOMS	•
VALET PARKING	•
RV PARK	—
ROOM SERVICE	•
FREE BREAKFAST	—
FINE DINING/TYPES	Steak, American, Mexican, Asian
COFFEE SHOP	•
24-HOUR CAFE	•
BUFFET	•
CASINO	•
LOUNGE	•
SHOWROOM	Production show
GIFTS/DRUGS/NEWS	•
POOL	•
EXERCISE ROOM	Health spa/tennis

Westin Lake Las Vegas ★★★★
101 Montelago Blvd.
Henderson, NV 89011
☎ 702-567-6000
FAX 702-567-6067
westinlakelasvegas.com

RACK RATE	$$$$
ROOM QUALITY	88
LOCATION	Henderson
NO. OF ROOMS	493
CHECKOUT TIME	11
NONSMOKING	•
CONCIERGE	•
CONVENTION FACIL.	—
MEETING ROOMS	•
VALET PARKING	•
RV PARK	•
ROOM SERVICE	•
FREE BREAKFAST	—
FINE DINING/TYPES	Steak, Japanese
COFFEE SHOP	•
24-HOUR CAFE	—
BUFFET	—
CASINO	—
LOUNGE	•
SHOWROOM	—
GIFTS/DRUGS/NEWS	•
POOL	•
EXERCISE ROOM	Health spa/tennis

Westin Las Vegas ★★★½
160 E. Flamingo Rd.
Las Vegas, NV 89109
☎ 702-836-5900
FAX 702-836-9776
TOLL-FREE 866-716-8132
starwoodhotels.com/westin

RACK RATE	$$$$-
ROOM QUALITY	80
LOCATION	Mid-Strip
NO. OF ROOMS	826
CHECKOUT TIME	Noon
NONSMOKING	•
CONCIERGE	•
CONVENTION FACIL.	•
MEETING ROOMS	•
VALET PARKING	•
RV PARK	—
ROOM SERVICE	•
FREE BREAKFAST	—
FINE DINING/TYPES	American
COFFEE SHOP	—
24-HOUR CAFE	•
BUFFET	• (Breakfast only)
CASINO	—
LOUNGE	•
SHOWROOM	—
GIFTS/DRUGS/NEWS	•
POOL	•
EXERCISE ROOM	Health spa

Wyndham Grand Desert ★★★★
265 East Harmon Ave.
Las Vegas, NV 89169
☎ 702-691-2626
FAX 702-691-2600
wyndhamgranddesert.com

RACK RATE	$$$$$$-
ROOM QUALITY	88
LOCATION	East of Strip
NO. OF SUITES	787
CHECKOUT TIME	10
NONSMOKING	Yes
CONCIERGE	•
CONVENTION FACIL.	—
MEETING ROOMS	•
VALET PARKING	—
RV PARK	—
ROOM SERVICE	•
FREE BREAKFAST	—
FINE DINING/TYPES	—
COFFEE SHOP	•
24-HOUR CAFE	—
BUFFET	—
CASINO	—
LOUNGE	—
SHOWROOM	—
GIFTS/DRUGS/NEWS	•
POOL	•
EXERCISE ROOM	Health spa

Wynn Encore ★★★★★
3121 Las Vegas Blvd. S.
Las Vegas, NV 89109
☎ 702-770-7000
FAX 702-770-1500
TOLL-FREE 888-320-7123
wynnlasvegas.com

RACK RATE	$$$$$+
ROOM QUALITY	96
LOCATION	Mid-Strip
NO. OF ROOMS	2,034
CHECKOUT TIME	Noon
NONSMOKING	•
CONCIERGE	•
CONVENTION FACIL.	•
MEETING ROOMS	•
VALET PARKING	•
RV PARK	—
ROOM SERVICE	•
FREE BREAKFAST	—
FINE DINING/TYPES	Italian, steak, seafood, Asian, American
COFFEE SHOP	•
24-HOUR CAFE	•
BUFFET	•
CASINO	•
LOUNGE	•
SHOWROOM	•
GIFTS/DRUGS/NEWS	•
POOL	•
EXERCISE ROOM	Health spa

Wynn Las Vegas ★★★★★
3131 Las Vegas Blvd. S.
Las Vegas, NV 89109
☎ 702-770-7000
FAX 702-770-1500
TOLL-FREE 888-320-7123
wynnlasvegas.com

RACK RATE	$$$$-
ROOM QUALITY	96
LOCATION	Mid-Strip
NO. OF ROOMS	2,716
CHECKOUT TIME	Noon
NONSMOKING	Floors
CONCIERGE	•
CONVENTION FACIL.	•
MEETING ROOMS	•
VALET PARKING	•
RV PARK	—
ROOM SERVICE	•
FREE BREAKFAST	—
FINE DINING/TYPES	French, Italian, seafood, Asian, American
COFFEE SHOP	•
24-HOUR CAFE	•
BUFFET	•
CASINO	•
LOUNGE	•
SHOWROOM	Production show
GIFTS/DRUGS/NEWS	•
POOL	•
EXERCISE ROOM	Health spa

PART TWO

ENTERTAINMENT
and NIGHTLIFE

LAS VEGAS SHOWS
and ENTERTAINMENT

LAS VEGAS CALLS ITSELF the "Entertainment Capital of the World." This is arguably true, particularly in terms of the sheer number of live-entertainment productions staged daily. On any given day in Las Vegas, a visitor can select from dozens of presentations, ranging from major production spectaculars to celebrity headliners, from comedy clubs to live music in lounges. The standard of professionalism and value for your entertainment dollar is very high. According to an annual census conducted by the consumer-oriented *Las Vegas Advisor*, the average price of a ticket to one of the major production shows approached $95. In 2018, there were 58 shows with some tickets priced above $100. However, the standard of quality for shows has likewise soared. And variety, well, there's now literally something for everyone. And believe it or not, the value is still there—maybe not in the grand showrooms and incessantly hyped productions, but in the smaller showrooms and lounges and in the main theaters of off-Strip hotels. There's more of everything now, including both overpriced shows and bargains. Regarding the former, you'll be blinded by their billboards all over town. As concerns the latter, you'll have to scout around, but you'll be rewarded with some great shows at dynamite prices. And there are always discount coupons floating around.

CHOICES, CHOICES, CHOICES

MOST LAS VEGAS LIVE ENTERTAINMENT offerings can be lumped into one of the following categories:

- Celebrity headliners • Elvis shows • Long-term engagements
- Magic and illusion shows • Broadway and off-Broadway shows
- Musical-tribute and nostalgia shows • Production shows
- Impersonator shows • Skin shows • Comedy-headliner shows
- Hypnosis shows • Comedy clubs • Lounge entertainment

Celebrity Headliners

As the name implies, these are concerts or shows featuring big-name entertainers on a limited-engagement basis, usually one to four weeks, but sometimes for one night. Performers such as David Copperfield and Jay Leno play Las Vegas regularly. Some even work on a rotation with other performers, returning to the same showroom for several engagements each year. Other stars, such as Barbra Streisand, Paul McCartney, and the Rolling Stones, play Las Vegas only rarely, transforming each appearance into a special event. While there are exceptions, the superstars are regularly found at the MGM Grand, the Mirage, Mandalay Bay, Caesars Palace, Planet Hollywood, Westgate Las Vegas, Bally's, Flamingo, Wynn Encore, the Hard Rock, the Park Theater, and T-Mobile Arena at The Park. Big-name performers in the city's top showrooms command premium admission prices. Headliners of slightly lesser stature play at various other showrooms.

There's a new category of headliners who are said to be "in residence." This means they are contracted to a particular venue but perform usually 35 or fewer shows a year. For example, Celine Dion is the primary headliner for the Colosseum at Caesars Palace, but when she's on break, Rod Stewart or Mariah Carey performs. Boyz II Men sub for Terry Fator at the Mirage, playing 78 shows, and Carlos Santana performs on 33 nights at Mandalay Bay. Others joining the residency ranks are Lionel Richie, Wayne Newton, The Righteous Brothers, and Gwen Stefani.

Long-Term Engagements

These are shows by the famous and once-famous who have come to Las Vegas to stay. Celine Dion is back and better than ever at Caesars Palace, and Marie and Donny Osmond continue to hold sway with the PG-preferred crowd at the Flamingo.

Broadway and Off-Broadway Shows

Las Vegas showrooms have dallied with Broadway shows for a long time. Some caught on, but most didn't, and many were signed for limited engagements. The tide has turned, however, and there are now a goodly number of shows that originated on Broadway or in London playing long-term engagements in Las Vegas. As of this writing, these include *Blue Man Group* and *Defending the Caveman*.

Production Shows

These are continuously running, Broadway-style theatrical and musical productions. Cast sizes run from a dozen performers to more than 100, with costumes, sets, and special effects spanning a comparable range. Costing hundreds of thousands, if not millions, to produce, the shows feature elaborate choreography and great spectacle. Sometimes playing twice a night, six or seven days a week, these shows often run for years.

Production shows generally have a central theme to which a more or less standard mix of choreography and variety acts (also called specialty acts) are added. Favorite central themes are magic and illusion, rock and roll retrospectives, and "best of Broadway." Defying categorization, Cirque du Soleil now offers seven shows.

Las Vegas puts its own distinctive imprint on all this entertainment, imparting a degree of homogeneity and redundancy to the mix of productions. The quality of Las Vegas entertainment is quite high, even excellent, but most production shows seem to operate according to a formula that fosters a numbing sameness. Particularly pronounced in the magic-illusion shows and the Broadway-style musical productions, this sameness discourages sampling more than one show from each genre. While it is not totally accurate to say that "if you've seen one Las Vegas production or magic show, you've seen them all," the statement comes closer to the truth than one would hope.

Sadly, *Jubilee!*, the only show that carried on the tradition of the *Ziegfeld Follies*–inspired grand production show, closed in late 2015. Before that, the Parisian *Folies Bergère* went dark permanently in 2009 after a 49-year run at the Tropicana. With *Jubilee!* ending its decades-long run, a fabled piece of Las Vegas history dies with it (though *Vegas! The Show* at the Miracle Mile Shops does an outstanding job of chronicling the evolution of production shows using the traditional ensemble number–specialty act formula).

While they share a common format, production shows, regardless of theme, can be differentiated by the size of the cast and by the elaborateness of the production. Other discriminating factors include the creativity of the choreography, the attractiveness of the performers, the pace and continuity of the presentation, and its ability to build to a crescendo. Strength in these last-mentioned areas sometimes allows a relatively simple, lower-budget show to provide a more satisfying evening of entertainment than a lavish, long-running spectacular.

Impersonator Shows

These are usually long-running production shows, complete with dancers, that feature the impersonation of celebrities, both living (Cher, Neil Diamond, Adele, Tina Turner, Madonna) and deceased (Marilyn Monroe, Elvis Presley, Liberace, Blues Brother John Belushi). In shows such as *Legends in Concert,* the emphasis is on the detail and exactness of the impersonation. In general, men impersonate male stars and women impersonate female stars (as you might expect). There are productions, however, featuring males impersonating female celebrities. But no one— dead or alive, male or female—is impersonated as frequently as The King. The Las Vegas Convention and Visitors Authority says there are at least 260 Elvis impersonators locally. We'd love to see them all in the same show. Wouldn't that be "a hunk-a hunk-a burnin' love"!

Comedy-Headliner Shows

These are stand-up comedy presentations usually featuring a warm-up comic followed by a well-known comedian. Though Jerry Seinfeld, Jay Leno, Ray Romano, and David Spade regularly play Las Vegas, this discussion is limited to the several comics who perform year-round. They're all good, and happily, all different in style, tone, personality, and delivery. Here is a chart showing the long-engagement comics and what they are known for. Reviews can be found later in this chapter.

CARROT TOP | Luxor	• The furious pace makes us dizzy. Highly dependent on props and sight gags. PG-13.
EDDIE GRIFFIN | SLS	• Specializes in very blue, very loud, racial humor.
RICH LITTLE | Tropicana	• Jokes, impersonations, stories, and songs in an autobiographical retrospective.
GEORGE WALLACE | Westgate	• Milks the irony of modern life, hitting youth especially hard by calling them "dum-dums on their smartphones."

Several top-name comics, such as Brad Garrett, have opened clubs of their own. These clubs charge a premium price on nights when the namesake comic is on the bill.

Comedy Clubs

Stand-up comedy has long been a tradition in Las Vegas entertainment. With the success of comedy clubs around the country and the comedy-club format on network and cable television, stand-up comedy in Las Vegas was elevated from lounges and production shows to its own specialized venue. Las Vegas comedy clubs are small- to medium-size showrooms featuring anywhere from two to five comedians per show. As a rule, the shows change completely each week, with a new group of comics rotating in. Each showroom has its own source of talent, so there is no swapping of comics from club to club. Comedy clubs are one of the few Las Vegas entertainments that draw equally from both the tourist and local populations.

Comedy Clubs pop up and disappear like dandelions, but there are usually six to eight clubs operating in any given year. Following were the choices when we went to press:

ACES OF COMEDY | Mirage	• Fri. and Sat., 9 or 10 p.m.
BRAD GARRETT'S COMEDY CLUB • MGM Grand	• Nightly, 8 p.m.
COMEDY CELLAR | Rio	• Wed.-Fri., 7 and 9 p.m.; Sat., 7, 9, and 11 p.m.
CONS OF COMEDY | Hooters	• Thurs.-Sun., 9 p.m.
JOKESTERS COMEDY CLUB | The D	• Nightly, 10:30 p.m.
L.A. COMEDY CLUB | Stratosphere	• Wed.-Mon., 6 and 10 p.m.; Tues., 10 p.m.
LAS VEGAS LIVE COMEDY CLUB | Miracle Mile Shops	• Nightly, 9 p.m.
LAUGH FACTORY | Tropicana	• Sun.-Thurs., 8:30 and 10:30 p.m.; Fri. and Sat., 8:30 p.m., 10:30 p.m., and midnight

The comedy club format is simple and straightforward. Comedians perform sequentially, and what you get depends on who's performing. The range of humor runs from slapstick to obscene to ethnic to topical to just about anything. Some comics are better than others, but all the talent is solid and professional. There's no way to predict which club will have the best show in a given week. In fact, there may not be a "best" show since response to comedy is a matter of individual sense of humor.

Among Las Vegas comedy clubs there are exceptions to the standard template. Brad Garrett has his own club at which he performs regularly. When he's off, the usual rotation of comics holds sway. Ticket prices vary depending on who's playing. The Mirage fields a number of top comics in its Aces of Comedy show. Regulars are Daniel Tosh, George Lopez, Wayne Brady, Jay Leno, and Kathleen Madigan, as well as Ray Romano and David Spade. Aces is performed in the 1,200-seat Terry Fator Theatre and usually showcases one famous comic each night, sometimes augmented by a warm-up act. Prices vary.

Performances at all clubs last about 70–75 minutes. Average prices run in the $50–$80 range, but there are half-price tickets available most nights from Tix4Tonight and coupons for discounts in the local visitor mags, as well as on websites such as lasvegasadvisor.com and bestofvegas.com.

Elvis Shows

Elvis has been a part of Las Vegas entertainment for years, first as a storied performer and subsequently as the inspiration of dozens of Elvis impersonators.

Elvis is alive and well in Las Vegas. Trent Carlini is the best Elvis impersonator in town. *All Shook Up* is an Elvis tribute show at Planet Hollywood's Miracle Mile Shops. If you don't want a whole show centering on Elvis, *Legends in Concert* at the Flamingo caps every performance with an excellent Elvis impersonator finale. For a free Elvis, and a good one at that, our favorite is Big Elvis (Pete Vallee), who had a gig at Bill's Gamblin' Hall for ages and can now be seen Monday, Wednesday, and Friday at The Piano Bar at Harrah's.

Off the stage, there are Elvises who can marry you and Elvises who are available to sing at your birthday party or other big event. For a guide to Elvis options in Las Vegas, see vegas.com/traveltips/guide /elvis.html. If you want to rent an Elvis, a good selection can be found at gigmasters.com. Finally, if you don't like your Elvis to gyrate, your best bet is the Elvis at Madame Tussauds Wax Museum at The Venetian. You can touch and pose with him, but he won't give you a scarf.

Magic and Illusion Shows

There are usually five to eight Las Vegas production shows dedicated to magic and illusion. The rage in these shows is to put unlikely creatures or objects into boxes or behind curtains and make them disappear. Some featured magicians repeat this sort of tiresome illusion as often as a dozen times in a single performance, with nothing really changing except the size of the box and the object placed into it. These box illusions are amazing the first time or two, but become less compelling after

COMEDY MAGIC		
**SHOW	HOTEL/ROOM SIZE • DESCRIPTION**		
NATHAN BURTON	Saxe Theater/Large • Frenetic pace, sexy showgirls; more magic than comedy.		
MIKE HAMMER	Fours Queens/Small • Quick-witted with sharp tongue and good sleight of hand.		
MAC KING	Harrah's/Small • Pioneer of the genre and best small-room act.		
PENN & TELLER	Rio/Large • Best (and bluest) big-room comedy magic act.		
MURRAY SAWCHUCK	Planet Hollywood/Small • Wild hair and a mischievous persona; turns comic stage mishaps into clever illusions.		
TOMMY WIND	NA/NA • Combines comedy, music, and good close-up work.		

TRADITIONAL MAGIC AND ILLUSION		
**SHOW	HOTEL/ROOM SIZE • DESCRIPTION**		
CRISS ANGEL	Luxor/Large • Talented and creative but self-aggrandizing; lowest rated Cirque du Soleil production.		
LANCE BURTON	NA/NA • Second only to Copperfield. Retired but young enough to come back.		
DAVID COPPERFIELD	MGM Grand/Large • The gold standard. Best magic and illusion show in Vegas.		
MAT FRANCO	LINQ/Medium • Season winner of *America's Got Talent* who does great close-up work and tries hard at being original.		
DAVID GOLDRAKE	Tropicana/Large • Las Vegas newcomer from Luxembourg. Easily establishes rapport with audience.		
SETH GRABEL	NA/NA • Talented newcomer from *America's Got Talent*. Excellent close-up work and sleight of hand.		
JEN KRAMER	Westgate/Small • First Las Vegas female magician since the 1990s. Specializes in close work, especially cards.		
XAVIER MORTIMER	Planet Hollywood/Small • Very artsy—weaves illusions into a story line that elevates the magic.		
RICK THOMAS	NA/NA • Longtime Vegas veteran. Another big-illusion, big-cat guy.		
MICHAEL TURCO	NA/NA • Competent execution of classic illusions. Upstaged by dancers.		
STEPHAN VANEL	NA/NA • 2011 Magician of the Year known for his sleight-of-hand and manipulation skills.		
STEVE WYRICK	NA/NA • Longtime Vegas veteran. Makes big things disappear (like airplanes!).		

that. After he had seen all of the illusion shows in Las Vegas, our reviewer commented that the only thing not seen vanishing from a box was his mortgage. Food for thought.

Most Las Vegas magic and illusion shows trot out variations of the same tricks. You'll see daring escapes (usually involving sharp objects or fire); the aforementioned box tricks; and an inexhaustible inventory of elaborate contraptions. All magicians have comely assistants, and large-stage productions throw in some dancers as well. Small stages can only accommodate small contraptions and thus are limited in the scale of the illusion. So, if you want to see big stuff disappear, try a production in a larger showroom. Sleight of hand and close work are perfect for small, intimate showrooms, but you usually won't find competent practitioners such as Joseph Gabriel and David Copperfield working there. For the foreseeable future, contraptions rule.

If you've never seen a Las Vegas magic and illusion show, you'll probably be very happy with whichever show you choose. Even in the small showrooms, the magician has to be a pro to play Las Vegas. If you have seen a Vegas magic show or two, you can expect more of the same, albeit with each performer adding a personal twist. Leaving aside magicians such as Joseph Gabriel, who performs short magic specialty acts in multifaceted Vegas extravaganzas, you have two genres of shows to choose from: traditional productions devoted to serious magic and illusion, and so-called "comedy magic shows." As concerns the latter, there's generally more comedy than magic, but what magic there is tends to be of high quality. The comedy magic shows are upbeat and lots of fun, but the comedic patter consumes most of the show.

The chart on the facing page lists the magicians and illusionists who regularly work Las Vegas showrooms with their own productions. Most of the shows are reviewed later in this chapter. If the past is any indicator, however, many of the featured magicians without a regular gig will turn up in other productions.

Musical Tribute and Nostalgia Shows

Musical tribute shows can be defined as contemporary musicians and vocalists recreating the sound and appearance of a legendary singer or group. Some musical tribute shows, such as *Legends in Concert,* present a whole lineup of performers, each impersonating a different musical superstar. Although several musical tribute shows, such as *Raiding the Rock Vault,* have transcended the genre to become fully realized production shows with story lines, elaborate sets, and eye-popping ensemble numbers, most tribute shows are very minimalist productions that simply try to capture the feel of hearing the famous singer or group in concert at a club or small theater. In other words, don't expect dancers, variety acts, and the like.

Though more than half of the musical tribute shows in Las Vegas honor a specific singer or group, others focus on a musical genre or period. *Human Nature Jukebox* at The Venetian and *Hitzville* at the Miracle Mile Shops, for example, reprise the Motown hits of the 1960s and 70s. Here the performers nail the Motown sound but identify themselves by their real names and do not pretend to be specific Motown stars. A musical tribute variation is the nostalgia show, where performers seek to capture the impersonated stars in a particular time and place. *The Rat Pack Is Back* takes the audience back to an early-1960s performance at the Copa Room in the Sands Hotel with Frank Sinatra, Dean Martin, Joey Bishop, and Sammy Davis Jr. Here the Copa Room setting is replicated and the impersonators stay in character throughout. The performers banter, smoke, and drink in a very effective recollection of the Rat Pack and the old Vegas club scene. In all shows the impersonators do their own singing and play their instruments. There are no recorded tracks or lip-syncing. Everything, in other words, is live.

Just about anyone will enjoy shows like *The Rat Pack Is Back*. It doesn't matter whether you're a Rat Pack fan. For other tribute shows, your enjoyment will probably pivot on how much you like the impersonated singer/group or musical genre. If you're not big on the Bee Gees or disco, it might be best to punt on *The Australian Bee Gees Show*. If you're a fan, however, you'll be as hyped up as a gnat in a glass of wine.

Several major shows have beefed up the genre. Cirque du Soleil's *Michael Jackson ONE,* at Mandalay Bay, celebrates the mystique, dance, and music of the late superstar with the most riveting choreography ever seen in Las Vegas.

Following are musical tribute and nostalgia shows that are likely to still be around when you visit. Absent are impersonator shows where the performers sing along with recorded tracks. All of the shows listed are high-quality productions. We don't rank them because your personal taste in music will largely dictate, with the exception of *Michael Jackson ONE,* which show you'll like best. Our personal favorites include *Purple Reign,* the Prince tribute show, for its energy; *The Rat Pack Is Back* for its retrospective of old Las Vegas; and *Human Nature* for its walk down Motown's memory lane. *Michael Jackson ONE* is in our top-10 list of Las Vegas shows irrespective of genre. Most of the shows are reviewed later in this chapter.

SHOW	HOTEL	TRIBUTE TO
• *All Shook Up*	**Miracle Mile Shops**	Elvis Presley
• *Australian Bee Gees*	**Excalibur**	Bee Gees
• *Beatleshow Orchestra*	**Miracle Mile Shops**	Beatles
• *The Bronx Wanderers*	**Bally's**	Multigenre retrospective
• *Hitzville*	**Miracle Mile Shops**	Motown
• *Human Nature*	**The Venetian**	Motown
• *Legends in Concert*	**Flamingo**	Various music legends
• *Michael Jackson ONE*	**Mandalay Bay**	Michael Jackson
• *MJ Live*	**Stratosphere**	Michael Jackson
• *Purple Reign*	**Tropicana**	Prince
• *Raiding the Rock Vault*	**Hard Rock**	History of rock retrospective
• *The Rat Pack Is Back*	**Tuscany**	The Rat Pack and old Las Vegas
• *Tenors of Rock*	**Harrah's**	History of rock retrospective

Skin Shows

There are six topless productions for male and mixed audiences, and three (occasionally four) beefcake shows for the ladies. Additionally, Cirque du Soleil's *Zumanity* at New York–New York, and *Absinthe* at Caesars Palace feature topless acts as part of extravagant multidimensional production shows. Most of the T&A efforts play in smaller showrooms albeit in large hotels. The intimacy of small rooms is a boon for the myopic, though in most productions the showgirls are covered as much, if not more, of the time as they're topless. Several showrooms have flat floors, meaning that shorter patrons need to sit up front. Most shows are reviewed later in this chapter.

SHOW	HOTEL	DESCRIPTION
• *Crazy Girls*	**Planet Hollywood**	Longest-running show by decades. The revamped edition features 6 out of 7 dancers with natural breasts. Flat-floored showroom.
• *Fantasy*	**Luxor**	Good choreography but not as steamy as *Zumanity*. Arguably the hottest showgirls. Very comfortable modern showroom.
• *SEXXY*	**Westgate**	Fast paced, athletic, and more erotic than most. All-female cast.
• *X Burlesque*	**Flamingo**	A teaser. Less erotic than athletic with excellent choreography. Flat-floored showroom.
• *X Country*	**Harrah's**	Topless hoedown and vignettes with a country/cowgirl twist.
• *X Rocks*	**Bally's**	The most sexual production next to *Zumanity*.

The beefcake shows for women are much rowdier than the topless revues because (1) admission is restricted to women; (2) women attend in large groups of friends; and (3) there's more interaction between the audience and the performers. You get a lot of "What Happens in Vegas Stays in Vegas" moments at these shows. The shows are reviewed later in this chapter.

SHOW	HOTEL	DESCRIPTION
• *Aussie Heat*	**Miracle Mile Shops (V Theater)**	Rippled Aussies. Best dancing of any beefcake show. Much audience interaction.
• *Chippendales*	**Rio**	Very sensual with simulated sex acts. Explores female fantasies. Tight dance routines.
• *Thunder From Down Under*	**Excalibur**	Guy-next-door types. Much tamer than *Chippendales*. Athletic more than sensual. Flat-floored showroom.

Hypnosis Shows

In hypnosis shows, volunteers from the audience are invited onto the stage to be hypnotized. The volunteers really do get hypnotized. We have had medical clinicians who use hypnosis in their practice review the shows and verify the authenticity of the trance. Folks that fake being under hypnosis or for whom the hypnotic state is marginal are quickly identified by the hypnotist and returned to their seats. To the best of our knowledge, there are no plants or ringers.

Most, if not all, of the Las Vegas hypnosis shows are very "blue." This means that volunteers may end up doing things which after the fact may embarrass them immensely. We've seen volunteers attempt to have sex with a folding chair, perform fellatio on imaginary objects, enjoy orgasms, and audition for a job as an exotic dancer. We should make it clear that the contestants do all of this fully clothed. Most showrooms record each performance and make a DVD available for sale after the show.

The quality (?) and relative outrageousness of any given performance depends on the number of volunteers and their susceptibility to hypnosis. So if you prefer to be a voyeur instead of a volunteer, your best chance for a really wild spectacle is to choose a show in a big hotel where the size of the audience is likely to be large. Marc Savard (Miracle Mile Shops) and Anthony Cools are the top hypnotists in town (oh, how we miss Dr. Naughty). We profile only the Anthony Cools hypnosis show at Paris Las Vegas and Frederic Da Silva's *Paranormal*, but these reviews are pretty representative of the genre.

Dance Lessons

Judging from our reader mail, there are a lot of ladies who are thinking about a new line of work. We asked our friend Camille Cannon to see what's up. Here's her report.

What's a lady to do with a little extra time and cash on her hands? Whether you're in town for a bachelorette party, divorce party, or something in between, pole-dance classes are a great way to spend some good old (err, naughty) bonding time with friends. Las Vegas, after all, has built its reputation on adult entertainment offerings—why not gather your gals and get in on the action? Unlike your losses at the craps table, your hotel towels, or the nightclub confetti that drifts into your cocktails, you can take your sexy new skills home with you. (Because, really, not everything that happens in Vegas has to stay here.)

Other cities might blush at the thought of such classes, but in Las Vegas, you've got several to choose from. All classes run an average of one hour long, and the differences are subtle.

Stripper 101 has an ultra-convenient location, tucked inside the V Theater at the Miracle Mile Shops. (You'll know you're close when you see the Amazonian statue marking the entrance to Showgirl Bar.) Classes are offered daily, and the full schedule is available at Stripper101.com. Purchasing tickets is easy ($44 per person for general admission, $77 for VIP perks), and online reservations are recommended to ensure space. After check-in at the box office and waiver signing—a standard for all pole-related coursework—you'll be escorted through the bar to a small gift shop where you may purchase branded hoodies, tees, and of course, panties. Farther down the hall, your exotic dance dungeon awaits.

The classroom is walled with mirrors, making it easy to observe your moves as you learn. (But be aware: No photos or videos are allowed during class.) After some hip-rotating warm-up maneuvers, the instructor leads the class in a sensual lap-dance routine. No detail goes unturned, as the strip expert explains (and demonstrates) how to move your legs around the chair, transition into a shimmy, and execute a proper "cookie dip" to entrance your dance recipient. Then, aided by sultry tunes on the sound system, students practice the full routine on empty chairs as the instructor offers one-on-one attention.

Next it's on to the poles. Instructors get specific with technique ("arms at boobie height," "booty arched"), emphasizing ease and safety when executing these vertical dance moves. Plus, the close detail makes it easier to recall the routine later. You'll start with a squat spin and progress to the more advanced fireman spin. After casual observation, the instructor will offer individual assistance. Before you know it, the whole room is gliding and riding the pole like a pro. After one last freestyle session, you'll pick up your souvenir "stripper license" and select a "stripper name." And yes, it's OK to use your own.

Coming in at the same price point but located off the Strip is **Vegas Girls Night Out** (vegasgirlsnightout.com), which offers a pole-dancing/stripper instruction program called Night School 4 Girls. The classes are sold as part of multi-activity packages and are conducted at Pole Fitness Studio (polefitnessstudio.com), a separate entity that provides space and instructors. If you're not interested in buying a package from Vegas Girls Night Out, you can book a party or class directly through Pole Fitness Studio; types of classes and times are listed on its website. When you arrive, you might see footage of pole pros on TVs in the waiting area. But don't let that intimidate you. Night School is all about letting loose.

From start to finish, music is bumping and lights are flashing around the room. Photos and videos are allowed—and encouraged—the entire time. This leads to some compromising positions caught on camera and never-ending giggles resonating throughout the room. At times it's difficult to hear the instruction over all of the laughter.

Nevertheless, the class begins with pole work. You'll learn the impressive fireman spin and—so long as you've got some lower body strength—how to climb the pole. Afterward, it's on to the floor to practice your come-hither crawls, booty pops, and twerk technique. (Don't even bother keeping a straight face as you grind against the hardwood floor.)

If your class is large enough, you'll be paired with a partner and practice your lap dance in an actual lap. That way, you'll know where to position yourself so as not to stab your subject with stilettos. After a few tries to music, the instructor will ask your group to gather around your bride-to-be/divorcée/birthday girl. It's her time to practice everything she's learned . . . on all of you. (If you all weren't close before, you certainly will be now.) As you exit, you'll be treated to a swag bag of apparel, party favors, and your Night School diploma. Then the receptionist will gladly arrange cabs to take you and your crew to your next adventure.

Afternoon Shows

Afternoon shows can be an affordable alternative to the high-priced productions playing in the major showrooms at night. Most cost under $50, and many can be enjoyed for even less by taking advantage of coupons and special offers found in local freebie visitor magazines. Because afternoon shows sprout and disappear like wildflowers (or weeds), it's not possible to review all of them in the *Unofficial Guide*. What we can do, however, is profile the ones that have demonstrated staying power.

Below is a chart listing the afternoon shows profiled later in this chapter. There has been a numbing proliferation of afternoon shows recently, and as you might expect, the shows vary immensely in terms of quality. Finding the good ones and avoiding the bad ones is not unlike threading your way through a minefield. The good ones are better than a lot of the high-ticket productions that hold down stages around town at night. But the bad ones . . . heaven help us.

REVIEWED AFTERNOON SHOWS (in alphabetical order)
• Beatleshow **MIRACLE MILE SHOPS**
• The Bronx Wanderers **BALLY'S**
• Hitsville The Show **MIRACLE MILE SHOPS**
• Mac King Comedy Magic Show **HARRAH'S**
• Menopause: The Musical **HARRAH'S**
• Murray: Celebrity Magician **PLANET HOLLYWOOD**
• Nathan Burton Comedy Magic **MIRACLE MILE SHOPS**
• Paranormal **BALLY'S**

Afternoon shows are often instrumental in giving new talent a chance to break into the Las Vegas entertainment scene. Talent incubators include the Miracle Mile theaters, the Plaza, Royal Resort, and The D.

Lounge Entertainment

Many casinos offer exceptional entertainment at all hours of the day and night in their lounges. For the most part, lounges feature musical groups. On a given day almost any type of music, from oldies rock to country to jazz to folk, can be found in Las Vegas lounges. Unlike the production and headliner showrooms and comedy clubs, no reservations are required to take advantage of most lounge entertainment. If you like what you hear, just walk in. Sometimes there is a one- or two-drink minimum for sitting in the lounge during a show, but just as often there are no restrictions at all. You may or may not be familiar with the lounge entertainers by name, but you can trust that they will be highly talented and very enjoyable. Lounge entertainment is a great barometer of a particular casino's marketing program; bands are specifically chosen to attract a certain type of customer.

To find the type of music you prefer, consult one of the local visitor guides available free from the front desk or concierge at your hotel. There are a number of online sites that offer lounge entertainment information, but most stick to opening hours and nuts-and-bolts stuff such as address and phone number. Many are hopelessly out of date (one still lists the lounge at the long-ago-imploded Stardust). A good site is lasvegasweekly.com/clubs, where there is some, but by no means comprehensive, information on scheduled performers.

unofficial **TIP**
In general, if you find a casino with lounge entertainment that suits your tastes, you will probably be comfortable lodging, dining, and gambling there also.

The best resource is blogger Evan Davis's evandavisjazz.com. Evan compiles a weekly list of who is playing where, mostly at venues that do not charge a cover.

As an alternative to high ticket prices in Las Vegas showrooms, several casinos have turned their nightclubs and lounges into alternative show venues with ticket prices in the $30–$60 range. We've seen a number of marginal or unsuccessful clubs turned into showrooms over the years, but this is the first time we've observed highly success-ful nightspots converted. In the main, we don't care for this trend. True, it offers some low-price shows, but at the cost of sacrificing some of the city's best lounges and nightclubs.

THEY COME AND THEY GO

LAS VEGAS SHOWS come and go all the time. Sometimes a particular production will close in one Las Vegas showroom and open weeks later in another. Some shows actually pack up and take their presentations to other cities, usually Reno/Lake Tahoe or Atlantic City. Other shows close permanently. The bottom line: It's hard to keep up with all this coming and going. Don't be surprised if some shows reviewed in this guide have bitten the dust before you arrive. Also do not be surprised if the enduring shows have changed or moved to another casino.

LEARN WHO IS PLAYING BEFORE YOU LEAVE HOME

ON THE INTERNET, check out vegas.com/shows. The site also pro-vides information and reviews on long-run headliners and production shows. The *Las Vegas Advisor* (see page 6) offers a complete listing of shows on its website lvahotels.com, along with pretty good discounts on tickets. The Las Vegas Convention and Visitors Authority publishes a free Official Visitors Guide that lists shows alphabetically according to host hotel, tells who is playing, provides appearance dates, and lists information and reservation numbers. You can view this publication at visitlasvegas.com.

SHOW PRICES AND TAXES

ADMISSION PRICES for Las Vegas shows range from around $12 all the way up to $310 per person. Usually show prices are quoted exclusive of entertainment and sales taxes. Also not included are server gratuities.

Once, there was no such thing as a reserved seat at a Las Vegas show. If you wanted to see a show, you would make a reservation (usually by phone) and then arrive well in advance to be assigned a seat by the showroom maître d'. Slipping the maître d' a nice tip ensured a bet-ter seat. Typically, the price of the show included two drinks, or there would be waitstaff service and you would pay at your table after you were served. While this arrangement is still practiced in a few show-rooms, the prevailing system is reserved seating. With reserved seat-ing, you purchase your tickets at the casino box office (or by phone or online in advance with your credit card). As at a concert or a Broadway play, your seats are designated and preassigned at the time of purchase, and your section, aisle, and seat number will be printed on your ticket. When you arrive at the showroom, an usher will guide you to your assigned seat. Reserved seating, also known as "hard" or "box office" seating, occasionally includes drinks but usually does not.

If there are two performances per night, the early show is often (but not always) more expensive than the late show. In addition, some shows add a surcharge on Saturdays and holidays. If, in a showroom without reserved seating, you tip your server a couple of bucks and slip the maître d' or captain some currency for a good seat, you can easily end up paying $47 or more for a $40 list-price show and $63 or more for a $50 list-price show.

BUYING TICKETS

AS WITH MANY OTHER THINGS, the internet has revolutionized how Las Vegas show tickets are sold. Now you can purchase all of your show tickets well in advance online before you leave home. Many sites have a seating chart of the theater to help choose where to sit. Sellers include the host casino's website; the Las Vegas Visitor and Convention Authority's visitlasvegas.com; sites offering discounts and special deals (seat upgrades, free drinks, etc.) such as lvahotels.com, bestofvegas.com, and vegas.com/shows; and national event and ticket-selling sites such as ticketmaster.com.

unofficial **TIP**
Avoid buying show tickets from independent brokers. They tack on extra surcharges.

Buying in advance is definitely recommended if you want to see a popular show or celebrity headliner on a weekend. As an example, tickets went on sale for Celine Dion's show a year before it opened. Every show for the first several months sold out in just a couple of days.

Many of the online ticket vendors sell only at full retail, while others offer modest discounts on some but not all shows. Few of the online discounts come close to matching those of half-price ticket outlets in Las Vegas described below, but with the latter you have to buy your ticket in person on the day of the show.

You can also purchase tickets in advance at the host casino's box office, either in person or by phoning and using your credit card. The main advantage of phoning or going to the box office is that you're able to discuss seating options with a live person. The main disadvantage is that the box offices are usually understaffed. Because each buyer takes up a lot of agent time asking questions and going over seating charts, your chances of being stuck on hold or in a long line are about 80%. We were once in line at the MGM Grand box office behind a tour operator who purchased show tickets for a group of 60 people—can't begin to tell you how long that took.

HOW TO SAVE BIG BUCKS ON SHOW TICKETS

THE EASIEST WAY TO SAVE is to see *Dr. Naughty X-Rated Hypnosis* instead of Celine Dion. OK, just kidding. Here are some practical tips:

1. Most of the high-price shows are in state-of-the art theaters, which often have several classifications of seats. You can see Celine Dion at Caesars Palace from a second-level mezzanine seat for far less than in a front orchestra seat at the same show.

2. Half-price ticket outlets. The preeminent half-price ticket seller in Las Vegas is **Tix4Tonight** (tix4tonight.com), with 9 locations (see the location chart on the facing page). Box offices open at 10 a.m., though show postings are available at

TIX4TONIGHT TICKET OUTLET LOCATIONS

- **BALLY'S** (Mid-Strip) • **CASINO ROYALE** (Mid-Strip)

- **FASHION SHOW MALL** (North Strip; ground floor by Neiman Marcus)

- **FOUR QUEENS** (Downtown) • **GIANT COKE BOTTLE** (Mid-Strip)

- **HAWAIIAN MARKETPLACE** (South Strip) • **PLANET HOLLYWOOD** (Mid-Strip)

- **SHOWCASE MALL** (South Strip) • **TOWN SQUARE CENTER** (South Strip)

9:30 a.m. Each morning shows with unsold seats make some of those seats available to the half-price sellers. Sometimes it's a lot of seats, and other times it's just a handful, or none, depending on the show. The sellers post the available shows for customers to choose from. Before the recession, tickets to the most popular productions, such as the Cirque du Soleil shows, and most major celebrity headliners, were almost never available. Now, however, it's possible to find discounted tickets for just about any show in town, though the number of tickets for sale may be quite limited, or on weekends nonexistent.

You have to go in person to one of the box offices the day of the show to purchase your tickets. If you're staying on the Strip, there's usually a discounter within a 15-minute walk. If you're driving, parking can be a hassle for the Strip locations but is usually not a problem for off-Strip box offices. Instead of an actual ticket, discounters will issue you a voucher that you can exchange for a ticket at the official box office of the show. If it's not terribly inconvenient, we recommend exchanging your voucher sometime during the day instead of waiting until just before showtime.

You can blow a fair amount of time buying half-price tickets. Strip discounter locations are almost invariably understaffed. This, coupled with each purchaser asking untold questions, can combine for a long, slow-moving queue. At the Four Queens Tix4Tonight location Downtown, one couple monopolized the sole staffer for 35 minutes. Seriously. The average processing time for a person who knows exactly what they want is just over 10 minutes and requires showing photo ID and signing multiple documents. Most people have questions, so it takes longer. A lot of folks are afraid Tix4Tonight is a scam (it's not), forcing the ticket seller to waste time presenting his bona fides. If you do use Tix4Tonight, save your receipt and show it to access their kiosks' VIP queues for the following three days.

Parking is difficult for most locations. Out of the way but perhaps the easiest location to access if you're driving is the Tix4Tonight at Town Square Shopping Center. This is where we usually purchase our discounted tickets. Head south on Las Vegas Boulevard South and turn right into the shopping center on Town Square Parkway. Park in the South Garage. Tix4Tonight faces centrally located Town Square Park and the Children's Park.

It's helpful to have one of the local freebie visitor magazines with you when shopping. These publications always list the non-discounted price for show tickets. If you know the non-discounted price, you can calculate what a half-price ticket should cost. It's not uncommon in Las Vegas today for shows to offer VIP seating at a premium price. Often discounters will sell you a VIP seat without letting you know if there are less expensive seats available. For almost all shows, paying extra for a VIP seat is a waste of money. Tix4Tonight charges a service fee of $4 per ticket for processing your purchase. Coupons for $2 off this charge are available on the Tix4Tonight website and also in freebie magazines.

We found that after buying tickets, the discounters tell you to arrive at the show much earlier than necessary. True, you might encounter a logjam at the box office when you show up to exchange your vouchers, but arriving an hour in advance should be more than sufficient.

We're often asked whether the seats you're assigned when exchanging your voucher are inferior to those sold at full price. The answer is often, but not always, yes. As discussed above, you can improve your assigned seating somewhat by exchanging your voucher well in advance of showtime. If seats at a showroom are first-come, first-served, or assigned on the spot by a maître d', your chances of scoring a primo seat are as good as anyone else's.

3. At Las Vegas Advisor's lvahotels.com, you can buy discounted tickets in advance. Because the Las Vegas Advisor is the best-selling Vegas periodical for gamblers and frequent visitors, hotels and show producers offer lvahotels.com some of the better deals available. On the menu bar at the top of the page, move your mouse over See & Do, then Entertainment, and then click on Show & Event Deals.

4. Showrooms, like other Las Vegas hotel and casino operations, sometimes offer special deals. Sometimes free or discounted shows are offered with lodging packages. Likewise, coupons from complimentary local tourist magazines or casino "fun books" (see page 6) provide discounts or two-for-one options. Since these specials come and go, your best bet is to inquire about currently operating deals and discounts when you call for show reservations. If you plan to lodge at a hotel-casino where there is a show you want to see, ask about room-show combo specials when you make your room reservations. When you arrive in Las Vegas, pick up copies of the many visitor magazines. Scour the show ads for discount coupons.

We should note that the free mags are not as numerous as they once were, and many casinos—especially the large ones on the Strip—often have only one available. Downtown and at some nongaming hotels, there's more of a selection. In addition to lvahotels.com, there a lot of discount-ticket websites, but often the discounts are for shows that hardly ever go for list price. Before using these sites, always check the host casino's website to find out the baseline price.

DINNER SHOWS

SOME DINNER SHOWS REPRESENT GOOD DEALS, others less so. Be aware that with all dinner shows, your drinks will be extra, and invariably expensive. Food quality at dinner shows varies. In general, it can be characterized as acceptable, but certainly not exceptional. What you are buying is limited-menu banquet service for 300–500 people. Whenever a hotel kitchen tries to feed that many people at once, it is at some cost in terms of the quality of the meal and the service.

At *Tournament of Kings,* all shows include a dinner of Cornish hen with soup, potatoes, vegetable, dessert, and choice of nonalcoholic beverage for about $77 per person, plus taxes and gratuities. *Tournament of Kings* is described in detail later in the chapter. For the murder mystery production *Marriage Can Be Murder* at the D and *Tony n' Tina's Wedding* at Bally's, the meal is integrated into the unfolding story line, and you're expected to role-play as the show demands.

Several casinos offer show-and-dinner combos where you get dinner and a show for a special price but dinner is served in one of the casinos' restaurants instead of in the showrooms. Many restaurants provide only coffee-shop ambience, but the food is palatable and a good deal for the money. At each casino, you can eat either before or after the early show.

Early Versus Late Shows

If you attend a late show, you'll have time for a leisurely dinner before the performance. For those who prefer to eat late, the early show followed by dinner works best. Both shows are identical, except that for some topless revues the early show may be covered and the late show is topless. On weekdays, late shows are usually more lightly attended. On weekends, particularly at the most popular shows, the opposite is often the case.

PRACTICAL MATTERS

What to Wear to the Show

While it is by no means required, guests tend to dress up a bit when they go to a show. For a performance in the main showrooms at Bellagio, Caesars Palace, Mandalay Bay, Wynn Las Vegas, Wynn Encore, Aria, Park MGM, The Venetian, The Palazzo, or the Mirage, gentlemen will feel more comfortable in sport coats, with or without neckties. Women generally wear suits, dresses, skirt-and-blouse/sweater combinations, and even semiformal attire. That having been said, however, you'll find a third to a half of the audience at any of these casinos dressed more casually than described.

Showrooms at the Luxor, Stratosphere, New York–New York, TI, the MGM Grand, Harrah's, Rio, Flamingo, Westgate Las Vegas, Paris Las Vegas, Tropicana, and Planet Hollywood are a bit less dressy (sport coats are fine, but slacks and sweaters or sport shirts are equally acceptable for men), while showrooms at the Excalibur, The LINQ, The Orleans, Sam's Town, Suncoast, Sunset Station, Texas Station, House of Blues at Mandalay Bay, Golden Nugget, and Hard Rock are the least formal of all (come as you are). All of the comedy clubs are informal, though you would not feel out of place in a sport coat or, for women, a dress.

Getting to and from the Show

When you make your reservations, always ask what time you need to arrive for seating, and whether you should proceed directly to the showroom or stop first at the box office. You are normally asked to arrive 1 hour before the curtain rises, though a half hour or even less will do if you already have your reserved-seat tickets (ticket will show a designated row and seat number). If you are driving to another hotel for a show and do not wish to avail yourself of valet parking, be forewarned that many casinos' self-parking lots are quite distant from the showroom. Give yourself an extra 20 minutes or more to park, walk to the casino, and find the showroom.

*un**official* **TIP**
After shows, patrons flood the valets. To avoid delays, your best bet is to use self-parking and give yourself some extra time, or use valet parking and plan to stick around the casino for a while after the show.

A show with a large seating capacity in one of the major casinos can make for some no-win situations when it comes to parking. At all of the megahotels except Wynn Las Vegas and Wynn Encore, self-parking is either way off in the boonies or in a dizzying multistory garage, so your inclination may be to use valet parking. After the show, however, 1,000–1,650 patrons head for home, inundating the valets, particularly after a late show.

Invited Guests and Line Passes

Having arrived at the casino and found the showroom, you will normally join other showgoers waiting to be seated. If the showroom assigns reserved seats, the process is simple: just show your tickets to an usher and you will be directed to your seats. At many showrooms, generally those without reserved seating, you will encounter two lines. One line, usually quite long, is where you will queue up unless you are an "invited guest." There is a separate line for these privileged folks that allows them to be seated without waiting in line or coming an hour early. Most invited guests are gamblers who are staying at the host casino. Some have been provided with "comps" (complimentary admission) to the show. These are usually regular casino customers or high rollers. If you are giving the casino a lot of action, do not be shy about requesting a comp to the show.

unofficial **TIP**
If you are an invited guest under any circumstances, always arrive to be seated for a show at least 30 minutes early.

Gamblers or casino-hotel guests of more modest means are frequently given line passes. These guests pay the same price as anyone else for the show but are admitted without waiting via the Invited-Guest line. To obtain a line pass, approach a floorman or pit boss (supervisory personnel are usually distinguished from dealers by their suits and ties) and explain that you have been doing a fair amount of gambling in their casino. Tell him or her that you have reservations for that evening's show and ask if you can have a line pass. Particularly if you ask on Sunday through Thursday, your chances of being accommodated are good.

Reservations, Tickets, and Maître d' Seating

If, like most guests, you do not have a line pass, you will have to go through the process of entering the showroom and being seated. A dwindling number of showrooms practice what is known as maître d' seating. This means that, except in the case of certain invited guests, no seats are reserved. If you called previously and made a reservation, that will have been duly noted and the showroom will have your party listed on the reservations roster, but you will not actually be assigned a seat until you appear before the maître d'.

At the comedy clubs and an increasing number of major showrooms, you will be directed to a window variously labeled "Tickets," "Reservations," "Box Office," or "Guest Services." The attendant will verify your reservation and ask you to go ahead and pay. Once paid, you will receive a ticket to show the maître d' upon entering the showroom. The ticket does not reserve you any specific seat; you still need to see the maître d' about that. Also, the ticket does not include gratuities for your server in the showroom unless specifically stated.

As discussed earlier, most showrooms have discarded maître d' seating in favor of "box office" or "hard" seating. Specific reserved-seat assignments are printed on each ticket sold, as at a football game or on Broadway.

Where to Sit

When it comes to show seating, there are two primary considerations: visibility and comfort. The newer main showrooms at Caesars Palace, Mandalay Bay, Bellagio, Mirage, TI, MGM Grand, The Venetian, The Palazzo, Paris, Luxor, Wynn Las Vegas, Wynn Encore, Aria, Planet Hollywood, Park MGM, New York–New York, and Westgate Las Vegas provide plush theater seats, many with drink holders in the arms. The best accommodations in older showrooms are roomy booths, which provide an unencumbered view of the show. The vast majority of seats in these showrooms, however, and all in some, will be at banquet tables—a euphemism for very long, narrow tables where a dozen or more guests are squeezed together so tightly they can hardly move much less eat. When the show starts, guests seated at the banquet tables must turn their chairs around in order to see. This requires no small degree of timing and cooperation, since every person on the same side of the table must move in unison.

Showrooms generally will have banquet-table seating right in front of the stage. Next, on a tier that rises a step or two, will be a row of plush booths. These booths are often reserved for the casino's best customers (and sometimes for big tippers). Many maître d's would rather see these booths go unoccupied than have high rollers come to the door at the last minute and not be able to give them good seats. Behind the booths and up a step will be more banquet tables. Moving away from the stage and up additional levels, the configuration of booths and banquet tables is repeated on each tier.

For a big production show on a wide stage (Cirque du Soleil shows or Celine Dion), you want to sit in the middle and back a little. Being too close makes it difficult to see everything without wagging your head back and forth. Also, many productions make use of the whole theater, so some of the action might take place behind, on the sides, and even above you. Likewise, at a concert by a band or musical celebrity headliner, partway back and in the center is best. This positioning provides good visibility and removes you from the direct line of fire of amplifiers and lights. This advice, of course, does not apply to avid fans who want to fling their underwear or room keys at the star. For smaller production shows on medium-size stages (*Penn & Teller, Legends in Concert,* and such), right up front is great. This is also true for headliners like Rita Rudner. For female impersonators the illusion is more effective if you are back a little bit.

Be aware that comedians often single out unwary guests sitting down front for harassment, or worse, incorporate them into the act.

At comedy clubs and smaller shows, there are really no bad seats, provided the showroom has tiered seating (seating that is arranged in sloping tiers so that spectators in the back can see over the heads of those in front). In flat-floored showrooms you might not be able to see much at all if a taller person is seated in front of you. A high stage helps in flat-floored showrooms but doesn't completely resolve the problem.

Seat Switching

As mentioned earlier, VIP tickets are almost never a good deal. We buy general admission and then enter the showroom just a minute or two before showtime. Because shows rarely sell out their VIP tickets, we waltz to the front of the showroom and plop down in one of the invariably unoccupied VIP seats. This works best in small showrooms and for one or two people. Don't expect to score four VIP seats together. Here's another strategy we use for small showrooms where seats are assigned: Be seated where directed but scope out the better unoccupied seats. About 5 or so minutes into the show, when it's not likely someone will show up and occupy the better seats, we move into them. One of our researchers who finds direct seat switching too brazen exits the theater as if going to the restroom and then scores a better seat when she reenters.

Getting a Good Seat at Showrooms with Maître d' Seating

1. ARRIVE EARLY No maître d' can assign you a seat that's already taken. This is particularly important for Friday and Saturday shows. We have seen comped invited guests (the casino's better customers) get lousy seats because they waited until the last minute to show up.

2. TRY TO GO ON AN OFF NIGHT (that is, Sunday through Thursday) Your chances of getting a good seat are always better on weeknights, when there is less demand. If a citywide convention is in town, weekdays also may be crowded.

3. TRY TO KNOW WHERE (AS PRECISELY AS POSSIBLE) YOU WOULD LIKE TO SIT. In showrooms with maître d' seating, it is always to your advantage to specifically state your seating preferences.

4. UNDERSTAND YOUR TIPPING ALTERNATIVES Basically, you have three options:

1. Don't tip. **2.** Tip the maître d'. **3.** Tip the captain instead of the maître d'.

DON'T TIP Politely request a good seat instead of tipping. This option actually works better than you would imagine in all but a few showrooms, particularly Sunday through Thursday. If the showroom is not sold out and you arrive early, simply request a seat in a certain area. Tell the maître d', "We would like something down front in the center." Then allow the captain (the showroom staff person who actually takes you to your seat) to show you the seats the maître d' has assigned. If the assigned seat is not to your liking, ask to be seated somewhere else of your choosing. The captain almost always has the authority to make the seat-assignment change without consulting the maître d'.

TIP THE MAÎTRE D' When you tip the maître d', it is helpful to know with whom you are dealing. First, the maître d' is the man or woman in charge of the showroom. The showrooms are their domain, and they rule as surely as battalion commanders. Maître d's in the better show-rooms are powerful and wealthy people, with some maître d's taking in as much as $1,650 a night. Even though these tips are pooled and shared in some proportion with the captains, it's still a lot of money.

When you tip a maître d', especially in the better showrooms, you can assume it will take a fairly hefty tip to impress him, especially on a busy night. The bottom line, however, is that you are not out to impress anyone; you just want a good seat. Somebody has to sit in the good seats, and those who do not tip, or tip small, have to be seated regardless. So, if you arrive early and tip $15–$20 (for a couple) in the major showrooms, and $5–$10 in the smaller rooms, you should get decent seats. If it is a weekend or you know the show is extremely popular or sold out, bump the tip up a little. If you arrive late on a busy night, ask the maître d' if there are any good seats left before you proffer the tip. Speaking of which, maître d's would argue that almost all of their seats are good seats. Therefore, it pays to be more specific. For example, "I'd like a seat in the middle and back 30 feet or so from the stage." You can also point to the area where you'd like to sit.

Have your tip in hand when you reach the maître d'. Don't fool around with your wallet or purse as if you are buying hot dogs and beer at the ball park. Fold the money and hold it in the palm of your hand, arranged so that the maître d' can see exactly how big the tip is without unfolding and counting the bills. State your preference for seating at the same time you inconspicuously place the bills in the palm of his hand. If you think all this protocol is pretty ridiculous, we agree. But style counts, and observing the local customs may help get you a better seat.

A variation is to tip with some appropriate denomination of the casino's own chips. Chips are as good as currency to the maître d' and implicitly suggest that you have been gambling with that denomina-tion of chips in his casino. This single gesture, which costs you noth-ing more than your cash tip, makes you an insider and a more valued customer in the eyes of the maître d'.

Many maître d's are warm and friendly and treat you in a way that shows they appreciate your business. These maître d's are approach-able and reasonable, and they will go out of their way to make you comfortable. There are also a number of maître d's and captains, unfortunately, who are extremely cold, formal, and arrogant. Mostly older men dressed in tuxedos, they usually have gray hair and an imperious bearing and can seem rather imposing or hostile. Do not be awed or intimidated. Be forthright and, if necessary, assertive; you will usually be accommodated.

TIP THE CAPTAIN Using this strategy, tell the maître d' where you would like to sit, but do not offer a tip. Then follow the captain to your assigned seats. If your seats are good, you have not spent an extra nickel. If the assigned seats are less than satisfactory, slip the captain a tip and ask if there might be something better. If you see seats you would like to have that are unoccupied, point them out to the captain. Remember, however, that the first row of booths is usually held in reserve.

Before the Show Begins

Some showrooms serve drinks, while others offer self-service. A few of the variations you will encounter: A cash bar and no table service; if you want a drink before the show, you walk to the bar and buy it. Drinks are included, but there is no table service; you take a receipt stub to the bar and exchange it for drinks. In other showrooms there is table service where you can obtain drinks from a server.

In showrooms with table service, the servers run around like crazy trying to get everybody served before the show. Because all the people at a given table are not necessarily seated at the same time, the server responsible for that table may make five or more passes before everyone is taken care of. If your party is one of the last to be seated at a table, stay cool. You *will* be noticed and you *will* be served.

Bladder Matters

Be forewarned that in most showrooms there is no restroom, and that the nearest restroom is invariably a long way off, reachable only via a convoluted trail through the casino. Since the majority of showgoers arrive early and consume drinks, it is not uncommon to start feeling a little pressure on the bladder minutes before showtime. If you assume that you can slip out to the restroom and come right back, think again. If you are at the Westgate Las Vegas or the Tropicana, give yourself more than 10 minutes for the round-trip, and prepare for a quest. If you get to the can and back without getting lost, consider yourself lucky.

At most other showrooms, restrooms are somewhat closer but certainly not convenient. The LINQ, Luxor, Planet Hollywood, Harrah's, Park MGM, New York–New York, MGM Grand, Stratosphere, The Venetian/Palazzo, Wynn Las Vegas, Aria, and Mirage, however, seem to have considered that show guests may not wish to combine emptying their bladders with a 5-mile hike. Showrooms in these casinos are situated in close and much-appreciated proximity to the restrooms.

SELECTING *a* SHOW

SELECTING A LAS VEGAS SHOW is a matter of timing, budget, taste, and schedule. Celebrity headliners are booked long in advance but may play only for a couple of days or weeks. If seeing Elton John or Jerry Seinfeld is a big priority for your Las Vegas trip, you will have to schedule your visit to coincide with their appearances. If the timing of your visit is not flexible, as in the case of conventioneers, you will be relegated to picking from those stars playing when you are in town. To find out which shows and headliners are playing before you leave home, visit lvcva.com, visitlasvegas.com, or lvahotels.com.

Older visitors are often more affluent than younger visitors. It is no accident that most celebrity headliners are chosen, and most production shows created, to appeal to the 40-and-over crowd. If we say a Las Vegas production show is designed for a mature audience, we mean that the theme, music, variety acts, and humor appeal primarily to older guests. Most Las Vegas production shows target patrons 40–50 years old and up, while a few appeal to audiences over 50 years of age.

The hippest, avant-garde show in town is *Blue Man Group* (Luxor), which targets younger audiences and is wild, loud, and conceptually very different from anything else in Las Vegas. A close runner-up is a rap and hip-hop production featuring the JABBAWOCKEEZ dance crew. For in-your-face raunch with an acrobatic twist, try *Absinthe* or *Opium,* hands-down favorites for under-40 Las Vegas locals. Another contender is *Miss Behave Gameshow,* a totally wild and nutso parody of a television gameshow.

If you are younger than 35 years old you will also enjoy the Las Vegas production shows, though for you their cultural orientation (and usually their music) will seem a generation or two removed. Several production shows, however, have broken the mold, in the process achieving a more youthful presentation while maintaining the loyalty of older patrons. Cirque du Soleil's *Mystère* (TI) is an uproarious yet poignant odyssey in the European tradition, brimming over with unforgettable characters. Ditto for the other Cirque shows, especially *Michael Jackson ONE.* And, again, the comedy clubs have a more youthful orientation.

LAS VEGAS SHOWS FOR THE UNDER-21 CROWD

AN EVER-INCREASING NUMBER of showrooms offer productions appropriate for younger viewers. Circus Circus provides complimentary high-quality circus acts about once every half-hour, and *Tournament of Kings* at the Excalibur is a family dinner show featuring jousting and other benign medieval entertainments. Other family candidates include *Legends in Concert,* a celebrity-impersonation show at the Flamingo, and all Cirque du Soleil shows except *Zumanity.* Most afternoon shows are also a good bet for families.

Many of the celebrity-headliner shows are fine for children. Of the topless production shows, some operate on the basis of parental discretion while others do not admit anyone under age 21. Comedy clubs and comedy theater usually will admit teenage children accompanied by an adult. All continuously running shows are profiled later in this section. The profile will tell you whether the show is topless or particularly racy. If you have questions about a given showroom's policy for those under age 21, call the showroom's reservation and information number listed in the profile.

CELEBRITY-HEADLINER ROOMS

CHOOSING WHICH CELEBRITY HEADLINER to see is a matter of personal taste, though stars like Cher and David Copperfield seem to have the ability to rev up any audience. Our point is to suggest that the talent, presence, drive, and showmanship of many Las Vegas headliners often exceed all expectations, and that adhering to the limitations of your preferences may prevent you from seeing many truly extraordinary performers. Las Vegas is about gambling, after all. Do not be reluctant to take a chance on a headliner who is not familiar to you.

Most of the major headliners play at a relatively small number of showrooms. Profiles of the major celebrity showrooms and their regular headliners follow. The list is not all-inclusive, but it will give you an idea of where to check if you are interested in a certain headliner. Long-running (that is, a year or more) celebrity-headliner shows, including Celine Dion, Terry Fator, and so on, are reviewed in depth in our coverage of continuously running shows later in this chapter.

David Copperfield Theater
RESERVATIONS AND INFORMATION ☎ 702-891-7777 or 800-929-1111; mgmgrand.com

Frequent headliners David Copperfield, Howie Mandel, and Tom Jones. **Usual showtimes** Varies. **Approximate admission price** $78–$240. **Showroom size** 740 seats.

DESCRIPTION AND COMMENTS A comfortable, modern showroom, with all front-facing seats, the Hollywood Theatre hosts a range of musical and celebrity-headliner productions for one- to three-week engagements.

CONSUMER TIPS Purchase tickets in advance online or by calling the MGM Grand's main reservations number. Children are allowed at most presentations (check first). If you are not staying at the MGM Grand, either arrive by cab or give yourself of extra time to park and make your way to the showroom.

Hard Rock Hotel—The Joint
RESERVATIONS AND INFORMATION ☎ 702-693-5000 or 800-693-7625; hardrockhotel.com

Frequent headliners Top current and oldies rock, pop, blues, folk, electronic, and world music stars. **Usual showtimes** 8 p.m. **Approximate admission price** $40–$600. **Showroom size** 4,000 persons.

DESCRIPTION AND COMMENTS The Joint, once an intimate concert venue, has been redesigned and more than doubled in size with a new, larger stage and cutting-edge lighting and video effects. The main floor of the multi-level venue can be configured for theater-type seating, lounge seating (two to four chairs around a small cocktail table), or for standing only. So versatile is The Joint that it can set up for professional prize fights. Lines of sight are super, as is the sound system. For bands with a video dimension, there are 36 monitors, including a huge high-definition screen on each side of the stage. Paul McCartney, one of the first to perform in the expanded facility, said, "It's good in here, isn't it?" The upper levels of The Joint provide standing-room-only balcony viewing as well as seating and

VIP accommodations. Acoustics are excellent with a feltlike material covering the walls to minimize echo and sound bleeds.

CONSUMER TIPS If you don't want to be put in balcony Siberia where you can hear well enough but see nothing, or pinned against the stage for the whole show by a crush of sweaty rowdies, don't buy standing-room tickets. Book early for reserved seating—or shrug and say, "Oh well."

The Hard Rock Hotel box office sells reserved seats to shows at The Joint. You can purchase tickets via phone using your credit card or online. Shows at The Joint are hot tickets in Las Vegas and sell out quickly, so buy your tickets as far in advance as possible.

Finally, the Hard Rock Hotel was sold in 2018 to Richard Branson and his Virgin Brand. Branson said Virgin will invest "hundreds of millions of dollars" overhauling and rebranding the property. The Hard Rock will retain its name until the changeover is complete in late 2019.

Mandalay Bay—House of Blues

RESERVATIONS AND INFORMATION ☎ 702-632-7600 or 877-632-7600; houseofblues.com/lasvegas

Frequent headliners Santana, as well as current and former pop, rock, R&B, reggae, folk, and country stars. **Usual showtimes** Varies. **Approximate admission price** $20–$100. **Showroom size** 1,800 seats.

DESCRIPTION AND COMMENTS House of Blues is a concert hall, almost more like an opera house, with low ceilings and multiple tiers, which gets the audience as close to the act as possible. To that end, the acoustics are fantastic, but HOB can get claustrophobic. Also, the sight lines are highly variable, even bizarre, especially for a modern room—it's almost as if the designers were modifying an old theater. And it doesn't seem to have much to do with how much you pay for a seat: some bad seats (in the nosebleed section and on the sides of the stage) don't cost much less than the best seats or much more than the cheapest tickets.

Live music is presented almost every night of the year. Major headliners appear once or twice a week at 8 p.m.; for these shows you must be 21 years old to attend. Performers have included Ted Nugent, Rusted Root, Santana, Violent Femmes, Al Green, and Frank Zappa. Filling in the booking gaps are minor shows; check the website. You must be 18 years or older for most shows.

CONSUMER TIPS The box office is open 9 a.m.–9 p.m. Headliner shows sell out extremely fast, though you can usually pick up standing-room-only tickets, where you'll be sardined in front of the stage (watch your wallet). If money is no object, try to get a VIP seat front and center in the balcony. If you can't, you might as well just opt for the cheap standing room, as the upper balcony and many of the loge seats aren't worth the extra money. Indeed, many people give up their bad reserved seats to move down to the floor where they can see the whole stage!

MGM Grand—Grand Garden Arena

RESERVATIONS AND INFORMATION ☎ 702-531-3826 or 800-929-1111; mgmgrand.com

Frequent headliners National acts, superstars, televised boxing, wrestling, and other sporting events. **Usual showtimes** Varies. **Approximate admission price** $30–$1,250. **Showroom size** 16,800 seats.

DESCRIPTION AND COMMENTS This 275,000-square-foot special-events center is designed to accommodate everything from sporting events and concerts to major trade exhibitions. The venue also offers auxiliary meeting rooms and ballrooms adjacent to the entertainment center. Barbra Streisand christened this venue with her first concert in more than 20 years on New Year's Eve 1993. Championship boxing events are favorite attractions at the Grand Garden Arena, as are the many big-name musical concerts.

CONSUMER TIPS Purchase tickets in advance online or by calling the MGM Grand numbers listed above. If you are not staying at the MGM Grand, either arrive by cab or give yourself plenty of extra time to park and make your way to the arena.

The Orleans—Orleans Showroom

RESERVATIONS AND INFORMATION ☎ 702-365-7111 or 800-675-3267; orleanscasino.com

Frequent headliners Clint Black, Michael Bolton, Air Supply, Four Tops, Kenny G, Bill Maher, and Dennis Miller. **Usual showtimes** Varies. **Dark** Varies. **Approximate admission price** $35–$70. **Showroom size** 850 seats.

DESCRIPTION AND COMMENTS This small but comfortable showroom offers tiered theater seats arranged in a crescent around the stage. Designed for solo performers and bands, The Orleans Showroom is an intimate venue for concerts with good visibility from anywhere in the house. The star lineup runs the gamut with a concentration on country-and-western singer celebrities.

CONSUMER TIPS This showroom features some great talent at bargain prices. All seats are reserved. Tickets can be purchased at the box office to the left of the showroom, online, or over the phone.

Park Theater

RESERVATIONS AND INFORMATION ☎ 844-600-PARK (7275) or 888-529-4828; parkmgm.com

Frequent headliners Lady Gaga, Bruno Mars, Ricky Martin, Stevie Nicks. **Usual showtimes** Varies. **Dark** Varies. **Approximate admission price** From a pittance to a fortune. **Showroom size** Up to 5,200 seats.

DESCRIPTION AND COMMENTS The Park Theater was the first major component in reinventing the Monte Carlo as The Park MGM. An attraction in itself, the theater has four seating levels that can be modified according to the needs of whatever is playing. Sight lines are excellent with no seat more than 150 feet from the stage, which stretches 135 feet wide. Cutting-edge technology includes 30K HD projectors and an 80-foot LED display along the back of the stage. Though almost any production could be staged, The Park Theater was designed primarily for headliners, touring concerts, and smaller boxing matches and UFC fights.

A concourse to the rear of each level offers food and beverage options, as well as restrooms in a design similar to that of a football stadium or ballpark. The theater derives its name from The Park, an outdoor entertainment and dining plaza that fronts both the Park Theater and the nearby T-Mobile Arena.

CONSUMER TIPS We recommend the center balcony as a near perfect combination of value and sight lines. Parking is a challenge. Park MGM garages are open but not nearly large enough to handle T-Mobile Arena and Park Theater crowds concurrently. For the time being, park at Bellagio and take the tram to Park MGM, with a stop at Crystals at CityCenter on the way.

Smith Center for the Performing Arts

RESERVATIONS AND INFORMATION ☎ 702-749-2000; thesmithcenter.com

Frequent headliners Touring Broadway musicals and dramas, classical and contemporary concerts, dance, and comedy. **Usual showtimes** Varies. **Approximate admission price** $24–$200. **Showroom sizes** 258–2,050 seats and an alfresco theater seating 2,500.

DESCRIPTION AND COMMENTS The zenith of Downtown's redevelopment is a world-class performance center in Symphony Park, presenting a mix of entertainment primarily developed for locals and disproving the adage that Las Vegas is a cultural abyss. The 61-acre campus includes three state-of-the-art theaters presenting major productions and artists: the Jazz Cabaret seating 258, the 300-seat Troesch Studio Theater, and the 2,050-seat Reynolds Hall. The fourth performance venue is an outdoor lawn seating up to 2,500 for starlight plays and concerts. The adjacent Boman Pavilion houses three resident companies: Nevada Ballet Theater, Las Vegas Contemporary Dance Theater, and The Las Vegas Philharmonic. The architectural design of the buildings pays homage to the 1935 Art Deco style of historic Hoover Dam, the genesis of Las Vegas's initial growth. The dam's towers are represented in the center's logo and replicated throughout the center, and the winged figures at the dam take flight in the Grand Lobby. Symphony Park itself is an open-air gallery of public art.

CONSUMER TIPS Moderately priced beverages and snacks are served in the Jazz Cabaret and in the lobbies of Reynolds Hall. Each level features restrooms and concession stands, eliminating long lines at intermission. Wheelchair seating is easily accessible. Free parking is available in the North Lot on City Parkway; valet parking is available in front of Reynolds Hall.

T-Mobile Arena

RESERVATIONS AND INFORMATION ☎ 702-692-1600; t-mobilearena.com

Frequent headliners Major stars like Barbra Streisand, the Rolling Stones, Coldplay, and Carrie Underwood, and events such as the PBR World Finals, boxing, Vegas Golden Knights NHL hockey, and basketball games. **Usual showtimes** Varies. **Approximate admission price** Varies considerably. **Showroom size** Up to 20,000 seats depending on the presentation.

DESCRIPTION AND COMMENTS The Strip's newest entertainment-and-sports complex is the majestic gold-and-copper T-Mobile Arena, strategically holding court on 16 acres between the New York–New York and Park MGM resorts. The facility flaunts five tiers: Event, Mezzanine, Suite, Upper Concourse, and Tower, each with steep unobstructed sight lines. In addition to standard seating for up to 20,000 and 44 tricked-out luxury suites, T-Mobile boasts a Hyde Lounge with a view of the area; admission is included with all tickets, or you can purchase stand-alone entry with bottle service to watch the show from a comfy couch. On the other end of the pricing spectrum, some acts open a standing-room-only party deck for a reduced price. Along with mega-screens throughout, a colossal video resolution screen suspended over the main floor brings the performers close-up. Moving platforms change seating configurations as needed. The complex includes a nightclub, six lounges, a smorgasbord of eateries, and an array of viewing choices, from standard stadium seats to private loge boxes. Each floor of the facility includes outdoor patios and balconies to showcase the Strip's dazzling lights. The adjoining 2-acre Toshiba Plaza is a tree-dappled open entertainment space with three stages hosting complimentary live performances and showcasing exhibits.

CONSUMER TIPS T-Mobile Arena is situated at the west end of Park Avenue, the narrow street separating the Park MGM and New York–New York resorts. The best and most hassle-free way to reach the complex is to walk or take the monorail, which stops behind six hotels along the Strip's east side. Disembark at the MGM Grand, Paris/Bally's, or The LINQ and cross the bridges over the Strip.

Free trams glide from the Bellagio to the Park MGM and from Mandalay Bay and Luxor to the Excalibur. From the tram stations, it's a quick 15-minute walk to the complex. Parking? The short answer is leave your wheels elsewhere, but if you prefer to drive, be aware traffic is massive. The Aria, Cosmopolitan, New York–New York, Park MGM, Bellagio, MGM Grand, and Tropicana garages are nearby, but paid parking will be in effect. A $10 prepaid parking pass can be reserved in advance at t-mobilearena.com; the cost doubles on event day. Avoid using valet service at neighboring hotels because everyone else will have the same idea. To avoid the Strip, take Frank Sinatra Drive, which extends from Russell Road to Caesars Palace and is used mostly by locals. That four-lane road to the west parallels Las Vegas Boulevard and delivers vehicles coming from the south or north to the eight west-of-Strip hotel parking garages along that corridor. MGM Resorts has constructed an immense 3,000-space parking garage just south of the arena at the Excalibur, directly across Tropicana Avenue. When completed, walkers can access the arena via the overpass above that congested east–west thoroughfare.

Zappos Theater at Planet Hollywood
RESERVATIONS AND INFORMATION ☎ 855-234-7469 or 866-693-2425; planethollywoodresort.com

Frequent headliners Britney Spears, Justin Bieber, Jennifer Lopez, Gwen Stefani, Jimmy Buffett, Backstreet Boys, charity events, beauty pageants. **Usual showtimes** 8 p.m. **Approximate admission price** $70–$855. **Showroom size** 4,500 seats.

DESCRIPTION AND COMMENTS Formerly The Axis, and before that The Aladdin Center for the Performing Arts, Zappos Theater is a 4,500-seat concert venue with three tiered sections of seating arrayed in a fan-shaped configuration facing a broad stage. The venue hosts concerts, charity events, and beauty pageants, including Miss America, Miss Universe (no one from Klingon has ever won), and Miss USA. Acoustics are good, though the decibel level of rock concerts, such as Britney Spears's *Piece of Me* show, is overwhelming. Sight lines are universally good, though the rear third of the theater is quite distant from the stage.

CONSUMER TIPS The Zappos Theater is the land of big productions, so center seats a little less than one third back usually serve best. All seats are plush theater chairs. Restrooms are located near the showroom. If you drive, park in the Miracle Mile Shops garage rather than at Planet Hollywood.

PRODUCTION SHOWS

LAS VEGAS PREMIER PRODUCTION SHOWS: COMPARING APPLES AND ORANGES

WHILE WE ACKNOWLEDGE THAT LAS VEGAS production shows are difficult to compare and that audiences of differing tastes and ages have different preferences, we have nevertheless rated the continuously running shows to give you an idea of our favorites. This is definitely an apples-and-oranges comparison (how can you compare *Zumanity* to *Blue Man Group?*), but one based on each show's impact, vitality, originality, pace, continuity, crescendo, and ability to entertain.

We would hasten to add that even the continuously running shows change acts and revise their focus periodically. Expect our ratings, therefore, to change from year to year. Also, be comforted by the knowledge that while some shows are better than others, there are only one or two real dogs. The quality of entertainment among the continuously running production shows is exceptional. By way of analogy, we could rank baseball players according to their performance in a given All-Star game, but the entire list, from top to bottom, would still be All-Stars. You get the idea.

A Word About Small Showrooms

During the past couple of years, we have seen a number of casinos convert their lounge into a small showroom. Though the stage in these showrooms is routinely about the size of a beach towel, productions are mounted that include complex choreography, animal acts, and, in one notable demonstration, an illusionist catching bullets in his teeth. In the case of musical revues, as many as four very thin or three average-size hula dancers can fit comfortably on the stage at one time.

A real problem with some smaller shows is that they often cost as much as productions in Las Vegas's major showrooms. Another problem is that small shows often play to even smaller crowds. We saw a performance of *That's Magic* at O'Shea's where the cast outnumbered the audience. Though the show featured talented illusionists, a good ventriloquist, and some dancers, the small facility made the production seem amateurish. It was heartrending to see professional entertainers work so hard for such a tiny audience. We felt self-conscious and uncomfortable ourselves, as well as embarrassed for the performers.

When it comes to smaller showrooms, simpler is better. That's why *Mac King* and *Purple Reign* work so well: both shows take a minimalist approach. Additionally, both shows play in casinos large enough to draw an audience. Little showrooms in smaller casinos that attempt to mount big productions create only parody and end up looking foolish. Better that they revert to offering lounge shows.

We've given up trying to cover the productions that play in these small showrooms, mostly because the shows are very short-lived. If a small-showroom production is exceptionally good and demonstrates staying power, however, we sometimes review it right along with the full-scale shows. (This discussion, by the way, does not apply to comedy clubs, which work best in small rooms.)

Gotta Keep on Movin'

If every player in major-league baseball were a free agent, the willy-nilly team-hopping would bear a close resemblance to the Las Vegas entertainment scene. If, after reading our show reviews, you discover that your preferred performer or production has disappeared from the listed showroom, don't despair. Chances are good that the show has moved to a different venue. Melinda, "The First Lady of Magic" (now retired), holds the all-time record, having played at almost a dozen different Las Vegas casinos during her career.

LAS VEGAS SHOW PROFILES

FOLLOWING IS A PROFILE of each of the continuously running shows, listed alphabetically by the name of the show. If you are not sure of the name of a show, consult the previous section. Comedy clubs and limited-engagement celebrity-headliner showrooms are profiled in separate sections. Prices are approximate and fluctuate about as often as you brush your teeth.

Following the alphabetized profiles are comments regarding a number of productions that for various reasons we elected not to profile. Reasons range from too few performances to redundancy to mediocrity or worse.

52 Fridays ★★★½

APPEAL BY AGE   **UNDER 21 ★★★**   **21-37 ★★★½**   **38-50 ★★★★**   **51+ ★★★★**

HOST CASINO AND SHOWROOM Golden Nugget—The Showroom;
☎ 886-946-5336; goldennugget.com/las-vegas

Type of show Weekly concert series with ever-changing headliner. **Admission** $19–$99. **Cast size** Varies by artist. **Usual showtimes** Friday only, 8 p.m. **Topless** No. **Duration of presentation** About 80 minutes (varies by artist).

DESCRIPTION AND COMMENTS Fans of the glory days of AM rock-and-roll radio strike it rich every Friday night at the Golden Nugget, which has given its 600-seat showroom over to musical acts who had their heydays in the 1960s through 1980s. Scheduled artists in 2018 ranged from Grammy award–winning artists and tribute bands to Country Music Hall of Famers, classic rock bands, R&B songstresses, and standout comedians.

The stage is flanked by undersize flat-screen TVs, which occasionally show video clips to accompany or introduce the songs, and scenic effects are limited to a color-changing backdrop and a handful of infrequently active moving lights. The visuals may have modest production values, but the focus is firmly on the music, which was rendered cleanly without excessive overamplification. Depending on who is on the bill, this could be a Baby Boomer's best bet for a Friday date night, but those under 30 are likely to say "Who was that?" to most of these headliners.

CONSUMER TIPS A low ceiling makes the showroom seem more intimate than its seat count would suggest. The stage is shallow but wide, with the audience arrayed in plush cinema-style seats (with cup-holders) on a slight rake. No booth seating is available. Photography is officially forbidden, but that didn't seem to stop our audience, who also spoke and sang along throughout the show.

Absinthe ★★★★

APPEAL BY AGE	18-21 ★★★★	21-37 ★★★★	38-50 ★★★	51+ ★★½

HOST CASINO AND SHOWROOM Caesars Palace—Spiegeltent on the Roman Plaza; ☎ 800-745-3000; ticketmaster.com or spiegelworld.com

Type of show Low-tech, low-brow circus. **Admission** $109–$200. **Cast size** 23. **Night of lowest attendance** Wednesday. **Usual showtimes** Wednesday–Sunday, 8 and 10 p.m. **Dark** Monday and Tuesday. **Special comments** No one under 18 admitted. **Topless** Yes (male), almost (female). **Duration of presentation** 90 minutes.

DESCRIPTION AND COMMENTS It's a silly, sultry, risqué interactive and participatory experience. Equal parts cabaret, burlesque, circus, and midway sideshow, *Absinthe* incorporates an impudent cast of slick professionals. The aerial and acrobatic performances are separated by repartee, tomfoolery, and other shtick hosted by an in-your-face ringmaster and his ditzy female assistant. Among the rotating acts are a quartet of tubby aerialists, an acrobat balancing on a tower of chairs, a chanteuse who sings and strips while surrounded by four guys in drag, a limber lady on ropes, two musclemen with exceptional equilibrium, and a trio of highly focused low-wire tightrope walkers. While the performers are skilled and execute wonders on a tiny circular stage, without fail each act features the artists disrobing, which gives you an idea of the general tenor of the goings-on. An exception is The Silicon Girls, three women who look like a cheerleading squad but demonstrate the strength, balance, and sex appeal of Gal Gadot. No need to shed clothes; they'd look totally hot in footie pajamas.

Occasionally, celebrity guests are featured. The show includes some audience participation. Expect raunch and lots of dirty jokes as the MC comments on the dress, physical attributes, proclivities, and vulnerabilities of the performers and audience members in the front rows and on the aisles. A libation or three will help you decide whether this is a clever lampoon of big-ticket gymnastic-infused performance art, a bawdy tour de farce, or a below-the-belt satire.

Outside of an Army barracks you'd be hard pressed to find language as raunchy as what you'll hear in *Absinthe*. And it doesn't stop there, visuals abound: consider a performer munching on a used Tampon. Yet this is perhaps the favorite show of Las Vegas locals under 40—the show they take out-of-town guests to see. There's definitely an age divide with *Absinthe*. Younger patrons more often than not love it, while those over 50 are frequently stunned to the point of being exceedingly uncomfortable. Unless you're going for shock value, this is probably not the show to see with your mom (or, for that matter, anyone who won't enjoy a lively discussion about vaginas, penises, breasts, and bowels).

CONSUMER TIPS The 600-seat venue is a round, circus tentlike pavilion with air-conditioning. Seating is in the round and very close to the stage, so close that a performer who screws up might literally fall in your lap. Be prepared to sit on a flat floor in folding chairs. Because the stage is elevated, however, there are good lines of sight from most seats. The pavilion is outside the casino on the southeast section of the Caesars property, near the pedestrian bridge over Flamingo Road.

There is no reserved seating except for those purchasing the VIP package. Box offices in the casino do not sell *Absinthe* tickets. The *Absinthe* box office is a small, stand-alone, tollbooth of a building situated in a beer garden adjacent to the show pavilion. There are not separate windows for ticket sales and will call, so everyone is forced to endure a lengthy queue. If it's possible, buy or pick up your tickets earlier in the day.

Anthony Cools ★★★½

APPEAL BY AGE	UNDER 21 –	21-37 ★★★★	38-50 ★★	51+ ★

HOST CASINO AND SHOWROOM Paris—Anthony Cools Theater; ☎ 702-946-7000 or 877-374-7469; parislasvegas.com or anthonycools.com

Type of show Uncensored hypnosis comedy. **Admission** $45–$110. **Cast size** 3 (+12 volunteers). **Night of lowest attendance** Tuesday. **Usual showtimes** Thursday–Sunday and Tuesday, 9 p.m. **Dark** Monday and Wednesday. **Topless** No. **Special comments** Must be 18 or older to attend. **Duration of presentation** 90 minutes.

DESCRIPTION AND COMMENTS If you must see a hypnotist show—and you don't mind incessant cursing and dirty talking—then this is the show. Unlike his thematic predecessor, the late and unlamented "Dr. Naughty," Anthony Cools is a slick, adroit manipulator and a truly devious creator of setups for his hypnotized zombie minions. Medical professionals who use hypnosis in their practice confirm that the volunteers really are hypnotized and are unconsciously obeying the bizarre suggestions by Cools. Some audience members volunteer as a lark and feign being hypnotized. Cools spots them almost immediately and shoos them back to their seats. The remaining subjects are put through their, mostly blue, paces, including being afflicted with burning nether regions, dealing with uncontrollably vocal genitals, and making sweet love to a chair, among other torments.

CONSUMER TIPS Obviously, this is not a show for the easily offended or intimidated. Salacious humor is the order of the day, and it's one of the bawdiest productions in town. Get in early if you want a seat near the front, and feel free to volunteer (or volunteer your friends). Taking photos during the show is encouraged; also, an instantly produced DVD of the show you just saw is available after it's over. Grade-A blackmail material. Hypnosis shows, including Anthony Cools, are only as good as the selection of volunteers. Try to catch a weekend show, when the audience is larger; this gives Cools more to work with. If the V Theater at Planet Hollywood/Miracle Mile Shops is more convenient than the showroom at Paris, try Marc Savard's hypnosis show, every bit the equal of Anthony Cool's.

The Australian Bee Gees Show ★★★

APPEAL BY AGE	UNDER 21 ★★½	21-37 ★★★	38-50 ★★★½	51+ ★★★

HOST CASINO AND SHOWROOM Excalibur—Thunder from Down Under Showroom; ☎ 702-597-7600; excalibur.com

Type of show Disco concert. **Admission** $55–$77. **Cast size** 5. **Night of lowest attendance** Tuesday. **Usual showtimes** Sunday–Friday, 7 p.m. **Dark** Saturday. **Topless** No. **Duration of presentation** 75 minutes.

DESCRIPTION AND COMMENTS I expected John Travolta to zip-line from the rafters Branson style. Such was my mindset as old disco movies fused with Alvin and the Chipmunks falsettos in a 75-minute recollection of Bee Gees discography. The concert covers the Bee Gees' career, mixing lesser-known compositions from the group's early days with their legendary hits. While Travolta's absence was a disappointment, I warmed to the music and soon found myself pumping an imaginary bass drum. I was actually grooving on a sound that gave me hives back in the day.

The music didn't change, but evidently I did. Or perhaps I was won over by a compelling live presentation courtesy of three talented vocalists from Australia. Michael Clift is the long-haired Barry Gibb. David Scott, as the only member of the five-piece group who doesn't play an instrument, is the late Robin Gibb. Scott and Clift carry most of the lead vocals, while Wayne Hosking, as the late Maurice Gibb, harmonizes and plays keyboard. The trio is backed by electric bass and drums. The impersonators stay in role throughout and refer to each other by their Bee Gees names. I had to go online for a memory jog of how the Bee Gees actually looked and was surprised by how much the Aussies resemble them—not dead ringers, but close enough. The Aussies' sound, however, is right on.

CONSUMER TIPS If you're a Bee Gees fan, you'll eat this up. Ditto for disco fans. For others, primarily due to there being so little visual stimulation, not so much. The showroom has a flat floor with no rise, but the stage is high enough that sight lines from most seats are good. The totally PG performance coupled with the opportunity to dance makes the Aussie Bee Gees a good selection for kids. Atypically, there are restrooms inside the showroom, a convenience we'd like to see everywhere. Excalibur valet parking is frequently full, so if you drive give yourself enough time to use self-parking if necessary.

Beatleshow Orchestra ★★★

APPEAL BY AGE	UNDER 21 ★★	21-37 ★★★	38-50 ★★★	51+ ★★★½

HOST CASINO AND SHOWROOM Miracle Mile Shops—Saxe Theater;
☎ 866-932-1818; vtheaterboxoffice.com

Type of show Musical impressionist and tribute act. **Admission** $60–70. **Cast size** 8 (4 Beatles, 2 actors, 2 dancers). **Night of lowest attendance** Tuesday. **Usual showtimes** Nightly, 5:30 p.m. **Dark** None. **Topless** No. **Duration of presentation** 90 minutes.

DESCRIPTION AND COMMENTS It's immediately obvious that the performers in this Beatles tribute group have honed their craft. The four artists play their own instruments onstage—no backing tapes or synthesized tracks—and they briefly sing a cappella to prove their musical chops. Vocally they are dead-on, and the audience gets especially charged up and rowdy during sing-alongs like "Twist and Shout."

The costumes and musical selections follow the Beatles' career, from the early 1960s through psychedelia and into the 1970s. Film clips from various eras (including BBC footage of Brits singing badly, and the chilling moment when Howard Cosell announced Lennon's assassination during Monday Night Football) add historical context. The Beatle-esque mannerisms and speech patterns are there, even if the physical resemblances are a bit loose; George is a dead ringer, and John and Paul look decent, but Ringo, who becomes the butt of most of the show's jokes, falls more into the "haircut impression" category. A pair of backup dancers put in intermittent appearances, and two impressionists (a good Ed Sullivan and an awful Austin Powers) help bridge the musical segments. Fans of the lads from Liverpool will get their money's worth.

CONSUMER TIPS The Saxe Theater is located in the Miracle Mile Shops at Planet Hollywood. Self-parking at Planet Hollywood funnels you directly into the Miracle Mile Shops not far from the theater. Arrive 40 minutes or more before show time if you are buying or picking up tickets or redeeming ticket vouchers. More expensive VIP tickets include assigned seating in the center of the modestly sized venue; cheaper general admission seats are in the back, but the view is nearly as good.

Blue Man Group ★★★★½

APPEAL BY AGE   **UNDER 21** ★★★★½   **21-37** ★★★★½   **38-50** ★★★★   **51+** ★★★

HOST CASINO AND SHOWROOM Luxor—Blue Man Theater;
☎ 702-262-4400; luxor.com

Type of show Performance-art production show. **Admission** $79–$158. **Cast size** 3 + a 15-piece band. **Nights of lowest attendance** Sunday and Monday. **Usual showtimes** Nightly, 7 p.m. and 9:30 p.m. **Dark** None. **Topless** No. **Special comments** Teenagers really like this show, but the blue guys, loud music, and dark colors could scare small children (we suggest 5 years as the minimum age). **Duration of presentation** 105 minutes.

DESCRIPTION AND COMMENTS *Blue Man Group* gives Las Vegas its first large-scale introduction to that nebulous genre called "performance art." If the designation "performance art" confuses you, relax—it won't hurt a bit. *Blue Man Group* serves up a stunning show that all kinds of folks ages 8–80 can appreciate.

The three blue men are just that—blue—and bald and mute. Wearing black clothing and skullcaps slathered with bright-blue greasepaint, their fast-paced show uses music (mostly percussion) and multimedia effects to make light of contemporary art and life in the information age. The Vegas act is just one expression of a franchise that started with three friends in New York's East Village. Now you can catch their zany, wacky, smart stuff in New York, Boston, Orlando, Chicago, Berlin, and Toronto.

The Las Vegas Blue Man Group show was overhauled recently, removing the clunky "Showbot" segment and its accompanying industrial robots and replacing them with giant insect puppets created by Michael Curry. Two recent additions include flying eyeball drones and high-tech video projection mapping in the preshow. The current production shares many elements with the Orlando version—including "GiPad" giant computer tablets and "2.5-D" neon animated characters—but enhances them with upgraded LED lighting effects and adds a couple of new tricks, such as kettle drums that launch smoke rings over the audience.

Funny, sometimes poignant, and always compelling, *Blue Man Group* hooks the audience even before the show begins with digital messages that ultimately spin performers and audience alike into a mutual act of joyous complicity. The trio pounds out vital, visceral tribal rhythms on complex instruments (made of PVC pipes) and makes seemingly spontaneous eruptions of visual art rendered with marshmallows and a mysterious goo. Their weekly supplies include 60 Twinkies, 996 marshmallows, and 9.5 gallons of paint. If all this sounds silly, it is, but it's also strangely thought-provoking about such various topics as the value of modern art, DNA, the way rock music moves you, and how we are all connected. (*Hint:* It's not the internet.)

Audience participation completes the Blue Man experience. The blue men often bring audience members on stage. And a lot of folks can't help standing up to dance—and laugh. Most fun of all is the finale, when the entire audience bats around illuminated exercise balls. Magicians for the creative spirit that resides in us all, *Blue Man Group* makes everyone a co-conspirator in a culminating joyous explosion. In July of 2017, the Blue Man Group franchise was acquired by Cirque du Soleil. We look forward to seeing the fruits of that combination.

CONSUMER TIPS This show is decidedly different and requires an open mind to be appreciated. It also helps to be a little loose, because everybody gets sucked into the production and leaves the theater a little bit lighter in spirit, judging by the rousing standing ovations. If you don't want to be pulled onstage to become a part of the improvisation, don't sit in the first half-dozen or so rows.

The Bronx Wanderers ★★★½

APPEAL BY AGE	UNDER 21 ★★½	21-37 ★★★	38-50 ★★★½	51+ ★★★★

HOST CASINO AND SHOWROOM Bally's—Windows Showroom;
☎ 702-777-2782; thebronxwanderers.com or caesars.com/ballys-las-vegas

Type of show Rock-and-roll oldies cover band. **Admission** $56–$83. **Cast size** 6. **Night of lowest attendance** Wednesday. **Usual showtimes** Nightly, 5:30 p.m. **Topless** No. **Duration** 75 minutes.

DESCRIPTION The stage musical *Jersey Boys* may have vacated Vegas, but The Bronx Wanderers are keeping the sounds of Frankie Valli and his *American Bandstand*–era contemporaries alive with this energetic, if eccentric, musical tribute to the golden age of rock and roll. This leather jacket–sporting sextet is a family affair fronted by father "Yo'Vinny" Adinolfi (who looks like the love child of Gene Simmons and Wayne Newton) and his two sons, Vinny "The Kid" and Nicky "Stix."

Dad is an incorrigible name-dropper, repeatedly referencing his early career producing Jim Croce records and his friendship with actor Chazz Palminteri, who encouraged the band's formation. Vinny's stories and video clips, which try to make the group seem like Arthur Avenue's answer to The Four Seasons, don't always strongly connect to the set list, which veers wildly from vintage doo-wop and surf rock to Billy Joel, Bruno Mars, and "Bohemian Rhapsody."

But while the patter and production values could use polishing, as musicians they put on a solid show with boundless energy and tight vocal harmonies; their take on the Beach Boys' "God Only Knows" will give you goose bumps. More important, the Wanderers win over the audience with their warm personalities, intimate interaction, and a bit of wedding reception-style audience participation. By the encore, expect to see the entire audience up on their feet dancing, artificial hips be damned.

CONSUMER TIPS In its current configuration, Bally's Windows Showroom is a fairly uncomfortable venue to catch a concert. The wide, shallow stage and mostly unraked seating results in terrible sight lines from the sides; we had trouble even seeing half the band from our extreme house-right seats. The band sticks around outside the showroom after each performance for photographs.

Carlos Santana ★★★★

APPEAL BY AGE	UNDER 21 ★★★	21–37 ★★★★	38–50 ★★★★	51+ ★★★★

HOST CASINO AND SHOWROOM Mandalay Bay—House of Blues; ☎ 702-632-7600 or 800-745-3000; houseofblues.com/lasvegas, ticketmaster.com

Type of show Guitar-centric rock concert. **Admission** $130–$350. **Cast size** 1 plus 10-piece band. **Night of lowest attendance** None. **Usual showtimes** Wednesday, Friday, and Sunday, 7 p.m. **Dark** Varies. **Topless** No. **Duration of Presentation** 115 minutes.

DESCRIPTION AND COMMENTS *An Intimate Evening with Santana: Greatest Hits Live!* The title just about sums up this show, which reaffirms why Santana richly deserves the #15 spot on *Rolling Stone*'s "Top 100 Greatest Guitarists of All Time" list, as well as membership in the Rock and Roll Hall of Fame. Fusing Latin beats, jazz, and blues, plus African rhythms and instruments, multiple Grammy winner and guitar virtuoso Carlos Santana rocks the 1,200-seat House of Blues. After three years at the Hard Rock's Joint showroom, this remodeled, more compact space at Mandalay Bay allows the six-stringer to interact more intimately with the audience while improvising his familiar classics. The show is purposely loose and unpredictable; there is no set list, and he frequently covers the music of personal favorites Bob Dylan, Marvin Gaye, or John Lennon. Occasionally a surprise vocal guest or jazz musician will join Santana on stage while his energetic band provides percussive back-up. Highlights are "Black Magic Woman," "Oye Como Va," and a vigorous extended take on "Smooth," with adrenaline running rampant. Throughout, the rear screen and monitors project vintage footage of his celebrated 1969 Woodstock performance, as well as highlights of a four-decade life in music.

CONSUMER TIPS Three seating choices are available. In addition to mosh-pit general admission and theater-style seats in the mezzanine, which is 150 feet from the stage, the venue has been reconfigured with VIP cabaret tables that place listeners alongside the band. Santana likes to jam with visiting musicians, so check who else is playing Las Vegas when you purchase tickets. There's a good chance you might see him mixing it up with performing pals at his gig. Santana's website or the hotel's will list performance dates. Must be 18 to attend the show.

Carrot Top ★★★

APPEAL BY AGE	UNDER 21 ★★★★	21–37 ★★★★	38–50 ★★★	51+ ★★

HOST CASINO AND SHOWROOM Luxor—Atrium Showroom; ☎ 702-262-4400 or 800-557-7428; luxor.com

Type of show Stand-up comedy. **Admission** $55, $77 with dinner buffet. **Cast size** 1. **Night of lowest attendance** Thursday. **Usual showtimes** Wednesday–Monday, 8 p.m. **Dark** Tuesday. **Topless** Only Carrot Top. **Special comments** Must be 18 or older to attend. **Duration of presentation** 1 hour 40 minutes.

DESCRIPTION AND COMMENTS Fans of comedian Carrot Top will love this fast-paced, high-energy, quick-spurting comedy orgy that strikes many mature themes. The redhead makes extensive use of the special effects, lighting, and sound capabilities of the room. These heighten the experience far beyond the boundaries of standard nightclub stand-up fare. Pulling from large crates and even a washing machine, Carrot Top relies heavily on "homemade" props. His basic routine runs to "look at this" as he pulls strange thing after strange thing from the containers.

His humor is highly topical: rednecks, rock musicians, NASCAR, etc. Many of his quips are tasteless and offensive to various groups and persuasions, but the delivery is so fast and so brief that it's hard to take offense. In fact, his full-tilt boogie onslaught makes it difficult to stay with him, and you find yourself tuning out just to give your brain a respite. The pacing may prompt recall of the comedic delirium of Robin Williams. But whereas Williams explores our common humanity, Carrot Top fires bullets past the head that never touch the heart. His routines could be described as quickwitted, but not brainy. The 100-minute show includes a 15-minute opening act with another comedian. Dedicated fans will be delighted, but the uninitiated may find that Carrot Top's comedy degenerates too quickly to the bottom drawer.

CONSUMER TIPS Alcohol is not served in the theater. The theater is tiered, and seats (all with good sight lines) are preassigned. Bring along a few aspirins—you'll need them for your headache after the show.

Celine Dion ★★★★½

APPEAL BY AGE   UNDER 21 ★★★   21–37 ★★★★★   38–50 ★★★★★   51+ ★★★★★

HOST CASINO AND SHOWROOM Caesars Palace—Colosseum;
☎ 702-731-7110 or 877-423-5463; caesars.com/caesars-palace

Type of show Celebrity headliner. **Admission** $55–$250. **Cast size** 1 plus 31-piece orchestra and 4 back-up singers. **Night of lowest attendance** Midweek. **Usual Showtimes** Nights vary, 7:30 p.m. **Topless** No. **Duration of presentation** 90 minutes.

DESCRIPTION AND COMMENTS It takes a big voice and a bigger personality to fill the 4,300-seat Colosseum at Caesars Palace. Celine Dion is blessed with both, which she amply demonstrates in her return to Las Vegas. She is emotional and energetic, graceful and glamorous, exquisitely gowned, and at the top of her very sophisticated game. Dion's show is dazzling, with an extravagance of spectacular visuals, lights, and music surrounding her versatile five-octave range.

The powerful 31-piece orchestra and four backup singers sit on five separate mobile stages that reconfigure based on the music. Sometimes it's just the horns; other times, just the strings, a quartet, or a quintet as accompaniment.

Light panels beneath the orchestra change color depending on mood or theme. On the sides of the stage and extending over the audience are screens that depict family scenes or blaze with vibrant patterns of fire and fireworks, flowers, stardust, and hundreds of other 3-D images exploding toward the audience.

The set list is 20 songs followed by a wildly popular encore, which she sings atop a fountain cascading water in stunning designs. Visually gorgeous and aurally breathtaking, this upbeat and refined event is a class act from initial downbeat to final note.

CONSUMER TIPS Dion's engagement runs for three years, and she is contracted for 70 shows per year. She performs for 3–4 weeks, goes on a short hiatus, then returns again. Check with Caesars Palace or celinein vegas.com for show dates. There are good sight lines from every seat. Plus, the enormity of the stage and scope of the production make sitting close to the stage less than desirable, unless you intend to chat up Dion on potato-pancake recipes or some such. If you drive to Caesars, use the valet parking at the adjoining Forum Shops rather than the hotel-casino valet service at Caesars' main entrance. There is also valet service, as well as self-parking, at the rear of the hotel, with an entrance convenient to the theater. Give yourself lots of extra time to process through the metal detectors and bag-purse search at the entrance to the theater.

Chippendales ★★★★

| APPEAL BY AGE | 18-20 ★★★★ | 21-37 ★★★★ | 38-50 ★★★★ | 51+ ★★★½ |

HOST CASINO AND SHOWROOM Rio—The Chippendales Theatre; ☎ 702-777-7776 or 888-746-7784; riolasvegas.com

Type of show Male revue. Admission $70–$101. Cast size 12. Night of lowest attendance Monday. Usual showtimes Nightly, 8:30 and 10:30 p.m. Topless Yes (male). Duration of presentation 75 minutes.

DESCRIPTION AND COMMENTS *Chippendales* strives to be the ultimate ladies' night out and succeeds. The show, which originated in Los Angeles and celebrates its 40th anniversary in 2018, is a mesmerizing erotic exploration of female fantasies. Performed by a cast of one dozen flawless model types, the men of *Chippendales* exude sex appeal while acting out a sequence of 11 vignettes. Most of the tightly synchronized dance routines are performed to contemporary R & B slow jams, creating a seductive and sensual atmosphere. Unlike the comparatively tame *Thunder from Down Under*, the *Chippendales* dancers feign sex acts and remove their G-strings entirely at several times during the show (albeit only when the guys have their backs turned to the audience). Large video screens surround the 600-or-more-person showroom, offering a close-up view of the dancers, who can be difficult to see at times from the general-admission seating. The dancers also venture into the audience at various points throughout the performance, although not as much as the *Thunder* cast. After the show, the men of *Chippendales* host a meet-and-greet session.

CONSUMER TIPS On weekends tables are removed from the VIP/floor section to provide more seating, requiring guests to hold their drinks (which can be pricey, so be careful not to spill). The bathroom is located next to the Masquerade Bar, diagonally across the casino. Paying extra for floor seats is well worth it for ladies seeking the best view. A seating chart is available online.

CIRQUE DU SOLEIL SHOWS

CIRQUE DU SOLEIL has taken Las Vegas by storm. As of 2018, there are seven Cirque du Soleil productions playing Las Vegas showrooms. First to open was *Mystère* at TI, followed some years later by *"O"* at the Bellagio. The third show to premier was *Zumanity* at New York–New York, with *KÀ* at the MGM Grand following close on its heels in 2005. *Cirque's* production *LOVE*, based on the music of the Beatles, opened in

June of 2006; *Criss Angel Believe* (now *Mindfreak*) opened in September of 2008; and Cirque's latest effort, *Michael Jackson ONE,* opened in 2013, celebrates the music and dance of Michael Jackson.

If you've never seen a Cirque du Soleil show, understand that Cirque productions completely redefine and elevate circus as a genre. They feature the best and most original circus acts you're ever likely to see, but those acts are woven into a whole that includes beloved characters, stunning costuming, deep symbolism, poignant drama, cutting-edge theatrical technology, and original musical scores. If you've seen a Cirque traveling production and were awed, you won't believe what Cirque is capable of in its Las Vegas custom-built theaters.

KÀ, Mystère, LOVE, and *"O"* are representative of Cirque shows everywhere, albeit on a grand scale, and are appropriate for all ages. Also appropriate for families is *Michael Jackson ONE,* an acrobatic and choreographic spectacular. *Zumanity,* an in-your-face celebration of everything sexual, is much different from the other productions. *Criss Angel* likewise breaks the mold and has only staging, lighting, and costumes in common with the other shows. All Cirque shows provide an awe-inspiring evening of entertainment, so you really can't go too wrong (assuming, in the case of *Zumanity,* that you're comfortable with the sexual content).

How to Choose a Cirque du Soleil Show

In choosing a Cirque show, I suggest you start with *Mystère.* That's where it all began, and it's still the best. From there, let your taste guide you. If you're really into the Beatles or Michael Jackson, see *LOVE* or *ONE* next. *"O"* and *KÀ* feature unique technological stagecraft that is totally captivating. *Zumanity* celebrates all manner of sex. It's a great show, and steamier than any topless production in town, but don't see it with anyone you wouldn't feel comfortable watching soft porn with. Tickets for *Mystère* and *Zumanity* sell at $25–$45 less than for the other Cirque productions, making them by far the best value. For discounts on all seven shows, see lasvegasadvisor.com.

Below you will find reviews of all the Las Vegas Cirque du Soleil shows. This information will help you refine your choice of productions.

Cirque du Soleil's *Criss Angel MINDFREAK Live!* ★★★

APPEAL BY AGE **UNDER 21** ★★½ **21-37** ★★★ **38-50** ★★½ **51+** ★★

HOST CASINO AND SHOWROOM Luxor—Luxor Showroom; ☎ 702-262-4400 or 800-557-7428; luxor.com

Type of show Magic and illusion. **Admission** $65–$197. **Cast size** Angel, plus 2 live musicians and a dozen assistants. **Night of lowest attendance** Wednesday. **Usual showtimes** Wednesday–Sunday, 7 and 9:30 p.m. **Dark** Monday and Tuesday. **Topless** No. **Special comments** Not suitable for those under 12 years of age. **Duration of presentation** 90 minutes.

DESCRIPTION AND COMMENTS Criss Angel is an illusionist who, as an adolescent, studied mysticism, music, martial arts, and dance. Angel made his television debut in the 1994 ABC special *Secrets* and gained notoriety for his spooky aesthetic and surreal stunts, such as being trapped underwater in Times Square. Angel also created and starred in the A&E network series *Criss Angel Mindfreak,* which ran from 2005 to 2010.

Angel's first Vegas outing was an ill-fated collaboration with Cirque du Soleil called *Believe.* When *Believe* premiered in 2008, it was about a dream that took the form of a little morality play, the standard good-versus-evil thing except the bad guys were bunnies (I'm not making this up). Critics and the audience balked. Some wanted more Cirque du Soleil, while others wanted more Criss Angel. The producers straddled the fence for a long time, trying to please everyone. Ultimately, they decided to largely jettison the uniquely Cirque stuff and zero in on Angel, his illusions, and his escape artistry.

The result of this refocusing is *MINDFREAK Live!,* which opened in the summer of 2016. Although Cirque has almost completely erased its involvement with the show, with the acrobatics and dancing severely downplayed, some original elements remain, including the giant bunny sculptures on the proscenium, a superb hand-balancing demonstration, and some lovely illuminated arboreal scenery. Cirque also left its impressive technology behind to costar, including state-of-the-art LED lighting, pyrotechnics, advanced video projection mapping, and lasers. There's more humor in *MINDFREAK Live!,* courtesy of comic actors Mateo Amieva and Penny Wiggins, who can be annoying as well as funny; Wiggins is best known as the daffy ex-sidekick of The Amazing Johnathan. Magician Chloe Crawford also makes a welcome cameo, performing an impressive canine illusion in addition to being easy on the eyes (she formerly performed in the *Fantasy* topless revue at the Luxor).

Unfortunately, the primary focus in *MINDFREAK Live!,* as it was in *Believe,* is still Angel. The new show is more varied and lighter, but there remains a lethal dose of self-adulation, which starts with an interminable hagiographic preshow video. Angel is an average illusionist, but he's a world-class cheerleader—for himself. He struts around the stage and into the audience inviting adoration, and he's pretty in-your-face about it: "What? I can't hear you! Louder!" Loud and self-aggrandizing, he is the antithesis of Cirque's trademark subtlety and grace.

Angel may have created some amazing illusions in his time, but they're not on display in *MINDFREAK Live!.* In fact, almost all of his effects are just slight variations on tricks other magicians have been doing for years, from the hoary "Metamorphosis"—which Angel repurposes repeatedly—to his signature flying finale, which is merely a modification of David Copperfield's decades-old method. Occasionally he'll acknowledge the masters he's copying, such as when he re-creates Lance Burton's sword-fight routine. But most of the time, he seemingly wants audiences to believe he invented birthday-party basics, simply because he dressed them up with some black eye makeup. The only sin worse than Angel's indifferent execution of his innovation-free illusions is his emotionally manipulative exploitation of critically ill kids (including his own) through a climactic trick themed around childhood cancer—again, I'm not making this up.

CONSUMER TIPS Sitting near the stage occasionally requires you to turn around in your seat to see things going on overhead or behind you, though there isn't as much happening in the house since Cirque was sidelined. Views from the side sometimes spoil the illusion by letting you see the apparatus behind the tricks. The Luxor Theater is split into a front section and a rear section separated by a broad aisle. The best seats are in the first 10 rows in the center of the rear section. Because of the location of the showroom, it's just as convenient to park in Luxor's self-parking lot as it is to use valet.

Cirque du Soleil's *KÀ* ★★★★½

APPEAL BY AGE **UNDER 21** ★★★★ **21–37** ★★★★★ **38–50** ★★★★★ **51+** ★★★★★

HOST CASINO AND SHOWROOM MGM Grand—KÀ Theater;
☎ 702-891-7777 or 866-774-7117; mgmgrand.com

Type of show Fearsome ballet as epic journey. **Admission** Adults, $76–$251; children, $38–$83 (no tax or fees included). *Note:* Wheelchair-accessible seating available at all ticket levels. **Cast size** 80. **Night of lowest attendance** Wednesday. **Usual showtimes** Saturday–Wednesday, 7 and 9:30 p.m. **Dark** Thursday and Friday. **Topless** No. **Special comments** Guests age 12 and under permitted only if accompanied by an adult; no children under age 5. **Duration of presentation** 90 minutes.

DESCRIPTION AND COMMENTS *KÀ* is a departure for Cirque du Soleil in many ways. Most striking is the menacing atmosphere of the *KÀ* Theater. It has the look of an enchanted Asian foundry from space complete with 30-foot bursts of flame, performers hanging batlike from girders and scampering along catwalks, and industrial clangs reverberating as you find your seat. You are shown to your seat by one of many hair-raising Gatekeepers, who also serve as security during the show. (This reviewer would not advise breaking theater rules; it will be a Gatekeeper who sees to your punishment.) At the center of the theater, a gaping pit lurks where the stage would rightfully be. The overall effect, while chilling, isn't off-putting, but the proscription against very young children makes good sense.

KÀ is also unique in that it is the first Cirque production that attempts to tell a linear story that follows twins who have been separated and must each make a journey to meet their destiny. That journey is the focus of the show, and the twins travel through beaches, mountains, forests, and blizzards, face warriors and whimsical sea and forest creatures, and witness remarkable feats of strength and agility. All these, of course, completely overshadow the storytelling and relegate the story to something you're vaguely conscious of from time to time, but nothing more.

If there is a single star of *KÀ*, it is the gantry stage. From the pit emerges a large deck, supported by a boom, that is manipulated with computer precision to spin, tilt, raise, and lower throughout the show, all with surprising fluidity and speed. Not to knock the performers, who are as lithe and powerful as any cast of humans has a right to be, but the stage is an incredible industrial achievement. In one of the most breathtaking scenes, the stage tilts fully vertical as warriors loose arrows toward it and their intended victims scramble to find purchase. The arrows appear to stick in the stage, giving the "attacked" performers the handholds they need to dance and spin and flip their way up the vertical wall. As the performers ascend the wall, the "arrows" (which are actually 80 retractable pegs built into the stage) retract and the stage appears to shrug off the performers like so much detritus—an effect that is both unforgettable and disturbing.

In short, *KÀ* is a spectacle, and arguably the most technologically complex show in Las Vegas. The story line fails, but the production as a whole doesn't suffer from the loss. *KÀ* is a new breed of Cirque show, though it still contains the elements of all Cirque productions: elaborate costumes, haunting scores, physical prowess and beauty, and acrobatic feats. If you've already fallen hard for *Mystère*, *KÀ* may not be quite what you expect of a Cirque performance. While *KÀ* does display some of the whimsy of *Mystère,* the overall impression is shock, awe, and menacing power. If you are in a show-going mood, you can easily see both *KÀ* and *Mystère* in a single vacation without feeling over-Cirqued. In fact, we recommend it. *KÀ* is a fearsome production, and an elegant foil for the playful *Mystère.*

CONSUMER TIPS *KÀ* is a fine show—as virile and stirring as anything on the Strip—but the tariff is steep. Comparatively, though, the mid-priced seats are a better deal than similar seats at *"O,"* because *KÀ* Theater was thoughtfully designed without "limited-visibility" seats. *Note:* there are wheelchair-accessible seats in all three of the theater's ticketed sections.

If you do see *KÀ* and if you can manage to remember this tip with menacing creatures dangling overhead, arrows zipping at the performers, and a stage that's come shouldering to life in front of you, try to spot the three "performers" on stage who are actually technicians in costume.

Cirque du Soleil's *LOVE* ★★★★★

APPEAL BY AGE	UNDER 21 ★★★	21–37 ★★★★	38–50 ★★★★	51+ ★★★★★

HOST CASINO AND SHOWROOM Mirage—LOVE Theater; ☎ 702-792-7777 or 800-963-9634; mirage.com or cirquedusoleil.com/love

Type of show Circus based on music of the Beatles. **Admission** $87–$251. **Cast size** 60. **Night of lowest attendance** Monday. **Usual showtimes** Thursday–Monday, 7 and 9:30 p.m. **Dark** Tuesday and Wednesday. **Topless** No. **Duration of presentation** 90 minutes.

DESCRIPTION AND COMMENTS *LOVE*, like most Cirque du Soleil shows, is nothing if not an overwhelming spectacle. But this latest Cirque extravaganza is a definite departure from what might be loosely called the norm. First, it's heavily multimedia, combining extensive video effects projected onto a variety of screens with dancers, acrobats, and aerialists in outlandish costumes and bizarre props, all driven by the most powerful soundtrack ever, perhaps, produced. And because music, especially familiar music, is the force behind the visuals and theatrics, *LOVE* is grounded in a reality that the audience shares, which renders this show unified and accessible in a way that *Mystère* approximates, but that *"O,"* *Believe,* and even *KÀ* with its loose plot line, can never be.

That's not to imply, however, that *LOVE* doesn't have its extreme flights of fancy. The teaming of Cirque and the Beatles is, simply put, a marriage made in psychedelic heaven. Only Cirque could so effectively choreograph, costume, and showcase the characters, images, themes, humor, whimsicality, and all-around 1960s optimism, exuberance, and magic that the Beatles continue, 60 years later, to embody.

The show opens with a rousing rendition of "Get Back." Then it flashes back to begin a loose retrospective based on the Beatles' meteoric rise to become the most influential rock-and-roll band in history. "Eleanor Rigby" is set to theatrical scenes of the devastation that World War II wrought on the Beatles' Liverpool. "I Want to Hold Your Hand" introduces the collective planetary hysteria of Beatlemania. By now you know what you're in for. The stage, in pieces controlled by individual hydraulics, rises and falls as necessary. Visuals range from actual Beatles concerts and appearances to paisleys and spirals guaranteed to give (some of) you flashbacks. The music, which has been digitized and remixed by the late Sir George Martin (the fifth Beatle) and his son Giles, isn't exactly the same as on the LPs, as you might expect, and it's fun to listen for the little differences. The soundtrack consists of full songs, medleys, snippets of tunes down to a bar or two that disappear as soon as you recognize them, along with Beatles banter and fragments from recording sessions, plus suitably surreal transitions holding it all together. One thing's for sure: The acoustics are outstanding. More than 6,000 speakers surround you, with one installed in the backrest of every seat in the house.

Song after timeless song parades by. "Something in the Way She Moves" is accompanied by an aerial ballet; "Lucy in the Sky with Diamonds" is similar. The skit around "Blackbird" is hilarious, with spastic birds learning to fly. For "Strawberry Fields," big bubbles are blown from the top of a grand piano. "Octopus's Garden" has airborne squids and anemones. If you pay close attention, you'll catch new lyrics at the end of "While My Guitar Gently Weeps." Four skaters perform acrobatics on steep ramps to "Help," "Lady Madonna," "Here Comes the Sun," "Come Together," "Revolution Number Nine," "Back in the USSR," and "A Day in the Life"—ultimately, *LOVE* passes the true test of psychedelia: it doesn't matter if your eyes are open or closed.

For the finale, umbrellas spread confetti all over the room to "Hey Jude" and predictably, the show ends on "Sgt. Pepper's Lonely Hearts Club Band": "We hope you have enjoyed the show and we're sorry but it's time to go." The audience is sorry too. An encore of "All You Need Is Love" caps the evening. LOVE celebrated its 10th anniversary in 2017 with a major refresh that included colorfully redesigned costumes, an even more immersive sound system, and cutting-edge digital projections that appear to interact with the dancers. "I Am the Walrus" was swapped out for "Twist and Shout," and more energetic choreography was added throughout the production, making the entire experience even more ebullient without altering its essence.

CONSUMER TIPS *LOVE* plays in the space where Siegfried and Roy used to perform, but the theater underwent a mere $120 million worth of renovations. There's not a bad seat in the 2,000-seat theater-in-the-round, but the top $250 ticket might be too close. Since all the action occurs on the elevated stages and above, the eye-level mid-priced seats are better. You can't see *LOVE* anywhere else on the planet, folks, so be sure to buy your tickets as far in advance as possible. The concession stand sells bottled water, beer, wine, popcorn, and overpriced cocktails with Beatles-esque names.

Cirque du Soleil's *Michael Jackson ONE*   ★ ★ ★ ★ ★

APPEAL BY AGE   UNDER 21 ★ ★ ★ ★   21-37 ★ ★ ★ ★ ★   38-50 ★ ★ ★ ★ ★   51+ ★ ★ ★ ★ ★

HOST CASINO AND SHOWROOM Mandalay Bay—Michael Jackson ONE Theater; ☎ 702-632-7777 or 888-505-5211; mandalaybay.com

Type of show Cirque production show based on the music and dance of Michael Jackson. **Admission** $76–$210. **Cast size** 63. **Night of lowest attendance** Tuesday. **Usual showtimes** Friday–Tuesday, 7 and 9:30 p.m. **Dark** Sunday, Wednesday, and Thursday. **Topless** No. **Duration of presentation** 90 minutes.

DESCRIPTION AND COMMENTS Michael Jackson moonwalked off this mortal coil almost a decade ago, but the multifaceted idol's legacy as the King of Pop lives on in Cirque du Soleil's high-concept production, *Michael Jackson ONE*. Commemorating his vision and over-the-top talent, the dynamic staging combines the Cirque du Soleil and Michael Jackson brands in a spectacle of dance, gymnastic arts, and, of course, the timeless music. The cursory plot (which is relatively coherent by Cirque's standards) involves a quartet of friends who gate-crash Neverland Ranch to liberate Michael's iconic talismans: shoes, hat, microphone, and bedazzled glove. Galvanized by MJ's magical musical objects, they replicate his agility, courage, whimsical spirit, and love in their own lives. The protagonists are pursued throughout by trench coat–clad baddies representing the press and paparazzi. The paranoid demonization of the media, who supposedly "distorted and manipulated" Jackson's image, will raise eyebrows with anyone who gave credence to the many allegations made against the singer, but as a dramatic device it's effective in the context of the show.

The supple cast eerily recreates the Gloved One's idiosyncratic hip-hop and urban dance choreography (including the signature "Smooth Criminal" 45-degree lean), while video clips and symbols race across huge screens. Production values are lavish, with the latest complex theatrical technologies allowing acrobats to soar over the audience's heads, and pyrotechnics to punctuate key climaxes. Each seat has three built-in speakers to enhance the clarity of lyrics and melody. The King of Pop's voice has been extracted from his recordings and is remixed with a live band, featuring a striking Lady Gaga–esque lead guitarist. Standouts include: "Billie Jean," with the performers in LED suits accompanied by Jackson in archival footage; ghouls interacting with the audience during the gothic "Thriller"; the Pilobolus-style oversize shadow puppets of "What About Us?"; and "The Way You Make Me Feel," spotlighting powerful females ignoring the guys chasing them. Dancers perform wondrous tricks juggling hats, acrobats fly off slack lines and bungee from a Ferris wheel–like contraption, and the focus of "Man in the Mirror" is an incomparable dancing hologram of MJ (created though the same Musion technology used in Universal's Harry Potter attractions). Costumes reflect his glitzy taste, with an abundance of silver, gold, and crystal flash. The bold and strenuous athletic dance is interspersed with quietly conveyed messages of love, unity, and harmony during the few restrained segments. The show is vigorous, whimsical, sentimental, and bittersweet.

CONSUMER TIPS *ONE* begins precisely at the scheduled time; late-comers will not be seated while acrobats perform among the audience. You'll miss the panorama if you sit too close to the stage. No one younger than 5 is admitted, and those under 18 must be accompanied by an adult. Though both shows were directed by choreographer Kenny Ortega (who also created the posthumous *This Is It* concert film), this is a completely different production than Cirque's *Michael Jackson Immortal* arena tour of recent years. That show was essentially a dance concert with some acrobatics, while *ONE* is a fully integrated Cirque experience with all-new acts and effects specifically designed for the show's permanent venue at Mandalay Bay.

Valet parking is available at the rear (west) entrance. Self-parking at Mandalay Bay is relatively convenient to the showroom. From the rear (west) entrance to the casino, bear left past several restaurants and then continue left, passing the sports book en route. Although there are restrooms just outside the theater and a bar in the theater lobby, you'll save time by using the restroom and bar facilities in the main casino. Hold on to your ticket stub, you'll need it to get back into the theater.

Cirque du Soleil's *Mystère* ★★★★★

HOST CASINO AND SHOWROOM TI—Mystère Theater; ☎ 702-894-7722 or 800-392-1999; treasureisland.com

Type of show Circus as theater. **Admission** $76–$137. **Cast size** 72. **Night of lowest attendance** Tuesday. **Usual showtimes** Saturday–Wednesday, 7 and 9:30 p.m. **Dark** Thursday and Friday. **Special comments** No table service (no tables!). **Topless** No. **Duration of presentation** 90 minutes.

DESCRIPTION AND COMMENTS *Mystère* was the first permanent Cirque production in Las Vegas and the one that set the standard for all that followed. It is a far cry from a traditional circus but retains all of the fun and excitement. It is whimsical, mystical, and sophisticated, yet pleasing to all ages. The action takes place on an elaborate stage that incorporates almost every part of the theater. The original musical score is exotic, like the show.

To categorize it as a circus does not begin to cover its depth, though its performers could perform with distinction in any circus on earth. Cirque du Soleil is much more than a circus. It combines elements of classic Greek theater, mime, the English morality play, Dalí surrealism, Fellini characterization, and Chaplin comedy. *Mystère* is at once an odyssey, a symphony, and an exploration of human emotions. If this sounds overly intellectual, not to worry, Mystère is also the most fun show in the Cirque lineup. The show pivots on its humor, which is sometimes black, and engages the audience with its unforgettable characters. Though light and uplifting, it is also poignant and dark. Simple in its presentation, it is extraordinarily intricate, always operating on multiple levels of meaning. As you laugh and watch the amazingly talented cast, you become aware that your mind has entered a dimension seldom encountered in a waking state. The presentation begins to register in your consciousness more as a seamless dream than as a stage production. You are moved, lulled, and soothed as well as excited and entertained. The sensitive, the imaginative, the literate, and those who love good theater and art will find no show in Las Vegas that compares with *Mystère* except Cirque's sister productions.

CONSUMER TIPS Be forewarned that the audience is an integral part of *Mystère* and that at almost any time you might be plucked from your seat to participate. Our advice is to loosen up and roll with it. If you are too rigid, repressed, hung over, or whatever to get involved, politely but firmly decline to be conscripted.

Because *Mystère* is presented in its own customized showroom, there are no tables and, consequently, no drink service. In keeping with the show's circus theme, however, spectators may purchase refreshments at nearby concession stands.

In 2018, Cirque invited the public to free open rehearsal of the show each Saturday (3:30–4 p.m.). If it's still offered when you visit, be sure to go. You'll also have the chance to purchase a pair of tickets for an actual performance at a discounted rate upon presenting a voucher from the open rehearsal at the box office. All ages are welcome to attend; for more information, call the box office at ☎ 702-894-7722.

Cirque du Soleil's *"O"* ★ ★ ★ ★

HOST CASINO AND SHOWROOM Bellagio—"O" Theater; ☎ 702-693-7722 or 888-488-7111; bellagio.com

Type of show Circus and aquatic ballet as theater. **Admission** $108–$213 plus $14 service charge. **Cast size 74. Night of lowest attendance** Sunday. **Usual showtimes** Wednesday–Sunday, 7 and 9:30 p.m. **Dark** Monday and Tuesday. **Topless** No. **Special comments** Guests age 18 and under permitted only if accompanied by an adult. **Duration of presentation** 1 hour and 45 minutes.

DESCRIPTION AND COMMENTS The title *"O"* is a play on words derived from the concept of infinity, with 0 (zero) as its purest expression, and from the phonetic pronunciation of *eau,* the French word for water. Both symbols are appropriate, for the production (like all Cirque shows) creates a timeless dream state and (for the first time in a Cirque show) also incorporates an aquatic dimension that figuratively and literally evokes all of the meanings, from baptism to boat passage, that water holds for us. The foundation for the spectacle that is *"O"* resides in a set (more properly an aquatic theater) that is no less than a technological triumph. Before your eyes, in mere seconds, the hard, varnished surface of the stage transforms seamlessly into anything from a fountain to a puddle to a vast pool. Where only moments ago acrobats tumbled, now graceful water ballerinas surface and make way for divers somersaulting down from above. The combined effect of artists and environment is so complete and yet so transforming that it's almost impossible to focus on specific characters, details, or movements. Rather there is a global impact that envelops you and holds you suspended. In the end you have a definite sense that you *felt* what transpired rather than having merely seen it.

Though *"O"* is brilliant by any standard and pregnant with beauty and expression, it lacks just a bit of the humor, accessibility, and poignancy of Cirque's *Mystère* at TI. Where *"O"* crashes over you like a breaking wave, *Mystère* is more personal, like a lover's arrow to the heart. If you enjoyed *Mystère,* however, you will also like *"O,"* and vice versa. What's more, the productions, while sharing stylistic similarities, are quite different. Though you might not want (or be able to afford) to see them both on the same Las Vegas visit, you wouldn't feel like you saw the same show twice if you did.

CONSUMER TIPS If you've never seen any of the Las Vegas Cirque du Soleil productions, we recommend catching *Mystère* first. It is more representative of Cirque du Soleil's hallmark presentation and tradition.

If you want to go, buy your tickets before you leave home. If you decide to see *"O"* at the spur of the moment, try the box office about 30 minutes before showtime. Sometimes seats reserved for comped gamblers will be released for sale.

Cirque du Soleil's *Zumanity* ★ ★ ★ ★

HOST CASINO AND SHOWROOM New York–New York—Zumanity Theatre; ☎ 702-740-6815 or 866-606-7111; newyorknewyork.com or zumanity.com

Type of show A risqué Cirque du Soleil. **Admission** $76–$191; duo sofas also available at $129 (sold in pairs). **Cast size 50. Night of lowest attendance** Wednesday. **Usual**

showtimes Friday–Tuesday, 7 and 9:30 p.m. **Dark** Wednesday and Thursday. **Topless** Yes. **Special comments** For ages 18 and over due to adult themes and nudity. **Duration of presentation** 90 minutes.

DESCRIPTION AND COMMENTS *Zumanity* is about love, emotional and physical, in all its unrequited, sated, comedic, tender, and lunatic dimensions. It is also the first Cirque production to chart a decidedly adult course. As it turns out, Cirque does love and sex as well as it does everything else, and *Zumanity* is a hell of a ride.

Zumanity is zany, raucous, and decidedly outrageous. It is lovable in its humor and insightful in its understanding of sex. The visually rich production blends its challenging theme with Cirque du Soleil's signature music, color, acrobatics, and dance. *Zumanity* is sometimes very tender but at other moments hard-edged. It urges us to look at how we define human beauty and makes a plea for the acceptance of differences. *Zumanity* delivers a powerful message.

Like all Cirque productions, *Zumanity* is hauntingly dreamlike. But where other Cirque shows operate on multiple levels of meaning and interpretation, *Zumanity* tells us in unambiguous terms that sex is amazing, infinitely varied, and wonderful. As the production unfolds, you witness an artful sequence of sexual vignettes celebrating heterosexual sex, gay sex, masturbation, sex between obese lovers, sex with midgets, group sex, sadomasochistic sex, and sex enjoyed by the very old. As the name *Zumanity* implies, sex (and the varied emotions we bring to it) is a defining element of our humanity. Sex is happy, sex is sad, sex is of the moment, sex is transcendent, sex is funny, sex is bewildering. And as *Zumanity* so ably demonstrates, sex is a window into our essential being.

Now, after digesting the above, you might be thinking that's one window you're uncomfortable peering into, that you really don't need to know all that much about our essential being. But there's also this nagging impulse to take a little peek. You might even want to take a big peek, but aren't sure it's a good idea with your wife, mother, or father-in-law sitting beside you. That's the genius of *Zumanity:* it forces you to confront your own sexuality, including your hangups—all in the presence of your friends, family, and possibly your own lover (plus, of course, 1,200 strangers). For some it's very disquieting, even frightening. Tension is palpable. Some shift continuously in their seats. They laugh a bit too loud at the jokes, try to appear unaffected by the orgasmic groaning, pretend they're quite accustomed to leather and whips, and attempt to will themselves not to be aroused. Most people, however, will find *Zumanity* to be exhilarating, and more than a few find it absolutely liberating.

CONSUMER TIPS *Zumanity* is brilliant, but clearly not for everyone. Certainly, it's not for prudes, the sexually repressed, or the sexually phobic. Equally, it's not for the gentlemen's-club set. *Zumanity* is altogether too complex, cerebral, and theatrical for their taste. Give some thought to who you see *Zumanity* with and make sure they know what they're getting into. Many readers have reported being so preoccupied with the reaction of their companion that they couldn't enjoy the show.

The production is staged in a 1,256-custom-seat, custom-designed showroom that facilitates a performer–audience intimacy remarkable for a theater so large and for a production of *Zumanity*'s scope. With the exception of some first-floor seats that make viewing aerial acts impossible, sight lines are excellent. The best seats are on the lower-floor center and about 12 rows or more back. As with all Cirque du Soleil shows, audience members are at risk of being hauled into the performance.

Clint Holmes and Earl Turner—*Soundtrack: Your Songs. Our Stories. The Show* ★★★½

APPEAL BY AGE	UNDER 21 ★★	21-37 ★★½	38-50 ★★★	51+ ★★★½

HOST CASINO AND SHOWROOM Westgate—Westgate International Theater; ☎ 800-222-5361; westgateresorts.com/hotels/nevada/las-vegas

Type of show Nostalgic music concert. **Admission $48–$98. Cast size** 3 plus 8 live musicians. **Night of lowest attendance** Thursday. **Usual showtimes** Thursday–Saturday, 7 p.m. **Dark** Sunday–Wednesday. **Duration of presentation** 90 minutes.

DESCRIPTION AND COMMENTS Earl Turner is a Las Vegas homie and a classy entertainer who sings, dances, and spins a good yarn. He has teamed up with longtime Vegas veteran Clint Holmes, whose signature is weaving heartfelt autobiographical storytelling into his show, including thoughts about his biracial identity. The show is a sweet reminiscence of songs that call up special memories. Holmes and Turner are augmented by songstress Serena Henry, who has performed with Gladys Knight, and a live eight-piece band. The show feels touchy-feely, and is, but it's laced with humor and is totally high-energy. The show features songs from Bruno Mars, Blake Shelton, Bill Withers, Irving Berlin, Michael Jackson, Prince, Stevie Wonder, and Al Green, among others.

CONSUMER TIPS This is a good family show, though younger viewers will not have the same emotional attachment to the music as older patrons. Westgate International Theater is a perfect venue for this kind of show. Also, the Westgate has a monorail station, so commuting from the east side of the strip is a breeze.

The Comedy Lineup ★★★

APPEAL BY AGE	UNDER 21 ★★★	21-37 ★★★½	38-50 ★★★	51+ ★★★

HOST CASINO AND SHOWROOM Harrah's—Harrah's Showroom; ☎ 855-234-7469 or 702-777-2782; caesars.com/harrahs-las-vegas

Type of show Stand-up comedy. **Admission $37–$99. Cast size** 2. **Night of lowest attendance** Monday. **Usual showtimes** Thursday–Monday, 10 p.m. **Dark** Tuesday and Wednesday. **Topless** No. **Duration of presentation** TBD.

DESCRIPTION AND COMMENTS Comedians Tom Green and John Caparulo have teamed up at Harrah's Showroom. Green performs Sunday and Monday nights, and Caparulo performs Thursday–Saturday.

Green, a groundbreaking prankster who was an MTV mainstay in the early 1990s, comes to Harrah's from a short-lived solo residency at Bally's. His set features a nostalgic look at video footage from his glory days, when he was making feature films and being name-dropped by Eminem, along with topical observations from his current career as a touring comic. Fans of Green should get a charge out of seeing rare clips, and his fresh material has some bite, but off-kilter pacing often quashes his jokes' momentum, and those who aren't longtime followers may find his reminiscing rather sad.

Caparulo, best known for his recurring role as the "under-dressed everyman" on E!'s *Chelsea Lately*, has appeared on *The Tonight Show* and *Jimmy*

Kimmel Live!, as well as hosted his own Netflix special. Caparulo tells personal stories about marriage and fatherhood, usually with a profane punchline.

CONSUMER TIPS All seats are preassigned, with theater-style seating close to the stage. Tables and booths toward the back are tiered for good sight lines.

Crazy Girls ★★★

APPEAL BY AGE	UNDER 21 –	21-37 ★★★½	38-50 ★★★½	51+ ★★★½

HOST CASINO AND SHOWROOM Planet Hollywood—Sin City Theater;
☎ 702-777-2782; caesars.com/planet-hollywood

Type of show Erotic dance and adult comedy. **Admission** $51–$91. **Cast size** 8. **Night of lowest attendance** Monday. **Usual showtimes** Thursday–Tuesday, 9:30 p.m. **Dark** Wednesday. **Topless.** Yes. **Duration of presentation** 75 minutes.

DESCRIPTION AND COMMENTS After celebrating its 28th anniversary, *Crazy Girls* relocated to Planet Hollywood in 2015 following the closure of the Riviera. The transition was complicated by the theft of *Crazy Girls*'s sets, props, and costumes. Fortunately, the show's primary assets are personal and always in the possession of their owners. As at the Riv, the Planet Hollywood version gets right to the point. This is a no-nonsense show for men who do not want to sit through trained dogs, magicians, and half the score from *Oklahoma!* before they see naked women. The focus is on seven engaging, talented, and athletically built young ladies who bump and grind through more than an hour of exotic dance and comedy. The choreography is pretty creative and set to a diverse soundtrack stretching from Peggy Lee and Sophie Tucker classics to Led Zeppelin and booty-shaking rap. Most numbers are lip-synced, but a handful (including *Crazy Girls*'s custom-written theme song) are sung live. The dancers are emceed by a crude comedian who brings the otherwise fast-paced show to a grinding halt with a mercifully brief magic act. *Crazy Girls* is a notch classier than the X family of striptease shows, and the girls exhibit a sense of humor along with their skin.

CONSUMER TIPS The show is not as risqué as the X burlesque shows; the nudity does not go beyond topless and G-strings, and for many segments those tops stay on until the last moment. While most of the show has little that would make women or couples uncomfortable, some of the later acts (obviously inserted to update the production) push the envelope further with lesbian action, bondage themes, and a giant ejaculating penis pillow. If hearing the explicitly zoophilic lyrics to Nine Inch Nails's "Closer" blasted at full volume makes you squirm, you have been warned.

Sin City Theater has a flat floor and a short runway bisecting the audience. Up-close VIP seating, available for old farts who forgot their glasses, gets you a priority entry line and a cocktail table. The girls line up for a photo op after the show, but you'll have to fork over $20 to use your own camera.

Criss Angel MINDFREAK Live! by Cirque du Soleil
(see pages 209–211)

David Copperfield ★★★★

APPEAL BY AGE	UNDER 21 ★★★★	21-37 ★★★★	38-50 ★★★★	51+ ★★★★

HOST CASINO AND SHOWROOM MGM Grand—David Copperfield Theater;
☎ 702 891-7777; mgmgrand.com

Type of show Illusion and magic. **Admission** $78–$240. **Cast size** 1. **Night of lowest attendance** Thursday. **Usual showtimes** Nightly, 7 and 9:30 p.m. plus 4 p.m. Saturday matinee. **Dark** None. **Topless** No. **Duration of presentation** 90 minutes.

DESCRIPTION AND COMMENTS David Copperfield has been the preeminent illusionist in Las Vegas for decades, including the Siegfried and Roy era. Lance Burton could give Copperfield a run for his money when it came to showmanship and sleight of hand, but Copperfield has always set the standard for originality and creativity. Magic and illusion shows in Las Vegas wrote the book on redundancy. Regardless whose name was on the marquee, one magic show was pretty much like the next. Production values varied wildly, ranging from Siegfried and Roy's extravaganzas to the modest Showgirls of Magic (whose show could fit on a 12-x-12-foot stage), but the content was largely the same. We reviewed show after show and could barely keep them straight. That is, except for Copperfield.

Copperfield performs as a celebrity headliner, so he isn't in town all the time. Whenever we review him, however, we know we're seeing the illusions that the other magicians will try to emulate a year or two down the road. Like the other guys, Copperfield puts things in boxes or behind curtains and makes them disappear. But jaded reviewers aside, audiences still love that stuff, and even here Copperfield tops the competition. In one such illusion he selects 13 audience members at random and puts them in what looks like a suspended jury box and then makes them vanish. If you're wondering about animals that eat people, Copperfield eschews them in favor of a modest white duck.

Another Copperfield trademark is making use of his audience, as many as 40 of them in a given performance! Sometimes he selects them individually, and sometimes he tosses a number of large inflatable balls into the audience—if you catch one consider yourself conscripted. Illusions range from passing through a steel plate, to making a vintage auto appear, to sleight of hand only inches from an audience volunteer. Elaborate illusions, including walking through an industrial fan and guessing a lottery number, are punctuated with simpler, less prop-dependent illusions. Copperfield works alone (except for a crew who moves his heavy contraptions) and engages the audience in a nearly continuous repartee and chatter. The pace is measured and includes several illusions with lengthy (and sometimes schmaltzy) narratives.

CONSUMER TIPS Copperfield works hard cranking out a full 90-minute show, including encores. The David Copperfield Theater, located along the south wall of the main casino, is a perfect venue for Copperfield with good sight lines supplemented by large LED screens showing all the action. Except for cushy high-roller booths, seating is cramped at banquet tables and little round four-tops. Waitstaff take orders for an extensive and expensive selection of drinks before the show. The nearest restroom is in another zip code away and gone in the casino.

David Goldrake *Imaginarium* ★★★★

APPEAL BY AGE	UNDER 21 ★★★★	21-37 ★★★★	38-50 ★★★★	51+ ★★★★

HOST CASINO AND SHOWROOM At press time, *Imaginarium* closed at The Trop, but we expect the show will find a new home soon.

Type of show Magic. **Admission** $46–$115. **Cast size** 5. **Night of lowest attendance** NA. **Usual showtimes** Pending relocation. **Dark** NA. **Topless** No. **Special comments** Kids age 12 and under admitted for free with paying adult. **Duration of presentation** 75 minutes.

DESCRIPTION AND COMMENTS Luxembourg native David Goldrake says his show "is not about being spectacular. It's about being beautiful and touching people." That's a pretty accurate assessment. *Imaginarium* isn't the edgiest or most innovative magic show on the Strip. Most of Goldrake's illusions are fairly formulaic—objects and people appear, disappear, and reappear inside other objects—but he has a few advantages over his conjuring competition. One, he's extremely personable and easily establishes rapport with his audience. Two, his production gets an A for aesthetics, with 3-D projection mapping augmenting the steampunk set for a mise-en-scène that evokes films such as *Moulin Rouge* and *The Imaginarium of Doctor Parnassus.* Three, Goldrake's quartet of assistants are far more than pretty faces who stand around waiting to be sawed in half; each is a talented dancer and acrobat, executing athletic choreography on the ground and in the air with flair. Finally, as stylish as the transitions are, Goldrake's variations on classic illusions are the real deal, highlighted by his heart-stopping re-creation of Houdini's water torture escape and a walking-through-a-wall effect that improves on David Copperfield's famous version. If you're looking for competence and showmanship, Goldrake has both, and he's blessedly not in your face like Criss Angel, making him our favorite new illusionist in town.

CONSUMER TIPS *Imaginarium* is a good family show (with an occasional PG-13 wink to the adults). Also, the show's previous host casino, the Trop, was a smaller and less-daunting hotel than the Luxor (Criss Angel) or MGM Grand (David Copperfield). Because of Goldrake's close work, the production works best in a medium to small venue. Raked seating is important, however. Wherever *Imaginarium* pops up, check to make sure the venue is not flat-floored.

Defending the Caveman ★★★½

APPEAL BY AGE	UNDER 21 ★★	21-37 ★★★★	38-50 ★★★★	51+ ★★★★

HOST CASINO AND SHOWROOM The D—The D Showroom;
☎ 702-328-1111; thed.com

Type of show Stand-up comedy. **Admission** $47–$78. **Cast size** 1. **Night of lowest attendance** Monday. **Usual showtimes** Nightly, 8:40 p.m. **Dark** None. **Topless** No. **Duration of presentation** 80 minutes.

DESCRIPTION AND COMMENTS Veteran stand-up comic Kevin Burke stars in this insightful and clever exploration of how men and women relate. Written by Rob Becker, *Defending the Caveman* was the longest-running solo play in the history of Broadway. In addition to the ongoing gig at The D, eight other comics take the production on the road all across the country. Great material coupled with flawless timing and super delivery make for an excellent evening's entertainment. Dealing with sexuality, contemporary feminism, masculine sensitivity, and why women have more shoes than men, it's *Men Are from Mars, Women Are from Venus* on laughing gas.

CONSUMER TIPS The show is a rare bargain among Las Vegas productions these days. Be forewarned that the show is pretty blue. If you're easily offended, you're better off with Donny and Marie. One detractor posted a comment on the internet that "Cave Man is a one-man show and all he does is talk about relationships." Well, hello? We can't think of another topic that offers a comedian more grist for the mill. Also, you will discover that your gender-influenced behaviors are not unique to you and will be trotted out in all their embarrassing dimensions. Throughout the show you'll hear people whisper, "George, that's exactly what you do!" or "Sally, he absolutely has you nailed."

Donny and Marie ★★★★

APPEAL BY AGE   UNDER 21 ★★★★   **21-37** ★★★★   **38-50** ★★★★½   **51+** ★★★★½

HOST CASINO AND SHOWROOM Flamingo—Flamingo Showroom;
☎ 702-733-3333 or 800-221-7299; caesars.com/flamingo-las-vegas

Type of show Celebrity headliner. **Admission** $95–$260. **Cast size** 19. **Night of lowest attendance** Wednesday. **Usual showtimes** Tuesday–Saturday, 7:30 p.m. **Dark** Sunday and Monday. **Topless** No. **Duration of presentation** 90 minutes.

DESCRIPTION AND COMMENTS Donny and Marie Osmond demonstrate the same chemistry that made them irresistible on TV in the 1970s and late 1990s—and both still have their chops. The production showcases their hits (mostly Donny's) like "Puppy Love," "Soldier of Love," and "Go Away, Little Girl," but also includes enough contemporary and Broadway tunes that you don't founder on Memory Lane. Marie provides the most surprises, strutting her stuff with torch songs and revealing her sensual side as she vamps around the stage. She even tosses in a little opera. There are lots of duets, but each also performs alone, and yes, they still do that brother-sister ribbing and arguing thing, and their fans still eat it up. They're backed by a nine-piece live band and eight very modestly attired dancers. Production values are high with compelling sets and a lot of nostalgic video footage.

CONSUMER TIPS The Flamingo Showroom is a good venue for this production, with good sight lines and the kind of intimacy desirable in a celebrity headliner show. The showroom has always had a hard time getting people in and seated expeditiously, so come prepared to wait in line to enter. As with Wayne Newton and other performers over the years, we've had readers recount being dragged to Donny and Marie by their spouse or friend and being blown away by the quality and energy of the performance. And, as you'd expect, Donny and Marie put on as squeaky clean a show as you'll find in Las Vegas, making it a great choice for the under-21 crowd.

Fantasy ★★★

APPEAL BY AGE   UNDER 21 -   **21-37** ★★★   **38-50** ★★★   **51+** ★★★

HOST CASINO AND SHOWROOM Luxor—Atrium Showroom;
☎ 702-262-4400 or 800-557-7428; luxor.com

Type of show Topless dance-and-comedy revue. **Admission** $43–$65. **Cast size** 13. **Night of lowest attendance** Tuesday. **Usual showtimes** Nightly, 10:30 p.m. **Dark** None. **Topless** Yes. **Special comments** Must be age 18 or older to attend. **Duration of presentation** 90 minutes.

DESCRIPTION AND COMMENTS Speculate on the anthropological reasons why the American appetite for female breasts is a cultural staple. *Fantasy,* possibly the Strip's most artistic topless show, satisfies this hunger in a tasteful, glamorous way in this smorgasbord of sexual scenarios. The cast consists of eight very adept dancers, power vocalist Jaime Lynch, and comedian Sean Cooper. Rubber bondage, dominatrix office-politics, and light lesbianism are a few of the erotic offerings, none of which ever reach raunchy, which is perhaps why the audience includes many women. Breasts are indeed revealed early on in the show, but not every number is topless. The office scene, for example, is performed chiefly in men's business suits. The Las Vegas feeling of high production values with sets, lights, smoke, and bass-filled sound is certainly there to support the well-executed Bob Fosse–style choreography. While the sexually suggestive theme runs strongly throughout, most of the numbers could stand on their own without the topless element. It should be noted that some *Fantasy* cast members depicted in ads are no longer with the show.

CONSUMER TIPS Staged in the same fairly intimate room as Carrot Top's show, you can be pulled on stage if you are a man sitting in the first row or two. Row D offers the most leg room.

Frank Marino's *Divas Las Vegas* ★★★

APPEAL BY AGE	UNDER 21 ★★½	21-37 ★★★½	38-50 ★★★½	51+ ★★★

HOST CASINO AND SHOWROOM At press time, Frank Marino closed at The LINQ Hotel & Casino, but we expect the show will find a new home soon.

Type of show Cross-dressing celebrity impersonator show. **Admission** $28–$109. **Cast size** 14. **Night of lowest attendance** NA. **Usual showtimes** Pending relocation. **Topless** No. **Duration of presentation** 75 minutes.

DESCRIPTION AND COMMENTS Frank Marino, who ages at the same rate as Tina Turner, has been heading boys-will-be-girls shows in Las Vegas for decades. Doing his signature impression of Joan Rivers, Marino presides over a high-tempo revue where the guys impersonate such stars as Cher, Diana Ross, Beyoncé, Britney Spears, Madonna, and Dolly Parton. A crew of dancers, also men playing dress-up, give the presentation the feel of a quirky production show.

Some of the impersonators are convincing and pretty enough to fool just about anyone. Their costumes reveal slender, feminine arms and legs and hourglass figures. Other performers, however, look like who they are—men in drag. The cast performs with great self-effacement and gives the impression that nobody is expected to take things too seriously. As one impersonator quipped, "This is a hell of a way for a 40-year-old man to earn a living."

Divas is solid entertainment. It is also pretty popular and plays to appreciative straight audiences. If you're broad-minded and looking for something different, give it a try.

CONSUMER TIPS This is a show where you want to pass on VIP seats—the illusion is much more effective if you are back a little. The production works best in a small showroom.

Gordie Brown Live ★★★½

HOST CASINO AND SHOWROOM Hooters—Hooters Night Owl Showroom;
☎ 866-LV-HOOTS; hooterscasinohotel.com

Type of show Impressions with music and comedy. **Admission** $55–$66. **Cast size** 8. **Night of lowest attendance** Wednesday. **Usual showtimes** Sunday, Monday, Wednesday, Thursday, and Saturday, 7 p.m. **Dark** Tuesday and Friday. **Topless** No. **Duration of presentation** 90 minutes.

DESCRIPTION AND COMMENTS Impressionists are almost as ubiquitous as showgirls in Las Vegas, so we weren't expecting anything special from Gordie Brown. *Wrong!* His is the operational definition of a sleeper show. Brown sets the house on fire with his impressions, musicianship, and humor. Backed by a turbo-energized live band, Brown moves along at a gallop impersonating such artists as Travis Tritt, Roy Orbison, Willie Nelson, Paul Simon, Billy Joel, Henry Fonda, MC Hammer, and Frank Sinatra. Aside from nailing the voices and mannerisms of his celebrity subjects, Brown has an uncanny chameleon-like ability to change his countenance to actually look like them. Brown is at his best when he's moving quickly. Unfortunately, he has a pronounced tendency, particularly with his comedy, to drive a routine into the ground. As you would expect, trying to ride a horse that's been dead for 10 minutes isn't good for a show's momentum. Sooner or later though, Brown will plug the holes in his act.

CONSUMER TIPS Gordie Brown earned his stripes at the Golden Nugget and, after gigs at the V Theater and Venetian, has settled into this inconspicuous showroom directly across from the Steak 'n Shake. The floor is flat, but the stage is high enough to compensate for the lack of seat risers.

Hitzville The Show ★★★

HOST CASINO AND SHOWROOM Miracle Mile Shops—V Theater;
☎ 866-932-1818; vtheaterboxoffice.com

Type of show Motown music concert. **Admission** $60–$75. **Cast size** 14. **Night of lowest attendance** Tuesday. **Usual showtimes** Monday–Saturday, 5:30 p.m. **Dark** Sunday. **Topless** No. **Duration of presentation** 80 minutes.

DESCRIPTION AND COMMENTS This no-frills production offers a tight playlist of Motown hits competently performed by the four-man group Fair Play and a female group of four featuring Jin Jin Reeves. Reeves, the show's headliner, is equally at home with a ballad or blowing out the windows with a Gladys Knight or Tina Turner classic. A live five-piece band backs all of the vocalists. It's well paced, well executed, and overall a good night's entertainment. It may be overpriced for a show with such minimalist production values, but the music won't disappoint.

CONSUMER TIPS The V Theater is in the Miracle Mile Shops adjacent to Planet Hollywood. The box office is routinely undermanned, so arrive early if you're buying tickets or collecting them from will call. If driving, park in the Miracle Mile Shops self-parking garage as close to the door leading into the shops as possible. After entering the shopping complex, turn right to the V Theater.

Human Nature Jukebox ★★★★

HOST CASINO AND SHOWROOM The Venetian—Sands Showroom;
☎ 702-414-9000; venetian.com

Type of show Motown musical tribute. **Admission** $73–$128. **Cast size** 10 including the band. **Night of lowest attendance** Wednesday. **Usual showtimes** Tuesday–Saturday, 7:30 p.m. **Dark** Sunday and Monday. **Topless** No. **Duration of presentation** 80 minutes.

DESCRIPTION AND COMMENTS *Human Nature* is an Australian vocal group, produced by Motown legend Smokey Robinson. Hugely popular down under, the group has racked up a number of multiplatinum albums and charted 17 Top-40 hits and 5 top-10 singles in wallaby land. Their first American album was released in 2009. Featuring the harmonies of Toby Allen, Phil Burton, Andrew Tierney, and Michael Tierney, *Human Nature* presents a high-energy musical field trip down Motown's Memory Lane. They nail the Motown sound as well as the smooth moves (their showmanship was honed opening for Celine Dion and Michael Jackson, respectively), a singular accomplishment for four white guys from Australia. They are backed by a live band.

CONSUMER TIPS The Sands Showroom is located on the main floor of the shopping plaza that connects The Venetian and The Palazzo. It's a perfect venue for *Human Nature Jukebox,* and the best seats can be found in the last four rows of the lower section. The showroom is convenient to Venetian self-parking, though finding your way from the garage to the theater can be challenging the first time.

Inferno: The Fire Spectacular ★★★★

HOST CASINO AND SHOWROOM Paris Las Vegas—Paris Theater;
☎ 855-234-7469; caesars.com/paris-las-vegas

Type of show Special effects tour de force supplementing magic and illusion. **Admission** $71–$165. **Cast size** 6 plus stage hands. **Night of lowest attendance** Wednesday. **Usual showtimes** Wednesday–Sunday, 9:30 p.m. **Dark** Monday and Tuesday. **Topless** No. **Duration of presentation** 75 minutes.

DESCRIPTION AND COMMENTS *Inferno* describes itself as a "a gasoline-soaked spectacular," which you'll understand isn't PR talk if you sit in the first 10 rows. At heart, *Inferno* is a magic-and-illusion production centered on the use of fire as the differentiating element. Starring Swedish illusionist Joe Labero, the show is a pyrotechnical rampage. Labero's illusions are classic, presented with wit and warmth (no pun intended), and deftly performed (Imagine Siegfried & Roy making an elephant disappear while it blows flames from its trunk—example only, no elephants involved). Ably assisting Labero, and sometimes stealing the show, are the Fuel Girls, who got their start touring Europe with punk rockers. Athletic and easy on the eye, they juggle flaming props, handle swords and whips engulfed in flames, and assist Labero with his illusions. A standout among the Fuel Girls is Teta Stone, who performs pointe ballet while twirling the fiery skeletal frame of an umbrella. For comic relief, Ronnie Nilsson portrays a Quasimodo-like character named Animal who is nuts for gasoline. His big trick is submerging in a tub of the stuff that the Fuel Girls (naturally) set ablaze.

CONSUMER TIPS Though flammable chemicals are a mainstay, fumes are negligible, barely noticeable even in the first row. The Paris Theater is a great showroom for any production show. Lines of sight are excellent, and the seats are plush and comfortable. Restrooms are handy in a corridor connecting the theater with the casino. If you use Paris paid self-parking, be aware that payments are processed at automated kiosks located near the garage elevators. The number of kiosks is totally insufficient to handle the wave of departing showgoers. Be prepared to wait as long as 30 minutes to pay.

JABBAWOCKEEZ ★★★★

APPEAL BY AGE UNDER 21 ★★★★ 21-37 ★★★★ 38-50 ★★★½ 51+ ★★½

HOST CASINO AND SHOWROOM MGM Grand—Jabbawockeez Theater;
☎ 702-891-3577; mgmgrand.com

Type of show Ultra-hip-hop dance production. **Admission** $55–$120. **Cast size** 12.
Night of lowest attendance Monday. **Usual showtimes** Thursday–Monday, 7 and 9:30
p.m. **Dark** Tuesday and Wednesday. **Topless** No. **Duration of presentation** 75 minutes.

DESCRIPTION AND COMMENTS JABBAWOCKEEZ is an all-male modern-dance troupe disguised, or more correctly, rendered indistinguishable by masks and loose-fitting clothes. The frenetic production features some of the best break and robotic dancing around. Sprinkle in some mime, humor, and a pulsing hip-hop score and you have one of the freshest and most energetic shows to hit Las Vegas in a long time.

The crew was introduced to a national audience on *America's Got Talent* and later won Season 1 of *America's Best Dance Crew.* The masks create an overall homogeneous appearance, more or less forcing you to zero in on the choreography as a whole as opposed to being seduced by the looks and talents of any individual performer. The troupe's name is derived from the nonsense-verse poem "Jabberwocky" by Lewis Carroll. Interestingly, as per the JABBAWOCKEEZ name, if you don't understand the show, then by George, you've got it! That's the idea, as expressed by the Lewis Carroll character Alice (from *Through the Looking Glass*) after reading "Jabberwocky."

"'It seems very pretty,' she said when she had finished it, 'but it's rather hard to understand!' (You see she didn't like to confess, even to herself, that she couldn't make it out at all.) 'Somehow it seems to fill my head with ideas—only I don't exactly know what they are!'"

Bottom line, don't burn out your circuits trying to make sense of JABBAWOCKEEZ, just enjoy.

CONSUMER TIPS Anyone who enjoys modern dance will like JABBAWOCKEEZ. Beyond that, however, appreciation divides along chronological lines, with those under 40 wildly enthusiastic and those older than 40 pretty much mystified.

Jen Kramer: *The Magic of Jen Kramer* ★★★★

APPEAL BY AGE UNDER 21 ★★★★ 21-37 ★★★★ 38-50 ★★★★ 51+ ★★★★

HOST CASINO AND SHOWROOM Westgate—Westgate Cabaret;
☎ 800-222=5361; westgateresorts.com/hotels/nevada/las-vegas

Type of show Magic and illusion. **Admission** $20–$30. **Cast size** 4. **Night of lowest attendance** Wednesday. **Usual showtimes** Wednesday–Saturday, 6 p.m. **Dark** Sunday–Tuesday. **Topless** No. **Duration of presentation** 70 minutes.

DESCRIPTION AND COMMENTS OK, the magic is top-notch, especially the close work and sleight of hand, but it's Jen Kramer's warm, cheery, and ebullient personality that will win your heart. She's the person with the contagious smile you could watch all night, doing just about anything. She probably won't follow you home, but you wish she would. In addition to magic, her show also features comedy, mentalism, and a heavy dose of audience participation. Fast-paced, and most of all fun, it's a super family show, but also wildly entertaining for adults.

CONSUMER TIPS The Westgate Cabaret, a smaller venue, is perfect for an artist specializing in close work. The seating is by maître d', so arrive early for a good seat. Restrooms are directly across the casino from the showroom or to the left at the restaurant promenade. If you drive, be aware that it's a long walk from the cavernous self-parking garages to the Cabaret. There's a monorail station at the Westgate, and it's the best option if you're staying on the east side of the Strip.

KÀ by Cirque du Soleil *(see pages 211–212)*

Legends in Concert ★★★½

APPEAL BY AGE	UNDER 21 ★★★	21-37 ★★★½	38-50 ★★★★	51+ ★★★★

HOST CASINO AND SHOWROOM Flamingo—Flamingo Showroom;
☎ 702-733-3111; caesars.com/flamingo-las-vegas

Type of show Celebrity-impersonator and musical-production show. **Admission** $53–$74 adult, $34 child. **Cast size** Approximately 20. **Night of lowest attendance** Tuesday. **Usual showtimes** Daily, 4, 7:30, and 9:30 p.m. **Dark** None. **Topless** No. **Duration of presentation** 90 minutes.

DESCRIPTION AND COMMENTS *Legends in Concert* is a musical-production show featuring a highly talented cast of impersonators who re-create the stage performances of such celebrities as Elvis, Cher, Jay Leno, Michael Jackson, and Aretha Franklin. Impersonators actually sing and/or play their own instruments, so there's no lip-syncing or faking. In addition to the impersonators, *Legends* features an unusually hot and creative company of dancers, much in the style of TV's *Solid Gold* dancers of yore. There are no variety acts.

   The impersonations are extremely effective, replicating the physical appearances, costumes, mannerisms, and voices of the celebrities with remarkable likeness. While each show features the work of about eight stars, with a roster that ensures something for patrons of every age, certain celebrities (most notably Elvis) are always included. Regardless of the stars impersonated, *Legends in Concert* is fun, happy, and upbeat. It's a show that establishes rapport with the audience.

CONSUMER TIPS In addition to the Las Vegas production, *Legends in Concert* also fields a road show. The second show makes possible a continuing exchange of performers between the productions, so that the shows are always changing. *Legends* is a good show for families.

Le Rêve ★★★★½

APPEAL BY AGE   UNDER 21 ★★½   21–37 ★★★★   38–50 ★★★★½   51+ ★★★★½

HOST CASINO AND SHOWROOM Wynn Las Vegas—Wynn Theater;
☎ 702-770-9966 or 888-320-7110; wynnlasvegas.com

Type of show Aquatic theater in the round. **Admission** $115–$205. **Cast size** 85.
Nights of lowest attendance Sunday and Monday. **Usual showtimes** Friday–Tuesday,
7 and 9:30 p.m. **Dark** Wednesday and Thursday. **Topless** No. **Special comments** No
seat is more than 42 feet from the stage. **Duration of presentation** 75 minutes.

DESCRIPTION AND COMMENTS Imagine a wet concoction of someone else's
dreams. The anchoring image is a nocturnal voyager in a red dress who
explores from her own bed of dreams. Her journey recalls images from
the swirling dark psychology of the fantastical movie *Brazil;* Busby
Berkeley's dance routines; swamp things with long tails; the rescuing
flights from *Angels in America;* "Baby Elephant Walk" from *Hatari!;* dancing flowers from *Fantasia;* the deft touch of Gene Kelly's *Singin' in the
Rain,* with a setting undercurrent of *Mad Max: Beyond Thunderdome.* All
this is a taste of the theatrical pastiche of Franco Dragone's specialty
production *Le Rêve* at Wynn Las Vegas.

The collaboration of hands-on Steve Wynn and Belgian Dragone, who
logged 10 years with Cirque du Soleil, including designing their watery
world of "*O,*" was highly anticipated. *Le Rêve* (French for "the dream") requires a specially constructed amphitheater seating 2,100 where no seat is
more than 42 feet from the action (audience members in the front rows are
given water-protective clothing). Performed in the round, the cast of more
than 70 internationally assembled gymnasts, acrobats, synchronized swimmers, and dancers execute their impressive routines within an expansive,
mysterious tank of water. Mechanical lifts hoist various configurations of
the stage out of the seemingly bottomless reservoir. The set is heightened
by fire, smoke, and dripping skin. At times the performers are atop a rising
column, and at other times they appear to walk on water with the "beach"
platform, as they call it, just below the water's surface. Sometimes they are
hoisted straight up into the dome's opening. Sometimes they swing on tra-
pezes or they dangle in suspended contortions like a Michelangelo version
of hell. Yet none of these descriptions can do justice to the physical display
that arises everywhere before your eyes.

Roman in its level of spectacle and operatic in its reach, *Le Rêve* is long
on sensuality but was initially criticized as short on narrative coherence.
Since opening, the plot has been radically overhauled, resulting in a whole
different (and better) show. The role of the "woman in red" is clarified with
a relatable romantic motivation, making for a much more straightforward
story line to support the still-thrilling spectacle. *Le Rêve's* storytelling is still
a bit light on logic, but perhaps that's appropriate, for who can make true
sense of another's dreams? The show's 10th anniversary in 2015 was also
occasion to add an explosive denouement, with ballroom dancers spinning
through a $3-million flame-spouting fountain. While some of the water and
Cirque-style elements originated in *O,* since the upgrades we find *Le Rêve*
to be the more involving and impressive of the two shows. The concepts
and physical feats invite a thinking person to reconsider the possibilities of
what it is to be human, making it an inspiring treat for the senses and soul.

CONSUMER TIPS Parking in Wynn's self-parking garage is more convenient than using valet parking, if you drive. In our opinion, the first 15 rows are too close and too low to take in the whole of this expansive production that makes use of the entire theater.

LOVE by Cirque du Soleil *(see pages 212–213)*

The Mac King Comedy Magic Show ★★★★

HOST CASINO AND SHOWROOM Harrah's—Harrah's Showroom; ☎ 855-234-7469 or 702-777-2782; caesars.com/harrahs-las-vegas

Type of show Mostly comedy with some magic thrown in. **Admission** $37–$47. **Cast size** 1. **Usual showtimes** Tuesday–Saturday, 1 and 3 p.m. **Dark** Sunday and Monday. **Special comments** Appropriate for children. **Duration of presentation** 1 hour.

DESCRIPTION AND COMMENTS Our pick for the best afternoon show in town, Mac King uses magic and illusion as a platform for his unique brand of comedy. His humor pokes fun at Las Vegas, other Vegas magicians, and at himself. The show is fresh and imaginative, and the illusions are good. But it's King's ability to work an audience, coupled with his sheer insanity, that keeps audiences rolling. If it's really magic you crave (as opposed to comedy), then *Nathan Burton,* described on page 235, is a better choice.

CONSUMER TIPS Harrah's runs two-fer and discount specials on *Mac King,* but they come and go. Unique among afternoon shows, *Mac King* frequently sells out. So purchase tickets in advance if possible.

Magic Mike Live Las Vegas ★★★

HOST CASINO AND SHOWROOM Hard Rock Hotel—Club Domina; ☎ 800-745-3000; magicmikelivelasvegas.com

Type of show Male revue. **Admission** $64–$160. **Cast size** 14. **Night of lowest attendance** Wednesday. **Usual showtimes** Wednesday–Sunday, 8 and 10:30 p.m. **Dark** Monday and Tuesday. **Topless** Yes (male). **Duration of presentation** 90 minutes.

DESCRIPTION Steven Soderbergh's hit 2012 film *Magic Mike* and its 2015 sequel reinvigorated interest in exotic male revues, with tribute acts inspired by the movies suiting up (and stripping down) across the country. In 2017, franchise star Channing Tatum, whose true-life story as a male dancer inspired the series, produced and codirected an authorized incarnation of *Magic Mike* that seeks to redefine the genre long dominated by Chippendales.

Tatum, working with film choreographer Alison Faulk, has transformed Hard Rock Hotel's old Body English nightclub into Club Domina from *Magic Mike XXL* and filled it with 13 talented dancers selected as much for their athletic prowess as their exceptional physiques. A female host makes clear from the start that this is a different sort of striptease, focused on fun and female empowerment rather than misogynistic clichés. There's even a bit of a story line, involving a member of the club's staff who wants to join the dancers onstage, to add a veneer of theatrical respectability to the erotic aerial acrobatics.

CONSUMER TIPS Club Domina's 360-degree setup features booth and cabaret-style seating that completely encircles a central stage. The cheapest tickets are for a couple of rows of theater-style seats in the far back of the room. The closer you are to the stage, the more opportunity you'll have to join in the frequent audience participation. Don't feel obligated to bring a pocketful of dollar bills; in lieu of singles, patrons are encouraged to "make it rain" on the performers with pink "you're welcome" slips. Note that Tatum himself does not perform in the show, though he may occasionally make surprise guest appearances.

Marriage Can Be Murder ★★★½

APPEAL BY AGE	UNDER 21 ★★½	21-37 ★★★½	38-50 ★★★½	51+ ★★★½

HOST CASINO AND SHOWROOM The D—Showroom at The D;
☎ 702-388-2111; thed.com

Type of show Mystery dinner theater. **Admission** $77–$110. **Cast size** 8. **Night of lowest attendance** Monday. **Usual showtimes** Nightly, 6:30 p.m. **Dark** None. **Topless** No. **Duration of presentation** 2 hours.

DESCRIPTION AND COMMENTS *Marriage Can Be Murder* is a well-paced, interactive murder mystery where you try to sniff out the real murderer from among those present. Think of it as a dinner-party version of the board game Clue. The brainchild of Jayne and Eric Post, who star, the production has improved immensely since its debut. Eric the cop grills audience members while keeping up a constant banter with Jayne's character, a hyperditzy blond named D. D. Other cast members pose as paying customers and intermingle with the real audience. It's all played for laughs, with puns and one-liners flying throughout. There's naturally some corniness, but the jokes have been sharpened to the point where you'll only groan and roll your eyes occasionally. Oh, did we mention it's great fun?

CONSUMER TIPS Not the great bargain it once was, the production costs upwards of $77 for general admission and includes dinner and a non-alcoholic beverage. The higher-priced VIP options also include premium seating, a souvenir T-shirt, and either one or two alcoholic beverages. You can fully participate in the sleuthing regardless of which admission you buy. Because you don't have to leave your seat, or mingle with other guests (except at your dinner table), you can enjoy the show even if you're a bit introverted. Plots change periodically throughout the year. Children age 8 and older are welcome, provided they can distinguish reality from theater—it is about murder after all.

Masters of Illusion ★★★

APPEAL BY AGE	UNDER 21 ★★★½	21-37 ★★★½	38-50 ★★★	51+ ★★★

HOST CASINO AND SHOWROOM Bally's—Jubilee Theater; ☎ 702-777-2782; caesars.com/ballys-las-vegas

Type of show Magic. **Admission** $37–$97. **Cast size** 16. **Night of lowest attendance** Wednesday. **Usual showtimes** Wednesday–Monday, 7 p.m. **Dark** Tuesday. **Topless** No. **Duration of presentation** 90 minutes.

DESCRIPTION AND COMMENTS Like the old "ten-in-one" circus sideshows, *Masters of Illusion* tries to draw in patrons with the lure of seeing five professionals for the price of one. But like the traveling carnival, there's the whiff of humbug from the moment you approach the theater's gift shop/entrance, where green screen souvenir photos are given the hard hustle. Once inside, it's soon apparent that this stage spinoff of the CW television show is less than the sum of its parts.

The good news is that with five different magicians trading off routines, there isn't much downtime between tricks. The bad news is that since original costar Jason Bird departed the production, Chris Randall is the only remaining member of the quintet with world-class material, performing both close-up sleight-of-hand and larger-scale musical illusions with charm and panache. The bottom of the bill finds Tommy Wind plying his "rock magician" shtick with obvious levitation effects that rely on heavy fog and black fabric. In the middle of the pack, Farrell Dillon coaxes chuckles with his comical straightjacket escape, while Greg Gleason's big move is making a mini-helicopter materialize.

Many of the individual tricks are competently executed, but with so many cooks this show never congeals into a coherent stew. There's no attempt at a thematic through-line, and the finale effect's pacing is somewhat anticlimactic, making the production paradoxically feel both ADD and overlong. Unless you're already a big fan of one particular performer on the bill (which may have already rotated again by the time you read this), this buy-one/get-four offer isn't the bargain it seems.

CONSUMER TIPS Even if the show isn't magical, at least we can take solace in the fact that *Jubilee!*'s former home is finally getting use again. The venue is fairly intimate for such a big room, and large video screens broadcast the small-scale illusions, but you'll want to sit down front for the best chances of being selected as an audience volunteer.

Mat Franco: *Magic Reinvented Nightly* ★★★★

APPEAL BY AGE	UNDER 21 ★★★★½	21-37 ★★★★	38-5 ★★★★	51+ ★★★½

HOST CASINO AND SHOWROOM The LINQ Hotel & Casino—LINQ Theater;
☎ 702-777-2782; caesars.com/linq

Type of show Magic and illusion. **Admission** $48–$108. **Cast size** 12. **Night of lowest attendance** Monday. **Usual showtimes** Daily, 7 and 9:30 p.m. **Topless** No. **Duration of presentation** 90 minutes.

DESCRIPTION AND COMMENTS Mat Franco, the first and only illusionist ever to win NBC's *America's Got Talent,* may just become the biggest thing in family-friendly magic to hit Vegas since Siegfried and Roy retired. Franco's got the goods, including a humorous, upbeat personality and a real knack for connecting with his audience. This skinny, self-deprecating sleight-of-hand genius is like an anti–Criss Angel, taking seemingly standard magic tricks and transforming them into inventive new effects without overbearing theatrics. Franco's forte is close work, especially with cards and coins, which he favors over flashy dance numbers or elaborate grande illusions. But he isn't afraid to bring out the big guns—literally, a giant card-firing cannon—when the time comes for his jaw-dropping finale. Franco's flawless dexterity, combined with his witty repartee and breezy youthful style, delivers one of the best all-ages traditional magic shows in town.

CONSUMER TIPS The LINQ Theater can be accessed via an escalator on the left side of the casino. It's a little large for Franco's close work, but he's built a production around his magic that makes full use of the room.

Seating is in tall chairs along long cocktail tables, set on elevated tiers. The "preferred seating" is still on the sides and rear, so it isn't worth paying extra for. The show features frequent audience participation, so don't panic if your iPhone is confiscated; it's sure to shortly reappear in an impossible place.

Menopause: The Musical   ★★★★

APPEAL BY AGE	UNDER 21 ★★	21–37 ★★★	38–50 ★★★★★	51+ ★★★★★

HOST CASINO AND SHOWROOM Harrah's—Harrah's Showroom; ☎ 855-234-7469 or 702-777-2782; caesars.com/harrahs-las-vegas

Type of show Off-Broadway musical comedy. **Admission** $56–$83. **Cast size** 4. **Night of lowest attendance** Wednesday. **Usual showtimes** Monday and Saturday, 4 and 7:30 p.m.; Tuesday–Friday, 7:30 p.m. **Dark** Sunday. **Topless** No. **Duration of presentation** 90 minutes.

DESCRIPTION AND COMMENTS This cabaret-style jewel was first launched in a 76-seat theater in Orlando in 2001. Now, it is a rollicking frolic, still packing in people in American cities and beyond. Yes, it really is about "the change," and, yes, about 10% of the audience were unabashed men who were also having an uproariously good time. But hands down and hot flashes up, this is a show for anyone approaching, in, or past menopause.

Many of the heads in the audience are silver, but the punch of estrogen is still palpable upon entering the theater. There was a preponderance of red and purple clothing in the house, perhaps because members of the Red Hat Society, the Red Hot Mamas, Heart Truth, and Minnie Pauz frequently attend the show in groups. Creator Jeanie Linders summed up the crux of the production: "Four women meet at a Bloomingdale's lingerie sale with nothing in common but a black lace bra, hot flashes, night sweats, memory loss, chocolate binges, not enough sex, too much sex, and more." The soap star, the earth mama, the power woman, and the Iowa housewife are each skillfully drawn and wonderfully executed. It would be hard to imagine how to improve upon the show we saw—the cast was perfect in physical style, comedic timing, and song-and-dance delivery.

The 90-minute production moves along by lyrically parodying 24 wonderful songs of the past, especially of the 1960s. For example, Aretha Franklin's "Chain of Fools" becomes "Change, Change, Change"; Irving Berlin's "Heat Wave" becomes "Tropical Hot Flash"; and "Looking for Love in All the Wrong Places" becomes "Looking for Food . . . ," with a chorus that begins "Now I'm packin' on pounds where I don't have spaces / Looking for food in too many places . . . " You get the idea.

You must be 14 years of age to attend, for some of the content is deemed "mature." It's basically a clean, if anatomically forthright show, but if the idea of mechanical "Good Vibrations" paired with "What's Love Got to Do with It?" bothers you, maybe it's time to hit the nickel slots again instead. That would be something of a shame, however, because *Menopause: The Musical* is clever, tons of fun, and very self-affirming. The synergy cycling in the room between the cast and the audience is a jubilant intoxicant that you shouldn't miss imbibing.

Finally for men, this show is a total hoot, especially if you've been married or close to a menopausal woman.

CONSUMER TIPS Alcohol is not served in the theater. The theater is tiered, and seats (all with good sight lines) are preassigned.

Michael Jackson ONE by Cirque du Soleil
(see pages 213–214)

Mike Hammer Comedy Magic Show ★★★

APPEAL BY AGE	UNDER 21 ★★★½	21-37 ★★★	38-50 ★★★	51+ ★★★

HOST CASINO AND SHOWROOM Four Queens—Canyon Club Showroom;
☎ 800-634-6045; fourqueens.com

Type of show Comedy magic. **Admission** $27–$39. **Cast size** 1. **Night of lowest attendance** Thursday. **Usual showtimes** Tuesday–Saturday, 7 p.m. **Dark** Sunday and Monday. **Topless** No. **Duration of presentation** 70 minutes.

DESCRIPTION AND COMMENTS Razor-sharp wit, a genial style, and competent close-up illusions distinguish this Downtown winner. Plus, it's a real bargain. Hammer warms up the crowd with videos of crashes and falls, such as you've seen on *America's Funniest Home Videos*. Then, recruiting "volunteers" for almost every trick, he launches a quickly paced 70-minute torrent of one-liners, asides, and exchanges with members of his audience. You've no doubt seen some of the illusions before, but not with the comic twist that is Hammer's signature. It's a minimalist production, devoid of contraptions, big cats, or comely assistants, but it exceeds expectations on both counts of comedy and magic.

CONSUMER TIPS The Canyon Club is located next to the hotel lobby in the back of the building. The room is set up club style, and though not tiered, it provides good sight lines. There's a bar (serving throughout the show) in the theater, as well as a restroom. Plan to arrive early and enjoy the videos.

Miss Behave Game Show ★★★★

APPEAL BY AGE	UNDER 21 NA	21-37 ★★★★½	38-50 ★★★★	51+ ★★★★

HOST CASINO AND SHOWROOM Bally's—The Back Room; ☎ 702-777-2782; caesars.com/ballys-las-vegas

Type of show Interactive comedy game show. **Admission** $78–$90. **Cast size** 2. **Night of lowest attendance** Wednesday. **Usual showtimes** Wednesday–Sunday, 8 p.m. **Dark** Monday and Tuesday. **Topless** No. **Duration of presentation** 90 minutes.

DESCRIPTION AND COMMENTS *Miss Behave* takes everything you know and love about game shows—valuable prizes, glamorous hosts, intellectual challenges—and chucks it out the window, instead delivering a deviously demented battle of wits that manages to draw even the most reticent audience members into its interactive mayhem. The evening begins with our English-accented hostess (who wears sequins and slings candy at patrons with minimal provocation) dividing the audience along the most crucial conflict in our culture: iPhone users versus Android. Thus divvied into teams, we're thrust into an hour and a half of barely controlled chaos, as Miss Behave conducts a randy rapid-fire pop-culture quiz using handwritten cue cards and a seemingly bottomless collection of sound clips. Between rounds, Behave's tattooed assistant, Tiffany, fills time with exuberantly campy yet impressively athletic dance numbers. The aesthetics are aggressively amateurish, with a scrap cardboard Vegas skyline figuring prominently in the no-budget production numbers.

What makes *Miss Behave* more than a glorified pub quiz is that the questions don't really matter: players are openly encouraged to cheat, with points awarded for shameless begging. Miss Behave's irony-drenched, apocalyptic absurdism conceals a subtext commenting on greed and societal disconnection. Think of her as a DIY Dadaist counterpoint to the Blue Man Group, only with a lot more cursing. If you're sober, it's fascinating to watch fellow audience members debase themselves for non-existent rewards. And if you've had a few in the brothel-like lounge beforehand, it's even more fun to join in. Though in many ways the exact opposite of what we usually expect from a Vegas production, *Miss Behave Game Show* is genuinely avant garde and one of the most delightful surprises on the Strip.

CONSUMER TIPS The Back Room's stage is the size of a postage stamp, with VIP booths in the back and general admission in folding chairs on the floor. Try to sit up front or on an aisle if you plan on getting involved.

MJ Live   ★★★

HOST CASINO AND SHOWROOM Stratosphere—Stratosphere Theater; ☎ 702-380-7777; mjliveshow.com

Type of show Tribute to Michael Jackson. **Admission** $73–$108. **Cast size** 12. **Night of lowest attendance** Monday. **Usual showtimes** Nightly, 7 p.m. **Dark** None. **Topless** No. **Duration of presentation** 70 minutes.

DESCRIPTION AND COMMENTS *MJ Live* is a tribute to Michael Jackson. Differentiated from Cirque do Soleil's *Michael Jackson ONE,* which doesn't have a Michael impersonator, *MJ Live* is centered on impersonation. The production has evolved more than most and may evolve more, but our viewing featured a three-piece band that sounded twice the size, eight dancers, and the impersonator (one of three that rotate, all excellent). The show rocks, slowing only briefly for a couple of down-tempo tunes. Impersonators are convincing. The music is legendary.

CONSUMER TIPS If you're into Michael, *MJ Live* is a mainline dose, unlike the more sentimental and less literal Cirque production. While most anyone enjoys the power, scale, and nuance of *Michael Jackson ONE,* it definitely helps to be a fan to get the most out of *MJ Live.* The Stratosphere Theater is set up like a nightclub, with seats surrounding cocktail tables. Take the escalator up one level from the casino floor.

Murray: Celebrity Magician   ★★½

HOST CASINO AND SHOWROOM Planet Hollywood—Sin City Theater; ☎ 702-777-6737; caesars.com/planet-hollywood or murraysawchuck.com

Type of show Magic and comedy. **Admission** $49 general; $60 VIP. **Cast size** 3. **Night of lowest attendance** Sunday. **Usual showtimes** Saturday-Monday, Thursday, Saturday, 4 p.m. **Dark** Tuesday, Wednesday, and Friday. **Topless** No. **Duration of presentation** 1 hour.

DESCRIPTION AND COMMENTS From his television appearances on *Pawn Stars* and *Reno 911,* Murray Sawchuck seems to be an affable, energetic, eccentric performer—all things you want to see in a stage magician. Sadly, in person Murray The Celebrity Magician proved to be apathetic, amateurish, and unable to fill Planet Hollywood's postage-stamp-size Sin City stage.

Murray screens clips of the large-scale illusions that landed him on *America's Got Talent,* but in this tiny room he's only able to produce birthday-party tricks of the "pick-a-card" variety, an uncomfortably large percentage of which go awry (intentionally or not, it's impossible to say).

With his blonde Yahoo Serious hair and "Salvation Armani" electric-blue suit, Sawchuck's Andy Warhol–meets–Beaker the Muppet appearance at least implies he should make a suitably zany host. But Murray delivers his patter in an incomprehensible mumble, lurching unevenly between effects and occasionally pausing to complain about what a lousy audience we are. Murray is actually upstaged by his assistants, with curvy Chloe elevating yet another average "lady-in-a-box" contraption with her cleavage, and Lefty the stagehand temporarily commandeering the show to demonstrate masterful card manipulations that far outshine any of Sawchuck's skills.

After slogging through poorly paced audience participation segments and a succession of gags you might find in any entry-level magic kit, Murray's big finale is a three-way variation on the ancient Metamorphosis illusion, which we've seen performed better by every other magician in town (including a guy working the sidewalk outside our hotel). After one badly botched trick, the bored-looking Sawchuck said, "Thank you for your pity." Take some pity on yourself—and any of your children who you don't want to grow up hating magic—and skip this stale show.

CONSUMER TIPS The small Sin City Theater has cramped cabaret-style seating and no rake to the floor. Sit close to the stage if you want to see well and be selected as a volunteer assistant. Better yet, don't.

Mystere by Cirque du Soleil *(see page 215)*

Nathan Burton Comedy Magic ★★★

APPEAL BY AGE	UNDER 21 ★★★½	21-37 ★★★	38-50 ★★★	51+ ★★★

HOST CASINO AND SHOWROOM Miracle Mile Shops—Saxe Theater;
☎ 866-932-1818 or 702-260-7200; vtheaterboxoffice.com or nathanburton.com

Type of show Comedy magic (duh!). **Admission** $60, $66 (but check Burton's website for discounted tickets). **Cast size** 6. **Usual showtimes** Tuesday–Sunday, 4 p.m. **Dark** Monday. **Special comments** Appropriate for children. **Duration of presentation** 1 hour.

DESCRIPTION AND COMMENTS The show begins with a collection of video clips on two large video screens flanking the stage (you may recognize Burton from his appearance on TV's *America's Got Talent,* which brought him a lot of attention). From there, he runs the magical gamut, from some baffling gimmick illusions to classic magic tricks. Burton doesn't break any new ground, but his illusions are current and represent the genre well. With a nod to magic's history, he performs Houdini's straitjacket escape with a modern twist—it's completely see through—and a levitation trick with what must be the world's largest hair dryer. High-energy (and very loud) music augments the upbeat pace of the show. Burton smiles his way through a production that is longer on magic than on comedy, but still, it all works well. If your primary interest is magic and illusion, Nathan Burton does a good job. If it's more comedy you crave, try Mac King at Harrah's.

CONSUMER TIPS The Saxe Theater in the Miracle Mile Shops is a perfect venue for Burton. From the Planet Hollywood casino, enter the Miracle

Mile shops and turn right, walking in a counterclockwise direction. From the parking garage, turn left and proceed in a clockwise direction. The box office is often undermanned, and long queues form. If you are buying tickets, picking up tickets, or exchanging Tix4Tonight vouchers, arrive 35 minutes or more before showtime.

"O" by Cirque du Soleil (see page 216)

Opium ★★★★

APPEAL BY AGE   UNDER 21 ★★★½   21-37 ★★★½   38-50 ★★★★   51+ ★★★

HOST CASINO AND SHOWROOM Cosmopolitan—Opium Theatre;
☎ 877-893-2003; cosmopolitanlasvegas.com

Type of show Comedy theater. Admission $79–$129. Cast size 10 plus 5-piece band. Night of lowest attendance Monday. Usual showtimes Monday and Wednesday, 8 p.m.; Thursday–Sunday, 8 and 10 p.m. Dark Tuesday. Topless No. Special comments Must be 18 to attend. Duration of presentation 85 minutes.

DESCRIPTION AND COMMENTS *Opium* was created by Spiegelworld, the same production company that fielded *Absinthe* at Caesars Palace. Like *Absinthe*, *Opium* is in-your-face insane, raunchy, and way over the top. It differs from *Absinthe* in that it has a story line, to wit, an interplanetary space flight that gets lost in the cosmos but ultimately finds its way to Las Vegas. The oversexed crew consists of Captain Ann Tennille, who takes no prisoners; Lieutenant Lou Tenant, given to belting out Queen with an S&M vibe; Chip, a clueless new recruit who's saving his virginity for someone special; and half-naked android Rob the Rumba 5000 Robot. Also included in the menagerie are such characters as crossdressing entertainer Dusty Moonboot and Doctor Regis, the flight surgeon and crew magician. And, of course, no crew would be complete without a Scottie to keep the toilets working. Finally, the space cadets travel with a hot five-piece band.

Plot notwithstanding, *Opium* is a kaleidoscope of quirky variety acts, punctuated by mostly dirty jokes (many about Uranus, natch) and sight gags. There's a portly hula hoop spinner, a sword swallower who will make your sphincters clench, assorted feats of strength, Chihuahua balancing, other-worldly dancing, and juggling, among other things. Our favorite cringe moment comes when a couple launches bananas into each other's mouth from across the room. Pace is a little uneven, but in the main *Opium* comes together pretty well. Oh, and did we mention, audience members can suddenly find themselves part of the show.

CONSUMER TIPS If you thought mom was uncomfortable at *Zumanity*, she won't survive this sucker. Definitely, like *Absinthe*, this is a show for the young or hip at heart. The audience is seated VERY close to the action, and there's frequent intermingling. The production is staged in the Opium Theater next to the Rose. Rabbit. Lie. restaurant. Dinner packages at Rose. Rabbit. Lie. or the Wicked Spoon Buffet start at $95.

Paranormal—The Mind Reading Magic Show ★★★★

APPEAL BY AGE   UNDER 21 ★★★★   21-37 ★★★★   38-50 ★★★★   51+ ★★★★

HOST CASINO AND SHOWROOM Bally's—Windows Showroom;
☎ 702-777-2782; caesars.com/ballys-las-vegas

Type of show Mentalism illusions. **Admission** $56 general, $71 VIP. **Cast size** 1. **Night of lowest attendance** Monday. **Usual showtimes** Sunday–Tuesday and Friday and Saturday, 4 p.m. **Dark** Wednesday and Thursday. **Topless** No. **Special comments** Appropriate for children. **Duration of presentation** 1 hour.

DESCRIPTION AND COMMENTS Illusionist Frederic Da Silva bills himself as a "mentalist," which means that instead of making rabbits or coins appear out of thin air, he prestidigitates thoughts. In his fast-paced, audience-participation-focused performance, Da Silva pulls off a jaw-dropping succession of mind-reading stunts that take the proverbial "power of suggestion" to startling new heights. After assuring his audience that absolutely no plants or stooges are employed in his effects, Da Silva proves it by using tossed Frisbees and other low-tech methods to select his volunteers, eventually roping in almost every single audience member. With their assistance, he plucks randomly selected words, numbers, and images from attendees heads, guessing the serial number from a dollar bill or the time on a stopped watch with eerily unerring accuracy.

Such parlor tricks are impressive, but we've seen plenty of similar pseudo-psychic acts over the years. It was Da Silva's signature "Invisible Touch" routine that really floored us: Two volunteers seated on opposite sides of the stage have their nervous systems "synchronized," so that one visibly reacts to Da Silva touching the other. This was by far the best bit in a filler-free hour of tricks that quickly flew by, leaving us scratching our skeptical heads. With his charming French accent and modest one-man production values, Da Silva doesn't dazzle like some other illusionists, but the mental spell he casts lingers much longer. Warning: You may annoy your friends for days afterward asking, "How did he do that?" If you figure it out, please write in and let us know.

A similar show worth considering is *The Mentalist* at the Miracle Mile Shops starring Gerry McCambridge, who mixes mind reading with magic and comedy. Where Da Silva presents a more serious and sophisticated show, McCambridge steers toward variety and laughs. Prices are comparable for both productions.

CONSUMER TIPS With five matinee performances a week, this is a great pick for an afternoon's entertainment. The Windows Showroom is on Bally's second floor. The front half of the room's seating has no rake, so arrive early to sit front and center. There is a cash bar at the theater entrance, but you may not bring in drinks purchased anywhere else (even water from the shop downstairs).

Penn & Teller ★★★½

| APPEAL BY AGE | UNDER 21 ★★★½ | 21-37 ★★★½ | 38-50 ★★★★ | 51+ ★★★★ |

HOST CASINO AND SHOWROOM Rio—Penn & Teller Theater; ☎ 702-777-7776 or 888-746-7784; riolasvegas.com or pennandteller.com

Type of show Magic and comedy. **Admission** $78, $120, $170. **Cast size** 4. **Night of lowest attendance** Wednesday. **Usual showtimes** Saturday–Wednesday, 9 p.m. **Dark** Thursday and Friday. **Topless** No. **Special comments** Sometimes they reveal secrets to their tricks. **Duration of presentation** 90 minutes.

DESCRIPTION AND COMMENTS OK, for starters, Penn is the big, loud one and Teller is the cute, passive little guy. They've been together for more than 30 years. The show is great fun, but long on talk (Penn's endless digressions tend to numb after 5 minutes or so), and short on magic. Well, not short actually. It's just that the setup for every illusion takes so much time that only a handful of tricks will fit in the allocated 90 minutes. But that's part of the show and provides the backdrop for Penn & Teller's playful tension and hallmark onstage chemistry. The illusions vary from the simple to the elaborate, with Penn & Teller sometimes sharing magician secrets of the trade along the way. Though most of the stuff, including Penn's occasionally blue monologues and the majority of the magic, is old hat to Penn & Teller followers, it works fine for the uninitiated.

CONSUMER TIPS Strictly speaking, this show is about two parts comedy to one part magic. If you're hot primarily for magic, you'll be happier at one of the other magic productions in town. Penn & Teller don't perform any illusions on the order of Siegfried and Roy of old or Steve Wyrick, so sitting up front is fine. Be aware that Penn & Teller are the whole show. There are no showgirls, singing, dancing, or warm-up acts: just the big guy and the little guy.

Piff the Magic Dragon   ★★★

APPEAL BY AGE	UNDER 21 ★★★½	21-37 ★★★	38-50 ★★★	51+ ★★½

HOST CASINO AND SHOWROOM Flamingo—Bugsy's Cabaret;
☎ 702-777-2782; caesars.com/flamingo-las-vegas-shows

Type of show Comedy magician. **Admission** $63–$103. **Cast size** 3, including the dog. **Night of lowest attendance** Wednesday. **Usual showtimes** Daily, 8 p.m. **Dark** None **Topless** No. **Duration of presentation** 75 minutes.

DESCRIPTION AND COMMENTS Las Vegas is lousy with magicians of every variety, but it's a safe bet that there's only one in the city—nay, the solar system—who performs with an impenetrable London accent while wearing a ridiculous full-body dragon costume and holding an adorable Chihuahua named Mr. Piffles. If you haven't caught Piff (real name John van der Put) on *Penn & Teller: Fool Us* or *America's Got Talent,* his schtick consists of performing snarky spins on standard illusions while affecting an obnoxiously disaffected persona, à la an English Larry David . . . in a dragon suit.

Piff uses household objects in his tricks—including a toaster, a MacBook, a can of dog food, and a live goldfish—to excellent effect, but he's really more of a prop comic than master prestidigitator; the best part of his performance is his increasingly prickly interactions with the audience. Years ago, this is the type of show you'd have to go to an underground comedy club or fringe theater festival to experience; now, Piff's avant garde apathy is available only steps away from the slot machines.

Piff's act is preceded by a funny and skillful juggling unicyclist, who inspires terror with his machete-wielding wobbling on the stage's edge.

CONSUMER TIPS Bugsy's Cabaret is a wide but shallow, flat-floored room with too many cabaret tables squeezed like sardines around the semicircular stage. Seating is by maître d' and is maddeningly slow and arbitrary.

A word of warning to parents: though the show is rated PG-13 (no one under 13 may attend), there are enough f-bombs dropped to push it firmly into R territory. Also, a warning to dog lovers: while Mr. Piffles is prominently featured in advertisements, he spends most of the show on the sidelines (in the lap of one lucky viewer) and is only prominently featured in the finale.

Purple Reign   ★★★½

HOST CASINO AND SHOWROOM Tropicana—Tropicana Theater;
☎ 800-829-9034; purplereign.net

Type of show Prince tribute show. **Admission** $50–$100. **Cast size** 8. **Night of lowest attendance** Sunday. **Usual showtimes** Tuesday–Sunday, 9 p.m. **Dark** Monday. **Topless** No. **Special comments** Loud! **Duration of presentation** 90 minutes.

DESCRIPTION AND COMMENTS The 1990s are in the rearview mirror but not forgotten by avid fans of Prince. Jason Tenner, Prince look-alike and sound-alike, backed by a tight (and very loud) live band, shake the house in this driving tribute show. The name of the show and much of its content is inspired by Prince's performance in the 1984 film *Purple Rain*. Tenner's resemblance to Prince is uncanny, and it's not hard to pretend you're hearing the real thing. While many tribute shows lapse into redundancy, *Purple Reign* goes from electric to acoustic, up-tempo to ballad, serious to humorous, and manages to keep things fresh throughout. A major assist comes midway when impersonators of Morris Day and Jerome Benton hammer out a short set of Morris Day and The Time's hits, all while demonstrating the fanciest footwork in the production. Even if you're not a fan or familiar with Prince's music, *Purple Reign* is a great night's entertainment and is sure to exceed your expectations. Prince lovers will find it all but impossible to stay in their seats.

CONSUMER TIPS You can almost always find discounted tickets for *Purple Reign* at the half-price ticket outlets.

Raiding the Rock Vault   ★★★★

HOST CASINO AND SHOWROOM Hard Rock Hotel—Vinyl;
☎ 800-473-7625; hardrockhotel.com or raidingtherockvault.com

Type of show Live rock music retrospective. **Admission** $48–$124. **Cast size** 9 plus guest stars. **Night of lowest attendance** Monday. **Usual showtimes** Saturday–Wednesday, 8:30 p.m. **Dark** Thursday and Friday. **Topless** No. **Special comments** Must be at least age 5 to attend. **Duration of presentation** 2 hours.

DESCRIPTION AND COMMENTS Veteran members of eight great rock groups, including Rock and Roll Hall of Fame member Howard Leese (Heart), Doug Aldrich (Whitesnake), Robin McAuley (Survivor), John Payne (Asia), Paul Shortino (Quiet Riot), Jay Schellen (Asia), Andrew Freeman (The Offspring), and Michael T. Ross (who played with Lita Ford), team up to crank out anthems from the birth of rock and roll to 1989. Rotating female vocalists Carol-Lyn Liddle and Stephanie Calvert (Starship), along with occasional special-guest musicians, add to the mix. Bands covered include The Rolling Stones, The Who, The Doors, Led Zeppelin, Jimi Hendrix, The Eagles, Queen, AC/DC, Van Halen, and Journey, among others.

To make this more than just a concert by the world's most overqualified cover band, a multilayered framing story has been added, with somewhat confusing results. First, there's an almost incomprehensible opening exposition about post-apocalyptic archaeologists in the year 2165 unearthing a Mayan temple containing a holographic history of 20th-century culture. That story line is swiftly abandoned and replaced by seriocomic skits between songs, tracing a baby boomer's journey from hippie stoner to Vietnam volunteer to yuppie salesman. The live music is also accompanied by historic news and concert footage, augmented by VH1 *Pop-Up Video*–style trivia subtitles. It's easy to see why this show is top-rated on internet travel sites; every song is a solid-platinum crowd-pleaser, and performed with note-perfect precision (even the epic "Stairway to Heaven") and pulse-pounding enthusiasm.

CONSUMER TIPS The show is loud (but exceptionally well balanced), as you might expect, so seats more than 10 rows back are recommended. The venue, Vinyl, is a multipurpose event space that can be configured as a theater or club.

The Rat Pack Is Back ★★★½

| APPEAL BY AGE | UNDER 21 – | 21-37 ★★★ | 38-50 ★★★½ | 51+ ★★★½ |

HOST CASINO AND SHOWROOM Tuscany—Copa Showroom;
☎ 702-947-5981; ratpackisback.com

Type of show Celebrity impersonation. **Admission** $60–$90. **Cast size** 17, including 12-piece band. **Night of lowest attendance** Wednesday. **Usual showtimes** Monday–Saturday, 7:30 p.m. **Dark** Sunday. **Topless** No. **Duration of presentation** 75 minutes.

DESCRIPTION AND COMMENTS The heart and soul of the original Rat Pack were crooners Frank Sinatra, Dean Martin, and Sammy Davis Jr., and comedian Joey Bishop. They all worked the Las Vegas showrooms of the 1960s, sometimes dropping in on each other's shows and sometimes working together. Their late-night antics at the old Sands, particularly, are among the richest of Las Vegas showroom legends.

The Rat Pack Is Back re-creates a night when the acerbic Bishop and hard-drinking Martin team up with Davis and Sinatra. Backed by piano, bass, drums, along with, get this, a nine-piece horn section, four talented impersonators take you back to a night at the Sands Copa Room in 1963. The impressionists are excellent: each impersonator captures his character's voice, singing style, and body language. The performers playing Bishop and Davis bear strong physical resemblances to the originals, and the Sinatra impressionist more or less squeaks by, but the Martin character looks more like an Elvis impersonator.

The casual interplay among the four effectively transports you back to the 1960s, and what you see is pretty much how it was. The humor was racist, sexist, and politically incorrect, the showroom packed and smoky, and the music, well . . . drop-dead brilliant.

CONSUMER TIPS There are usually discount coupons for *The Rat Pack Is Back* in the local tourists mags.

Rich Little ★★★

| APPEAL BY AGE | UNDER 21 ★★ | 21-37 ★★½ | 38-50 ★★★ | 51+ ★★★½ |

HOST CASINO AND SHOWROOM Tropicana—The Laugh Factory;
☎ 800-829-9034; troplv.com

Type of show Celebrity impersonator. **Admission** $39.95–$59.95. **Cast size** 2 (Little plus a keyboardist). **Usual showtimes** Sunday–Wednesday, 7 p.m. **Dark** Thursday–Saturday. **Topless** No. **Duration of presentation** 60 minutes.

DESCRIPTION AND COMMENTS From Johnny Carson to John Wayne, Rich Little has now outlived most of the superstars whose voices he made a career out of impersonating, but that doesn't seem to have slowed him down. Looking and sounding spry for 77, Little is still mimicking Jack Benny, Henry Fonda, George Burns, and other giants from the Golden Age of Television and Hollywood who have long since passed from this earth, or at least the popular consciousness.

During his hour-long monologue, occasionally backed by barely there musical accompaniment, Little leads the audience through his life in show-biz, letting slip which of his dozens of celebrity targets were fans (Ronald Reagan once let Little take over a real press conference), which ones couldn't handle the mocking (Paul Lynde), and which ones (Ed Sullivan) were just plain stupid. The act is equal parts stand-up set, autobiographic monologue, and gossip session; a lifelong artist, Little even shares some of the celebrity portraits he has sketched.

If you happen to have been frozen in amber since 1992, Little's act will seem devastatingly topical. His vocal mimicry skills are still sharp enough to show why he was such a big hit in his day, and he winks at salacious topics without treading far across the PG-13 barrier. In other words, this is comedy nirvana for those who remember and pine for the era of Dean Martin's roasts and Carnac's mystical envelopes. But popular culture has passed his repertoire by; Bill Clinton is his most recent fully developed character, and despite the ripe material in present politics, both Obama and Trump get only glancing mentions.

CONSUMERS TIPS The Laugh Factory club is dark and cavelike, with a low ceiling, flat floor, and a few booths in the back. Most of the audience, which skews older and female, is seated at cabaret tables around the small, slightly elevated stage. Sight lines from the sides are substandard due to several obstructing poles; try to maneuver yourself within view of one of the scattered video screens, which are used frequently throughout Little's presentation.

SEXXY ★★★½

APPEAL BY AGE	UNDER 21 NA	21-37 ★★★½	38-50 ★★★½	51+ ★★★½

HOST CASINO AND SHOWROOM Westgate—Westgate Cabaret;
☎ 702-555-1212 or 800-222-5361; sexxyshow.com

Type of show Topless revue. **Admission** $54–$75. **Cast size 7. Night of lowest attendance** Wednesday. **Usual showtimes** Wednesday–Saturday, 10 p.m. **Dark** Sunday-Tuesday. **Topless** Yes. **Special comments** Must be 18 to attend. **Duration of presentation** 65 minutes.

DESCRIPTION AND COMMENTS Producer-choreographer Jennifer Romas has assembled her ideal burlesque show at the Westgate, and while the production doesn't break any new ground, *Sexxy* has managed to stand out in a city of formulaic flesh parades thanks to Romas's energetic, sensually muscular movements. The performers are way buff and dauntingly athletic, including Romas herself, who sets a new standard for pole dancing and performs a violent bathtub routine that puts pommel horse Olympians to shame. The cast is all female, including a belting vocalist, who also goes topless by the end, and an acrobatic specialty act. The song list includes both old-school ("Feeling Good," "Put a Spell on You") and Top 40 ("Bang Bang," "Runaway Baby"), and the show is enhanced by peppy pacing and a dynamic fog-assisted lighting design.

Topless Vegas Online's Arnold Snyder rates *Sexxy* as "the sexiest of the Vegas topless production shows." Those whose tastes favor the demure and delicate may find the show more intimidating than arousing. But if you are intrigued by the idea of a powerful woman who could crush your skull between her thighs without missing a dance beat, then this is the skin show you've been searching for.

CONSUMER TIPS Westgate Cabaret is an intimate venue with maître d' seating, so arrive early to score a good spot. The front row will give you a stiff neck from looking up; aim for a cocktail table toward the center instead. Another option is to sit on a high stool at the bar. The sight lines are great, but you're back a bit from the action. Restrooms are all the way across the casino or around the corner in the restaurant arcade. *Sexxy* attracts an audience with a surprisingly high number of women and couples.

Solid Gold Soul ★★★½

APPEAL BY AGE   UNDER 21 ★★★   21–37 ★★★½   38–50 ★★★★   51+ ★★★★

HOST CASINO AND SHOWROOM Bally's—Windows Showroom; ☎ 702-777-2782; caesars.com/ballys-las-vegas

Type of show Motown tribute concert. **Admission** $89–$111. **Cast size** 12. **Night of lowest attendance** Monday. **Usual showtimes** Thursday–Sunday, 6 p.m. **Dark** Monday–Wednesday. **Topless** No. **Duration** 90 minutes.

DESCRIPTION Much like *Hitzville* at the Miracle Mile, *Solid Gold Soul* is a Motown tribute concert that tries to re-create the experience of seeing several soul legends in person. With icons like Ray Charles, Smokey Robinson, and Sam Cooke on the bill, that's setting an impossibly high bar, but this show comes impressively close given the limitations of its intimate venue. Producer/choreographer Nannette Barbera also serves as emcee, fronting the live three-piece band and introducing a parade of faux R&B superstars. Each act is accompanied on a handful of signature tunes by a quartet of nubile dancing backup singers, whose skimpy costumes would never have passed the 1960s censors.

Falling somewhere in between a cover band and full impersonation, many of *Solid Gold Soul*'s singers bear scant physical resemblance to their subjects beyond an invariably embarrassing wig, but all excel at capturing the spirit and sound of the original artists. The catalog of megahits covered ranges from Jackie Wilson's "Higher and Higher" and The Four Tops' "I Can't Help Myself" to James Brown's "It's a Man's Man's Man's World," complete with choreographed cape tossing. Because so many shows use this venue, production values are minimal at best: stage effects consist of a balky fog machine and two wobbly doors, and the show needs video interludes to ease the transitions. But the performers, several of whom have won awards and performed alongside genuine Motown greats, deliver every number with nonstop energy that gets their baby boomer audience on its feet dancing to song after song.

CONSUMER TIPS *Solid Gold Soul* would be a much better value if it weren't crammed into Bally's 300-seat Windows Showroom, where a large pole ruins sight lines for much of the right side of the audience. If you aren't in the VIP cocktail seating up front, ask for a seat in the rear center instead of the sides.

Tenors of Rock ★★★★

HOST CASINO AND SHOWROOM Harrah's—Harrah's Showroom; ☎ 855-234-7469 or 702-777-2782; caesars.com/harrahs-las-vegas

Type of show Rock retrospective concert. **Admission** $53–$102. **Cast** 5 vocalists, live band, and 4 dancers. **Night of lowest attendance** Monday. **Usual showtimes** Wednesday-Monday, 8 p.m. **Dark** Tuesday. **Topless** No. **Duration of presentation** 90 minutes.

DESCRIPTION AND COMMENTS Starring five Brits (Welsh, Scottish, and English), most of whom look like nightclub bouncers, *Tenors of Rock* is a tapestry of forceful harmonies organized around a retrospective of rock music. The Tenors, far from being a cover band, reimagine rock's greatest anthems, adding nuance, vocal complexity, and power. Individually or collectively, the Tenors' formidable delivery transcends the songs themselves. In addition, each Tenor is unique and establishes a singular stage presence that makes the production as much about the men as about the music. Speaking of which, it's varied to say the least, and though it features the work of such iconic bands as Bon Jovi, Aerosmith, Queen, Guns N' Roses, and the Stones, there are also renditions of ballads and even Broadway show tunes. Add the musicians—who are as talented as the vocalists—and extra oomph supplied by the dancers, and you have a production at the top of its genre.

CONSUMER TIPS First, this show is really LOUD, so sitting back a ways is better. Harrah's Showroom is located two escalator flights up from the front of the casino. Drinks are available in the showroom lobby, and restrooms are just outside the showroom entrance. Harrah's, like all Caesars properties, charges for parking, so the monorail is your best bet if you're staying on the east side of the Strip.

Terry Fator ★★★★

HOST CASINO AND SHOWROOM Mirage—Terry Fator Showroom; ☎ 702-792-7777; mirage.com and terryfator.com

Type of show Voice-impersonation ventriloquism. **Admission** $66–$154. **Cast size** 2 plus live band. **Night of lowest attendance** Wednesday. **Usual showtimes** Monday–Thursday, 7:30 p.m. **Dark** Friday-Sunday. **Topless** No. **Duration of presentation** 90 minutes.

DESCRIPTION AND COMMENTS As stated on Fator's website, it took him "32 years to become an overnight sensation." The catalyst was taking first place (and a million bucks) in the *America's Got Talent* television show. Though the talent-show win was long in coming, Fator's arrival in one of Las Vegas's most prestigious showrooms was near meteoric.

Terry Fator brings so many talents to the Mirage that his show is tough to categorize. He's a superb and versatile vocalist, a consummate comedian, a world-class ventriloquist, and an imaginative puppeteer. Fator can mimic virtually any voice, male or female, and during his ventriloquism routines, pulls it off with his mouth closed. His quirky puppet costars are what you might have expected from Jim Henson had he designed puppets for adults. Topping the list is Winston, the Impersonating Turtle, inspired by Henson's Kermit the Frog. Winston sings a duet of "Wonderful World" with

Louis Armstrong—one of the most magical moments in the show. Other puppet characters include Walter T. Airedale, a country singer; lovable and sassy Emma Taylor; Maynard Thomkins, an Elvis impersonator who doesn't know any Elvis songs; Julius, an African American soul singer who nails Marvin Gaye; Johnny Vegas, a lounge singer who impersonates the likes of Dean Martin and Tony Bennett; and Dougie Scott Walker, a hippy dippy heavy-metal dude. The latest addition is Vikki "The Cougar," a cut-up with a big mouth and plenty of attitude.

Ventriloquism isn't what usually comes to mind when you're shopping for a Las Vegas show, but ventriloquism is only the tip of Terry Fator's iceberg. Consider his ventriloquism and puppets as icing on some of the best voice impersonation and edgy humor you're likely to find. When he trots out a perfect duet between Garth Brooks and Michael Jackson, you won't believe what you're hearing. Never mind that he's belting it out with his mouth closed! Fator is backed by a seven-piece live band and a comely assistant. The show has great energy throughout and runs the gamut from zany to poignant. The puppets are a little hard to see from the seats in back, but large LED screens flanking the stage monitor the action. The main problem we'd like to see corrected is that of the band overwhelming the vocals.

CONSUMER TIPS Terry Fator's humor is definitely adult but not often blue, so the show is OK for those under 18, though they might not dig the music. Because of the location of the showroom, you're better off using Mirage self-parking rather than valet parking.

Thunder from Down Under ★★★

APPEAL BY AGE	UNDER 21 ★★★	21–37 ★★★	38–50 ★★★	51+ ★★★

HOST CASINO AND SHOWROOM Excalibur—Thunder from Down Under Showroom; ☎ 702-597-7600; excalibur.com or thunderfromdownunder.com

Type of show Male revue. **Admission** $45–$104. **Cast size** 10. **Night of lowest attendance** Monday. **Usual showtimes** Sunday–Thursday, 9 p.m.; Friday and Saturday, 9 and 11 p.m. **Dark** None. **Special comments** Must be 18 or older to attend (guests ages 18–20 must be accompanied by an adult). **Topless** Yes (male). **Duration of presentation** 75 minutes.

DESCRIPTION AND COMMENTS Thunder from Down Under offers a naughty night of ladies' fun—a girls' night out that won't cause complete embarrassment for the conservative set. These Aussies are the guys next door—friendly and cute, but not the Chippendales dancers. Thunder is suggestive but not explicit, much tamer, in fact, than its American-based competitor. The scantily clad cast performs upbeat dance, acrobatics, and martial-arts routines, with a few comedy sketches tossed in. Acts are performed to a varied soundtrack, resulting in a high-energy—but not always sexy—show.

There's lots of audience interaction as the Thundermen constantly pull girls out of the crowd and onto the stage. If you're shy and want to remain inconspicuous, try sitting in the back, where the lighting is also softer (our reviewer experienced light-blindness a few times from harsh overheads above her front-center seat in the 400-person showroom). After the show, cast members stick around to mingle with guests and offer photo opportunities.

Although there's lots of teasing and suggestion, the Thundermen never fully remove their G-strings (unlike the Chippendales guys). Thunder seemingly presumes that women can't appreciate blatantly risqué entertainment.

Our female reviewer also got the distinct impression that the guys of *Thunder* would be more interested in each other than any of the hundreds of girls in the audience, which for some may diminish the show's sex appeal.

CONSUMER TIPS The Thunder from Down Under Showroom is located on the "Medieval" level, above the casino. Conveniently, there's a restroom within the showroom. Drinks must be purchased directly from the bar (no at-the-table cocktail service).

Tony n' Tina's Wedding ★★★½

APPEAL BY AGE   **UNDER 21 ★**   **21-37 ★★★½**   **38-50 ★★★½**   **51+ ★★★**

HOST CASINO AND SHOWROOM Bally's—Buca di Beppo Italian restaurant; ☎ 855-234-7469; caesars.com/ballys-las-vegas

Type of show Interactive dinner theater. **Admission** $120–$155. **Cast size** 20. **Night of lowest attendance** Tuesday. **Usual showtimes** Sunday–Wednesday, Friday, and Saturday, 7 p.m. **Dark** Thursday. **Topless** No. **Duration of presentation** 2 hours.

DESCRIPTION AND COMMENTS Have you ever been to a wedding or wedding reception where you really didn't know anyone? Well, that's the premise for *Tony n' Tina's Wedding*. You're a wedding guest, welcomed into a large banquet hall and seated at a dinner table with total strangers. There you sit befuddled and somewhat uncomfortable as members of the bride's family (actors) stop to say hello and reminisce about Tony and Tina. And this is just the beginning. If you thought you could sit passively and watch a show, you're quite mistaken. During the course of a panicky few minutes, you become acutely aware that you are being sucked into the cast of this strange piece of theater, or if you can suspend your disbelief, this wedding. First there's the ceremony, then obligatory toasts, then dancing, then dinner followed by more toasts, and the tossing of the bouquet and the garter. As it unfolds, you are taken back to all those weddings in your life where one of the bridesmaids gets drunk, where an uninvited guest makes a 5-minute toast, and where the best man wants to sing with the band. Inevitably it's you that the inebriated bridesmaid wants to spin around the dance floor, you who are pushed into the conga line, and you who are pulled into the throng to vie for the bouquet or garter.

There's a story line, of course, plus enough subplots to give Robert Ludlum a run for his money. The families don't get along well, and each in its own way tries to monopolize the reception. The strain is almost too much for the happy couple and for a while their minutes-old marriage hangs in the balance.

CONSUMER TIPS Is this fun? At the show we attended, we observed a pretty diverse range of audience reaction. Some really got into it, danced to every tune, and role-played right along with cast. Others kept as much as possible to themselves, refusing to the extent possible to be drawn in. With some difficulty, we warmed to the proceedings but nonetheless kept a wary lookout for the sloshed bridesmaid. It was impossible not to admire how exactly the production nailed every wedding cliché, and how, if you weren't familiar with the family members as individuals, you had met their characters at similar events dozens of times in real life. If it helps you make up your mind, we'll tell you that the dinner was passable, sort of a pasta buffet, and that you had one chance to go through the line and load up your plate. The only alcohol served was a splash of Champagne for one of the toasts, though there was a cash bar (where we spent a goodly sum trying to improve our attitude).

Tournament of Kings ★★★

HOST CASINO AND SHOWROOM Excalibur—King Arthur's Arena;
☎ 702-597-7600 or 877-750-5464; excalibur.com

Type of show Jousting and medieval pageant. **Admission** $45–$73 with dinner. **Cast size** 35 (with 38 horses). **Night of lowest attendance** Monday. **Usual showtimes** Monday and Friday, 6 p.m.; Wednesday, Thursday, Saturday, and Sunday, 6 and 8:30 p.m. **Dark** Tuesday. **Topless** No. **Duration of presentation** 75 minutes.

DESCRIPTION AND COMMENTS *Tournament of Kings* is a retooled version of *King Arthur's Tournament,* which logged 6,000 performances. It's basically the same show, with a slightly different plot twist. If you saw one, the other will come as no surprise.

The idea is that Arthur summons the kings of eight European countries to a sporting competition in honor of his son Christopher. Guests view the arena from dinner tables divided into sections; a king is designated to represent each section in the competition. Ladies-in-waiting and various court attendants double as cheerleaders, doing their best to whip the audience into a frenzy of cheering for their section's king. The audience, which doesn't require much encouragement, responds by hooting and pounding on the dinner tables. Watch your drinks—all the pounding can knock them over.

Soup is served to the strains of the opening march. The kings enter on horseback. Precisely when the King of Hungary is introduced, dinner arrives (big Cornish hen, small twice-baked potato, bush of broccoli, dinner roll, and dessert turnover). The kings engage in contests with flags, dummy heads, javelins, swords, and maces and shields and joust a while, too. The horse work, fighting, and especially the jousting are exciting, and the music (by a three-man band) and sound effects are well executed.

Right on cue, Mordred the Evil One crashes the party, accompanied by his Dragon Enforcers. Arthur is mortally slain and all the kings are knocked out, leaving Christopher to battle the forces of evil and emerge— surprise!—victorious in the end.

Except that . . . it's not over. The coronation is the culmination, after some acrobatics and human-tower stunts from a specialty act. Finally, the handsome new king goes out in a (literal) blaze of glory. It's a bit anticlimactic and bogged down, which helps hurry you out so the crew can quickly set up for the second show or clean up and go home.

CONSUMER TIPS One of the few Las Vegas shows suitable for the whole family, and one of the fewer dinner shows, *Tournament of Kings* enjoys great popularity and often plays to a full house. Reserved seats can be purchased online or at the Excalibur box office, which opens at 8 a.m.

No matter where you sit, you're close to the action—and the dust and stage smoke. The air-conditioning system is steroidal, so you might consider bringing a wrap. Seating is reserved, so you can walk in at the last minute and don't have to tip any greeters or seaters.

Dinner is served without utensils and eaten with the hands, so you might want to wash up beforehand. Eating a big meal is a bit awkward with the show going on and all the cheering duties, so you might consider bringing some aluminum foil and a bag to take out the leftover bird. Beverage is limited to soda with dinner, but the food server will bring you water, and a cocktail waitress will bring you anything else. Service is adequate; no one tips, so you'll be a hero if you do. The Excalibur is hell-bent on ditching all the elements that made it appealing to the family market. It's possible *Tournament of Kings* will be the next casualty.

V: The Ultimate Variety Show ★★★★

APPEAL BY AGE	UNDER 21 ★★★½	21–37 ★★★	38–50 ★★★	51+ ★★½

HOST CASINO AND SHOWROOM Miracle Mile Shops—V Theater;
☎ 702-892-7790; vtheaterboxoffice.com

Type of show A hodgepodge of variety acts. **Admission** $80–$100. **Cast size** About 12 (varies). **Nights of lowest attendance** Monday and Wednesday. **Usual showtimes** Nightly, 7 and 8:30 p.m. **Special comments** Some of Las Vegas's quirkiest acts; great fun. **Topless** No. **Duration of presentation** 75 minutes.

DESCRIPTION AND COMMENTS In quite a few headlining Las Vegas shows, old and new, intermissions are handled by variety acts—comics, jugglers, acrobats, magicians, ventriloquists, and more. And in several of these cases (particularly the older ones), these variety acts become more entertaining than the headliners. The advantage of *V* is that the cast consists of a rotating stable of variety acts culled from Vegas and elsewhere. This means that no act lasts longer than a few minutes; it's the show for the short-attention-span set. Most of the acts are quite good. The emcee is a hilariously flamboyant and aggressive comic-magician, and when we visited, there was also an amusingly abusive juggler, a few species of acrobats, and a bizarre ventriloquist who uses audience volunteers as his "dummies," among others.

CONSUMER TIPS The V Theater is located in the Miracle Mile Shops at Planet Hollywood. Self-parking at Planet Hollywood funnels you directly into the Miracle Mile Shops not far from the theater. Because there are only a couple of windows at the box office, arrive 35 minutes or more before showtime if you are buying or picking up tickets, or redeeming ticket vouchers. The split-level showroom has a bar on a mezzanine floor and most seating on ground level. Because the V Theater is a multifunctional facility, there's no vertical rise from front to back for the seating. If you sit behind someone tall, in other words, your line of sight will be majorly obstructed. Also be aware that the available restrooms are totally inadequate for the size of the audience.

Vegas! The Show ★★★★

APPEAL BY AGE	UNDER 21 ★★★½	21–37 ★★★★	38–50 ★★★★	51+ ★★★★

HOST CASINO AND SHOWROOM Miracle Mile Shops—Saxe Theater;
☎ 866-932-1818 or 702-260-7200; vtheaterboxoffice.com

Type of show Las Vegas production show. **Admission** $100–$120. **Cast size** 29. **Night of lowest attendance** Monday. **Usual showtimes** Nightly, 7 and 9 p.m. **Topless** No. **Duration of presentation** 90 minutes.

DESCRIPTION AND COMMENTS *Vegas!* is a quintessential Las Vegas production show with feathered showgirls and lavish ensemble routines punctuated by myriad specialty acts. Cleverly presented as a reminiscence of "old Las Vegas," the show couples Las Vegas history with the evolution of the production show genre. Sets depict neon marquees of long-gone hotels such as the Stardust, Dunes, Sands, and Desert Inn, while music and choreography capture the essence of classic Vegas productions such as *Lido de Paris* and *Folies Bergère*. Though not topless, the statuesque showgirls and dancers successfully recreate the feel of the extravagant Ziegfeld-type shows. Add some great vocalists (Reva Rice and Josh Strickland) recalling iconic Vegas showroom personalities, and you have one hot and memorable show. Everything is live—no recorded tracks or lip-synching. Music is courtesy of a tight 11-piece band. Continuity is sustained by a film montage of Vegas past.

In the better production shows of old, specialty acts sometimes stole the show, transcending their utilitarian function of killing time while the next big number was being set up. So too with *Vegas!*—the specialty acts really grab you. Though acts change from performance to performance, the recent line-up has included Professor Wacko and his comedy trampoline, the roller skating duo of Bill and Yana, and former Cirque du Soleil gymnast Tamara Yeroffyeva.

CONSUMER TIPS Saxe Theater operations are a little different. The queue to enter the showroom starts on the ground level next to the bar, so neither the bar nor the queue functions efficiently. Compounding the congestion is the location of the restrooms next to the bar. Once you unscramble the folks in the queue from the barflies and the potty-goers, the queue winds up a staircase several stories and enters the theater at the top rear. From there an insufficient number of ushers help you find your seat. All seats are reserved, so you may as well relax at the bar until most of the queue has disappeared from the staircase (there's an elevator for non-ambulatory patrons).

Half-price tickets are usually available at the discount ticket outlets and sometimes coupons are available for *Vegas!* in the local visitor magazines. Discounted tickets are harder to score for the early show (which often sells out) than for the 9 p.m. performance. Park in the Miracle Mile Shops self-parking. Once you enter the mall proceed to the first intersection and turn left to the theater. The box office is routinely overwhelmed before the early show, so arrive 35 minutes or so in advance if you're buying tickets, exchanging vouchers, or picking up tickets at will call.

WOW ★★★

APPEAL BY AGE	UNDER 21 ★★★★	21-37 ★★★½	38-50 ★★★	51+ ★★½

HOST CASINO AND SHOWROOM Rio—Rio Showroom; ☎ 855-234-7469; caesars.com/rio-las-vegas

Type of show Variety. **Admission** $39–$173. **Cast size** 22. **Night of lowest attendance** Tuesday. **Usual showtimes** Tuesday–Sunday, 5, 7, and 9 p.m. **Dark** Monday. **Topless** No. **Duration of presentation** 80 minutes.

DESCRIPTION *WOW* stands for "Worlds of Wonder," and it's also what you'll exclaim upon entering the Rio Showroom, which has been decked out with a circular stage and swimming pool, surrounded by 180 degrees of stunning floor-to-ceiling digital displays. Once the show begins, you'll be further dazzled by holographic projections, remote-controlled watercraft, curtains of falling water, and other high-tech feats of stagecraft.

Unfortunately, all the special-effects wizardry in the world can't conceal the flaws in this colorful but misguided attempt to ape Cirque du Soliel's "O" and Le Rêve.

The large cast is certainly enthusiastic and acrobatic enough, and some demonstrate impressive aerial and aquatic maneuvers. Pole climbers, roller skaters, and plate spinners join the party, along with America's Got Talent semifinalist Sylvia Silvia, who uses a chain reaction of crossbows to shoot an apple off her own head (eat your heart out, William Tell). But their valiant efforts are largely lost among cluttered staging and a nonsensical plot, which leaps from mermaids and pirates to the Titanic, Atlantis, and New York, with no rhyme or reason.

WOW's biggest problem is Alberto, the clownlike character who serves as a linking device between acts. He's more annoying than Jerry Lewis and Austin Powers put together, without any of their charm or comic talent, and his recurring presence repeatedly kills whatever momentum or good will his costars can generate. Without Alberto, this show would be more than tolerable as a family-friendly successor to old-school variety productions like Jubilee!; with him, WOW becomes an exercise in enduring aural torture.

CONSUMER TIPS Seats are preassigned, with rows of chairs on three circular tiers and private booths in the middle rear. To avoid hypothermia and for good sight lines, you don't want to sit up front. If you prefer a similar but more nuanced and artistic show, with a compelling story line and memorable characters, go with "O" or Le Rêve instead.

Xavier Mortimer's Magical Dream ★★★★

APPEAL BY AGE   UNDER 21 ★★★½   21-37 ★★★★   38-50 ★★★★   51+ ★★★★

HOST CASINO AND SHOWROOM Planet Hollywood—Sin City Theater;
☎ 702-777-6737; caesars.com/planet-hollywood

Type of show Avant-garde comedy magic. **Admission** $60-$85. **Cast size** 2 onstage, plus hidden assistants. **Night of lowest attendance** Tuesday. **Usual showtimes** Saturday-Thursday, 7 p.m. **Dark** Friday. **Topless** No. **Duration** 60 minutes.

DESCRIPTION French television star Alex Goude, who fronted the ill-fated Twisted Vegas variety show at Westgate, stepped into the director's chair to help fellow countryman Xavier Mortimer adapt his magical miming for an American audience. Unique among Vegas illusionists, Magical Dream doesn't simply present a series of tricks but also weaves impressive effects into a simple but effective story line about Mortimer's hapless pursuit of a "fantasy girl," played by baby-voiced Lauren Metter, a practiced prestidigitator herself. We follow Mortimer's romantic quest through a fast-paced series of scenarios that effortlessly integrate magical illusions with dance, physical comedy, and ingenious interactive videos that give new meaning to the phrase "magic mirror."

The dreamlike result is closer to Charlie Chaplin meets Cirque du Soleil (which Mortimer performed with) than David Copperfield, which is not to dis his sleight-of-hand skills. Mortimer makes classic mind reading and "Metamorphosis" gags feel fresh again, and his levitation finale—performed while jumping rope in front of a full-length mirror—will make you wonder for weeks afterward. Between Mortimer's adorably impenetrable accent and his extremely European sense of absurdity, Magical Dream may be a bit too "artsy-fartsy" for folks who just want their magicians to make stuff disappear. But if you're on his wavelength, Mortimer will make you believe there's still room left for innovation in the art of illusion.

CONSUMER TIPS Sin City Theater's cabaret setup could be charitably described as cozy, or more honestly as sardine-like. Sight lines from the unelevated general-admission seats are hit-or-miss, but you must upgrade to VIP to get a cocktail table up front (where most of the audience volunteers are picked from), even if some are empty.

X Burlesque ★★★

APPEAL BY AGE	UNDER 21 -	21-37 ★★	38-50 ★★½	51+ ★★½

HOST CASINO AND SHOWROOM Flamingo—X Showroom; ☎ 702-733-3333 or 800-221-7299; caesars.com/flamingo-las-vegas or xshowslasvegas.com

Type of show Topless revue. **Admission** $62–$95. **Cast size** 8. **Night of lowest attendance** Tuesday. **Usual showtimes** Nightly, 10 p.m. **Dark** None. **Topless** Yes. **Duration of presentation** 90 minutes.

DESCRIPTION AND COMMENTS Less erotic than athletic, *X Burlesque* features a half dozen skilled dancers performing highly choreographed routines to songs ranging from Broadway standards to techno. Some numbers feature all the dancers, while others involve only one or two. The dancers wear tops as often as not, and their bodies are lithe and toned rather than top-heavy, so guys looking for a hot and juicy T&A show may want to look elsewhere. Those seeking more subtle eroticism won't be disappointed. The audience sits at round tables, nightclub-style, and the comely dancers strut on and off the stage and through the tables, sometimes taking a swing on a pole near the back of the room. The variety of music, the lights and costumes, and the sensual images flashing on large screens at either side of the small stage give the show a charged energy that captures the crowd. Given the general tone of the show, the appearance of the stand-up comic constitutes a real interruption. In X's defense, however, it should be pointed out that a bit of stand-up comedy is pretty routine in topless revues as well as in many strip joints.

CONSUMER TIPS X Showroom is small, giving the production an appropriate intimacy, and most of the tables are set up near the stage on a flat floor. The music is loud, the images bright and quick, and the choreography often frenetic, so expect a full sensory experience. Pun intended.

X Country ★★★

APPEAL BY AGE	UNDER 21 ★★★½	21-37 ★★★½	38-50 ★★★	51+ ★★★

HOST CASINO AND SHOWROOM Harrah's—Harrah's Cabaret; ☎ 855-234-7469; caesars.com/harrahs-las-vegas or xshowslasvegas.com

Type of show Country-themed topless revue. **Admission** $47.94–$72.95. **Cast size** 6 (5 girls, plus a comic). **Usual showtimes** Sunday–Saturday, 10 p.m. **Dark** None. **Topless** Yes. **Duration of presentation** 65 minutes.

DESCRIPTION AND COMMENTS The X family of topless shows has taken off in Vegas, to the point that you may be confused as to which of the brand's erotic dance revues you are actually attending. Fear not—here's how to figure it out: if the girls onstage are wearing (or removing) corsets to vintage bump-and-grind tunes, you're at *X Burlesque;* if they're in black leather gyrating to Black Sabbath, you're at *X Rocks;* and if you see Daisy Dukes and cowboy hats, and hear Molly Hatchet and Gretchen Wilson, it must be *X Country.*

Much like its sister shows, *X Country* doesn't mess around with high-falutin plot or dialogue, but rather dives right into the boot-scooting and bare boobs. The girls—mostly blondes, and mostly natural—frequently wear half-shirts that are erotic in a girl-next-door sort of way and are given plenty of props—baseball bats, bullwhips, and a pair of bathtubs—to play with. The playlist includes both kinds of music (country and western) and spans the genre's history from Patsy Cline to the Dixie Chicks; the cast even recorded a custom music video for good measure.

As with the other X shows, the pace is propulsive with minimal filler, and the obligatory stand-up comedian performs only a single 8-minute intermission. *X Country* may not have the pedigreed history of *Crazy Girls,* nor the extreme athleticism of *Sexxy,* nor the intense energy of *X Rocks,* but for proud rednecks it is currently the tastiest slice of country-fried cheesecake in town.

CONSUMER TIPS *X Country*'s audience demographic is middle-age and middle-class, looking more like the crowd at a state fair than your typical Sin City show. Harrah's Cabaret stage is just barely big enough for the half dozen cast members to strut on without stumbling off into the crowd. Most of the seating is on the flat floor, with some elevated tables toward the rear. The girls appear after the show to take photos.

X Rocks ★★★½

APPEAL BY AGE	UNDER 21 –	21-37 ★★★½	38-50 ★★★½	51+ ★★★½

HOST CASINO AND SHOWROOM Bally's—The Back Room; ☎ 702-777-2782; caesars.com/ballys-las-vegas or xshowslasvegas.com

Type of show Topless revue. **Admission** $53–$81. **Cast size** 6. **Night of lowest attendance** Sunday. **Usual showtimes** Thursday–Sunday, 10 p.m. **Dark** Monday-Wednesday. **Topless** Yes. **Duration of presentation** 70 minutes.

DESCRIPTION AND COMMENTS Las Vegas topless revues rarely offer anything new or innovative. Thus, we were taken by surprise by *X Rocks.* First, the production features beautiful, skilled, and majorly athletic dancers, with choreography that makes the most of their talent. Second, the show is edgy and hot, the most sensual show of its kind save Cirque du Soleil's *Zumanity.* But what really grabbed us is the pace of the show—it comes at you in a blitz of 2- to 4-minute vignettes. Most topless shows can't get the dancers on and off stage in that amount of time. You literally don't have a chance to catch your breath between numbers. The staccato pace, all driven home by a backing track of classic rock, from Black Sabbath to the Beatles, leaves you wanting more of the act that just concluded and hyped in anticipation for the one to follow. It's high intensity all the way.

CONSUMER TIPS Bottom line, the show's great but the venue is crappy. *X Rocks* deserves better. Seating is on a non-tiered flat floor, and the stage is too low to see the performers if they're not standing. Acoustics are good, though, as is lighting. Just don't sit behind anyone taller than you.

Zombie Burlesque ★★★★

APPEAL BY AGE	UNDER 21 ★★★★½	21-37 ★★★★	38-50 ★★★★	51+ ★★★½

HOST CASINO AND SHOWROOM Miracle Mile Shops—V Theater; ☎ 702-260-7200 or 866-932-1818; zombieburlesqueshow.com

Type of show Zombie-style variety burlesque. **Admission** $80–$100. **Cast size** 8 performers and a 7-piece live band. **Night of lowest attendance** Tuesday or Wednesday. **Usual showtimes** Monday–Friday, 8:30 p.m.; Saturday, 8:30 and 10 p.m. **Dark** Sunday. **Topless** Yes. **Special comments** Must be 16 or older to attend. **Duration of presentation** 80 minutes.

DESCRIPTION AND COMMENTS Burlesque and zombies both blew up so big in recent years, making it seem inevitable these two overexposed pop culture clichés should join forces in Las Vegas, where all cutting-edge trends go to die. So it was no small shock that producer David Saxe's *Zombie Burlesque* has much more bite and brains than one might expect from such an opportunistic mash-up. The year is 1958, and the living and lurching alike are welcome at Club Z, the hippest joint in the post-apocalypse, where undead emcee Zenoch (Enoch Augustus Scott) keeps his troupe of decaying dancers from eating the live band by feeding them prisoners for lunch. The athletic cast, lathered in latex makeup that's more goofy than gory, deliver all the traditional burlesque pleasures, only with a perverse twist. The featured females each perform tightly choreographed strip-teases with carousel poles, pointe shoes, and aerial straps, accentuated by elaborate video backdrops and kinky S&M accessories. To cleanse your palate between gangrenous gams, chew on specialty acts such as bone-breaking contortionist Alonzo "Turf" Jones, drag cartoonist Steve "Tiny Bubbles" Daly, and a cross-dressing fan dancer who defies description.

The tone of Zombie Burlesque is irreverently macabre without becoming Walking Dead–grim, with copious references to B-grade sci-fi films. Zenoch proves an adept emcee, deftly controlling the often-rowdy crowd through participatory segments such as a Newlywed Game knockoff. His zombie puns may be groaners, but the "real music, real singing, and real boobs" are genuinely entertaining, from comic-book opening credits to the gospel finale. (The free vodka-spiked Jell-o shots distributed to the audience don't hurt either.) Our only complaint is that the band's amplification packs such a punch that they often overwhelm the clever lyrics. Zombie Burlesque may have a cast of corpses, but this is one of the liveliest, lustiest shows on the Strip.

CONSUMER TIPS The theater is fairly narrow but deep, with a steep rake for seats in the back half. VIP ticket holders sit up front and are the most likely to be selected for audience participation.

Zumanity by Cirque du Soleil *(see pages 216–218)*

REGARDING SHOWS NOT PROFILED

THE FOLLOWING ARE SHOWS that you may have heard of or seen advertised. They were not profiled in the preceding section for various reasons, ranging from too few performances to unpredictable schedules to mediocrity or worse. Once again, the shows are listed alphabetically.

- *ALL SHOOK UP* **(V THEATER AT MIRACLE MILE SHOPS)** This Elvis tribute features an excellent impersonator, Travis Allen, backed by a live band, who runs through a repertoire of Elvis's big hits. Straightforward, unembellished, and well done. For more on this show and the work of other E. P. impersonators around town, see gigmasters.com/search/elvis-impersonator-las-vegas-nv.

• **THE BACKSTREET BOYS, GWEN STEFANI, AND LIONEL RICHIE (PLANET HOLLYWOOD'S ZAPPOS THEATER)** The foregoing alternate residencies here. The Backstreet Boys, the best-selling boy band in history, showcase their polyphonic harmonies as they sing their greatest hits. Four-time Grammy-winner Lionel Richie entertains with all of his hits, while music and style icon Gwen Stefani is the latest star to take up residency here. For more information, call ☎ 855-234-7469 or visit caesars.com /planet-hollywood/shows.

• **BOYZ II MEN (MIRAGE)** Grammy Award–winning R&B group Boyz II Men performs a limited number of shows in their Mirage mini-residency filling in for Terry Fator in the Terry Fator Theatre. For more information, call ☎ 702-792-7777 or see mirage.com.

• **MARIAH CAREY, ROD STEWART, REBA MCENTIRE, BROOKS AND DUNN, JERRY SEINFELD, AND OTHERS (COLOSSEUM AT CAESARS PALACE)** All the foregoing do mini-residencies when Celine Dion is away. Mariah Carey has opened a new residency with her The Butterfly Returns production. An unusually intimate show for the mammoth Colosseum, Carey reprises the most beloved songs of her journey from ballad diva to hip-hop queen. For appearance dates, see caesars.com/caesars-palace.

• *MARILYN! THE NEW MUSICAL* This original production explores the mystique of a true American icon, Marilyn Monroe. The upbeat, biographical show tells the story of Monroe from troubled youth Norma Jeane to becoming a sex icon in the '50s and early '60s. Ruby Lewis stars, er . . . starred as Marilyn. Favorable reviews notwithstanding, the show closed after only 23 performances. It was good enough, however, that we think it likely to come back, probably renamed and revamped.

• **MATT GOSS (MIRAGE)** British crooner and frequent Las Vegas lounge act Matt Goss has recruited some dancers (The Dirty Virgins, no less) and set up shop at the 1 OAK nightclub at the Mirage. The playlist is eclectic but best suited to older patrons.

• **NITRO CIRCUS VEGAS (BALLY'S)** Opening in spring 2019, Nitro Circus will feature the best athletes in the world in FMX, BMX, skate, and scooter. The show is produced by Travis Pastrana, who in 2018 bested Evel Knievel's Vegas records by jumping over 52 crushed cars, 16 Greyhound buses, and the Caesars Palace fountain.

• *SEX TIPS FOR STRAIGHT WOMEN FROM A GAY MAN* **(ANTHONY COOLS SHOWROOM AT PARIS LAS VEGAS)** Starring Katie Kenner and Katch Gray, much of the advice in this show, not surprisingly, is about fellatio.

• **TAPE FACE (HARRAH'S)** New Zealander and *America's Got Talent* alum Sam Wills, aka Tape Face, performs stand-up comedy with tape over his mouth, relying on grunts, noises, props, and mime, but not speech. Most routines employ conscripted audience members. He's all over YouTube .com if you want to see his stuff. For more information, call ☎ 855-234-7469 or 702-777-2782 or visit caesars.com/harrahs-las-vegas.

LAS VEGAS NIGHTLIFE

IN SO MANY WAYS, Las Vegas's nightlife scene closely resembles the city's many buffets: amid the chaos, there's something for everybody. Today, Las Vegas makes billions as America's go-to city for dining, nightlife, shopping, and entertainment, but this was not always the case.

In the Rat Pack era, it was gaming that raked in the big bucks, with steakhouses and 99¢ breakfasts positioned as loss leaders, keeping players near the action at all times. Entertainment took the form of big-room shows with Elvis, Liberace, and Sinatra and the boys, and smoky lounges where the booze flowed endlessly. Disco wasn't even a twinkle in anyone's eye. Cut to 1988, when local bars Tramps and the Shark Club began—gasp—charging cover at the door. The 1990s brought the rise and subsequent demise of rave music and underground parties (much of which centered around Las Vegas's electronic-music trailblazers, Utopia nightclub and the Cande Factory), but by the Millennium the casinos themselves were creating nightlife worth getting off the couch and dressing up for: Club Rio, Studio 54, C2K, Ra....

Today, creating fulfilling party opportunities for tourists, locals, and everyone in between is big business for the casinos. And it's only intensifying. Electronic dance music currently dominates the club scene, with Top 40 and hip-hop (often called "open-format") occupying what balance remains. Celebrity nightclub appearances are waning, as the dominant draw today is the celebrity DJ: Tiësto, Calvin Harris, Zedd, and so on. (Don't worry if you don't know who these artists are—you soon shall.) Gone are the days of the DJ booth; DJs perform live on centrally located stages complete with confetti cannons, light shows, custom-choreographed entrances, and LED screens worthy of a stadium. And the word "residency" has come to mean everything from an in-house DJ who opens and closes nightly to the headliner who shows up just once each quarter. (That said, there is already a counter-movement in favor of live music. EDM lovers: this is a wait-and-see situation.)

The annual spate of trendy new venues on the Strip has slowed dramatically since the arrival of The Cosmopolitan in 2010, with casinos favoring rebranding over new construction. Downtown continues its rebirth with myriad bars and lounges, live music venues, coffee roasters, microbreweries, and independent restaurants. Las Vegas is again a buyer's market, with more clubs than tourists to fill all of them. Every visitor is ravenous for a piece of it, and every club wants to sell you something, anything to get you into *their* VIP booth rather than their neighbor's. Call it the upside. So keep your wits about you, and we'll show you how to reap the many benefits of the nightlife buffet.

Trend Alert! Brunch fever has utterly consumed Las Vegas: hot people, cool music, bottomless drinks. Sounds like a nightclub or lounge, but it's brunch. Try **STK's Sunday Brunch Club** during holiday weekends at The Cosmopolitan, **Lavo Party Brunch** at The Palazzo (seasonal), and **Herringbone** at Aria. For something truly out there, try the Italian "dim sum" brunch at **GIADA** in The

Cromwell. If you prefer something more traditional, **Bouchon** in The Venetian and **La Cave** in the Wynn scratch that itch. Also consider heading to the pools: **Marquee Dayclub, Drai's Beachclub, Encore Beach Club, Liquid, Bare, Wet Republic, Daylight, Tao Beach,** and **The Aquatic Club** all serve up exceptional poolside fare.

LAS VEGAS NIGHTLIFE BESTIARY

THE KEY TO UNLOCKING LAS VEGAS'S dizzying club scene is to do your homework *before* you arrive. You're already reading this handy guide, so that puts you light years beyond those who show up clueless, only to be preyed upon for being so unsavvy. But don't be discouraged if you de-plane at McCarran with little more of a clue than when you left home. Here's a quick-and-dirty rundown of just some of the categories of nightlife activity available to you.

CASINO BARS It's said that making a strong first impression is important. The same goes for the Strip resorts' casino, lobby, and center bars—they serve as your official welcome to the property. These establishments lure you in with curated soundtracks and sleek design, and then they win you over with expertly crafted cocktails and thoughtful beer and wine lists.

While receiving your room key quickly used to be enough to introduce you to your Hotels.com decision, you'll remember your inaugural cocktail long after your front desk representative's efficiency and cheerful demeanor.

These venues are generally open 24/7 and have one thing in common: speedy access to a good drink. Some even count among the city's finest beverage programs. Requirements for entry? A valid ID, a pulse, and an appreciation of cocktails. You're in Las Vegas—why not start the party at check-in?

Ones to try: Throw a rock and you'll hit one. Every casino has a bar, and most have several. Seek out Rojo Lounge (Palms); Lobby Bar, Cocktail Lounge, and Alto Bar (Caesars Palace); Bound (The Cromwell); Franklin (The Delano); Bond and Vesper (The Cosmopolitan); Aurora and Flight (Luxor); Rouge and Centrifuge (MGM Grand); Eyecandy Sound Lounge (Mandalay Bay); Center Bar (Hard Rock Hotel); and Petrossian Bar (Bellagio).

RESTAURANT BARS AND PUBS Las Vegas has become an international dining destination, and in a town known for cocktail carousing, it's no surprise that the epicurean expertise has extended to the drink menus. Restaurant bars and pubs occupy the gap between the too-casual casino bar and the swanky party lounge. They're less stringent about dress code than ultralounges and clubs, often feature a robust mixology program, and sometimes have live entertainment. Restaurant bars and pubs are a perfect place for dates, as well as large groups (with reservations, of course). Cover charges here are extremely rare, and speed of entry is usually gauged by capacity (expect a wait for any party size at Strip-side venues on the weekend).

Ones to try: Beerhaus and Sake Rok (The Park); Scotch 80 Prime (Palms); Chica, Delmonico Steakhouse, and Lagasse's Stadium (The Venetian); Libertine Social (Mandalay Bay); Starboard Tack and Herbs and Rye (Downtown Environs); 7th & Carson and Carson Kitchen (Downtown); Sparrow + Wolf (Chinatown); Nine Fine Irishmen (New York–New York); McFadden's (Town Square); The Pub (Crystals); Yard House (Town Square, Red Rock Resort, and the LINQ Promenade); Firefly and Tacos & Beer (Central Environs); and Beer Park (Paris).

COCKTAIL BARS AND LOUNGES Remember your first taste of Las Vegas on the big or small screen? When you saw crooners commanding a cocktailing crowd in a smoky, swanky spot? Well, those moments are few and far between in 21st-century Las Vegas. But if you want a taste of yesteryear, cocktail bars and lounges will give you the closest to what you're looking for. Whether Downtown, Center Strip, or off-Strip, lounges offer a heavy dose of class and ambience, forgoing the velvet rope dance in favor of getting you inside with a drink in your hand. Plush, open seating, elegant lighting, intriguing cocktails, and a possible small bites menu are the calling cards of a proper lounge. The town being so spread out, Las Vegas locals are accustomed to having to come together in the middle; lounges being so plentiful and accessible, they are at the heart of the "meet market" singles scene. Locals love their happy hours (which usually last 2–4 hours), so expect an after-work crowd early and a pre-club party later. Ease of entry is generally dependent upon the day of the week, conventions, and holidays; sometimes cover charges appear for special events. High-end restaurants also tend to have killer bars and lounges for cocktails and small bites.

Ones to try: Alexxa's Bar (Paris); The Dorsey (The Venetian); Rosina (The Palazzo); Bond and Chandelier (The Cosmopolitan); Vista Cocktail Lounge (Caesars Palace); Mandarin Bar (Mandarin Oriental); Parasol Up and Down (Wynn); Encore Players Lounge (Encore); Atomic Liquors, Downtown Cocktail Room, Mike Morey's Sip 'n' Tip, Oak & Ivy, The Laundry Room, and Velveteen Rabbit (Downtown); Rhumbar (The Mirage); and SkyFall (The Delano).

ULTRALOUNGES This was a specious marketing term invented by Las Vegas promoters quite a few years back, but "ultralounge" serves as well as anything to describe high-end venues that charge dearly both at the door and at the bar. Such places are immaculately designed and furnished, staffed with gorgeous servers (and ogrelike security), and policed to ensure compliance with a snappy dress code. With the rise of the megaclub, they're something of a dying breed. But if you're looking for a nightclub experience without all the pomp and circumstance, consider an ultralounge.

Ones to try: Alibi Ultra Lounge (Aria); Lily (Bellagio); Clique (The Cosmopolitan); Hyde Lounge (T-Mobile Arena); and Level Up (MGM Grand).

BOUTIQUE/INTIMATE NIGHTCLUBS Fed up with being pigeonholed as fashions trended toward smaller size, clubs for a time became "intimate" and "boutique" to differentiate themselves, taking advantage of hot hotel and travel buzzwords and thumbing their noses at ultralounges and the ever-swelling megaclub. Some boutique clubs are actually located *inside* of larger clubs! Don't be fooled, though—these venues regularly book some of the biggest names to command the DJ decks or light up the club with electrifying live performances.

Ones to try: Hyde Bellagio (Bellagio); 1 OAK (The Mirage); Chateau Nightclub & Rooftop (Paris); Ling Ling Lounge & Club inside Hakkasan (MGM Grand); Heart of Omnia inside Omnia (Caesars Palace); and the Living Room inside Intrigue (Wynn).

COUNTRY AND COUNTRY-CROSSOVER As country music keeps on infiltrating today's mainstream music charts, it's no surprise that venues dedicated to it have started to sprout up in numbers here in Las Vegas. Line dancing to today's Top-40 hits? VIP bottle service and Stetsons? The latest trend to take root is the country-crossover nightclub, where you might find yourself two-stepping to the Black Eyed Peas, Kenny Chesney, and Justin Timberlake, then riding a mechanical bull to the sounds of crossover artists Taylor Swift, Keith Urban, and Carrie Underwood.

Ones to try: Stoney's Rockin' Country (Town Square); PBR Rock Bar (Miracle Mile Shops); Rockhouse (The Venetian); Coyote Ugly (New York–New York); Toby Keith's I Love This Bar & Grill (Harrah's); and Gilley's Saloon (TI).

NIGHTCLUBS/MEGACLUBS Resorts now customarily spend tens of millions on nightlife, so you can expect the best in everything from the attractive staff and the stylish digs to the internationally renowned DJs and the celebrity contingent. These sprawling labyrinths may cover several floors and include dance room(s), side lounges, bars, a restaurant, VIP rooms, and possible access to a pool. They might even have multiple entrances. Count on long lines at every entrance regardless. Expect to wait an hour or more to get in, if ever. Inside, you'll find massive crowds of beautiful people, dressed to the nines and ready to party, plus a half dozen ways to entertain yourself—DJs, dance troupes, novelty performers, you name it. The time, distance, and expense effectively kill the idea of club-hopping, but with all this on offer, you probably won't need anything else. Promoters use every trick in the books to assemble the most attractive clientele in one place. Bottle service is king, and everyone else is there to merely fill in the spaces between the most valuable real estate. Check your ego at the door unless you intend to spend heavily to keep up with the wealthiest of the Joneses, and that means both once you are inside the ropes as well as just to make it through them. These days, nightclubs have more in common with live concerts and EDM music festivals than they do with the hot spots of the city's past, so there's no shame in buying tickets online in advance. It saves everyone time and gets you inside faster.

Ones to try: XS (Encore); Tao (The Venetian); Marquee (The Cosmopolitan); Light (Mandalay Bay); Hakkasan (MGM Grand); Drai's

Nightclub (The Cromwell); Omnia (Caesars Palace); Intrigue (Wynn); and Jewel (Aria).

AFTERHOURS When the clubs close, the staff doesn't exactly rush home and go to bed, nor does the party crowd. Those wishing to test the limits of their endurance can do so at one of a few dedicated late-night joints offering after-hours parties. Doors open as early as midnight or as late as 4 a.m., but all keep the music and drinks flowing till dawn, and often well beyond that. Music usually tends toward house, trance, and electronica, but some offer hip-hop occasionally. While there is almost always a cover charge, lines are not so much a problem here as parking. But at 6 a.m., should you really be driving anyway?

Ones to try: Afterhours Lounge at The Artisan (1501 W. Sahara Ave.) and Drai's After Hours (The Cromwell).

POOL PARTIES Incredible to think there was ever a time when such an animal didn't exist in Las Vegas. That is, until Rehab came on the scene in 2004, turning day into nightlife. When Wet Republic Ultra Pool opened in 2008, it finished what Rehab started, cementing the term "daylife" in the party lexicon. Just about every casino these days invests in the holy trinity of nightclub, ultralounge, and the hip dining experience loosely called "dining with a scene" or the less appetizing "vibe dining." But during the summer—roughly from March into October—adults-only party pools pop up, joining the trinity and boasting every amenity the clubs do, only without the roof: bottle service, VIP hosts, cocktail servers, DJ music. Just add water, cabanas, hot tubs, and, in some cases, European bathing (read: topless). As with nightclubs, you can snag tickets to such venues, but admittance to this flesh parade is at the doorman's discretion and is very much determined by appearance and the maintenance of a healthy female-to-male ratio.

unofficial **TIP**
Pool parties don't just happen by day, and daylife doesn't necessarily happen by pools! Check out Night-Swim at XS (Encore) and Eclipse at Daylight (Mandalay Bay). And in the off-season, Lavo Brunch (The Palazzo); climate-controlled pool and pool-side parties at Marquee's Dayclub Dome (The Cosmopolitan); and Encore Beach Club (Encore) keep partiers occupied.

Ones to try: Aquatic Club (The Palazzo); Bare (The Mirage); Daydream (M Resort); Daylight (Mandalay Bay); Drai's Beachclub (The Cromwell); Encore Beach Club (Encore); Retro and Foxtail (SLS); Liquid (Aria); Marquee Dayclub (The Cosmopolitan); European Pool (Artisan); Rehab (Hard Rock); Tao Beach (The Venetian); Venus European Pool Lounge (Caesars Palace); and Wet Republic (MGM Grand).

What NOT to bring to a pool party:

- **Large backpacks:** Small purses and bags are OK but will likely be searched.
- **Valuables:** Unless you have a cabana with a safe (and many of the newer ones do), take only what you need.
- **Liquids:** All beverages must be purchased after going through security.
- **Medications:** Paramedics are almost always on hand, so leave all pills and

potions behind. You can argue for inhalers, insulin syringes, and EpiPens, but be prepared for a fight.

- **Weapons** of any and all kinds. Duh.
- **Glass:** Again—duh.

CELEBRITIES

THEY'RE EVERYWHERE, and it isn't by happenstance. Celebrity sightings are rarely just coincidental; more often than not, they are arranged in advance by ambitious nightclub promoters, publicists, and sponsors. Stars of film, music, and TV are regularly booked to tip their hat, make a toast, pose with their (often fake!) birthday cake, or belt out a tune or two. For a club to bill a star as a "guest performer" is to subject itself to a mandatory live-entertainment tax (LET) or casino-entertainment tax (CET). Many do this, but just as many do not, and prefer instead to keep a live mic on hand, you know, *just in case*. Billed as "hosts" or "special guests," some of today's hottest artists can be seen performing a quick two- or three-song set. Just be prepared to wait—sometimes these performances don't happen until the wee hours of the morning.

If you party a little too hearty and wake up feeling the worse for wear, **Hangover Heaven** (3281 S. Highland Drive, Suite 806, 702-850-4297, **hangoverheaven.com**) offers restorative vitamin IVs and amino acid cocktails starting at $159–$259. Treatments are available Monday–Thursday 8 a.m.–4 p.m. and Friday–Sunday 8 a.m.–6 p.m. at their walk-in office, in your hotel room, and aboard the Hangover Heaven Bus, their mobile clinic. The clinic was founded by anesthesiologist Dr. Jason Burke, and all treatments are administered by registered nurses and nurse practitioners, who will arrest your retching and rehydrate you in time to head back out and do more damage.

INSIDER ADVICE

LAS VEGAS—NOT JUST FOR WEEKENDS ANYMORE Vegas was, is, and always will be a weekend destination—one that hits its stride at about 8 p.m. on Friday and doesn't stop to take a breath until early Monday morning. It's a given that the town's bars, lounges, and clubs will be filled to the brim on Friday and Saturday nights. But what all locals (and an increasing number of tourists) know is that Sunday–Thursday the clubs don't close their doors; they just refocus. The secret to midweek partying is knowing which night each club holds its local-industry night, thus avoiding the tourist traps that will take anyone off the street—Birkenstocks, shorts, and all. Expect gratuitous contests, costumes, gimmicky promotions, and hordes of locals partying like it's Mardi Gras. While there, get on everyone's email list, bring business cards, and if someone says he's a VIP host from another venue (as many will on industry nights), buy him a shot—he's your new best friend. Reap the benefits later with easy access to his venue and maybe a few other perks (drink tickets, etc.).

Ones to try: Sundays at NightSwim at XS (seasonally, Encore); Mondays at Marquee (The Cosmopolitan) and Jewel (Aria); Tuesdays at Hyde (Bellagio), Drai's Beachclub (The Cromwell), and Omnia (Caesars Palace); Wednesdays at Intrigue (Wynn) and 1 OAK (The Mirage); and Thursdays at Tao (The Venetian), Hakkasan (MGM Grand), and NightSwim at Encore Beach Club (seasonally, Encore).

GETTING IN Showing up is half the battle, so do so nice and early. For any party size or gender mix other than two attractive young ladies by themselves, save yourself and your guests the agonizing, soul-crushing velvet-rope experience by doing some of the work ahead of time. At the rope, the uninitiated and uninformed can expect a long wait (30 minutes to upwards of 2 hours), a complete lack of eye contact, and even possible ridicule. Sometimes doormen employ intimidation and humiliation to pressure a group's point man into investing his life savings in bottle service or huge tips to pass through the pearly gates. Or worse, a doorman might keep you in line for an eternity only to finally grant you entry . . . into a half-empty club. Consider yourself warned.

Your best bet for getting into your club of choice is to contact the club directly. You can consult jackcolton.com for the lead VIP hosts' direct email address and cell numbers. As previously mentioned, doing your research and buying tickets in advance will also save some time.

TIME IS MONEY Ah yes, bottle service. If the dutifully paying customers who line the bars and walls of a club are the meat and potatoes of the industry, bottle-service patrons are the dessert. But nightclubs like to have dessert first, so you will see bottle-service patrons waiting far less time to get in. But remember that these patrons are paying a great deal more for that privilege. The bottom line is you will spend time or money. In other words, if you want to spend very little money, you can get in for just the cover charge, but you might wait a long time. Or, consider investing in bottle service (that is, buying a bottle—or, likely, multiple bottles—of liquor to get a VIP table or booth) to bypass the line entirely, thus spending very little time outside the club. The real estate itself is a perk for ladies looking to rest their stiletto-strapped feet, and it's also somewhere to store pesky belongings (clutches, purses, coats, etc.)—just make sure someone in your party stays at the table (and stays moderately sober) to keep an eye out. Bottles can go up to the high hundreds, thousands, and even into the tens of thousands for rare champagnes, cognacs, or special packages. Some bottle-service packages even come with elaborate displays (think: sparklers, employees parading out with signs, and presentations themed to the current holiday weekend).

unofficial **TIP**
Look closely at that bill! If you're doing bottle service, inquire beforehand what taxes and gratuities will be added. When the bill comes, make sure you're not adding gratuity on top of the server's "auto-grat" (unless you mean to), and be careful not to put the total onto the sneaky extra line sometimes added below the customary server tip line for tipping your busser (unless you mean to).

While a liter of Grey Goose is obtainable at any neighborhood liquor store for about $40, it's not what's inside the bottle you're paying for. It's the valuable real estate of having a private booth or table, the attention of an attractive cocktail server, a busser to clean up spills and refresh ice, and likely even a neighboring thug of a security guard to keep an eye on your prize. Bottle service is unique to each club: one table's price might be determined by location, while another's is by the number of people (usually three to four people per bottle). Be prepared for a possible shakedown; you might find yourself being walked to an undesirable table, past better ones, only to be told that those tables cost extra—cash preferably, payable right now to your host. If this happens, stand firm and ask to see other available tables within your price range. Once you have the table, take your time with your bottles and resist your alluring server's offers to pour you shots, as you may find yourself required to order more bottles or else shove off to make room for another party. Milk that bottle for all it's worth!

COMFORT ZONES A place for everyone, and everyone in their place. Vegas has it. Just as there are clubs, bars, and lounges where everyone can feel comfortable, there are some where not everyone would. The top clubs target a 21-to-45 age range, and though guests of any age (over 21) are welcome to try their luck at the rope or make a reservation, they may find that it's the other patrons who might make a club unfriendly to someone over that hump. Tight confines, loud music, inebriated neighbors, and little to no elbowroom might make for an uncomfortable evening.

But some venues make it easier for patrons of any age to enjoy themselves. The city's many dueling piano bars, such as Napoleon's in Paris, play everything from the best of the 1980s to today in a convivial environment that is inclusive rather than exclusive. **Downtown Cocktail Room** and **Mike Morey's Sip 'n' Tip** will appeal to the sophisticated imbiber from any age bracket. Even from Hakkasan Group—which has Hakkasan and Omnia, two of Vegas's hottest clubs—**Lily** is small and approachable without giving up the Vegas excitement you came for. Just about every casino has something that will appeal to the 35-and-over set; they want to keep you on property and will do just about anything to satisfy, and that includes providing nightlife venues for every age group.

DRESS CODES Inside every club you will witness flagrant violations of dress code—hats, sneakers, T-shirts, ripped jeans, and more. Attempt to emulate this behavior and you may find yourself left on the wrong side of the ropes. The only people who can get away with this sort of rebellion are celebrities, well-known local socialites, and the DJ. Even if you think you are on close, personal terms with a doorman or VIP host, you might see him go pale and cold when you show up in tennis shoes and a ball cap. Gentlemen, pack dress shoes, a nice pair of jeans, and remember that a sport coat (thrown over anything) cures most ills. Ladies, you pretty much have carte blanche, but think practical—comfiest heels (don't be the girl walking through the casino barefoot later!) and your smallest effective purse.

TIPPING Vegas is a tipping town, so keep plenty of small bills handy to do just that. Aside from the valet and the coat-check girl, tip anyone who goes out of their way for you. The doorman who looked the other way about your scuzzy loafers, the VIP host who walked you past the line, the bathroom attendant who got the cranberry juice out of your shirt . . . all are deserving of your monetary gratitude. Bartenders and cocktail servers can usually be tipped on a bill if you're charging your round. Otherwise, cash tips are highly recommended lest you find yourself high and dry the rest of the night.

If your queuing situation is looking hopeless, you can try to encourage (read: tip, grease, bribe) a doorman or VIP host to expedite the process. A good rule of thumb is $20–$25 per head, but with so many trying the same thing, it's not so much the amount as the ease of his slipping you through that will help or hurt the situation. A doorman letting in 10 guys will get a stern look from his boss, while a doorman letting in six ladies and four guys might get a mere eyebrow raise. Gentlemen, pad your group heavily with women and keep the guy count low. Be discreet (don't wave money around), but make your presence and your willingness to play (read: pay) known.

THE DOWNTOWN RENAISSANCE Downtown Las Vegas is back in a big way! Fremont Street is the original Las Vegas Strip. It caps off the current or "New" Strip like a T, with a covered pedestrian entertainment zone called The Fremont Street Experience to the west of Las Vegas Boulevard and the Fremont East Entertainment District to the east. Tourists are generally drawn to the bright lights of "The Old Strip" like moths to the Luxor light, but savvy travelers are finally beginning to follow the locals' example and venture into Fremont East territory. There you will find the sophisticated and cocktail-centric **Downtown Cocktail Room** and **Mike Morey's Sip 'n' Tip** within, the cavelike hipster haven **The Griffin** (complete with fire pits inside—making it a fabulous winter option), as well as **Atomic Liquors, Vanguard Lounge,** irreverent and dive-y music spot **Beauty Bar,** and piano bar **Don't Tell Mama** (where the bartenders pour drinks just as well as they belt out Broadway classics and modern favorites). There's also the whiskey-centric **Oak & Ivy** (in Downtown Container Park), **Park on Fremont** (which boasts a killer patio for al fresco cocktailing), gastropub **The Smashed Pig,** and **Commonwealth,** with the speakeasy-esque **Laundry Room** within. For coffee, vinyl records, modern art, and even a beer (after 7 p.m.), visit **PublicUs** on East Fremont at Maryland Parkway. For a bite with your beverage, stop into **Carson Kitchen, 7th & Carson, Atomic Kitchen, Le Thai, Le Pho,** or **Evel Pie.** Venture just north of the Fremont Street Experience to find **Triple George Grill, Pizza Rock,** and **Mob Bar,** before letting your hair down and perhaps donating a bra to the impressive collection found at gritty biker bar **Hogs & Heifers.** In the nearby 18 blocks that make up Las Vegas's Arts District are **Artifice, Mundo at Mingo, Velveteen Rabbit,** local brewery **Hop Nuts Brewing Co.,** and, most recently, **Rebar** and **Jammyland.** In the greater Downtown area, **Starboard Tack** is the city's new rum-focused late-night place, **Herbs and Rye** is the cocktail bar that brought the city's mixology scene to the world stage, **Tenaya Creek Brewery** is definitely worth a pint or two on a hot day, and **Sparrow + Wolf** in Chinatown is a recent cocktail spot everyone is talking about.

If you can't find something to do every night in Las Vegas, you're just not trying that hard.

Note: All clubs profiled below can be found on the maps in Part 4, Dining and Restaurants, pages 368–379.

NIGHTCLUB PROFILES

1 OAK

New York's one-of-a-kind club is now two of a kind

The Mirage, 3400 Las Vegas Blvd. S.; ☎ 702-693-8300; 1oaklasvegas.com
MID-STRIP AND ENVIRONS

Cover Wednesday, Friday, and Saturday, $30 and up men; locals free on Wednesday; prices may vary. **Mixed drinks** $15 and up. **Wine** $12 and up. **Beer** $10 and up. **Dress** Upscale fashionable attire. **Food available** None. **Hours** Wednesday, Friday, and Saturday, 10:30 p.m.–close.

WHO GOES THERE Socialites in training, celebrity gawkers, and people somehow still looking for Jet Nightclub, the space's previous incarnation.

WHAT GOES ON A raucous party focusing on the clubber as the main attraction, with occasional celebrity hosts (think Nick Cannon, Mariah Carey, and the Kardashian clan) and guest DJs spinning Top 40, hip-hop, and house.

SETTING AND ATMOSPHERE A sexy yet unpredictable environment, 1 OAK merges art and fashion, the famous and the infamous, cutting edge and the established, providing a visually stunning destination that plays for a one-of-a-kind experience. Visitors to the previous Jet Nightclub will be delighted to see the signature stripper poles and dance floor pit are still among the architectural features, but with updated design elements and a modern edge.

IF YOU GO As with any Las Vegas hot spot, lines can be lengthy, so arrive early, and maybe even stop by during the day to make friends with the promoter stationed at the door on day duty. This might give you a chance to be put on his or her guest list for that night to possibly reduce your cover charge and bump you up to the shorter guest list line.

ALSO TRY Hyde Bellagio (☎ 702-693-8700, hydebellagio.com).

Alexxa's Bar

Sip on sangria at this Strip-side space

Paris Las Vegas, 3655 Las Vegas Blvd. S.; ☎ 702-331-5100; alexxasbar.com
MID-STRIP AND ENVIRONS

Cover None. **Mixed drinks** $15 and up. **Wine** $9 and up. **Beer** $8 and up. **Dress** Stylish casual. **Food available** Sharable plates like dips, fries, and sliders are complemented with flatbreads and delectable desserts. **Hours** 24/7.

WHO GOES THERE Tourists looking for quick preclub or show bites, Strip-side barhoppers lured in by the welcoming vibe, and local winos who want a break from suburban imbibing.

WHAT GOES ON Quickly after its opening, the venue branched out from being just a bar with numerous weekly entertainment offerings. Alexxa's features both DJs and live music from locals and touring acts.

SETTING AND ATMOSPHERE With warm wood and black metal features, firefly-inspired light fixtures, and accents of sunshine yellow, Alexxa's walks the line between rustic chic and cozy contemporary. Did we mention the Strip-side patio with views of the Bellagio fountains?

IF YOU GO Take advantage of the location and snag a table on the patio. Then order a glass of sangria or a punch bowl for the table and enjoy the aquatic show—and the Strip's often-hilarious people-watching.

ALSO TRY In search of a good glass of wine on the Strip? Try **La Cave Wine & Food Hideaway** at the Wynn (☎ 702-770-7000, wynnlasvegas.com).

Apex Social Club

Rooftop revelry at its finest

Palms, 4321 W. Flamingo Road; ☎ 702-944-5980; palms.com
MID-STRIP AND ENVIRONS

Cover $25 females, $50 males. **Mixed drinks** $14 and up. **Wine** $12 and up. **Beer** $10 and up. **Dress** Stylish casual. **Food available** None. **Hours** Thursday–Sunday, 5 p.m.–late.

WHO GOES THERE Millennials seeking selfies at the city's newest nightclub. Actually, anyone seeking selfies at the city's newest nightclub.

WHAT GOES ON Apex has been host to some of the biggest names in music, some supplying sound and others simply presiding over the party as its official host—rapper Nas, DJ Questlove (from The Roots and *The Tonight Show Starring Jimmy Fallon*), and Travis Barker have all stepped inside Las Vegas's latest nightlife offering.

SETTING AND ATMOSPHERE Futuristic in design, Apex looks like a nightclub you'd find on *Star Trek*'s Starship Enterprise. With luxe leather couches, sleek lines, and glass-encased sculptures that look like embalmed aliens, Apex is like nothing you've ever seen in Las Vegas—and that's really cool.

IF YOU GO Be sure to take in the near-360-degree view of the city, as Apex stands 55 floors high on the rooftop of the Palms tower. And snag a selfie with one of those sculptures—your Instagram will blow up with "what's that?" inquisitions.

ALSO TRY Looking for a party with a view? Try **Foundation Room** at the top of Mandalay Bay (☎ 702-632-7631, houseofblues.com/lasvegas).

Artisan Afterhours

The city's hottest underground afterhours

Artisan, 1501 W. Sahara Ave.; ☎ 702-214-4000; artisanhotel.com
NORTH STRIP AND ENVIRONS

Cover None. **Mixed drinks** $10 and up. **Wine** $10 and up. **Beer** $6 and up. **Dress** Stylish casual. **Food available** None. **Hours** Friday and Saturday, midnight–7 a.m.

WHO GOES THERE Vampires, party monsters, night crawlers, and off-duty industry members blowing off steam before (and even after) the next day dawns. Birthday boys and girls; book your group in advance to enjoy buy-one-get-one-free bottle service.

LAS VEGAS NIGHTCLUBS

NAME OF CLUB | TYPE OF CLUB

1 OAK | New York's one-of-a-kind club is now two of a kind

Alexxa's | Sip on sangria at this Strip-side space

Apex Social Club | Rooftop revelry at its finest

Artisan Afterhours | The city's hottest underground afterhours

Bound | Lobby bar dripping with style

The Chandelier | Dazzling three-story pre-post cocktail bar

Chateau Nightclub & Rooftop | Opulent indoor-outdoor nightlife

Clique | Your girl's favorite lounge

Commonwealth | Downtown's largest nightlife hub

The Dorsey | Fête in fashion at this swanky Strip spot

Downtown Cocktail Room & Mike Morey's Sip 'n' Tip | Cozy mixology mecca

Drai's Beachclub & Nightclub | The Strip's highest rooftop megaclub and pool complex

Encore Beach Club at Night | Party outside under the stars and inside with them

The Foundry | The ideal cross between concert venue and club

Hakkasan | 60,000 square feet of party potential, plus celebrity DJs

House of Blues | Cover bands, live rock, and headliners in a casual scene

Hyde Bellagio | Boutique-y L.A.-style club with an A-List view

Intrigue | A safe bet on the element of surprise

Jewel | Aria's glittering nightlife treasure

Light | Las Vegas's legendary hot spot is resurrected

Lily Bar & Lounge | Central gathering spot at the heart of Bellagio

Marquee | Glamorous megaclub and DJ magnet

Omnia | The nightlife mothership of Caesars Palace

Rí Rá | Authentic Irish music, food, drinks, and *craíc*

Rosina | The Jazz Age gets an update at The Palazzo

Sayers Club | The hot, younger sibling of Hollywood's famous outpost

Tao | A labyrinthine restaurant, lounge, and megaclub

XS | Excessively beautiful, inside and out

WHAT GOES ON When the restaurants close and the clubs are already hitting their stride, the evening is just getting started at the Artisan. Early birds enjoy bottle specials, and those who simply can't call it a night at 4 a.m. enjoy the ultimate people-watching, plus friendly bartenders. Special guest DJs bring true underground electronic music to a party that often spills over to the patio and pool deck in summer.

SETTING AND ATMOSPHERE Tucked away just minutes from the Strip, the Artisan Hotel is in the midst of a cosmetic transition from quirky, artsy locals hideaway to sophisticated, modern European-style boutique oasis. Inside, the Artisan Bar & Ultralounge off the main lobby has unique decor with luxurious dark woods and leather couches.

IF YOU GO Go late. *Really* late. Why not? Plenty of clubs will help you see 4 a.m., maybe 5 a.m., but few can see you through till dawn with such ease and little hassle at the door. The party is usually hopping inside until well after the sun is up. If that's not your style, Artisan Amplified goes off from a more civilized 6–10 p.m., with live musicians performing in the space Monday–Friday.

ALSO TRY Drai's Afterhours in The Cromwell (☎ 702-737-0555, draisafter hourslv.com); **Crazy Horse III** (☎ 702-673-1700, crazyhorse3.com); and wherever Afterhours happens to be operating at the moment—most recently, that would be **The Sahara Lounge** (☎ 702-907-6669, 1000 E. Sahara Ave., afterlasvegas.com).

Bound

Lobby bar dripping with style

The Cromwell, 3595 Las Vegas Blvd. S.; ☎ 702-777-3777; caesars.com/cromwell
MID-STRIP AND ENVIRONS

Cover None. **Mixed drinks** $17 and up. **Wine** $13 and up. **Beer** $8 and up. **Dress** Casual. **Specials** None. **Food available** Small plates and antipasti such as salumi picante pizzette and cacciatore-style chicken wings from GIADA, also in The Cromwell. **Hours** Monday–Thursday, 4 p.m.–midnight; Friday–Sunday, noon–2 a.m.

WHO GOES THERE For resort guests, passersby, and locals alike, Bound is a see-and-be-seen spot. Located just inside the valet doors and off the main lobby of the Strip's first boutique hotel, this is a mixology vortex into which everyone on property will at some point be pulled.

WHAT GOES ON Whether it's after work, before dinner, or before the night really gets going, a cocktail here sets a sophisticated tone for whatever's to follow. Bound couples lively classic and original libations with live music nightly. Try a classic or signature cocktail, then wander over to the Liquid History cabinet to see what rare bottles are currently on display.

SETTING AND ATMOSPHERE The distinctive circular bar serves as a centerpiece for this elegant space. Dark gold and amber tones and subtle lighting impart a feeling of warmth and intimacy throughout. Plush seating and curtains surround the bar, allowing guests to step away from the madness of the Strip and enjoy themselves in a classy, relaxing atmosphere.

IF YOU GO Pregame for a long night with one of the espresso cocktails, made from espresso that's infused during the brewing process with liqueurs, beer, champagne, and even Red Bull, then served in frozen Italian Moka coffee pots.

ALSO TRY Petrossian in Bellagio (☎ 888-987-6667, bellagio.com); **Vesper** in the Cosmopolitan (☎ 702-698-7000, cosmopolitanlasvegas.com); and **The Barrymore** in the Royal Resort (☎ 702-407-5303, barrymorelv.com).

The Chandelier

Dazzling three-story pre-post cocktail bar

The Cosmopolitan, 3708 Las Vegas Blvd. S.; ☎ 702-698-7000; cosmopolitanlasvegas.com **MID-STRIP AND ENVIRONS**

Cover None. **Mixed drinks** $16 and up. **Wine** $12 and up. **Beer** $7 and up. **Dress** Casual. **Food available** None. **Hours** Level 1: 24/7; Level 1.5: 6 p.m.–2 a.m.; Level 2: 11 a.m.–4 a.m.

WHO GOES THERE Couples grabbing cocktails before or after dinner, groups fueling up before (or instead of) heading to the clubs.

WHAT GOES ON Whether for sheer convenience and location's sake, or because they heard there was a top-notch beverage program to be sampled, bodies pile up at The Chandelier by evening time, when everyone kind of just joins together as one giant party.

SETTING AND ATMOSPHERE A thing of certain beauty: Multiple bar levels are stacked vertically within a massive three-story chandelier constructed of more than two million glass crystals, which dominates the center of the casino. Stairs and elevators connect Levels 1, 1.5, and 2, which cumulatively serve as a center bar, a stand-alone hot spot, and a central meeting point for Marquee Nightclub's VIP hosts and their would-be patrons.

IF YOU GO Find seats first, then either send emissaries to the bar or send up flares to attract the attention of a cocktail server. From the menus, go for classics and award-winning cocktails on Level 1, flirty and feminine notions on Level 2, and avant-garde (read: experimental) mixology in between on Level 1.5.

ALSO TRY The Cosmopolitan's other fine jewels: **Vesper** just off the lobby, **Bond** by the Strip entrance, the **Talon Club** (The Cosmopolitan's high-stakes gaming room, which offers bespoke cocktails and a self-serve whiskey bar for players), and **Clique,** a chic lounge across the way from Vesper; cosmopolitanlasvegas.com.

Chateau Nightclub & Rooftop

Opulent indoor-outdoor nightlife

Paris Las Vegas, 3655 Las Vegas Blvd. S.; ☎ 702-776-7770; chateaunights.com **MID-STRIP AND ENVIRONS**

Cover $30 men, $20 ladies; local ladies always get in free. **Mixed drinks** $14 and up. **Wine** $12 and up. **Beer** $9 and up. **Dress** Fashionable; no sports jerseys, tank tops on men, tennis shoes, or athletic wear of any kind. **Food available** None, but the club sits directly above Hexx Kitchen and Bar, which serves 24/7. **Hours** Wednesday–Saturday, 10:30 p.m.–close.

WHO GOES THERE Tourists from all over, overjoyed to partake in the mass gawking at the usual suspects from this group's stable of celebrities, including hot hip-hoppers, famous athletes, and young Hollywood.

WHAT GOES ON The Rooftop, perched directly beneath the Eiffel Tower Restaurant, offers magnificent views of the Strip and is French party central, with DJs playing Top 40 and French maids fetching bottles and parading sparklers to tables.

SETTING AND ATMOSPHERE Think *Alice in Wonderland,* assuming Wonderland was located in France. Here, nightlife coexists with its host casino in theme-y cooperation: oversize gilt and silver mirrors, exaggerated furniture, cocktail staff in French maid unis, one DJ booth atop a fireplace, another atop a bar, and so on. But implied Francophilia gives way to out-and-out luxury outside, where private VIP cabanas overlook the Strip and directly oppose the Bellagio fountains.

IF YOU GO Begin the evening downstairs with dinner and gourmet chocolate at Hexx. Steal a quick look at the inside of the club, but then make an immediate beeline for the outdoors to dance the night away under the Eiffel Tower—the Las Vegas version, of course.

ALSO TRY **1923 Bourbon Bar** in Mandalay Bay (☎ 702-912-4001, 1923lv.com).

Clique

The Cosmopolitan, 3708 Las Vegas Blvd. S.; ☎ 702-698-7939; cliquelv.com
MID-STRIP AND ENVIRONS

Cover None, but depending on the event, there may be a food and beverage minimum. **Mixed drinks** $18 and up. **Wine** $15 and up. **Beer** $12 and up. **Dress** Trendy, chic, and upscale. **Food available** Chef Brian Massie's kitchen puts out craveable, shareable items such as signature wings, mini sliders, and sushi. **Hours** Daily, 4 p.m.–3 a.m.

WHO GOES THERE Clique is an ideal spot for groups to gather before moving on to the evening's main course, but there's also enough of a scene and a lively enough bar to keep one's attention all night. Local DJs, the likes of Kid Conrad, Stretch, Neva, and D-Miles, cycle through keeping the vibe fresh, while industry locals mix and mingle.

WHAT GOES ON Hip-hop, Top 40, and classic rock sounds dominate, drawing passersby from the casino floor like a Siren's song, though certainly there are worse fates than a plush couch and attractive neighbors. Major sporting events are another huge draw.

SETTING AND ATMOSPHERE Intimate and opulent, as you might expect from a major casino lounge, but with zero kitsch. This is the "little black dress" of lounges—everyone looks like a million bucks in it.

IF YOU GO Do not order your usual! More attention has been paid to the beverage program here than the typical pre-post watering hole. Try any of the twists on classic cocktails and party-ready shooters, or, as a fun alternative to bottle service, have showy cocktails prepared tableside from a cart by your (momentarily) private mixologist (Bow Street Banana for the win!).

ALSO TRY **Hyde Bellagio** (☎ 702-693-8700, hydebellagio.com) and **Lily Bar & Lounge** (☎ 702-693-8300, lilylasvegas.com).

Commonwealth

525 Fremont St.; ☎ 702-445-6400; commonwealthlv.com **DOWNTOWN**

Cover $5 downstairs, $20 rooftop after 10 p.m. Friday and Saturday. **Mixed drinks** $12 and up. **Wine** $9 and up. **Beer** $9 and up. **Dress** Fashionable. **Specials** Happy hour Wednesday–Friday, 7–9 p.m. **Food available** None. **Hours** Tuesday–Thursday, 7 p.m.–2 a.m.; Friday and Saturday, 6 p.m.–2 a.m.

WHO GOES THERE Hipsters, students, off-duty DJs, and diehard fashionistas. Don't be turned off by the velvet rope and tattooed doorman; Fremont Street is the epicenter of the Downtown Las Vegas revival, so there is still a rough element that occasionally needs bouncing.

WHAT GOES ON The owners cringe a little to hear it, but this antique-y, Boston-inspired bar and pub frequently becomes something of a nightclub. Fortunately, it's Downtown's hottest one. On any given night, you'll find everything from rooftop music and playful signature cocktails to live music, DJs, and special events—it's almost never a dull scene at the bar.

SETTING AND ATMOSPHERE Awash in warm incandescent light, Commonwealth's downstairs bar is all dark, grainy wood and exposed brick. Artwork and photos are of the vintage and ironic variety. And, no, you're not hallucinating—that is indeed an albino peacock welcoming you to the bar. Crystal chandeliers are nicely juxtaposed against the worn, industrial ambience, much of it genuine, as this building was once the laundry facility for the nearby landmark El Cortez. Upstairs, one of Downtown's many rooftop bars offers 360-degree views of the area's burgeoning scene.

IF YOU GO Text your name, number in your party, and requested date and time to ☎ 702-701-1466 to inquire about getting a seat in the Laundry Room, the tiny speakeasy that used to be part of the laundry facility; walk-ups are handled on a first-come, first-served basis. Inside, a lone mixologist stirs up classic and original cocktails to a soundtrack of Prohibition-era jazz and standards. The Laundry Room operates nightly from 7 p.m. till late.

ALSO TRY **Park on Fremont** at 506 Fremont Street (☎ 702-834-3160, parkonfremont.com).

The Dorsey

Fête in fashion at this swanky Strip spot

The Venetian, 3355 Las Vegas Blvd. S.; ☎ 702-414-1945; venetian.com
MID-STRIP AND ENVIRONS

Cover None. **Mixed drinks** $15 and up. **Wine** $17 and up. **Beer** $8.50 and up. **Dress** Casual. **Food available** None. **Hours** Nightly, 3 p.m.–4 a.m.

WHO GOES THERE Foodies looking for an after-dinner nightcap spot, following a fabulous meal at one of The Venetian's many spectacular culinary collection destinations. The lounge is also popular among cigar connoisseurs (just ask for a casino hostess to bring you a selection of stogies) and conventioneers hoping to score a deal over drinks.

WHAT GOES ON Reserved revelry. The Dorsey attracts a crowd that's done with the *Hangover*-style Las Vegas experience but still wants to enjoy a cocktail or two at an opulent mid-Strip spot—either after dinner or before a night spent at the tables.

SETTING AND ATMOSPHERE The Dorsey looks like your grandfather's study, and the atmosphere is just the same—refined yet reserved and upscale yet cozy. With dark wood finishes, bookshelves filled with real titles to pull, and an opportunity to warm up next to the Strip's most famous fireplace (spoiler alert: it's not real), this is the best spot to cozy up with a good book (or friend)—cocktail in hand, of course.

IF YOU GO Find a spot in the library section, hopefully near the fireplace—it's the perfect place to converse over cocktails. If cigar smoke bothers you, stick to the bar and adjacent lounge couches, where the tobacco toking is minimal. Oh, and order the Penicillin, The Dorsey's go-to signature drink.

ALSO TRY If you dig the study room environs but also want to dance the night away to EDM's finest, check out **Marquee** (and its Library room) at The Cosmopolitan (☎ 702-333-9000, marqueelasvegas.com).

Downtown Cocktail Room & Mike Morey's Sip 'n' Tip

Cozy mixology mecca

111 Las Vegas Blvd. S.; ☎ 702-880-3696; downtowncocktailroom.com
DOWNTOWN

Cover None. **Mixed drinks** $12 and up. **Wine** $8 and up. **Beer** $3 and up. **Dress** Fashionable and retro/vintage–friendly. **Specials** Happy hour Monday–Friday, 4–7 p.m. with reduced drinks. **Food available** None. **Hours** Monday–Friday, 4 p.m.–2 a.m.; Saturday, 7 p.m.–2 a.m.

WHO GOES THERE Artists, musicians, writers, off-duty bartenders, Zappos employees, and dilettantes.

WHAT GOES ON With the arrival of Downtown Cocktail Room, Las Vegas was made nearly whole. What has long been missing was an oasis to draw in the artists, writers, cognoscenti, and whiskey-bottle philosophers. Small-time filmmakers, big-time dreamers, and those who just like to be in a creative atmosphere flock to the corner of Las Vegas Boulevard and East Fremont Street (opposite the pedestrian-only, covered Fremont Street Experience).

SETTING AND ATMOSPHERE Showing up is half the battle, especially when faced with a puzzle at the door. The first hurdle here is locating it. Inside, regulars chuckle as tourists and first-timers attempt to manipulate the glass panels to get in, completely ignoring the scuffed metal sheet that is the actual door; just push. Once inside, darkness pervades except for pin spotlights and flickering red candles. Partake of the open seating on chaises and leather-couch groupings, at the cement bar, or in the back room, a bar-within-a-bar called Mike Morey's Sip 'n' Tip. The cozy, candlelit room is the perfect spot for a craft beer and a shot of Irish whiskey, also called a Boilermaker.

IF YOU GO Keep an open mind. The seasonal cocktail list is the focal point of the bar program here, as are classic cocktails and absinthe (once again legal in the United States). Get your Red Bull–and–vodka fixes elsewhere. Soak up the groovy vibes (music tends toward down-tempo, along with sexy vocal and instrumental house music), listen to a live singer-songwriter, or strike up a conversation with the bleary-eyed Hunter S. Thompson–looking fellow on the next barstool. He probably painted the art you were so admiring on the walls.

ALSO TRY Herbs and Rye at 3713 W. Sahara Avenue (☎ 702-982-8036, herbsandrye.com); **Velveteen Rabbit** at 1218 S. Main Street (☎ 702-685-9645, facebook.com/velveteenrabbitlv); **Oak & Ivy** in Container Park (☎ 702-359-9982, oakandivy.com); and **Atomic Liquors** at 917 Fremont Street (☎ 702-982-3000, atomiclasvegas.com).

Drai's Beachclub Nightclub

The Strip's highest rooftop megaclub and pool complex

The Cromwell, 3595 Las Vegas Blvd. S.; ☎ 702-777-3800; draislv.com
MID-STRIP AND ENVIRONS

Cover Generally $20–$60, but prices vary by event and gender. Caesars Entertainment property guests receive complimentary entry into Drai's Beachclub. **Mixed drinks** $15 and up. **Wine** $12 and up. **Beer** $10 and up. **Dress** Upscale and fashionable attire—dress to impress. Collared shirts and dress shirts are encouraged. No baggy clothing, athletic wear, athletic sneakers, ball caps, men's shorts, men's sandals, or ripped pants. **Food available** A menu of gourmet items is available at Drai's Café daily, 11 a.m.–6 p.m. **Hours** Nightclub: Thursday–Sunday, 10:30 p.m.–4 a.m.; After Hours: Thursday–Sunday, 1 a.m.–8 a.m.; Beachclub: Friday–Sunday, 11 a.m.–6 p.m.

WHO GOES THERE High net worth-y individuals with a taste for the finer things in life—or at the very least a desire to make other people think they have money and/or taste. Either way, when a true baller throws down for one of the insane bottle packages that include the Sparktacular, everyone wins.

WHAT GOES ON Contrary to what they might tell you, no nightclub has truly "reinvented" nightlife in Las Vegas since the days of the firsts: first club on the Strip, first club in a casino, first club in a casino on the Strip. . . . But with each successive major nightclub opening, the bar gets hoisted higher with regard to architecture, opulence, technology, vastness (or intimacy), DJ talent, and bottle service. And Drai's hits all the notes with pitch-perfection. The Drai's LIVE series offers full-length concert performances by huge names in music.

SETTING AND ATMOSPHERE Located atop the Strip's first freestanding boutique hotel, Drai's new spot—a beach club by day, nightclub thereafter—delivers on the promise of his reputation in Las Vegas and Los Angeles and is replete with his signature touches (hey, the guy loves red) and a sexy indoor-outdoor French Riviera feel. Drai's After Hours resides in its original location in the resort's basement.

IF YOU GO Arrange your visit in advance. No, you don't have to throw down for the $737,000 package that includes a flight on a Boeing 737 and a fireworks display the entire Valley can enjoy, but you can book your table or buy tickets at draislv.com. Unless you know someone (we suggest someone with the last name Drai), this is not the place to try out newly minted velvet-rope swagger. The best time to arrive to the beach club is 11:30 a.m., nightclub 10:30 p.m., and afterhours 3 a.m.

ALSO TRY **Marquee Nightclub & Dayclub** in The Cosmopolitan (☎ 702-333-9000, marqueelasvegas.com).

Encore Beach Club at Night

Party outside under the stars and inside with them

Encore, 3131 Las Vegas Blvd. S.; ☎ 702-770-7300; wynnsocial.com
MID-STRIP AND ENVIRONS

Cover $35 and up. **Mixed drinks** $19 and up. **Wine** $20 and up. **Beer** $12 and up. **Dress** Resort casual and nightclub chic; no athletic gear or street clothes. **Food available** None, but dining at Andrea's—the hip Asian, dining-by-DJ joint next door—is highly encouraged. **Hours** Thursday–Saturday, 10:30 p.m.–close.

WHO GOES THERE Local tastemakers, casino guests, and tourists with the wherewithal to try anything Steve Wynn is backing.

WHAT GOES ON By day, Encore Beach Club offers 55,000 square feet of lush oasis with three tiered pools, daybeds, 26 cabanas, and a walk-up grill (Friday–Sunday, 11 a.m.–7 p.m.), but by night the smallish club (about 5,000 square feet) envelops the Beach Club into its embrace and offers a unique, climate-controlled combined 60,000 square feet of party acreage. Experience the best of both worlds at NightSwim, which takes place seasonally. Fans of European-style electronic music and DJs will definitely want to make a pilgrimage, as Encore Beach Club keeps an impressive stable of renowned resident DJs, including The Chainsmokers, Diplo, David Guetta, and Kygo, as well as fresh talent on tap, mostly in the electronic-dance-music genre.

SETTING AND ATMOSPHERE High ceilings, 20-foot-tall windows, wide-open spaces, and dramatic views of the pool deck create the "wow" factor.

Playing on the theme of original sin, fabric and feature colors are eye-popping yellows, chrome is abundant, and the carpets leopard print—subtlety is for wusses.

IF YOU GO Consider stopping in during the day and introducing yourself to the VIP host–looking fellows (they'll be the ones texting furiously on their smartphones) who will likely offer to help you out in returning that night.

ALSO TRY If you like the all-in-one club and pool complex, check out **Drai's Beachclub Nightclub** in The Cromwell (☎ 702-737-0555, draislv.com); **Marquee** in The Cosmopolitan (☎ 702-333-9000; marqueelasvegas .com); **XS** in Encore (☎ 702-770-0097, wynnsocial.com); and **Tao** (☎ 702-388-8588, taolasvegas.com).

The Foundry

The ideal cross between concert venue and club

SLS, 2535 Las Vegas Blvd. S.; ☎ 702-761-7764; foundrylv.com
NORTH STRIP AND ENVIRONS

Cover Varies per show. **Mixed drinks** $13 and up. **Wine** $11 and up. **Beer** $8 and up. **Dress** No dress code. **Food available** None. **Hours** Vary by event.

WHO GOES THERE Fans of whichever act is booked for the night.

WHAT GOES ON The Foundry embraces eclectic offerings for nearly every taste: Alt-pop priestess Santigold, rockers X-Ambassadors and AWOLNATION, and rappers the likes of Kid Cudi and Lil Wayne have all graced the custom-built, elevated stage. The raised bar area makes for easy simultaneous sipping (there are three full bars) and people-watching, and every spot in the general admission standing pit has a great view.

SETTING AND ATMOSPHERE While its programming focus has broadened beyond dance music, this 1,800-capacity concert hall still retains some of its nightclub charm and boasts state-of-the-art technology, including cutting-edge acoustics, a 25-foot-by-65-foot stage, impressive lighting, full-motion graphics production capabilities, and more. The bar stretches all along the back wall and stays busy servicing thirsty attendees. Those who'd rather stay seated can book a VIP table in front of the bar or tucked behind either side of the stage—depending on whether you're there to see or be seen. Vintage-inspired speaker panels decorate the side walls, an aesthetic reinforcement of the venue's affinity for live entertainment.

IF YOU GO Know what you're getting into by checking the website's event calendar. If the evening's entertainment suits you, purchase tickets in advance to avoid waiting at the door.

ALSO TRY **House of Blues** at Mandalay Bay (☎ 702-632-7607, houseof blues.com/lasvegas).

Hakkasan

60,000 square feet of party potential, plus celebrity DJs

MGM Grand, 3799 Las Vegas Blvd. S.; ☎ 702-891-3838; hakkasanlv.com
SOUTH STRIP AND ENVIRONS

Cover $30 and up men, $20 and up ladies. **Mixed drinks** $14 and up. **Wine** $16 and up. **Beer** $10 and up. **Dress** Upscale fashionable; collared shirts required for men; no hats, sandals, sneakers, hard-soled shoes or boots, ripped or oversize clothing, or athletic wear. **Food available** None in the club, but downstairs you'll find Hakkasan Restaurant, open nightly. **Hours** Thursday–Sunday, 10:30 p.m.–close.

WHO GOES THERE As an all-encompassing nightlife experience, Hakkasan is a nightlife wonder that simply must be seen to be believed. The parent company, Hakkasan Group, is well known and respected in the nightlife, culinary, and hospitality world, with properties from Mumbai to Miami.

WHAT GOES ON The biggest electronic-dance-music DJs in the world call Hakkasan home. They're paid royally to do so, so expect lavish, spectacular sets with lighting and production teams giving the night's headliner the full festival treatment.

SETTING AND ATMOSPHERE A tangle of hallways, stairs, and elevators connects the first-level restaurant to the second level's private dining rooms. The next layer holds the open-format Ling Ling Club and the eclectic Ling Ling Lounge, a perfect respite for when the fourth level's spaceshiplike Main Room, Pavilion (straight outta *Kill Bill*), and electronic music get to be too much. The fifth-level mezzanine is the best way to experience the main room without going elbow-to-nose with everyone who came out to see Calvin Harris, Tiësto, or Steve Aoki and those floor-to-ceiling LED screens.

IF YOU GO Ladies, wear reasonably comfortable shoes (you might as well see the whole place!), and everyone should consider bringing earplugs; the better these sound systems are getting, the more efficient they are at wreaking havoc on your eardrums with nearly concussive bass. As with all Las Vegas nightclubs, it's always a good idea to purchase tickets online in advance to expedite entry.

ALSO TRY **Omnia** in Caesars Palace (☎ 702-785-6200, omnianightclub.com).

House of Blues

Cover bands, live rock, and headliners in a casual scene

Mandalay Bay, 3950 Las Vegas Blvd. S.; ☎ 702-632-7607; houseofblues.com/lasvegas   **SOUTH STRIP AND ENVIRONS**

Cover Live entertainment nightly, no cover. **Mixed drinks** $10 and up. **Wine** $9 and up. **Beer** $8 and up. **Specials** Happy hour daily, 2–5 p.m.; reverse happy hour Sunday–Thursday, 9 p.m.–midnight. **Dress** Casual. **Food available** Southern-inspired Crossroads restaurant is open breakfast, lunch, and dinner, plus Sunday Gospel Brunch in the main music hall at 10 a.m. and 1 p.m. **Hours** Daily, 5 p.m.–midnight or 1 a.m., depending on event.

WHO GOES THERE Locals, tourists, music lovers.

WHAT GOES ON House of Blues encompasses three venues: the 1,800-seat Music Hall downstairs, Crossroads Restaurant & Bar upstairs (casino level), and the Foundation Room restaurant-lounge on the top floor (more on that later). In this review, we're talking about the live music that takes place in the restaurant nightly, when blues, rock, and local performers take the stage under lights that spell out "Have Mercy, Las Vegas." It's a cool, casual, and not-too-cacophonous scene, with an eclectic audience grooving to some hot licks.

SETTING AND ATMOSPHERE House of Blues is one of the more evocative dining rooms in town, set to resemble an outdoor courtyard in the middle of a small bayou village, with a huge tree in the center and tables on a stone floor under and around it, as well as up on patio-style wooden decks. Wrought-iron railings, stone walls, etched and stained glass, and the facades of swamp shacks extend the theme, all under dim lighting. (They also account for the good acoustics.) The only incongruity is the collection of TV monitors on various walls throughout.

IF YOU GO Anything seems to go here during the music: big tables of beer-drinking college kids; couples (and singles) dancing all around the room; unreconstructed barefoot hippies in peasant blouses and patchouli perfume praising the Lord; lead singers or guitarists roaming the room wireless and interacting directly with the audience. It's best on nights when there's no concert downstairs in the main House of Blues Music Hall, and only those in the know are upstairs, enjoying some of the best bargain (free) entertainment in town.

ALSO TRY Foundation Room at House of Blues on the 63rd floor in Mandalay Bay, open nightly from 5 p.m., with dining from 6 p.m. and DJs from 10 p.m.; ☎ 702-632-7631.

Hyde Bellagio

Boutique-y L.A.-style club with an A-List view

Bellagio, 3600 Las Vegas Blvd. S.; ☎ 702-693-8700; hydebellagio.com
MID-STRIP AND ENVIRONS

Cover $30 men, $20 ladies, locals free on Tuesdays. **Mixed drinks** $17 and up. **Wine** $12 and up. **Beer** $9 and up. **Dress** Fashionable nightlife attire. **Food available** Italian small plates from LAGO 5–9 p.m. **Hours** Lounge open 5–10 p.m. nightly; club hours Tuesday, Wednesday, Friday, and Saturday, 10:30 p.m.–5 a.m.

WHO GOES THERE Tourists looking to start their night early, partiers looking for a gorgeous environment and unparalleled view of Bellagio's fountains rather than big-name DJs and celebs. Rub elbows with the industry crowd and snag a few business cards for future outings during Hyde's Industry Tuesdays insiders night.

WHAT GOES ON The newest addition to the nightclub's weekend lineup, Sunday's Stereo Hyde boasts a VIP experience with delicious drinks and beats by skillful DJs. Guests can revel until the early-morning hours at this weekly party—all to the hottest EDM tracks in an opulent lakeside setting.

SETTING AND ATMOSPHERE Hyde boasts a seamless indoor-outdoor patio, floor-to-ceiling windows, an expansive terrace showcasing Las Vegas's most celebrated landmark, the Bellagio fountains, plus multiple bars, 40 comfy VIP tables, and a diverse rotation of DJs and live performances.

IF YOU GO Did we mention the view?

ALSO TRY Hyde at T-Mobile Arena (☎ 702-818-3425, hydetmobilearena.com).

Intrigue

A safe bet on the element of surprise

Wynn, 3121 Las Vegas Blvd. S.; ☎ 702-770-7300; wynnsocial.com
MID-STRIP AND ENVIRONS

Cover $30 and up men, $20 and up ladies. **Mixed drinks** $16 and up. **Wine** $15 and up. **Beer** $10 and up. **Dress** Upscale; no baggy clothing, jeans, or athletic wear. **Food available** None. **Hours** Wednesday, Friday, and Saturday, 10:30 p.m.–4 a.m.

WHO GOES THERE This 1,200-capacity club attracts a savvy clientele who trust the Wynn Resorts team to deliver service and entertainment par excellence. Performers are not announced in advance, so an open mind is just as important as the right pair of shoes. Stars who have flocked here include Rihanna, Gigi Hadid, Justin Bieber, Ashton Kutcher, Leonardo DiCaprio, Las Vegas hometown hero Ne-Yo, and Kate Hudson.

WHAT GOES ON Offering a more intimate and exclusive experience than the resort's other poplar nightlife concepts XS and Encore Beach Club, Intrigue's cream palette provides the perfect canvas on which to create a dramatic and sensual experience enhanced by thoughtfully articulated lighting, lasers, and applied projection technology. The circular layout has been designed for you to soak up the room, socialize with your neighbors, and actually dance on the dance floor.

SETTING AND ATMOSPHERE The beloved Tryst-era waterfall remains as the backbone of the 14,000-square-foot indoor-outdoor sanctuary. Snag a table on the patio for fresh air and a front-row seat for the color-changing water fountains or play on the plush white booths in the main room. Either option presents plenty of gorgeous photo opportunities.

IF YOU GO Let your mind wander as to what—or who—is in the private VIP room. The 1,200-square-foot enclave—which features private bottle lockers, a 1,000 vinyl record collection, and maintains a strict no-social media policy—is only open to 50 VIP cardholders.

ALSO TRY Encore Beach Club at Night (☎ 702-770-7300, wynnsocial.com) and XS (☎ 702-770-0097, xslasvegas.com) in Encore.

Jewel

Aria's glittering nightlife treasure

Aria, 3730 Las Vegas Blvd. S.; ☎ 702-590-8000; jewelnightclub.com
MID-STRIP AND ENVIRONS

Cover $30 and up men, $20 and up women; prices may vary. **Mixed drinks** $15 and up. **Wine** $15 and up. **Beer** $12. **Dress** Upscale fashionable; collared shirts required for men; no hats, sandals, sneakers, hard-soled shoes or boots, ripped or oversize clothing, or athletic wear. **Food available** None. **Hours** Friday, Saturday, and Monday, 10:30 p.m.–close.

WHO GOES THERE With an emphasis on intimacy and VIP amenities, Jewel's crowd ranges from high rollers transitioning from the craps table to table service to young, sophisticated partiers looking for the hottest dance floor and dance partners.

WHAT GOES ON Performances by some of the most popular artists are often on the club's calendar. Past musical guests have included actor-singer Jamie Foxx, DJ duo The Chainsmokers, and Drake. That small sample is pretty indicative of the weekly lineups here. While its sister properties rely almost entirely on EDM DJs, this gem incorporates live performers and emcees.

SETTING AND ATMOSPHERE At 24,000 square feet, Jewel is about half the size of Omnia but packs just as much wow factor per square inch. Designed by New York–based architecture firm Rockwell Group, the club will have your jaw dropping before you even get your first drink thanks to a staircase entryway decked out in LED paneling. But the most striking feature? That goes to the 1,400 feet of LED "ribbon" hugging the walls—swirling panels that can shift the mood as quickly as a scratch of the vinyl.

IF YOU GO Do wander upstairs. The mezzanine level is where you'll find five VIP suites, each with its own individual theme, such as the speakeasy-esque Blind Tiger and European-inspired photography in the Gallery. Don't feel like splurging? The rest of the floor is roam-friendly GA space, where you ·can catch a prime view of the action below, sans premium.

ALSO TRY **Omnia** in Caesars Palace (☎ 702-785-6200, omnianightclub.com) and Hakkasan in MGM Grand (☎ 702-891-3838, hakkasanlv.com).

Light

Las Vegas's legendary hot spot is resurrected

Mandalay Bay, 3950 Las Vegas Blvd. S.; ☎ 702-675-7884; thelightvegas.com
SOUTH STRIP AND ENVIRONS

Cover Starts at $30 men, $20 ladies, but goes up to $50 men, $30 ladies depending on the event. **Mixed drinks** $17 and up. **Wine** $12 and up. **Beer** $10 and up. **Dress** Upscale chic. **Food available** None. **Hours** Wednesday, Friday, and Saturday, 10:30 p.m.–4 a.m.

WHO GOES THERE Herds of hotties, hip-hop heads, electronic-dance-music aficionados, staff of other nightclubs, and friends of the DJ.

WHAT GOES ON Light's raison d'être is its stable of resident talent, joining the Heavy-Hitters Club that also includes Wynn Resorts' Encore Beach Club at Night, XS, and Intrigue; Tao Group's Marquee Nightclub & Dayclub; Hakkasan Group's Omnia, Hakkasan, Wet Republic, and Jewel; and Drai's Beachclub Nightclub.

SETTING AND ATMOSPHERE Today's Light has huge shoes to fill, and does so by merging cutting-edge productions (that is, video mapping, lighting, sound, and special effects by experts, Moment Factory) with nightlife, as well as avant-garde costumes and unique choreography.

IF YOU GO The club has a large dance floor right in front of the DJ booth, so the DJ's fans can be front and center, even if they don't have a VIP table. Follow Light on its social media outlets to find out about upcoming contests and shows.

ALSO TRY Nighttime pool parties at **Daylight Beach Club,** also in Mandalay Bay (☎ 702-693-8300, daylightvegas.com); **Hakkasan** in MGM Grand (☎ 702-891-3838, hakkasanlv.com); and **Omnia** in Caesars Palace (☎ 702-785-6200, omnialasvegas.com).

Lily Bar & Lounge

Central gathering spot at the heart of Bellagio

Bellagio, 3600 Las Vegas Blvd. S.; ☎ 702-693-8300; lilylasvegas.com
MID-STRIP AND ENVIRONS

Cover None. **Mixed drinks** $16 and up. **Wine** $16 and up. **Beer** $9 and up. **Dress** Stylish nightlife attire. **Food available** Small plates from neighboring FIX Restaurant & Bar. **Hours** Daily, 5 p.m.–close.

WHO GOES THERE Nightclub pre-partiers and industry professionals touting their latest side project. Bellagio guests and anyone who isn't necessarily looking for the full-on club vibe, but who might appreciate a well-crafted cocktail in comfortable surroundings.

WHAT GOES ON Live music on Tuesdays, DJs all weekend long, and major sporting event broadcasts.

SETTING AND ATMOSPHERE Located in the center of Bellagio, Lily offers a sophisticated atmosphere shielded from the bustling casino floor, including imported Spanish stone tabletops and plush leather couches.

IF YOU GO Pre-party for a price as the creations from Lily's bartenders will delight with more than a standard vodka-and-Red Bull.

ALSO TRY **Hyde Bellagio** (☎ 702-693-8700, hydebellagio.com) and **Vista Lounge** at Caesars Palace (☎ 702-731-7852, vistacocktaillounge.com).

Marquee Nightclub & Dayclub

Glamorous megaclub and DJ magnet

The Cosmopolitan, 3708 Las Vegas Blvd. S.; ☎ 702-333-9000; marqueelasvegas.com **MID-STRIP AND ENVIRONS**

Cover Monday: men $35, ladies $25, locals free; Friday and Saturday: men $45, ladies $25. **Mixed drinks** $15 and up. **Wine** $10 and up. **Beer** $8 and up. **Dress** Stylish nightlife attire required; collared shirts for men. **Specials** Locals free on Marquee Mondays. **Food available** None. **Hours** Monday, Friday, and Saturday, 10:30 p.m.–5 a.m.

WHO GOES THERE Everyone. No, seriously—everyone.

WHAT GOES ON Thanks to Marquee's killer roster of today's top DJs—both residents and guests—the scene at the door is a cattle call of unthinkable proportions, the dance floor a sea of beautiful bodies, and the stairwells connecting the main room to the Boom Box Room and the Library surging arteries. So, why would you want to throw yourself into such a mix? Please refer back to "Who goes there" above. And check out Marquee's online calendar to see who will be manning the decks.

SETTING AND ATMOSPHERE Featuring similar attention to detail as big sister Tao (though without the Asian influence), Marquee makes luxury its theme. The circular main room is a well-appointed house-music amphitheater, perfectly arranged so that even someone in back can see the celebrity DJ jump up on the rig and feel the rush of wind as confetti cannons fire overhead. The Boom Box Room packs bodies in around the DJ and bar like a subway car, so New Yorkers should feel right at home. Upstairs in the Library, a fire roars, sexy librarians pop bottles, and a vintage pool table awaits your attention.

IF YOU GO Strategy is a must. Dine nearby at Holsteins or China Poblano. From there you can keep an eye on the velvet ropes. When the bodies begin to stack up, get the check and a to-go cocktail, and get in line. Being among the first through the door that night, you will have the rare opportunity to see how beautiful the rooms are (and get to the bar) before all hell breaks loose. When you finally emerge, check out the late-night breakfast joint Eggslut across the hall. And don't miss out on Marquee Dayclub, open daily 11 a.m.–sunset in season.

ALSO TRY **Drai's Beachclub Nightclub** in The Cromwell (☎ 702-737-0555, draislv.com).

Omnia

The nightlife mothership of Caesars Palace

Caesars Palace, 3570 Las Vegas Blvd. S.; ☎ 702-758-6200; omnianightclub.com **MID-STRIP AND ENVIRONS**

Cover $40 and up men, $20 and up women; prices may vary. **Mixed drinks** $16 and up. **Wine** $16 and up. **Beer** $12 and up. **Dress** Upscale fashionable. No hats, sandals, sneakers, hard-soled shoes or boots, ripped or baggy clothing, or athletic wear. Collared shirts are required for men. **Specials** None. **Food available** No, but dine next door at Searsucker, by chef Brian Malarkey and Hakkasan Group, for the complete experience. **Hours** Tuesday and Thursday–Sunday, 10 p.m.–late.

WHO GOES THERE Young money may be Omnia's target market, but the megaclub attracts everyone from the typical bachelor/bachelorette crowd and international tourists to locals and suits cutting loose, while Hakkasan Group practically prints money in the footprint of the former mothership, Pure Nightclub.

WHAT GOES ON In its simplest form, "Omnia" means "all," and the club does not fall short of its predecessor's reputation. Omnia uses its various environments to cater to each of its guests and the sheer force of its gravitational pull to attract the world's most in-demand DJ talent. Spanning numerous genres, the destination nightclub hosts a variety of electronic music artists, as well as renowned open-format talent. Pour over the calendar before you go to find out who will be creating the soundtrack to your night.

SETTING AND ATMOSPHERE Conceptualized around the elements of opulence and modern technology, Omnia is an interactive, immersive nightlife experience. The 75,000-square-foot, multilevel club encompasses a seductive ultralounge, Heart of Omnia; a high-energy main club with its surrounding balconies; and the venue's famous outdoor Terrace, which showcases panoramic views of the Las Vegas Strip.

IF YOU GO Take the full tour of all three venues within the venue before deciding where to make your stand for the evening. You might find that the breezy Terrace or the intimate Heart of Omnia (formerly Pure's main room, just to give you an idea of the scale of this place!) appeals most.

ALSO TRY Vista Cocktail Lounge is just a stone's throw away from Omnia's doors in Caesars Palace (☎ 702-731-7852, vistacocktaillounge.com).

Rí Rá Las Vegas

Authentic Irish music, food, drinks, and _craic_

The Shoppes at Mandalay Place, 3930 Las Vegas Blvd. S.; ☎ 702-632-7771; rira.com/las-vegas   **SOUTH STRIP AND ENVIRONS**

Cover None. **Mixed drinks** $12 and up. **Wine** $10 and up. **Beer** $6 and up. **Dress** Casual. **Food available** Authentic Irish cuisine with a hint of American flair; a wide selection of appetizers, sandwiches, and entrées 7 days a week. **Hours** Monday–Friday, 8 a.m.–3 a.m.; Saturday and Sunday, 9 a.m.–3 a.m.

WHO GOES THERE Eireophiles, Celtic music fans, and footy fiends.

WHAT GOES ON Deceiving from the outside, the seemingly endless interior of this lively, casual gastropub and bar is actually a buzzing hive of nearly constant activity. Bands Irish and beyond play for the exuberant crowd, those that are not entranced by a football game (that's soccer to the rest of us) showing on one of the many flat-panel TVs that dot the space. The food is tasty and interesting, especially the generous fish-and-chips and the house-made soda bread; here, every Guinness is well poured.

SETTING AND ATMOSPHERE No expense was spared in bringing a whole lotta Ireland to Sin City. Professionals salvaged authentic 19th-century materials, millwork, and bric-a-brac from all over the Emerald Isle, including artifacts dating back to 1890 from the Olympia Theater in Dublin and a 500-pound carved statue of St. Patrick from 1850.

IF YOU GO Try not to be in a hurry; so much of pub life is about leaving the world out on the doorstep, or in this case, in the mall. Take time to experience and appreciate the individual personality of each room, as well as the entertainment—this can mean the live music variety, the stars of sport, and the friendly Irish staff.

ALSO TRY **McMullan's Irish Pub** at 4650 W. Tropicana Avenue (☎ 702-247-7000, mcmullansirishpub.com) and **Nine Fine Irishmen** in New York–New York (☎ 702-740-6463, newyorknewyork.com).

Rosina

The Jazz Age gets an update at The Palazzo

The Palazzo, 3325 Las Vegas Blvd. S.; ☎ 702-607-1945; palazzo.com
MID-STRIP AND ENVIRONS

Cover None. **Mixed drinks** $14 and up. **Wine** $22 and up. **Beer** $8 and up. **Dress** Casual. **Food available** None. **Hours** Nightly, 4 p.m.–3 a.m.

WHO GOES THERE As Rosina is the Strip's newest cocktail bar, the clientele is quite varied, but that shouldn't deter you from stopping by the latest lounge on Las Vegas Boulevard. From the pregaming club crews and aperitif-seeking diners to businessmen and women brokering partnerships post-convention, it's a mixed (and delightful) crowd at Rosina.

WHAT GOES ON Cocktail carousing at its very finest. Rosina's menu features all the classics: Negronis, Manhattans, Dark and Stormys. Did we mention the Champagne call button? One click and a new flute is in your hand within minutes.

SETTING AND ATMOSPHERE If you don't feel like Jay Gatsby or Daisy Buchanan when you're at Rosina, you might want to revisit F. Scott Fitzgerald's masterpiece. With Art Deco elements, plush booths, and shining chandeliers, Rosina looks like a 1920s speakeasy. And with a soundtrack chock-full of dancey disco and soulful R&B, the vibe is then-meets-now in all the right ways.

IF YOU GO With a significant other? Snag one of the booths flanking the bar for an intimate start (or end) to your night out on the town. And whether you're with a partner, group, or flying solo, skip your usual vodka-soda order. Rosina's handcrafted vintage cocktails are some of the best in town—class it up with a French 75, featuring Champange, gin, and freshly squeezed lemon juice.

ALSO TRY Looking for classic cocktails and a modern soundtrack all in a luxe setting? You can find a similar vibe to Rosina's at **Franklin** at the Delano (☎ 702-632-7888, delanolasvegas.com).

Sayers Club

The hot, younger sibling of Hollywood's famous outpost

SLS, 2535 Las Vegas Blvd. S.; ☎ 702-761-7618; thesayersclublv.com
NORTH STRIP AND ENVIRONS

Cover None. **Mixed drinks** $15 and up. **Beer** $8 and up. **Dress** Upscale casual. **Specials** Happy hour 6–9 p.m., featuring two-for-one cocktails and domestic beers. **Food available** None. **Hours** Thursday–Saturday, 6 p.m.–1 a.m.

WHO GOES THERE Open-minded tourists and locals heading to or from Downtown.

WHAT GOES ON Anything, really. Programming at this refined-yet-raw space is part nightclub, part speakeasy, making it ideal for meeting friends or a significant other for happy hour, late-night cocktails, and everything in between. This 4,700-square-foot chameleon has seen country nights, DJs, and a high-caliber mix of local and touring bands—not to mention the occasional after-party for concerts at The Foundry.

SETTING AND ATMOSPHERE Walking in feels like you're stumbling upon the coolest 1970s-era den your friends' parents never had: Dim lighting casts a golden glow over plush, tufted leather couches. The fully stocked bar resembles a bookcase you'd actually want to study from. And while the vibe changes from night to night, the view of the Strip from the outdoor patio is always spectacular.

IF YOU GO Check the website to see what flavor of Sayers Club is being served that night.

ALSO TRY **Foundation Room** at HOB (☎ 702-632-7631, houseofblues.com).

Tao

A labyrinthine restaurant, lounge, and megaclub

The Venetian, 3377 Las Vegas Blvd. S.; ☎ 702-414-1000; taolasvegas.com
MID-STRIP AND ENVIRONS

Cover Thursday: $25 men, $10 ladies, locals free; Friday: $25 men, $20 ladies; Saturday: $35 men, $20 ladies. **Mixed drinks** $14 and up. **Wine** $12 and up. **Beer** $8 and up. **Dress** Upscale casual; collared shirts or blazers for men. **Specials** Thursday is local/industry night. **Food available** Pan-Asian cuisine and sushi available downstairs in the restaurant, daily 5 p.m.–midnight. **Hours** Lounge: Sunday–Wednesday, 5 p.m.–midnight; Thursday–Saturday, 5 p.m.–1 a.m; nightclub: Thursday–Saturday, 10:30 p.m.–5 a.m.

WHO GOES THERE Hard-core club crawlers, pretty people, young Hollywood, sexpots, the scantily clad, and hedonists.

WHAT GOES ON The Venetian finally hit the jackpot with Tao, after misfiring with several nightlife venues. A huge combination of restaurant, lounge, and nightclub, Tao offers highly sought-after dinner reservations, a cool lounge space, and a labyrinthine club that packs 'em in from the moment the velvet rope drops. Hordes of casino patrons and Strip-walkers swarm Tao. Entertainment is keyed to the hottest dance music and meant to move the most flesh as quickly as possible, en masse. It's meat-market central for the young, sweaty, and on the make.

SETTING AND ATMOSPHERE The pretty but minimally decorated lounge serves mainly as an air lock and chill-out space for the upstairs club space, which includes several bars, two levels of VIP cells, a recessed dance floor, several dancer showcase platforms, and a tiny bit of Strip-side balcony. Various Buddhas sit in nooks and crannies or in placid groups. Vaguely exotic and certainly sexy, Tao's look and feel is downright aphrodisiacal when the crowd is right.

IF YOU GO Go early or go with your celebrity friends. The line will be long, but it does move, and everyone really does get a chance to get in eventually. Front-of-line passes available from various websites or other sources would come in handy here, and if you have (or are) a group of attractive females, your chances of skipping the line or portions thereof will be dramatically improved. The V.I.We Package grants you access ($50 ladies, $100 gents) to a sort of communal VIP bottle service area where you can party it up on the cheap(er). Remember: A stranger is just a friend you haven't raged with yet.

ALSO TRY **Light** in Mandalay Bay (☎ 702-693-8300, thelightvegas.com) and **Marquee** in The Cosmopolitan (☎ 702-333-9000, marqueelasvegas.com).

XS

Excessively beautiful, inside and out

Encore, 3131 Las Vegas Blvd. S.; ☎ 702-770-0097; wynnsocial.com
MID-STRIP AND ENVIRONS

Cover $30 and up men, $20 and up women. **Mixed drinks** $18 and up. **Wine** $20 and up. **Beer** $13 and up. **Dress** Upscale casual; no athletic wear of any kind (no flip-flops, tennis shoes, shorts, hats, etc.); no baggy jeans or jeans with holes; swimwear encouraged at NightSwim parties. **Food available** None. **Hours** Friday–Sunday, 10 p.m.–4 a.m.

WHO GOES THERE With 13,000 square feet of indoor space for bars, a dance floor, and VIP seating, and 27,000 square feet of exterior space for more bars, 170 additional VIP tables, an illuminated pool, a gaming pavilion, and 30 poolside cabanas, XS is naturally a magnet for the well-heeled and wannabe-well-heeled.

WHAT GOES ON Supernatural beauty is rewarded by XS's cast of stunning servers and VIP hosts. Guests are encouraged to make use of the VIP table backs for elevated seating—all the better to view and be viewed. XS enjoys the collaborative buying power of Wynn's nightlife contingent (which also includes Encore Beach Club and Intrigue) to keep top DJs in its stable, from The Chainsmokers and David Guetta to Kygo and Diplo.

SETTING AND ATMOSPHERE Las Vegas's most beautiful nightclub was inspired by the sexy curves of the human body and boasts more than 10,000 individual light sources, including a disco chandelier and 14 stripper poles thinly disguised as lamps. Focal features include gold-leaf body forms, an illuminated outdoor pool (open some summer nights for the Nightswim pool party), and a large circular dance floor surrounded by VIP tables.

IF YOU GO Bring your A-game and break out the good shoes. Long before you pass through XS's gilded gates, you will have to navigate a maze of admission lines and pass through multiple sets of eyes critical of your attitude, dress, comportment, and entourage. A Darwinian process ensues, culling the herd down to the haves and the have-nots. Leave embarrassing in-laws, cousins, and friends in the casino, and expect to throw down a mortgage payment for a table and more bottles than your group could ever realistically consume.

ALSO TRY The other big kids on the Strip include **Drai's Beachclub Nightclub** in The Cromwell (☎ 702-737-0555, draislv.com); **Marquee Nightclub** in The Cosmopolitan (☎ 702-333-9000, marqueelasvegas.com); **Hakkasan** in MGM Grand (☎ 702-891-3838, hakkasanlv.com); and **Omnia** in Caesars Palace (☎ 702-785-6200, omnianightclub.com).

LAS VEGAS *Below the* BELT

DON'T WORRY, BE HAPPY

IN MANY WAYS, LAS VEGAS is a bastion of hedonism. Simply being there contributes to a loosening of inhibitions and a partial discarding of the rules that apply at home. Las Vegas exults in its permissiveness and makes every effort to live up to its image and to bestow upon its visitors the freedom to have fun. Las Vegas has a steaminess, a cosmopolitan excitement born of superabundance, an aura of risk and reward, a sense of libertine excess. The rules are different here; it's all right to let go.

Behind the illusion, however, is a community, and more particularly, a police department that puts a lot of effort into making it safe for visitors to experience the liberation of Las Vegas. It is hard to imagine another city where travelers can carry such large sums of money so safely. A tourist can get robbed or worked over in Las Vegas, but it is comparatively rare, and more often than not is due to the visitor's own carelessness or naivete. The Strip and Downtown, especially, are well patrolled, and most hotels have very professional in-house security forces.

In general, a tourist who stays either on the Strip or Downtown will be very safe. Police patrol in cars, on foot, and, on mountain bikes. The bikes allow the police to quickly catch pickpockets or purse snatchers attempting to escape down sidewalks or through parking lots. Cross-streets that connect the Strip with Paradise Road and the Las Vegas Convention Center are also lighted and safe. When tourists get robbed, they are commonly far from Downtown or the Strip and often in pursuit of drugs or sex.

ORGANIZED CRIME AND CHEATING

FEW VISITORS WALK THROUGH a casino without wondering if the games are rigged or if the place is owned by the Mafia. During the early days of legalized gambling, few people outside of organized crime had any real experience in managing gaming operations. Hence, a fair number of characters fresh from eastern gangs and crime families came to work in Nevada. Since they constituted the resource pool for experienced gambling operators, the state suffered their presence as a necessary evil. In 1950, Tennessee senator Estes Kefauver initiated an attack on organized crime that led (indirectly) to the formation of the Nevada Gaming Commission and the State Gaming Control Board. These agencies, in conjunction with federal efforts, were ultimately able to purge organized crime from Las Vegas, or at least from the casinos. This ouster, coupled with the Nevada Corporate Gaming Acts of 1967 and 1969 (allowing publicly held corporations such as Hilton, Holiday Inn, and MGM to own casinos), at last brought a mantle of respectability to Las Vegas gambling.

Today the Gaming Control Board oversees the activities of all Nevada gaming establishments, maintaining tight control through frequent unannounced inspections of gambling personnel and equipment. If you ever have reason to doubt the activity or clout of the Gaming

Control Board, try walking around the Strip or Downtown in a dark business suit and plain black shoes. You will attract more attention from the casino management than if you entered with a parrot on your head.

Ostensibly, cheating exists in Las Vegas gambling to a limited degree. But a case of a Nevada casino cheating customers hasn't been publicized for decades. "Gaffing" the games is seldom perpetrated by the house itself. In fact, most cheating is done at the expense of the house, though honest players at the cheater's table may also get burned. Sometimes a dealer, working alone or with an accomplice (posing as a player), will cheat, and there are always con artists, grab-and-run rip-off artists, and rail thieves ready to take advantage of the house and legitimate players.

SKIN GAMES—SEX IN LAS VEGAS

THOUGH NUDITY, PROSTITUTION, and pornography are regulated more tightly in Las Vegas than in many Bible Belt cities, the town exudes an air of sexual freedom and promiscuity. Las Vegas offers a near-perfect environment for marketing sex. More than 50% of all visitors are men, most ages 21–59. Some come to party, and many, particularly convention-goers, are alone and ready for action. Almost all have time and money on their hands.

Las Vegas evolved as a gambler's city, projecting the image of a trail town where a man could be comfortable and just about anything could be had for a price. It was not until strong competition developed for the gambling dollar that hotels sought to enlarge their market by targeting women and meetings. Today, though there is something for everyone in Las Vegas, its male orientation remains unusually strong.

STRIPPING ON THE STRIP Compared to the live adult entertainment in many cities, skin shows in Las Vegas, both Downtown and on the Strip, are fairly tame. In some of the larger showrooms, this is an accommodation to the ever-growing percentage of women in the audience. More often, however, it is a matter of economics rather than taste, the result of a curious City of Las Vegas law that stipulates that you can offer totally nude entertainment or you can serve alcoholic beverages, but not both.

MALE STRIPPERS Economics and the market have begun to redress (or undress) the inequality of women's erotic entertainment in Las Vegas. Spearheaded by the Rio, which features (*Chippendales*) male strippers for lengthy engagements, and empowered by the ever-growing number of professional women visiting Las Vegas for trade shows and conventions, the rules for sexual objectification are being rewritten. Today in Las Vegas, if watching a young stud flex his buns is a woman's idea of a good time, that experience is usually available. In addition to the Rio, *Thunder from Down Under,* the Australian male revue, plays at the Excalibur, and *Aussie Heat* plays at the Miracle Mile Shops.

Where the Girls Are

Below we describe some of the better-known strip joints. If you want the whole scoop, check out **Arnold Snyder's Topless Vegas** at toplessvegasonline.com. In a city where it's easy to spend $400 at a topless club, Snyder's free site can save you a bundle. It tells you where the most beautiful dancers are; how to have a great strip-club experience for $30 or less; topless-club etiquette (there's more to this than you might imagine); lap dancing A–Z; and how to avoid taxi scams and scams at the clubs. There are detailed rankings and reviews of all-nude clubs and topless clubs, all topless shows at the casinos, and all of the city's topless pools. Straight talk is Snyder's trademark, so you can count on him to address just about any question you can think of, including those you'd be too embarrassed to ask. The site also encourages feedback, where visitors discuss such topics as the relative merits of fully nude versus topless clubs. One poster thought topless clubs superior because, as he put it, "I've never had anything contagious leap off a boobie at me." All righty, then.

Strip clubs are not the homogeneous experience you might expect. As a quick dichotomy, some clubs specialize in presentations where the focal point is one or several performing dancers on a central stage with the usual theatrical elements of music and lighting. The stage is the focal point, and seating is arrayed around it. In other clubs, the action is decentralized, and though there will be strippers performing somewhere (for example, in disco cages or on a bar top), there's no single stage at the center of the action. The breadwinning products of these clubs are lap dancing and shows in private or semiprivate rooms. Clubs can also be categorized as topless clubs or clubs offering full nudity. Concerning the latter, only the Palomino Club in North Las Vegas (see below) is licensed for total nudity and alcohol consumption. In case you're wondering, refreshments at the other all-nude clubs consist of froufrou (and outrageously expensive) fruit drinks.

Finally, if you're a nonlocal and arrive by cab, you'll be hit with a higher cover charge to pay a kickback to the driver. Taxi drivers get a kickback for delivering you to a particular gentlemen's club. Do not let a taxi driver talk you out of your chosen destination and take you someplace he recommends.

THE PALOMINO CLUB (☎ 702-642-2984, palominolv.com) At the Palomino Club, 10 minutes from Downtown, the customer can have it all. The Palomino Club is not inexpensive, but at least they're up front about what they're selling. Before 9 p.m. admission is free; after 9 it's $30. Things don't heat up till around 11 p.m., so you'll have to do a lot of sitting (and drinking) to beat the entrance fee. Still, though you have to be 21 to get in, dancers have to be only 18 to work there, so the scenery, if you're into youngish girls, is easy on the eyes.

An average of seven professionals dance nightly, performing in rotation and stripping nude. Most of the women are attractive and athletic. The Palomino delivers some of the best erotic dancing in town for about the same cost as a production show on the Strip.

LITTLE DARLINGS (1514 Western Ave., ☎ 702-366-1141, dejavu .com) If you can do without alcohol, Little Darlings is our pick for the best nude stage show in the state. Not only are the dancers stunningly gorgeous, but many of them are extremely athletic. Unlike many topless and nude shows where the performers pretty much clamber around the stage, Little Darlings' showgirls can dance. Beverage service is limited to non-alcoholic drinks. Cover is $40 for nonlocals, $29 for VIP admission, and $15 for locals.

TOPLESS BARS The main difference between a topless bar and a totally nude nightclub (aside from the alcohol regulations) is a G-string. If you have more than a few drinks, the topless bars aren't less expensive than the Palomino but are often more conveniently located.

With two lower-level stages and an L-shape runway stage on the second level, **Larry Flynt's Hustler Club** (6007 Dean Martin Drive, ☎ 702-795-3131, vegashustlerclub.com) is our top-ranked topless club for stage shows. The upper level houses a roof-top bar with comfortable seating and great views of Las Vegas. Dancers are stunning, and drink prices reasonable. Cover charge for nonlocals is $30; locals enter free.

The **Sapphire Club** (3025 Industrial Road, ☎ 702-796-6000, sapphire lasvegas.com) claims 6,000 women in its lineup of strippers (insiders say it's closer to 2,000, which is still plenty). By observation, the later you arrive in the evening, the better-looking the dancers. Though the club claims to be the largest of its kind in the world, much of the space is allocated to private rooms and VIP areas. Sapphire is upscale but doesn't seem all that big. Admission is $40.

A club with a pedigree and a long-running history is **Sophia's Gentlemen's Club** (3500 W. Naples Drive, ☎ 702-982-6777, sophiasvegas .com), formerly OG and Olympic Gardens. It caters to out-of-town men, and its prices are a dead giveaway: a $40 cover charge and up to $500 for a half hour in the VIP room.

Boxer Floyd Mayweather brought an upscale, luxury concept to the topless club scene with **Girl Collection** (2580 S. Highland Drive, ☎ 702-410-9999, girlcollection.com). With the highest entry fee of any club, $50, the fighter is angling for VIP exclusivity. Beer is $14, and all tables are reserved for bottle service.

EROTIC HERITAGE MUSEUM (3275 Sammy Davis Jr. Drive, ☎ 702-794-4000, eroticmuseumvegas.com) Located just north of Desert Inn Road next door to the Déjà Vu all-nude club, this 17,000-square-foot museum exhibits a small part of the erotic art of two collectors who between them own whole warehouses full of the stuff. The permanent collection includes all the mid- to late-20th-century films that launched the sexual revolution; bondage paraphernalia from the famous bondage inventor Gord; arcade peep machines and other fetish equipment; a display devoted to Larry Flynt and the First Amendment; the work of urban sex artists; and much more. The boutique sells reproductions and posters of erotic art, classic erotic DVDs, books, T-shirts, and the like. Admission is a $30 donation, $10 for locals, students, and military. The EHM is open Monday–Wednesday 11 a.m.–7 p.m. and Thursday–Sunday 11 a.m.–10 p.m.

PART THREE

GAMBLING

The WAY IT IS

GAMBLING IS THE REASON LAS VEGAS (in its modern incarnation) exists. It is the industry that fuels the local economy, paves the roads, and gives the city its identity. To visitors and tourists, gambling may be a game. To those who derive their livelihood from gambling, however, it is serious business.

There is an extraordinary and interesting dichotomy in the ways gambling is perceived. To the tourist and the gambler, gambling is all about luck. To those in the business, gambling is about mathematics. To the visitor, gambling is a few hours a day, while to the casinos, gambling is 24/7. The gambler *hopes* to walk away with a fortune, but the casinos *know* that in the long run that fortune will belong to the house. To visitors, gambling is recreation combined with risk and chance. To the casinos, gambling is business combined with near-certainty.

The casino takes no risk in the games themselves. In almost all cases, in the long run the house will always win. The games, the odds, and the payoffs are all carefully designed to ensure this outcome. Yet the casino does take a chance and is at risk. The casino's bet is this: that it can entice enough people to play.

Imagine a casino costing hundreds of millions of dollars, with a staff numbering in the thousands. Before a nickel of profit can be set aside, all the bills must be paid, and the payroll must be met. Regardless of its overwhelming advantage at the tables, the house cannot stay in business unless a lot of people come to play. The larger the casino, the more gamblers are required. If the casino can fill the tables with players, the operation will succeed and be profitable, perhaps spectacularly so. On the other hand, if the tables sit empty, the casino will fail.

The gambling business is competition personified. All casinos sell the exact same product. Every owner knows how absolutely critical it is to get customers (gamblers) through the door. It is literally the *sine qua non*: no players, no profit. The casinos are aggressive and creative when it comes to luring customers, offering low-cost buffets, $2 shrimp cock-tails, stage shows, lounge entertainment, free drinks, gambling tourna-ments, and players clubs.

The most common tactic for getting customers through the door is to package the casino as a tourist attraction in its own right. Take the Mirage. There are exploding volcanoes in the front yard, palm trees in the living room, and live sharks in the parlor. Who, after all, wants to sip their free drink in a dingy red-Naugahyde-upholstered catacomb when they can be luxuriating in such a resplendent tropical atrium?

THE SHORT RUN

ASK A MATHEMATICIAN OR A CASINO OWNER if you can win gambling in a casino, and the truthful answer is yes, but almost always only in the short run. Unless you're a professional player who only plays with the long-term edge on your side, the longer you play, the more certain it is that you will lose.

I (Bob here) learned about the short run (and the long run) on a road trip when I was in the fifth grade. My family lived in Kentucky, and every year we were fortunate enough to take a vacation to Florida. This particular year I was allowed to invite a schoolmate, Glenn, along.

As the long drive progressed, we became fidgety and bored. To pass the time, we began counting cars traveling in the opposite direction. Before many miles had passed, our counting evolved into a betting game. We each selected a color and counted the cars of that color. Whoever counted the most cars of his chosen color would win.

Glenn chose blue as his color. I was considering red (my favorite), when I recalled a conversation between my mother and a car sales-man. The salesman told my mother that white was by far the most popular color "these days." If this were true, I reasoned, there should be more white cars on the road than blue cars. I chose white.

As we rumbled through the hilly Kentucky countryside between Bowling Green and Elizabethtown, my friend edged ahead. This puz-zled me and I began to doubt the word of the car salesman. By the time we made it to Bowling Green, Glenn was ahead by seven cars. Because I was losing, I offered to call it quits and pay up (a nickel for each car he was ahead). Glenn, not unexpectedly, was having a high time and insisted we continue playing.

By the time we crossed the Tennessee line I had pulled even. Once again I suggested we quit. Glenn would have none of it. Gloating enormously, he regained a three-car lead halfway to Nashville. Slowly, however, I overtook him, and by Nashville I was ahead by four cars. Tired of the game, I tried once more to end it. Since he was behind, Glenn adamantly demanded that we play all the way to Atlanta. We did, and by the time we got there, Glenn owed me almost $4.

After a night in Atlanta and a great deal of sulking on Glenn's part, we resumed our travels. To my amazement, Glenn demanded the opportu-nity to win back his previous day's losses. There would be one great "do-or-die battle, blues against whites," he said, all the way to our destination

(St. Augustine, Florida). As we drove south, I went ahead by a couple of cars, and then Glenn regained the lead by a small margin. By the time we reached St. Augustine, however, Glenn owed me another $5.40.

Outraged (and broke), Glenn exercised the only option remaining—he complained to my parents. Shaking his head, my father said, "Give Glenn his money back. Everybody knows that there are more white cars than blue cars." Not so. Glenn didn't.

While Glenn's behavior is not unusual for a preadolescent, you would assume that adults have better sense. Everybody knows there are more white cars than blue cars, remember? In Las Vegas, however, the casinos are full of Glenns, all over age 21, and all betting on blue cars.

I nailed Glenn on the cars because I knew something that he didn't. In casino games, patrons either do not understand what they are up against, or alternatively (and more intelligently), they do understand, but chalk up their losses as a fair price to pay for an evening's entertainment. Besides, in the short run, there's a chance they might actually win.

Glenn's actions on our trip mirrored almost exactly the behavior of many unfortunate casino gamblers:

1. He did not understand that the game was biased against him.
2. He did not take his winnings and quit when he was ahead in the short run.
3. On losing, he continued playing and redoubled his efforts to pull even or win, ultimately (in the long run) compounding his losses.

EAGLES AND ROBINS

IF ON OUR DRIVE I HAD SAID, "Let's count birds. You take eagles and I'll take robins," Glenn would have laughed in my face, instantly recognizing that the likelihood of spotting an eagle was insanely remote. While the casinos will not offer a fair game (like betting even money on the flip of a coin), they do offer something a bit more equitable than eagles and robins.

I had another friend growing up who was big for his age. Whenever I went to his house to play, he would beat me up. I was not a masochist, so I finally stopped going to his house. After a few days, however, he asked me to come back, offering me ice cream and other incentives. After righteously spurning his overtures for a time, I gave in and resumed playing at his house. True to his word, he gave me ice cream and generously shared his best toys, and from that time forward he beat me up only once a week.

This is exactly how the casinos operate, and why they give you a better deal than eagles versus robins. The casinos know that if they hammer you every time you come to play, sooner or later you will quit coming. Better to offer you little incentives and let you win every once in a while. Like with my big friend, they still get to beat you up, but not as often.

THE BATTLE AND THE WAR

IN CASINO GAMBLING, the short run is like a battle, and either player or casino can win. However, the casino almost always wins the war. The American Indians never had a chance against the continuing encroachment of white settlers. There were just too many settlers and too few Indians for the outcome ever to be in doubt. Losing the war, however, did not keep the Indians from winning a few big battles. So it goes in casino gambling. The player struggles in the face of overwhelming odds. If he keeps slugging it out, he is certain to lose. If, on the other hand, he hits and runs, he may come away a winner.

 Gambling is like a commando raid: the gambler must get in, do some damage, and get out. Hanging around too long in the presence of superior forces can be fatal.

To say that this takes discipline is an understatement. It's hard to withdraw when you are winning, and maybe even harder to call it quits when you are losing. Glenn couldn't do either, and a lot of gamblers are just like Glenn.

THE HOUSE ADVANTAGE

IF CASINOS DID ENGAGE in fair bets, they would win about half the bets and lose about half the bets. In other words, the casino (and you), on average, would break even, or at least come close to breaking even. While this arrangement would be more equitable, it would not, as a rule, generate enough money for the casino to pay its mortgage, much less foot the bill for the dancing waters, lounge shows, $8 steaks, and free drinks.

HOUSE ADVANTAGES	
BACCARAT 1.17% on bank bets, 1.36% on player bets	**ROULETTE** 5.26%–7.89%, depending on the bet
BLACKJACK 0.5%–5.9% for most games	**SLOTS** 2%–25% (average 4%–14%)
CRAPS 1.4% to almost 17%, depending on the bet	**VIDEO POKER** 0.2%–12% (average 4%–8%)
KENO 20%–35%	**WHEEL OF FORTUNE** 11%–24%

To ensure sufficient income to meet their obligations and show a profit, casinos establish rules and payoffs for each game to give the house an advantage. While the house advantage is not strictly fair, it is what makes bargain rates on rooms, meals, and entertainment possible.

There are three basic ways in which the house establishes its advantage:

1. THE RULES OF THE GAME ARE TAILORED TO THE HOUSE'S ADVANTAGE In blackjack, for instance, the dealer by rule always plays his own hand last. If any player busts (attains a point total over 21), the dealer wins by default before having to play out his hand.

2. THE HOUSE PAYS OFF AT LESS THAN THE ACTUAL ODDS Imagine a carnival wheel with 10 numbers. When the wheel is spun, each number has an equal chance of coming up. If you bet a dollar on number 6, there is a 1-in-10 chance you will win and a 9-in-10 chance you will lose. Gamblers express odds by comparing the likelihood of losing to the likelihood of winning. In this case, 9 chances to lose and 1 to win, or 9–1. If the game paid off at the correct odds, you would get $9 every time you won (plus the dollar you bet). Each time you lost you would lose a dollar.

Let's say you start with $10 and do not win until your tenth try, betting your last dollar. If the game paid off at the correct odds, you would break even. Starting with $10, you would lose a dollar on each of your first nine attempts. In other words, you would be down $9. Betting your one remaining dollar, you win. At 9–1, you would receive $9 and get to keep the dollar you bet. You would have exactly the $10 you started with.

As we have seen, there is no way for a casino to play you even-up and still pay the bills. If, therefore, a casino owner decided to install a wheel with 10 numbers, he would decrease the payoff. Instead of paying at the correct odds (9–1), he might pay at 8–1. If you won on your last bet and got paid at 8–1 (instead of 9–1), you would have lost $1 overall. Starting with $10, you lose your first nine bets (so you are out $9) and on your last winning bet you receive $8 and get to keep the dollar you bet. Having played 10 times at the 8-to-1 payoff, you have $9 left, for a total loss of $1. Thus the house's advantage in this game is 10% (one-tenth).

The house advantage for actual casino games ranges from less than 1% for certain betting situations in blackjack to 35% on keno. Although 1% doesn't sound like much of an advantage, it will get you if you play long enough. Plus, for the house it adds up.

Because of variations in game rules, the house advantage for a particular game in one casino may be greater than the house advantage for the same game in another casino. In most Las Vegas casinos, for instance, the house has a 5.26% advantage in roulette. At European casinos, however, because of the elimination of 00 (double zero) on certain roulette wheels, the house advantage is pared down to about 2.7%.

The rule variations in blackjack swing the house advantage from almost zero in single-deck games (surrender, doubling on any number of cards, dealer stands on soft 17, etc.) to more than 6% in multiple-deck games with draconian rules, such as a recent wrinkle at blackjack, where a natural 21 pays off at 6–5 rather than the age-old 3–2. Quite a few mathematicians have taken a crack at computing the house's advantage in blackjack. Some suggest that the player can gain an advantage over the house by keeping track of cards played. Others claim that without counting cards, a player utilizing a decision guide known as "basic strategy" can play the house nearly even. The reality for 95% of all blackjack players, however, is a house advantage of between 0.5% and 5.9%, depending on rule variations and the number of decks used.

Getting to the meat of the matter: blackjack and some video poker played competently, baccarat, and certain bets in craps minimize the house advantage and give the player the best opportunity to win. Keno and wheel of fortune are outright sucker games. Slots, other video poker, and roulette are only marginally better.

How the house advantage works in practice causes much misunderstanding. In most roulette bets, for example, the house holds a 5.26% advantage. If you place a dollar on black each time the wheel is spun, the house advantage predicts that, on average, you will lose 5.26 cents per dollar bet. Now, in actual play you will either lose one whole dollar

THE INTELLIGENCE TEST

If you have been paying attention, here is what you should understand by now:

1. That all gambling games are designed to favor the house, and that in the long run the house will always win.

2. That it costs a lot to build, staff, and operate a casino, and that a casino must attract many players in order to pay the bills and still make a profit.

3. That casinos compete fiercely for available customers and offer incentives ranging from 99-cent hot dogs to free guest rooms to get the right customers to their gaming tables.

QUESTION: Given the above, what kind of customer gets the best deal?
Answer: *The person who takes advantage of all the incentives without gambling.*

QUESTION: What kind of customer gets the next best deal?
Answer: *The customer who sees gambling as recreation, gambles knowledgeably, makes sensible bets, sets limits on the amount he or she is prepared to wager, and enjoys all of the perks and amenities, but stays in control.*

QUESTION: What kind of customer gets the worst deal?
Answer: *The person who thinks he or she can win. This person will foot the bill for everyone else.*

or win one whole dollar, so it's not like somebody is making small change or keeping track of fractional losses. The longer you play, however, the greater the likelihood that the percentage of your losses will approximate the house advantage. If you played for a couple of hours and bet $1,000, your expected loss would be about $53.

All right, you think, that doesn't sound too bad. Plus, you're thinking: I would never bet as much as $1,000. Oh, yeah? If you approach the table with $200 and make 20 consecutive $10 bets, it is not very likely that you will lose every bet. When you take money from your winning bets and wager it, you are adding to your original stake. This is known as "action" in gambling parlance, and it is very different from bankroll. Money that you win is just as much yours as the stake with which you began. When you choose to risk your winnings by making additional bets, you are giving the house a crack at a much larger amount than your original $200. If you start with $200, win some and lose some, and keep playing your winnings in addition to your original stake until you have lost everything, you will have given the house (on average) about $3,800 worth of action. You may want to believe you lost only $200, but every penny of that $3,800 was yours.

3. THE HOUSE TAKES A COMMISSION In all casino poker games and in certain betting situations in table games, the house will collect a commission on a player's winnings.

Sometimes the house combines its various advantages. In baccarat, for instance, rules favor the house; payoffs are less than the true odds; and in certain betting situations, the house collects a commission on the player's winnings.

GAMES OF CHANCE AND THE LAW OF AVERAGES

PEOPLE GET FUNNY IDEAS ABOUT the way gambling works. In casinos there are games of chance (roulette, craps, keno, bingo, slots, baccarat) and games of chance *and* skill (poker, blackjack, video poker).

A game of chance is like flipping a coin or spinning a wheel with 10 numbers. What happens is what happens. A player can guess what the outcome will be but cannot influence it. Games of chance operate according to the law of averages. If you have a fair coin and flip it 10 times, the law of averages leads you to expect that approximately half of the tosses will come up heads and the other half tails. If a roulette wheel has 38 slots, the law of averages suggests that the ball will fall into a particular slot one time in 38 spins.

The coin, the roulette ball, and the dice, however, have no memory. They just keep doing their thing. If you toss a coin and come up with heads nine times in a row, what are your chances of getting heads on the tenth toss? The answer is 50%, the same chance as getting heads on any toss. Each toss is completely independent of any other toss. When the coin goes up in the air that tenth time, it doesn't know that tails has not come up for a while, and certainly has no obligation to try to get the law of averages back into whack.

Though most gamblers are familiar with the law of averages, not all of them understand how it works. The operative word, as it turns out, is "averages," not "law." If you flip a coin a million times, there is nothing that says you will get 500,000 heads and 500,000 tails, no more than there is any assurance you will get five heads and five tails if you flip a coin 10 times. What the law of averages *does* say is that, *in percentage terms,* the more times you toss the coin, the closer you will come to approximating the predicted average.

If you tossed a coin 10 times, for example, you would not be surprised to get six tails and four heads. Six tails is only one flip off the five tails and five heads that the law of averages tells you is the probable outcome. By percentage, however, tails came up 60% (6 of 10) of the time, while heads came up only 40% (4 of 10) of the time. If you continued flipping the coin for a million tries, would you be surprised to get 503,750 tails and only 496,250 heads, a difference of 7,500 more tails than heads? The law of averages stipulates that the more we toss (and a million tosses are certainly a lot more than 10 tosses) the closer we should come to approximating the average, but here we are with a huge difference of 7,500 more tails. What went wrong?

Nothing went wrong. True, after 10 flips, we had only two more tails than heads, while after a million flips we had 7,500 more tails than heads. But in terms of percentage, 503,750 tails is 50.375% of one million, only about one-third of a measly percent from what the law of averages predicts. The law of averages is about percentages. Gambling is about dollars out of your pocket. If you had bet a dollar on heads each toss, you would have lost $2 after 10 flips. After a million flips you would have lost $7,500. The law of averages behaved just as mathematical theory predicted.

Games of Chance and Skill

Blackjack, poker, and video poker are games of chance and skill, meaning that the knowledge, experience, and skill of the player can have some influence on the outcome. All avid poker players or bridge players can recall nights when they played for hours without being dealt a good hand. That's the chance part. In order to win, you need good cards. There is usually not much you can do if you are dealt a bad hand.

If you are dealt something to work with, however, you can bring your skill into play and try to make your good hand even better. In casino poker, players compete against each other in the same way they do at Uncle Bert's house back home. The only difference is that in the casino the house takes a small percentage of each winning pot as compensation for hosting the game (are you listening, Uncle Bert?). Although not every casino poker player is an expert, your chances of coming up against an expert in a particular game are good.

 Our advice on casino poker: if you're not a tough fish, better not try to swim with the sharks.

Blackjack likewise combines chance and skill. In blackjack, however, players compete against the house (the dealer). Players have certain choices and options in blackjack, but the dealer's play is completely bound by rules. Much has been written about winning at blackjack. It's been said that by keeping track of cards played (and thereby knowing which cards remain undealt in the deck), a player can raise his or her bets when the deck contains a higher-than-usual percentage of aces, tens, and picture cards. In practice, however, the casino confounds efforts to count cards by combining several decks together, "burning" cards (removing undisclosed cards from play), and keeping the game moving at a fast pace. If an experienced gambler with extraordinary memory and power of concentration is able to overcome these obstacles, the casino will simply throw out this person.

In blackjack, as in every other casino game, it is ludicrous to suggest that the house is going to surrender its advantage. Incidentally, a super-gambler playing flawlessly and keeping track of every card will gain only a nominal and temporary advantage over the house. On top of playing perfectly and being dealt good cards, the super-gambler must also disguise his play and camouflage his betting so the house won't know what he's up to. It's not impossible, but very few players who try ever pull it off successfully.

MILLENNIALS

CASINOS HAVE BURNED A LOT OF BRAIN RUBBER figuring out how to get Millennials to gamble. Millennial visitors to Las Vegas have spiked in recent years and are likely to account for 34% and up of overall visitors in the years to come. Problem is, Millennials haven't shown much interest in the games casinos offer. Consequently, game manufacturing companies have been trying to develop games more like those Millennials play on their phones and laptops, usually fast-paced games that combine elements of chance and skill. It turns out, however, that this is a lot harder than it sounds. Several games, including a few that involve team play, have had a field trial. Some have seen promising action, but not from Millennials. Some take too long to play for the casino to realize adequate return for the investment of floor space. Others have favored skill over chance, which whittles away the house advantage, and a few have garnered favor with younger players, but with wagers on the anemic side. Many new high-tech games offer virtual reality, as with blackjack dealt by a VR dealer rather than a live one. All new games must be approved by the Nevada Gaming Control Board, no easy feat. Keep your eyes peeled for new games and skill-based twists on traditional machine games. They're coming.

PLAYING IT SMART

EXPERIENCED, NONCOMPULSIVE, recreational gamblers typically play in a disciplined, structured manner. Here's what they recommend:

1. **Never gamble when you are** tired, depressed, or sick. Also, watch the drinking. Alcohol impairs judgment (you play badly) and lowers inhibitions (you exceed prudent limits).

2. **Set a limit before you leave home** on the total amount you are willing to lose gambling. No matter what happens, do not exceed this limit.

3. **Decide which game(s) interest you and get the rules down before you play.** If you are a first-timer at craps or baccarat, take lessons (offered free at the casinos most days). If you are a virgin blackjack player, buy a good book and learn basic strategy. For all three games, spend an hour or two observing games in progress before buying in. Stay away from games like keno and wheel of fortune, in which the house advantage is overwhelming.

4. **Decide how long you want to play** and work out a gambling itinerary consistent with the funds you set aside for wagering. Let's say you plan to be in Las Vegas for two days and want to play about five hours each day. If you have $500 in gambling money available for the trip, that's $250 a day. Dividing the $250 a day by five hours, you come up with $50 an hour.

   Now, forget time. Think of your gambling in terms of playing individual sessions instead of hours. You are going to play five sessions a day with $50 available to wager at each session.

5. **Observe a strategy for winning and losing.** On buying in, place your session allocation by your left hand. Play your allotted session money only once during a given session. Anytime you win, return your original bet to the session-allocation stack (left hand), and place your winnings in a stack by your right hand. Never play any chips or coins you have won. When you have gone through your original allocation once, pick up the chips or coins in your winning stack (right hand) and quit. The difference between your original allocation and what you walk away with is your net win or loss for the session.

   During the session, bet consistently. If you have been making $1 bets and have lost $10, do not chase your losses by upping your bets to $10 in an effort to get even in a hurry.

   If you were fortunate and doubled your allocated stake during the session (in this case, walked away with $100 or more), take everything in excess of $100 and put it aside as winnings, not to be touched for the remainder of your trip. If you won, but did not double your money, or if you had a net loss (quit with less than $50 in your win stack), use this money in your next playing session.

6. **Take a break between sessions.** Relax for a while after each session. Grab a bite to eat, enjoy a nap, or go for a swim.

7. **When you complete** the number of sessions scheduled for the day, stop gambling. **Period.**

GAMING INSTRUCTION AND RESOURCES

MOST CASINO GAMES ARE ACTUALLY FAIRLY SIMPLE once you know what's going on. A great way to replace inexperience and awkwardness with knowledge and confidence is to take the free gaming lessons offered by the casinos. Going slowly and easily, the instructors take you step by step through the play and the betting without you actually wagering any money. Many casinos feature low-minimum-bet "live games" following the instruction. We also recommend the lessons to nonplaying companions of gamblers. For folks who usually spend a fair amount of time as spectators, casino games, like all other games, are more interesting if you know what is going on.

 We highly recommend the free gaming lessons offered by casinos. They introduce you not only to the rules but also to the customs and etiquette of the respective games.

No matter how many books you have read, take a lesson in craps before you try to play in a casino. You don't need to know much to play baccarat, but *understanding* it is a different story. Once again, we strongly recommend lessons. Though you can learn to play blackjack by reading a book and practicing at home, lessons will make you feel more comfortable.

A list of free gambling lessons currently offered in Las Vegas can be found at lvahotels.com. Click on "Gambling Advisor" at the top right of the page. A great website for gambling odds, playing strategies, practice games, and general information is Michael Shackleford's wizardofodds.com.

WRITTEN REFERENCES AND THE GAMBLERS BOOK CLUB Most libraries and bookstores offer basic reference works on casino gambling. If you can't find what you need at home, call the **Gamblers Book Club** at ☎ 800-522-1777 for a free catalog. If you would like to stop in and browse while in Las Vegas, the club's store is located at 800 S. Main St. (between Charleston and Fremont). The local phone is ☎ 702-382-7555, and visit online at gamblersbookclub.com. For those of you who visited the club at its Eastern Avenue location, it moved to share space with the Gamblers General Store (☎ 702 382-9903, gamblersgeneralstore.com), the one-stop shop for all things gambling. Gamblers Book Shop, incidentally, sells single issues of the *Las Vegas Advisor,* quoted below.

WHERE TO PLAY

WE RECEIVE A LOT OF MAIL FROM READERS asking which casino has the loosest slots, the most favorable rules for blackjack, and the best odds on craps. We directed the questions to veteran gambler and tournament player Anthony Curtis, publisher of the *Las Vegas Advisor.* Here's Anthony's reply:

ANTHONY'S RECOMMENDED BEST PLACES TO PLAY

BLACKJACK EL CORTEZ

El Cortez steadfastly continues to offer several single-deck games with a 3-2 payoff on naturals, and at low ($5) minimums. Add in the good promotions here and you have the best place in town to play low-stakes blackjack. As a novelty, Hooters deals a $1-minimum game 24/7, but it has weak rules and is one table only.

QUARTER SLOTS RAMPART

Since you can't tell definitively whose slots pay best (they can't be analyzed like video-poker machines), picking a casino with strong player benefits and an overall policy of liberal gambling is as good a way to choose as any. Rampart fits that bill. And in addition to being one of the best gambling houses in Las Vegas, the Rampart also has excellent comp deals, so your players points from quarter slots will go farther here.

DOLLAR SLOTS PALMS

Evidence continues to point to the Palms as another casino that's among the loosest for slots in general. Almost nothing has changed here since a sale to Station Casinos—lots of promotions and a good slot club make it the pick at the dollar level (though video poker provides much better returns). Dollar slot players earn comps fast, and this is one of the best places in town to use them, especially after an extensive makeover that has brought the resort back to its previous status as one of Las Vegas's coolest hangs.

CRAPS THE CROMWELL

The Cromwell is the only casino in Las Vegas dealing 100X odds. It's offered on all tables for bets of $10 up to the table max. This generous odds multiple makes it the best in town in this category, and at center-Strip, no less.

QUARTER VIDEO POKER FOUR QUEENS

Lots of high-return schedules, including several quarter progressives at the bars that are often at or above 100% returns. Save your players club points for a splurge in the excellent Hugo's Cellar.

DOLLAR VIDEO POKER SOUTH POINT

Hundreds of machines here pay at the 9/6 Jacks or Better level (99.54%) or better. Add the generous South Point slot club and other benefits and you're playing at a 100% theoretical return 24/7. Plus, whereas many casinos reduce players club benefits on machines with the best schedules, South Point pays full benefits on all machines.

ROULETTE CLUB FORTUNE

Since the town's single-zero wheels all have high minimums, the better move is to play double-zero games for lower stakes. One of the best is the wheel at Club Fortune in Henderson. It's open only in the evenings, but you can play with 25¢ chips for $1 minimum bets (inside) and $2 (outside).

BACCARAT PALACE STATION

Action around the clock at oversized mini baccarat tables. Minimums are low. If you get hungry, they'll deliver food to your table.

KENO JERRY'S NUGGET

In a comparison of 10-spots at every keno room in town, Jerry's Nugget came in with the lowest house edge of 25.10%, about 5% less than the standard edge for live keno. For best video keno returns, hit the bar at the Downtown Grand.

BINGO PLAZA

The only bingo room downtown offers lots of the features bingo players like, including guaranteed payouts, daily progressives, and good electronic specials. The Plaza runs good gambling promotions in general, so check the players club booth between sessions.

POKER ARIA

Aria is the most consistently busy room in town, offering a good mix of games, lots of tournaments, and a strong comp structure relative to competing rooms. There's also a discounted "poker rate" on rooms for players. On the high end, some of the biggest games in town run regularly out of the "Ivey Room."

ANTHONY'S RECOMMENDED BEST PLACES TO PLAY (continued)

RACE AND SPORTS BETTING WESTGATE LAS VEGAS

The Super Book at the Westgate is the easy call here. It takes big action, is first out with proposition bets on big games, and runs the SuperContest, the most prestigious handicapping tournament in the world. Look for –105 pricing (bet $105 to win $100, as opposed to the standard $110/100) during football season on Thursdays.

LET IT RIDE FOUR QUEENS

Not much separates one Let It Ride game from another, so a low-minimum-bet requirement is a good feature. The Four Queens usually has a game in action with a $5 minimum. Show your players card—this casino's mailing list is a good one to be on.

CARIBBEAN STUD THE VENETIAN

Caribbean Stud games are getting harder to find. Of the diminishing number of casinos that still deal the game, the Venetian is the best bet to find one that's open.

PAI GOW POKER GOLD COAST

Lots of tables cater to lots of action at any hour. As a favorite of local pai gow players, the Gold Coast usually has several tables with low minimums in play.

Where's the best casino in Las Vegas to play blackjack, video poker, and the rest of the gambling games? It could be almost any place on any given day due to spot promotions and changing management philosophies. A few casinos, however, have established reliable track records in specific areas. Absent a special promotion or change in policy, I recommend the casinos in the chart above as the best places for the games listed.

Players Clubs

Most Las Vegas casinos now have loyalty programs, known as players clubs. The purpose of these clubs is to foster increased customer loyalty among gambling patrons by providing incentives. Even if you're not a gambler, or only gamble a little, you should sign up. This will get you on the casino's mailing/email lists identified as a gambler, and ensure that you receive special offers and discounts on rooms, shows, dining, and more.

You can join a club by signing up at the casino or (at most casinos) by applying through the mail or online. There is neither a direct cost associated with joining nor any dues. You are given a plastic membership card that resembles a credit card. This card can be inserted into a special slot on any gambling machine in the casino. As long as your card is in the slot, you are credited for the amount of action you put through that machine. Programs at different casinos vary, but in general, you are awarded points based on how long you play and how much you wager. All clubs award points for slot play; some also use the card at the tables to input hours played and average bets into the player-tracking database. As in an airline frequent-flyer program, accumulated points can ultimately be redeemed for rewards. Rewards range from casino logo apparel to discounts and comps on meals, shows, and rooms.

Las Vegas is dominated by large casino companies such as Caesars Entertainment, MGM Resorts International, and local companies such as Boyd Gaming and Station Casinos. These major stakeholders respectively offer a players club card that can be used in any of their casinos. The following casinos' players club cards can be acquired online:

• Aria • Bally's • Bellagio • Boulder Station • Caesars Palace
• California • The Cosmopolitan • The Cromwell • Downtown Grand
• Ellis Island • Excalibur • Fiesta Henderson and Rancho • Flamingo
• Fremont • Gold Coast • Golden Gate • Green Valley Ranch • Hard Rock
• Harrah's • LINQ Hotel & Casino • Luxor • Main Street Station
• Mandalay Bay • MGM Grand • Mirage • MonteLago Village Resort
• New York–New York • The Orleans • Palace Station • Palazzo • Palms
• Paris • Park MGM • Planet Hollywood • Plaza • Rampart
• Red Rock Resort • Rio • Sam's Town • Silverton • SLS • South Point
• Suncoast • Sunset Station • Texas Station • Venetian • Westgate LV

Players clubs are evolving into programs where nongambling spending on rooms, dining, entertainment, and shopping is tracked in addition to gambling action. As discussed in the introduction to this guide, gaming revenue has slipped into second place behind nongaming revenue at many casinos, so this metamorphosis makes sense.

Most Strip casinos, except Circus Circus, Stratosphere, TI, Tropicana, Wynn, and Encore, track and reward all spending. At most off-Strip casinos, only spending on gaming is rewarded. Exceptions are the Hard Rock and the Rio.

One good thing about players clubs is that they provide a mechanism for slot players to obtain some of the comps, perks, and extras that have always been available to table players. The bad thing about a players club is that it confines your play. In other words, you must give most of your business to one or two casinos in order to accumulate enough points to reap rewards, though you will nonetheless receive the special offers mentioned earlier. If you are a footloose player and enjoy gambling all around town, you may never accrue enough points in any one casino to redeem a comp.

CHANGES IN ATTITUDE, CHANGES IN LATITUDE

MOST PEOPLE WHO LOVE TO GAMBLE are not motivated solely by greed. Usually it is the tension, excitement, and anticipation of the game that they enjoy. Misunderstanding this reality has led many naive and innocent people into the nightmare of addictive gambling.

Ed was attending a convention on his first visit to Las Vegas. One evening, he decided to try his luck at roulette. Approaching the table, Ed expected to lose ("I'm not stupid, after all"). His intentions were typical. He wanted to "try" gambling while in Nevada, and he was looking for an adventure. What Ed never anticipated was the emotional impact gambling would have on him. It transcended winning and losing. It was the *playing* that mattered. The "action" made him feel alive, involved, and terribly sophisticated. It also made him crazy.

The "high" described by the compulsive gambler closely parallels the experience of drug and alcohol abusers. In fact, there is a tendency for chemical addiction and gambling compulsion to overlap. The compulsive gambler attempts to use "the action" as a cure for a variety of ills, in much the same way that people use alcohol and drugs to lift them out of depression, anxiety, or boredom, and make them feel more "in control."

Some people cannot handle gambling, just as some people cannot handle alcohol. The problem, unfortunately, is compounded by the attitude of our society. As we profess to admire the drinker who can "hold his liquor," we reinforce the gambler who beats the odds in Las Vegas. By glamorizing these behaviors we enable afflicted individuals to remain in denial about the destructive nature of their problem. The compulsive gambler blames circumstances and other people for the suffering occasioned by his or her affliction. One may hear excuses like: "I didn't get enough sleep; I couldn't concentrate with all the noise; I lost track of the time; I'm jinxed at this casino."

If this sounds like you or someone you love, get help. In Las Vegas there is a meeting of **Gamblers Anonymous** almost every Tuesday night. Call ☎ 855-222-5542 or check the web at gamblersanonymous.org. If, like Ed, you catch something in Las Vegas and take it home with you, Gamblers Anonymous is listed in your local *White Pages* or online.

RULES *of the* GAMES

SLOT MACHINES

SLOT MACHINES, INCLUDING VIDEO POKER, have long eclipsed table games in patron popularity. Few Las Vegas casinos remain that have not allocated half or more of their available floor space to various types of slot machines.

The popularity of slots is not difficult to understand. First, slots allow a person to enjoy casino gambling at low or high stakes. Except at the oldest and lowest-tier casinos, all slot machines are now multi-denominational, meaning you can play them for a penny, nickel, dime, quarter, dollar, and up. You don't need change to do so; slot machines no longer have slots. You load them up with bills, then play at your chosen denomination. Higher-stakes players can find machines that accept bets of $1–$500 ($2,500 to load up a $500 video poker machine).

Second, many people like the slots because no human interaction is required. Absent in slot play is the adversarial atmosphere of the table games. Machines are less intimidating—at least more neutral—than dealers and pit bosses. A patron can sit at a machine for as long as his stamina and money last and never be bothered by a soul.

Finally, slot machines are simple, or at least ostensibly so. Although there are a number of things you should know before you play the slots, the only thing you have to know is how to put money (mostly bills) into the machine and press the spin button (it's the rare slot machine that still has a handle).

What You Need to Know Before You Play Slot Machines

Starting at the beginning: All slot machines have a slot for inserting either coins, bills, or machine tickets, a button to push to activate the machine, a visual display where you can see the reels spin and stop or video symbols line up on each play, and a coin tray or machine-ticket dispenser out of which you hope some winnings will come. Today, almost all slot machines are essentially computers attached to a monitor. Gone are the mechanical reels, replaced by an electronic depiction of reels or other symbols illustrated on the monitor.

While slot machines used to have three mechanical reels, most today have been replaced by either three or four electronic reels or video screens with up to 12 depictions of reels. Each reel has some number of "stops," positions where the reel can come to rest. On each reel at each stop (or resting position) is a single slot symbol (a cherry, bar, themed symbol, etc.). What you hope will happen (when the video reels stop spinning) is that paying symbols will line up. If this happens, you win some number of coins or credits based on the bet and particular symbols. With the old slot machines things were pretty simple. There was one coin slot, one handle to pull, and a display with one pay line. Symbols either lined up or they didn't. The newer machines are much more complex. All modern machines accept more than 1 coin per play (usually 3–5 but up to 250). No matter how many coins the machine will take, it requires only one to play. If you put in additional coins (bet more), you will buy one of the following benefits:

1. **Payoff schedules** On some slot machines, the payoff schedule is posted on the glass above the screen; on others, you have to press the See Pays button to determine the winning combinations. If you study these schedules you will notice that by playing extra coins you can increase your payoff should you win the grand jackpot. Usually there is a straightforward increase. If you play two coins, you will win twice as much as if you play one coin. If you play three coins, you will win three times as much as if you play one coin, and so on. Some machines, however, have a jackpot that will pay off only if you have played the maximum number of coins. If you line up the symbols for the jackpot but have not played the maximum number of coins, you will not win the maximum amount possible. The machines with three or four reels, such as the venerable Red, White, and Blue; Double Diamonds; and Blazing Sevens, are easy to understand, with the payout schedules posted prominently on the glass screen above the reels. Video (also known as Australian) slots, on the other hand, which come in hundreds of different themes, are much more complicated. You can press the Help button at the bottom of the screen to bring up three or four additional screens that explain the machine. But most slot players don't bother, and it's not necessary to comprehend all the ins and outs. Just slip your money into the bill acceptor, press the button with the number of coins you want to play, and spin the reels; the machine does the rest.

   Though most casino slot machines are kept in good working order, watch to make sure the machine credits you for every coin you play and for all the winnings due to you.

Slot Machine Pay Lines

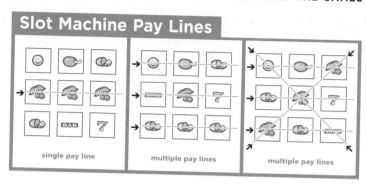

single pay line

multiple pay lines

multiple pay lines

2. Multiple pay lines When you play your first coin, you buy the usual pay line, right in the center of the display. By playing more coins, you can buy additional pay lines.

Each pay line you purchase gives you another way of winning. Instead of being limited to the center line, the machine will pay off on the top, center, or bottom lines, and five-coin machines will pay winners on diagonal lines. Australian machines pay off on a dozen lines or more, criss-crossing symbols all over the screen. If you play machines with multiple pay lines, make sure that each pay line you buy is acknowledged by a light before you push the button.

An irritating feature of many multiple-line machines are "blanks" or "ghosts." A blank is nothing more than an empty stop on the reel—a place where you would expect a symbol to be but where there is nothing. As you probably know, you cannot hit a winner by lining up blanks.

NONPROGRESSIVE VS. PROGRESSIVE SLOT MACHINES Nonprogressive slot machines have fixed payoffs. You can read the payoff schedules posted on the machine and determine exactly how much you will get for each winning combination for any number of coins played.

 The nonprogressive machine is for the player who likes plenty of action, who gets bored when credits aren't rising on the meter every four or five spins. The progressive machine is for the player who is willing to forgo frequent small payouts for the chance of hitting a really big one.

A second type of machine, known as a progressive, has a top jackpot that grows and grows until it's hit. After the top prize has been won, the jackpot is reset and starts to grow. While individual machines can offer modest progressive jackpots, the really big jackpots (up to tens of millions of dollars) are possible only on machines linked in a system to other machines. Sometimes an "island," "carousel," or "bank" of machines in a given casino is hooked up to create a progressive system. The more these machines are played, the faster the progressive jackpot grows. The largest progressive jackpots come from huge multicasino systems that sometimes cover the entire state. Players have won more than $30 million by hitting these jackpots.

While nothing is certain in slot play, it is generally accepted that nonprogressives pay more small jackpots, while progressives offer an opportunity to strike it really rich, but they give up fewer interim wins.

How Slot Machines Work

Almost all slot machines used in casinos today are controlled by microprocessors. This means the machines can be programmed and are more like computers than mechanical boxes composed of gears and wheels. During the evolution of the modern slot machine, manufacturers eliminated the traditional spinning reels in favor of a video display, and replaced the pull handle with a spin button. Inside the newer machines, there is a device that computer people call a "random number generator" and that we refer to as a "black box." What the black box does is spit out hundreds of numbers each second, selected randomly (that is, in no predetermined sequence). The black box has about four billion different numbers to choose from, so it's very unusual (but not impossible) for the same number to come up twice in a short time.

The numbers the black box selects are programmed to trigger a certain set of symbols on the display, determining where the reels stop. What most players don't realize, however, is that the black box pumps out numbers continuously, regardless of whether the machine is being played or not. If you are playing a machine, the black box will call up hundreds or thousands of numbers in the few seconds between plays while you sip your drink, put money in the slot, and push the button.

Why is this important? Try this scenario: Mary has played the same quarter machine for hours, pumping an untold amount of money into it. She cashes out and gets up to stretch her legs for a few minutes, thinking she'll come back afterwards and keep playing. In the meantime, a man walks up to Mary's machine and hits the jackpot. Mary is livid. "That's my jackpot!" she screams. Not so. While Mary took her walk, thousands of numbers and possible symbol combinations were generated by the black box. The only way Mary could have hit the jackpot (even if the man had not come along) would have been to activate the machine at that same exact moment in time, right down to a fraction of a millisecond.

Another slot myth is that a machine is "overdue to hit." Each spin of the reels on a slot machine is an independent event, just like flipping a coin. The only way to hit a jackpot is to activate the machine at the exact moment that the black box randomly coughs up a winning number. If you play a slot machine as fast as you can, pushing the spin button like a maniac, the black box will still spew out more numbers (and possible jackpots) between each try than you will have spins in a whole day of playing.

CHERRY, CHERRY, ORANGE The house advantage is known for every casino game except slots. With slot machines, the house advantage is whatever the casino programs it to be. In Atlantic City the maximum legal house advantage is 17%. Nevada's limit for slot machines is a hold of 75%. This means that Nevada slot machines can have a house advantage of up to 25%. Interviews with ex–casino employees suggest, however, that the house advantage on casino slots in Las Vegas ranges from about 2.5% to 25%, with most machines giving the house an edge of between 4% and 14%.

Casinos advertise their slots in terms of payout or return rate. If a casino states that its slots return up to 97%, that's another way of saying that the house has a 3% advantage. Some casinos advertise machines that pay up to 98%, and on special-promotion occasions, a casino might advertise slots that pay more than 100%.

SLOT QUEST A slot machine that withholds only a small percentage of the money played is referred to as "loose," while a machine that retains closer to the maximum allowable percentage is called "tight." "Loose" and "tight" are figurative descriptions and have nothing to do with the condition of the machine. Because return rates vary from casino to casino, and because machines in a given casino are programmed to withhold vastly differing percentages of the money played, some slot players devote much time and energy to finding the best casinos and the loosest machines. Exactly how to go about this is the subject of much discussion.

In terms of choosing a casino, several theories have at least a marginal ring of truth. Competition among casinos is often a general indicator for finding loose slots. Some say that smaller casinos, which compete against large neighbors, must program their slots to provide a higher return. Alternatively, some folks will play slots only in casinos patronized predominantly by locals, such as Gold Coast, Sam's Town, and Arizona Charlie's, among others. The reasoning here is that these casinos vie for regular customers on a continuing basis and must therefore offer extremely competitive win rates. Downtown Las Vegas is likewise cast in the "we try harder" role, because smaller Downtown casinos must go head-to-head with the Strip to attract patrons.

Extending the logic, machines located in supermarkets, restaurants, convenience stores, airports, and lounges are purported to be very tight. In these places, some argue, there is little incentive for management to provide good returns, because the patrons will play regardless (out of boredom or compulsion or simply because the machine is there).

Veteran slot players have many theories when it comes to finding the loose machines in a particular casino. Some will tell you to play

---

LAND OF THE LOOSE SLOTS

MOST RECREATIONAL SLOT PLAYERS play at the casino where they're staying, even if they know there are looser machines elsewhere. Those who are serious about finding the loosest slots, however, should check out *Casino Player Magazine*'s **casinocenter.com.** According to its findings, the best machines, located at the Hard Rock, Palms, Orleans, and Silverton, return 94.64% of the money played. A tiny 1/4th of 1 percent behind are the Boulder Highway casinos, Boulder Station, Sam's Town, and Arizona Charlie's East. Strip casino slots are tight, and there's no data to rate Downtown, but its video poker schedules are superior to those of Strip casinos, so maybe their slots are better as well. Bear in mind, however, that a 94.64% return rate is just about the same house edge as double zero roulette. Not great.

the machines by the door or in the waiting area outside the show-room. By placing the loose machines in these locations, the theory goes, the casino can demonstrate to passersby and show patrons that the house has loose slots. Perhaps the most accurate way to judge the relative looseness of reel slots is to monitor the payouts for video poker. As explained in the next section, knowledgeable players who know how to interpret video poker pay schedules can determine the payback percentage to thousandths of percentage points. It's safe to assume (as safe as it is to assume anything) that a casino with loose video poker machines will have loose slots as well.

I have had a slot manager admit to me that his quarter machines are looser than his nickel machines and that his dollar and five-dollar machines are the loosest of all. Tight or loose, however, all slots are programmed to give the casino a certain profit over the long run. It is very unlikely, in any event, that you will play a machine long enough to experience the theoretical payoff rate. What you are concerned about is the short run. In the short run anything can happen, including winning.

MAXIMIZING YOUR CHANCES OF WINNING ON THE SLOTS If you play less than the maximum number of coins on a progressive, you are simply contributing to a jackpot that you have no chance of winning. If you don't want to place a maximum bet, play a nonprogressive machine.

Slot-Machine Etiquette and Common Sense

Regardless of whether you are playing a slot machine, a video-poker machine, or any other type of electronic or mechanical gambling device, there are some things you need to know:

1. Realize that avid slot players sometimes play more than one machine at a time. Do not assume that a machine is not in use simply because nobody is in front of it. Slot players can be fanatically territorial.

2. Before you start to play, check out the people around you. Do you feel safe and comfortable among them?

3. Read the payout schedule of any machine you play; if you don't understand it completely, don't worry.

4. Almost all machines have credit meters; be sure to cash out your credits before you abandon the machine.

5. If the casino has a players club, join (this usually takes less than 5 minutes on-site, but can be accomplished through the mail or online prior to your trip). Use the club card whenever you play. When you quit, don't forget to take your club card with you.

6. Never play more machines than you can watch carefully. Be particularly vigilant when playing machines near exits and corridors. If you're asleep at the switch, you're vulnerable to victimization by thieves and scam artists, who have plenty of nefarious tricks up their sleeves to relieve you of your lucre. They even have ways of absconding with payout tickets issued from the machine while you're playing!

7. Keep your purse and your money in sight at all times. Never put your purse on the floor behind you or to the side.

8. If you line up a big winner and nothing happens, don't panic. Slot machines lock up when a jackpot exceeds the tax-reporting requirement. Any winning combination of more than $1,200 on a slot or video poker machine must be "hand paid" directly by a slot floorperson. If you're lucky and hit a big enough jackpot that tax paperwork needs to be filled out, the "candle" (light fixture) atop the machine will blink or some other indicator of a jackpot will manifest, summoning a slot attendant. Don't wander off to look for one; sit patiently and one will show up shortly.

9. If the appropriate payout sections or pay lines fail to illuminate when playing multiple coins, do not leave or activate the machine (push the button) until you have consulted an attendant.

Slot Hold by Reporting Area, January 2004 to April 2018

Slot hold is understood as the average slot hold percentage (or percentage going to the house) for the period in question as released by the Nevada Gaming Control Board. A slot that has a 94% payout rate would over the long term have a slot hold percentage of 6%. The lower the slot hold rate, the better for the player.

REPORTING AREA AVERAGE HOLD	
• Las Vegas Strip **7.3%**	• North Las Vegas **5.94%**
• Downtown Las Vegas **6.61%**	• Boulder Strip **5.35%**
• Statewide **6.27%**	• Reno **5.08%**

The Future of Slot Machines

The bandits have always been stand-alone machines with individual controls, from mechanical cogs and gears in the early days to central-processing units in the electronic age. So in order to change a slot's games, denominations, or payback percentages, a slot technician has had to manipulate the circuitry of the machine itself. However, a new generation of slots, known as "server-based" machines, are all networked to a central back-office computer system; the machines on the floor essentially become dumb monitors dressed up in slot cabinets, into which (with the click of a back-room mouse) different games, denominations, payback percentages, bonuses, and so on can be downloaded.

From the casino's point of view, server-based slots allow managers, with a few keystrokes, to tailor their games to player preferences. Perhaps the casino needs more slots during the day and more video poker at night. Or maybe weekday crowds prefer penny games and free spins, while weekend players like quarter games and second-screen bonuses. Operators can also increase denominations, say from nickels to quarters and quarters to dollars, at prime time on Saturday nights. In short, casinos are able to adapt to changing conditions on the fly.

In addition, with the use of the player-tracking system, managers can record a player's preferred game, then offer those games on a machine as soon as a player inserts the card. The casino can also contact players right at the machine in real time. For example, a message that you've earned a free buffet or discounted show tickets could be sent to the display terminal on the machine.

From the player's perspective, server-based slots have to overcome a long-cherished myth: that casinos can change the payback of a machine at the flip of a switch, tightening games during busy times, then loosening them again when the crowds go home. Downloadable slots will certainly have that capability. Thus, the onus will be on the casinos and gaming regulators to make the process as transparent as possible, so that when a player suddenly goes from hot to cold, he won't suspect that a computer has just changed the payback percentage from 98% to 82%. For example, the machine's screen might display a "modification-in-progress" message, followed by, say, 5 minutes of down time.

Early adopters of server-based slots in Las Vegas include Aria and The Cosmopolitan. Stay tuned.

VIDEO POKER

NEVER IN THE HISTORY of casino gambling has a game become so popular so quickly. What's the allure of video poker? More people are familiar with poker than with any other casino game. The video version affords average folks an opportunity to play a game of chance and skill without going up against professional gamblers. Also, like slot machines, video poker is fast; you can play 300, 400, 500 hands per hour. And like blackjack, it's skilled, so you can study and become an expert player and gain an edge over the house. Finally, it's hypnotic; many people find it hard to get up from a video poker machine (if that's you, you might think twice about playing too much and becoming compulsive).

In video poker you play against a machine. The object is to make the best possible five-card-draw poker hand. In the most common rendition, you insert your money and push a button marked "deal." Your original five cards are displayed on the screen. Below the screen and under each of the cards pictured are "hold" buttons. After evaluating your hand and planning your strategy, designate the cards you want to keep by pressing the appropriate hold button(s). If you hit the wrong button or change your mind, simply "unhold" your choices by pushing the buttons again. If you do not want to draw any cards (you like your hand as dealt), press all five hold buttons. When you press the hold button for a particular card, the word "hold" will appear over that card on the display. Always double-check the screen to make certain the cards you intend to hold are marked before proceeding to the draw.

When you are ready, press the button marked "draw" (on many machines it is the same button as the deal button). Any cards you have not designated to be held will be replaced. As in live draw poker, the five cards in your possession after the draw are your final hand. If the hand is a winner (a pair of jacks or better on most non-wild-card machines), you will be credited the appropriate winnings on the credit meter on the video display. These are actual winnings that can be retrieved, mostly via a machine ticket, by pressing the "cash-out" button. If you choose to leave your winnings on the credit meter, you may use them to bet, eliminating the need to physically insert more money into the machine. When you are ready to quit, simply press the cash-out button and collect your coins from the tray or a ticket from the dispenser.

As with other slot machines, you can increase your payoffs and become eligible for bonus jackpots by playing the maximum number of coins. Note that some machines have jackpots listed in dollars, while others are specified in coins. Obviously, there is a big difference between $4,000 and 4,000 nickels.

Playing video poker is vastly different from playing live poker. There's no psychology involved. You can't bluff the machine. You can show all the emotion you want. In most games, you don't hold kickers. All you need to know to play is the hierarchy of winning poker hands (pair, two-pair, three-of-a-kind, straight, and so on). All the winning hands with their respective payoffs are enumerated on or above the video display.

But to play video poker well, you need two additional skills: selecting the right machine and playing the proper strategy. The first skill requires the ability to decipher the pay schedules posted prominently on the face-plates of every machine. Some machines have a high payback percentage, even higher than 100%, while others pay less. You're looking for the highest paying schedules within each variation of video poker—and there are dozens of variations, but you have to know only a few of them.

Two of these are Jacks or Better (JoB) and Double Bonus. The highest paying version of JoB is called 9/6, meaning it pays 9-for-1 per coin played when you hit a full house, and 6-for-1 when you hit a flush. When you check the payout schedule for a single coin played, it could read 8 for a full house and 5 for a flush, even 7 or 6 for a full house. But unless you're returned 9 for the full house and 6 for the flush, you might as well play any random slot machine. The payback percentage for 9/6 JoB is 99.5%, almost break-even.

The other schedule to look for is 10/7 Double Bonus. Again, this means 10-for-1 on a full house and 7-for-1 on a flush. You'll see lower paybacks, but it's only 10/7 that we play, which pays back 100.7%, a positive game.

Other payback schedules are also playable, such as Deuces Wild and Joker Wild. But you have to recognize the highest-paying versions, which you can learn easily and quickly. Read a few pages of a good gambling primer, such as *The Frugal Gambler, More Frugal Gambling, or Frugal Video Poker* by Jean Scott, and you'll be locating the beatable machines like a pro.

Learning the proper playing strategies requires a bit more work. Luckily, the tools are readily available, inexpensive, easy to use, and completely effective. In fact, the first tool, the computer tutorial, is also fun. These software programs, such as *Frugal Video Poker* and *Video Poker for Winners,* teach you "computer-perfect strategy" by alerting you to and correcting strategy mistakes as you play on your home or office computer. Programming yourself with the proper plays takes only four or five enjoyable hours; this is time extremely well spent for preparing to take on the casino with real money.

Problem is, you can't take the computer into the casino. That's where strategy cards come into play—the best video-poker aids of all. These $6.95 handy-dandy trifold pocket-size color-coded laminated cards use a sort of shorthand to list every decision by which you can possibly be confronted at a machine; they pay for themselves in one playing session with the saving gained by avoiding costly mistakes. And the best thing is, other than spending a few minutes deciphering the shorthand when you first receive them, you don't have to do anything with them, except remember to put them in your pocket and refer to them while you play.

The edge at video poker ranges from more than 10% on the worst schedules up to positive 1% (a player advantage) on the best.

 A computer tutorial and handy strategy cards will give you an edge in video poker.

An Example of Video-Poker Strategy

Each hand in a video-poker game is dealt from a fresh 52-card deck. Each hand consists of 10 cards, with a random number generator or "black box" selecting the cards dealt. When you hit the deal button, the first five cards are displayed face up on the screen. Cards 6–10 are held in reserve to be dealt as replacements for cards you discard when you draw. Each replacement card is dealt in order off the top of the electronic deck. The microprocessor "shuffles" the deck for each new game. Thus on the next play, you will be dealt five new and randomly selected initial cards, and five new and randomly selected draw cards to back them up. In other words, you will not be dealt any unused cards from the previous hand.

THE POWER OF THE ROYAL FLUSH In video poker, the biggest payout is usually for a royal flush. This fact influences strategy for playing the game. Simply put, you play differently than you would in a live poker game. If in Jacks or Better video poker you are dealt

A♣ Q♣ 10♣ A♠ J♣

you would discard the ace of spades (giving up a paying pair) to go for the royal flush. Likewise, if you are dealt

5♠ A♠ K♠ Q♠ J♠

you would discard the 5 of spades (sacrificing a sure spade flush) in an attempt to make the royal by drawing the 10 of spades. If you are dealt

J♥ Q♥ K♥ 4♥ 6♣

draw two cards for the royal flush as opposed to one card for the flush.

The payoff for the royal flush is so great that it is worth risking a sure winning hand. The payoff for a straight flush, however, does not warrant risking a pat flush or straight.

OTHER SITUATIONS If you are dealt

Q♦ A♣ 4♥ J♠ 4♣

hold the small pair. But if you are dealt

K ♦   A ♣   4 ♥   J ♣   3 ♠

hold the ace of clubs and the jack of clubs to give yourself a long shot at a royal flush. Similarly, if you are dealt

K ♣   A ♣   4 ♥   J ♣   3 ♠

hold the ace of clubs, king of clubs, and jack of clubs.

DRAW POKER If you are playing draw poker (no wild cards), with a pair of jacks or better required to win, observe the following:

1. Hold a jacks-or-better pair, even if you pass up the chance of drawing to an open-end straight or to a flush. If you have

Q ♣   4 ♠   6 ♠   2 ♠   Q ♠

or

Q ♥   9 ♦   10 ♣   J ♠   Q ♣

in each case keep the pair of queens and draw three cards.

2. Split a low pair to go for a flush. If you are dealt

2 ♦   4 ♣   4 ♦   8 ♦   10 ♦

discard the 4 of clubs and draw one card to try and make the flush.

3. Hold a low pair rather than drawing to an inside or open-end straight.

4. A "kicker" is a face card or an ace you might be tempted to hang onto along with a high pair, low pair, or three-of-a-kind. If you are dealt, for example,

5 ♣   5 ♦   8 ♠   10 ♠   A ♥

or

2 ♣   2 ♣   2 ♥   8 ♠   A ♥

hold the pair or the three-of-a-kind, but discard the kicker (the ace).

LIVE POKER

POKER, A GAME OF SKILL and chance, has come a long way from the kitchen table. In its most elemental form, it's a simple game, one that children can easily grasp. Played recreationally by adults, the game admits more strategic play. At the highest level, poker combines psychology, probability theory, laser focus, steely calculation, and a universe of nuance.

The game has enjoyed a renaissance over the past decade, with tele-vised poker tournaments, such as the World Series of Poker, and an unending profusion of poker apps, websites, and books. It has become the subject of higher mathematics and academic research. Today, the complexity of the game in all of its manifestations requires a player to study poker in the same way that serious chess players study chess.

Poker embodies essential elements of other card games. Like bridge (depending on the game dealt), it's necessary to keep track of cards played and not played. It's necessary to pay close attention to the playing style and decisions of your opponents, and to disguise your own playing style to render it unpredictable. Poker requires that you understand the psychology and utility of bluffing, including under what circumstances and with whom to do it. Also key is the importance of managing the game rather than being swept away by it. Most of all, poker demands a well-considered reason for everything you do. It's about maximizing skill and minimizing chance.

In casino play, a variety of poker and poker derivative games are dealt, including Caribbean Stud, Let It Ride, Three Card poker, Crazy 4 poker, 3-5-7 poker, and the Asian favorite, Pai Gow poker. Though all have their advocates, by far the most popular game is no-limit Texas Hold'em, both in ring games (a "live" poker game where actual money is in play) and tournaments (buy-ins for tournament chips). The combination of procedures, strategy and tactics, and psychology can take a lifetime to perfect, but the rules of no-limit Texas Hold'em can be learned from an hour of study and another hour of practice.

I recommend studying the game, then playing the free games online at poker sites such as **partypoker.com.** You should also take a lesson, played with free chips, offered by some casino poker rooms. Then, when you're ready for a live game, look for one with the lowest mandatory bets (called blinds), such as $1 to $2 and $2 to $4. As your skills improve, you can move up in denomination, all the way to $25,000 buy-in tournaments. If you're just playing for fun, you'll have little to worry about in low-minimum-blind games.

Following are the basic steps in a round of no-limit Texas Hold'em:

There are two types of bets: blinds and antes. Antes are rare in hold 'em ring games, but they're usually imposed in the later rounds of tournaments. Blinds, a forced bet that one or more players, typically to the left of the dealer, make before any cards are dealt are always used. This starts the action on the first round of betting.

The game begins when the two players to the left of the dealer make initial bets, also known as "posting the blinds." The player to the immediate left of the dealer is the small blind; he puts up a bet equal to half the lowest allowable bet. The player two to the left of the dealer is the big blind; his bet is equal to the lowest allowable bet. If it's a $10–$20 game, the small blind bets $5 and the big blind bets $10.

Each player is dealt two cards facedown, known as hole (or pocket) cards. The first round of betting, "pre-flop," begins with the player to the left of the big blind. The betting structures can get a bit complicated, but to keep it simple, in our $10–$20 game, you'll bet $10 at a time in pre-flop rounds. You can bet four times per betting round. In other words, the initial bet can be "raised" by $10 three times. So if you initially bet $10, to stay in the pre-flop round, you might have to put up $30 more. "Checking" means you don't bet but keep open your options of "calling" (betting an equal amount; not raising), raising, or folding later in the betting round if your prospects look dim.

At the end of the pre-flop betting rounds, the dealer "burns" (discards) the top card, then deals three cards faceup on the table. This is known as "the flop." These three cards are combined with each player's two hole cards to form the initial five-card poker hand. Then there's another round of betting, starting with the player to the left of the dealer.

At the end of the post-flop betting, the dealer burns the top card, then deals one card faceup on the table: "the turn." Players can now use this fourth community card to improve their five-card poker hand. Another round of betting ensues. Often, this is where the lowest allowable bet doubles. So in our $10–$20 game, initial bets can be $20.

At the end of the turn betting, the dealer burns the top card, then deals one card faceup on the table: "the river." Players can now combine any of the five community cards with their two pocket cards to make the best five-card hand. One more round of betting follows, beginning with the player to the left of the dealer.

Finally, the "showdown" occurs, when players reveal their hands. The player with the best hand wins the pot. The dealer, a casino employee, rakes the house's cut (in a ring game), collects the cards, and another round begins.

A critical dimension of no-limit Texas Hold'em is position, or expressed differently, where you sit relative to the dealer. In professional or casino Texas Hold'em games, the players don't deal the cards themselves. Instead, a house dealer sits in the middle of the layout. To establish position, a round disc with "dealer" or "button" written on it is passed to the left after each round to denote where the dealer would be if the deck were actually being passed from player to player. In this case, the most favorable position is to be "on the button," i.e., in the dealer position. Here, seeing all your opponents play before you play gives you a great advantage. Conversely, the player to the immediate left of the button is in the worst position and must play without seeing the actions of his opponents. Much no-limit Texas Hold'em strategy is predicated on your position. If in one round you have a pair of 8s as hole cards but are seated just to the left of the button (worst position), you'd probably play that hand differently than if you held the same cards and are on the button. Going clockwise, or left, the farther you are from the button the better.

Although it might sound like a cousin of 7-Card Stud, there's a lot of protocol and jargon to no-limit Texas Hold'em. Again, I highly recommend reading up on the game, then participating in the free tournaments at poker websites, before taking a lesson in a casino poker room. These steps can (and probably will) save you a certain amount of grief when you start playing for real money, even in the lowest-limit games. The best book on Texas Hold'em is Annie Duke's *Decide To Play Great Poker: A Strategy Guide to No-Limit Texas Hold'em* (Huntington Press, 448 pages, $34.95). Less-experienced players, however, might find Duke's exposition a bit over their heads. For a more basic guide to Texas Hold'em, try *Small Stakes No-Limit Hold'em* by Ed Miller (Dimat Enterprises, 376 pages, $25.99).

BLACKJACK

MANY BOOKS HAVE BEEN PUBLISHED about the game of black-jack. The serious gamblers who write these books will tell you that black-jack is a game of skill and chance in which a player's ability can actually turn the odds of winning in his favor. While that is true, we also know the casinos wouldn't keep the tables open if they were taking a beating.

The methods of playing blackjack skillfully involve being able to count all the cards played and flawlessly manage your own hand, while mentally blocking the distraction of the casino. The ability to master the prerequisite tactics and to play under casino conditions is so far beyond the average (never mind beginning) player that any attempt to track cards is, except for a talented and disciplined few, exhausting and futile.

This doesn't mean that you should not try blackjack. It is a fun, fast-paced game that is easy to understand, and you can play at low-minimum-wager tables without feeling intimidated by the level of play. Moreover, most people already have an understanding of the game from playing "21" at home. The casino version is largely the same, only with more bells and whistles.

In a game of blackjack, the number cards are worth their spots (a 2 of clubs is worth two). All face cards are worth 10. The ace, on the other hand, is worth either 1 point or 11, whichever you choose. In this manner, an ace and a 5 could be worth 6 (hard count) or 16 (soft count). The object of the game is to get as close to 21 as you can without going over (called "busting"). You play only against the dealer, and the hand closest to 21 wins the game.

The dealer will deal you a two-card hand, then give you the option of taking another card (called a "hit") or stopping with the two cards you have been dealt (called "standing"). For example, if your first two cards are a 10 and a 3, your total would be 13, and you would normally ask for another card to get closer to 21. If the next card dealt to you was a 7, you would have a total of 20 points and you would "stand" with 20 (that is, not ask for another card).

It makes no difference what the other players are dealt, or what they choose to do with their hands. Your hand will win or lose only in comparison to the hand that the dealer holds.

The dealer plays his hand last. This is his biggest advantage. All the players who go over 21 points, or bust, will immediately lose their cards and their bet before the dealer's turn to play. What this means in terms of casino advantage is that while the player has to play to win, the only thing the dealer has to do is not lose. Every time you bust, the casino wins. This sequence of play ensures a profit for the casino.

 Take time to observe a few hands before you play blackjack. This will give you the opportunity to find a friendly dealer and to check out the minimum-bet signs posted at each table.

Be sure to check the minimum-bet signs posted at each table. They will say something like: MINIMUM BET $2 TO $500. This means the minimum wager is $2, and the maximum wager is $500. If you sit down at a blackjack table and begin to bet with insufficient cash or the wrong denomination chip, the dealer will inform you of the correct minimum wager, whereupon you may either conform or excuse yourself.

A blackjack table is shaped like a half-circle, with the dealer inside the circle and room for five to seven players around the outside. Facing the dealer, the chair on the far right is called "first base." The chair on the far left is called "third base." The dealer deals the cards from first base to third, and each player plays out his hand in the same order.

 If you can, try to sit at third base or as close to it as you can get. This gives you the advantage of watching the other players play out their hands before you play.

To buy in, find an empty seat at a table with an agreeable minimum wager and wait until the hand in progress is concluded. Though you can bet cash, most players prefer to convert their currency to chips. This is done by placing your money on the table *above* the bettor's box. Because blackjack is one of the many games in the casino in which the dealer is allowed to accept cash bets, he will assume that any money placed in the bettor's box is a wager.

Your dealer will take the cash, count out your chips, and push the money through a slot cut in the top of the table. Because he cannot give you change in cash, the total amount you place on the table will be converted to chips. You may at any time, however, redeem your chips for cash from the casino cashier. Once you have been given chips and have bet, you will be included in the next deal.

To confound a player attempting to count cards, many casinos deal blackjack with four to eight (two-hand held) decks shuffled together. This huge stack of cards is rendered manageable by dealing from a special container known as a shoe.

The dealer will shuffle the decks and may offer the cards to you to cut. The dealer offers you a plastic card stop. Place the card stop halfway or so into the deck, leaving the stop sticking out. The dealer will cut the deck at that point and put it into the shoe.

After he cuts a single deck, or puts the multiple deck into the shoe, the dealer will "burn" one or more cards by taking them off the top and putting them into the discard pile. This is yet another tactic to inhibit players from keeping track of cards dealt. Also to the advantage of the casino is the dealer's right to shuffle the cards whenever he pleases. Usually the dealer will deal from the shoe until he reaches the plastic stop card and then he will "break the deck," which means reshuffle and recut before dealing the next hand. In a single-deck game, the dealer will usually reshuffle about three-quarters through the deck.

Because the dealer always plays his hand last, you must develop your strategy by comparing your card count to what you assume (based on his visible card) the dealer has. The rule of thumb for most situations is to play your hand as if the dealer's down card has a value of 10. The principles governing when or when not to take a hit are known as "basic strategy" (see charts on pages 315, 317, and 318). If you elect to

The Blackjack Table

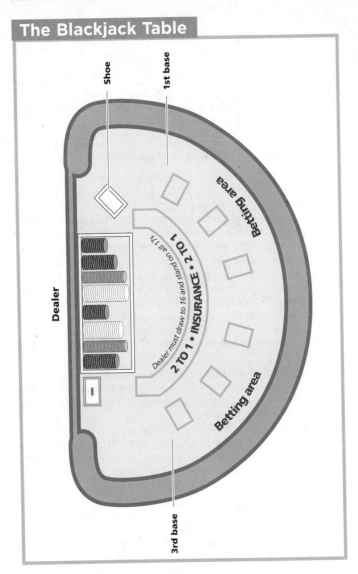

Shoe

1st base

Betting area

Dealer must draw to 16 and stands on all 17s

2 TO 1 • INSURANCE • 2 TO 1

Dealer

Betting area

3rd base

take a hit and go over 21 (bust), you lose. If you stand with your original two cards or take a number of hits without going over 21, you can relax for a few seconds while the dealer continues on around the table, repeating the same process with the other players. When the other players finish, the dealer exposes his "down" card and plays out his hand according to strict rules. He must take a hit on any total of 16 or less and must stand on any total of 17 or more. When he finishes his hand,

BASIC STRATEGY

THE DEALER IS SHOWING:		2	3	4	5	6	7	8	9	10	Ace
YOUR TOTAL IS:	4–11	H	H	H	H	H	H	H	H	H	H
	12	H	H	S	S	S	H	H	H	H	H
	13	S	S	S	S	S	H	H	H	H	H
	14	S	S	S	S	S	H	H	H	H	H
	15	S	S	S	S	S	H	H	H	H	H
S = STAND H = HIT	16	S	S	S	S	S	H	H	H	H	H

the dealer goes from third base to first, paying off each winning player and collecting chips from the losers who didn't bust.

If you're closer to 21 than the dealer, you win. If he is closer (or if you busted), he wins. If there is a tie, neither hand wins. When you tie, the dealer will knock on the table above your bet to indicate that the hand is a tie, or a "push." You may leave your bet on the table for the next hand, or change it.

There is a way for you to win automatically, and that is to be dealt exactly 21 in the first two cards. This can be done with an ace and any 10-value card. Called a blackjack, or a natural, this hand is an automatic winner, and you should turn your cards face up immediately. The dealer will look to see if he ties you with a blackjack of his own; this is one of the only times a dealer will look at his cards before all the players have played. If the dealer does not have a blackjack, he will pay you immediately at 3-to-2 odds (or a punitive six-to-five payoff in most Strip single-deck or Super Fun 21 games), so your $5 bet pays off $7.50 and you keep your original wager. If the dealer has a blackjack too, then only you and any other players at the table with a natural will tie him. The rest lose their bets, and the next round will begin.

 Fun fact: The correct term for the suit symbols on playing cards is "pips."

SOFT-HAND STRATEGY*

THE DEALER IS SHOWING:		2	3	4	5	6	7	8	9	10	Ace
YOUR TOTAL IS:	Ace, 9	S	S	S	S	S	S	S	S	S	S, H
	Ace, 8	S	S	S	S	S	S	S	S	S	S
	Ace, 7	S	D	D	D	D	S	S	H	H	S
	Ace, 6	H	D	D	D	D	S	H	H	H	H
	Ace, 5	H	H	D	D	D	H	H	H	H	H
	Ace, 4	H	H	D	D	D	H	H	H	H	H
	Ace, 3	H	H	H	D	D	H	H	H	H	H
	Ace, 2	H	H	H	D	D	H	H	H	H	H
S = Stand H = Hit D = Double down											

*The charts reflect basic strategy for multiple-deck games. For single-deck games, a slightly different strategy prevails for doubling and splitting.

Nothing beats a natural. If the dealer has a 4 and a 6, then draws an ace, his 21 will not beat your blackjack. A blackjack wins over everything and pays the highest of any bet in the game. Just as you can win automatically, you may lose just as fast. When your count goes over 21 and you bust, you must turn your cards over. The dealer will collect your cards and your bet before moving on to the next player.

Hitting and Standing

When dealing, whether from the shoe or from a single deck in his hand, the dealer will give two cards to each player. Most casinos will deal both cards facedown, though some casinos, especially those that use large multiple decks, will deal both cards faceup. There is no advantage to either method. Most players are more comfortable with the secrecy of the facedown deal, but the outcome will not be affected either way. Starting with the player at first base, the dealer will give you cards to play out your hand. After the initial deal, you have two basic options: either stand or take a hit. If you are satisfied with your deal, then you elect to stand. If your cards were dealt facedown, slide them under the chips in the bettor's box with one hand, being careful not to touch your chips or conceal them from the dealer. If the cards were dealt faceup, wave your hand over the top, palm down, in a negative fashion, to signal the dealer not to give you another card.

Sometimes you will improve your hand by asking for another card. You signal for a hit by scratching the bottom of your cards toward you on the felt surface of the table. In a faceup game, scratch your fingers toward you in the same fashion. You may say, "Hit me," or "I'll take a hit," depending on the mood at your table, but use the hand gestures also. Because of noise and distractions, the dealer may misinterpret your verbal request.

The card you request will be dealt faceup, and you may take as many hits as you like. When you want to show that you do not want another card, use the signals for standing. If you bust, turn your cards faceup right away so the dealer can collect your cards and chips. He will then go to the next player. There are times when the dealer stands a good chance of busting. At these times, it is a good idea to stand on your first two cards even though your total count may seem very low. The basic strategy chart on page 315 shows when to stand and when to take a hit. It is easy to follow and simple to memorize. The decision to stand or take a hit is made on the value of your hand and, once again, the dealer's up card, and is based on the probability of his busting. Although following basic strategy won't win every hand, it will improve your odds and take the guesswork out of some confusing situations.

Basic strategy is effective because the dealer is bound by the rules of the game. He must take a hit on 16 and stand on 17. These rules are printed right on the table so that there can be no misunderstanding. Even if you are the only player at the table and stand with a total of 14 points, the dealer with what would be a winning hand of 16 points *must* take another card.

There is one exception to the rule: Some casinos require a dealer to take a hit on a hand with an ace and a 6 (called a "soft 17"). Since the ace can become a 1, it is to the casino's advantage for the dealer to be allowed to hit a soft 17.

Bells and Whistles

Now that you understand the basic game, let's look at a few rules in the casino version of blackjack that are probably different from the way you play at home.

DOUBLING DOWN When you have received two cards and think that they will win with the addition of one and *only* one more card, then double your bet. This "doubling down" bet should be made if your two-card total is 11, since drawing the highest possible card, a 10, will not push your total over 21. In some casinos you may double down on 10, and some places will let you double down on any two-card hand.

DOUBLING DOWN											
THE DEALER IS SHOWING:		2	3	4	5	6	7	8	9	10	Ace
YOUR TOTAL IS:	11	D	D	D	D	D	D	D	D	D	H
	10	D	D	D	D	D	D	D	D	H	H
	9	H	D	D	D	D	H	H	H	H	H
H = Hit D = Double down											

To show the dealer that you want to double down, place your two cards touching each other faceup on the dealer's side of the betting box. Then place chips in the box that equal your original bet. Now, as at all other times, don't touch your chips once the bet is made.

SPLITTING Any time you are dealt two cards of the same value, you may split the cards and start two separate hands. Even aces may be split, though when you play them, they will each be dealt only one additional card. If you happen to get a blackjack after splitting aces, it will be treated as 21; that is, paid off at one to one and not three to two or six to five.

Any other pair is played exactly as you would if you were playing two consecutive hands, and all the rules will apply. Place the two cards *apart from each other* and above the betting box, so the dealer won't confuse this with doubling down. Then add a stack of chips equal to the original bet to cover the additional hand. Your two hands will be played out one at a time, cards dealt faceup.

You will be allowed to split a third card if it is the same as the first two, but not if it shows up as a later hit. Always split a pair of eights, since they total 16 points, the worst total. *Never* split two face cards or tens, since they total 20 and are probably a winning hand.

Some casinos will let you double down after splitting a hand; if you're unsure, ask the dealer. Not all blackjack rules are posted, and they can vary from casino to casino, and even from table to table in the same casino.

SPLITTING STRATEGY

THE DEALER IS SHOWING:		2	3	4	5	6	7	8	9	10	Ace
YOUR TOTAL IS:	2, 2	H	H	SP	SP	SP	SP	H	H	H	H
	3, 3	H	H	SP	SP	SP	SP	H	H	H	H
	4, 4	H	H	H	H	H	H	H	H	H	H
	5, 5	D	D	D	D	D	D	D	D	H	H
	6, 6	H	SP	SP	SP	SP	H	H	H	H	H
	7, 7	SP	SP	SP	SP	SP	SP	H	H	H	H
	8, 8	SP	SP	SP	SP	SP	SP	SP	SP	SP	SP
	9, 9	SP	SP	SP	SP	SP	S	SP	SP	S	S
	10, 10	S	S	S	S	S	S	S	S	S	S
	Ace, Ace	SP	SP	SP	SP	SP	SP	SP	SP	SP	SP

S = Stand   H = Hit   SP = Split   D = Double down

INSURANCE When the dealer deals himself an ace as his second, faceup card, he will stop play and ask, "Insurance, anyone?" Don't be fooled. You're not insuring anything. All he's asking for is a side bet that he has a natural. He must make the insurance bets before he can look at his cards, so he doesn't know if he has won or not when he asks for your insurance bets.

 Insurance is a bad move for the basic-strategy player, because the odds are against the dealer actually having a natural.

The insurance wager can be up to half the amount of your original bet. Place the chips in the large semicircle marked "insurance." As it says, it pays off two to one. If your original bet was $10 and you bet $5 that the dealer had a natural, you would be paid $10 if he actually did. Depending on your cards, you would probably lose your original $10 bet, but break even on the hand. If the dealer does not have a 10-value card, you lose your $5 insurance bet, but your $10 bet still can win.

This sounds deceptively easy, but you will lose this bet more often than you will win it, though the dealer may suggest it to you as a smart move. The dealer might also tell you to insure your own blackjack, but this should never be done. The odds are always against the insurance bet. When you insure your blackjack, you can be paid off for it at one to one, as if it were 21, instead of the three to two or six to five that you would normally be paid for the blackjack. Even though you may occasionally tie with the dealer, you will more than make up for it with the three-to-two or six-to-five payoffs on the blackjacks you don't insure.

Avoiding Common Pitfalls

1. Always check the minimum bets allowed at your table before you sit down. Flipping a $5 chip into a $25-minimum game can be humiliating. If you make this mistake, simply excuse yourself and leave. Happens all the time.

2. Keep your bet in a neat stack, with the largest value chips on the bottom and the smallest on top. A mess of chips can be confusing if you want to double down, and your dealer will get huffy if he has to ask you to stack your chips.

3. Never touch the chips once the bet is down. Cheaters do this, and your dealer may assume you're cheating. It's too easy for a player to secretly up his bet once he's seen his cards or lower it if the cards are bad. Do not stack a double-down bet or split bets on top of the original bet. Place them beside the original bet and then keep your hands away.

4. Along the same lines, don't touch a hand if the cards are dealt faceup. Use the hand signals to tell the dealer that you stand or that you want a hit. Never move your cards below the level of the table, where the dealer can't see them. When you brush your cards for a hit, do so lightly so that the dealer won't think that you are trying to mark them by bending them.

5. Take your time and count your cards correctly. The pace of the game in the casino can pick up to a speed that is difficult for a beginner. It's perfectly all right to take your time and recount after a hit. One hint: count aces as 1 first, then add 10 to your total. An ace and a 4 is equal to 5 or 15. Once you have this notion in your head, you won't make a mistake and refrain from hitting a soft hand. If you throw down an ace, a 10, and a 9 in disgust, for example, many dealers will simply pick up your cards and your bet, even though your 20 might have been a winning hand. If you are confused about your total, do not be embarrassed to ask for help.

6. Know the denomination of the chips that you are betting. Stack them according to denomination, and read the face value every play until you know for sure which chips are which color. Otherwise you might think you are betting $5 when you are actually throwing out a $25 chip on every hand.

7. Be obvious with your hand signals to the dealer. The casinos are loud and busy, and the dealer may be distracted with another player. Don't leave any room for misinterpretation. If some problem does arise, stop the game immediately; the dealer will summon a boss to mediate.

8. If cards fly off the table during the deal, pick them up slowly using two fingers. See number four, above.

9. Tip the dealer at your discretion if he or she has been friendly and helpful. One of the better ways to tip the dealer is to bet a chip for him on your next hand and say, "This one is for you." If you win, so does he. Never tip when a dealer has been rude or uncooperative. Finish your hand and leave. Period.

CRAPS

OF ALL THE GAMES OFFERED IN CASINOS, craps is by far the fastest and, to many, the most exciting. It is a game in which large amounts of money can be won or lost in a short amount of time. The craps table is a circus of sound and movement. Yelling and screaming are allowed—even encouraged—here, and the frenetic betting is bewildering to the uninitiated. Don't be intimidated, however; the basic game of craps is easy to understand. The confusion and insanity of craps have more to do with the pace of the game and the amazing number of betting possibilities than with the complexity of the game itself.

The Basic Game

Because it is so easy to become confused at a crowded and noisy craps table, we highly recommend that beginning players study this section, read a more detailed book, and take advantage of the free lessons

The Craps Table

offered by most of the casinos. Once you understand the game, you will be able to make the most favorable bets and ignore the rest.

In craps, one player at a time controls the dice, but all players will eventually have an opportunity to roll or refuse the dice. Players take turns in a clockwise rotation. If you don't want the dice, shake your head, and the dealer will offer them to the next player.

All the players around the table are wagering either with or against the shooter, so the numbers he throws will determine the amount won

ACTUAL-ODDS CHART

NUMBER	WAYS TO ROLL	ODDS AGAINST REPEAT
4	3	2-1
5	4	3-2
6	5	6-5
8	5	6-5
9	4	3-2
10	3	2-1

or lost by every other player. The casino is covering all bets, and the players are not allowed to bet among themselves. Four casino employees run the craps table. The boxman in the middle is in charge of the game. His job is to oversee the other dealers, monitor the play, and examine the dice if they are thrown off the table.

There are two dealers, one placed on each side of the boxman. They pay off the winners and collect the chips from the losers. Each dealer is in charge of half of the table.

The fourth employee is the stickman, so called because of a flexible stick he uses after each roll to retrieve the dice. His job, among other things, is to supply dice to the shooter and to regulate the pace of the game. When all bets are down, the stickman pushes several sets of dice toward the shooter. The shooter selects two dice, and the stickman removes the others from the table. Occasionally the stickman and boxman check the dice for signs of tampering.

The shooter then throws the dice hard enough to cause them to bounce off the wall at the far end of the table. This bounce ensures that each number on each die has an equal probability of coming up.

THE PLAY When it is your turn to throw the dice, pick out two and return the other to the stickman. After making a bet (required), you may throw the dice. You retain control of the dice until you throw a 7 ("seven out") or relinquish the dice voluntarily.

Your first roll, called the come-out roll, is the most important. If you roll a 7 or an 11 on your come-out roll, you are an immediate winner. In this case, you collect your winnings and retain possession of the dice. If your come-out roll is a 4, 5, 6, 8, 9, or 10, that number becomes "the point." A marker (called a puck or buck) is placed in the correspondingly numbered box on the layout to identify the point for all players at the table. In order to win the game, this number (the point) will have to be rolled again before you roll a 7.

Thus, if you roll a 5 on your first roll, the number five becomes your point. It doesn't matter how long it takes you to roll another 5, as long as you don't roll a 7 first. As soon as you roll a 7, you lose, and the dice are passed to another player.

Let's say 5 is your point, and your second roll is a 4, your third roll is a 9, and then you roll another 5. You win because you rolled a 5 again without rolling a 7. Because you have not yet rolled a 7, you retain possession of the dice, and after making a bet, you may initiate a new game.

Your next roll is, once again, a come-out roll. Just as 7 or 11 are immediate winners on a come-out roll, there are immediate losers, too. A roll of 2, 3, or 12 (all called "craps") will lose. You lose your chips, but you keep the dice because you have not yet rolled a 7.

If your first roll is 2, for example, it's craps, and you lose your bet. You place another bet and roll to come-out again. This time you roll a 5, so 5 becomes your point. Your second roll is a 4, your third is a 9, and then you roll a 7. The roll of 7 means that you lose and the dice will be passed to the next player.

This is the basic game of craps. The confounding blur of activity is nothing more than players placing various types of bets with or against the shooter, or betting that a certain number will or will not come up on the next roll of the dice.

THE BETTING   Of the dozens of bets that can be made at a dice table, only two or three should even be considered by a novice crap player. Keeping your bets simple makes it easier to understand what's going on, while at the same time minimizing the house advantage. Exotic, long-shot bets, offering payoffs as high as 30–1, are sucker bets and should be avoided.

The line bets: pass and don't pass   Pass and don't pass bets combine simplicity with one of the smallest house advantages of any casino game, about 1.4%. If you bet pass, you are betting that the first roll will be a 7 or 11 or a point number, and that the shooter will make the point again before he rolls a 7. If you bet don't pass, you are betting that the first roll will be a 2, 3, or 12, or, if a point is established, that the shooter will seven out and throw a 7 before he rolls his point number again. The 2 and 3 are immediate losers, and the casino will collect the chips of anyone betting pass. A roll of 12, however, is considered a standoff ("push") where the shooter "craps out" but no chips change hands for the "don't" bettor. Almost 90% of casino crap players confine their betting to the pass and don't-pass line.

Come and don't come   Come and don't-come bets are just like pass and don't-pass bets, except that they are placed *after* the point has been established on the come-out roll. Pass and don't-pass bets must be placed before the first roll of the dice, but come and don't-come bets may be placed before any roll of the dice *except* come-out rolls. On his come-out roll, let's say, the shooter rolls a 9. Nine becomes the shooter's point. If at this time you place your chips in the come box on the table, the next roll of the dice will determine your "come number." If the shooter throws a 6, for example, your chips are placed in the box marked with the large 6. The dealer will move your chips and will keep track of your bet. If the shooter rolls another 6 before he rolls a 7, your bet pays off. If the shooter sevens out before he rolls a 6, then you lose. If the shooter makes his point (that is, rolls another 9), your come bet is retained on the layout.

If you win a come bet, the dealer will place your chips from the numbered box back into the come space and set your winnings beside it. You may leave your chips there for the next roll or you may remove them entirely. If you fail to remove your winnings before the next roll, they may become a bet that you didn't want to make.

Don't-come bets are the opposite of come bets. A 7 or 11 loses, and a 2 or 3 wins. The 12 is again a push. The don't-come bettor puts his chips in the don't-come space on the table and waits for the next roll to determine his number. His chips are placed *above* the numbered box to differentiate it from a come bet. If the shooter rolls his point number before he rolls your number, your don't-come bet is retained on the layout. You are betting against the shooter; that is, that he will roll a 7 first. When he rolls 7, you win. If he rolls your don't-come number before he sevens out, you lose.

The come and don't-come bets have a house advantage of about 1.4% and are among the better bets in craps once you understand them.

Odds bets When you bet the pass/don't pass or the come/don't come, you may place an odds bet *in addition* to your original bet.

Once it is established that the come-out roll is not a 7 or 11, or craps, the bettor may place a bet that will be paid off according to the actual odds of a particular number being thrown.

The Actual-Odds Chart on page 321 shows the chances against a number made by two dice being thrown. For example, the odds of making a 9 are three to two. If you place an odds bet (in addition to your original bet) on a come number of 9, your original come bet will pay off at even money, but your odds bet will pay off at three to two.

Because this would make a $7.50 payoff for a $5 bet, and the tables don't carry 50-cent chips, you are allowed to place a $6 bet as an odds bet. This is a very good bet to make, and betting the extra dollar is to your advantage.

To place an odds bet on a line bet, bet the pass line. When (and if) the point is established, put your additional bet behind the pass line and say, "Odds."

To place an odds bet on a come bet, wait for the dealer to move your chips to the come number box, then hand him more chips and say, "Odds." He will set these chips half on and half off the other pile so that he can see at a glance that it's an odds bet.

Etiquette of Craps

When you arrive at a table, find an open space and put your cash down in front of you. When the dealer sees it, he will pick it up and hand it to the boxman. The boxman will count out the correct chips and give them to the dealer, who will pass them to you.

A craps table holds from 12 to 20 players and can get very crowded. Keep your place at the table. Your chips are in front of you, in the rail and on the table, and it is your responsibility to watch them.

After you place your bets, your hands must come off the table. It is bad form to leave your hands on the table when the dice are rolling.

Stick to the good bets listed here, and don't be tempted by bets that you don't understand. The box in the middle of the layout, for example, offers a number of sucker bets.

BACCARAT

ORIGINALLY AN ITALIAN CARD GAME, baccarat (pronounced bah-kah-rah) gets its name from the Italian word for "zero," which refers to the value of all the face cards in the game.

Because baccarat involves no player decisions, it is an easy game to play, yet a very difficult game to understand. Each player must decide to make a bet on either the bank or the player. That's it. There are no more decisions until the next hand is dealt. The rules of playing out the hands are ridiculously intricate, but beginning players need not concern themselves with them, because all plays are predetermined by the rules, and the dealer will tell you exactly what happened.

All cards, ace through 9, are worth their spots (the 3 of clubs is worth three). The 10, jack, queen, and king are worth zero. The easiest way to count at baccarat is to add all card totals in the hand, then take only the number in the ones column.

If you have been dealt a 6 and a 5, then your total is 11, and taking only the ones column, your hand is worth 1 point. If you hold a 10 and a king, your hand is worth zero. If you have an 8 and a 7, your point total is 15, and taking the ones column, your hand is worth 5. It doesn't get any simpler than this.

In baccarat, regardless of the number of bettors at the table, only two hands are dealt: one to the player and one to the bank. The object of the game is to be dealt or draw a hand closest to nine without going over. If the first two cards dealt equal nine (a 5 and a 4, for example), then you have a natural and an automatic winner. Two cards worth eight are the second best hand and will also be called a natural. If the other hand is not equal to or higher than eight, this hand wins automatically. Ties are pushes, and neither bank nor player wins, though a longshot bet on the tie (the third wager at baccarat) does.

If the hands equal any total except nine or eight, the rules are consulted. These rules are printed and available at the baccarat table. The hands will be played out by the dealer whether you understand the rules or not.

The rules for the player's hand are simple. If a natural is not dealt to either hand, and if the player holds 1, 2, 3, 4, 5, or 10 (zero), he will always draw a card. He will stand on a total of 6 or 7. A total of 8 or 9, of course, will be a natural.

The bank hand is more complicated and is partially determined by the third card drawn by the player's hand. Though the rules don't say so, the bank will always draw on zero, one, or two. When the hand is worth three or more, it is subject to the printed rules.

If you study a few hands, the method of play will be clear:

FIRST HAND The player's hand is worth three, and the bank's is worth four. The player always goes first. Looking at the rules for the player, we see that a hand worth three points draws a card. This time he draws a 9, for a new total of 12 points, which has a value of two. The bank, having four points, must stand when a player draws a 9. The bank wins four to two.

The Baccarat Table

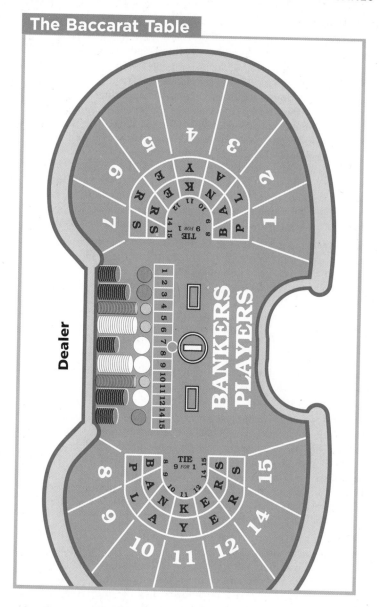

SECOND HAND The player's hand is worth six points, and the bank has two queens, for a total of zero. The player must stand with six points, while the bank must draw with zero. The bank gets another card, a 4. Player wins, six to four.

The Atmosphere

Casinos try to attract players by making baccarat seem sophisticated. The section is roped off from the main casino, and the dealers are often dressed in tuxedos instead of the usual dealer's uniforms. Don't be put off by glamorous airs; everyone is welcome to play.

Because the house wants baccarat to be appealing to what they consider to be their upper-crust clientele, the table minimums are usually very high in baccarat—usually $100 to $15,000. This means that the minimum bet is $100, and the maximum bet is $15,000.

Even the shuffle and deal of the deck is designed to perpetuate an exotic feeling. Elaborately cut and mixed by all three dealers, the cards are cut by one player and marked with the plastic card stop. The dealer will then separate the cards at the stop, turn the top card over, and discard, or burn, the number of cards equal to the face value of the upturned card. The cards are then placed in a large holder called the shoe.

THE PLAY If the game has just begun, the shoe will be passed to the player in seat number one, who is then called the bank. Thereafter, whenever the bank hand loses, the shoe is passed counterclockwise to the next player, until it reaches seat number 15, where it is passed to seat number one again.

When all bets are down, one of the three dealers will nod to the holder of the shoe, who will then deal out four cards in alternating fashion—two for the player and two for the bank.

The player's hand is passed (still facedown) to the bettor who has wagered the most money on the player's hand. He looks at the cards and passes them back to the dealer. The dealer then turns both hands faceup and plays out the game according to the rules.

THE BETTING In baccarat, you must back either the player or the bank. You do this by putting your chips in the box in front of you marked "player" or "bank." Once the bets are down, the deal will begin.

The house advantage on baccarat is quite low: 1.36% on player wagers and 1.17% on bank bets. Because the bank bet has such an obvious advantage, the house extracts a commission when you win a bank bet. This is not collected with each hand, but must be paid before you leave the table.

MINIBACCARAT Some casinos offer a version of baccarat in the main pit, usually near the blackjack games. The tables are smaller and lower than normal baccarat tables, with each table seating seven players. The dealers dress in the standard casino floor uniform and the table minimums (and maximums) are much lower than the more common high stakes version. It's the same game with the same house advantage, except that in minibaccarat, the shoe is never passed. In fact, the dealer places the cards right-side-up on the table and the players never touch them at all. Also, the dealer is always the banker.

All of the rules of baccarat apply to the mini version: eight decks are used; face cards and 10s count as zero and aces count as one; the casino collects a 5% commission on a winning banker hand (when the player is ready to leave). The minimum bet is $10, though sometimes you can find $5 minimums. However, since there's much less ritual and fewer players, the speed of the game is very fast, so often more is bet at a $10 minibaccarat table than a $25 baccarat table.

Some experts believe that because minibaccarat lacks the atmosphere of the big table, the game loses its charm and becomes redundant and boring. That could explain why minibaccarat is one of the least popular table games in the casino.

ROULETTE

A QUIET GAME WHERE WINNERS merely smile over a big win and losers suffer in silence, roulette is very easy to understand. The dealer spins the wheel, drops the ball, and waits for it to fall into one of the numbered slots on the wheel. The numbers run from zero to 36, with a zero and double zero thrown in for good measure. You may bet on each individual number, on combinations of numbers, on all black numbers, all red numbers, and many more. All possible bets are laid out on the table (see illustration on the next page).

In 2018, the Venetian, New York–New York, and Planet Hollywood all ran triple zero tables, which increase the house advantage from 5.26% to 7.69%. This is a blatant under-the-radar ploy to jack up the house's take. If you're determined to play roulette, check the wheel to make sure there are only two slots that are not red or black. The MGM Grand, Mandalay Bay, Aria, Wynn, Encore, Mirage, and Bellagio offer European roulette where there is only a single zero with a house advantage of 2.65%. These games return half of the even-money wagers if the ball lands on zero. Four other casinos offer single zero roulette but not European rules, meaning no money is returned if the ball lands on zero. Find this game at the Cromwell, Venetian, Palazzo, and Caesars Palace. European rules or no, most of these games require a high ($50 and up) minimum bet.

Special chips are used for roulette, with each bettor at the table playing a different color. To buy in, convert cash or the casino's house chips to roulette chips. When you are ready to cash out, the dealer will convert your special roulette chips back to house chips. If you want cash, you must then take your house chips to a casino cashier.

ROULETTE BET AND PAYOFF CHART			
BET	**PAYOFF**	**BET**	**PAYOFF**
Single number	35–1	Six numbers	5–1
Two numbers	17–1	12 numbers (column)	2–1
Three numbers	11–1	1st 12, 2nd 12, 3rd 12	2–1
Four numbers	8–1	1–18 or 19–36	1–1
Five numbers	6–1	Odd or even	1–1
Six numbers	5–1	Red or black	1–1

The Roulette Table

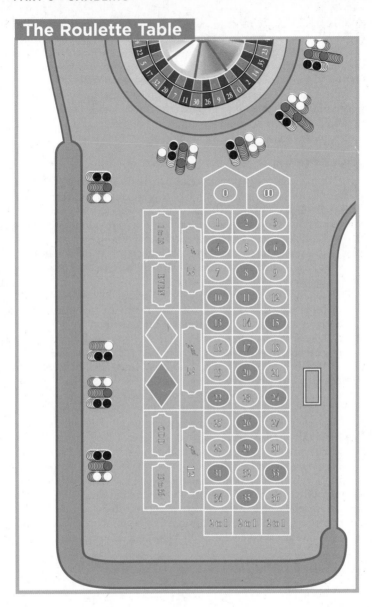

To place a bet, put your chips inside a numbered square or choose one of the squares off to the side. A chip placed in "1st 12," for example, will pay off if the ball drops into any number from 1 to 12. The box marked "odd" is not for eccentrics—it pays when the ball drops into an odd-numbered slot.

Roulette is fun to play, but expect to pay! The house advantage on most bets is a whopping 5.26%, and on some wagers it can be 7%. Most American roulette wheels have both a zero and a double zero, while European wheels have a single zero, which cuts the house edge for red and black bets to 2.7%. Single zero wheels in Las Vegas are the exception, but there are always a couple to be found. For a list of casinos operating single zero wheels, see lasvegasadvisor.com /inforoul.cfm.

SPORTS BETTING

CONSIDER THE SUPER BOWL. Historically there's been more money bet on that game than any other American sporting event. While much of the betting is casual and among friends, there's a flabbergasting amount wagered with sports books and online bookmakers. Though bets among friends are pretty straightforward, laying bets with sports books and bookmakers is anything but.

Any discussion of sports betting can wind up in the weeds pretty fast. Odds making, the spread, prop bets, overs and unders, parlays: It's about as clear as accounting in a third-world bureaucracy. We're going to try, however, to blow away the fog one small puff at a time, and hopefully, in the process, illuminate the arcane mysteries of sports betting.

1. It all starts with a game. Usually there is a favorite and an underdog. Just common sense and following sports gives most folks a sense of which team is more likely to win. Let's say, for example, next September the Alabama Crimson Tide will play the Blue Raiders of Middle Tennessee University. Anything can happen in sports, but most would agree that the probability of Middle Tennessee pulling off an upset is slim to none. If a Blue Raiders alum wants to make a straight-up bet for even money that his team will beat the Tide, he can do it, but it wouldn't be the smartest thing he ever did.

2. Enter the bookmaker. If you were a bookie covering straight-up win/lose bets, you'd get creamed because most bettors would bet on Alabama and very few on Middle Tennessee. As it happens, the bookie actually doesn't care who wins. What he wants is a low-risk scenario when approximately the same amount of money is wagered on each team. When betting with a sports book or bookie, you're charged what amounts to a commission (in gambling terms "vigorish") for handling the bets. Or, in other words, you'll have to bet $11 to win $10. The extra $1, from losing bets, goes to the bookie regardless of the outcome of the game. If an equal amount is bet on each team, the bookie uses the money bet by the losers to pay off the winners and pockets the vig. Balancing the amount wagered on each team, however, is very difficult, and a bookmaker who makes the wrong adjustments to the line can lose a bundle.

3. Let's hear it for the underdog. So how does the bookmaker get people to bet on the underdog? He gives them a little help. In our example, he would say, "If you'll bet on Middle Tennessee, I'll add 35 extra points to their actual score. If the Blue Raiders rack up 7 points in the game and the bookie adds 35, their total score as far as the bet is concerned would be 42. If you bet with the bookie on Alabama, the Tide would have to

score 43 or more points for you to win your bet. Theoretically, if the bookie offers enough points to the underdog to make betting on it attractive, the same amount of money will be bet on each team. The number of points the bookie allows the underdog is what determines the "line," also referred to as the "spread."

Points accorded the underdog are usually pretty much the same from one bookmaker to another, but it's still worthwhile to shop around. If one bookmaker gives Middle Tennessee only 32 points instead of 35, that makes a bet on Alabama easier to win, because they need only to score 40 points rather than 43. If you're betting on Alabama and deciding with which bookie or sports book to place your bet, the one offering 32 points increases the probability of you winning the bet.

A few years ago, when the NFL conference championships were decided and we learned the Seattle Seahawks would play the New England Patriots in the Super Bowl, sports books announced the opening line, or the number of points allowed the underdog. But guess what? The sports books at Westgate Las Vegas and Caesar Entertainment properties thought the teams were so evenly matched that they didn't give points to either team. This is known as a "pick 'em." But an opening line is just that. Let's say that because more people live in New England than in Washington, more money is wagered on the Pats than on the Seahawks. In this case, bookies would give a point or two to the Seahawks to even up the amount bet on both sides. Thus the line would fluctuate somewhat right up until game time. It's unlikely that the Super Bowl betting line closes as a "pick 'em." It's never happened before, according to vegasinsider.com's history, and would be unprecedented.

THERE ARE SEVERAL TYPES OF SPORTS BETS The different odds, point spread (the line), and payoffs for the most popular wagers are encapsulated in two lines of figures per game on an electronic sports board display in a casino or an online sports book's internet site. The figures are not explained—it's up to you to know what they mean. Because the referenced Super Bowl is a "pick 'em" or close to it, we'll look at a board-display entry from the past that offers more differentiation.

COWBOYS	-8	-400
CHIEFS	42	+300

We should pause here to say this discussion applies to two teams going head-to-head and is different from how odds are presented for multi-contestant events such as horse races.

POINT SPREAD BETS The Cowboys are the favorite and -8 is the number of points you would subtract from their score, or expressed differently, tack onto the actual score of the underdog Chiefs. So if you bet the Chiefs, and the score turned out to be Cowboys 14, Chiefs 7, adding the 8 points to the Chiefs would give them a score of 15 (7 +8) and you would win the bet.

OVER/UNDER BETS The 42 is for over and under bets. Here you bet that the two teams' scores added together would either be over or under 42.

If the game's a defensive battle and the final score is Cowboys 10, Chiefs 7, the total score for the game would be 17 (10 + 7), and bets on "under" would win.

MONEY-LINE BETS The -400 and +300 are for money-line bets. Money-line bets are simply on whom will win straight up without any consideration of the line. However, the probability of one team winning over another is incorporated into the payouts for winning bets. The way this is stated on the odds board is a little counterintuitive and confuses many people. Each minus figure (-400) indicates how much you'd have to bet to win $100. So if you bet on the Cowboys, you'd have to put down $400 to win $100. Betting on the Chiefs, a plus figure (+300) means the wager pays off at more than 1 to 1. If you risk $100, a winning bet would pay $300.

PROP BETS "Prop," or proposition bets can be made covering a whole range of things that may or may not occur in a game. For the Super Bowl, for example, you can bet on which team will win the coin toss, which team will score first, the distance in yards of the longest touchdown of the game, and so on. The number of prop bets available is simply numbing. For a look at some of the Super Bowl prop bets and their respective odds, check out LVAsports.com around Super Bowl time.

PARLAYS AND TEASER BETS Parlay bets link separate bets together. You have to win all bets for the parlay to pay off. Let's say that by game time the line adjusts to the Patriots being a 3.5-points favorite. Half points, as in 3.5, eliminate the possibility of a tie, or "push," as it's called in gambling. Because there's no way to score a half point on the field, it takes at least 4 points to beat the spread. Thus, betting on the Seahawks, the underdog, you add 3.5 points to their score. So the Pats must win by at least 4 points (more than 3.5) for you to lose your bet. Then, hooking another bet to the first in a parlay, you bet that the final sum of the two teams' scores will be under 48.5 points. To win your parlay, the Hawks must win the game by holding the Pats to a four or fewer points difference, AND the total score must be under 48.5 points. In this example, a total score of 48 points would be a winner.

Simply put, a teaser bet involves an adjustment of the spread to increase your odds of winning. Teasers are "offered," so to speak. For instance, you might be offered an adjustment (teaser) of the line of 6 or 6.5 or 7 points. If you select 7 points, those are added to the spread of the first bet of the parlay. So if the spread on the first bet of the parlay was 3.5, and then you add the 7 points teaser, the adjusted spread is 3.5 + 7 = 10.5, which means that New England must win by 11 points instead of the original 4 in the parlay for you to lose. Likewise, 7 points are added to the second bet of the parlay for the under bet, so 48.5 + 7= 55.5. For the teaser to win, the Patriots cannot win by more than 10.5 points, AND the total score must be under 55.5.

Why would you want to bet a teaser? Probably because it took you a month just to understand it, but also because it improves your chances of winning. The enhanced probability, however, comes at a price. The payoff for the teaser will be less than that of the parlay.

LEGALITY OF SPORTS BETTING IN THE UNITED STATES Certainly you can place a sports bet in person at licensed casinos with sports books. Legal sports betting online, however, is convoluted and tricky. The bottom line is that it's illegal, but lots of people do it and nobody's been busted. **USA Online Sports Books** (usaonlinesportsbooks.com/is-sports-betting-legal-in-the-united-states.html) has a good, if somewhat self-serving, and qualified summary of the legality of sports betting in the United States. In 2018, the US Supreme Court ruled that outlawing sports betting altogether is unconstitutional but left it to each state to determine how it would apply and what laws would govern it.

Watching the Big Game in Las Vegas

Nongamblers sometimes use the casino as a resource, as in the case of those looking for a good place to watch a sporting event. Casino sports books have high-definition video screens, giant LED walls, and comfortable seating, and they offer the opportunity to join other enthusiastic fans in a partylike atmosphere. There's simply no place better than a sports book to watch a big game, but are those who don't wager welcome, or are they looked upon as party crashers?

The day before the game, you scope out your casino's sports book. You'll marvel at all the screens and be impressed by the general plushness. But then you notice that many, if not all, of the seats have a little private cubicle with a desk and often a small monitor. It dawns on you that the seating is designed for serious sports bettors and that their action makes this incredible venue possible. What will happen, you think, if you as a nongambler occupy one of those seats? Will the house require you to wager, ask you to leave, or worse, escort you out?

Happily, the answer is none of the above. Needless to say, the sports book is a business and would prefer a gambler in every seat, but in practice a nonbetting guest is welcome. The house doesn't monitor whether you bet or not. In fact, a number of casinos have a downloadable app that enables a bettor to place wagers using a smartphone instead of going to the betting window. Bottom line is that the casino doesn't know if you're betting or not, so there's no reason to be anxious.

For regular season college and professional football, basketball, and baseball games, just walk in and claim a vacant seat. For major sporting events, such as pro and college play-offs and Triple Crown horse racing, getting a seat can be a challenge. Though most sports books reserve a small number of seats for their best customers, remaining seats are filled on a first-come, first-serve basis. For really big games, some queues set up as early as 4 a.m. the day of the game, but a slightly less daunting 6 or 7 a.m. is more typical. All sports books offer standing room after all the seating is filled.

If you arrive early and your efforts are rewarded with a seat, that's only half the battle. Holding on to the seat is the other half. Obviously, you'll need to leave your seat to obtain food and drinks, and to use the restroom. The best way to guard your turf is to sit next to a friend, so one of you is always there. If you're alone and don't want to find a squatter in your place, you'll need to unambiguously demonstrate that the seat is taken. My suggestion is to bring something personal but expendable to leave on, or pin to, your seat (I use a small reporter's notebook and a pack of gum). Also, use your computer at home to create a nice-looking sign that reads "Reserved," along with your name (for example, "Reserved—W. L. Smith").

Regarding betting, you'll feel more a part of the action if you have a bet down. It doesn't have to be a big bet, rather just enough to sweeten the overall experience.

The better sports books are at the Westgate (best in town), Mirage, Caesars Palace, MGM Grand, Green Valley Ranch, Palms, Cosmopolitan, Wynn, Bellagio, Orleans, Mandalay Bay, and Red Rock Resort. Downtown, the Golden Nugget offers the largest and most technologically advanced sports book.

Many casinos host parties in conjunction with big games or races. Though some of these events are free, it's common for casinos to charge a fee of $25–$200. The fee allows you to partake in all the festivities, including watching the game and consuming the food and drinks being served. Parties without a fee serve food and beverages at bargain prices, such as $1.50 hot dogs and $2 beers, as well as margarita and Bloody Mary specials. Parties are usually held in an ancillary ballroom, in meeting rooms, or in a side bar instead of in the sports book proper. Generally, the projection screens in these rooms are only a slight step down from the sports book screens, so you can count on a high-quality broadcast. Party rooms are large enough to accommodate a great throng of fans, and there are almost always enough seats for all who attend.

No matter how you play it, celebrating a major sporting event at a Las Vegas casino is about as good as it gets. As an addendum, there are plenty of high-tech, multiscreen sports bars around town, but they're often as packed as the casino sports books.

PART FOUR

DINING *and* RESTAURANTS

DINING IN LAS VEGAS

LAS VEGAS TOURISM continues to grow, as old players and new investors—both intent on providing tourists with new sights and experiences—continue to pump money into fresh ideas on the Strip and Downtown. In this changing landscape, dining remains a major attraction and an important source of revenue, and even frequent visitors are guaranteed to find brand-new breakfast, lunch, and dinner options to satisfy their tastes the next time they visit, from internationally renowned celebrity chefs and passionate young upstarts alike. Lucky for us, there's no sign of this expansion slowing down anytime soon.

DOWNTOWN

THE DOWNTOWN LAS VEGAS revival flourishes, thanks in large part to Zappos CEO Tony Hsieh and his **Downtown Project.** But more and more independent entrepreneurs have entered the fray, expanding the urban renewal efforts both to the south and the east. As a result, Downtown dining now consists of multiple vibrant and independent scenes.

Carson Avenue has become Downtown's established restaurant row, and it now complements East Fremont's monopoly on the Downtown cocktail culture. The recently expanded **Carson Kitchen** remains the hottest restaurant on that stroll for dinner, while **Eat** remains the go-to spot for breakfast and lunch. In the block or so between the two, **VegeNation** is Downtown's undisputed leader in plant-based dining, while **7th & Carson** has stepped in to take over the corner spot that was previously home to Glutton. In the meantime, the main drag of East Fremont (located just a block to the north) has replaced the popular coffee shop The Beat with a chain restaurant called **Eureka!** that actually offers some interesting beers and whiskeys. And a tiny operation called **Food Junky,** operating out of the ticket booth of Inspire Theater during its off hours, provides delivery to kitchen-less watering holes in the neighborhood such as **Corduroy** and **Banger Brewing.**

Walking east, **Downtown Container Park** has replaced The Perch with **Downtown Terrace.** But sadly, the loss of Chow has left a serious gap in dining choices farther down this street until you hit East Fremont's **PublicUs,** on the corner of Maryland Parkway.

A bit to the north, check out the new location for James Beard Award nominee Sheridan's Su's **Flock & Fowl,** located inside The Ogden high-rise. And the Gold Spike's tiny eatery **Fiddlestix** has been wowing people with quirky offerings such as Unicorn Grilled Cheese (it's not on the menu—you have to know to ask for it) and a boozy milkshake large enough for eight people.

Outside Zappos's sphere of influence, the Arts District has emerged as an even more exciting and independent pocket of Downtown culture. The brand-new Italian spot **Esther's Kitchen** has quickly emerged as one of the city's hottest restaurants and most difficult reservations to get. The nearby reggae lounge **Jammyland** offers Downtown's only Jamaican kitchen.

Pawn Stars star Rick Harrison's Pawn Plaza shopping center— adjacent to his Gold & Silver Pawn Shop—lost most of its original food and beverage tenants early on and has been trying to rebuild its offerings. **Rollin Smoke Barbeque** remains its anchor tenant. But the new **Good Pie** has added to Downtown's reputation as the city's pizza capital, thanks to amazing renditions of Long Island–style "grandma pie" and Detroit-style square pizzas, as well as some of the city's best gluten-free crusts. (For a full Downtown pizza tour, make sure to also hit **Pizza Rock, Evel Pie, Naked City Pizza**'s new location inside the El Cortez, and The Plaza's **Pop Up Pizza.**)

AROUND THE STRIP

BIG CULINARY CHANGES have been happening here as well—we'll address them starting at the north end of the Strip and then proceed south. Another sale of the **SLS/W Hotel** has left the future of its restaurants in doubt. But its two best offerings, José Andrés's **Bazaar Meat** and the Mediterranean concept **Cleo,** both appear to be secure.

In the meantime, just off Las Vegas Boulevard on West Sahara Avenue, the closure of **Lucky Dragon** casino has left a hole in the Chinese dining options. Also on West Sahara, **Palace Station** is in the midst of a major renovation that will undoubtedly affect its restaurant lineup. The first big announcement is the addition of Long Island's **BBD's,** which will specialize in burgers, craft beer, and desserts.

The **Wynn** resorts are the latest hotel group to decide curbside shopping and dining are an easy way to lure customers in off the streets, so they're hard at work trying to find tenants for the new **Wynn Plaza.** New York's **Cipriani** will be among the first food and beverage projects to sign on.

The **Mirage** has continued the restaurant reboot that began with re-christening its Japanese restaurant as **Otoro,** with little modification of the concept. Of much more interest is the closing of the high-end Italian

CELEBRITY CHEFS

CHEF	ORIGINAL RESTAURANT	LAS VEGAS RESTAURANT(S)
José Andrés	Jaleo, Minibar, Café Atlántico (Washington, D.C.)	Bazaar Meat (SLS); China Poblano, é by José Andrés, and Jaleo (The Cosmopolitan)
David Chang	Momofuku Noodle Bar (New York)	Momofuku (The Cosmopolitan)
Michael Chow	Mr. Chow (London)	Mr. Chow (Caesars Palace)
Tom Colicchio	Craft (New York)	Craftsteak (MGM Grand); Heritage Steak (Mirage)
Scott Conant	Scarpetta (New York)	Masso Osteria (Red Rock)
Alain Ducasse	Louis XV (Monte Carlo, Paris)	Rivea (Delano)
Susan Feniger	Border Grill (Los Angeles)	Border Grill (Mandalay Bay and Forum Shops)
Guy Fieri	Johnny Garlic's (Santa Rosa)	El Burro Borracho (Rio); Guy Fieri's Vegas Kitchen & Bar (LINQ Hotel & Casino)
Bobby Flay	Mesa Grill (New York)	Bobby's Burger Palace (Crystals); Mesa Grill (Caesars Palace)
Pierre Gagnaire	Pierre Gagnaire (Paris)	Twist (Mandarin Oriental)
Lorena Garcia	Food Café (Miami)	Chica (Venetian)
Hubert Keller	Fleur de Lys (San Francisco)	Fleur and Burger Bar (Mandalay Bay)
Thomas Keller	French Laundry (Yountville, CA) Per Se (New York)	Bouchon (Venetian)
Emeril Lagasse	Emeril's (New Orleans)	Delmonico (Venetian); Emeril's New Orleans Fish House (MGM Grand); Lagasse's Stadium (Palazzo)
Giada De Laurentiis	N/A	GIADA (The Cromwell); Pronto by Giada (Caesars Palace)
Nobu Matsuhisa	Matsuhisa (Beverly Hills)	Nobu (Caesars & Hard Rock)
Shawn McClain	Spring (Chicago)	Sage and Five50 Pizza (Aria); Libertine Social (Mandalay Bay)

eatery Portofino and the addition of a more casual Italian coastal concept called **Osteria Costa** in the spot that used to house Samba Brazilian steakhouse.

Across the street, **The Venetian** and **The Palazzo** faced a huge hole in its dining lineup when they announced the closing of all three of Mario Batali's restaurants in the wake of the chef's scandals. So far, there's no word on what will replace Carnevino or OTTO Enoteca e Pizzeria, but L.A.'s **Factory Kitchen** will take the place of B&B Ristorante. On a more positive note, The Palazzo has replaced Emeril's Table 10 with a new Japanese-tinged Peruvian restaurant called **Once** that may end up being the most exciting and underappreciated restaurant to open on Las Vegas Boulevard in 2018. That opening also adds another touch of

CELEBRITY CHEFS (continued)

CHEF	ORIGINAL RESTAURANT	LAS VEGAS RESTAURANT(S)
Mary Sue Milliken	**Border Grill** (Los Angeles)	**Border Grill** (Mandalay Bay and Forum Shops)
Michael Mina	**Aqua** (San Francisco)	**Bardot Brasserie** (Aria); **Michael Mina** (Bellagio); **Michael Mina PUB 1842** (MGM Grand); **Strip Steak** (Mandalay Bay)
Rick Moonen	**Oceana** (New York)	**RM Seafood** and **RX Boiler Room** (Mandalay Bay)
Masaharu Morimoto	**Morimoto** (Philadelphia)	**Morimoto** (MGM Grand)
Wolfgang Puck	ORIGINAL RESTAURANT: **Spago** (Los Angeles) LAS VEGAS RESTAURANTS: **Cucina by Wolfgang Puck** (Crystals); **CUT** (Palazzo); **Lupo** (Mandalay Bay); **Spago** (Bellagio); **Wolfgang Puck Bar & Grill** (MGM Grand); **Wolfgang Puck Bar & Grill** (Downtown Summerlin)	
Gordon Ramsay	**Restaurant Gordon Ramsay** (London)	**Gordon Ramsay Burger** (Planet Hollywood); **Gordon Ramsay Fish & Chips** (LINQ); **Gordon Ramsay Hell's Kitchen** (Caesars); **Gordon Ramsay Pub & Grill** (Caesars); **Gordon Ramsay Steak** (Paris LV)
Joël Robuchon	**Jamin, Joël Robuchon** (Paris)	**L'Atelier de Joël Robuchon** and **Joël Robuchon** (MGM Grand)
Chris Santos	**Stanton Social** (New York)	**Beauty & Essex** (The Cosmopolitan)
Guy Savoy	**Restaurant Guy Savoy** (Paris)	**Brioche** and **Restaurant Guy Savoy** (Caesars Palace)
Julian Serrano	**Masa's** (San Francisco)	**Julian Serrano** (Aria); **Lago** (Bellagio); **Picasso** (Bellagio)
Christina Tosi	**Momofuku Milk Bar** (New York)	**Milk Bar** (The Cosmopolitan)
Buddy Valastro	**Carlo's Bakery** (Hoboken, NJ)	**Carlo's Bakery** and **Buddy V's** (Palazzo)
Jean-Georges Vongerichten	**JoJo** (New York)	**Jean-Georges Steakhouse** (Aria); **Prime** (Bellagio)
Roy Yamaguchi	**Roy's** (Hawaii)	**Roy's** (Flamingo Road)

Latin flare to the two resorts, which were already home to **SushiSamba, Sugarcane Raw Bar & Grill,** and Lorena Garcia's **Chica.**

Over at **Caesars Palace,** Gordon Ramsay's fifth Las Vegas restaurant. **Gordon Ramsay Hell's Kitchen,** was an overnight success and is packed just about every night. And the Forum Shops have two new buzz-worthy spots on the calendar for the coming months: California's **Water Grill** chain is moving into the old Spago space, while San Francisco's Charles Phan is importing his **Slanted Door** Vietnamese concept to the shopping complex.

Bellagio has managed to score a major coup by stealing Wolfgang Puck's flagship restaurant, **Spago,** away from The Forum Shops. The new locale, which boasts a patio overlooking the fountains, is located in the shopping promenade on the north side of the building in the space that was previously home to Olive's. (If you're driving, park in the side valet located off Flamingo Road.) **Michael Mina** has also revamped his namesake local flagship with a redesigned lounge, new private dining room overlooking the Bellagio conservatory and a menu that takes the place back to its seafood roots.

Cosmopolitan is preparing to put the final touches on its restaurant reboot with the addition of an "urban dining hall." While the project seems a bit like a high-end food court, the resort has cherry-picked some major players from around the country to participate. They include Portland's **Lardo** sandwich shop and **Pok Pok Wings** (by James Beard Award–winner Andy Ricker), as well as **District: Donuts. Sliders. Brew.** from New Orleans, a local incarnation of the New York tequila and mezcal bar **Ghost Donkey, Hattie B's Hot Chicken** from Nashville, and the locally conceived **Tekka Bar: Handroll & Sake.**

Aria finally pulled the trigger on the long-rumored closure of Masa Takayama's extraordinary-but-expensive sushi experience BarMasa. It's being replaced by the popular L.A. and New York City sushi and steak concept **Catch.** And Todd English is no longer associated with the pub concept that straddles the border between the hotel lobby and the Crystals shopping mall. As a result, it's been renamed **The Pub at The Shops.**

The **Monte Carlo's** transition into **Park MGM** is complete, although the attached boutique property **NoMad** and the restaurant of the same name are still works in progress. For the present time, hungry visitors will have to be content with the addition of the famed Chicago steakhouse **Bavette's** and the new breakfast, lunch, and dinner spot **Primrose.** The outdoor market and dining collection **Eataly** is expected in late 2018 or early 2019.

Over at Mandalay Bay, Border Grill's Susan Feniger and Mary Sue Milliken have expanded across the hallway with a new Mexican barbecue concept called **BBQ Mexicana.**

Moving off the Strip, the **Hard Rock's** transformation into a Virgin property is just getting started, and there's no word yet on what that will mean for the dining collection. Changes at the **Palms,** however, have been happening fast and furiously since Station Casinos bought it. The new **Scotch 80 Prime** steakhouse is already open, and new restaurants from **Chris Santos, Bobby Flay, Marc Vetri,** and **Michael Symon** are all coming soon. And they won't be the only celebrity chefs in the Station Casinos roster. **Scott Conant** has opened an Italian spot called **Masso Osteria** at the company's Red Rock resort.

THE SUBURBS

THE DINING BOOM in the 'burbs has continued for yet another year. The trend of talented casino chefs leaving high-profile gigs to set up shop outside the city core means some of the best and most interesting restaurants in the area are no longer located on Las Vegas Boulevard or even Downtown, thus requiring you to jump in a car or taxi to experience them. The good news is that Vegas is geographically compact, so the cost in both time and dollars is usually more than made up for by the savings on your check. And, by heading outside the city core, you get the added benefit of having tried a place that none of your friends back home have visited yet. Many of these spots also make great stops on your way to or from more-remote tourist attractions such as the area's two water parks, Mount Charleston, the Las Vegas Motor Speedway, Hoover Dam, or Red Rock Canyon.

The area around Spring Mountain Road known as Chinatown continues to be the single hottest location for cool and trendy restaurants. But it's finally beginning to attract talented chefs who want to do something other than Asian cuisine. **Sparrow + Wolf** proved the area could sustain innovative, high-end cuisine that draws on influences from around the globe. And its success has inspired more edgy new concepts, such as the French fine-dining spot **Partage,** which specializes in multicourse tasting menus and mildly exotic ingredients, and a new wine bar called **Mordeo** that offers Latin and Spanish small plates.

On West Flamingo Road, the relocation in 2016 of the popular **Nora's Italian Cuisine** to a new building 900 feet closer to The Strip had left a vacancy at its much-loved original location. Giovanni Mauro, one of the three sons in the family that ran the original, has filled that vacancy with the opening of **Pizzeria Monzu,** which specializes in the Pizza alla Pala that's popular in Rome, as well as small antipasti plates.

Heading a bit farther south and west, **The Black Sheep** serves amazing Vietnamese cuisine with a fine-dining touch on the corner of Warm Springs Road and Durango Drive. And just around the corner, a funky little spot called **Paid in Full** is impressing adventurous foodies with its spin on Japanese Street food.

The Downtown Summerlin outdoor mall continues to have the heaviest concentration of restaurants in the deep suburbs. In fact, some might argue there are too many options and the herd could stand some thinning. So far, however, the largest casualty has been the suburban incarnation of the Brazilian steakhouse Fogo de Chao. That said, there are some serious standouts in every price range, and the vast majority are pet-friendly.

Just next door to Downtown Summerlin you'll find the Red Rock Resort, which recently added celebrity chef Scott Conant's new restaurant **Masso Osteria** (see above, under The Palms).

But the most popular restaurant in this neighborhood during hockey season is, without a question, **MacKenzie River Pizza.** But that's not a result of its pizza and sandwiches, which are quite good. It's because it's located in the **Vegas Golden Knights'** practice facility, **City National Arena,** where the Western Conference Champions hold open practices and every home and away game is guaranteed to be on every TV screen.

A bit farther out in Henderson, Natalie Young has opened a suburban outpost of her tremendously successful Downtown breakfast and lunch spot **Eat.**

On the opposite end of the valley, in Henderson, the short-lived Standard & Pour is being replaced with a new breakfast, lunch, and brunch concept from Hell's Kitchen veteran Scott Commings called **The Stove.**

The Las Vegas restaurant scene is forever reinventing itself, but one thing remains constant: This is an exciting city for dining and a world-class destination for anyone who cares about food, wine, and a good time.

THE TOP 25

WE KNOW THAT NOT EVERYONE has the desire or ability to drop $500–$1,000 on a meal while visiting Las Vegas, so we present a broad range of restaurants for all different tastes and price points. Accordingly, the value of a restaurant is reflected in its overall rating. Still, the simple fact is, when we're asked about Las Vegas's absolute top restaurants, a lot of our choices are going to be in the "money is no object" category. But the relatively recent migration of many Strip chefs to the suburbs—where they can find cheaper spaces and concentrate on simpler food—has helped reduce the incredible dominance of expensive and very expensive restaurants on our lists. You can detect this change on page 341, where a chart rating and ranking the top 25 restaurants in town includes spots that anyone can afford. All restaurants are profiled later in this chapter.

BUFFETS

TO SAY THAT THE BUFFET HAS BEEN ELEVATED would be an understatement. What used to be considered a cost-effective and valuable way to feed guests looking more for a filling meal than a dining experience has evolved into something that satisfies both those who care only about stuffing their bellies and food aficionados alike.

You could conceivably eat your three squares a day at the buffet of the same property where you rest your head (and wouldn't your hotel love that!). Caesars Entertainment has even created a 24-hour pass, **The Buffet of Buffets,** that allows you to dine at each of its properties, including Harrah's, Bally's, Rio, Paris, and, of course, Caesars Palace.

LAS VEGAS'S 10 BEST BUFFETS

RANK	BUFFET	QUALITY RATING
1.	BACCHANAL BUFFET (Caesars)	99
2.	WICKED SPOON (The Cosmopolitan)	99
3.	THE BUFFET AT WYNN	98
4.	BUFFET BELLAGIO	97
5.	THE BUFFET AT ARIA	96
6.	CRAVINGS (Mirage)	94
7.	LE VILLAGE BUFFET (Paris)	93
8.	FEAST BUFFET (Green Valley Ranch/Texas Station)	92
9.	STUDIO B (M Resort)	89
10.	TREASURE ISLAND BUFFET (Treasure Island)	88

TOP 25 LAS VEGAS RESTAURANTS

RESTAURANT	CHEF	OVERALL RATING	PRICE RATING	HOST HOTEL
1. JOËL ROBUCHON	Joel Robuchon	★★★★★	Very Expensive	MGM Grand
2. RESTAURANT GUY SAVOY	Guy Savoy	★★★★★	Very Expensive	Caesars Palace
3. TWIST	Pierre Gagnaire	★★★★★	Very Expensive	Mandarin Oriental
4. YUI EDOMAE SUSHI	Gen Mizoguchi	★★★★★	Very Expensive	None
5. BAZAAR MEAT	José Andrés	★★★★★	Very Expensive	SLS
6. L'ATELIER DE JOËL ROBUCHON	Steve Benjamin	★★★★★	Very Expensive	MGM Grand
7. SAGE	Shawn McClain	★★★★½	Very Expensive	Aria
8. ESTIATORIO MILOS	Costas Spiliadis	★★★★½	Very Expensive	The Cosmopolitan
9. PICASSO	Julian Serrano	★★★★½	Very Expensive	Bellagio
10. LE CIRQUE	Wilfried Bergerhausen	★★★★½	Very Expensive	Bellagio
11. SPARROW + WOLF	Brian Howard	★★★★½	Expensive	None
12. TOP OF THE WORLD	Claude Gaty	★★★★½	Very Expensive	Stratosphere
13. JALEO	José Andrés	★★★★	Moderate/ Expensive	The Cosmopolitan
14. RAKU	Mitsuo Endo	★★★★	Moderate/ Expensive	None
15. BARDOT BRASSERIE	Michael Mina	★★★★	Expensive/ Very Expensive	Aria
16. THE BLACK SHEEP	Jamie Tran	★★★★	Moderate/ Expensive	None
17. CARSON KITCHEN	John Courtney	★★★★	Moderate/ Expensive	None
18. NOBU CAESARS	Tommy Buckley	★★★★	Very Expensive	Caesars Palace
19. EDGE STEAKHOUSE	Steve Young	★★★★	Expensive/ Very Expensive	Westgate
20. CLEO	Danny Elmaleh	★★★★	Moderate	SLS
21. OTHER MAMA	Dan Krohmer	★★★★	Moderate	None
22. FLOCK & FOWL	Sheridan Su	★★★★	Inexpensive	None
23. PIZZA ROCK	Tony Gemignani	★★★½	Inexpensive/ Moderate	None
24. EAT	Natalie Young	★★★½	Inexpensive	None
25. BOUCHON	Thomas Keller	★★★½	Expensive	The Venetian

But be warned: If you want to add on the **Bacchanal Buffet** at Caesars, that will cost you an extra $20–$40.

When **The Cosmopolitan** opened, it raised the bar for the Vegas aesthetic, a development that included elevating the concept of the buffet. **Wicked Spoon,** the hotel's $20 million offering, was modeled after food

KNIGHT TIME DINING

IT WOULD HAVE BEEN UNIMAGINABLE just a few years ago, but NHL hockey has become one of the hottest tickets on the Las Vegas Strip. The Vegas Golden Knights packed T-Mobile Arena throughout their first season, and their improbable run to the Stanley Cup finals almost guarantees that trend will continue. (If you're coming in a visiting team's jersey, have no fear: Las Vegas is a hospitality-driven town, and Knights fans are usually pretty welcoming of tourists supporting their home team.) Fortunately, if you're headed to a game, grabbing a bite before, during, or after the game will not be a problem.

Options inside the arena itself include national chains, outposts of popular neighborhood spots, and concepts created specifically for the venue. The former includes **Pink's Hotdogs** and **Shake Shack.** (Be aware, however, that the T-Mobile Shake Shack has a more limited menu than the chain's other locales, and it doesn't participate in most national promotions.) Among the local businesses that have locations here are the award-winning **Rollin Smoke Barbeque, Pizza Forte** (from the family behind Ferraro's Italian Restaurant), the sushi burrito spot **Tail & Fin,** and **Chronic Tacos.** As you wander the main concourse, you'll also find fresh-carved sandwiches from **The Carvery**'s mobile carts, while fans in the upper level can grab snacks from original concepts like **Loaded Chip, eNVy Pizza,** and **Lucky Dog.**

There are also certain dining and drinking spots reserved for specific ticketholders. We won't bother listing everything available to the owners of the private suites because the sky is basically the limit for that select group. But fans who buy club tickets (lower level, center ice) will have access to specialty cocktails by famed mixologist Tony Abou-Ganim, as well as high-quality food in the gastropubs of **The Jack Daniels Lounge** (sections 5 and 6) and **The Bud Light Lounge.** Fans with "glass seat" tickets anywhere in the arena (generally the first two or three rows on the ice) get access to a free buffet and cocktails in a special VIP lounge accessible through a special elevator. (The food tends to be the type of sliders-and–chicken fingers menu you'd find on midlevel casino catering menu, although the desserts are usually a

courts in Asia, with food portioned for individual servings rather than served from giant trays in steam tables behind sneeze glass. In a nutshell, Cosmo classed up the buffet with grown-up dishes such as bone marrow, oysters Rockefeller, and short rib cavatelli. The single-serving pulled pork eggs Benedict are mandatory for breakfast, as are the chicken-apple sausages. At $36 for brunch and $49 for dinner, Wicked Spoon is reasonably priced for a dining experience of this caliber.

But while Wicked Spoon may have been the rising tide that lifted all ships, **Bacchanal Buffet** at Caesars Palace has sailed ahead of the fleet. Bacchanal embodies both quality and quantity, with more than 500 items offered each day spread over three main dining rooms. Live-action stations include a smoked barbecue line and a rotating *comal*, or tortilla griddle, for the Mexican cuisine. Like **Wicked** bit more impressive.) On the flip side, the nosebleed area surrounding The Fortress (where the Drum Line and Golden Aces dancers perform, The DJ spins music, and the game announcer introduces special guests) offers standing-room-only tickets that include unlimited beer, wine, hotdogs, bratwursts, popcorn, and chips. And at the opposite end of the rafters, you'll find T-Mobile's spin-off of Bellagio's **Hyde Lounge,** offering nightclub-style service and seating to any ticket-holder in the house—although securing a table with a view usually means you'll have to meet a food-and-beverage minimum. (You can call ahead to reserve a spot, or just wander up.)

For pre- and postgame action, nothing beats The Park—the outdoor area right next to the arena's Toshiba Plaza. Dining options there include sushi and other Japanese cuisine in the funky **Sake Rok,** a **California Pizza Kitchen** and the waffle restaurant **Bruxie.** If you don't have a ticket, any one of these is a great spot for watching the game on TV. But the best game-viewing spot outside the arena is **Beer Haus,** which not only shows every game on multiple TVs while offering craft beer, sandwiches, and snacks, but also hosts game-related TV and radio broadcasts from its patio.

One experience even a casual Golden Knight fan won't want to miss on game day is the pregame parade. Led by team mascot Chance, the official Golden Knight character, the drum, cheer, and dance squads descend an escalator onto the New York–New York casino floor about an hour before the puck drops and wind their way outside to Toshiba Plaza for a pregame rally. To get a good view, and maybe a chance to high-five Chance, grab a seat near the windows of Nine Fine Irishmen, on the patio of Tom's Urban in the casino, outside the New York–New York Shake Shack, or on the patios of one of The Park's restaurants.

Of course, all of the restaurants in New York–New York or the new Park MGM also offer good game-adjacent options for a meal. And once **Eataly** opens at Park MGM, it will have plenty of additional outdoor places to grab a bite.

Spoon, Bacchanal offers dishes in individual portions, such as servings of fried chicken or sweet potato fries in miniature paper-lined wire baskets. Even more interesting are the ever-evolving specials—almost unheard of when you're cooking in bulk. But Bacchanal's back of the house—which, for a buffet operation, has a surprising number of toques from Michelin-starred kitchens—puts out around 15 daily, seasonal specials, such as chilled pea soup with crab and chicken Marsala. Desserts are legendary, if tiny, so that you can eat many of them, including cookies, cake pops, tarts, and cupcakes, plus a fun assortment of gelato. True bacchanalia—festivals in honor of the Greek god Bacchus, god of wine—never come cheap, and neither does this

Continued on page 348

DOWNTOWN DINING

THOUGH WE PROFILE ONLY A HANDFUL OF DOWNTOWN RESTAURANTS in this guide, we want to make it clear that the restaurant scene here has gotten both diverse and dynamic. You'll find steakhouses, sushi, seafood, buffets, vegetarian offerings, and a broad selection of ethnic cuisines, including Japanese, Hawaiian, Thai, Mexican, Chinese, and Italian. There are places that specialize in barbecue, hamburgers, shrimp cocktails, pizza, and chili dogs, as well as funky little spots intent on creating their own styles of cooking that defy description. Restaurant settings range from luxurious to clubby to hole-in-the-wall. Moreover, the best offerings are no longer concentrated in two or three tiny areas.

The heart of the Downtown revival remains the block of Fremont just east of the Fremont Street Experience canopy. And that area saw another boom over the past year when it comes to food. The pioneer of the area is **Le Thai,** which has a tiny dining room but an expansive walled patio with pergola, heaters, and misters; its menu features such dishes as Three Color Curry and Short Rib Fried Rice. Around the corner is **La Comida,** which serves an updated urban Mexican menu with such dishes as Mexican street corn and ahi tostadas in a casual mix-and-match atmosphere reminiscent of a Baja beach bar. And next to that, there's the sushi spot **Bocho.**

Back on the main drag is **Park on Fremont,** which is pretty much whimsy from start to finish, from the picket fence–enclosed alfresco dining area out on the street to the herringbone-floored front entrance to the glam-hunting-lodge decor to the walled rear garden complete with seesaw. The gastropub menu includes such dishes as Mac & Cheese Balls, Fried Egg Burger, and Strawberry Summer Salad.

A bit farther east, you'll see the Evel Knievel–themed pizza place **Evel Pie,** followed by **Therapy,** which is the most upscale place to eat on this block. On the corner, **Eureka!** offers a chain-restaurant spin on innovative American cuisine with a serious craft beer and whiskey program. (Where else will you find Pappy Van Winkle in a chain restaurant?)

Don't leave the block until you've popped your head into a couple of other restaurants on the south side of the street. **The Smashed Pig** offers up English pub grub. Chef Martin Swift's menu is packed with Brit dishes like mini–Yorkshire puddings, fish and chips, and bangers and mash, but he also parlays his experience as a sushi chef in the Nobu empire with daily sashimi specials. And if you want a quick burger, check out **Flippin' Good Burgers & Shakes.** Yes, it's fast food. And yes, it's a chain. Sometimes, though, that hits the spot.

But don't stop your tour of the area at Fremont and Sixth Street. Stroll down a block to **Container Park,** a popular hangout for tourists, local families, and hipsters alike. Dining offerings there include **Big Ern's BBQ, Cheffini's** for hot dogs, more-sophisticated fare at **Downtown Terrace,** vegan cuisine at **Simply Pure,** and sweets at **Waffelato** and **Sweet Spot Candy Shop.**

If you want a more formal experience on this block, head across the street from the park to the new upscale Indian joint **Turmeric.** The back room is a high-end modern restaurant, the front is a more casual lounge, and the second-floor patio is a prime party spot overlooking Downtown's hottest intersection.

Keep traveling east and you'll come to the area's coolest bar, **Atomic Liquor,** which has upgraded the food at the adjoining **Atomic Kitchen** from bar grub to destination dining.

If you're feeling really brave, venture farther down Fremont to Maryland Parkway, where you'll find the coffee shop/casual restaurant **PublicUs.** Their cold salads, sandwiches, and entrées all boast gourmet touches. While the looks of the neighborhood may take some people aback, like most of Downtown, it's generally very safe due to a strong Metro Police and private security presence.

Fremont Street is no longer the only place to dine well in this area. Pioneered by **Eat** and solidified by the award-winning **Carson Kitchen,** Carson Avenue, one block to the south, has developed a wonderful collection of restaurants in a short two-block span.

At the recently expanded **Carson Kitchen** (see also pages 373–374), you'll find traditional comfort food updated with contemporary flavors. The menu has an emphasis on shared plates, such as tempura green beans with pepper jelly and cream cheese and bacon jam with baked Brie and toasted baguette. The sandwich selection includes short rib sliders, a jerk turkey burger, and grilled cheese with apples and caramelized onion.

Just down the street from Carson Kitchen, at Seventh Street and Carson Avenue, is **Eat** (see also page 378). This Downtown pioneer caters to a different crowd, serving only breakfast and lunch, which includes such dishes as shrimp and grits, free-range chicken, and the Killer Grilled Cheese, which truly lives up to its name.

The area between Carson Kitchen and Eat has some other offerings that also have people buzzing. California import **Donut Bar** has replaced O Face Donuts as the local sweets spot, and **VegeNation** offers the neighborhood a meat-free experience. (Another good spot for Downtown vegetarians is the **Bronze Café** at The Market grocery store.) Unfortunately, two other spots on this block, Glutton and Zydeco Po' Boys, recently closed their doors. The former has been replaced by an eclectic little spot called **7th & Carson.**

The centerpiece of the blocks to the north of Fremont is **The Ogden,** a luxury condo building. In its previous incarnation as an apartment building, it served as a makeshift dorm for Zappos employees working nearby—so much so that the company bought the Gold Spike hotel across the street and turned it into a sort of clubhouse for them and other local residents. Today, The Ogden is prime real estate, and its preferred dining destination is the new location of **Flock & Fowl** (see also pages 382–383). At Gold Spike, **Fiddlestix** has some interesting options as well.

DOWNTOWN DINING (continued)

Across Sixth Street from The Ogden is the venerable **El Cortez Hotel & Casino,** which extends from Ogden Avenue to Fremont Street and Sixth to Seventh Streets. The El Cortez dates to 1941 and was once run by Benjamin "Bugsy" Siegel. Its restaurant, **Siegel's 1941,** is a 24-hour vintage-themed coffee shop that's a playful nod to the notorious mobster. Siegel's took over the Flame Steakhouse space in 2015, but it has kept such popular selections as the prime rib and seasonal stone crab. For something more casual, try the newest location of popular local chain **Naked City Pizza,** which serves square Buffalo, New York–style slices.

Another older hot spot in the new Downtown is the **Arts District.** At its heart, in the Arts Factory building that gave the area its name and identity, you'll find bar food at the indoor-outdoor bar **Urban Lounge** and Mexican cuisine at the adjacent **Tacos Huevos.** On the other side of Charleston Boulevard, while maybe not technically in the district, is the old guard of the area's dining scene, **Lola's,** where the cooking is 100% New Orleans–style.

Just across the street in the rear of the Arts Factory, you'll now find the popular bar **Artifice,** as well as **Mingo Kitchen & Lounge,** which offers high-end hot dogs, burgers, and egg sandwiches in a plush, chic lounge setting.

The most interesting new development in the Arts District is its extension south across Charleston. Directly on Charleston proper you can find the new location of the **Cornish Pasty Co.,** which features traditional English dough pockets packed with American, British, Indian, and Italian cuisine—and a nice vegetarian selection to boot. The huge space is also rumored to be adding live music sometime soon.

Turn down Main Street or the surrounding blocks, and you'll find antiques shops, galleries, trendy bars, and even a brewery. For a bite to eat, the coffee shop **Makers and Finders** has wonderful Latin cuisine and a quaint sidewalk patio. When you finish your meal, hop next door for a handcrafted beer at **Hop Nuts Brewing.** Across the street, a new reggae lounge called **Jammyland** is offering up amazing rum, handcrafted cocktails, and Jamaican cooking.

The most buzzed-about place in all of Downtown, however, is just around the corner from those spots. There, with its entrance on California Avenue but a Casino Center Boulevard address, you'll find the red-hot Italian eatery **Esther's Kitchen.** Trying to score a reservation here can be tough. But chef James Trees usually keeps a few tables open for walk-ins, so don't be afraid to drop by if you're in the area.

As exciting as the expansion of Downtown development is, the area on and around Downtown's classic casino corridor is certainly not to be ignored. A block north of the Fremont Street Experience, you'll encounter the **Downtown Grand** and its adjacent **Downtown 3rd** area. Inside the casino, check out the 24-hour restaurant/performance space **Freedom Beat** for some live music and food from *Hell's Kitchen* alumnus Scott Commings.

Downtown 3rd is perhaps best known for **Triple George Grill,** a knock-off of a classic San Francisco restaurant; it boasts excellent sourdough, fresh fish, steaks, and comfort foods. Almost adjacent is **Pizza Rock** (see pages 395–396), an offering from former World Pizza Cup Champion Tony Gemignani. The restaurant has pizza ovens heated to four different temperatures to properly prepare numerous styles of pizza.

But back to Fremont—specifically the offerings under the canopy. When the old Fitzgeralds hotel, which extends from Fremont to Carson Street and Third to Fourth Streets, was renovated and updated as **The D,** the Detroit-centric owners brought in **Andiamo Steakhouse** from Detroit restaurateur Joe Vicari, who has 10 restaurants in the Motor City. The Las Vegas Andiamo may be relatively new, but it carries an old-world feel, with a brick-lined vaulted entrance, curtained booths, and attentive service augmenting a classic menu of steaks and chops. The D is also home to Detroit favorite **American Coney Island,** which serves chili dogs.

Just across Third Street from The D is the **Four Queens,** site of the landmark **Hugo's Cellar.** A rarity in Southern Nevada, Hugo's really is in a sort of cellar—brick-lined and below street level—and is a bastion of old-time elegance (so much so that it's frequently cited as the most romantic restaurant in town). Its hallmarks include a red rose for each female customer; old-school table-side preparations of Caesar salad, bananas Foster, and cherries Jubilee; and a menu heavy on dishes such as Chateaubriand and rack of lamb.

Continuing west on Fremont Street is the **Golden Nugget,** with **Vic & Anthony's,** an updated steakhouse; the **Chart House,** a seafood place complete with 75,000-gallon aquarium; **Lillie's Asian Cuisine;** and the **Grotto** for classic Italian.

Andiamo Steakhouse, Hugo's Cellar, and Vic & Anthony's are all excellent Downtown choices if you want the feel of old Vegas. But be prepared to open your wallet because they can be pricey.

At the intersection of Fremont and Main Street, you'll find **The Plaza.** The iconic building houses **Oscar's Steakhouse,** named in honor of former mayor Oscar Goodman. In an elevated circular structure at the mouth of Fremont Street, Oscar's offers one of the best views of the Fremont Street Experience. But in a town loaded with astounding steaks, this place is more about the ambience than the beef. Other dining options at The Plaza include the indoor-outdoor **Beer Garden, Hash House A Go Go,** and **Pop Up Pizza.**

A few blocks west is **Main Street Station,** site of **Triple 7,** one of the city's most established brewpubs—and one that's known for excellent sushi (because of a large Hawaiian clientele), along with more-beer-friendly foods like burgers and steaks.

Also off the Fremont Street Experience you'll find the **California** and the **Fremont.** The recently renovated California, in particular, attracts a heavily Hawaiian clientele and is home to **Aloha Specialties,** offering the flavors of the islands. The venerable Pasta Pirate is now the **California Noodle House,** serving Thai, Japanese, Vietnamese, and Chinese noodle dishes. Also at the Cal is the **Redwood Steakhouse,** an old-school Las

DOWNTOWN DINING (continued)

Vegas gourmet room that serves steak and seafood. Good value also can be found at the Fremont's Pacific Rim–centric **Second Street Grill** and at **Binion's** next door, where the 24th-floor **Top of Binion's Steakhouse** offers an epic view along with old-Vegas food and service.

One of the few stand-alone restaurants Downtown with a true old-Vegas vibe is **Chicago Joe's,** in business since 1975 in a house built in the 1930s at 820 South Fourth Street. (Las Vegas Boulevard would be Fifth, so this is one block to the west). Chicago Joe's serves old-school Italian and reportedly was a hangout for Oscar Goodman back in his mob-attorney days, along with such notorious clients as Tony Spilotro. And if you decide to visit the famous Gold & Silver Pawn from TV's *Pawn Stars*, you can grab a bite at the adjoining Pawn Plaza's **Rick's Rollin Smoke Barbeque** or **Good Pie** pizza shop.

Finally, a recent development in Downtown dining has been the arrival of some restaurants in the high-rises (and not just The Ogden). At **The Juhl,** you'll find the wonderful modern Vietnamese restaurant **Le Pho.** And the ground floor of the **SoHo Lofts** is now the new home of popular sandwich spot the **Goodwich** (see also pages 384–385).

Continued from page 343

one: Breakfast has been discontinued and rolled into a brunch that costs $40 weekdays and $50 on weekends. Dinner will set you back $60 Monday–Thursday, $70 on weekends.

There's been an interesting shake-up at **The Buffet at Wynn,** where the excellent breakfast buffet has been discontinued. Also, no more are the champagne brunch and the gourmet dinner. The offerings have been consolidated and simplified, so there's now a daily brunch from 7:30 a.m. to 3:30 p.m. for $28.99 weekdays and $36.99 weekends; dinner is 3:30–9:30 p.m. for $49.99 weekdays and $52.99 weekends.

As one of the first true luxury resorts in Las Vegas, the Bellagio has always set a high standard for its **Buffet Bellagio,** with lots of seafood, unique salads, and fresh-baked bread. Gourmet dinner service on Fridays and Saturdays breaks out the fish eggs, as in fine caviar with accoutrements, fresh-rolled sushi, and ahi tuna cones. And, to keep itself relevant, Bellagio's all-you-can-eat has added a VIP experience that includes a chef's table. VIP guests bypass the (usually) long line and are seated at a private table with a menu created especially for the party by a team of chefs that might include charcuterie, caviar, and table-side preparations of fresh salads or carvings of leg of lamb or prime rib. (And yes, you still get to graze the buffet as well.) Breakfast is easy at $25, with lunch and dinner setting you back $28 and $39, respectively; weekend brunch is $34, or $49 with bottomless champagne. If you're looking for more luxury on your plate, the gourmet dinner service is $44, while the chef's table costs $69 per person.

BUFFET SPEAK	
ACTION FORMAT	Cooking food to order in full view of patrons
GLUTTONY	A Las Vegas buffet tradition that carries no moral stigma
GROANING BOARD	A buffet table that "groans" beneath the weight of its bounty
ISLAND	Serving area for a particular cuisine or specialty—salads, desserts, Mexican, and the like)
SHOVELIZER	Diner who prefers quantity over quality
FORK LIFT	A device used to remove shovelizers

Thanks to a renovation that brightened the decor and added some ethnic options, **The Buffet at Aria** is now one of the city's more diverse buffets. With one of the few tandoor ovens on the Strip, this is an unsung spot for Indian food, and you can watch as fresh naan bread is baked for you in the oven, along with kabobs and other Indian fare. Mediterranean cuisine goes beyond Greece, including bites from North Africa and the Middle East, while even the humble pizza enjoys multiple preparations: deep-dish, New York–style, and Stromboli. There's even variety during breakfast, with made-to-order classic, snow crab, or salmon eggs Benedict. While the pricing—$25 for breakfast, $29 for weekday brunch and $34 on weekends, $39 and $44 for dinner on weekdays and weekends, respectively, Buffet at Aria—might make it seem like a middle-of-the-road buffet, Buffet at Aria excels in freshness and service and delivers lots of bang for the buck.

Treasure Island Buffet, remodeled in 2018, features perhaps fewer items than other buffets described but offers more made-to-order dishes, including salads, pasta, sushi, and even deli sandwiches and wraps. Seafood, including Dungeness crabs, snow crabs, and lobster ravioli, is a specialty. Likewise, the carving station is first class. Wood-fired pizza is also a strong item, as are Chinese selections. The buffet avoids the cavernous impersonal feel of many buffets by dividing the space into small, cozier rooms, and the service is good. We like the TI Buffet more for dinner than for breakfast or lunch.

It's safe to characterize **Cravings at The Mirage** along the same lines as the TI Buffet, though their cuisine is perhaps slightly more diverse. Both feature chefs cooking dishes to order at every station.

Le Village Buffet at Paris Las Vegas combines French provincial preparations from Provence, Savoie, Burgundy, Brittany, and Alsace, and made-to-order crepes, both sweet and savory. The latter are made with cheese, ham, and chicken, among other ingredients. At dinner prime rib and snow crab legs are featured items. Breakfast runs $22 on weekdays and $24 on weekends. Brunch (served 10 a.m.–3 p.m.) and dinner are both $31.

Farther south down Las Vegas Boulevard, **M Resort** offers one of the better off-Strip buffets. **Studio B** is the Vegas buffet in its purest

Continued on page 352

CHINATOWN

LAS VEGAS HAS A VIBRANT CHINATOWN, but it's really a misnomer. Unlike other large cosmopolitan cities, such as Los Angeles and New York, which have concentrated areas associated with specific Asian countries (Chinatown, Koreatown, Little Saigon, Little Tokyo, or Japantown), in Las Vegas everything's lumped together.

The traditional capital of Las Vegas's Chinatown is the **China Town Plaza,** at 4215 Spring Mountain Road, between Valley View and Decatur Boulevards, a few blocks west of the Strip. China Town Plaza is the most visible symbol of the community, with a towering gateway and gilded statue, and it annually has one of the city's most colorful celebrations of the Chinese New Year, complete with a Lion Dance. All of this action can be quite a surprise to anyone who's just stopping by 99 Ranch Market for some frozen banana leaves or fresh fish.

Despite the "China" in its name, the China Town Plaza is reflective of the melting-pot nature of the Asian community in southern Nevada. It's currently home to restaurants serving food from Vietnam (**Mr. Sandwich** and **Pho Vietnam**), Taiwan (**The Little Kitchen Cafe**), the Philippines (**Kapit Bahay**), Korea (**Mother's Korean Grill**), and Japan (**Volcano Tea House**), as well as regional Chinese cuisines such as Hong Kong-style (**Sam Woo BBQ Restaurant**), Cantonese (**Harbor Palace Seafood**), Yunnan (**Spicy City**), and southern Chinese (**Capital Seafood Restaurant**).

How authentic are these restaurants? Many people think of this area as a tourist draw, but it's not the usual tourist—it's not uncommon to see busloads of visitors from China parading into one of the Plaza restaurants . It's also not uncommon to encounter a server who, faced with a table of Western customers, must fetch someone who speaks English. And while the servers will—sometimes shamefacedly—slip a fork to a Westerner, most of the tables are set only with chopsticks.

Fifteen years ago, a motorist who saw the prominent CHINA TOWN exit sign along I-15, which parallels the Strip, might have been surprised to see things pretty much confined to the Plaza, but the Asian district has grown greatly since then, with Asian businesses (some of them with signs only in their native languages) lining multiple blocks of Spring Mountain Road and the streets that lead off of it. On the far western extreme, at Rainbow Boulevard, is **Koreatown Plaza,** which has yet to establish its identity.

Chinese—and Japanese, and Korean, and Vietnamese, and on and on—restaurants are sprinkled throughout the Las Vegas Valley; don't assume that the best ones are confined to the Chinatown area. But here are a few noteworthy spots in the district.

- **ABRIYA RAKU OR JUST RAKU** (5030 Spring Mountain Road) In its early days, this place was a magnet for area chefs, who were drawn to its authentic Japanese specialties (including many grilled items—but no sushi) and late-night, after-work hours. Today, those same chefs have a hard time getting into the tiny place. A specialty is house-made *agedashi* tofu. You never knew tofu could taste so good. (See also page 397.)

- **CHINA MAMA** (3420 S. Jones Blvd.) China Mama, which is in an old bank building, almost reached cult status early on for its impeccable execution of steamed juicy pork buns, dumpling-like shapes with broth and seasoned pork inside. But the green-onion pancake is excellent as well, as is the creamy chicken-corn soup. (See also page 374.)

- **DISTRICT ONE** (3400 S. Jones Blvd.) This pan-Asian restaurant has become a popular spot for local restaurant and nightlife employees getting off work and other denizens of the wee hours, thanks to its 2 a.m. closing time. But chef Khai Vu's mastery of Vietnamese and Japanese cuisine, plus a selection of fresh seafood that changes daily, makes it worth a visit any time of day. His lobster pho is a treat for the eyes as well as the taste buds.

- **HONEY PIG** (4725 Spring Mountain Road) This Korean barbecue joint is best known for its all-you-can-eat fare, including brisket, pork belly, and *bulgogi,* and the unusual round grills on which you cook the meat.

- **HONG KONG GARDEN** (5300 Spring Mountain Road) Formerly Jade, Hong Kong Garden is one of the longest-standing restaurants in Chinatown—even though it's not in the China Town Plaza—and draws its share of tour buses, in part for its storied dim sum, which focuses on shrimp. There's an à la carte menu, as well, though it doesn't attract much attention. What does is a surprisingly good view of the Strip.

- **HUE THAI** (5115 Spring Mountain Road) Despite the "Thai" in its name, Hue Thai is most well known for its excellent execution of the Vietnamese banh mi, the layered sandwich on a crisp-crusted baguette that is a nod to the French influence in that country (think of it as a Saigon sub). The house special is a winner, as is the char-broiled pork.

- **ICHIZA** (4355 Spring Mountain Road) Ichiza is one of the Japanese restaurants in Las Vegas's Chinatown that's beloved by locals, especially for their Honey Toast, a dessert of crisp-edged sweet bread drizzled with honey and topped with vanilla ice cream. Remember to save room as you're partaking of the fried tofu and miso-based ramen. And remember to call ☎ 702-367-3151 to make reservations.

- **JOYFUL HOUSE** (4601 Spring Mountain Road) Joyful House was founded in 1996, which makes it a landmark by Las Vegas standards. Just west of the China Town Plaza, it's one of the city's most elegant Chinese restaurants, known for its live seafood and shark fin in various preparations, some of which must be ordered in advance.

- **KABUTO** (5040 Spring Mountain Road) For a few years this was considered the finest sushi restaurant in Las Vegas, and possibly one of the best in the country. We still love it. But the departure of head chef Gen Mizoguchi to open Yui Edomae Sushi (profiled on page 405) has prompted us to put this super-pricey spot on our watch list for a while to see how it handles the change. We're encouraged that preliminary reports have been good. So if you can't get into Yui, this is a good fall-back for mind-blowing raw fish and other Japanese delicacies.

CHINATOWN (continued)

- **KUNG FU THAI AND CHINESE RESTAURANT** (3505 S. Valley View Blvd.) Tucked away at the east end of the China Town Plaza, Kung Fu is a venerable place dating to 1973, which goes a long way toward explaining the name. Its proprietors are Thai, but they opened in Downtown Las Vegas before that cuisine became popular in the United States, so the emphasis has long been Chinese; regardless, they make a wonderful pad thai and a nice *tom kha* chicken soup.

- **MONTA JAPANESE NOODLE HOUSE** (5030 Spring Mountain Road) If your idea of ramen is limited to the cheap, salty packets you lived on in college, it's time for a welcome awakening. The ramen at Monta is limited to four basic styles: *tonkotsu* (pork), shoyu (chicken and vegetables), *tonkotsu*-shoyu (a combination of the two), and miso (nice and smoky). Get a bowl of *tonkotsu* and you'll be served a creamy, smoky, slightly buttery broth with lots of noodles and two slices of *chashu,* rolled and sliced pork that brings to mind nothing more than butter. And you can add vegetables, egg, whatever, if you feel a need to gild the lily. (See also pages 392–393.)

- **MOTHER'S KOREAN GRILL** (4215 Spring Mountain Road) Mother's is a classic Korean barbecue spot in the downstairs of the China Town Plaza with rectangular grills built into the tables. It's open 24 hours and attracts a large native clientele who like its authentic dishes, such as *dolsot bibimbap* and *bulgogi.* Of particular note are the *banchan* condiments—side dishes to the grilled meats, including a truly stellar (and well-balanced) kimchi.

- **PHO KIM LONG** (4023 Spring Mountain Road) The racy name—racy, anyway, if you know that pho is pronounced "fuh"—might indicate a

Continued from page 349

form: nothing fancy, just high-quality, free-flowing crab legs, prime rib, cocktail shrimp, oysters, and Asian specialties such as Korean *kalbi* and oxtail. There's also a live-action cooking studio, where chefs on display prepare dishes made to order. Top it off with a huge spread devoted to seafood on weekends and reasonable prices ($17 lunch, $25 dinner, $42 seafood buffet on weekends and Friday dinner) that include unlimited beer, wine, and champagne, and you've got a buffet worth the trek—from anywhere.

Among other off-Strip options, the **Feast Buffets** at the Station Casinos, which include Red Rock Resort, Sunset Station, and Fiesta, are favorites among locals, not only because they're located in locals-friendly casinos but also because there's something that makes each of them special (even though they all share a name). On Seafood Fridays at the **Feast at Green Valley Ranch,** for example, people line up with plates piled high with crab legs for the "Mama Sarah" treatment:

lack of seriousness on the part of this restaurant, located in a shopping center between the China Town Plaza and the Strip. But it's one of the best places in town to get a bowl of pho, the soup you build yourself from a basic meat broth and a veritable garden of fresh vegetables. Try the Rare Steak Noodle Soup or the Cantonese Roast Duck with Egg Noodle Soup.

• **PING PANG PONG** (Gold Coast, 4000 W. Flamingo Road) Its Flamingo Road location technically removes Ping Pang Pong from the Chinatown area, but it's just a few blocks away down Valley View Boulevard, and the Gold Coast has a huge proportion of Chinese guests—so many that the restaurant employs hosts who speak Mandarin and Cantonese. Ping Pang Pong is considered one of the best Chinese restaurants in town; a particular favorite is its dim sum, which draws a large contingent of expatriates.

• **SWEETS RAKU** (5040 Spring Mountain Road) When a place gets you started with an edible menu, you know there are lots of surprises in store, and that's true at this offshoot of Abriya Raku. Don't miss the Mount Fuji Chestnut Cream Cake.

• **SAM WOO BBQ** (4215 Spring Mountain Road) One of the longest-standing tenants of the China Town Plaza, Sam Woo BBQ, as the name indicates, is known for its *char siu*, or Chinese barbecued pork, which has levels of flavor that most American pit masters can only dream about, including hints of star anise and fennel. But the egg drop soup is also one of the best in town.

• **VEGGIE HOUSE** (5115 Spring Mountain Road) Whether you're a vegetarian or not, you'll probably find something to like at Veggie House, including a variety of faux-meat dishes.

The crab legs are tossed onto the flat top; coated with butter, herbs, and chiles; and then thwacked with a metal spatula to crack open the shells, allowing the seasonings to seep in—a preparation perfected by Louisiana-born line cook "Mama" Sarah Jamerson. **Feast at Texas Station** is renowned for the tacos *al pastor* made to order at its Mexican station; they're created from a nearly 90-year-old family recipe handed down to chef Jaime Montes.

Downtown, Main Street Station, the Golden Nugget, and the Fremont offer palatable buffets at reasonable prices. Garden Court buffet at Main Street Station claims the most attractive venue.

Seafood Buffets

Several casinos feature these on certain days. **The Orleans**'s **Main Street Station**'s, **Green Valley Ranch**'s, and **Golden Nugget**'s are on Friday, while the **Fremont**'s Paradise Buffet features seafood on Tuesday and Friday. The piscatory repasts at the **Cannery** (Thursday) and **Suncoast** (Friday) are worth trying as well.

Buffet Line Strategy

Popular buffets develop long lines. The best way to avoid the crowds is to go Sunday–Thursday and get in line before 6 p.m. or after 9 p.m., but we recommend going early, when the food is fresher. If you go to a buffet on a weekend, arrive extra-early or extra-late. If a large trade show or convention is in town, try to hit the buffets of casinos that don't draw big convention business. Good choices among the highly ranked buffets include **Texas Station,** the two **Fiestas, Green Valley Ranch, Boulder Station, Gold Coast, The Orleans, Suncoast,** and the **Fremont.**

BRUNCHES

UPSCALE, EXPENSIVE SPREADS with reserved tables, imported champagne, sushi, and seafood have made an impact on the local brunch scene. Although there is a plethora of value-priced brunches, the big-ticket shindigs attract diners who are happy to pay a higher tab for fancy food and service at a place that takes reservations so they can avoid a wait. In general, the higher the price, the better the champagne or other beverages served. **Bally's, Bellagio,** the **MGM Grand,** and **Wynn Las Vegas** serve decent champagne; California sparkling wine, mimosas, and Bloody Marys are the norm at the others. Reservations are accepted at all of the following:

• Bardot Brasserie Aria; ☎ 702-590-8610; michaelmina.net. Michael Mina has responded to his romantic French bistro's overnight success by adding a brunch option on the weekend. This à la carte affair might break your heart by forcing you to decide among delicious options like a foie gras parfait, gloriously simple escargot in pastry shells, brioche French toast with vanilla mascarpone and almond brittle, and a Nutella sticky bun. But hey, you can drown your sorrows with never-ending rosé for an extra $25; Saturday and Sunday, 9:30 a.m.–1:30 p.m.; reservations suggested.

• Border Brunch Border Grill, Mandalay Bay and The Forum Shops; ☎ 702-632-7403 and 702-854-6700; bordergrill.com/border-brunch. Mary Sue Milliken and Susan Feniger offer the best brunch bargain in town with their Saturday and Sunday Mexican feasts. All dishes are made to order and range from traditional brunch fare to whimsical Mexican treats. Beverage choices include fresh-squeezed juices, $15 bottomless mimosas and a $20 bottomless mimosa, *michelada,* and Bloody Mary combo. $39 at Mandalay Bay, $35 at Caesars Palace; Saturday and Sunday, 10 a.m.–3 p.m. at Mandalay Bay; 10 a.m.–2 p.m. at The Forum Shops.

• CHICA Venetian; ☎ 702-805-8472; venetian.com. The hot new brunch on the block is from celebrity chef Lorena Garcia, and it features a mixture of several Latin American cuisines served in a party atmosphere. À la carte; Saturday and Sunday, 10 a.m.–4 p.m.; reservations recommended.

• Gospel Brunch House of Blues, Mandalay Bay; ☎ 702-632-7777; houseofblues.com /lasvegas. Praise the Lord and pass the biscuits! This is the most raucous and joyous Sunday brunch in town. Grammy-winning gospel legend Kirk Franklin recently joined forces with House of Blues to custom-tailor the gospel performance in each city to suit its particular audience. The food is soulful as well: cornbread muffins and maple butter, Creole chicken and shrimp jambalaya, chicken and waffles, carving stations, plus create-your-own Bloody Mary and mimosa bars. Purchase tickets at the House of Blues box office: adults, $55; children ages 3–11, $28. Seatings at 10 a.m. and 1 p.m.

• **Herringbone Aria;** ☎ 877-230-2742; aria.com. If a gourmet brunch overlooking the pool is your favorite way to start the day, Aria's second-floor seafood restaurant is the place to do it, thanks to the outdoor patio seating. New executive chef Marty Lopez has changed up the brunch format a little, offering an all-you-can-eat combination of made-to-order items from the kitchen and several chef-attended stations. Offerings change weekly, but don't be surprised to find a whole roast duck or two types of salmon at the carving station, or lobster tails at the raw bar. $59 plus $35–$95 for assorted boozy beverage packages; Saturday and Sunday, 10 a.m.–3 p.m.; reservations recommended.

• **Sterling Brunch BLT Steak, Bally's;** ☎ 702-967-7999; ballyslasvegas.com. This place pioneered the Vegas brunch trend. And it just got a much-needed makeover: Bally's converted the old Bally's Steakhouse that housed it into the sleekly redesigned BLT Steak. At $105 per person, plus tax (children ages 7–10, $53 plus tax; under age 6, free), it's still the big ticket, but there's no shortage of diners who love it. The lavish selections include smoked salmon, freshly made sushi, real lobster salad, seafood, sturgeon caviar, and unlimited Perrier-Jouët champagne. The dessert selection is awesome. Entrée selections change weekly. Sunday, 9:30 a.m.–1:30 p.m.; reservations required.

Other good brunches can be found at **Bellagio, The Cromwell, Downtown Summerlin, Container Park,** and **Mandalay Place.**

MEAL DEALS

IN ADDITION TO BUFFETS, many casinos offer special dining deals that include New York strip and porterhouse steaks, prime rib, crab legs, lobster, and combinations of the foregoing, all at giveaway prices. You'll also find breakfast specials, burgers, hot dogs, and shrimp cocktails.

While the meal deals generally deliver what they promise in the way of an entrée, many of the extras that contribute to a high-quality dining experience are missing. With a couple of notable exceptions, the specials are served in big, bustling restaurants with all the atmosphere of a high-school cafeteria. When you're eating at closely packed Formica tables under lighting bright enough for brain surgery, it's difficult to pretend you're engaged in fine dining.

Our biggest complaint, however, concerns the lack of attention paid to the meal as a whole. We've had nice pieces of meat served with tired, droopy salads; stale bread; mealy, microwaved potatoes; and tasteless canned vegetables. How can you get excited about your prime rib when it's surrounded by the ruins of Pompeii?

Deke Castleman, a contributor to this book and editor of the *Las Vegas Advisor,* has given some thought to the meal deal. In his view, discount dining actually isn't about food at all:

> A "quality dining experience" is not really what Las Vegas visitors are looking for, in my humble opinion, when they pursue an $8 steak, $12 prime rib, or $24 lobster. To me what they're after is twofold: (1) a very cheap steak, prime rib, or lobster—damn the salad, vegetable, and Formica; and (2) a cool story to take home about all the rock-bottom prices they paid for food.

Finally, it's hard to take advantage of many of the specials: They're offered only in the middle of the night, or require an hour wait for a table, or force you to eat dinner at 3:30 in the afternoon. In restaurants all over town, in and out of the casinos, you'll find plenty of good food served in pleasant surroundings at extremely reasonable prices. Honestly, we don't think saving $5 on a meal is worth the hassle.

Because Las Vegas meal deals often come and go, it's impossible to cover them adequately in a book. To stay abreast of them, your best bet is to subscribe to the *Las Vegas Advisor,* a monthly newsletter that provides independent, critical evaluations of meal deals, buffets, brunches, and drink specials. To order, call ☎ 800-244-2224 or visit lvahotels.com. If you're already in town and you want to pick up a copy, head to the **Gamblers Book Club** (800 S. Main St.; ☎ 702-382-7555 or 800-522-1777; gamblersbookclub.com).

STEAK Though specials constantly change, a few have weathered the test of time. **Ellis Island Casino** (☎ 702-733-8901; ellisislandcasino .com), attached to the Super 8 motel on Koval Lane near East Flamingo Road, serves an excellent $8 New York strip dinner complete with salad, baked potato, green beans, and microbrewed beer or root beer. It's available 24 hours, but it's not on the menu. To obtain the rock-bottom price, you must print out two coupons from an EI kiosk, the second after playing at least $5 in any slot machine with your club card inserted. The **Hard Rock Hotel** (☎ 702-693-5000; hardrockhotel.com) has a steak-and-shrimp "Gambler's Special," served 24 hours a day in Mr. Lucky's coffee shop for about $10, also not on the menu. Someone at the table must have a Hard Rock Players' Club card to take advantage of this special.

PRIME RIB One of the best prime rib specials in a town glutted with them is available Downtown at the California's **Market Street Cafe** (☎ 702-385-1222; thecal.com), where you can get a good cut of meat between 4 p.m. and 11 p.m. for $9.99; it comes with soup or salad, vegetable, carb of choice, and cherries Jubilee for dessert.

South Point (☎ 702-796-7111; southpointcasino.com), at the far south end of the Strip, serves a big slab of prime rib prepared to order, with soup or salad, potato, rolls, and au jus, plus tear-inducing horseradish, if you ask. It's available 11 a.m.–11 p.m. in the **Coronado Cafe** for $14.95. For $5 more, you can enjoy the same dinner at the upscale **Primarily Prime Rib** restaurant on the second floor, where salads are mixed table-side and there's always a featured wine on sale for a bargain price. Primarily Prime Rib is open Wednesday–Sunday for dinner only. For reservations, call ☎ 702-797-8075.

LOBSTER AND CRAB LEGS Lobster-and-steak (surf-and-turf) combos and crab leg deals no longer appear as regularly as they once did on casino marquees around Las Vegas. The best place for crab legs is at the gourmet buffets. **Aria, Bellagio, M Resort, Planet Hollywood,** and **Wynn Las Vegas** serve all-you-can-eat cold king crab nightly.

SHRIMP COCKTAILS Peddled at nominal prices, these seafaring snacks are frequently used to lure gamblers into the casinos. The shrimp are the tiny bay variety, usually drowned in cocktail sauce. The best and cheapest shrimp cocktail has traditionally been found at the **Golden Gate** (☎ 702-385-1906; goldengatecasino.com), a small Downtown casino that's been serving this special for more than 50 years. The price: $3.99, having been raised a dollar in 2010, 2012, and 2013 after costing 99¢ for nearly 20 years. In 2017, the Golden Gate closed the restaurant serving the shrimp cocktails. Management insists that the cocktail is only taking a breather and will return, but nothing has happened yet. Reviving the Golden Gate's tradition, however, is the Fremont, as well as the **Skyline** on Boulder Highway, with a 99¢ cocktail. Other contenders are served at the **Four Queens** ($10) and **Palace Station** (coffee shop; $13).

PASTA AND PIZZA A good pizza play is to hit up satellite outlets—fast-food counters attached to the Italian restaurants—at **Boulder Station** and **Sunset Station** for a quickie slice. You can also get a good slice of New York–style pizza at the Rio's **Sports Deli. Metro Pizza** at Ellis Island wins local-media popularity contests, while the Red Rock and Green Valley Ranch food courts have good options with **Villa Pizza** and **Pizza Rock,** respectively. The best pizza on the Strip, though, is now found at the no-name hidden pizza place on the third floor of **The Cosmopolitan.**

BREAKFAST SPECIALS The best ham-and-eggs specials are found at the **Gold Coast, Arizona Charlie's Decatur,** and **Boulder Station.** All offer terrific prices, usually around $9. Arizona Charlie's Decatur also has decent steak and eggs for $7.77. Other worthwhile breakfast deals include the buffets at **Sam's Town, The Orleans,** and the **Rio.**

TASTING MENUS

DON'T LET THE PHRASE "TASTING MENU" throw you—it's probably one of the most cost-effective ways to get to know a restaurant. For a set price, diners are guaranteed a certain number of courses (anywhere from a standard three, such as lunch at **Milos,** to 12 or more, as in the *dégustation* at **Joël Robuchon**) that usually include signature dishes for which the restaurant is best known. Multiple courses usually mean smaller portions, but after six or seven, all those bites add up to a full belly—without breaking the bank.

- Sage Aria This contemporary American restaurant by chef Shawn McClain at Aria offers a six-course signature tasting for $150 (with additional wine pairing for $100) as well as a five-course vegan version for $90. All of those courses give you the chance to fully experience the clean, simple flavors that McClain and his team do best. While dishes change seasonally, recent offerings have included sturgeon and caviar, Alaskan king crab with sea urchin cream and caviar, and a grilled rib eye cap with bone marrow.

- L'Atelier de Joël Robuchon MGM Grand One of Las Vegas's most formal temples of fine dining, **Joël Robuchon at MGM Grand,** with its 12-dish, five-course dégustation, will set you back $445 per person—and that's without wine. That can be a little hard to swallow, so the next best thing is to head to the more casual concept next door, L'Atelier de Joël Robuchon, which has counter dining where you can watch the chefs prepare your meal. While no less a fine-dining restaurant than Joël Robuchon, its more egalitarian neighbor, L'Atelier has a more comfortable feel and an easier check average for the seven-course *Le Plates En Petites Portions Dégustation* (that's its Menu of Small Tasting Portions, if your French is a little rusty), and two pre-theater menus at significantly lower price points. And you shall discover the finest of Robuchon, from his elegant langoustines cooked in green curry and coconut milk to his famous roasted quail stuffed with foie gras and legendary purée *de pommes*.

• **Estiatorio Milos The Cosmopolitan** There are few prix-fixe lunch menus on the Strip, but Milos gives new meaning to the term "power lunch." The midday meal—three courses for $29—is considered one of the best deals in town. Begin your Greek journey with a choice of meze, such as ripe tomato salad, grilled octopus, or dips like *taramasalata* and hummus. Your second course showcases what Milos is known for: fresh seafood, flown in straight from the Mediterranean daily. Choose from a whole *lavraki* (grilled sea bass, dressed simply with good olive oil and lemon) or shrimp *saganaki*—or even a lamb chop. Finish it off with true Greek yogurt or fresh fruit. It's a simple, elegant meal, but the price alone is enough to make you say, "Opa!"

• **Restaurant Guy Savoy Caesars Palace** At $385 per person (plus $200 or $375 for optional wine pairings), the Prestige Menu is not cheap. But considering that appetizers alone range from $60 to $95 à la carte, this 14-course menu might be considered a steal. This is actually one of the restaurant's midrange tasting menus, with others priced at $170, $500, and $555.

• **Partage 3839 Spring Mountain Road** A French restaurant offering three different tasting menus in the heart of Chinatown? It's certainly a risky move, but with a pair of chefs who are both veterans of Michelin-starred establishments in France, all eyes are on this audacious newcomer. And with five-, seven-, and nine-course options available for between $80 and $130, it's worth the short trip from The Strip to give it a shot.

THE HOLE-IN-THE-WALL GANG

"IT'S JUST A LITTLE HOLE IN THE WALL." When applied to restaurants, this description usually means a personal favorite, a little-known treasure, some unpretentious place with knockout food that transcends its humble appearance. Avid diners, including us, comb Las Vegas looking for these below-the-radar jewels. Most are barely known outside of Las Vegas and offer unique dining experiences, the kind of restaurants that leave friends asking, "How on earth did you find this place?" So sharpen up your appetite—here are a whole lot of holes.

• **Rollin Smoke Barbeque 3185 S. Highland Dr.; ☎ 702-836-3621; rollinsmokebarbeque .com.** Located down the street from the Spearmint Rhino topless bar and next to the Diamond Cabaret strip club, Rollin Smoke is defined by its Southern dry-rubbed meats cooked ever-so-slowly over hickory fires. The beef ribs are the house specialty, but the pork and chicken are also something special. For a walk on the wild side, try the smoked meat loaf. No alcoholic beverages are served, but you can consume your own beer or wine as long as it's in a cup. Inexpensive.

• **Fat Choy Eureka Casino, 595 E. Sahara Ave.; ☎ 702-794-3464; fatchoylv.com.** The former coffee shop of the low-rent Eureka "casino" now serves amazing but inexpensive Asian food by a chef who formerly worked at Robuchon (MGM Grand) and Comme Ça (Cosmopolitan). Serving both American diner food like cheeseburgers and what the chef calls Asian comfort food, including Peking duck *bao* and roasted marrow, Fat Choy is open for lunch and dinner. Inexpensive.

- Merkato Ethiopian 4970 S. Arville St., Ste. 104; ☎ 702-776-6769. Sample a wide assortment of dishes by ordering a meat/vegetarian combination platter arrayed on spongy injera bread. It comes with a sweet Ethiopian smile. If the joint is packed, there's probably a meeting of the cab drivers' union. Open daily, 11 a.m.–2 a.m. Inexpensive.

- Naked City Pizza 3240 S. Arville St.; ☎ 702-243-6277; nakedcitylv.com. There are now four Naked City operations scattered throughout the valley, plus outposts at the Las Vegas Motor Speedway and at Cashman Field during 51s games. But for the full experience, try the one inside a dive bar called Moon Doggie's on Arville, just north of West Desert Inn Road. You can't go wrong with any of the pies here, but our favorite is the Fatboy, which is like the best antipasto you've ever eaten served hot on a pizza. Moderate.

- Chicago Joe's 820 S. Fourth St.; ☎ 702-382-JOES (5637); chicagojoesrestaurant .com. Located in what looks like a 1950s-built single-family brick home a couple blocks off South Las Vegas Boulevard near Downtown, Joe's flies the traditional red-checkered-tablecloth flag. Carb up on a wide selection of pasta preps or go for house specialties such as pasta with snails in garlic butter, veal Angelo, or pasta with mussels. Don't worry; the usual standbys are available too. Open for lunch and dinner most days. If you go for lunch, take a whack at the Italian sub. Moderate.

OFF-STRIP DINING

EVIDENTLY, OPENING A RESTAURANT IN LAS VEGAS is on the bucket list of every celebrity chef. Their haunts on the Strip are all excellent—and extremely pricey. You're paying for the label, plus a pretty space in some of the most expensive real estate on Earth.

OK, now let's talk about cars. Not the segue you were expecting? Bear with me. If you're staying on the Strip or Downtown but want to visit the veritable galaxy of amazingly good eateries located away from those areas, make sure you have the Uber and Lyft apps installed on your phone. Because for anyone who has flown into town, the obscene pay parking policies of the Strip make renting a car during your visit totally impractical. Las Vegas taxis are notoriously unreliable outside of the main tourist corridors, which means they'll take you from the Strip to the 'burbs—but don't count on them to get you back. The only visitors who will benefit from having a car are those who have driven into town (depending on their resort's parking policy) and those staying with their own wheels in an off-Strip resort.

Once you've gotten to the suburbs, you'll find a brave new world of Las Vegas dining. The resident chef might not be a household name, but he or she can turn out some singularly remarkable dishes. Even better, these dishes can be had at a fraction of the price you'd pay at one of the brand-name Strip restaurants.

Note: If you're thinking about lodging on the Strip anywhere from Mandalay Bay to the Stratosphere and you want to dine off-Strip, try to stay on the west side of the Strip. Hotels here are easier for coming and going due to a network of side streets that connect to the casinos' rear. (New York–New York, Excalibur, and Bellagio are exceptions to this.) On the east side of the Strip, your best bets if traveling by car are Wynn Las Vegas, Wynn Encore, MGM Signature, and the Tropicana.

Here are some off-Strip restaurants we love, but not quite enough for a full profile in the next section:

- Abyssinia (Ethiopian) 4780 W. Tropicana # 108, West of Strip; ☎ 702-220-5304; abyssinialasvegas.com. If you find a friendlier eatery, let us know. Sample a wide assortment of dishes by ordering a meat/vegetarian combination platter atop injera bread. Inexpensive.

- Crab Corner Maryland Seafood House (Seafood) 6485 S. Rainbow Blvd., West of Strip; ☎ 702-489-4646; crabcornerlv.com. This unprepossessing Westside sports bar serves Maryland-style seafood specialties such as crab cakes, hard-shell blue crabs, raw oysters, littleneck clams, and black mussels. Moderate.

- India Palace (Indian) 505 E. Twain Ave., East of Strip; ☎ 702-796-4177; indiapalacelv .com. This small, cozy, and quiet family-owned restaurant serves specialties from both northern and southern India. A great choice for vegetarians, there's plenty here for carnivores too. The lunch buffet is rated one of the best in the city. Moderate.

- Lindo Michoacán (Mexican) 2655 E. Desert Inn Road, East of Strip; ☎ 702-735-6828; lindomichoacan.com. Big and noisy, with flamboyant decor. Michoacán favorites like birria (stewed goat) are rustled up alongside the usual cast of burritos, tacos, and such. Be sure to try Tío Raul's flan. Inexpensive to moderate.

- Primarily Prime Rib (American) South Point Casino, 9777 Las Vegas Blvd. S., South of Strip; ☎ 702-797-8075; southpointcasino.com. Capturing the feel of the plush Las Vegas gourmet rooms of yesteryear, this surprisingly affordable prime rib restaurant prepares salads and desserts table-side. A featured wine of the day is available by the bottle for about what you would pay at retail. Moderate.

- Table 34 (American) 600 E. Warm Springs Road, Southeast of Strip; ☎ 702-263-0034; table34lasvegas.com. This hip Henderson eatery offers seasonal menus supplemented by standards like chef Wes Kendrick's signature soups and house-smoked salmon on a crisp potato pancake. Also try the grilled rack of pork with chipotle potatoes. Moderate to expensive.

THE RESTAURANTS
OUR FAVORITE LAS VEGAS RESTAURANTS

WE'VE DEVELOPED DETAILED PROFILES for the best restaurants (in our opinion) in town. Each profile features an easily scanned heading that allows you, in just a second, to check out the restaurant's name, cuisine, overall rating, cost category, quality rating, and value rating.

OVERALL RATING This encompasses the entire dining experience: style, service, and ambience, in addition to taste, presentation, and food quality. Five stars is the highest rating possible and connotes the best of everything. Four-star restaurants are exceptional, three-star restaurants well above average, two-star restaurants good. One star indicates an average restaurant that demonstrates an unusual capability in some area of specialization—for example, an otherwise unmemorable place that serves great barbecued chicken.

COST Our expense description provides a comparative sense of how much a complete meal will cost. A complete meal for our purposes consists of an entrée with vegetable or side dish, plus a choice of soup or salad. Appetizers, desserts, drinks, and tips are excluded.

INEXPENSIVE	Below $15 per person
MODERATE	$16–$35 per person
EXPENSIVE	$36–$60 per person
VERY EXPENSIVE	$61+ per person

QUALITY RATING Beneath each heading appear a quality rating and a value rating. The quality rating is based expressly on the taste, freshness of ingredients, preparation, presentation, and creativity of food served; price is not a consideration. If you are a person who wants the best food available, and cost is not an issue, you need look no further than the quality rating. The quality ratings are defined as:

★★★★★	Exceptional quality
★★★★	Good quality
★★★	Fair quality
★★	Somewhat-subpar quality
★	Subpar quality

VALUE RATING If, on the other hand, you're looking for both quality and value, then you should check the value rating. Value ratings are a function of the overall rating, price rating, and quality rating:

★★★★★	Exceptional value; a real bargain
★★★★	Good value
★★★	Fair value; you get exactly what you pay for
★★	Somewhat overpriced
★	Significantly overpriced

LOCATION Beneath the value rating is an area designation. For ease of use, we divide Las Vegas into seven geographic areas:

• East of Strip	• Downtown	• Mid-Strip and Environs	• North Strip and Environs
• South Strip and Environs	• Southeast Las Vegas–Henderson	• West of Strip	

OUR PICKS FOR THE BEST LAS VEGAS RESTAURANTS

BECAUSE RESTAURANTS OPEN and close all the time in Las Vegas, we try to confine our list to those establishments with a proven track record over a fairly long period of time. Also, the list is highly selective. Exclusion of a particular place doesn't necessarily indicate that the restaurant is bad, only that we felt it wasn't among the best in its genre. Note that some restaurants appear in more than one category.

Continued on page 364

THE BEST LAS VEGAS RESTAURANTS

CUISINE	OVERALL RATING	PRICE	QUALITY RATING	VALUE RATING
AMERICAN				
CARSON KITCHEN	★★★★	Mod/Exp	★★★★	★★★★
HONEY SALT	★★★★	Moderate	★★★★	★★★★
SAGE	★★★½	Very Exp	★★★★½	★★★★
TOP OF THE WORLD	★★★½	Expensive	★★★★½	★★★½
BEER PARK	★★★½	Inexp/Mod	★★★★	★★★★½
PUBLIC HOUSE	★★★½	Moderate	★★★★	★★★★
KITCHEN TABLE	★★★½	Inexp/Mod	★★★★	★★★½
GORDON RAMSAY HELL'S KITCHEN	★★★½	Exp/V. Exp	★★★★	★★½
EAT	★★★½	Inexpensive	★★★½	★★★½
BEAUTY & ESSEX	★★★½	Expensive	★★★	★★★
FAT CHOY´	★★½	Inexpensive	★★★★	★★★★★
HAUTE DOGGERY	★★½	Inexpensive	★★★★	★★★½
GOODWICH	★★	Inexpensive	★★★	★★★½
ASIAN/PACIFIC RIM				
FLOCK & FOWL	★★★★	Inexp/Mod	★★★★½	★★★★★
ANDREA'S	★★★★	Very Exp	★★★★	★★★½
BRAZILIAN				
FOGO DE CHÃO	★★★½	Mod/Exp	★★★★	★★★★
CHINESE				
CHINA MAMA	★★★	Inexpensive	★★★★	★★★★
CHINA POBLANO	★★★	Moderate	★★★★	★★★★
FAT CHOY	★★½	Inexpensive	★★★★	★★★★★
CONTINENTAL/FRENCH				
TWIST BY PIERRE GAGNAIRE	★★★★★	Very Exp	★★★★★	★★★★★
L'ATELIER DE JOËL ROBUCHON	★★★★★	Very Exp	★★★★★	★★★
JOËL ROBUCHON	★★★★★	Very Exp	★★★★★	★★★
RESTAURANT GUY SAVOY	★★★★★	Very Exp	★★★★★	★★★
LE CIRQUE	★★★★½	Very Exp	★★★★½	★★½
PICASSO	★★★★½	Very Exp	★★★★	★★½
BARDOT BRASSERIE	★★★★	Exp/V. Exp	★★★★	★★★★
MARCHÉ BACCHUS: FRENCH BISTRO AND WINE SHOP	★★★★	Moderate	★★★★	★★★★
BOUCHON	★★★½	Expensive	★★★★	★★★★
FLEUR	★★★½	Mod/V. Exp	★★★★	★★★½
MON AMI GABI	★★★½	Mod/Exp	★★★★	★★★½
EASTERN EUROPEAN				
FORTE	★★★	Moderate	★★★	★★★★
ECLECTIC				
SPARROW + WOLF	★★★★½	Expensive	★★★★★	★★★★½
RX BOILER ROOM	★★★½	Exp/V. Exp	★★★★	★★★½
GERMAN				
HOFBRÄUHAUS	★★★	Moderate	★★★½	★★★★

THE BEST LAS VEGAS RESTAURANTS *(continued)*

CUISINE	OVERALL RATING	PRICE	QUALITY RATING	VALUE RATING
GREEK				
ESTIATORIO MILOS	★★★★★	Very Exp	★★★★★	★★★★
ITALIAN				
GIADA	★★★½	Expensive	★★★★	★★½
RAO'S	★★★	Expensive	★★★★	★★
SINATRA	★★★	Expensive	★★★	★★
JAMAICAN/NEW MEXICAN				
DW BISTRO	★★★	Moderate	★★★½	★★★★
JAPANESE *(see also Sushi)*				
YUI EDOMAE SUSHI	★★★★★	Very Exp	★★★★★	★★★
MORIMOTO	★★★★	Very Exp	★★★★★	★★★½
NOBU CAESARS PALACE	★★★★	Very Exp	★★★★★	★★★½
RAKU	★★★★	Moderate	★★★★	★★★★
MIZUMI	★★★★	Very Exp	★★★★	★★★
KYARA	★★★½	Moderate	★★★★	★★★★★
TRATTORIA NAKAMURA-YA	★★★½	Moderate	★★★	★★★
MONTA JAPANESE NOODLE HOUSE	★★½	Inexp	★★★★	★★★★★
MEDITERRANEAN				
CLEO	★★★★	Moderate	★★★½	★★★★★
MEXICAN				
CHINA POBLANO	★★★	Moderate	★★★★	★★★★
PIZZA				
PIZZA ROCK	★★★½	Inexp/Mod	★★★★	★★★
SETTEBELLO	★★★½	Moderate	★★★★	★★★
SEAFOOD				
OTHER MAMA	★★★★	Moderate	★★★★★	★★★★
TODD'S UNIQUE DINING	★★★★	Mod/Exp	★★★★	★★★★
HERRINGBONE	★★★½	Expensive	★★★★	★★★½
EMERIL'S NEW ORLEANS FISH HOUSE	★★★½	Expensive	★★★	★★★
SOUTH AMERICAN				
VIVA LAS AREPAS	★★★½	Inexp	★★★½	★★★★
SOUTHERN				
YARDBIRD SOUTHERN TABLE & BAR	★★★½	Expensive	★★★★½	★★
SPANISH				
PICASSO	★★★★½	Very Exp	★★★★	★★½
JALEO	★★★★	Mod/Exp	★★★★	★★★★
JULIAN SERRANO	★★★★	Expensive	★★★★	★★★★
STEAK				
BAZAAR MEAT	★★★★★	Very Exp	★★★★★	★★★
EDGE STEAKHOUSE	★★★★	Exp/V. Exp	★★★★	★★★★½
TODD'S UNIQUE DINING	★★★★	Mod/Exp	★★★★	★★★★
GORDON RAMSAY STEAK	★★★★	Very Exp	★★★★	★★★½

THE BEST LAS VEGAS RESTAURANTS (continued)

CUISINE	OVERALL RATING	PRICE	QUALITY RATING	VALUE RATING
STEAK (continued)				
OLD HOMESTEAD STEAKHOUSE	★★★★	Very Exp	★★★★	★★★½
PRIME STEAKHOUSE	★★★★	Very Exp	★★★★	★★½
SUSHI (see also Japanese)				
OTHER MAMA	★★★★	Moderate	★★★★★	★★★★
MORIMOTO	★★★★	Very Exp	★★★★★	★★★½
NOBU CAESARS PALACE	★★★★	Very Exp	★★★★★	★★★½
MIZUMI	★★★★	Very Exp	★★★★	★★★
SEN OF JAPAN	★★★½	Mod/Exp	★★★★	★★★½
THAI				
LOTUS OF SIAM	★★★★	Moderate	★★★★	★★½
VIETNAMESE				
THE BLACK SHEEP	★★★★	Mod/Exp	★★★★½	★★★★
VEGETARIAN				
VEGENATION	★★★	Inexp/Mod	★★★	★★★
ROOMS WITH A VIEW				
TOP OF THE WORLD	★★★½	Expensive	★★★★½	★★★½

Continued from page 361

MORE RECOMMENDATIONS

The Best Bakeries

• Bouchon Bakeries 3355 Las Vegas Blvd. S. (The Venetian); ☎ 702-414-6203; bouchonbakery.com. Pastries, cookies, macaroons, breads, and sandwiches at these three Venetian locations offer a taste of Thomas Keller's Bouchon without the formality of a sit-down meal.

• Carlo's Bake Shop 3327 Las Vegas Blvd. S. (The Venetian); ☎ 702-607-2356; venetian .com. People line up before celebrity chef Buddy Valastro's shop opens for the best pick of his cookies, cannoli, and cakes.

• Freed's Bakery 9815 S. Eastern Ave.; ☎ 702-456-7762; freedsbakery.com. This longtime locals' secret has become a tourist attraction, thanks to the success of Food Network's *Vegas Cakes.* But it's still one of the best spots in the valley for a custom wedding cake or a tasty snack—and the only spot we know of where you can take a cake decorating class taught by a real, live TV star.

• Great Buns Bakery 3270 E. Tropicana Ave.; ☎ 702-898-0311; greatbunsbakery.net. This place has both a commercial and a retail business; fragrant rosemary bread, sticky buns, and apple loaf are good choices. More than 400 varieties of breads and pastries are offered.

• Suzuya Pastries and Crêpes 7225 S. Durango Dr.; ☎ 702-432-1990; suzuyapastries .com. Sweet crepes, cakes, and truly original Japanese pastries in a small Westside setting.

• Tsp. Baking Co. 6120 N. Decatur Blvd.; ☎ 702-331-9265; tspbakingcompany.com. Former Retro Bakery partner Kari Garcia is serving the same neighborhood with her mini-cupcakes and signature fairy rolls.

The Best Brewpubs and Gastropubs

• Aces and Ales 3740 S. Nellis Blvd.; ☎ 702-436-7600; acesandales.com. Located just behind Boulder Highway, the original Aces and Ales location has a rotating selection of 50 beers on tap with more than 150 rare and vintage selections in bottles. The second location (2801 N. Tenaya Way, ☎ 702-683-2337) has almost as many, and they both have a great selection of innovative bar food made from scratch.

• Gordon Biersch Brewery Restaurant 3987 Paradise Road (Hughes Center); ☎ 702-312-5247; gordonbiersch.com. This upbeat brewpub has a contemporary menu and surprisingly good food at reasonable prices.

• Hop Nuts Brewing 1120 S. Main St.; ☎ 702-816-5371; hopnutsbrewing.com. Downtown Las Vegas's newest brewery is on a quickly developing stretch of Main Street and has an outdoor patio prime for people-watching.

• Pub 1842 3799 Las Vegas Blvd. S. (The MGM Grand); ☎ 702-891-3922; mgmgrand .com. Try more than 50 beers, craft cocktails, and Michael Mina's take on casual pub fare.

• Public House 3355 Las Vegas Blvd. S. (The Venetian); ☎ 702-407-5310; publichouse lv.com. More than 200 craft brews, including a rotating selection of cask beers, are served alongside French, Canadian, and English cuisine.

• Triple 7 Restaurant and Brewery 200 N. Main St. (Main Street Station); ☎ 702-387-1896; mainstreetcasino.com. Go for the late-night happy hour with bargain beers and food specials.

The Best Delis

• The Bagel Cafe 301 N. Buffalo Dr., Summerlin; ☎ 702-255-3444; thebagelcafelv.com. They actually slice the lox by hand at this popular local deli. The pastry case is filled with traditional Jewish-bakery faves, such as black-and-white cookies and hamantaschen.

• Carnegie Deli at Mirage 3400 Las Vegas Blvd. S.; ☎ 702-791-7371; mirage.com. This outpost of the famous New York deli has the best pastrami and corned-beef sandwiches in town—so big you can barely pick them up with one hand.

• Harrie's Bagelmania 855 E. Twain Ave. (at Swenson); ☎ 702-369-3322; bagelmanialv .com. Breakfast and lunch only. Full-service bagel bakery and deli. The best bagels in the city are baked in this down-at-the-heels café—the only bagels in town with an actual crust. Tuesdays, buy bagels by the dozen at half price.

• Siena Deli 9500 W. Sahara Ave.; ☎ 702-736-8424; sienaitalian.com. Everything here is Italian and homemade. Excellent bread is baked every morning; many of the area's Italian restaurants serve it. For the home cook, the selection of olive oils, tinned tomatoes, and balsamic vinegars is extensive and worthwhile.

• Weiss Deli Restaurant Bakery 2744 N. Green Valley Pkwy., Henderson; ☎ 702-454-0565; restaurantwebx.com/WeissRestaurant/. Home cooking by chef Michael Weiss is just like your Yiddish mama made, including terrific meat loaf, giant matzo balls, and rye bread baked on the premises.

The Best Espresso and Dessert

• The Coffee Bean & Tea Leaf 4550 S. Maryland Pkwy.; ☎ 702-944-5029; coffeebean .com. With many more locations around the city, this is a California-based chain of specialty coffeehouses.

• Coffee Pub 2800 W. Sahara Ave., Ste. 2A; ☎ 702-367-1913. This great breakfast and lunch location serves an imaginative menu.

• Sambalatte Torrefazione 750 Rampart Blvd., Summerlin; ☎ 702-272-2333; samba latte.com. Many call this the best coffee in Vegas. Brazilian Luiz Oliveira sources all his coffee from plantations in Brazil and brews them in various ways: in Japanese siphon pots, in Chemex pots, and individually. His pastries and sandwiches are top-notch too.

The Best Oyster and Clam Bars

• Bouchon 3355 Las Vegas Blvd. S. (The Venetian); ☎ 702-414-6200; bouchonbistro .com/lasvegas. French Laundry chef Thomas Keller sources the highest-quality seafood possible.

• Emeril's New Orleans Fish House 3799 Las Vegas Blvd. S. (MGM Grand); ☎ 702-891-7374; tinyurl.com/emerilsfish. Check out the 2–6 p.m. happy hour, where you can get $11 oyster specials, and don't miss the banana cream pie after you've finished.

• Morels Steakhouse 3225 Las Vegas Blvd. S. (The Palazzo); ☎ 702-607-6333; morelslv .com. On any given day, you'll find at least six varieties of oysters at the iced seafood bar, as well as one of the town's best selections of gourmet cheese.

• Other Mama 3655 S. Durango Dr. (West of Strip); ☎ 702-463-8382; othermamalv .com. Chef Dan Krohmer has mad skills in the kitchen. But he doesn't have to show them off on his rotating selection of oysters, which are delicious all on their own.

• The Oyster Bar 4949 N. Rancho Dr. (Santa Fe Station); ☎ 702-515-4385; santafestation .sclv.com. While fans wait to see how the renovations at Palace Station affect its Oyster Bar, this sister restaurant is keeping people happy in the 'burbs.

• The Oyster Bar 4455 Paradise Road (Hard Rock); ☎ 702-693-5000; hardrockhotel .com. This tiny addition to the Hard Rock's HRH all-suite tower offers all of the gumbos, chowders, and pan roasts you'd expect from a place of this style.

• RM Seafood 3950 Las Vegas Blvd. S. (Mandalay Bay); ☎ 702-632-9300, mandalaybay .com. Try a rotating selection of oysters from around the world from celebrity chef Rick Moonen.

The Best Pizza

• Dom DeMarco's Pizzeria & Bar 9875 W. Charleston Blvd.; ☎ 702-570-7000; domdemarcos.com. This offshoot of Di Fara Pizza in Brooklyn has many devotees. The meatballs and sausage are made on the premises.

• Good Pie 725 S. Las Vegas Blvd.; ☎ 702-844-2700; goodpie.com. Former Evel Pie pizzaiolo Vincent Rotolo offers New York–style round pies as well as Long Island–style square "grandma pies" and rectangular Detroit versions in this relatively new establishment, located next door to the pawn shop featured on TV's *Pawn Stars*.

• Metro Pizza 1395 E. Tropicana Ave.; ☎ 702-736-1955; metropizza.com. This place has fast service and is generous with the cheese. Try the Olde New York with thick-sliced mozzarella, plum tomatoes, and basil on a rich, hearty tomato sauce.

• Naked City Pizza 3240 S. Arville St.; ☎ 702-243-6277; nakedcitylv.com. Former Strip chef Chris Palmeri offers up gooey, square Buffalo, New York–style pizzas with some crazy toppings. He's taken the brand and the product to numerous locations around the valley, but the original location inside a grungy west side dive bar (featured on *Diners, Drive-Ins and Dives*) is still the best.

• Pizza Rock 201 N. Third St. and 2300 Paseo Verde Pkwy. (Green Valley Ranch); ☎ 702-385-0838 and 702-616-2997; pizzarocklasvegas.com. Nine different kinds of pizza are served in a nightclub-style environment.

• Settebello 140 S. Green Valley Pkwy., Henderson, and 9350 W. Sahara Ave., Summerlin; ☎ 702-222-3556 and 702-901-4877; settebello.net. Here, real Neapolitan-style pizzas are cooked in a wood-fired stone oven—and it's the only place in town certified by the group in Naples that oversees authenticity.

Restaurants with a View

- Eiffel Tower Restaurant 3655 Las Vegas Blvd. S. (Paris Las Vegas); ☎ 702-948-6937; tinyurl.com/eiffeltowerlv. Fancy French food is served in a drop-dead-gorgeous setting that towers over the Strip. The spectacular view encompasses the fountains at Bellagio.

- Foundation Room 3950 Las Vegas Blvd. S. (Mandalay Bay); ☎ 702-632-7631; houseofblues.com/lasvegas/fr. This private club and lounge run by the House of Blues has a public restaurant and patios with a great northward view of the Strip.

- Lago 3600 Las Vegas Blvd. S. (Bellagio); ☎ 866-259-7111; bellagio.com. Julian Serrano offers Italian small plates with an outdoor patio overlooking the Bellagio fountains.

- Marche Bacchus 2620 Regatta Drive; ☎ 702-804-8008; marchebacchus.com. This French bistro and wine shop sits on a gorgeous man-made lake in the suburbs.

- Picasso 3600 Las Vegas Blvd. S. (Bellagio); ☎ 702-693-7223; bellagio.com. With highly original food and glorious original artwork by the master himself, this is as good as it gets . . . unless you eat at Le Grand Véfour in the Louvre.

- Rivea 3940 Las Vegas Blvd. S. (Delano); ☎ 702-632-9500; delanolasvegas.com. Alain Ducasse's top-floor small-plates restaurant, featuring dishes from Southern France and Italy, offers a stunning north-facing view of the Strip.

- Top of the World Restaurant 2000 Las Vegas Blvd. S. (Stratosphere); ☎ 702-380-7711; topoftheworldlv.com. This revolving dining room with excellent food has the highest and best views of any of the restaurants in this list.

- VooDoo Steak & Lounge 3700 W. Flamingo Road (Rio); ☎ 702-777-7800; tinyurl .com/voodoosteak. At the top of the Masquerade tower, VooDoo offers a complete view of the city, steaks and French-Creole dishes, and a late-night lounge.

RESTAURANT PROFILES

Andrea's ★★★★

PAN-ASIAN	VERY EXPENSIVE	QUALITY ★★★★	VALUE ★★★½

Wynn Encore Resort, 3131 Las Vegas Blvd. S.; ☎ 702-770-7000; wynnlasvegas.com **MID-STRIP AND ENVIRONS**

Customers Visitors, locals. **Reservations** Essential. **When to go** Anytime. **Entrée range** $22–$148. **Payment** All major credit cards. **Service rating** ★★★★½. **Friendliness rating** ★★★★½. **Parking** Valet, lot. **Bar** Full service. **Wine selection** Excellent. **Dress** Upscale casual. **Disabled access** Yes. **Hours** Sunday–Thursday, 6–10:30 p.m.; Friday and Saturday, 6–11:30 p.m.

SETTING AND ATMOSPHERE The sensuous, color-shifting eyes that flash over the bar at this Asian-fusion restaurant at Wynn Encore belong to Steve Wynn's wife, Andrea. The chic decor by Todd-Avery Lenahan features an airy cream-and-gold space with windows that open to Encore Beach Club. The ceiling is studded with geometric rows of crystal teardrops. It's all quite impressive.

HOUSE SPECIALTIES Chef Joseph Elevado used to cook for Nobu, so don't be surprised to find sashimi, sushi, and loads of Japanese specialties on his menu. Many Asian bases are covered here, though. *Tom kha gai,* a creamy chicken soup with coconut and ginger, is distinctly Thai. One could argue that the chef's whole crispy fish in a tomato-and-egg broth is Filipino.

OTHER RECOMMENDATIONS Sixty-nine bucks may seem a lot for a steak, but chef Elevado does a Snake River Farms filet worth the indulgence. Five-spice garlic

Dining and Nightlife on the South Strip

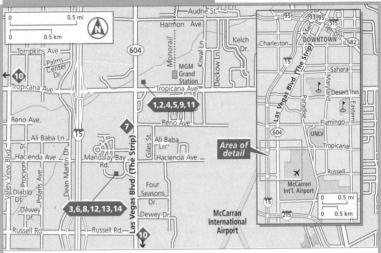

RESTAURANTS
1. L'Atelier de Joël Robuchon
2. Emeril's New Orleans Fish House
3. Fleur
4. Jöel Robuchon
5. Morimoto
6. Rx Boiler Room

Buffets:
7. Buffet at Luxor's
8. Mandalay Bay's Bayside Buffet
9. MGM Grand Buffet
10. Orleans Medley Buffet

NIGHTLIFE
11. Hakkasan
12. House of Blues
13. Light
14. Rí Rá Las Vegas

lobster, served with long beans, is also great, in spite of another hefty price tag. And for reluctant converts to a meat-free diet, try Wynn's exclusive Impossible Burger sliders, the trendy new meat substitute that actually "bleeds" as it cooks.

SUMMARY AND COMMENTS This restaurant may seem redundant because the resort has three other Asian restaurants: **Mizumi** (see pages 391–392), **Wing Lei**, and **Wazuzu**, a sushi-and-noodle house. But because Andrea's targets the nightclub crowd, it seems like a smart addition, as guests can slide effortlessly to Encore Beach Club next door.

L'Atelier de Joël Robuchon ★★★★★

FRENCH	VERY EXPENSIVE	QUALITY ★★★★★	VALUE ★★★

MGM Grand, 3799 Las Vegas Blvd. S.; ☎ 702-891-7358; mgmgrand.com
SOUTH STRIP AND ENVIRONS

Customers Visitors, locals. **Reservations** A must. **When to go** Anytime. **Entrée range** $70–$230. **Payment** All major credit cards. **Service rating** ★★★★½. **Friendliness rating** ★★★. **Parking** Valet, garage. **Bar** Full service. **Wine selection** Excellent. **Dress** Upscale casual. **Disabled access** Yes. **Hours** Daily, 5–10 p.m.

SETTING AND ATMOSPHERE Chef Joël Robuchon's casual concept offers guests a view into his culinary workshop, thanks to an open-air kitchen that dissolves the boundaries between kitchen and dining room. Chic and contemporary, with shades of black and red, L'Atelier is more laid-back than his fine-dining **Joël Robuchon Restaurant** next door (see pages 388–389) and more interactive with the staff, if you sit at the bar around the open kitchen.

HOUSE SPECIALTIES *Caille au* foie gras: tender roast quail stuffed with foie gras and served with Robuchon's famous mashed potatoes, equal parts butter and potato.

OTHER RECOMMENDATIONS To get the full experience, opt for the tasting menu, which changes seasonally and offers L'Atelier's best dishes in a thoughtful progression. Those with theater tickets will find an early-bird menu featuring an appetizer and the roast of the day for $58.

SUMMARY AND COMMENTS L'Atelier is fun—a less buttoned-up way to enjoy fine dining. Dining aficionados will appreciate watching the silent orchestra of chefs and cooks in their element, as well as the care it takes to create one of Robuchon's masterly dishes.

Bardot Brasserie ★★★★

FRENCH	EXPENSIVE/VERY EXPENSIVE	QUALITY ★★★★	VALUE ★★★★

Aria, 3730 Las Vegas Blvd. S.; ☎ 877-230-2742; michaelmina.net
MID-STRIP AND ENVIRONS

Customers Visitors, locals. **Reservations** Recommended. **When to go** Whenever you want to feel transported to classic Paris. **Entrée range** $26–$100. **Payment** All major credit cards. **Service rating** ★★★½. **Friendliness rating** ★★★★. **Parking** Valet, garage. **Bar** Full service. **Wine selection** Good. **Dress** Business casual to formal. **Disabled access** Yes. **Hours** Daily, 5:30–10:30 p.m.; Monday–Friday lunch, 11 a.m.–2:30 p.m.; Saturday and Sunday brunch, 9:30 a.m.–1:30 p.m.

SETTING AND ATMOSPHERE This large, elegant space is meant to transport diners back to Paris of the 1920s. The decor relies heavily on dark wood and glass, with an ornate bar area. The food may be the simplest that celebrity chef Michael Mina has ever attempted in a fine-dining restaurant, relying on impeccably prepared French classics.

HOUSE SPECIALTIES Start with garlicky escargot wrapped in pastry dough, or a beautifully seasoned steak tartare. From there, keep it casual with a classic croque madame, or go more formal with a beautifully baked heritage chicken with mushroom bread pudding.

OTHER RECOMMENDATIONS Mina and his crew get a bit creative with duck wings à l'orange and a decadently rich French onion soup with Périgord truffle, braised oxtail, and a soft poached egg.

SUMMARY AND COMMENTS Mina continues to be one of Las Vegas's most important celebrity chefs because he allows each of his restaurants to take on its own personality. Bardot is just the latest example. And the brunch is among the best in town.

Bazaar Meat ★★★★★

STEAK	VERY EXPENSIVE	QUALITY ★★★★★	VALUE ★★★

The SLS, 2535 Las Vegas Blvd. S.; ☎ 855-761-7757; slsvegas.com
NORTH STRIP AND ENVIRONS

Customers Visitors, locals. **Reservations** Recommended. **When to go** When you want a new twist on a steakhouse. Steaks range $26–$160/lb. **Payment** All major credit cards. **Service rating** ★★★★½. **Friendliness rating** ★★★★. **Parking** Valet, garage. **Bar** Full service. **Wine selection** Extensive. **Dress** Business casual. **Disabled access** Yes. **Hours** Sunday–Thursday, 5:30–10 p.m.; Friday and Saturday, 5:30–11 p.m.

SETTING AND ATMOSPHERE Architect Philippe Starck designed José Andrés's temple to carnivorism to resemble a plush hunting lodge. The walls are adorned with tapestries and alligator heads, and you can sit at a private table or make new friends at either the raw-meat bar or a large communal table in the center of the room.

HOUSE SPECIALTIES Steaks are fantastic, as are the whole suckling pigs carved table-side. But don't miss the chef's avant-garde specialties such as cotton candy foie gras and liquefied olives.

OTHER RECOMMENDATIONS While meats are the star of the show, there's also a great raw-seafood bar, as well as very good vegetable dishes.

SUMMARY AND COMMENTS Much more than a steakhouse, this is a tribute to meat.

Beauty & Essex   ★★★½

AMERICAN	EXPENSIVE	QUALITY	★★★	VALUE	★★★

Cosmopolitan Resort, 3708 Las Vegas Blvd. S.; ☎ 702-737-0707; beautyandessexlv.com   **MID-STRIP AND ENVIRONS**

Customers Visitors, locals, celebrities. **Reservations** Essential. **When to go** Anytime. **Entrée range** $19–$125. **Payment** All major credit cards. **Service rating** ★★★½. **Friendliness rating** ★★★½. **Parking** Valet, lot. **Bar** Full service. **Wine selection** Good. **Dress** Hip casual. **Disabled access** Yes. **Hours** Sunday–Wednesday, 5–11 p.m.; Thursday–Saturday, 5 p.m. –midnight.

SETTING AND ATMOSPHERE Hidden behind a pawn shop that sells rescued antiques, this restaurant has a sexy, trendy, elegant, and hip vibe. Partiers, celebrities, and assorted beautiful people relax in plush booths alongside walls of hanging lockets and beneath a ceiling of strung beads. If a rock star and a supermodel were having an affair, this would be where they'd dine before retiring to their suite.

HOUSE SPECIALTIES Small plates are the order of the day, with an entire section of the menu dedicated to gourmet toasts. For something wild, try the tomato soup dumplings. For something more traditional, the burger will never fail you.

OTHER RECOMMENDATIONS The peanut butter pie sundae is one of the best desserts in Las Vegas.

SUMMARY AND COMMENTS Atmosphere is the selling point here, and it would be hard for any food to match the restaurant's performance in that department. But celebrity chef Chris Santos and his team deliver quality on the plate—probably more than they have to.

Beer Park   ★★★½

AMERICAN	INEXPENSIVE/MODERATE	QUALITY	★★★★	VALUE	★★★★½

Paris Las Vegas, 3655 Las Vegas Blvd. S.; ☎ 702-444-4500; beerpark.com
MID-STRIP AND ENVIRONS

Customers Visitors. **Reservations** No. **When to go** To relax and catch a game. **Entrée range** $8–$26. **Payment** All major credit cards. **Service rating** ★★★★½. **Friendliness rating** ★★★★½. **Parking** Valet, lot. **Bar** Full service. **Wine selection** Excellent. **Dress** Upscale casual. **Disabled access** Yes. **Hours** Sunday–Thursday, 11 a.m.–11 p.m.; Friday and Saturday, 11 a.m.–2 a.m.; closing time varies by season and event.

Dining and Nightlife Mid-Strip

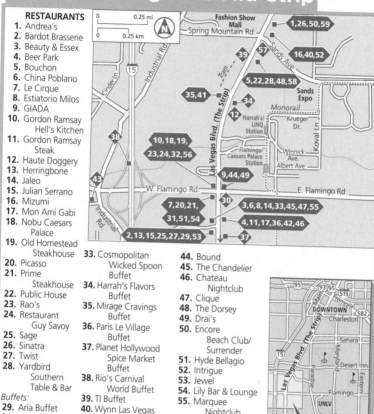

RESTAURANTS
1. Andrea's
2. Bardot Brasserie
3. Beauty & Essex
4. Beer Park
5. Bouchon
6. China Poblano
7. Le Cirque
8. Estiatorio Milos
9. GIADA
10. Gordon Ramsay Hell's Kitchen
11. Gordon Ramsay Steak
12. Haute Doggery
13. Herringbone
14. Jaleo
15. Julian Serrano
16. Mizumi
17. Mon Ami Gabi
18. Nobu Caesars Palace
19. Old Homestead Steakhouse
20. Picasso
21. Prime Steakhouse
22. Public House
23. Rao's
24. Restaurant Guy Savoy
25. Sage
26. Sinatra
27. Twist
28. Yardbird Southern Table & Bar

Buffets:
29. Aria Buffet
30. Bally's Sterling Brunch
31. Bellagio Buffet
32. Caesars Bacchanal Buffet
33. Cosmopolitan Wicked Spoon Buffet
34. Harrah's Flavors Buffet
35. Mirage Cravings Buffet
36. Paris Le Village Buffet
37. Planet Hollywood Spice Market Buffet
38. Rio's Carnival World Buffet
39. TI Buffet
40. Wynn Las Vegas Buffet

NIGHTLIFE
41. 1 Oak
42. Alexxa's Bar
43. Apex Social Club
44. Bound
45. The Chandelier
46. Chateau Nightclub
47. Clique
48. The Dorsey
49. Drai's
50. Encore Beach Club/ Surrender
51. Hyde Bellagio
52. Intrigue
53. Jewel
54. Lily Bar & Lounge
55. Marquee Nightclub and Dayclub
56. Omnia
57. Rosina
58. Tao
59. XS

SETTING AND ATMOSPHERE This second-floor spot with artificial turf flooring, a retractable glass roof, and an outdoor smoker manages to recreate an outdoor picnic in the heart of Las Vegas, right down to the acrylic glassware and china that look exactly like red Solo cups and paper plates. Games are displayed on the numerous TVs, and the picnic tables have built-in beer coolers. You can shoot pool or play shuffleboard, table tennis, or oversize Connect Four and Jenga. And the ledge seating on the Strip side provides an incredible view of the Bellagio fountains.

HOUSE SPECIALTIES Barbecue, brats, and *chile verde* nachos.

Dining and Nightlife on the North Strip

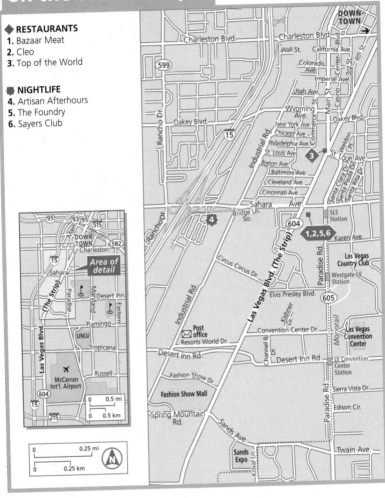

◆ **RESTAURANTS**
1. Bazaar Meat
2. Cleo
3. Top of the World

■ **NIGHTLIFE**
4. Artisan Afterhours
5. The Foundry
6. Sayers Club

OTHER RECOMMENDATIONS The smoked prime rib is the most expensive item on the menu at $26, but it's a bargain for one of the best cuts of beef around that's served a perfect medium-rare (or however you like it) and so tender that you can cut it with a butter knife. And the accompanying crinkle-cut garlic fries with bacon-fat dijonnaise are addictive.

SUMMARY AND COMMENTS Because this venture is a partnership with Budweiser, its products are used to flavor everything from the Shock Top bratwurst to the house hot sauce. Even the smoker uses the brewery's beechwood. But the 100 beers, including 36 taps, aren't limited to Anheuser-Busch products.

The Black Sheep ★★★★

MODERN VIETNAMESE MODERATE/EXPENSIVE QUALITY ★★★★½ VALUE ★★★★

8680 W. Warm Springs Road; ☎ 702-954-3998; blacksheepvegas.com
WEST OF STRIP

Customers Locals. **Reservations** Recommended. **When to go** Casual meal or special occasion. **Entrée range** $15–$32. **Payment** All major credit cards. **Service rating** ★★★★. **Friendliness rating** ★★★★½. **Parking** Lot. **Bar** Full service. **Wine selection** Very good. **Dress** Casual. **Disabled access** Yes. **Hours** Daily, 5–10 p.m.

SETTING AND ATMOSPHERE A small, nicely decorated, single-room dining room in a suburban strip mall.

HOUSE SPECIALTIES Bao sliders of house-recipe pork sausage, pan-seared salmon with forbidden rice, slow-cooked short rib with polenta.

OTHER RECOMMENDATIONS The whole rainbow trout doesn't get a lot of attention here, but the preparation in a ginger and rice wine vinegar sauce is one of the most original things on the menu.

SUMMARY AND COMMENTS Chef Jamie Tran learned her fine French technique in high-end restaurants such as Aureole and Daniel Boulud's now-closed Venetian brasserie before applying it to the recipes she learned from her Vietnamese family. The result is meticulously prepared Asian comfort food.

Bouchon ★★★½

FRENCH BISTRO EXPENSIVE QUALITY ★★★★ VALUE ★★★★

The Venetian, 3355 Las Vegas Blvd. S.; ☎ 702-414-6200;
bouchonbistro.com/lasvegas **MID-STRIP AND ENVIRONS**

Customers Visitors, locals. **Reservations** A must on weekends. **When to go** Anytime. **Entrée range** $19–$59. **Payment** All major credit cards. **Service rating** ★★★★½. **Friendliness rating** ★★★★½. **Parking** Valet, garage. **Bar** Full service. **Wine selection** Very good. **Dress** Upscale casual. **Disabled access** Yes (elevator). **Hours** Daily, 7 a.m.–1 p.m. and 5–10 p.m.; Friday–Sunday brunch, 7 a.m.–2 p.m.; Oyster Bar and Lounge, 3–10 p.m.

SETTING AND ATMOSPHERE Chef-owner Thomas Keller and renowned restaurant and hotel designer Adam Tihany have created a Belle Époque room filled with ornate floor tiles and brass. You could easily be on a Paris boulevard.

HOUSE SPECIALTIES Fresh seafood *plateaus*—grand plates with an assortment of freshly shucked raw items and shrimp and lobster; superb oysters (selection changes seasonally); country pâté served with cornichons and radishes; roast leg of lamb with flageolet beans in thyme jus.

OTHER RECOMMENDATIONS Salmon rillettes in a glass jar; herb-roasted flat-iron steak or grilled New York strip with fries; endive salad with Roquefort, apples, walnuts, and walnut vinaigrette; white sausage with potato purée and caramelized apples.

SUMMARY AND COMMENTS The most requested tables are on the outdoor terrace; they're difficult to get but worth a try. Many à la carte options are available at a moderate cost.

Carson Kitchen ★★★★

COMFORT FOOD MODERATE/EXPENSIVE QUALITY ★★★★ VALUE ★★★★

124 S. Sixth St.; ☎ 702-473-9523; carsonkitchen.com **DOWNTOWN**

Customers Visitors, locals. **Reservations** Recommended. **When to go** When you want the best that trendy Downtown has to offer. Small plates and sandwiches range $9–$20. **Payment** All major credit cards. **Service rating** ★★★½. **Friendliness rating** ★★★★. **Parking** Street. **Bar** Full service. **Wine selection** Small but varied. **Dress** Casual. **Disabled access** Yes. **Hours** Sunday–Wednesday, 11:30 a.m.–10 p.m., Thursday–Saturday, 11:30 a.m.–11 p.m.

SETTING AND ATMOSPHERE While the technical address is Sixth Street, the final restaurant that local hero Kerry Simon created before his untimely death is actually on Carson Avenue, along Downtown's hottest restaurant row. The vibe is casual, urban, and funky, with the chefs cooking in an exposed kitchen and the young, beautiful staff wearing rock-and-roll T-shirts. The rooftop patio and outside courtyard are top spots for hanging out in nice weather.

HOUSE SPECIALTIES Comfort food is given a gourmet twist in dishes like Coca-Espresso New York strip and fried chicken skins with smoked honey.

OTHER RECOMMENDATIONS Don't miss the bacon jam with Brie.

SUMMARY AND COMMENTS If you're going to tour Downtown—and you really should—this is the go-to spot for lunch or dinner.

China Mama ★★★

CHINESE	INEXPENSIVE	QUALITY ★★★★	VALUE ★★★★

3420 S. Jones Blvd.; ☎ 702-873-1977; chinamamavegas.com **WEST OF STRIP**

Customers Locals. **Reservations** Accepted. **When to go** Anytime. **Entrée range** $11–$29. **Payment** All major credit cards. **Service rating** ★★★. **Friendliness rating** ★★★★½. **Parking** Lot. **Bar** No. **Wine selection** None. **Dress** Casual. **Disabled access** Yes. **Hours** Daily, 11 a.m.–9:30 p.m.

SETTING AND ATMOSPHERE Just off the main drag of Las Vegas's Chinatown, China Mama is bright and welcoming.

HOUSE SPECIALTIES Shanghai soup dumplings (called juicy pork dumplings on the menu) are dough-wrapped pockets of meat with steaming soup in the middle. Carefully bite off the top, slurp out the delicious, savory broth, and then add a bit of the Chinese black vinegar and ginger that accompanies the dish. Pot stickers are also done very well.

OTHER RECOMMENDATIONS The beef roll; fish filet poached in a fiery red-chile oil and served in a giant clay pot—perfect with a bowl of rice.

SUMMARY AND COMMENTS Most dishes here have authentic flavors you won't find in most other American Chinese restaurants. The Shanghai soup dumplings—ubiquitous in Asia—are finally done right here.

China Poblano ★★★

CHINESE/MEXICAN	MODERATE	QUALITY ★★★★	VALUE ★★★★

The Cosmopolitan, 3708 Las Vegas Blvd. S.; ☎ 702-698-7000; chinapoblano.com **MID-STRIP AND ENVIRONS**

Customers Locals, hotel guests, conventioneers. **Reservations** Accepted. **When to go** Anytime. **Entrée range** $3.95–$45. **Payment** All major credit cards. **Service rating** ★★★★½. **Friendliness rating** ★★★★½. **Parking** Valet, garage. **Bar** Full service. **Wine selection** Fair. **Dress** Casual. **Disabled access** Yes. **Hours** Sunday–Thursday, 11:30 a.m.–11 p.m.; Friday and Saturday, 11:30 a.m.–11:30 p.m.

SETTING AND ATMOSPHERE Ultramodern, almost wacky decor features communal benches, conceptual art with Asian themes, and wall-mounted LCD

Dining East of Strip

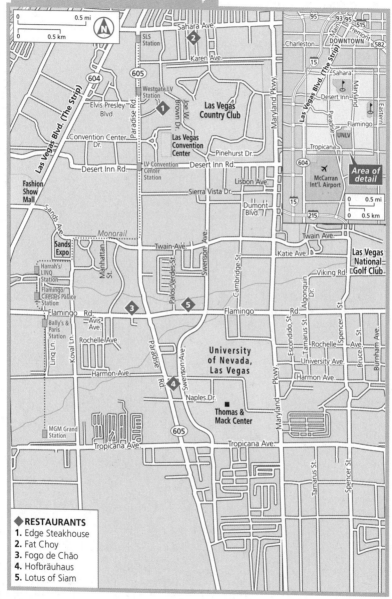

◆ RESTAURANTS
1. Edge Steakhouse
2. Fat Choy
3. Fogo de Chão
4. Hofbräuhaus
5. Lotus of Siam

Dining West of Strip

◆ **DINING**
1. The Black Sheep
2. China MaMa
3. DW Bistro
4. Forte

5. Honey Salt
6. Kyara
7. Marché Bacchus:
   French Bistro
   and Wine Shop

8. Monta
9. Other Mama
10. Raku
11. Sen of Japan
12. Settebello

13. Sparrow + Wolf
14. Trattoria
    Nakamura-ya
15. Yui Edomae Sushi

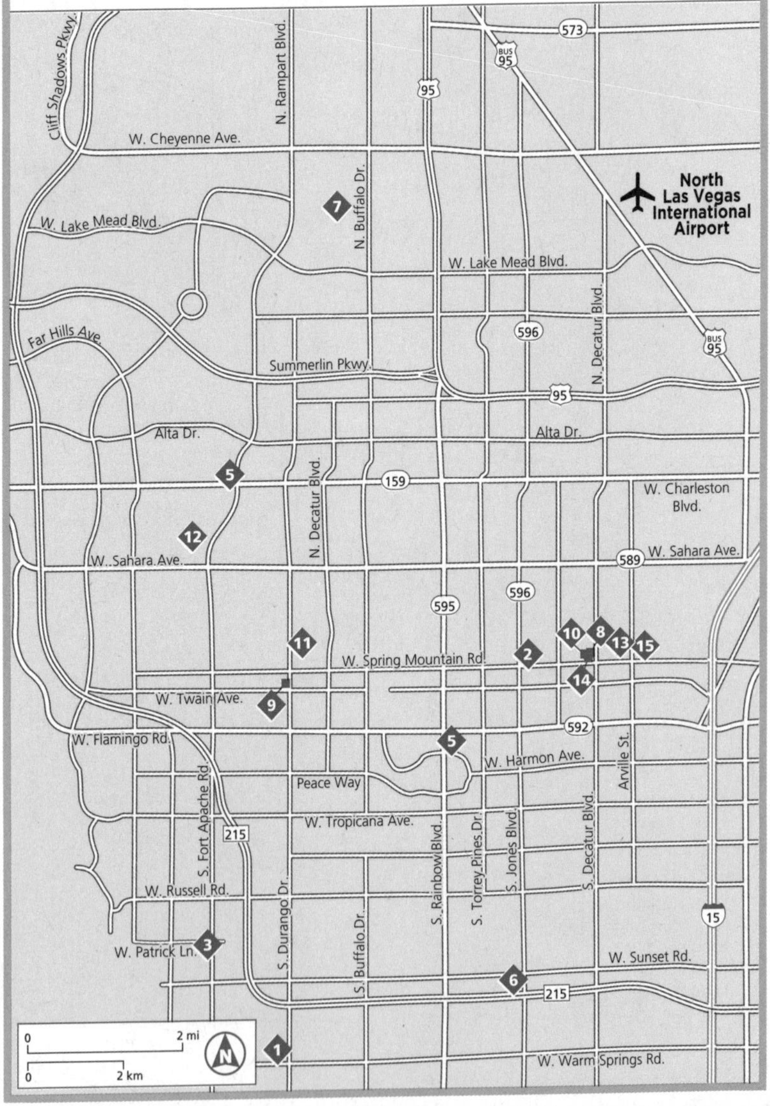

panels streaming head shots of famous Asians. There are separate noodle and tortilla bars.

HOUSE SPECIALTIES Hand-rolled noodles with *dan dan* sauce; made-to-order dim sum; crispy quail; tacos such as the Cochinita (Yucatán-style barbecued pork) and the evocatively named Silencio (duck tongue with lychee); various rice plates; seaweed salad; conceptual desserts such as chocolate-enrobed statues representing the famed terra-cotta warriors of Xi'an, China, filled with peanut butter–chocolate mousse.

OTHER RECOMMENDATIONS The rolled pancakes with beef and onions are wonderful, as are a number of oddball China-meets-Mexico dishes that you'll have to see (and try) to understand.

SUMMARY AND COMMENTS This is a groundbreaking restaurant in terms of creativity, with a concept new to the planet. Chef José Andrés is a wonder, and so are these prices. This has to be the least expensive place to eat in the entire Cosmopolitan.

Le Cirque ★★★★½

FRENCH	VERY EXPENSIVE	QUALITY	★★★★½	VALUE	★★½

Bellagio, 3600 Las Vegas Blvd. S.; ☎ 702-693-7223; bellagio.com
MID-STRIP AND ENVIRONS

Customers Visitors, locals. **Reservations** A must. **When to go** Special occasion. **Entrée range** Prix-fixe menus, $72–$350. **Payment** All major credit cards. **Service rating** ★★★★½. **Friendliness rating** ★★★★½. **Parking** Valet, garage. **Bar** Full service. **Wine selection** Excellent. **Dress** Upscale. **Disabled access** Yes. **Hours** Tuesday--Sunday, 5–10 p.m.

SETTING AND ATMOSPHERE Designer Adam Tihany built this room to resemble a circus tent; the theme even extends to the plates with frolicking monkeys. But despite those playful touches, this is one of the most elegant dining experiences in town. And the view of the Bellagio fountains is amazing.

HOUSE SPECIALTIES Selections on all of the 3-course, 5-course, and 10-course menus change seasonally. One classic, dating to the original New York location, is Mediterranean sea bass encrusted in potatoes. A more-modern classic you won't want to miss is the gold-crusted quail stuffed with foie gras.

SUMMARY AND COMMENTS Many expected this restaurant, which has been a shining star since it opened, to drop off when the Maccioni family decided to forgo hands-on operation. But it's as good today as it ever was, thanks in no small part to the creativity of young new chef Wilfried Bergerhausen.

Cleo ★★★★

MEDITERRANEAN	MODERATE	QUALITY	★★★½	VALUE	★★★★★

SLS Resort, 2535 Las Vegas Blvd. S.; ☎ 702-761-7612; slsvegas.com
NORTH STRIP AND ENVIRONS

Customers Visitors. **Reservations** Recommended. **When to go** Anytime. **Entrée range** $10–$22. **Payment** All major credit cards. **Service rating** ★★★. **Friendliness rating** ★★★★½. **Parking** Valet, lot. **Bar** Full service. **Wine selection** Very good. **Dress** Upscale casual. **Disabled access** Yes. **Hours** Sunday, Monday, and Thursday, 5–10:30 p.m.; Friday and Saturday, 5–11 p.m.

SETTING AND ATMOSPHERE Named after Cleopatra, the restaurant offers both a casual and a more formal area. White Lebanese crystal-style chandeliers hang from the ceiling, while books, photos, and other antiquities line shelves along the walls throughout. Up front, sit at the counter (lined with herbs and spices) that surrounds the central open kitchen. Or ask for a table or plush booth in the back of the restaurant for something a bit more serious.

HOUSE SPECIALTIES The mezes are great for creating a meal of shared small plates with friends. Highlights include a nice selection of dips, dolmas (stuffed grape leaves), and sausages.

OTHER RECOMMENDATIONS If you want a full entrée, you can't go wrong with the lamb tagine.

SUMMARY AND COMMENTS If you're celebrating something, tell your waiter and he'll get the entire restaurant to clap for you and yell "Opa!" as you smash a plate on the floor.

DW Bistro ★★★

JAMAICAN/NEW MEXICAN   **MODERATE**   **QUALITY ★★★½**   **VALUE ★★★★**

9275 W. Russell Road (The Gramercy); ☎ 702-527-5200; dwbistro.com
WEST OF STRIP

Customers Locals. **Reservations** Recommended for weekend brunch. **When to go** Anytime. **Entrée range** $10–$26. **Payment** All major credit cards. **Service rating** ★★★. **Friendliness rating** ★★★★½. **Parking** Lot. **Bar** Full service. **Wine selection** Average. **Disabled access** Yes. **Dress** Casual. **Hours** Tuesday–Thursday, 11 a.m.–9 p.m.; Friday, 11 a.m.–10 p.m.; Saturday, 10 a.m.–10 p.m.; Sunday, 10 a.m.–4 p.m.

SETTING AND ATMOSPHERE The new location is a single open room with minimal modern decor and a bar in front.

HOUSE SPECIALTIES Two separate cuisines, those of Jamaica and New Mexico, are done expertly here, but it would be wrong to think of this as a fusion restaurant. A bowl of killer red New Mexican slow-cooked pork contrasts with a terrific Jamaican chicken-curry soup, which brims with chopped chicken.

OTHER RECOMMENDATIONS Come for weekend brunch; the jerk pork hash is one of the most compelling dishes in the city. From the more upscale dinner menu, try an irresistible plate of the jerk lamb chops.

SUMMARY AND COMMENTS This place has become a de facto social club for locals, who gather at the bar several times a week. Incidentally, desserts, such as a Jamaican carrot cake, are the bomb.

Eat ★★★½

AMERICAN   **INEXPENSIVE**   **QUALITY ★★★½**   **VALUE ★★★½**

707 Carson Ave.; ☎ 702-534-1515; eatdtlv.com **DOWNTOWN**

Customers Locals. **Reservations** Suggested. **When to go** Anytime. **Entrée range** $5–$15. **Payment** All major credit cards. **Service rating** ★★★. **Friendliness rating** ★★★★. **Parking** Street. **Bar** No. **Wine selection** None. **Dress** Casual. **Disabled access** None. **Hours** Monday–Friday, 8 a.m.–3 p.m.; Saturday and Sunday, 8 a.m.–2 p.m.

SETTING AND ATMOSPHERE Natalie Young's joint makes a big statement in a small space. Reclaimed furniture, such as orange metal chairs and green banquettes, blends well with a deconstructed duct ceiling and a dark cement floor. It can get noisy at lunch, but somehow it manages to be relaxing.

HOUSE SPECIALTIES The ticket here is American comfort food—anything from the best hotcakes in the city to the occasional fried-chicken special that chef Nat, as her friends call her, serves from time to time. Young also makes lots of

Dining and Nightlife Downtown

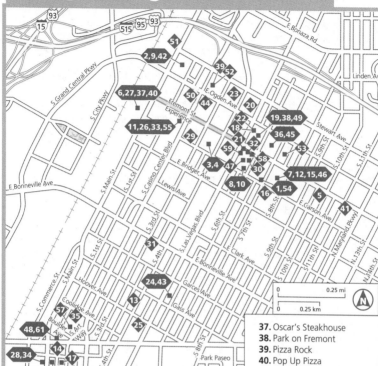

◆ **RESTAURANTS**
1. 7th & Carson
2. Aloha Specialties
3. American Coney Island
4. Andiamo Steakhouse
5. Atomic Kitchen
6. Beer Garden
7. Big Ern's BBQ
8. Bocho
9. California Noodle House
10. Carson Kitchen
11. Chart House
12. Cheffini's Hot Dogs
13. Chicago Joe's
14. Cornish Pasty Co.
15. Downtown Terrace
16. Eat
17. Esther's Kitchen
18. Eureka!
19. Evel Pie
20. Fiddlestix
21. Flippin Good Burgers & Shakes
22. Flock & Fowl
23. Freedom Beat
24. Good Pie
25. Goodwich
26. Grotto
27. Hash House A Go Go
28. Hop Nuts Brewing
29. Hugo's Cellar
30. La Comida
31. Le Pho
32. Le Thai
33. Lillie's Asian Cuisine
34. Makers & Finders
35. Mingo Kitchen & Lounge
36. Naked City Pizza
37. Oscar's Steakhouse
38. Park on Fremont
39. Pizza Rock
40. Pop Up Pizza
41. PublicUs
42. Redwood Steakhouse
43. Rick's Rollin Smoke Barbeque
44. Second Street Grill
45. Siegel's 1941
46. Simply Pure
47. The Smashed Pig
48. Tacos Huevos
49. Therapy
50. Top of Binion's Steakhouse
51. Triple 7
52. Triple George Grill
53. Turmeric
54. VegeNation
55. Vic & Anthony's
56. Viva Las Arepas

🌸 **NIGHTLIFE**
57. Artifice
58. Commonwealth
59. Downtown Cocktail Room
60. Jammyland
61. Urban Lounge

homey soups, salads, and sandwiches, but surprisingly, no burger. You'll dream about her mustard seed–driven potato salad, one of the best anywhere.

OTHER RECOMMENDATIONS For early risers, Young's breakfasts are even better than her lunches. Try the shrimp and grits, golden-brown omelets, and *huevos motuleños*. Her posole soup at lunch is a legend, and she makes a variety of terrific grilled-cheese sandwiches to console those who come in looking for burgers.

SUMMARY AND COMMENTS Eat is a large part of the Downtown eating renaissance. Young had many fans when she cooked at P.J. Clarke's at Caesars, and she is clearly happy in her new digs, which have become a regular breakfast and lunch hangout for Downtown office workers, lawyers, and city officials. This is, to put it simply, down-home fare at its best. A second location opened in Summerlin in summer 2017.

Edge Steakhouse ★★★★

STEAK   EXPENSIVE/VERY EXPENSIVE   QUALITY ★★★★   VALUE ★★★★½

Westgate, 3000 Paradise Road; ☎ 702-550-0850; westgatedestinations.com   **EAST OF STRIP**

Customers Conventioneers, locals. **Reservations** Recommended. **When to go** For a steak or an unexpected fine-dining treat. **Entrée range** $30–$105. **Payment** All major credit cards. **Service rating** ★★★★½. **Friendliness rating** ★★★★½. **Parking** Valet, lot. **Bar** Full service. **Wine selection** Good. **Dress** Upscale casual. **Disabled access** Yes. **Hours** Tuesday–Saturday, opens at 5 p.m.

SETTING AND ATMOSPHERE The circular, classical-meets-modern main dining room is surprisingly upscale for this lower-budget convention center–adjacent casino, with marble columns and a hip chandelier. Even the old Elvis artwork, a nod to the building's onetime resident performer, is given a gilded upgrade by housing it behind intricate gold frames. But the entrance bar is downright modern and sleek.

HOUSE SPECIALTIES This is, at its heart, a steakhouse, so the beef here is top-of-the-line. But up-and-coming chef Steve Young trained at Robuchon, and he's always looking to show off his globally influenced gourmet chops. So pay special attention to the appetizers and pastas, where surprises can be found.

OTHER RECOMMENDATIONS Don't overlook the beef Wellington, an out-of-place classic that gives Gordon Ramsay's interpretation a run for its money.

SUMMARY AND COMMENTS There aren't a lot of well-kept secrets in Las Vegas casinos, but chef Steve is still on that very short list. That won't last, and it's only a matter of time before serious foodies begin competing with convention crowds for a table here. Now's your chance to be ahead of the curve.

Emeril's New Orleans Fish House ★★★½

SEAFOOD/NEW ORLEANS   EXPENSIVE   QUALITY ★★★   VALUE ★★★

MGM Grand, 3799 Las Vegas Blvd. S.; ☎ 702-891-7374; mgmgrand.com
SOUTH STRIP AND ENVIRONS

Customers Visitors, locals. **Reservations** Always. **When to go** Avoid convention times. **Entrée range** $26–$55. **Payment** All major credit cards. **Service rating** ★★★★½. **Friendliness rating** ★★★★½. **Parking** Valet, lot, garage. **Bar** Full service. **Wine selection** Excellent. **Dress** Upscale casual; no sleeveless shirts for men. **Disabled access** Yes, through casino. **Hours** Daily, 11:30 a.m.–10 p.m.; happy hour daily 2–6 p.m. and 9:30–10 p.m.

SETTING AND ATMOSPHERE "A bit of New Orleans" is how Emeril Lagasse describes his beautiful restaurant. The main room is comfortable and handsome, with fine appointments and accessories. And a recent remodel has returned the famed raw bar in front, perfect for casual snacking.

HOUSE SPECIALTIES The always-changing tasting dinners at the chef's table are a fine way to sample small portions of many dishes; some are special recipes being considered for the menu. Emeril's New Orleans–style barbecue shrimp is delicious. You can rely on the good gumbos, the fresh Gulf oysters, and the banana cream pie, which is the best anywhere. Emeril's homemade Worcestershire sauce is addictively good.

SUMMARY AND COMMENTS Emeril's trades heavily on the celebrity of the chef, but you have about a one-in-a-hundred chance of seeing Emeril. The faithful don't seem to care.

Estiatorio Milos ★★★★★

GREEK	VERY EXPENSIVE	QUALITY ★★★★★	VALUE ★★★★

The Cosmopolitan, 3708 Las Vegas Blvd. S.; ☎ 702-698-7000; milos.ca/restaurants/las-vegas **MID-STRIP AND ENVIRONS**

Customers Visitors, locals. **Reservations** Always. **When to go** Avoid convention times. **Entrée range** $22–$141. **Payment** All major credit cards. **Service rating** ★★★★½. **Friendliness rating** ★★★★½. **Parking** Valet, garage. **Bar** Full service. **Wine selection** Excellent. **Dress** Upscale casual. **Disabled access** Yes. **Hours** Daily, noon–3:30 p.m.; Sunday–Thursday, 4–11 p.m.; Friday and Saturday, 4 p.m.–midnight.

SETTING AND ATMOSPHERE A dramatic, classically designed room filled with Greek urns and stonework. There is a classy bar area toward the front and a patio with Strip-facing views in the rear. Diners visit the fish market next to the open kitchen, where they choose the fresh live seafood they will eat for dinner.

HOUSE SPECIALTIES Milos flies in fresh seafood daily from the Aegean, as do sibling Milos restaurants in New York City, Miami, and Montreal. Standouts include octopus, red mullet, Aegean sea bass, and a host of other fish. All are prepared simply and impeccably in the classic Greek manner.

OTHER RECOMMENDATIONS If you've never tasted a proper avgolemono, Greece's egg-lemon soup, Milos's is a must, made with jasmine rice, organic eggs, Meyer lemon, and capon broth. Meat dishes, such as lamb chops grilled with oregano and garlic, are also superb. Desserts, such as the Greek yogurt with walnuts and thyme honey or the textbook baklava, are simple but satisfying.

SUMMARY AND COMMENTS Upon opening, Milos instantly rocketed to cult status in Vegas; it was the first high-end Greek restaurant in town, and one of the best in the country. Owner Costas Spiliadis is proud of his product, and rightly so. This is a not-to-be-missed experience, and the $29 three-course lunch, offered weekdays, is an amazing deal.

Fat Choy ★★½

ASIAN-AMERICAN	INEXPENSIVE	QUALITY ★★★★	VALUE ★★★★★

Eureka Casino, 595 E. Sahara Ave.; ☎ 702-794-0829; fatchoylv.com
EAST OF STRIP

Customers The Downtown crowd. **Reservations** No. **When to go** Anytime. **Entrée range** $8–$15. **Payment** All major credit cards. **Service rating** ★★★★½. **Friendliness rating** ★★★★½. **Parking** Lot. **Bar** Full service. **Wine selection** Minimal.

Dress Casual. **Disabled access** Yes. **Hours** Monday–Thursday, 11 a.m.–10 p.m.; Friday and Saturday, 11 a.m.–midnight; Sunday brunch, 9 a.m.–10 p.m.

SETTING AND ATMOSPHERE Formerly a coffee shop in a low-rent casino, Fat Choy has been nicely renovated—but it still feels a bit like a coffee shop in a low-rent casino.

HOUSE SPECIALTIES Any of the three *bao* sandwiches: Peking duck, pork belly, or tofu and mushroom; short rib grilled-cheese sandwich; Fat Choy burger.

OTHER RECOMMENDATIONS Duck rice; sesame noodles.

SUMMARY AND COMMENTS Chef Sheridan Su worked at Joël Robuchon and the late Comme Ça on the Strip before striking out on his own, and he was later featured in *The New York Times* for selling *bao* in the lobby of a hair salon. Locals love both of his current restaurants, the other being **Flock & Fowl** (see below). Fat Choy has a larger menu that mixes up his signature Asian fare with a few basic American sandwiches for longtime Eureka customers.

Fleur ★★★½

TAPAS/FRENCH MODERATE/VERY EXPENSIVE	QUALITY ★★★★	VALUE ★★★½

Mandalay Bay, 3950 Las Vegas Blvd. S.; ☎ 702-362-9400; mandalaybay.com
SOUTH STRIP AND ENVIRONS

Customers Tourists, conventioneers. **Reservations** Essential. **When to go** Anytime. **Entrée range** $9–$95. **Payment** All major credit cards. **Service rating** ★★★★½. **Friendliness rating** ★★★½. **Parking** Valet, lot, or garage. **Bar** Full service. **Wine selection** Excellent, eclectic list. **Dress** Casual. **Disabled access** Yes. **Hours** Monday–Thursday, 11 a.m.–10 p.m.; Friday–Sunday, 11 a.m.–10:30 p.m.

SETTING AND ATMOSPHERE A large bar area with patio tables protrudes out onto the Mandalay Bay pedestrian walkway area. The intimate dining room features leather chairs and banquettes and lamps that look like sea anemones.

HOUSE SPECIALTIES Celebrity chef Hubert Keller is a creative force, serving ahi tuna tacos, white onion soup velouté, clams and white beans, and spicy Thai chicken wings on a menu that features small plates from four different countries, plus several full entrées and a nice selection of steaks.

OTHER RECOMMENDATIONS The bartenders and the pastry chef like to use liquid nitrogen here to make frozen treats. Make sure to check out some of them.

SUMMARY AND COMMENTS Keller's through doing fancy-schmancy food in Vegas. This is the man who launched the burger craze with Burger Bar, and in spite of his classical French training, he remains terminally hip.

Flock & Fowl Downtown ★★★★

ASIAN INEXPENSIVE/MODERATE	QUALITY ★★★★½	VALUE ★★★★

150 N. Las Vegas Blvd.; ☎ 702-272-2222; flockandfowl.com **DOWNTOWN**

Customers Locals, tourists, serious foodies, off-duty chefs. **Reservations** Yes. **When to go** Dinner or weekend brunch. **Entrée range** $10–$26. **Payment** All major credit cards. **Service rating** ★★★★½. **Friendliness rating** ★★★★★. **Parking** Lot. **Bar** Full with excellent cocktail program. **Dress** Casual. **Disabled access** Yes. **Hours** Monday–Thursday, 5–11 p.m.; Friday, 5 p.m.–1 a.m.; Saturday, 11 a.m.–1 a.m.; Sunday, 11 a.m.–11 p.m.

SETTING AND ATMOSPHERE Hip and modern in the coolest condo tower in town, The Ogden.

HOUSE SPECIALTIES While the menu has expanded since they opened this more upscale location, the dish that earned chef Sheridan Su James Beard Foundation recognition at the original spot is still the dish to get: Hainanese chicken rice. It combines chicken-flavored rice, marinated cucumbers, mustard greens, a trio of house-made sauces, and your choice of chicken. Skip the tenders and resist the temptation of the roasted spring chicken: The poached and deboned Mary's Free Range bird is the way to go.

OTHER RECOMMENDATIONS Salt and pepper chicken wings and bang bang chicken noodle salad (if you like spicy food).

SUMMARY AND COMMENTS Locals love all of chef Sheridan Su's current restaurants. Be sure to check out page 358 in our "Hole in the Wall" section and pages 381–382 for his other restaurant, Fat Choy.

Fogo de Chão ★★★½

BRAZILIAN **MODERATE/EXPENSIVE** **QUALITY** ★★★★ **VALUE** ★★★★

360 E. Flamingo Road; ☎ 702-431-4500; fogodechao.com **EAST OF STRIP**

Customers Visitors, locals. **Reservations** Essential. **When to go** Lunch or dinner. **Entrée range** $27–$55. **Payment** All major credit cards. **Service rating** ★★★. **Friendliness rating** ★★★★. **Parking** Lot. **Bar** Full service. **Wine selection** Excellent. **Dress** Casual. **Disabled access** Yes. **Hours** Daily, 11:30 a.m.–2 p.m.; Monday–Thursday, 5–10 p.m.; Friday, 5–10:30 p.m.; Saturday, 2–10:30 p.m.; Sunday, 2–9 p.m.

SETTING AND ATMOSPHERE This is an enormous place, with plush booths, amber chandeliers, nine private dining rooms, and an abundance of wood. Walls are decorated with color-splashed murals. Wines are kept in a glass cellar visible from the floor of the dining room. The room's centerpiece is a giant salad bar stocked with everything from homemade chicken salad and fresh mozzarella to asparagus and sun-dried tomatoes.

HOUSE SPECIALTIES This is, in our opinion, the best place in Las Vegas to experience churrasco, or Brazilian-style barbecue—in this case, 15 cuts cooked on a fire and sliced table-side from skewers by a team of gauchos (their term for food servers). You'll also be plied with hot cheese rolls, sort of mini-popovers that are insidiously seductive. Save room for the meat, though.

OTHER RECOMMENDATIONS We don't have room to describe all the meats, but each is well seasoned, and many are crusted with garlic, pepper, salt, and other spices. *Picanha*, prime sirloin, is the real house specialty. *Costela de porco* are pork ribs, and the *frango*, or chicken, which comes in the form of moist leg meat or bacon-wrapped breasts, is amazing.

SUMMARY AND COMMENTS They want you to fill up on side dishes such as black beans, rice, and mashed potatoes, as well as *farofa*, the fried cassava flour that Brazilians religiously sprinkle on everything. Don't be sucked in. If you come at lunch, the feast is $18 less than dinner.

Forte ★★★

TAPAS/EASTERN EUROPEAN **MODERATE** **QUALITY** ★★★ **VALUE** ★★★★

4180 S. Rainbow Blvd.; ☎ 702-220-3876; barforte.com **WEST OF STRIP**

Customers Visitors, locals. **Reservations** Not necessary. **When to go** Anytime. **Entrée range** $7–$22. **Payment** All major credit cards. **Service rating** ★★★½. **Friendliness rating** ★★★★. **Parking** Lot. **Bar** Full service. **Wine selection** Fair. **Dress** Casual. **Disabled access** Yes. **Hours** Monday, 5–10 p.m.; Tuesday–Saturday, 11 a.m.–10 p.m.

SETTING AND ATMOSPHERE This small neighborhood restaurant has moderate furnishings and funky paintings on the walls.

HOUSE SPECIALTIES While Forte bills itself as a tapas restaurant and has a nice selection of Spanish small plates, what draws fans from across the valley is the Eastern European menu. Bulgarian charcuterie and egg come in a clay pot; dumplings include the potato variety, *vareniki*, served with fried onions, and Russian beef pelmeni, sprinkled with fresh dill and sour cream.

OTHER RECOMMENDATIONS Don't miss the *ajarski khachapuri:* a traditional Georgian bread boat filled with two types of pickled cheese and a cracked egg. And check out the imported caviar and ham selections offered exclusively at the bar, as well as the casual breakfast and lunch menu.

SUMMARY AND COMMENTS Forte is a family-run operation unlike anything else in Las Vegas, which has made it a favorite of expatriates from Eastern Europe and many other serious foodies.

GIADA ★★★½

ITALIAN	EXPENSIVE	QUALITY	★★★★	VALUE	★★½

The Cromwell, 3595 Las Vegas Blvd. S.; ☎ 877-735-5690; caesars.com/cromwell **MID-STRIP AND ENVIRONS**

Customers Visitors, locals, Food Network viewers. **Reservations** Very highly recommended. **When to go** Business dinners or family meals. **Entrée range** $25–$83. **Payment** All major credit cards. **Service rating** ★★½. **Friendliness rating** ★★★½. **Parking** Valet, garage. **Bar** Full service. **Wine selection** Excellent. **Dress** Business casual. **Disabled access** Yes. **Hours** Friday–Sunday, 9 a.m.–3 p.m.; Monday–Thursday, 5–10:30 p.m.; Friday–Sunday, 5–10:45 p.m.

SETTING AND ATMOSPHERE Food Network star Giada De Laurentiis conceived this restaurant to make guests feel like they were in her home. An open antipasto bar is the first thing you see. Movie posters from the films of her grandfather Dino De Laurentiis line the walls. And the wraparound windows (which can be opened in nice weather) offer one of the best views in town of the Strip.

HOUSE SPECIALTIES The restaurant is known for the star's take on family-style Italian cooking. It's easy to share a bunch of small plates—which range from cured meats, cheeses, and crostini to small pizzas—with a large group. Or grab something larger, like a chicken cacciatore for two carved table-side. Either way, don't be deceived by small price tags, which add up quickly thanks to similarly small portions.

OTHER RECOMMENDATIONS To truly sample the full range of GIADA's offerings, ask about the four-course tasting menu.

SUMMARY AND COMMENTS De Laurentiis's star power has made this one of the toughest reservations in town since the day it opened. Make sure to call ahead—far ahead!

Goodwich ★★

SANDWICHES	INEXPENSIVE	QUALITY	★★★	VALUE	★★★½

SoHo Lofts, 900 Las Vegas Blvd. S.; ☎ 702-910-8681; thegoodwich.com **DOWNTOWN**

Customers Locals. **Reservations** No. **When to go** Anytime. **Entrée range** $7–$10. **Payment** All major credit cards. **Service rating** ★★★. **Friendliness rating** ★★★★. **Parking** Valet, garage. **Bar** No. **Wine selection** None. **Dress** Casual. **Disabled access** Yes. **Hours** Daily, 11 a.m.–11 p.m.

SETTING AND ATMOSPHERE A modern industrial spot on the ground floor of one of Downtown's first high-rises, it features counter service and a modern mural of vintage Vegas neon by Downtown's painter laureate, Jerry Misko. A sidewalk patio area provides alfresco dining.

HOUSE SPECIALTIES The Reuben-ish (corned beef, Swiss, fennel kraut, and Thousand Island dressing); falafel.

OTHER RECOMMENDATIONS Check out the Pig o' the Week special pork sandwich.

SUMMARY AND COMMENTS This has been almost universally hailed as Las Vegas's top sandwich spot since it was just a walk-up kiosk in a dive-bar parking lot.

Gordon Ramsay Hell's Kitchen ★★★½

AMERICAN   EXPENSIVE/VERY EXPENSIVE   QUALITY ★★★★   VALUE ★★½

Caesars Palace, 3667 Las Vegas Blvd. S.; ☎ 702-731-7373; caesars.com/caesars-palace **MID-STRIP AND ENVIRONS**

Customers Gordon Ramsay's TV fans. **Reservations** Essential. **When to go** Anytime. **Entrée range** $32–$62. **Payment** All major credit cards. **Service rating** ★★★★. **Friendliness rating** ★★★★. **Parking** Valet, garage. **Bar** Full service. **Dress** Casual to business casual. **Disabled access** Yes. **Hours** Sunday–Thursday, 11 a.m.–10 p.m.; Friday and Saturday, 11 a.m.–11 p.m.

SETTING AND ATMOSPHERE Chef Gordon Ramsay's brand-new flagship is a tribute to the TV show of the same name, with chefs from the series in the kitchen and a wide-open main dining room to offer an unobstructed view. The decor—pitchfork light fixtures, video walls with images of flames, and windows opening onto the neon of the Strip—is guaranteed to wow you.

HOUSE SPECIALTIES People come for dishes like beef Wellington and risotto they know from the TV show.

OTHER RECOMMENDATIONS Make it a point to sample the cocktail selection, which includes one drink smoked table-side in a glass box.

SUMMARY AND COMMENTS If you only want to sample Ramsay's cooking, try one of his other places. His steakhouse is a fine-dining jewel, and his burger and fish-and-chips spots are far more affordable, while offering rock-solid execution of comfort food classics. If you are a serious fan of his TV shows, however, this is a Las Vegas destination you'll find as entertaining as Cirque or Celine, with food that's much better than it needs to be to keep the reservation book full.

Gordon Ramsay Steak ★★★★

STEAKHOUSE   VERY EXPENSIVE   QUALITY ★★★★   VALUE ★★★½

Paris Las Vegas, 3655 Las Vegas Blvd. S.; ☎ 702-944-4224; parislasvegas.com **MID-STRIP AND ENVIRONS**

Customers Visitors, locals. **Reservations** Essential. **When to go** Anytime. **Entrée range** $32–$321. **Payment** All major credit cards. **Service rating** ★★★★½. **Friendliness rating** ★★★★½. **Parking** Valet, garage. **Bar** Full service. **Wine selection** Upscale. **Dress** Upscale. **Disabled access** Yes, valet or elevator. **Hours** Sunday–Thursday, 4:30–10:30 p.m.; Friday and Saturday, 4:30 p.m.–midnight.

SETTING AND ATMOSPHERE You enter this steakhouse through the "Chunnel," a makeshift replica of the tunnel under the English Channel, thus going from "France" to "England" (wink-wink, nudge-nudge). Stenciled on the ceiling, alongside the Union Jack, is a pop sculpture of the master's two hands in motion. Seating is elegant; an upstairs mezzanine holds private rooms.

HOUSE SPECIALTIES The specialty here is beef: gaudy steaks presented on an eccentrically designed mirrored trolley. Pat LaFrieda, the legendary New York City butcher, is responsible for the excellent product, which doesn't come cheap. Expect to pay $52 for an 8-ounce American Wagyu skirt steak, and upward from there.

OTHER RECOMMENDATIONS Ramsay does a great beef Wellington, substituting a delicate mushroom duxelles for the out-of-favor foie gras, and lots more. His pricey fish-and-chips employs sea bass and is easily the best—and most expensive—version in the city. One of the best starters here is the English ale-and-cheese soup. It's hard to go wrong on Ramsay's menu.

SUMMARY AND COMMENTS The dining room is a bit noisy, and a few of the service gimmicks, such as an interactive iPad for ordering wines, seem gratuitous. But if you can afford it, this rivals Wolfgang Puck's CUT for the best all-around steakhouse on the Strip.

Haute Doggery ★★½

HOTDOGS	INEXPENSIVE	QUALITY ★★★★	VALUE ★★★½

The LINQ, 3545 Las Vegas Blvd. S.; ☎ 702-430-4435; hautedoggerylv.com
MID-STRIP AND ENVIRONS

Customers Visitors. **Reservations** No. **When to go** For a quick bite. **Entrée range** $6–$12. **Payment** All major credit cards. **Service rating** ★★★½. **Friendliness rating** ★★★. **Parking** Valet, lot. **Bar** Beer. **Wine selection** None. **Dress** Casual. **Disabled access** Yes. **Hours** Sunday–Thursday, 10 a.m.–midnight; Friday and Saturday, 10 a.m.–2 a.m.

SETTING AND ATMOSPHERE This is an upscale hot dog stand with limited seating at the end of the LINQ shopping plaza closest to the Strip.

HOUSE SPECIALTIES The signature work of decadence is the Billionaire Dog: a Kobe beef frank adorned with a foie gras torchon, port-onion marmalade, and truffle mayo. The Rising Sun features the same wiener topped with crispy yam, *nori furikake* seasoning, teriyaki glaze, and a tempura-fried avocado. For something more down-and-dirty, try a Tijuana Dog or a Jersey Ripper.

OTHER RECOMMENDATIONS These guys have also jumped on the poutine bandwagon and do a pretty decent job at it. The burgers aren't half-bad either.

SUMMARY AND COMMENTS This spot does for hot dogs what the slew of gourmet-burger joints on Las Vegas Boulevard try to do for hamburgers: take them to new and completely unexpected heights through either the bizarre nature or the sheer number of toppings that adorn them.

Herringbone ★★★½

SEAFOOD	EXPENSIVE	QUALITY ★★★★	VALUE ★★★½

Aria Resort, 3730 Las Vegas Blvd. S.; ☎ 702-590-9898; herringboneeats.com/las-vegas **MID-STRIP AND ENVIRONS**

Customers Visitors, locals. **Reservations** Recommended. **When to go** Anytime. **Entrée range** $34–$155. **Payment** All major credit cards. **Service rating** ★★★½. **Friendliness rating** ★★★★½. **Parking** Valet, lot. **Bar** Full service: excellent cocktail program, good beer selection. **Wine selection** Limited but varied. **Dress** Upscale casual. **Disabled access** Yes. **Hours** Sunday, 10 a.m.–10 p.m.; Monday–Thursday, 11 a.m.–10 p.m.; Friday, 11 a.m.–11 p.m.; Saturday, 10 a.m.–11 p.m.

SETTING AND ATMOSPHERE This place is part lounge, part patio, with no proper dining room in between. That's because this Aria space was formerly home to the Gold Lounge, and the main room still has that vibe. Outside dining on the patio is a bit more traditional, though it does boast some nice cabanas overlooking the pool area.

HOUSE SPECIALTIES Local favorite Geno Bernardo has turned over the reins of this kitchen to take a job in the company's corporate kitchen. But he's left it in the capable hands of chef Nick Aoki, who has redesigned the menu to add his own touch. Knockout additions include Buffalo-style octopus and decadent oysters Rockefeller.

OTHER RECOMMENDATIONS Come for the all-you-can-eat weekend brunch.

SUMMARY AND COMMENTS Celebrity chef Brian Malarkey opened Herringbone and his other local restaurant, Searsucker at Caesars Palace, less than a year apart. Both are laid-back, but with its secluded second-floor location at Aria and its funky layout, Herringbone has a more sophisticated feel.

Hofbräuhaus ★★★

GERMAN	MODERATE	QUALITY	★★★½	VALUE	★★★★

4510 Paradise Road; ☎ 702-853-2337; hofbrauhauslasvegas.com
EAST OF STRIP

Customers Visitors, local German community, beer enthusiasts. **Reservations** Requested for main dining room. **When to go** Anytime. **Entrée range** $13–$28. **Payment** All major credit cards. **Service rating** ★★★½. **Friendliness rating** ★★★½. **Parking** Valet, large lot. **Bar** Limited. **Wine selection** Small. **Dress** Casual. **Disabled access** Ramp. **Hours** Sunday–Thursday, 11 a.m.–11 p.m.; Friday and Saturday, 11 a.m.–midnight.

SETTING AND ATMOSPHERE This mini-replica of Munich's Hofbräuhaus flies in communal tables and oompah bands monthly, putting the *din* in dinner, yet the crowds love it. Comely fräuleins dressed in dirndls hoist as many as eight steins without a tray.

HOUSE SPECIALTIES Tennis ball–size dumplings that accompany the pork stew and a few other braised dishes; sauerbraten that can be on the dry side (the beer makes it go down easier); pretzels baked throughout the day—the dough is shipped from Germany, then shaped and baked in the kitchen.

OTHER RECOMMENDATIONS Perfect apple strudel—just delicious.

SUMMARY AND COMMENTS Hofbräuhaus serves the best beer in Las Vegas, and it's let go the notion that you shouldn't drink it cold. Take advantage of the discount coupons available in most hotels and taxis. Request to sit in the faux gardens behind the main dining room.

Honey Salt ★★★★

AMERICAN	MODERATE	QUALITY	★★★★	VALUE	★★★★

1031 S. Rampart Blvd.; ☎ 702-445-6100; honeysalt.com **WEST OF STRIP**

Customers Locals. **Reservations** Essential. **When to go** Anytime. **Entrée range** $11–$36. **Payment** All major credit cards. **Service rating** ★★★★½. **Friendliness rating** ★★★★½. **Parking** Lot. **Bar** Full service. **Wine selection** Interesting selection of boutique American wines. **Dress** Casual. **Disabled access** Yes. **Hours** Monday–Thursday, 11 a.m.–9 p.m.; Friday, 11 a.m.–10 p.m.; Saturday, 10:30 a.m.–10 p.m.; Sunday, 10:30 a.m.–9 p.m.

SETTING AND ATMOSPHERE Local decorator Randy Apel uses lime-green banquettes, funky mirrors, a chic bar, and an interior brick wall to provide hip, eccentric charm.

HOUSE SPECIALTIES The menu is as eclectic as the decor. You might find New England Fry, a lightly breaded combination of Ipswich clams and calamari from owner Elizabeth Blau's native Connecticut, alongside Nana's Tiffin Chicken Curry, reflective of the background of her husband and chef, Kim Canteenwalla, who has his roots on the Indian subcontinent.

OTHER RECOMMENDATIONS There are a host of delicious, approachable dishes here. Buttermilk fried chicken is one; roast swordfish with artichokes and sweet peppers is another. Almost everyone orders the turkey meatballs, as well, one of the few dishes that chef Kim held over from his tenure at the Society Café in Wynn Las Vegas.

SUMMARY AND COMMENTS It's impossible to state the importance of this restaurant, which has been doing a brisk business with locals since day one. It brings fine dining at reasonable prices to the suburbs and is well worth the trip from Strip casinos if you're looking for an authentic local dining experience.

Jaleo ★★★★

SPANISH/TAPAS	MODERATE/EXPENSIVE	QUALITY ★★★★	VALUE ★★★★

The Cosmopolitan, 3708 Las Vegas Blvd. S.; ☎ 702-698-7000; jaleo.com/las-vegas **MID-STRIP AND ENVIRONS**

Customers Visitors, locals. **Reservations** A must. **When to go** Anytime. **Entrée range** $8–$95. **Payment** All major credit cards. **Service rating** ★★★. **Friendliness rating** ★★★. **Parking** Valet, garage. **Bar** Full service. **Wine selection** Very good. **Dress** Informal. **Disabled access** Yes. **Hours** Sunday–Thursday, noon–11 p.m.; Friday and Saturday, noon–midnight.

SETTING AND ATMOSPHERE This colorful, open restaurant is filled with contemporary art from Spanish painters and sculptors. Small tables on one side of the room and communal wooden tables for multiple parties provide the seating.

HOUSE SPECIALTIES Creative tapas from chef José Andrés, the man who imported this genre from his native Spain. Excellent chicken *croquetas.* Catalan sausage stew with braised onion and mushrooms is not to be missed. Excellent selection of Iberian hams and boutique cheeses. Imaginative desserts.

OTHER RECOMMENDATIONS Don't miss the paellas, cooked over olive and orange wood–burning fires in an open cooking area. The best choice is probably the paella *valenciana,* which features rabbit and chicken, but the seafood paella is also quite wonderful. Avant-garde Spanish cuisine is served in an intimate setting in the attached é by José Andrés, one of the best-kept secrets in Las Vegas. Make sure to call well ahead for details on that.

SUMMARY AND COMMENTS José Andrés once cooked with Ferran Adrià at elBulli in Roses, Spain, so he's comfortable with both traditional and cutting-edge Spanish cuisine. The *patatas bravas*—small, blistered potatoes served with a salt crust—come with a pair of exotic sauces from the Canary Islands. A most memorable experience.

Joël Robuchon Restaurant ★★★★★

FRENCH	VERY EXPENSIVE	QUALITY ★★★★★	VALUE ★★★

MGM Grand, 3799 Las Vegas Blvd. S.; ☎ 702-891-7925; mgmgrand.com **SOUTH STRIP AND ENVIRONS**

Customers Visitors, locals. Reservations A must. When to go Special occasion. Entrée range Prix-fixe menus, $127–$445. Payment All major credit cards. Service rating ★★★★½. Friendliness rating ★★★. Parking Valet, garage. Bar Full service. Wine selection Excellent. Dress Formal. Disabled access Yes. Hours Daily, 5:30–10 p.m.

SETTING AND ATMOSPHERE Small and intimate, this dining room whisks guests out of the Vegas experience and into a regal one. Adorned in hues of plush purple and gold, the room is elegant yet warm and inviting.

HOUSE SPECIALTIES Expect high-quality gourmet ingredients and treatments. *La langoustine truffée et cuite en ravioli* (truffled langoustine ravioli) is luxurious and divine. The simple sounding Caviar Imperial reaches new levels of elegance by setting the pristine roe on a delicate gelée infused with the essence of crab and adorned with precisely allocated dots of cauliflower.

OTHER RECOMMENDATIONS For the full experience, opt for the degustation menu ($445 per person). There are also less-expensive and more-accessible abbreviated menus, starting in the low $100s.

SUMMARY AND COMMENTS Joël Robuchon is one of the most innovative chefs in the world (he was named "Chef of the Century" by *Gault & Millau*), and a meal here is no small feat. Next door, **L'Atelier de Joël Robuchon** (see pages 368–369) features a slightly more casual atmosphere where guests can watch chefs prepare their meals in an open kitchen.

Julian Serrano ★★★★

SPANISH/TAPAS	EXPENSIVE	QUALITY ★★★★	VALUE ★★★★

Aria at CityCenter, 3730 Las Vegas Blvd. S.; ☎ 702-590-7111; aria.com
MID-STRIP AND ENVIRONS

Customers Visitors, locals. Reservations Recommended. When to go Anytime. Entrée range $8–$50. Payment All major credit cards. Service rating ★★★★½. Friendliness rating ★★★★½. Parking Valet, lot. Bar Full service. Wine selection Excellent. Dress Casual. Disabled access Yes. Hours Sunday–Thursday, 11:30 a.m.–10:30 p.m.; Friday and Saturday, 11:30 a.m.–11 p.m.

SETTING AND ATMOSPHERE Contemporary Spanish decor with large open spaces and pastel colors and earth tones. Some guests prefer to sit at the long tapas bar, where they can watch the chefs putting together the small plates.

HOUSE SPECIALTIES Chicken croquettes; stuffed peppers; *albóndigas* (Spanish meatballs); *jamón ibérico* and *jamón serrano* (two types of Spanish ham); paella *valenciana; crema catalana.*

OTHER RECOMMENDATIONS Many of the small plates are irresistible, but the star dish is the paella, a rice casserole cooked in an iron pan. The *valenciana*, stocked with chorizo, chicken, and rabbit, and redolent of saffron, is simply sensational. And check out the weekend brunch menu.

SUMMARY AND COMMENTS Julian Serrano is a native of Madrid, French-trained, and chef at Picasso in the neighboring Bellagio, but his native cuisine is his first love. Vegas has several tapas bars, but Serrano and Jaleo are really the Spanish restaurants the city has been waiting for.

Kitchen Table ★★★½

AMERICAN	INEXPENSIVE/MODERATE	QUALITY ★★★★	VALUE ★★★½

1716 Horizon Ridge Pkwy., Henderson; ☎ 702-478-4782; kitchentablelv.com **SOUTHEAST LAS VEGAS–HENDERSON**

Customers Locals. **Reservations** No. **When to go** Breakfast or lunch. **Entrée range** $11–$30. **Payment** All major credit cards. **Service rating** ★★★. **Friendliness rating** ★★★★. **Parking** Lot. **Bar** Craft beer and sparkling wines. **Wine selection** Limited. **Dress** Casual. **Disabled access** Yes. **Hours** Monday–Friday, 7:30 a.m.–3 p.m.; Saturday and Sunday, 7:30 a.m.–3:30 p.m.

SETTING AND ATMOSPHERE Strip vets Anthony Nunez and Javier Chavez have created a cool urban enclave reminiscent of Seattle or downtown Brooklyn in the corner of a Henderson shopping center. The outdoor patio, where they smoke their own meat, is a beautiful option when the weather's nice.

HOUSE SPECIALTIES This may be the only place in town to offer foie gras on any breakfast entrée. Try it on the Amaretto French toast with caramelized pears and candied nuts. House-smoked pigs are used several delicious ways.

OTHER RECOMMENDATIONS Croque madame; Monte Cristo; duck-and-cheese omelet with house-made mac and cheese.

SUMMARY AND COMMENTS If traveling all the way to Henderson sounds like a hike for breakfast or lunch, well, it is. But we wouldn't recommend it if it weren't the best place in the valley serving those meals seven days a week.

Kyara ★★★½

JAPANESE	MODERATE	QUALITY ★★★★	VALUE ★★★★★

6555 S. Jones Blvd.; ☎ 702-434-8856; kyaravegas.com   **WEST OF STRIP**

Customers Locals, chefs. **Reservations** Recommended. **When to go** Dinner or late night. **Entrée range** $9–$18. **Payment** All major credit cards. **Service rating** ★★★. **Friendliness rating** ★★★. **Parking** Lot. **Bar** Beer, wine, a selection of sakes. **Wine selection** Good. **Dress** Casual. **Disabled access** Yes. **Hours** Daily, 5 p.m.–2 a.m.; Monday–Friday, 11 a.m.–3 p.m.

SETTING AND ATMOSPHERE This small place features a rabbit warren of semiprivate rooms that are fronted by white-birch slats. Tables are lacquered to a high gloss, and there are tiny white stones, *hashi-oki* in Japanese, on which your wooden chopsticks can rest, so as not to make contact with the table. There is also a counter at which to sit and watch the chefs ply their trade, but this is emphatically not a sushi bar.

HOUSE SPECIALTIES The idea is Japanese tapas: deep-fried, steamed, stir-fried, simmered, and skewered items. *Yamakake,* grated mountain potato served in a hot iron plate framed by a wooden platter, is astonishingly delicious. So is *agedashi* tofu, deep-fried tofu in Japanese broth, and *jidori tori kara,* a basket of delicately fried chicken.

OTHER RECOMMENDATIONS *Nikujaga,* a Japanese stew composed of sukiyaki beef, potato, and carrot, is a revelation. Ayu, a small fish in the trout family, salt-broiled, is wonderful when available. *Nankotsu* is soft shark's bone on thin slices of fresh cucumber. Skewers of charbroiled asparagus, chicken skin, beef tongue, and *tsukune* (soy-glazed chicken meatballs) are also a must.

SUMMARY AND COMMENTS Yasuo Komada, who owns Naked Fish, is the mastermind behind this place, which attracts many local chefs after their shifts. It's fun to watch the chefs turning skewers on the hibachis, shielded by a glass wall behind the counter. This place has become a veritable clubhouse for local foodies. As in Japan, beer, wine, and sake flow like a mountain stream.

Lotus of Siam ★★★★

THAI	MODERATE	QUALITY ★★★★	VALUE ★★½

620 E. Flamingo Road; ☎ 702-735-3033; lotusofsiamlv.com   **EAST OF STRIP**

Customers Locals, visitors. **Reservations** Recommended. **When to go** Anytime. **Entrée range** $9–$30. **Payment** All major credit cards. **Service rating** ★★★½. **Friendliness rating** ★★★★½. **Parking** Lot. **Bar** Wine. **Wine selection** Excellent. **Dress** Casual to casually elegant. **Disabled access** Yes. **Hours** Daily, 5:30–10 p.m.; Lunch Monday–Friday, 11 a.m.–2:30 p.m.

SETTING AND ATMOSPHERE A flood of the original location prompted a move to this larger, modern location in a much nicer neighborhood.

HOUSE SPECIALTIES Beef jerky Isan-style—crisp yet tender marinated beef served in a spicy sauce; *som tam*—green-papaya salad with salted crab; salmon pan-ang—charbroiled fresh salmon, served Thai-style in a thick, creamy sauce laced with curry.

OTHER RECOMMENDATIONS Sticky rice steamed in a bamboo basket; crispy rice salad; sausages made in-house. Ask the staff to show you the Northern Thai menu, featuring specialties from the chef's hometown, Chiang Mai. *Khao soi,* Myanmar-inspired noodles, and *nam prik noom,* a fiery green-chile dip, are just two of them.

SUMMARY AND COMMENTS The Isan specialties come from the region of that name in the northeastern corner of Thailand, bordering Cambodia and Laos. These dishes are even hotter and more highly seasoned than most Thai food, but the chef-owner will temper the heat to suit your taste. Gentle, caring service and one of the best lists of Austrian and German wines in this country are bonuses.

Marché Bacchus: French Bistro and Wine Shop ★★★★

FRENCH BISTRO	MODERATE	QUALITY	★★★★	VALUE	★★★★

2620 Regatta Dr., Ste. 106; ☎ 702-804-8008; marchebacchus.com
WEST OF STRIP

Customers Locals. **Reservations** Suggested weekends. **When to go** Anytime. **Entrée range** $17–$145. **Payment** All major credit cards. **Service rating** ★★★★½. **Friendliness rating** ★★★★½. **Parking** Large lot. **Bar** Full service. **Wine selection** Extensive. **Dress** Casual. **Disabled access** On lower level. **Hours** Monday–Thursday, 11 a.m.–9 p.m.; Friday and Saturday, 11 a.m.–10 p.m.; Sunday, 10 a.m.–9 p.m.

SETTING AND ATMOSPHERE Walk through the wine shop to the adjacent bistro, or dine on the terrace with its gorgeous view of artificial Regatta Lake. Simply furnished, this neighborhood eatery is an escape from the cares of the day.

HOUSE SPECIALTIES In addition to French-bistro classics, such as escargot in garlic butter and mussels in white wine, you'll find flavorful andouille sausage gumbo. And Italian touches shine throughout the menu.

OTHER RECOMMENDATIONS The adjoining wine shop is dazzling. Any wine can be purchased to enjoy with dinner for only $10 over retail.

SUMMARY AND COMMENTS Wines by the glass are terrific here, as is the charcuterie, made on premises. The terrace is favored by local sommeliers, who bring winemakers and chefs to relax here, making it a great place for networking.

Mizumi ★★★★

JAPANESE	VERY EXPENSIVE	QUALITY	★★★★	VALUE	★★★

Wynn Las Vegas, 3131 Las Vegas Blvd. S.; ☎ 702-770-7000; wynnlasvegas.com **MID-STRIP AND ENVIRONS**

Customers Visitors, locals. **Reservations** Essential. **When to go** Anytime. **Entrée range** $18–$165. **Payment** All major credit cards. **Service rating** ★★★★½. **Friendliness rating** ★★★★. **Parking** Valet, garage. **Bar** Full service. **Wine selection**

Excellent. **Dress** Upscale. **Disabled access** Yes. **Hours** Sunday–Thursday, 5:30–10 p.m.; Friday and Saturday, 5:30–10:30 p.m.

SETTING AND ATMOSPHERE Wynn chief designer Roger Thomas created a lavish extravaganza featuring dozens of Noh masks, walls of mock gold brick, a wall draped in antique Japanese sashes, and a private dining room with direct views of Wynn's fabled waterfall.

HOUSE SPECIALTIES Creative Hawaiian-born chef Devin Hashimoto is one of the most talented cooks on the Strip. He excels at many genres, but you won't want to miss his *robatayaki,* a method of cooking meats on wooden skewers over hot coals; seafood *bibimbap* rice bowl, inspired by his Korean-American wife; and wonderful fresh, grilled seafood in season.

OTHER RECOMMENDATIONS Spicy king crab tacos and yellowtail sashimi with jalapeño gelée are both exemplary; so is a toothsome Wagyu-beef tartare, topped with a creamy quail egg.

SUMMARY AND COMMENTS Mizumi is a luxury experience on every level. Service commences with an elegant tea selection, and the sushi and sashimi are absolutely first-rate. If you have the bucks, the restaurant's Floating Pagoda Table, the city's most elegant place to sit, will cost a few thousand to reserve.

Mon Ami Gabi ★★★½

CONTINENTAL/FRENCH MODERATE/EXPENSIVE QUALITY ★★★★ VALUE ★★★½

Paris Las Vegas, 3655 Las Vegas Blvd. S.; ☎ 702-944-4224; monamigabi.com
MID-STRIP AND ENVIRONS

Customers Visitors, locals. **Reservations** Requested for dining room, not accepted for patio. **When to go** Anytime. **Entrée range** $13–63. **Payment** All major credit cards. **Service rating** ★★★½. **Friendliness rating** ★★★½. **Parking** Valet, garage. **Bar** Full service. **Wine selection** All French. **Dress** Upscale casual. **Disabled access** Yes. **Hours** Sunday–Thursday, 7 a.m.–11 p.m.; Friday and Saturday, 7 a.m.–midnight.

SETTING AND ATMOSPHERE This handsome brasserie has black leather booths and tables. The main dining room leads to a wonderful, plant-filled patio and a marvelous sidewalk café with a view of the Strip.

HOUSE SPECIALTIES Steak *frites,* thin-sliced steak and fries; an excellent selection of seafood and hors d'oeuvres; mussels *marinière*; daily specials. Filet mignon and New York strip are among the regular steak selections.

OTHER RECOMMENDATIONS Crêpes; omelets, and sandwiches at lunch.

SUMMARY AND COMMENTS Mon Ami Gabi is a charming dining place. Everyone wants to dine at the sidewalk café, but you'll have to come early to get a table (no reservations). The *frites* are actually curly fries, not steak fries, but they're crisp and good: so what if they're not authentic? Everything else is right on the mark. And for those whose dinner isn't complete without a good bottle of wine, there's a separate list of fine reserve ones.

Monta Japanese Noodle House ★★½

RAMEN   INEXPENSIVE   QUALITY ★★★★   VALUE ★★★★★

5030 W. Spring Mountain Road, Ste. 6; ☎ 702-367-4600; montaramen.com
WEST OF STRIP

Customers Local Japanese. **Reservations** Not accepted. **When to go** Lunch or late dinner. **Entrée range** $7–$10. **Payment** Cash only. **Service rating** ★★★. **Friendliness rating** ★★. **Parking** Lot. **Bar** Beer, wine. **Wine selection** Limited.

Dress Casual. **Disabled access** None. **Hours** Sunday–Thursday, 11:30 a.m.–11 p.m.; Friday and Saturday, 11:30 a.m.–1 a.m.

SETTING AND ATMOSPHERE There's rabbit warren–size ramen bar where the chefs toil behind a counter. Seating is cramped, on wooden chairs, with tables crowded closely together. A Japanese-speaking clientele predominates.

HOUSE SPECIALTIES The specialty here is ramen—long, wheat-based noodles slurped from giant bowls of broth. There are essentially two types: miso ramen, in a piquant broth made from fermented soybeans, and shoyu ramen, based on soy sauce. The flavorful broth is slow-cooked and tastes it, and the noodles are perfectly al dente.

OTHER RECOMMENDATIONS Don't miss the melt-in-your-mouth, thinly sliced pork topping—slices so light they literally float to the top of the broth. Corn, egg, and several other toppings enhance the ramen experience. There are also bowls of fried rice and several types of house-made Japanese pickles.

SUMMARY AND COMMENTS This place has some of the most authentic Japanese food in town, even more so than the so-called sushi palaces. Be prepared to wait in line. Monta is always in demand, and the restaurant is small.

Morimoto ★★★★

JAPANESE FUSION	VERY EXPENSIVE	QUALITY ★★★★★	VALUE ★★★½

MGM Grand, 3799 Las Vegas Blvd. S.; ☎ 702-891-3001; mgmgrand.com
SOUTH STRIP AND ENVIRONS

Customers Tourists and celebrity chef fans. **Reservations** Recommended. **When to go** Special occasions. **Entrée range** $26–$75. **Payment** All major credit cards. **Service rating** ★★★★. **Friendliness rating** ★★★★. **Parking** Valet, garage. **Bar** Full service. **Dress** Casual. **Disabled access** Yes. **Hours** Sunday–Thursday, 5–10 p.m., Friday and Saturday, 5–10:30 p.m.

SETTING AND ATMOSPHERE The restaurant is separated into four experiences: lounge, sushi bar, main dining room, and teppanyaki tables. The entire menu, however, is available in nearly all of them, with the exception of certain teppan dishes that require guests sit at those tables. The decor throughout is chic and modern.

HOUSE SPECIALTIES The sushi here is as good as it gets, and there's no substitute for classic hot dishes like miso black cod. There's also a nice selection of beef available, if someone in your party wants a simple steak dinner.

OTHER RECOMMENDATIONS If you want a bit of everything, try one of the omakase tasting menus. But brace yourself for the hefty price tag.

SUMMARY AND COMMENTS The Iron Chef is a master, and this is everything you'd expect from him.

Nobu Caesars Palace ★★★★

JAPANESE/SUSHI	VERY EXPENSIVE	QUALITY ★★★★★	VALUE ★★★½

Nobu Hotel at Caesars Palace, 3570 Las Vegas Blvd. S.; ☎ 877-346-4642 (reservations); caesars.com/caesars-palace **MID-STRIP AND ENVIRONS**

Customers Visitors, celebrity chef fans. **Reservations** Essential. **When to go** Anytime. **Entrée range** Sushi and sashimi, $12–$90; tasting dinners $125–$225; hot and cold dishes, $24–$70; *teppan* dinners, $125 and $155. **Payment** All major credit cards. **Service rating** ★★★★½. **Friendliness rating** ★★★½. **Parking** Valet, lot, garage. **Bar** Full service. **Wine selection** Excellent. **Dress** Upscale casual. **Disabled access** Yes. **Hours** Sunday–Thursday, 5–11 p.m.; Friday and Saturday, 5 p.m.–midnight.

SETTING AND ATMOSPHERE Architect David Rockwell has taken an enormous space—12,775 square feet—and somehow made it feel intimate. This is the largest of superstar chef Nobuyuki Matsuhisa's Nobu restaurants in the United States, using semicircular banquettes, partially sequestered *teppan* tables, and an enormous sushi counter, where a team of up to 10 chefs makes magic while you watch.

HOUSE SPECIALTIES The menu is a reflection of Japanese technique and precision with South American ingredients and influence. Signature dishes include black cod with miso glaze, an exquisite chicken baked in a clay vessel, and *hamachi kama* (broiled yellowtail collar), which is one of the menu's best values.

OTHER RECOMMENDATIONS *Tiraditos,* South American takes on ceviche and sashimi, are top-drawer here, though you pay for them—upward of $35.

SUMMARY AND COMMENTS Matsuhisa is the man who globalized the cuisine of his native Japan, with locations in such diverse ports-of-call as Budapest, Hungary; Cape Town, South Africa; Dubai; and Perth, Australia. A second Vegas location is located at the Hard Rock, but for a few dollars more, you can eat at this more glamorous, more creative outpost—so why not?

Old Homestead Steakhouse ★★★★

AMERICAN/STEAK	VERY EXPENSIVE	QUALITY ★★★★	VALUE ★★★½

Caesars Palace, 3570 Las Vegas Blvd. S.; ☎ 877-346-4642; caesars.com/caesars-palace **MID-STRIP AND ENVIRONS**

Customers Visitors, locals. **Reservations** Essential. **When to go** Anytime. **Entrée range** $28–$110. **Payment** All major credit cards. **Service rating** ★★★★½. **Friendliness rating** ★★★★½. **Parking** Valet, garage. **Bar** Full service. **Wine selection** Excellent. **Dress** Business casual. **Disabled access** Yes. **Hours** Sunday–Thursday, 4:30–10 p.m.; Friday and Saturday, 4:30–10:30 p.m.

SETTING AND ATMOSPHERE Just across Cleopatra's Way from **Nobu** (see above), this clubby, masculine room, filled with high-backed leather banquettes and black-and-white shots of bridge girders in Manhattan and Brooklyn, attempts to recall dining in the Big City.

HOUSE SPECIALTIES Meat is the ticket at this Vegas outpost of the legendary New York meatery. The good cuts come from Pat LaFrieda, a top butcher in New York's Meatpacking District. Steaks here are dry-aged a minimum of 30 days, a number of them on the bone. It ain't cheap, of course: Steaks start at $54 for an 8-ounce petite filet mignon.

OTHER RECOMMENDATIONS Appetizers, soups, and salads are done well here. The beefy, cheese-topped French onion soup is a hit, as are vine-ripened tomatoes with mozzarella and fresh basil. Don't miss the thick-cut applewood-smoked bacon, which feels like a bargain at about $8 a slice.

SUMMARY AND COMMENTS Most Strip steakhouses are similar in quality and price, yet this place manages to stand out in the crowd.

Other Mama ★★★★

SEAFOOD	MODERATE	QUALITY ★★★★★	VALUE ★★★★

3655 S. Durango Dr.; ☎ 702-463-8382; othermamalv.com **WEST OF STRIP**

Customers Locals, off-duty chefs. **Reservations** No. **When to go** Anytime. **Entrée range** $20–$30. **Payment** All major credit cards. **Service rating** ★★½. **Friendliness rating** ★★★★½. **Parking** Lot. **Bar** Full service. **Wine selection** Limited. **Dress** Casual. **Disabled access** Yes. **Hours** Daily, 5–11 p.m.

SETTING AND ATMOSPHERE This is a homey combination of oyster bar, sushi bar, and seafood grill with an open kitchen.

HOUSE SPECIALTIES Rotating selection of oysters; daily sushi catch; pork kimchi.

OTHER RECOMMENDATIONS Whole branzino; caviar and French toast; oyster–foie gras Rockefeller; fried rice.

SUMMARY AND COMMENTS Thanks to chef Dan Krohmer's background of cutting sushi for celebrity chef Masaharu Morimoto, he has amazing connections that provide some of the best cuts of fish available. The oysters are also top-notch. And the cocktail program is among the best you'll find in the suburbs. There's a reason this has been a hit among the foodie "in crowd" from the moment it opened its doors.

Picasso ★★★★½

FRENCH/SPANISH	VERY EXPENSIVE	QUALITY ★★★★	VALUE ★★½

Bellagio, 3600 Las Vegas Blvd. S.; ☎ 702-693-7223; bellagio.com
MID-STRIP AND ENVIRONS

Customers Visitors, locals. **Reservations** A must. **When to go** Anytime you can get a reservation. **Entrée range** Prix-fixe menus, $75–$132. **Payment** All major credit cards. **Service rating** ★★★★½. **Friendliness rating** ★★★★½. **Parking** Valet, garage. **Bar** Full service. **Wine selection** Excellent. **Dress** Casually elegant, jackets recommended. **Disabled access** Elevator. **Hours** Wednesday–Monday, 5:30–9:30 p.m.

SETTING AND ATMOSPHERE This is arguably the most beautiful dining room in Las Vegas, with original Pablo Picasso art adorning the walls. The flower displays throughout the restaurant are exquisite. A wall of windows gives most tables a full view of Bellagio's dancing fountains.

HOUSE SPECIALTIES Selections on both the five-course degustation and the four-course prix-fixe menus change regularly according to the whim of the chef. The warm lobster salad, sautéed foie gras, sautéed medallions of swordfish, and aged-lamb roti with truffle crust appear often. The roast pigeon (squab) is outstanding. Chef Julian Serrano sometimes offers a sensational amuse-bouche: a tiny potato pancake topped with crème fraîche and osetra caviar.

SUMMARY AND COMMENTS This exceptional restaurant is grand yet unpretentious. Allow enough time to enjoy the experience. After dinner, have a drink on the terrace. Where else but in Las Vegas can you have a view of Lake Como as well as one of the Eiffel Tower?

Pizza Rock ★★★½

PIZZA	INEXPENSIVE/MODERATE	QUALITY ★★★★	VALUE ★★★

201 N. 3rd St.; ☎ 702-385-0838; pizzarocklasvegas.com **DOWNTOWN**

Customers Visitors, locals. **Reservations** Recommended. **When to go** Anytime. **Entrée range** $15–32. **Payment** All major credit cards. **Service rating** ★★★½. **Friendliness rating** ★★★½. **Parking** Street. **Bar** Full service. **Wine selection** Excellent. **Dress** Casual. **Disabled access** Yes. **Hours** Sunday–Thursday, 11 a.m.–midnight; Friday and Saturday, 11 a.m.–2 a.m.

SETTING AND ATMOSPHERE From the cab of a semitruck that doubles as a DJ booth to an overall rock-and-roll vibe, this place screams party spot. Yet it's also family friendly, with crayons for the kids.

HOUSE SPECIALTIES Tony Gemignani is a 12-time World Pizza Champion and a master of every style. Here, he offers nine varieties of pizza, each distinguished by different dough and cooking temperature, even the style of oven in which they're made. If you have time for only one, get the New Yorker.

OTHER RECOMMENDATIONS The calzones here are easy to overlook. Do yourself a favor and don't.

SUMMARY AND COMMENTS This place takes pizza to a world-class level and should be part of any serious foodie's Las Vegas dining itinerary.

Prime Steakhouse ★★★★

STEAK	VERY EXPENSIVE	QUALITY	★★★★	VALUE	★★½

Bellagio, 3600 Las Vegas Blvd. S.; ☎ 702-693-7223; bellagio.com
MID-STRIP AND ENVIRONS

Customers Visitors, locals. **Reservations** Requested. **When to go** Avoid convention times. **Entrée range** $44–$125. **Payment** All major credit cards. **Service rating** ★★★★½. **Friendliness rating** ★★★★½. **Parking** Valet, garage. **Bar** Full service. **Wine selection** Excellent. **Dress** Casually elegant, jackets preferred. **Disabled access** Elevator. **Hours** Daily, 5–10 p.m.

SETTING AND ATMOSPHERE With dazzling powder-blue-and-chocolate carpets and wall hangings in a setting seldom seen for a steakhouse, it's gorgeous. In keeping with Bellagio's fine arts policy, there's plenty of original art to view here. Have a drink at the elegant bar and take it all in.

HOUSE SPECIALTIES Prime aged steaks and seafood; lamb chops in balsamic syrup; filet mignon with tomatoes; veal chop in pineapple chutney. There's also a choice of a variety of sauces and excellent side dishes.

SUMMARY AND COMMENTS Prime is on the lower level of the shopping corridor beside **Picasso** (see page 395), which shares an outdoor patio. Both restaurants get their share of lookers, but the staff keeps them from disturbing diners. Service here rarely misses a beat.

Public House ★★★½

AMERICAN	MODERATE	QUALITY	★★★★	VALUE	★★★★

The Venetian, 3355 Las Vegas Blvd. S.; ☎ 702-285-5544;
publichouselv.com   **MID-STRIP AND ENVIRONS**

Customers Locals, chefs. **Reservations** Essential. **When to go** Dinner or late night. **Entrée range** $14–$109. **Payment** All major credit cards. **Service rating** ★★★★. **Friendliness rating** ★★★★. **Parking** Valet, garage. **Bar** Beer, wine. **Wine selection** Extensive. **Dress** Casual. **Disabled access** Yes. **Hours** Daily, 11 a.m.–11 p.m.

SETTING AND ATMOSPHERE Local restaurant chain Block 16's gastropub at The Venetian is impressive. The space is modern and spacious, thanks to a ceiling composed of giant wooden cubes, banquettes of tufted dark-brown leather, and a burnished-mahogany parquet floor. Tables have handsome cherrywood surfaces.

HOUSE SPECIALTIES Chef Anthony Meidenbauer has created an impressive menu of snacks, savories, and large plates to go along with the pub's more than 200 brews and imaginative wine list. Meidenbauer's house-made charcuterie, Welsh rarebit, and house pickles are three items not to miss. The rarebit is an eccentric cheese toast with a bite—delicious. The pickles are wickedly sharp.

OTHER RECOMMENDATIONS Try the poutine, a French-Canadian dish composed of fries, cheese curds, brown gravy, and, here, a rotating assortment of specialty ingredients including duck confit. Potted farm egg comes in a casserole with lots of cheese sauce and a heap of sautéed mushrooms, the perfect comple-ment to wedges of crusty house bread. Fried quail served on waffles and lamb pierogi shows off chef Meidenbauer's awesome range.

SUMMARY AND COMMENTS Ask the restaurant's Cicerone (beer sommelier) to turn you on to one of the brews on tap.

Raku ★★★★

JAPANESE	MODERATE	QUALITY	★★★★	VALUE	★★★★

5030 Spring Mountain Road; ☎ 702-367-3511; raku-grill.com   **WEST OF STRIP**

Customers Visitors, locals. **Reservations** Recommended. **When to go** Anytime. **Entrée range** $15–$30. **Payment** All major credit cards. **Service rating** ★★★★½. **Friendliness rating** ★★★★½. **Parking** Lot. **Bar** Full service. **Wine selection** Fair. **Dress** Casual. **Disabled access** Yes. **Hours** Monday–Saturday, 6 p.m.–3 a.m.

SETTING AND ATMOSPHERE This small (seats 60), minimalist space is decorated in dark woods with burgundy walls.

HOUSE SPECIALTIES Don't expect sushi at this Japanese restaurant; it's a *sakaba,* or sake bar, where small, salty dishes meant to encourage thirst are served. A Japanese lump charcoal–fired grill is the source of the wonderfully smoky flavor imparted to meats such as pork cheek, Kobe beef tendon, bacon-wrapped enoki mushrooms, and whole fish. House-made tofu is silky and creamy, especially when paired with fresh tomato and seaweed, a sort of Japanese take on a caprese salad.

OTHER RECOMMENDATIONS Check the nightly specials board for seasonal addi-tions. Traditional Japanese flavors and techniques are the ticket. For dessert, walk a few doors down to sister restaurant Sweets Raku.

SUMMARY AND COMMENTS Raku is an off-Strip standout, garnering the attention of critics, locals, and, most important, other chefs in town. Chef Mitsuo Endo finds himself cooking for some of the biggest culinary names in Vegas after they get off work, so the restaurant is open late. A true Japanese *izakaya* (drinking–dining) experience, round after round of Raku's grilled small plates go well with beer, wine, or sake.

Rao's ★★★

ITALIAN	EXPENSIVE	QUALITY	★★★★	VALUE	★★

Caesars Palace, 3570 Las Vegas Blvd. S.; ☎ 877-346-4642; caesars.com/caesars-palace   **MID-STRIP AND ENVIRONS**

Customers Visitors, locals. **Reservations** Suggested. **When to go** Anytime. **Entrée range** $25–$53. **Payment** All major credit cards. **Service rating** ★★★★½. **Friend-liness rating** ★★★★½. **Parking** Valet, garage. **Bar** Full service. **Wine selection** Very good. **Dress** Casual. **Disabled access** Yes. **Hours** Sunday–Thursday, 5–10 p.m.; Friday and Saturday, 5–10:30 p.m.

SETTING AND ATMOSPHERE The Las Vegas outpost of Rao's is nearly three times the size of the tiny New York original, but you can still feel the heart of this family-owned business. Christmas lights and decorations hang year-round, and the walls are adorned with framed photographs of Rao's customers old and new. Dark woods along the bar and dining room evoke a classic, tradi-tional feel. Don't be surprised if you hear Italian-American classics such as "Volare" interspersed with covers by Michael Bublé from the jukebox; this restaurant is all about intermingling old and new traditions.

HOUSE SPECIALTIES Southern Italian red-sauce classics such as meatballs, gnocchi with Bolognese sauce, and Uncle Vincent's Lemon Chicken have been on the menu since the original restaurant opened in 1896. You'll also find some fresh seafood dishes and lighter pastas.

SUMMARY AND COMMENTS Rao's is a family-run joint—always has been and always will be. Owner and partner Frank Pellegrino Jr. now splits his time between here and L.A., but whether he's in the building or not, the front of the house feels like a family affair.

Restaurant Guy Savoy ★★★★★

FRENCH   VERY EXPENSIVE   QUALITY ★★★★★   VALUE ★★★

Caesars Palace, 3570 Las Vegas Blvd. S.; ☎ 877-346-4642; caesars.com/caesars-palace **MID-STRIP AND ENVIRONS**

Customers Visitors, locals. **Reservations** A must. **When to go** Special occasion. **Entrée range** À la carte, $80–$120; prix-fixe menus, $150–$500. **Payment** All major credit cards. **Service rating** ★★★★½. **Friendliness rating** ★★★★. **Parking** Valet, garage. **Bar** Full service. **Wine selection** Excellent. **Dress** Upscale. **Disabled access** Yes. **Hours** Wednesday–Sunday, 5:30–9:30 p.m.

SETTING AND ATMOSPHERE Clean lines and modern sophistication are the theme. You'll find the same elegance and refinement you would expect from the original Paris restaurant. Top-notch French dining is alive and well in Las Vegas.

HOUSE SPECIALTIES The artichoke-and-black-truffle soup is one of Guy Savoy's signature items all the way from his Paris restaurant. Served with toasted mushroom brioche and truffle butter, it's one of the most decadent dishes ever.

OTHER RECOMMENDATIONS As a starter, try Savoy's amazing Colors of Caviar—a layered caviar dish that looks like a dessert—or oysters in ice gelée. The salmon "iceberg," "cooked" on dry ice and served with warm consommé, is truly jaw-dropping.

Summary and Comments To get the full experience without breaking the bank, try either the four-course TGV prix-fixe menu or grab a seat in the Cognac Room for a rare spirit and one or two of Savoy's amazing appetizers.

RX Boiler Room ★★★½

ECLECTIC   EXPENSIVE/VERY EXPENSIVE   QUALITY ★★★★   VALUE ★★★½

Mandalay Bay, 3960 Las Vegas Blvd. S.; ☎ 702-632-7200; rxboilerroom.com **SOUTH STRIP AND ENVIRONS**

Customers Locals, visitors. **Reservations** Not necessary. **When to go** Anytime. **Entrée range** $24–$58. **Payment** All major credit cards. **Service rating** ★★★★. **Friendliness rating** ★★★★. **Parking** Valet, lot. **Bar** Full service; excellent cocktail menu. **Wine selection** Limited. **Dress** Casual. **Disabled access** Yes. **Hours** Daily, 5–10 p.m.

SETTING AND ATMOSPHERE The steampunk theme features Victorian-era sci-fi decor. It looks like a luxurious laboratory, and the waitresses dress in corsets.

HOUSE SPECIALTIES Celebrity chef Rick Moonen branches out beyond the sustainable seafood he's known for by giving crazy tweaks to comfort food. Small plates include bacon-wrapped bacon with quail egg, chicken-potpie nuggets, and Buffalo fried oysters, while entrées include Guinness-braised short rib and Maine lobster ravioli.

OTHER RECOMMENDATIONS Those bubbling and steaming potions behind the bar aren't for show; the bartenders use them to infuse original flavors into their cocktails. Make sure to try a few.

SUMMARY AND COMMENTS This is one of the coolest, most original spots in town, and it's worth a visit, even if you don't know what steampunk is.

Sage ★★★½

AMERICAN	VERY EXPENSIVE	QUALITY ★★★★½	VALUE ★★★★

Aria at CityCenter, 3730 Las Vegas Blvd. S.; ☎ 877-230-2742; aria.com
MID-STRIP AND ENVIRONS

Customers Visitors. **Reservations** Essential. **When to go** Anytime. **Entrée range** À la carte, $37–$105; prix fixe, $59–$150. **Payment** All major credit cards. **Service rating** ★★★★½. **Friendliness rating** ★★★★½. **Parking** Valet, lot. **Bar** Full service; excellent cocktail menu. **Wine selection** Excellent. **Dress** Upscale. **Disabled access** Yes. **Hours** Monday–Thursday, 6–10:30 p.m.; Friday and Saturday, 6–11 p.m.

SETTING AND ATMOSPHERE You enter through an elegant bar. The high-ceilinged dining room is dark, clubby, and formal. Appointments, such as stemware and table settings, are first-rate.

HOUSE SPECIALTIES Chicago's Shawn McClain (Spring) cooks smart American fare with hints of almost everywhere on the planet. He refers to his cooking as "refined American cuisine," and we're apt to agree. Kusshi oysters from Vancouver Island are topped with Tabasco sorbet and aged tequila. Don't miss the foie gras custard brûlée, the chef's signature.

OTHER RECOMMENDATIONS Main courses not to miss include roasted loin of Iberian pork, short ribs braised in Belgian ale, and roast Sonoma chicken with a *maitake*-mushroom persillade. The chef offers a small but imaginative vegetarian menu. Slow-poached organic farm egg and Bellwether Farms sheep's-milk ricotta gnocchi are so good that you would swear off meat to eat them.

SUMMARY AND COMMENTS Other than Bradley Ogden, Shawn McClain may be the best example of an American talent who sources the best American products.

Sen of Japan ★★★½

SUSHI	MODERATE/EXPENSIVE	QUALITY ★★★★	VALUE ★★★½

8480 W. Desert Inn Road; ☎ 702-871-7781; senofjapan.com **WEST OF STRIP**

Customers Locals. **Reservations** Recommended. **When to go** Anytime. **Entrée range** À la carte, $16–$45; *omakase* tasting menus, $60–$90. **Payment** All major credit cards. **Service rating** ★★★. **Friendliness rating** ★★★. **Parking** Lot. **Bar** Beer, wine, sake. **Wine selection** Limited. **Dress** Casual. **Disabled access** None. **Hours** Monday–Saturday, 5 p.m.–1:30 a.m.; Sunday, 5–11:30 p.m.

SETTING AND ATMOSPHERE A pleasant but generic room in a mini-mall, the restaurant features a sushi bar and a comfortable dining area.

HOUSE SPECIALTIES *Omakase,* or chef's choice, is definitely the way to go here. Tell the server what you want to spend, and then let chef Hiro Nakano rock and roll. The salmon-skin salad is superb, and the quality of the chef's sushi rice, the ne plus ultra for a Japanese gourmet, is the best around.

OTHER RECOMMENDATIONS *Tsukune*, delicious meatballs of chicken with a soy glaze served on wooden skewers; shishito, grilled Japanese green pepper; and tempura, served with a grated-radish dipping sauce, are wonderful.

SUMMARY AND COMMENTS This is some of Las Vegas's best sushi, and prices are about half what they would be in comparable sushi restaurants on or near the Strip, such as Nobu at the Hard Rock (where Nakano was previously head chef). If you're on the Westside and craving sushi, this place is a must.

Settebello ★★★½

PIZZA	MODERATE	QUALITY ★★★★	VALUE ★★★

140 Green Valley Pkwy., Henderson; ☎ 702-222-3556; settebello.net
SOUTHEAST LAS VEGAS–HENDERSON

9350 W. Sahara Ave.; ☎ 702-901-4877; settebello.net **WEST OF STRIP**

Customers Visitors, locals. **Reservations** Recommended. **When to go** Anytime. **Entrée range** $8–$30. **Payment** All major credit cards. **Service rating** ★★★. **Friendliness rating** ★★★. **Parking** Lot. **Bar** Beer, wine. **Wine selection** Good. **Dress** Casual. **Disabled access** Yes. **Hours** Daily, 11 a.m.–10 p.m.

SETTING AND ATMOSPHERE The restaurant has a decidedly neighborhood feel, but those who've discovered the joys of Settebello's pizza find themselves trekking all the way to Green Valley for a slice.

HOUSE SPECIALTIES Settebello serves quite possibly the best pizza in Las Vegas, made according to the tenets of the Associazione Verace Pizza Napoletana, an Italian organization dedicated to the preservation of true Neapolitan pizza. The crust (which takes only about 45–60 seconds to cook in Settebello's beautiful 950°F imported wood-fired oven) is crisp on the bottom from the high heat, yet somewhat soft enough to tear. Toppings, such as the simplest tomatoes, mozzarella, and olive oil, are mostly imported—pure ingredients that taste fresh and wholesome.

SUMMARY AND COMMENTS Settebello has a cult following in Las Vegas. Chef Theo Schoenegger of **Sinatra** (see below) says it's his favorite pizza place. Owner Brad Otton, who was trained as a pizzaiolo in Italy, oversees the place himself and greets regulars and newcomers on a daily basis.

Sinatra ★★★

ITALIAN	EXPENSIVE	QUALITY ★★★	VALUE ★★

Wynn Encore Resort, 3131 Las Vegas Blvd. S.; ☎ 702-248-3463; wynnlasvegas.com **MID-STRIP AND ENVIRONS**

Customers Visitors. **Reservations** Suggested. **When to go** Anytime. **Entrée range** $17–$98. **Payment** All major credit cards. **Service rating** ★★★★½. **Friendliness rating** ★★★. **Parking** Valet, garage. **Bar** Full service. **Wine selection** Very good. **Dress** Business casual. **Disabled access** Yes. **Hours** Daily, 5:30–10 p.m.

SETTING AND ATMOSPHERE Nothing says Las Vegas quite like Frank Sinatra, and Ol' Blue Eyes has his own restaurant at Encore. The room—more evocative of George Clooney's *Ocean's Eleven* than Sinatra's—is a blend of modern and midcentury, in natural hues of brown and green. Five custom-made olive-green chandeliers are composed of eco-friendly hemp rope and burlap. Frequent reminders of Sinatra's influence include his Oscar for *From Here to Eternity* and his Grammy for "Strangers in the Night," as well as gold albums and personal letters between him and his Rat Pack pals.

HOUSE SPECIALTIES The menu is a twist on Italian classics, some of which were Sinatra's favorites, along with some signature dishes such as *zuppa di fagioli* (made with borlotti beans); agnolotti with ricotta, herbs, and winter truffles; and Osso Bucco "My Way," with risotto Milanese and gremolata.

SUMMARY AND COMMENTS Michelin-starred chef Theo Schoenegger portrays his Italian roots in creative, modern ways for this menu. To be fair, we'd eat his food even if it didn't have an icon's name next to it.

Sparrow + Wolf ★★★★½

ECLECTIC/EXPERIMENTAL **EXPENSIVE** **QUALITY** ★★★★★ **VALUE** ★★★★½

4480 Spring Mountain Road; ☎ 702-790-2147; sparrowandwolflv.com
WEST OF STRIP

Customers Locals and visiting foodies. **Reservations** Recommended. **When to go** Date night or other special occasion. **Entrée range** Small plates $10–$25. **Payment** All major credit cards. **Service rating** ★★★★½. **Friendliness rating** ★★★★★. **Parking** Lot. **Bar** Full service. Wine Very good. **Dress** Upscale. **Disabled access** Yes. **Hours** Wednesday–Monday, 5–11 p.m.

SETTING AND ATMOSPHERE The casual atmosphere has upscale design features throughout. A graffiti-style mural over the bar adds a modern, urban touch.

HOUSE SPECIALTIES Beef cheek and bone marrow dumplings and the "campfire duck" combination of breast, foie gras, and broth with wood ear mushrooms and salted cucumber.

OTHER RECOMMENDATIONS The house-made charcuterie selection changes frequently but is always worth an inquiry.

SUMMARY AND COMMENTS Chef Brian Howard worked at numerous top Strip restaurants before setting up this small-plate experience in Chinatown. And while his original plans were to mix elevated and casual fare, the latter hasn't caught on as well as the former. As a result, this is a place for adventurous eaters to have an unforgettable meal for much less than you'd pay for a similar experience in a casino.

Todd's Unique Dining ★★★★

STEAK/SEAFOOD **MODERATE/EXPENSIVE** **QUALITY** ★★★★ **VALUE** ★★★★

4350 E. Sunset Road, Henderson; ☎ 702-259-8633; toddsunique.com
SOUTHEAST LAS VEGAS–HENDERSON

Customers Locals. **Reservations** Recommended. **When to go** Anytime. **Entrée range** $31–$60. **Payment** All major credit cards. **Service rating** ★★★. **Friendliness rating** ★★★★½. **Parking** Lot. **Bar** Full service. **Wine selection** Small. **Dress** Casual. **Disabled access** Yes. **Hours** Monday–Saturday, 4:30–9:30 p.m. (last seating)

SETTING AND ATMOSPHERE A small storefront among big-chain restaurants in Henderson, Todd's Unique Dining is homey, casual, and comfortable. A favorite with Green Valley residents, chef Todd Clore, a veteran of corporate Strip restaurants, makes his mark with this neighborhood restaurant.

HOUSE SPECIALTIES Mainly a seafood restaurant, Todd's Unique definitely has some Asian influence. Standards like the goat-cheese wontons are a surprising bite of pungent goat cheese balanced with an herby raspberry-and-basil sauce. Seared ahi tuna with wasabi and mashed leeks reveals a touch of East-meets-West, as does the Kobe skirt steak with black bean–chili sauce.

SUMMARY AND COMMENTS Clore has elevated neighborhood dining for Green Valley, garnering local regulars night after night. It's solid, high-end cuisine without the prices, or pretensions, that plague many Strip restaurants.

Top of the World ★★★½

AMERICAN **EXPENSIVE** **QUALITY** ★★★★½ **VALUE** ★★★½

Stratosphere Tower, 2000 Las Vegas Blvd. S.; ☎ 702-380-7711;
topoftheworldlv.com **NORTH STRIP AND ENVIRONS**

Customers Visitors, locals. **Reservations** Required. **When to go** Anytime. **Entrée range** $44–$119; four-course tasting menu, $49–$102. **Payment** All major credit cards. **Service rating** ★★★★½. **Friendliness rating** ★★★½. **Parking** Valet, garage, lot. **Bar** Full service. **Wine selection** Excellent. **Dress** Business casual. **Disabled access** Elevator. **Hours** Daily, 11 a.m.–11 p.m.

SETTING AND ATMOSPHERE Top of the World offers one of the most beautiful views of the city. The restaurant revolves as you dine, giving a panoramic spectacle of the surrounding mountains. One complete revolution takes an hour and 20 minutes. The dining room is elegant and sophisticated.

HOUSE SPECIALTIES Shrimp cocktail, four-course tasting menu, foie gras, Moroccan lamb, and many small plates from French chef Claude Gaty.

OTHER RECOMMENDATIONS Fresh Atlantic salmon encrusted with fresh sage and prosciutto di Parma; lobster ravioli; the towering vacherin dessert; tiramisu or panna cotta.

SUMMARY AND COMMENTS The food is excellent but still takes a back seat to the view. You must check in at a podium, go through security, and ride an elevator to the top. Arrive before sunset for an unforgettably romantic experience.

Trattoria Nakamura-ya ★★★½

JAPANESE	MODERATE	QUALITY	★★★	VALUE	★★★

5040 W. Spring Mountain Road; ☎ 702-251-0022; nakamurayalv.com
WEST OF STRIP

Customers Locals, chefs. **Reservations** Recommended. **When to go** Dinner. **Entrée range** $13–$30. **Payment** All major credit cards. **Service rating** ★★★. **Friendliness rating** ★★★. **Parking** Lot. **Bar** Beer, wine, a variety of sakes. **Wine selection** Good. **Dress** Casual. **Disabled access** Yes. **Hours** Daily, 11:45 a.m.–11:30 p.m.

SETTING AND ATMOSPHERE Nakamura-ya is the first Vegas outpost of Italian-Japanese cuisine—classic Italian dishes like spaghetti carbonara and pasta with creamy walnut sauce, each done in ways rarely seen outside Japan. Be prepared for a delightful experience in this dark, matchbox-size room, where chef Kengo Nakamura does magic tricks in an open kitchen.

HOUSE SPECIALTIES Fritto misto—octopus, calamari, shrimp, and zucchini on wooden skewers—is accompanied by a pair of homemade dipping sauces. Manila clams, swimming in a rich broth with wine and enough garlic to end the *Twilight* franchise, is in reality the very Japanese dish called *asari sakamushi*.

OTHER RECOMMENDATIONS Fried Jidori chicken, the meat cut into bits only slightly larger than popcorn-chicken nuggets, is matchless and a tribute to the skill of the chef. Pasta and sea urchin in tomato cream sauce is a beautiful blend of Italian and Japanese cuisine. Miso carbonara is textbook, if you don't mind miso paste mixed into the eggs, bacon, and cheese blanketing the noodles.

SUMMARY AND COMMENTS The Japanese are obsessed with *itaria-ryori,* what they call Italian food. Tokyo has literally thousands of restaurants in which to eat this cuisine, characterized by light tomato sauce, scandalous amounts of garlic (a component conspicuously absent in Japanese cooking), and various riffs in the key of noodle, masquerading as pasta.

Twist by Pierre Gagnaire ★★★★★

FRENCH	VERY EXPENSIVE	QUALITY	★★★★★	VALUE	★★★★★

Mandarin Oriental Las Vegas, 3752 Las Vegas Blvd. S.; ☎ 702-590-8888; tinyurl.com/twistvegas **MID-STRIP AND ENVIRONS**

Customers Visitors. **Reservations** Essential. **When to go** Dinner. **Entrée range** À la carte, $44–$220; prix fixe, $85–$777. **Payment** All major credit cards. **Service rating** ★★★★½. **Friendliness rating** ★★★★½. **Parking** Valet. **Bar** Full service. **Wine selection** Reasonably priced list of upscale wines. **Dress** Upscale. **Disabled access** Yes. **Hours** Tuesday–Thursday, 6–10 p.m.; Friday and Saturday, 6–10:30 p.m.

SETTING AND ATMOSPHERE On the 23rd and top floor of the chichi Mandarin Oriental Hotel, the modern dining room is tastefully elegant and decorated with glass globes and decorative art. Tables look out onto the Strip.

HOUSE SPECIALTIES Colorful, creative canapés, such as gelée made from Guinness, are a calling card, as are the swank tasting menus. The food of Pierre Gagnaire is among the most creative of the world's chefs. It's food that not only have you not seen before, but also food that most have never even imagined. Menus are seasonal, so dishes may differ from those listed here.

OTHER RECOMMENDATIONS Langoustine five ways is a standout. The chef also does tricks with fish and game, incorporating flavors you don't expect, such as lavender or licorice, in combinations that work like magic. Save room for the wonderful desserts.

SUMMARY AND COMMENTS If you don't wish to order a tasting menu, just order an entrée à la carte and still experience all the bells and whistles, such as canapés and petit fours, without spending a fortune. However you dine, nothing here is for the unadventurous eater.

VegeNation   ★★★

PLANT-BASED	INEXPENSIVE/MODERATE	QUALITY	★★★	VALUE	★★★

616 Carson Ave.; ☎ 702-366-8515; vegenationlv.com   **DOWNTOWN**

Customers Downtown residents, vegetarians, and vegans. **Reservations** Not required. **When to go** Breakfast, lunch, or dinner. **Entrée range** $10–$13. **Payment** All major credit cards. **Service rating** ★★★★. **Friendliness rating** ★★★★½. **Parking** Street. **Bar** Juice cocktails, beer, and wine. **Dress** Casual. **Disabled access** Yes. **Hours** Sunday–Thursday, 8 a.m.–9 p.m.; Friday and Saturday, 8 a.m.–10 p.m.

SETTING AND ATMOSPHERE This casual, hip place lies on the outskirts of Downtown's popular Fremont East district. Original photography, often with mildly political themes, hangs on the walls.

HOUSE SPECIALTIES Shitake and spinach dumplings, "save the tuna" veggie sushi rolls in forbidden rice, jackfruit tacos, and Thai curry vegetable bowl.

SUMMARY AND COMMENTS Chef Donald Lemperle is as dedicated to being a part of the Downtown community as he is to offering serious, plant-based cuisine. As a result, his restaurant has become nearly as popular among Downtown ominvores who come here for the cool vibe and delicious food as it is among vegan and vegetarian tourists and far-flung valley residents who want a bit less animal protein in their diets. Moreover, while his faux meats are as good as you'll find anywhere, plenty of dishes are content to let plants be plants.

Viva Las Arepas   ★★★½

SOUTH AMERICAN	INEXPENSIVE	QUALITY	★★★½	VALUE	★★★★

1616 Las Vegas Blvd. S., Ste. 120; ☎ 702-366-9696; vivalasarepas.com
DOWNTOWN

Customers Locals. **Reservations** Not necessary. **When to go** Anytime. **Entrée range** $4.50–$24. **Payment** All major credit cards. **Service rating** ★★½. **Friendliness rating** ★★★½. **Parking** Limited lot, on street. **Bar** No. **Wine selection** None.

Dress Casual. **Disabled access** Yes. **Hours** Sunday–Thursday, 8 a.m.–10 p.m.; Friday and Saturday, 8 a.m.–midnight.

SETTING AND ATMOSPHERE This unprepossessing, cafeteria-like room specializes in the *arepa,* a Venezuelan corn cake that is typically cut in half and stuffed with savory fillings. Eaten in a burger-style wrapper, one makes a satisfying meal; two constitute a trencherman's feast. Order from the counter and take your seat—you aren't here for the atmosphere.

HOUSE SPECIALTIES Arepas are what most people come for. The most popular one is carne asada—pounded, marinated rib eye finished on hickory and charcoal, as are all meats here. One of the more unusual choices is *reina pepiada,* its minced-chicken filling redolent of garlic and cilantro. *Arepa perico* is a South American Egg McMuffin, filled with ham and egg. Garlic-shrimp arepas are downright addictive. Owner Felix Arellano prepares some of the city's best barbecued meats, cooked on a wood grill as well.

OTHER RECOMMENDATIONS Empanadas and *pastelitos,* snack turnovers made from wheat or corn flour with savory fillings, are also a treat here. Arellano's mixed grill—sausages, pork ribs on the bone, amazing grilled chicken, and pounded steak—is one of the city's best values at under $15. If you fancy tropical beverages, try passion fruit, soursop (*guanabana* in Spanish), or other fruit drinks served over ice. The house rice-and-vegetable medley is another must.

SUMMARY AND COMMENTS This Venezuelan restaurant's authenticity is beyond reproach. It's a meeting place for locals from many South American countries, and the price point and wide variety of snacks and main dishes have made an indelible impression on Anglos.

Yardbird Southern Table & Bar ★★★½

SOUTHERN	EXPENSIVE	QUALITY	★★★★½	VALUE	★★

Venetian Resort, 3355 Las Vegas Blvd. S.; ☎ 702-297-6541; runchickenrun.com
MID-STRIP AND ENVIRONS

Customers Visitors. **Reservations** Recommended. **When to go** When you want to kick back. **Entrée range** $21–$65. **Payment** All major credit cards. **Service rating** ★★★. **Friendliness rating** ★★★½. **Parking** Valet, lot. **Bar** Full service. **Wine selection** Better known for whiskeys and cocktails. **Dress** Casual. **Disabled access** Yes. **Hours** Monday–Friday, 11 a.m.–11 p.m.; Saturday and Sunday, 10 a.m.–11 p.m.

SETTING AND ATMOSPHERE This Miami import tries to channel slow life in the American South with familiar comfort foods and good hooch in this very large, fun, and bustling outpost.

HOUSE SPECIALTIES Many will tell you that the only thing you need to worry about is the naturally raised, braised-for-27-hours fried chicken. Do you get it alone, with waffles, or on buttermilk biscuits? It's a tough decision.

OTHER RECOMMENDATIONS The fried green tomato BLT comes with house-smoked pork belly, tomato jam, and pimento cheese. The Swine Burger 2.0 may be the most decadent burger you eat this year. And make sure to save room for dessert because pastry chef Keris Kuwana shows off her fine-dining experience by putting an elegant spin on classic down-home sweets.

SUMMARY AND COMMENTS These guys do Southern much better than you'd ever expect in a Las Vegas casino—but it comes with a hefty price tag.

Yui Edomae Sushi ★★★★★

3460 Arville St.; ☎ 702-202-2408; yuisushi.com **WEST OF STRIP**

Customers Visitors, locals, sushi fanatics. **Reservations** Very strongly recommended. **When to go** For the sushi experience of a lifetime. Tasting menu range $68–$210. **Payment** All major credit cards. **Service rating** ★★★★½. **Friendliness rating** ★★★★. **Parking** Lot. **Bar** Limited. **Wine selection** Limited. **Dress** Upscale casual. **Disabled access** Yes. **Hours** Monday–Saturday, 6–10:30 p.m. (last seating)

SETTING AND ATMOSPHERE Gen Mizoguchi, who made a name for himself by bringing the Las Vegas suburbs world-class sushi at Kabuto, has created another modern temple to the art form. The stark white interior—accented in light wood grains—holds no more than 10 at the sushi bar, where you can observe Mizoguchi-san and his two apprentices painstakingly prepare your meal, and three four-person booths.

HOUSE SPECIALTIES This is sushi of the highest order, available at only three price points: $68, $120, and $160. The daily selection of species the chef flies in from Japan probably won't be familiar to you, though the Japanese A-5 Wagyu beef will. Have no fear: Put yourself in the chefs' hands, trusting that they know everything there is to know about each fish—most importantly, exactly how to prepare it.

SUMMARY AND COMMENTS This restaurant is exclusively for those who appreciate sushi at the absolute highest level. If you love the film *Jiro Dreams of Sushi,* you'll be telling stories of this meal for years to come. If you've never seen the movie and you like Screaming Orgasm rolls with hot sake shots, this will be a complete waste of your money.

PART FIVE

SHOPPING *and* SEEING *the* SIGHTS

SHOPPING *in* LAS VEGAS

EVERY HOTEL-CASINO HAS A RETAIL CENTER, large or small—some are extravagant, with high-fashion boutiques, such as Bellagio and Wynn, while others, such as the Miracle Mile Shops and Stratosphere Tower Shops, are midpriced and more affordable. Aside from guests purchasing sundries and souvenirs, hotel retailers are most often patronized by casino players cashing in their chips or curious vacationers conducting reconnaissance visits. Discounts and special sales are sporadic, depending on the vendors' need to move or replace merchandise.

With the renaissance of Downtown Las Vegas, more merchants have ventured there and to the surrounding blocks, opening smallish shops and cafés, although the gigantic Premium Outlets North supersedes all else. As Las Vegas's population has increased, so have large malls in the suburbs, several of which are included here.

Shopping overload is symptomatic of Las Vegas, with opportunities everywhere 24/7. The average amount spent per trip on shopping by Las Vegas visitors was $157 in 2017. To maximize shopping opportunities, before you leave be sure to check hotel, mall, and store websites for additional coupons and noteworthy promotions.

To find out what's in store for you, check out the high-profile shopping opportunities listed by area and then alphabetically below.

On or Near the Strip

Bellagio Shops

Bellagio, 3600 Las Vegas Blvd. S.; ☎ 702-693-7111; bellagio.com

Hours Daily, 10 a.m.–midnight (some stores close earlier). **Number of stores** 22. **Number of restaurants** 4. **Anchor stores** Giorgio Armani, Chanel. **Free self-parking** No. **Valet parking** Yes. **Other shopping venues within a 15-minute walk** Grand Bazaar, Bally's Avenue, Le Boulevard, Miracle Mile Shops, Cosmopolitan Shops, Crystals, Showcase Mall, Hawaiian Marketplace.

SETTING The Via Bellagio Shops are just inside the point where three pedestrian bridges crossing the Strip and Flamingo Road meet; consequently, there is heavy foot traffic in the arcade. The stylish retailers are top-shelf and cater to high rollers, although the hoi polloi are more than welcome.

SHOPS OF NOTE Bottega Veneta, Harry Winston, Breguet, Prada, Gucci, Tiffany & Co., Dior, Bella Dona.

RESTAURANTS OF NOTE Prime, Picasso, Yellowtail, Lago, Le Cirque.

ATTRACTIONS AND ENTERTAINMENT Bellagio Gallery of Fine Art, the beautiful dancing fountains next to the mall entrance, Dale Chihuly Gallery, Botanical Garden, the Conservatory, Cirque du Soleil's "O".

CONSUMER TIPS Six more shops are located on the Promenade near the pool entrance, and the Via Fiore includes three boutiques around the Conservatory and Botanical Garden.

Circus Circus Promenade

Circus Circus, 2880 Las Vegas Blvd. S.; ☎ 702-734-0410; circuscircus.com

Hours Daily, 9 a.m.–11 p.m. **Number of stores** 27. **Number of restaurants** 5. **Anchor stores** Vegas Young, Old Time Photos. **Free self-parking** Yes. **Valet parking** Yes. **Other shopping venues within a 15-minute walk** Stratosphere Tower Shops, Fashion Show Mall.

SETTING At family-friendly Circus Circus, there are two areas with shops: downstairs in the corridor between the lobby and the casino are 16 retailers and restaurants, and upstairs via an escalator are 11 more. For the most part, offerings are inexpensive imported items. Bling and rhinestones prevail.

SHOPS OF NOTE City Life USA, Shoes & More, Vegas Young.

RESTAURANTS OF NOTE The Steak House, Westside Deli, Circus Buffet, Blue Iguana, Vince Neil's.

ATTRACTIONS AND ENTERTAINMENT Neighboring the Promenade Shops upstairs is the Adventuredome, a fully enclosed theme park. Aerial and acrobatic acts perform hourly in the celestial space above the casino.

CONSUMER TIPS Expect continual noise and pandemonium in both shopping areas, the result of joyous kids and their families entertained by the hotel's Big Top attractions.

Cosmopolitan Shops

Cosmopolitan, 3708 Las Vegas Blvd. S.; ☎ 702-698-7000; cosmopolitanlasvegas.com

Hours Daily, 10 a.m.–11 p.m. **Number of stores** 13. **Number of restaurants** 4. **Anchor stores** Jason of Beverly Hills. **Free self-parking** No. **Valet parking** Yes. **Other shopping venues within a 15-minute walk** Crystals, Miracle Mile Shops, Le Boulevard, Bally's Avenue, Grand Bazaar, Showcase Mall, Hawaiian Marketplace, Forum Shops.

SETTING The second-level cavalcade of shops features retailers with no brick-and-mortar stores elsewhere in Las Vegas. These are on-trend shops with attitude, just like the Cosmopolitan itself. Along with restaurants and the Boulevard Pool complex, the arcade is in the east tower overlooking the Strip.

SHOPS OF NOTE Molly Brown's Swimwear, Stitched, Jason of Beverly Hills, All Saints, CRSVR Sneaker Boutique, and Monogram.

RESTAURANTS OF NOTE China Poblano, Holsteins, Va Bene Café Due, Wicked Spoon Buffet.

Las Vegas Strip
Shopping and Attractions

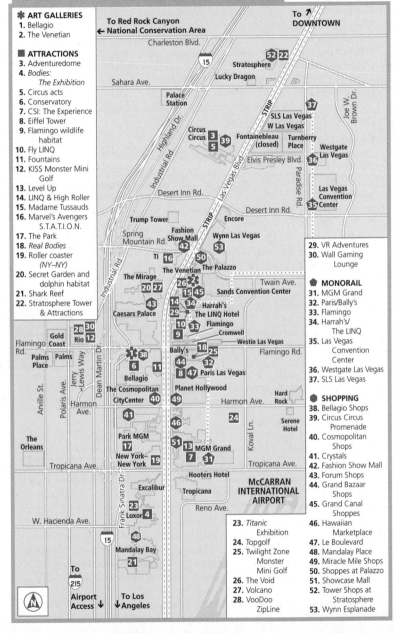

✳ ART GALLERIES
1. Bellagio
2. The Venetian

■ ATTRACTIONS
3. Adventuredome
4. *Bodies:*
   The Exhibition
5. Circus acts
6. Conservatory
7. CSI: The Experience
8. Eiffel Tower
9. Flamingo wildlife
   habitat
10. Fly LINQ
11. Fountains
12. KISS Monster Mini
    Golf
13. Level Up
14. LINQ & High Roller
15. Madame Tussauds
16. Marvel's Avengers
    S.T.A.T.I.O.N.
17. The Park
18. *Real Bodies*
19. Roller coaster
    (NY–NY)
20. Secret Garden and
    dolphin habitat
21. Shark Reef
22. Stratosphere Tower
    & Attractions

23. *Titanic*
    Exhibition
24. Topgolf
25. Twilight Zone
    Monster Mini
    Golf
26. The Void
27. Volcano
28. VooDoo
    ZipLine
29. VR Adventures
30. Wall Gaming
    Lounge

● MONORAIL
31. MGM Grand
32. Paris/Bally's
33. Flamingo
34. Harrah's/
    The LINQ
35. Las Vegas
    Convention
    Center
36. Westgate Las Vegas
37. SLS Las Vegas

● SHOPPING
38. Bellagio Shops
39. Circus Circus
    Promenade
40. Cosmopolitan
    Shops
41. Crystals
42. Fashion Show Mall
43. Forum Shops
44. Grand Bazaar
    Shops
45. Grand Canal
    Shoppes
46. Hawaiian
    Marketplace
47. Le Boulevard
48. Mandalay Place
49. Miracle Mile Shops
50. Shoppes at Palazzo
51. Showcase Mall
52. Tower Shops at
    Stratosphere
53. Wynn Esplanade

ATTRACTIONS AND ENTERTAINMENT The Race and Sports Book is adjacent and next to the famous Chandelier Bar.

CONSUMER TIPS Pedestrian bridges across the Strip and Harmon Avenue enter the hotel at the shopping level, resulting in a rush of looky-looks.

Crystals at CityCenter

3720 Las Vegas Blvd. S.; ☎ 702-590-9299 or 866-754-2489; crystalsatcitycenter.com

Hours Monday–Thursday, 10 a.m.–11 p.m.; Friday–Sunday, 10 a.m.–midnight. **Number of stores** 44. **Number of restaurants** 4. **Anchor stores** Prada, Louis Vuitton, Dolce & Gabbana, Tom Ford. **Free self-parking** Yes. **Valet parking** Yes. **Other shopping venues within a 15-minute walk** Cosmopolitan Shops, Via Bellagio, Miracle Mile Shops, Forum Shops, Le Boulevard, Bally's Avenue, Grand Bazaar, Hawaiian Marketplace, Showcase Mall.

SETTING Crystals is a 500,000-square-foot retail center at CityCenter, wedged between Aria, Veer, and the Strip. Conceived as an urban park, Crystals features exterior landscapes inside beneath a cubic crystalline roof. Deciduous trees line walkways, while displays throughout reflect the four seasons over an all-white backdrop. Über-posh, the offerings are well-recognized international luxury brands, and the restaurants are helmed by celebrity chefs. There are several bilevel flagship stores.

SHOPS OF NOTE Stella McCartney, Balenciaga, Van Cleef and Arpels, Christian Dior, Hermès, Versace, Fendi, Yves Saint Laurent, Céline, Lalique, Lanvin.

RESTAURANTS OF NOTE Mastro's Ocean Club, The Pub, Cucina by Wolfgang Puck.

ATTRACTIONS AND ENTERTAINMENT There are two extraordinary water features within Crystals: Glacia, a movable feast of carved ice columns with changing patterns responding to colorful lighting and music; and Halo, angled, brightly lit clear tubes containing churning water—great for selfie backgrounds. Between the Mandarin Oriental and Aria resorts is Crystals Place, a 4,200-square-foot annex and collection of several art galleries displaying the artwork, designs, and furniture of the CityCenter architects and artists.

CONSUMER TIPS Seating is sparse for relaxing or gawking. Don't expect coupons or deep discounts—the choices are higher than high-end. Most retailers will mail your purchases home. The concierge services desk is centrally located in the trunk of the avant-garde wooden-slat tree house sculpture. The hard-to-miss entrance is right on the Strip between Harmon Road and CityCenter Place. There is another entry inside CityCenter near Veer Towers and the tram station. Crystals is the intermediate stop on the tram, which carries visitors between the Bellagio Spa Tower and Park MGM. Valet parking is on the west side by Aria's porte cochere, and all self-parking is underground.

Fashion Show Mall

3200 Las Vegas Blvd. S.; ☎ 702-369-8382; thefashionshow.com

Hours Daily, 10 a.m.–9 p.m. **Number of stores** 250. **Number of restaurants** 10 plus food court. **Anchor stores** Dillard's, Macy's, Saks Fifth Avenue, Neiman Marcus, Forever 21, Nordstrom. **Free self-parking** Yes. **Valet parking** Yes, 5 locations. **Other shopping venues within a 15-minute walk** Wynn and Encore Esplanades, Grand Canal Shoppes, Shoppes at the Palazzo, Forum Shops.

SETTING There is no theme here—no Roman columns or canals with gondolas; it's shiny but, aside from the Strip entrance, architecturally unimaginative. Shopping is king here. Although there is no shortage of boutiques or designer shops, the presence of the big department stores defines the experience for most customers. The selection is immense, and most retailers are familiar and well known.

SHOPS OF NOTE Lush, The Lego Store, Lululemon, Hugo Boss, Clarks, Microsoft, ABC Stores, Kate Spade.

unofficial **TIP**

The Fashion Show Mall is the place to go for that new sport coat, tie, blouse, or skirt at a reasonable price.

RESTAURANTS OF NOTE Capital Grille, El Segundo Sol, Maggiano's Little Italy, Kona Grill.

ATTRACTIONS AND ENTERTAINMENT The mall houses three art galleries. To underscore the name, the mall stages free fashion shows from noon to 6 p.m. on most weekend afternoons.

CONSUMER TIPS This supersized mall sits at the intersection of Las Vegas Boulevard South and Spring Mountain Road. Added services include hotel delivery, personal shoppers, and favorable return policies. Foreign currency exchange is available.

The Forum Shops

3500 Las Vegas Blvd. S.; ☎ 702-893-4800; caesars.com/caesars-palace

Hours Sunday–Thursday, 10 a.m.–11 p.m.; Friday and Saturday, 10 a.m.–midnight. **Number of stores** 130. **Number of restaurants** 12. **Anchor stores** Brooks Brothers, Niketown, Express, Banana Republic. **Free self-parking** No. **Valet parking** Yes. **Other shopping venues within a 15-minute walk** Via Bellagio, Crystals, Grand Bazaar Shops, Bally's Avenue, Le Boulevard, Miracle Mile Shops, Fashion Show Mall, Grand Canal Shoppes, Shoppes at the Palazzo, Wynn and Encore Esplanades.

SETTING The Forum Shops is a *très chic* (*et très cher*) shopping complex situated between Caesars Palace and the Mirage. Connected to the Forum Casino in Caesars Palace, the extensive mall offers a Roman market–themed shopping environment. Executed on a scale that is extraordinary even for Caesars, The Forum Shops replicates the grandeur of Rome at the height of its glory. Shops and restaurants line an ancient Roman street punctuated by plazas and fountains. More retailers and eateries populate the three-story Appian Way on the north end, where a stunning statue of David oversees the Strip entrance.

SHOPS OF NOTE H&M, Baccarat, Ermenegildo Zegna, Burberry, Jimmy Choo, Tory Burch, Rolex, Elie Tahari, Gucci, M Missoni, Lacoste, Tumi.

RESTAURANTS OF NOTE Joe's Stone Crab, Border Grill, Sushi Roku, Trevi, Carmine's, The Palm, Planet Hollywood.

ATTRACTIONS AND ENTERTAINMENT Though indoors, clouds, sky, and celestial bodies are projected on the vaulted ceilings to simulate the actual time of day outside. Statuary in The Forum is magnificent; some is even animatronic. As in Rome, shopping neighborhoods are separated by plazas and fountains.

CONSUMER TIPS Expect heavy pedestrian traffic—overall, you'll find more walkers than shoppers. The mall has three levels, but to cover the complex, the second level is the way to go. Valet parking is underground by Caesars.

Grand Bazaar Shops

3635 Las Vegas Blvd. S.; ☎ 702-736-4988; grandbazaarshops.com

Hours Sunday–Thursday, 10 a.m.–10 p.m.; Friday and Saturday, 10 a.m.–11 p.m. **Number of stores** 85. **Number of restaurants** None. **Anchor stores** Mixx, Swatch. **Free self-parking** Yes. **Valet parking** Yes. **Other shopping venues within a 15-minute walk** Bally's Avenue, Le Boulevard, Forum Shops, Miracle Mile Shops, Crystals, Hawaiian Marketplace, Showcase Mall.

SETTING Juxtaposed on Bally's front corner at one of the busiest pedestrian intersections in the United States, the two-acre lower plaza is home to a Las Vegas version of an international outdoor marketplace. Cute metal cubicles vend goods from many countries. Mosaic patterns highlight walkways and colorful tentlike roofs with an essence of Arabian Nights.

SHOPS OF NOTE LOLO, Tokyo Nail Art, Swarovski, Lindbergh, Pascanoush, Havaianas, Sunset Case.

RESTAURANTS OF NOTE Wahlburgers, Blue Ribbon Fried Chicken, Giordano's, Ramen-Ya, Sin City Brewing Co.

ATTRACTIONS AND ENTERTAINMENT An LED show with flashing patterns on the hexagonal canopies is featured every night. Reliving New Year's Eve twice a night, at 9 p.m. and midnight, a 4,000-pound Swarovski crystal starbust dazzles spectators with a musical light show.

CONSUMER TIPS Fifteen shops offer international street foods. You can design your own wearable art and cosmetics at several workshops. Plenty of valet parking and free self-parking are available at the Bally's and Paris hotel garages and all hotels in the vicinity.

Grand Canal Shoppes

Venetian, 3377 Las Vegas Blvd. S.; ☎ 702-414-4525; grandcanalshoppes.com

Hours Sunday–Thursday, 10 a.m.–11 p.m.; Friday and Saturday, 10 a.m.–midnight. **Number of stores** 70. **Number of restaurants** 7 plus food court (11 counters). **Anchor stores** Cuadra, Horologio, Johnston & Murphy. **Free self-parking** Yes. **Valet parking** Yes. **Other shopping venues within a 15-minute walk** Shoppes at the Palazzo, Fashion Show Mall, Forum Shops, Wynn and Encore Esplanades, Grand Bazaar, Le Boulevard, Bally's Avenue.

SETTING Grandiose Venetian architecture with a retail deluge, the Grand Canal Shoppes are similar to The Forum Shops in terms of the realistic theming, but this time the setting is the modern-day canals of Venice. The shops, restaurants, boutiques, and cafés are arrayed beside a quarter-mile-long Venetian street flanking the canal. A 70-foot ceiling (more than six stories high) with simulated sky enhances the openness and provides perspective. The centerpiece is a replica of St. Mark's Square, without the pigeons. Gondolas navigating the canal add a heightened sense of commerce and activity.

SHOPS OF NOTE Na Hoku, Pearl Factory, Houdini's Magic Shop, Chapel Hats.

RESTAURANTS OF NOTE Canaletto, Tao Asian Bistro, Buddy V's Ristorante.

ATTRACTIONS AND ENTERTAINMENT Gondoliers provide canal rides while singing operatic arias. "Streetmosphere" is a troupe of costumed musical performers in St. Mark's Square—classical rather than pop prevails. Living statues throughout defy gravity. Evenings feature strolling musicians. Tao Nightclub is nearby. Check out *Human Nature Jukebox* if you're in the mood for a show. Madame Tussauds Wax Museum is on the Strip side of the Venetian.

CONSUMER TIPS The complex is convoluted, so follow the canal and you won't get lost. Most of the restaurants and the food court are located together off the south parking garage in an area separated slightly from the retail shops. If you're fond of Italian cuisine and gelatos, you'll find abundant choices throughout the complex.

Las Vegas Premium Outlets South

7400 Las Vegas Blvd. S.; ☎ 702-896-5599; premiumoutlets.com

Hours Monday–Saturday, 9 a.m.–9 p.m.; Sunday, 9 a.m.–8 p.m. **Number of stores** 145. **Number of restaurants** 2 food courts. **Anchor stores** Nike, Ann Taylor, VF Outlet, Guess, Reebok, Ralph Lauren, Coach, Tommy Hilfiger. **Free self-parking** Yes. **Valet parking** No. **Other shopping venues within a 15-minute walk** Town Square.

SETTING Located 3 miles south of Tropicana Avenue, Premium Outlets South is very similar to its sister mall Downtown; however, it is an air-conditioned indoor mall and popular with locals. The retailers represented are a combo of high-end and low-end.

SHOPS OF NOTE Michael Kors, DKNY, Perry Ellis, Timberland, Brooks Brothers, Kitchen Collection, Lane Bryant, OshKosh B'gosh, Crocs.

RESTAURANTS OF NOTE Casual restaurants located outside the mall along the west perimeter of the parking lot include Buffalo Wild Wings, Raising Cane's Chicken Fingers, IHOP, Roberto's Tacos, Smashburger, Jersey Mike's Subs, L&L Hawaiian BBQ, Joe's NY Pizza, and Panda Express.

ATTRACTIONS AND ENTERTAINMENT More shopping and snacking.

CONSUMER TIPS The easiest way to get there is to drive south on Las Vegas Boulevard. The mall is on the left (east) side just south of Warm Springs Road. There is also public transit service from the Strip. Be sure to check in at the information desk at the north end for the VIP discount coupon book. More savings are available on the website by clicking "In-Store Promotions."

Le Boulevard

Paris Las Vegas, 3655 Las Vegas Blvd. S.; ☎ 702-946-7000; caesars.com/paris-las-vegas

Hours Daily, 9 a.m.–11 p.m. **Number of stores** 20. **Number of restaurants** 6. **Anchor stores** Misura, Pérola, Paris Line, Les Eléments. **Free self-parking** No. **Valet parking** Yes. **Other shopping venues within a 15-minute walk** Grand Bazaar Shops, Bally's Avenue, Miracle Mile Shops, Crystals, Forum Shops, Via Bellagio, Cosmopolitan Shops, Hawaiian Marketplace, Showcase Mall.

SETTING Le Boulevard is an avenue of French-themed boutiques along the posterior of Paris Las Vegas, linking it with Bally's via a short promenade. Cobblestone streets, mansard roofs, and French music and signage transport shoppers across the Atlantic to the real City of Lights.

SHOPS OF NOTE La Cave Gourmet, Perfume de Paris, Misura, Glitz to Go, Travel+, Les Eléments.

RESTAURANTS OF NOTE Martorano's Café Bleu, Le Village Buffet, La Creperie, Yong Kang Street, Café Belle Madeleine.

ENTERTAINMENT AND ATTRACTIONS Napoleon's Dueling Pianos, hypnotist Anthony Cools, and the Eiffel Tower Experience.

CONSUMER TIPS From Paris's parking garage, take the elevator down: Le Boulevard is at the bottom of the escalator bank.

Miracle Mile Shops

Planet Hollywood, 3663 Las Vegas Blvd. S.; ☎ 702-866-0703; miraclemileshopslv.com

Hours Sunday–Thursday, 10 a.m.–11 p.m.; Friday and Saturday, 10 a.m.–midnight. **Number of stores** 150. **Number of restaurants** 17. **Anchor stores** Guess, Shoe Palace. **Free self-parking** Yes. **Valet parking** Yes. **Other shopping venues within a 15-minute walk** Grand Bazaar Shops, Bally's Avenue, Le Boulevard, Crystals, Cosmopolitan Shops, Forum Shops, Hawaiian Marketplace, Showcase Mall.

SETTING Meandering at the south and rear sides of Planet Hollywood Resort, the Miracle Mile Shops is a 450,000-square-foot shopping and entertainment complex. The venue features street scenes in a concourse that stretches around the periphery of the Zappos Theater. Shop facades sit beneath an arched ceiling painted and lighted to simulate the evening sky. Miracle Mile shops offer primarily midprice boutique shopping.

SHOPS OF NOTE Urban Outfitters, True Religion, Quicksilver, Brighton, Victoria's Secret, GNC.

RESTAURANTS OF NOTE Lombardi's, Oyster One, Pampas Grille, Cabo Wabo Cantina, Earl of Sandwich.

ATTRACTIONS AND ENTERTAINMENT Two daily shows captivating audiences are an indoor rainstorm, plus a light-and-sound show staged 10 a.m.–11 p.m. on the hour. Two theaters, The V and Saxe, present a roster of shows. The Zappos Theater schedules headliners throughout the year.

CONSUMER TIPS The mall is lively and noisy, and much of the affordable merchandise tends toward the flashy and glamorous. A pedestrian bridge situated mid-Strip from the Cosmopolitan provides accessibility over busy Las Vegas Boulevard. A coupon book is available at the information center. Access valet parking and the parking garage from Harmon Avenue. Several of the mall's bars and restaurants are open beyond midnight after retail hours.

The Shoppes at Mandalay Place

3950 Las Vegas Blvd. S.; ☎ 702-632-7777; mandalaybay.com

Hours Daily, 10 a.m.–11 p.m. **Number of stores** 26. **Number of restaurants** 7. **Anchor stores** Store on the Green, Elton's, Peter Lik Gallery. **Free self-parking** No. **Valet parking** Yes. **Other shopping venues within a 15-minute walk** Crystals, Hawaiian Marketplace, Showcase Mall.

SETTING Situated on the second-level Sky Bridge, this mall with flair serves as the pedestrian connector linking Mandalay Bay and Luxor. The retailers seem more diverse and selectively chosen than at many other venues, making the shopping interesting even for those not hooked on shopping.

SHOPS OF NOTE Shoe Obsession, Guinness, Ron Jon Surf Shop, The Art of Shaving, Nora Blue, Cariloha.

RESTAURANTS OF NOTE RM Seafood, Rx Boiler, Hussong's Cantina, Burger Bar, Ri Ra Irish Pub.

ATTRACTIONS AND ENTERTAINMENT Cirque du Soleil's *Michael Jackson ONE,* House of Blues Concert Hall. Several bars and lounges in the casino surround the escalator leading up to the shops.

CONSUMER TIPS A mall coupon booklet is available online. Inside Mandalay Bay Resort, the House of Blues Shop features musical gifts.

The Shoppes at the Palazzo

Palazzo, 3327 Las Vegas Blvd. S.; ☎ 702-414-4525; palazzo.com

Hours Sunday–Thursday, 10 a.m.–11 p.m.; Friday and Saturday, 10 a.m.–midnight. **Number of stores** 60. **Number of restaurants** 7. **Anchor stores** Barneys, Coach, Roberto Cavalli. **Free self-parking** Yes. **Valet parking** Yes. **Other shopping venues within a 15-minute walk** Grand Canal Shoppes, Fashion Show Mall, Forum Shops, Wynn and Encore Esplanades, Grand Bazaar, Le Boulevard, Bally's Avenue.

SETTING The Palazzo Resort is the Venetian's sister property. Although connected to the Grand Canal Shoppes by a walkway, The Shoppes at the Palazzo are tonier, and many are upscale Italian brands, with jewelry well represented. The complex is essentially unthemed.

SHOPS OF NOTE Guerlain, St. Croix, Bauman Rare Books, Canali, Links of London, Christian Louboutin, Montblanc, Prosecco.

RESTAURANTS OF NOTE CUT, Grimaldi's, Table 10, Sushi Samba.

ATTRACTIONS AND ENTERTAINMENT Madame Tussauds Wax Museum. The lobby level of The Shoppes at the Palazzo borders a lovely waterfall and garden with seasonal florals and foliage.

CONSUMER TIPS Bring your high-limit credit cards. There are two Strip pedestrian entrances. The best parking entrance is on the north side off Spring Mountain/Sands Road.

Stratosphere Tower Shops

Stratosphere, 2000 Las Vegas Blvd. S.; ☎ 702-380-7777; stratospherehotel.com

Hours Sunday–Thursday, 10 a.m.–10 p.m.; Friday and Saturday, 10 a.m.–11 p.m. **Number of stores** 30. **Number of restaurants** 4. **Anchor stores** Stratosphere Gifts, China +. **Free self-parking** Yes. **Valet parking** Yes. **Other shopping venues within a 15-minute walk** Circus Circus Promenade.

SETTING The Tower Shops are part midway and part strip mall, extending along a narrow passageway on the hotel's second floor. Shoppers will find an affordable mixture of figurines, costume jewelry, leather, clothing, hats, cell phone accoutrements, and magic. Exhibiting a sense of irony, the oxygen bar is between the daiquiri bar and a smoke shop.

SHOPS OF NOTE $10 Boutique, Amazing Perfume, D'eor, Las Vegas Magic Shop.

RESTAURANTS OF NOTE El Nopal Grille, Nunzio's Pizzeria, Chicago Food House.

ATTRACTIONS AND ENTERTAINMENT Haunted Arcade, Sky Jump.

CONSUMER TIPS Easiest access is up the escalator from the casino. The arcade is near the hotel's main showroom, so shops are busier in the evening.

Town Square

6605 Las Vegas Blvd. S.; ☎ 702-269-5000; mytownsquarelasvegas.com

Hours Monday–Thursday, 10 a.m.–9 p.m.; Friday and Saturday, 10 a.m.–10 p.m.; Sunday, 11 a.m.–8 p.m. **Number of stores** 95. **Number of restaurants** 20. **Anchor stores** The Container Store, Sephora, Abercrombie & Fitch, Staples, Saks Off 5th, Whole Foods Superstore. **Free self-parking** Yes. **Valet parking** Yes. **Other shopping venues within a 15-minute walk** Premium Outlets South.

SETTING Just 0.75 mile south of Mandalay Bay, Town Square is comprised of 26 low-rise buildings and is designed as a multiblock village with streets, sidewalks, and even a park with a playground. There is an extensive selection of merchandise, restaurants, and entertainment venues. The largest cluster of retailers is on the north side. A locals' favorite.

SHOPS OF NOTE Apple, Tommy Bahama, Victoria's Secret.

RESTAURANTS OF NOTE Blue Martini, Fleming's Steakhouse, Brio Tuscan Grille, Kabuki Japanese, Texas de Brazil, California Pizza Kitchen, Miller's Ale House.

ATTRACTIONS AND ENTERTAINMENT GameWorks, AMC 18 multiplex theater, Baobab Stage live.

CONSUMER TIPS Get a map! The side streets are packed with shops, but overhead signage is difficult to read, camouflaged by foliage, hanging lamps, and other obstacles. Bring plenty of quarters for streetside metered parking, although free parking is available in large lots and garages on the periphery. Parking cards for the meters are available at the concierge desk for up to $20; parking is $1 per hour, with a limit of 2 hours per swipe. Complimentary shuttles from the Strip run 11 a.m.–8 p.m. daily. Call ☎ 702-269-5001 for schedules and pick-up points.

Wynn Esplanade/Encore Esplanade/Wynn Plaza

3131 Las Vegas Blvd. S.; ☎ 702-770-7000; wynnlasvegas.com

Hours Sunday–Thursday, 10 a.m.–11 p.m.; Friday and Saturday, 10 a.m.–midnight. **Number of stores** Wynn, 17; Encore, 7. **Number of restaurants** 9. **Free self-parking** No. **Valet parking** Yes. **Other shopping venues within a 15-minute walk** Fashion Show Mall, Shoppes at the Palazzo, Grand Canal Shoppes, Forum Shops.

SETTING Resort entrepreneur Steve Wynn selected the epitome of high-end designers for the two exclusive malls, which feature an insanely expensive array of upscale shops and boutiques. Wynn Esplanade surrounds the Lake of Dreams near the Atrium. Encore Esplanade is across from XS nightclub along the connectway linking the Wynn and Encore Resorts. The 24 boutiques are the zenith of luxury shopping and are the stratospheric brands celebrities wear and fashionistas fantasize about.

Expanding the considerable empire, Wynn Resorts is building a charming bilevel luxury shopping addition to the Encore and Wynn Resorts. Fronting the Strip, Wynn Plaza, the new 70,000-square-foot arcade with a French flair, resembles Paris's Avenue Matignon and doubles the area and inventory of high-end fashion brands on-site.

SHOPS OF NOTE *Chez Wynn:* Alexander McQueen, Givenchy, Graff, Dior, Chopard, Brioni. *Chez Encore:* Hermès, Loro Pana, Chanel, Christian Louboutin. *Wynn Plaza:* Cipriani, Urth Caffé, SoulCycle, Céline, Balmain, Loewe, James Perse, Cotton Citizen, Marie France Van Damme, Vitra Eyewear.

RESTAURANTS OF NOTE *Wynn:* Lakeside, Costa di Mare, Sinatra, Mizumi, SW Steakhouse. *Encore:* Andrea's, Wazuzu.

ATTRACTIONS AND ENTERTAINMENT Lake of Dreams special-effects show, Conservatory Garden, *Le Rêve*.

CONSUMER TIPS Personal shoppers are available.

Downtown

Bridge Shops at the Cal

California, 12 E. Ogden Ave.; ☎ 702-385-2222; thecal.com

Hours Daily, 8 a.m.–11 p.m. **Number of stores** 6. **Number of restaurants** 1. **Free self-parking** Yes. **Valet parking** Yes. **Other shopping venues within a 15-minute walk** Container Park.

SETTING Catering to the sizeable numbers of Pacific Islanders visiting the hotel, Downtown's California bills itself as "The 9th Island," with stores reflecting the tastes and interests of that market. The shops are located on the mezzanine-level bridge over Main Street, which links the hotel to its sister property Main Street Station.

SHOPS OF NOTE Ethel M Chocolates, Vegas 808.

RESTAURANTS OF NOTE Redwood Steakhouse, Aloha Specialties, Market Street Cafe, California Noodle House, Lappert's Gourmet Ice.

ATTRACTIONS AND ENTERTAINMENT Golden Arm Wall of Fame, Kids' Arcade.

CONSUMER TIPS Early risers will find several shops open at dawn.

Container Park
707 Fremont St.; ☎ 702-359-9982; downtowncontainerpark.com

Hours Sunday–Saturday, 11 a.m.–9 p.m. **Number of stores** 19. **Number of restaurants** 4. **Free self-parking** No. **Valet parking** No. **Other shopping venues within a 15-minute walk** Fremont Street Experience, Pawn Plaza.

SETTING Located in the Fremont East Entertainment District, the open-air Container Park is an innovative concept in architecture; the petite boutiques and galleries are prefab shipping cubes stacked as storefronts. The operative steel decor is ubiquitous, from the fire-breathing praying mantis sculpture greeting visitors to the abundant chairs and tables on multilevel outdoor decks.

SHOPS OF NOTE Gamblers General Store, Athena's Jewelry Box, Kappa Toys, Lovo Cigars, JinJu Chocolates.

RESTAURANTS OF NOTE Big Ern's BBQ, Downtown Terrace, Cheffini's Hot Dogs.

ATTRACTIONS AND ENTERTAINMENT For climbers there's a kids' playground overseen by a four-level tree house and 30-foot slide. An open-air theater presents a range of free concerts, as well as a parkour show daily.

CONSUMER TIPS There are several parking options in the vicinity: free and metered street parking for several blocks surrounding Container Park, and valet and free parking in hotels along Fremont Street. The Fremont Street Experience is three blocks west.

Las Vegas Premium Outlets North
875 Grand Central Pkwy.; ☎ 702-474-7500; premiumoutlets.com

Hours Monday–Saturday, 9 a.m.–9 p.m.; Sunday, 9 a.m.–8 p.m. **Number of stores** 180. **Number of restaurants** 1 plus food court (6 counters). **Anchor stores** Disney Outlet, Ralph Lauren, Timberland, Nike, Tommy Hilfiger, Brooks Brothers, Banana Republic, Michael Kors. **Free self-parking** Yes. **Valet parking** Yes. **Other shopping venues within a 15-minute walk** None.

SETTING So many shops . . . so little time! Premium Outlets North is a clone of other Premium Outlet malls across the United States but much larger. Apparel shops predominate and range from low- to high-end. The complex truly lives up to its reputation as an outlet, with designer labels at discounted prices. Especially abundant are jewelry and shoe sources.

SHOPS OF NOTE Crocs, Dunhill, Carolina Herrera, Diane von Furstenberg, Johnston & Murphy, TAG Heuer, Van Heusen, Clarks, Diesel.

RESTAURANTS OF NOTE Cheesecake Factory, Shake Shack.

ATTRACTIONS AND ENTERTAINMENT Shopping and snacking.

CONSUMER TIPS North of Charleston Boulevard, between I-15 and Downtown, the main entrance is on Grand Central Parkway, although there are ancillary entrances on the south and north ends near the two parking garages. For coupons, visit the information desk in the southwest plaza for discounts. Valet parking is $6; stands are on the west access street and on the north side off Bonneville Avenue by Saks Off 5th. Foreign currency exchange is available through Travelex, located in the food court. Parts, but not all, of the mall walkways are shaded, so walking between stores can be exceptionally hot from June through mid-September.

Pawn Plaza

725 Las Vegas Blvd. S.; ☎ 702-385-7912; gspawn.com

Hours Daily, 9 a.m.–9 p.m. **Number of stores** 16. **Number of restaurants** 4. **Anchor store** Gold & Silver Pawn. **Free self-parking** No. **Valet parking** No. **Other shopping venues within a 15-minute walk** Fremont Street Experience, Container Park.

SETTING Pawn Plaza is a two-level Rubik's Cube of modular units created by the Harrison family, featured on the History Channel's reality show *Pawn Stars.*

SHOPS OF NOTE Gold & Silver Pawn Shop.

RESTAURANTS OF NOTE Rick's Rollin' Smoke BBQ, Good Pie.

CONSUMER TIPS Pawn Plaza was created to entertain the 4,000 visitors waiting daily to enter the Gold & Silver Pawn Shop, site of the popular TV series. The show's stars seldom venture outside because they are mobbed by fans. There is limited free parking in the lot adjacent to the pawn shop, but you must provide your name and contact information; there's also metered street parking in the residential neighborhood to the east. If you want to shop in the pawn store, arrive before 11 a.m. or be prepared to wait in a long line to enter. In case you were planning on hocking your wedding ring for some quick craps cash, interest rates run around 13% per month.

In the Burbs

The District

2225 Village Walk Drive, Henderson; ☎ 702-564-8595; shopthedistrictgvr.com

Hours Monday–Saturday, 10 a.m.–9 p.m.; Sunday, 11 a.m.–6 p.m. **Number of stores** 30+. **Number of restaurants** 14. **Anchor stores** Pottery Barn, Jos. A. Bank, REI, Loft. **Free self-parking** Yes. **Valet parking** No. **Other venues within a 15-minute walk** The District Green.

SETTING Eleven miles southeast of the Strip and adjacent Green Valley Ranch Resort & Spa, The District resembles a Georgetown, Washington, D.C., commercial and residential street. The central pedestrian plaza has been eliminated in favor of free street parking, but the leafy landscape shading abundant tables and benches remains. The shopping mix includes casual restaurants, many apparel shops, and a couple dozen specialty stores.

SHOPS OF NOTE Soma Intimates, Williams-Sonoma, White House/Black Market, Anthropologie, The Walking Company, Janie and Jack, REI.

RESTAURANTS OF NOTE Elephant Bar, Lucille's Smokehouse Bar-B-Que, P.F. Chang's, King's Fish House.

ATTRACTIONS AND ENTERTAINMENT Spring and fall farmer's market.

CONSUMER TIPS On Sunday, some stores are open later, depending on foot traffic. The District Green slightly east includes Bella Bridesmaids (by appointment), West Elm, Whole Foods, Cheesecake Factory, and more.

Downtown Summerlin

I-215 Beltway at Sahara Ave.; ☎ 702-832-1000; downtownsummerlin.com

Hours Monday–Saturday, 10 a.m.–9 p.m.; Sunday, 11 a.m.–7 p.m. **Number of stores** 105. **Number of restaurants** 12. **Anchor stores** Dillard's, Macy's, Nordstrom's Rack,

Sports Town. **Free self-parking** Yes. **Valet parking** Yes. **Other shopping venues within a 15-minute walk** None.

SETTING Located on the affluent west side of Las Vegas, Downtown Summerlin resembles a modern urban city center and sits at the northeast corner of the West 215 Beltway and West Sahara Avenue, just south of Red Rock Resort. Thirty buildings are surrounded by hectares of free parking along the perimeters, as well as on-street parking in front of your favorite store.

SHOPS OF NOTE Sur La Table, Charlotte Russe, Francesca's, Trader Joe's, J. Jill, Off-Broadway Shoe Warehouse, Torrid, Old Navy, Sunglass Hut, Kay Jewelers.

RESTAURANTS OF NOTE Grape Street, Andiron Steak & Sea, CRAVE, Trattoria Reggiano, Wolfgang Puck Bar & Grill, and 11 quick-food outlets.

ATTRACTIONS AND ENTERTAINMENT A five-screen Regal Theater with lounge chairs and bar service.

CONSUMER TIPS The 26-acre site is a narrow two-thirds of a mile of stores from south to north, so wear comfortable shoes. Several restaurants are clustered around a park on the northeast side.

Fashion Outlets of Las Vegas Mall

32100 Las Vegas Blvd. S., Primm; ☎ 702-874-1400; fashionoutletlasvegas.com

Hours Daily, 10 a.m.–8 p.m. **Number of stores** 70. **Number of restaurants** Food court (8 counters). **Anchor stores** Williams-Sonoma Marketplace, Polo, Calvin Klein, Gap. **Free self-parking** Yes. **Valet parking** No. **Other shopping venues within a 15-minute walk** None.

SETTING A quick 40 miles southwest on I-15 in Primm and connected to the Primm Valley Resort, this indoor mall features trendy goods with irresistible prices because of its way-out location.

SHOPS OF NOTE Aéropostale, Le Creuset, Hollister, Levi's, Lee, Michael Kors, H&M.

RESTAURANTS OF NOTE Carl's Jr., Flat Top's, Lotus Express.

ATTRACTIONS AND ENTERTAINMENT The adjacent 624-room Primm Valley Resort includes a casino, showroom with weekend headliners, and two golf courses. Two sister properties nearby are Buffalo Bill's, which features a roller coaster, and Whiskey Pete's, across I-15. A free hotel shuttle takes visitors underneath I-15 and across to Whiskey Pete's every hour.

CONSUMER TIPS Pick up a coupon book at the information desk by the food court for discounts. For a $15 round-trip, the Shoppers Shuttle runs customers to Primm from three Strip locations: Fashion Show Mall, Miracle Mile Shops, and the MGM Grand (call ☎ 888-424-6898 to schedule). Fare includes a discount card.

Tivoli Village

440 S. Rampart Blvd.; ☎ 702-570-7400; tivolivillagelv.com

Hours Monday–Thursday, 10 a.m.–8 p.m.; Friday and Saturday, 10 a.m.–9 p.m.; Sunday, 11 a.m.–6 p.m. **Number of stores** 19. **Number of restaurants** 10. **Free self-parking** Yes. **Valet parking** Yes. **Other shopping venues within a 15-minute walk** Boca Park, Rampart Commons.

SETTING Thirteen miles west of the Las Vegas Strip via I-95 North and Summerlin Parkway, this open-air Mediterranean-style complex features both an arcade of mid- to upscale shops and Market LV, a seperate bilevel retail center featuring an eclectic mash of small boutiques and specialty foods. The urban souk offers 15-plus vendors of clothing, accessories, candy, desserts, and gifts in distinctive shops. At night, the surrounding decorative cherry trees are lit with 5,000 LED bulbs, enveloping the complex in a cerise glow.

SHOPS OF NOTE Charming Charlie, Kidville, Paper Source, ANGL, Vasari, Restoration Hardware.

RESTAURANTS OF NOTE Brio Tuscan Grille, Echo & Rig, Leone Café, Waffle Bar.

ATTRACTIONS AND ENTERTAINMENT Saturday farmer's market.

CONSUMER TIPS Located in the suburban Queensridge neighborhood, Tivoli Village provides plenty of above- and below-ground free parking. Two golf courses are nearby, so spouses can shop while golfers swing.

UNIQUE SHOPPING OPPORTUNITIES

ART Las Vegas is a great place to shop for contemporary and nontraditional art and sculpture, with galleries in the Fashion Show Mall, The Forum Shops, the Grand Canal Shoppes, and elsewhere around town. Do not, however, expect any bargains.

If you're yearning to own artwork by Picasso, Dalí, Lichtenstein, Chagall, Miró, Murakami, Erté, or other popular 20th-century artists, visit the sophisticated **Martin Lawrence Gallery** in The Forum Shops. An immense vertical electric sign with the red letters A R T at the entrance lets you know what is for sale. Dealing in originals and limited-edition graphic prints, this sizable showcase presents fine art by the masters you know from art-history class and museum heists. Some pieces are surprisingly affordable . . . and some not so. There is an extensive rear area devoted to Andy Warhol's work. Browsers are welcome to stroll through the circuitous exhibits since today's gazer could be tomorrow's collector. Open Sunday–Thursday, 10 a.m.–11 p.m.; Friday and Saturday, 10 a.m.–midnight; ☎ 702-991-5990.

On the first Friday of every month from 5 to 11 p.m., the visual arts are celebrated in Las Vegas. In an eight-block area, generally bound on the north and south by Hoover and Wyoming Streets and on the west and east by Commerce and Third Streets, lies the Arts District. Eclectic and eccentric, the area is abundant with art galleries, restaurants and bars, gift emporiums, vintage couture, antiques shops, and malls of memorabilia; quality ranges from exceptional to godawful. With free parking at the Clark County Government Center, complimentary trollies transport arts lovers and the curious to this venerable commercial neighborhood. The lively **First Friday** festival (☎ 702-384-0092, ffflv .org) incorporates local bands, food, artist demonstrations, clairvoyants, and street performers. It's great for people-watching, and more than 60 businesses participate.

BOOKS **The Writer's Block** (1020 Fremont St. #100, ☎ 702-550-6399, thewritersblock.org) is Las Vegas's only independent bookstore. They stock an eclectic selection of current fiction, children's classics, and niche subjects and are associated with a nearby print-on-demand publisher that can produce thousands more titles in just five minutes. The shop is open Monday–Saturday 10 a.m.–7 p.m. and Sunday 11 a.m.–5 p.m.

SWEDISH-FURNITURE FANS, REJOICE!

IKEA (☎ 888-888-4532, ikea.com/us/en/store/las_vegas) has opened shop in Las Vegas, with one of the larger footprints in the retail chain. Admirers of the celebrated design superstar will be delighted with this new US location at 6500 Ikea Way near South Durango and West Sunset alongside the South 215 Beltway. The 351,000-square-foot emporium's circuitous route through 45 mini-showrooms displays the brand's 10,000 affordable products. Representing the Swedes' desire to furnish America, Ikea is designed to explore in a linear manner that encompasses both floors. A quick walk-through of the whole route takes at least 45 minutes. You'll see every household item that you ever heard of, as well as plenty that you haven't. The challenge is stopping in for one item. You can escape the linear routing via connecting passages. There are also interior maps, but you'll still probably have to ask a salesperson for directions. As far as finding your way back out, we recommend dropping breadcrumbs. Staff is available to demonstrate the art of furniture assembly. On-site are a huge 450-seat restaurant, grocery, and bistro takeout offering popular Swedish delicacies (lingonberries, gravlax, and especially meatballs). Hours are Monday–Saturday 10 a.m.–9 p.m. and Sunday, 10 a.m.–8 p.m.

ETHNIC SHOPPING At the southwest corner of Spring Mountain and Wynn Roads is **Las Vegas Chinatown Plaza** with 20 outlets (☎ 702-221-8448, lvchinatownplaza.com). This location offers Asian-theme shopping and Asian restaurants.

For American Indian art, crafts, books, music, and attire, try the **Las Vegas Indian Center** at 2300 W. Bonanza Road (☎ 702-647-5842). And 25 minutes north of Las Vegas in Moapa, Nevada, you'll find the **Moapa Tribal Enterprises Casino and Gift Center** (☎ 702-864-2600). Take I-15 north to Exit 75.

GAMBLING STUFF As you would expect, Las Vegas is a shopping mecca when it comes to anything gambling related. If you are in the market for a roulette wheel, a blackjack table, or some personalized chips, try the **Gamblers General Store** at 800 S. Main St. (☎ 702-382-9903 or 800-322-CHIP outside Nevada, gamblersgeneralstore.com). For books and periodicals on gambling, we recommend the **Gamblers Book Shop,** now located inside the Gamblers General Store (☎ 702-382-7555 or 800-522-1777, gamblersbookclub.com).

HEAD RUGS The next time you go to a Las Vegas production show, pay attention to the showgirls' hair. You will notice that the same woman will have a different hairdo for every number. Having made this observation, you will not be surprised that the largest wig and hairpiece retailer in the United States is in Las Vegas. At 4515 W. Sahara Ave., **Serge's Wigs** inventories more than 7,000 hairpieces and wigs, made from both synthetic materials and human hair. In addition to serving the local showgirl population, Serge's Wigs also specializes in assisting chemotherapy patients. A catalog and additional information can be obtained at ☎ 702-207-7494 or sergeswigs.com.

MUSIC With a three-level inventory of 500,000-plus recordings, **Wax Trax** (2909 S. Decatur Blvd., ☎ 702-362-4300, waxtraxonline.com) is a treasure chest of underground, indie, new wave, country, classic jazz, rock, and soul music. In this museum/mausoleum, the discs are scarce and pricey gems. The owner is an encyclopedic music visionary who sells *and* buys vintage records, CDs, sheet music, and posters, and he will search out rarities for customers. Open daily, 11 a.m.–4 p.m.

SHOES If smoking stunted your growth, increase your height with custom-made platforms, boots, and high heels from **Red Shoes** (4011 W. Sahara Ave., Unit 1, ☎ 702-889-4442). For a great selection of cowboy boots, try **Cowtown Boots** (1080 E. Flamingo Road, ☎ 702-737-8469, cowtownboots.com).

WINE AND LIQUOR Though not centrally located, **Lee's Discount Liquors** (9110 Las Vegas Blvd. S., ☎ 702-269-2400, leesliquorlv.com), just south of Blue Diamond Road, offers the best selection of wine, liquor, and beer within easy access of the Strip. Unless your hotel is south of Tropicana, take I-15 to the Blue Diamond Road exit and then head south on Las Vegas Boulevard South. If your hotel is south of Tropicana you're just as well off taking Las Vegas Boulevard South the whole way. Though Lee's Discount Liquors has 10 locations around Las Vegas, the stores vary in size and selection. None are particularly convenient to the Strip or Downtown, but we can recommend the 3480 E. Flamingo Road and the 4230 S. Rainbow Blvd. locations in addition to the store mentioned above.

SEEING *the* SIGHTS

RESIDENTS OF LAS VEGAS are justifiably proud of their city and are quick to point out that it has much to offer besides gambling. Quality theater, college and professional sports, dance, concerts, art shows, museums, and film festivals contribute to making Las Vegas a truly great place to live. In addition, there is a diverse and colorful natural and historical heritage. What Las Vegas residents sometimes have a difficult time understanding, however, is that the average business and leisure traveler doesn't really give a big hoot. Las Vegas differs from Orlando and Southern California in that it does not have any major tourist attractions except Hoover Dam. Nobody drives all the way to Las Vegas to visit the Neon Museum, interesting as it is. While there have always been some great places to detox from a long trade show or too many hours at the casino, they are totally peripheral in the minds of most visitors.

However, if you're game to explore, read on. You'll find plenty of attractions, tours, and experiences in and near Las Vegas to keep you busy. If you are a serious sightseer, consider the **Las Vegas Power Pass.** It allows entry into more than 30 Las Vegas–area attractions. Passes are available for one, two, three, or five days and range in cost from $89 for a one-day adult pass to $279 for a five-day adult pass;

children's passes range from $79 to $269. For more information and discounts on passes, visit lasvegaspass.com.

STRIP ATTRACTIONS

Bally's

Real Bodies at Bally's (☎ 702-777-2782, realbodiesatballys.com) is an edifying stroll through human anatomy, featuring more than 200 actual preserved human bodies and organs. *Real Bodies* is organized in a series of galleries, each focusing on the role of a particular bodily system. The specimens are posed in active positions that reveal the muscular/skeletal and circulatory contribution to the depicted activity. The exhibit is tasteful, respectful, and not at all gory, or in any way sensational. Many organs, such as heart, lungs, kidneys, brain, and abdominal organs, are accorded their own dedicated display. Some organs are displayed as both healthy and diseased. For example, one exhibit features a healthy lung alongside a smoker's lung. Allow 1½–2 hours to take in everything. Open daily at 10 a.m. to all ages. Tickets run about $30 for adults and $18 for children ages 3–12. Discounts are available to military personnel, seniors, students, and locals with proper identification at the box office. *Real Bodies* is very similar to *Bodies . . . The Exhibition* at Luxor (see page 424). Visit whichever is most convenient.

Right next to the *Real Bodies* exhibit is **Twilight Zone Monster Mini Golf** (☎ 702-333-2121, syfyminigolf.com), an indoor putt-putt based on the classic Rod Serling TV series. The compact 18-hole course wraps around larger-than-life statues representing iconic characters from the show—such as Willie the ventriloquist's dummy and Mr. Dingle's two-headed Martian—but there are no moving obstacles or special effects. Twilight Zone is open daily 10 a.m.–midnight and costs $11.95 per player. A pint-size bowling alley ($5 per game) and a sci-fi–themed party room for birthdays or weddings are also available.

Bellagio

The big draw at the Bellagio is the **Gallery of Fine Art,** which hosts temporary traveling exhibits. Tickets run about $19 for adults, $16 for seniors and Nevada residents, and $14 for children, teachers, and military; children age 12 and under are admitted free. For information, call ☎ 702-693-7871 or visit bellagio.com.

A very worthwhile and free attraction is the **Bellagio Conservatory and Botanical Gardens.** Located adjacent to the hotel lobby, the display features more than 10,000 blooming flowers, a diverse variety of plants, and even trees. The flora is changed periodically to reflect the season of the year or the theme of upcoming holidays.

Bellagio's free outdoor spectacle is a choreographed **fountain show** presented on the lake in front of the hotel (which stretches the length of three football fields). At the bottom of the eight-acre lake over 1,000 water jets and 4,000-plus individually programmable white lights are harnessed in choreography to "dance," if you will, to music.

The waters are capable of reaching 240 feet into the air (approaching a football field's length), undulating in graceful S-curves, or cascading open like a gigantic surrendering lotus. The magical waters of the Bellagio are for all to enjoy on the half hour every Saturday, Sunday, and holidays from noon to 8 p.m. and every 15 minutes from 8 p.m. to midnight. Weekdays the schedule begins at 3 p.m. The view from the street is assuredly wonderful, but many of the rooms at Caesars and the Cosmopolitan can also offer a visual feast.

Bellagio's dramatic three-story, glass-domed botanical garden provides a quiet oasis.

Circus Circus

To further appeal to the family market, Circus Circus opened a small but innovative amusement park in August of 1993. Situated directly behind the main hotel and casino, the park now goes by the name of **Adventuredome**. Architecturally compelling, the entire park is built two stories high atop the casino's parking structure and is totally enclosed by a huge glass dome. From the outside, the dome surface is reflective, mirroring its surroundings in hot tropical pink. Inside, however, the dome is transparent, allowing guests in the park to see out. Composed of a multilayer glass-and-plastic sandwich, the dome allows light in but blocks ultraviolet rays. The entire park is air-conditioned and climate-controlled 365 days a year.

Adventuredome is a fun way to escape the heat of a Vegas summer day.

The park is designed to resemble a classic Western desert canyon. From top to bottom, hand-painted artificial rock is sculpted into caverns, pinnacles, steep cliffs, and buttes. Set among the rock structures are the attractions: two roller coasters, an array of spinning amusements, and some rides for small children. Embellishing the scene are a replica of Pueblo cliff dwellings, a rock-climbing wall, and a small stage featuring free magic and clown shows. Hidden in the center of the complex are a black-light laser tag arena and Batman-themed obstacle course. Finally, and inevitably, there is an electronic games arcade. As far as theme parks go, it can't compete with the world-class ones a few hours west in Anaheim, but it's a big improvement over your local bare-bones family entertainment center, and certainly offers enough to occupy a full afternoon of fun.

Adventuredome's premier attractions are the **Canyon Blaster,** the only indoor, double-loop, corkscrew roller coaster in the United States, which resembles a scaled-down sibling to Busch Gardens Williamsburg's classic Loch Ness Monster, and **El Loco,** an unconventional wild-mouse-on-steroids steel coaster, with drops that exceed vertical and extended inversions that leave you hanging upside-down, secured only by a surprisingly comfortable lap-bar. Canyon Blaster and El Loco both wind in, around, and between the rocks and cliffs.

Other carnival-style thrill rides include **Sling Shot,** where you're shot vertically up a tower at 4 g's; **Inverter,** a pirate ship–style pendulum ride; **Chaos,** a vertical Tilt-A-Whirl that hauls riders randomly through three dimensions; and **Disk'O,** which has rocking motion and then spins you and about 20 other folks like a human discus. Adventuredome also features a simulator ride and the **Pacific Rim Motion Movie Experience.**

Guests can reach the theme park by proceeding through the rear of the main casino to the entrance and ticket plaza situated on the mezzanine level. Circus Circus has changed the admission policy so many times we have lost track. You can choose between paying for each attraction individually ($6–$12) or opting for an all-inclusive day pass ($33 adults, $19 juniors). For exact admission prices on the day of your visit, call ☎ 702-794-3939 or visit adventuredome.com.

Circus Circus also has water park, called **Splash Zone,** featuring three slides from a 50-foot-tall tower. Alas, at least for now, Splash Zone is open only to Circus Circus guests.

Excalibur

Excalibur's basement features a 4-D theater showing short 3-D movies with physical effects like wind, water, and shaking seats. Three movies are shown in rotation, with a new one starting every 15 minutes. Tickets are $10 for one, $13 for two, or $15 for all three. The *Lego Movie* has the sharpest script, while *San Andreas* (starring The Rock) has the best effects; give *Journey 2 the Mysterious Island* (also starring The Rock) a miss.

Luxor

The Luxor offers two continuously running gated (paid admission) attractions inside the pyramid on the level above the casino. *Bodies . . . The Exhibition* (☎ 702-262-4000, bodiestheexhibition.com) is an extraordinary introduction to human anatomy through authentic, preserved human bodies. Though somewhat grisly sounding, the exhibit is extremely tasteful and respectful. Arranged sequentially, *Bodies* takes you through every part of the human body, explaining its many systems. Though most of the exhibit deals with the anatomy of healthy people, there is some discussion of disease. One of the more arresting displays is that of a normal lung side-by-side with the lung of a smoker. *Bodies . . . The Exhibition* is very similar to *Real Bodies* at Bally's (see page 422). Visit whichever is most convenient. A second Luxor attraction is *Titanic: The Artifact Exhibition,* which takes guests on a chronological odyssey from the design and building of the ocean liner to life on board to its sinking (☎ 702-262-4400 or 800-557-7428, luxor.com). Allow a minimum of 2 hours to see *Bodies* and 90 minutes to take in *Titanic*. General admission for either exhibit is $32 adults, $24 children (ages 4–12).

Mandalay Bay

The big draw at Mandalay Bay is the **Shark Reef** aquarium (☎ 702-632-4555, sharkreef.com), featuring sharks, rays, sea turtles, venomous stonefish, and dozens of other denizens of the deep in a 1.3-million-gallon tank.

If you don't like fish, separate exhibits showcase rare pythons, golden crocodiles, and a huge komodo dragon. In excess of 2,000 animals, covering 100 different species including 15 species of shark, are on display. The animal enclosures look (and smell) like they are well maintained, with excellent water clarity throughout, and the environment is as well themed as any walkthrough you'll find at SeaWorld. The only problem is that it's a bit too short for the price; even if you go slowly, reading the informative plaques and interacting with the stingray touch tank, you'll still be done in about half an hour. Mandalay Bay sometimes includes limited-time exhibits with Shark Reef admission, extending guests' stay by 10–15 minutes. Most recently, **Polar Journey** offered interactive education displays about Arctic environments, such as a polar bear photo op and a touchable iceberg, concluding with a short stand-up motion simulator. These are a nice added bonus for aquarium visitors but not worth going out of your way for on their own. The Shark Reef tour is open Sunday–Thursday 10 a.m.–8 p.m. and Friday and Saturday 10 a.m.–10 p.m. (last admission is 1 hour prior to close). Admission is about $25 for adults, $19 for children age 12 and under, and free for those age 3 and under.

MGM Grand

The MGM Grand sent its signature lion habitat packing, but it still offers two attractions. Originally developed by the Fort Worth Museum of Science and History with a grant from The National Science Foundation, **CSI: The Experience** (csitheexperience.org) gives you the opportunity to play the role of a crime-scene investigator, learning scientific principles and real investigative techniques as you try to solve the case. Two state-of-the-art crime labs will help you piece together the evidence. Hands-on science combines with special effects to create an exciting, realistic, and educational experience. Players can choose from three different crime scenes to investigate. CSI: The Experience is self-guided and takes about an hour for most people. It is open daily, 9 a.m.–9 p.m. Tickets are $32 for adults and $25 for children ages 4–11. From our observation, it's pretty much a waste of money to take children younger than 11.

Also at the MGM Grand, **Topgolf Las Vegas** (☎ 702-933-8458, topgolf.com/us/las-vegas) opened in 2016 and is situated to the rear of the property, about a 10-minute walk from the middle of the MGM casino. A shuttle service is available between the casino and Topgolf. Barely five minutes into our tour of Topgolf we were ready to take up the sport. Inside this warehouse-size facility is a modern take on a golf driving range, with four floors and more than 100 individual practice bays. Each bay is configured like a deluxe cabana you'd find poolside at your resort hotel, with cool air vents, televisions, couches, and an attentive waitstaff to bring drinks and food. There's also a complete set of Calloway clubs in each, if you don't want to use your own.

Our favorite part of Topgolf may be the technology. Practice balls are delivered by swinging your club over a motion sensor near your practice tee. With each swing, a computer monitors your shot's trajectory on a nearby computer monitor, showing you how close you came to the hole you were aiming for.

Topgolf is set up for families and large groups. Those who don't want to golf can try the site's pools, lounge in the sun, or watch television on cinema-size monitors behind the tees. We saw lots of kids practicing with their parents, but nongolfers in your group could easily spend a couple of hours lounging here while you ironed out the kinks in your swing.

Prices vary by weekday, time of day, and floor. The cheapest is a $30-per-hour, first- or second-floor bay between 9 a.m. and noon, Monday through Thursday. That goes to $90 per hour for an upper-floor bay after 5 p.m. on Friday or Saturday. Reservations are recommended.

Mirage

The **volcano** at the Mirage goes off Sunday–Thursday at 8 and 9 p.m. and Friday and Saturday at 8, 9, and 10 p.m. provided the weather is good and winds are light. With an exclusive soundtrack composed by Grateful Dead drummer Mickey Hart, the volcano fires massive fireballs more than 12 feet into the air, and eruptions of fiery "lava" flow down the mountain's fissures. Usually, getting a good railside vantage point is not too difficult. If you want to combine the volcano with a meal, grab a window table at the second-floor restaurant in the Casino Royale across the street.

The Mirage also has a nice dolphin exhibit, plus the **Secret Garden** next to the dolphin habitat, a small zoo with Siegfried and Roy's white and Bengal tigers, white lions, an Indian elephant, and more. Both are open daily 10 a.m.–4 p.m. The dolphin and Secret Garden exhibit cost $22 for adults and $17 for children. (Children age 3 and under get in free.) For more information, call ☎ 702-791-7111 or visit mirage.com.

Paris Las Vegas

The big draw at Paris is, of course, the 540-foot-tall replica of the **Eiffel Tower.** Requiring 10 million pounds of steel and more than two years to erect, the Las Vegas version is a little more than half the size of the original. Just below the top (at 460 feet) is an observation deck accessible via two 10-passenger glass elevators. It costs $16 to ride during the day, and the cost increases to $22 starting at 7:15 p.m. (express passes are available for $35), but that's just the beginning of the story. You must first line up to buy tickets. Your ticket will show a designated time to report to the escalator. (That's right: *escalator.* You must take an escalator to reach the elevators.) If you're late you'll be turned away, and there are no refunds. The escalator will deposit you in yet another line where you'll wait for the elevator. The elevators run from 10 a.m. until 12:30 a.m. (1 a.m. weekends), except when it's raining.

unofficial **TIP**

If accessing Paris's observation platform seems like too much work, take the separate elevator that serves the restaurant and bar on the 11th floor of the tower. You don't need reservations to patronize the bar, but you must be nicely dressed (no jeans, T-shirts, tank tops, or sandals). The bar is open 11:30 a.m.–midnight and serves lunch.

Though all this hopping from line to line is supposed to take 5–20 minutes, we found 40–60 minutes more the norm. Here's the rub: The observation deck holds fewer than 100 persons, and once people get up there, they can stay as long as they want. Hence, when the observation deck is at max capacity, nobody can go up unless someone comes down. Because the tower affords such a great view of the Bellagio across the street, gridlock ensues several times nightly while people squeeze on the observation deck overlong to watch Bellagio's dancing-waters show.

Rio

Joining the Las Vegas zip line craze, the Rio offers **VooDoo ZipLine,** an 845-foot zip line launched from the popular nightspot VooDoo Lounge, 490 feet in the air. Up to two riders at a time are strapped in a ski lift–style seat and slide forward at speeds of 33 mph to the Rio's 200-foot Ipanema Tower below, before being hauled backward to the starting point at 20 mph, for a total ride time of about 2 minutes. The proximity of a fully stocked bar and copious quantities of alcohol is not accidental. VooDoo ZipLine is open daily, noon–midnight. Cost is $28; photos start at $22. There is a 48-inch height minimum, and after 7:30 p.m. the attraction is 21 and older only.

Also at the Rio is **KISS Monster Mini Golf,** an 18-hole glow-in-the-dark miniature golf course with a KISS-themed games arcade, a memorabilia exhibit, a wedding chapel, and music spun by a live DJ. The golf course itself is fairly basic with no moving obstacles or elevation changes; there are giant boots to putt around, and the final hole naturally features Gene Simmons's giant tongue. KISS Army veterans will appreciate the blacklight murals recounting major milestones in the band's history (such as the infamous comic book printed with the musicians' blood) and displays of tour costumes, instruments, and even a vintage Porsche. Open 10 a.m.–midnight, mini golf costs $11.95, but the exhibits and arcade are free to enter.

New in 2018, the **Wall Gaming Lounge** (☎ 800-752-9746, caesars .com/rio) is a 24,000-square-foot space featuring 30 state-of-the-art Alienware gaming PCs in addition to a number of console gaming stations. Local Lock In, MOBA, FPS, Battle Royal, FGC, and Twitch are among the tournament games played. The Wall Gaming Lounge is located in the Masquerade Village area. Players under 21 are welcome. With plush and comfy graffiti-inspired decor, the venue is open Thursday–Sunday, 4 p.m.–2 a.m.

Stratosphere

The Stratosphere Tower stands 1,149 feet tall and offers an unparalleled view of Las Vegas. You can watch aircraft take off simultaneously from McCarran International Airport and Nellis Air Force Base. To the south, the entire Las Vegas Strip is visible. To the west, Red Rock Canyon seems practically within spitting distance. North of the Tower, Downtown glitters beneath the canopy of the Fremont Street Experience. By day, the rich geology of the Colorado Basin and Spring Mountains merge in an earth-tone and evergreen tapestry. At night, the dark desert circumscribes a blazing strand of twinkling neon.

A 12-level pod crowns the futuristic contours of three immense buttresses that form the Tower's base. Level 12, the highest level, serves as the boarding area for **X-Scream**, a dangle-daddy; **Insanity**, a sort of Tilt-A-Whirl in the sky; and the **Big Shot**, an acceleration–free-fall thrill ride. Latest to join the lineup is **SkyJump**, a parachute ride with an 855-foot "controlled" free-fall descent. Oh, did we forget to mention that there's no parachute? Instead you're hooked up to a zip line on the 108th floor of the tower where you heave yourself over the side of a platform. Happily, after reaching speeds of 40 mph, you'll be slowed to a comfortable landing. The price to jump off a perfectly good building instead of taking the elevator is $120 and up. It's said the views on the descent are stupendous if you happen to open your eyes.

Levels 11 and 10 are not open to the public. An outdoor observation deck is Level 9, with an indoor observation deck directly beneath it on Level 8. Level 7 features a 220-seat lounge, and Level 6 houses an upscale revolving restaurant. Levels 4 and 3 contain meeting rooms, and the remaining levels—1, 2, and 5—are not open to the public.

The view from the Tower is so magnificent that we recommend experiencing it at different times of the day and night. Sunset is particularly stunning, and a storm system rolling in over the mountains is a sight you won't quickly forget. Be sure to try both the indoor and outdoor observation decks.

The rides are a mixed bag. The Big Shot is cardiac arrest. Sixteen people at a time are seated at the base of the skyward-projecting needle that tops the pod. You are blasted 160 feet straight up in the air at 45 mph and then allowed to partially free-fall back down. At the apex of the ascent, it feels as if your seat belt and restraint have mysteriously evaporated, leaving you momentarily hovering 100-plus stories up in the air. The ride lasts only about a half-minute, but unless you're accustomed to being shot from a cannon, that's more than enough.

If you're having difficulty forming a mental image of the Big Shot, picture the carnival game where macho guys swing a sledgehammer, propelling a metal sphere up a vertical shaft. At the top of the shaft is a bell. If the macho man drives the sphere high enough to ring the bell, he wins a prize. Got the picture? OK, on the Big Shot, you are the metal sphere.

In X-Scream, you ride in a large gondola attached to a huge steel arm. The arm dangles the gondola over the edge of the Tower, then releases it to slide forward a few feet as if the gondola is coming unglued from the arm. All and all, it's pretty dull.

The third ride, Insanity, is a little harder to describe. It consists of an arm that extends 64 feet over the edge of the Tower. Passengers are suspended from the arm in beefed-up swing seats and spun at up to three g's. As the ride spins faster and faster, the riders are propelled up to an angle of 70 degrees, at which point they're pretty much looking straight down.

unofficial **TIP**
If you visit the Tower on a weekend, go in the morning as soon as it opens.

The Stratosphere touts the ride as providing "a great view of historic Downtown Las Vegas."

The elevators to the Tower are at the end of the shopping arcade on the second floor of the Stratosphere, above the casino. Get tickets for the Tower at the ticket center in the elevator lobby on the second floor or at various places in the casino. Tower tickets cost about $20–$25 for adults and $14–$18 for children. Packages including the Tower and the rides run $25–$40, depending on the day and number of rides included. You can purchase individual tickets for the rides at a cost of $15, in addition to your Tower admission.

Expect big crowds at the Tower on weekends. Once up top, the observation levels are congested, as are the lounge, snack bar, restrooms, and gift shops. If you want to try the rides, expect to wait an additional 20–40 minutes for each on weekends. When you've had your fill of the Tower and are ready to descend, you'll have another long wait before boarding the elevator. However, if you walk down to the restaurant (you'll take the emergency staircase; ask an attendant where to find it), you can catch the down elevator with virtually no wait at all.

Another way to see the Tower without a long wait is to make a reservation for the **Top of the World** restaurant. To be safe, make reservations at least two weeks in advance. When you arrive, inform the greeter in the elevator lobby that you have a dinner reservation and give him your confirmation number. You will be ushered immediately into an express elevator. The restaurant is pricey, but the food is good and the view is a knockout, and you do not have to pay the Tower admission. If you want to try the Big Shot or the High Roller, purchase ride tickets before taking the elevator to the restaurant. Finally, be aware that most folks dress up to eat at Top of the World.

On weekdays, it is much easier to visit the Stratosphere Tower. Monday–Thursday, except at sunset, the wait to ascend is usually short. Waits for the rides are also short. Tower hours are Sunday–Thursday 10 a.m.–1 a.m. and Friday and Saturday 10 a.m.–2 a.m. For more information, call ☎ 702-380-7711 or visit stratospherehotel.com.

Treasure Island

Marvel's Avengers S.T.A.T.I.O.N. (Scientific Training and Tactical Intelligence Operative Network) is a walk-through exhibit focusing on the history and capabilities of every major character in the Marvel Cinematic Universe, plus many of the secondary characters. Your tour of the facility includes rooms dedicated to Captain America, the Incredible Hulk, Iron Man, Thor, and more. Most rooms are set up with large video monitors, which provide backstory for the props and costumes (all replicas, not actually screen-used) on display. Interactive stations scattered throughout the rooms allow you to test your reflexes against Kree warriors, trigger the Tesseract, or try on Tony Stark's suit. The games are well done and fun when they work, but there are too few of them, and some frequently malfunction. If you're a huge fan of the Marvel movies, Avengers S.T.A.T.I.O.N. is a must-visit, and even those only casually familiar with the characters should enjoy admiring the movie-quality environments. You'll need an Apple or Android smartphone to use the Avengers S.T.A.T.I.O.N. trivia app that accompanies this experience; download it in advance to save time, and get a 50% discount on photos in the extensive gift shop if you score high enough. iPods with the app preinstalled are available to rent, too, for $5, or free with a Groupon. It's open daily, 10 a.m.–10 p.m., with self-guided tours taking about 60–75 minutes. The last admission of the night is at 9 p.m. Cost is $34 for adults and $24 for children ages 4–11; children age 3 and under enter free.

The Venetian

As with New York–New York down the Strip, it can be argued that the entire Venetian is an attraction, and there's a lot to gawk at even if you limit your inspection to the streetside Italian icons and the Grand Canal Shoppes. But there's more. The Venetian is host to the first **Madame Tussauds Wax Museum** (☎ 702-862-7800, madametussauds.com/las vegas) built in the United States. Covering two floors and 28,000 square feet, the museum is about half the size of the original London exhibit. More than 100 wax figures are displayed in themed settings. Some, like Frank Sinatra and Tom Jones, were central to the development of the entertainment scene in Las Vegas. Unlike at most wax museums, here you can touch and pose, and, in some cases, drape yourself over the statues; as a result, the figures aren't as pristine as those seen at other locations, with some showing significant wear. Wax figures rotate among other Madame Tussauds, but the collection here focuses on pop-culture celebrities to the general exclusion of historical figures.

The original "haunted dungeon" finale was replaced by a new 4-D Marvel Superheroes show, with in-theater effects (water spritzes, falling bubbles, leg ticklers, and the like) accompanying a computer-animated short film in which Spider-Man, Tony Stark, and their super-pals battle baddies Doctor Doom and Loki. It's all-ages appropriate, unlike the tour's old ending, but anyone who has experienced Universal Orlando's Marvel attractions, or seen *Marvel Super Heroes* in IMAX 4-D, is unlikely to be impressed by the clunky script and chunky graphics. The museum opens daily at 10 a.m., and the self-guided tour takes about 50 minutes. Admission is $30 per adult and $20 per child, with $10-off coupons often available; there is a discount for tickets bought online.

Free Stuff on the Strip

The **water-and-laser show at Caesars' Forum Shops** is worthy of consideration. Staged daily on the hour beginning at 11 a.m., the show combines animatronic statues with fire and laser effects. Outdoor productions at Bellagio and the Mirage (described earlier) are also free.

The multistory **M&M's World** (mmsworld.com) features a free 3-D movie with in-theater special effects, similar to the 4-D attractions found at Disney and Universal. The 10-minute film screens every 20 minutes from 10:20 a.m. to 6 p.m. Tuesday–Thursday and until 8 p.m. Friday–Monday. There are also live meet-and-greets with costumed characters daily noon–8 p.m.

Strip Entertainment Districts

THE LINQ PROMENADE At Center Strip, tucked into the corridor between the LINQ and Flamingo Hotels, is **The LINQ Promenade,** a conveniently walkable urban entertainment zone created by Caesars Entertainment. Low-rise buildings house 32 mostly casual food and beverage venues and on-trend retail shops. Stylish tenants include **Goorin Bros.** headware and **Chilli Beans** sunspecs, plus eateries **Flour & Barley** (pizza), **Chayo Cocina** (Mexican), **Gordon Ramsay Fish & Chips,** and **Haute Doggery.** Nightlife includes **Purple Zebra** and the bowling-dining-concert mecca **Brooklyn Bowl.** Revelers will love the critical mass of outdoor restaurants, open-air drinking establishments, and late-night hot spots. Concerts are staged at the circular midpoint plaza, and a compact **O'Shea's Casino** rejoins the assemblage, preserving its prestige as beer pong central.

All of this is overseen by an extraordinary attraction, the world's tallest observation wheel, appropriately named the **High Roller** (more on that below). Located at the opposite end of the LINQ Promenade from the High Roller is the 122-foot-tall launch tower of **Fly LINQ,** featuring 10 side-by-side zip lines capable of simultaneously launching all riders. You can choose to ride in either a "Superman" or seated position. The launch tower is accessible via elevator and offers magnificent views of the Strip. After soaring 1,080 feet above LINQ Promenade, riders disembark near the base of the High Roller. Queuing and gear-fitting take place on the launch deck. The flight lasts 35 seconds and approaches speeds of 35 miles per hour.

Valet parking adjacent to the wheel is accessed going north on Linq Lane off Flamingo Avenue or west on Winnick Avenue from Koval Lane. The Venetian/Harrah's rear access road south of the Sands Expo also gets you there. Surface lots are behind (east of) The LINQ, along with neighboring parking garages, which are a quick trek from the Flamingo and LINQ Hotels. Signage is small, so drivers must pay attention.

A FERRIS WHEEL . . . OR SOMETHING Ask anybody having something to do with the **High Roller,** and you'll get, "It's NOT a Ferris wheel! It's an *observation wheel!*" OK, fine, it's an observation wheel (that bears a very close resemblance to every Ferris wheel you've ever seen). We'll go to our graves believing that the High Roller came from the same gene pool as the Ferris wheel, but here is the press-release difference: On a Ferris wheel you take a ride in the sense that you go around and around. On an observation wheel, you get on, slowly rotate one full circuit (which takes 30 minutes to an hour, giving you plenty of time to "observe"), and get off. No round and round. Also size counts—the average Ferris wheel would come up to an observation wheel's ankle.

The 550-foot **High Roller** is situated on the eastern end of The LINQ entertainment district. Each of the statuesque wheel's 28 transparent, spherical, climate-controlled globes can ferry 40 people aloft per rotation. Once aboard, you'll inch your way up and then back down, never stopping. For about half the rotation you'll be high enough to enjoy uncluttered views all around.

The High Roller has its own ticket booth and is open 11:30 a.m.–2 a.m. 365 days a year. A ride costs adults $27 from noon to 5:50, and $37 from 6 p.m. until closing. Children ages 13–18 pay $17 before 6 p.m. and $27 after. Children ages 12 and under ride free. In addition to the ticket price, there's a hidden and aggravating $2 "service charge" per ticket. You can order tickets online at caesars.com/thelinq or buy them on-site from kiosks or the main ticket booth. You must ride within 30 minutes of purchasing your ticket. This holds equally for online purchasers who must designate a date and specific time of day in order to complete the transaction. To ride at a time of your own choosing, you'll have to pony up for a one- or three-day "flex ticket" at $45 and $55, respectively.

The boarding process is very Disneyesque. First, tickets are scanned before you're dispatched up an escalator. Next, each person or group is photographed in front of a green screen. In the final version your photo is digitally enhanced with scenes of the High Roller. Then, departing slightly from the Disney model, you are ushered into the bar (!!), where you can buy drinks to take on the ride. Drinks bought outside are also ok, provided they're in plastic cups. From the bar there are more escalators to the next room, where a half dozen or so cartoons and quirky videos play on a 270-degree screen. This is like Disney's preshow rooms. Here, you'll also get some instruction from your guide. Finally, it's on to the loading platform, where the wheel rotates continuously at about half normal walking speed. Getting on is no harder than stepping onto an escalator, except that if you screw it up you'll fall several feet off the loading platform into a convenient net. Wheelchairs and strollers are welcome, and the ride actually stops to position a ramp for wheelchairs. Stroller jockeys are on their own, and must board while the wheel is in motion like everyone else. If you think you might have issues, speak to a boarding/disembarking supervisor.

Once you're on board, there are benches for about 16 riders, but most people prefer to stand. The High Roller is built to withstand hurricane-force winds, plus it rotates so slowly that it's hard to tell you're moving. Motion sickness is not a factor here. There are views to the east and limited views to the west as soon as you board. Views north and south become visible approximately from clock positions 9 to 3. There's a recorded mix of witty and educational narration from your guide, plus some peppy tunes, but if the pod is more than half full, it will likely all be drowned out by conversation. The pods are temperature-controlled and are not the least claustrophobic. Sunsets are special, but with all the preboarding rigmarole, it's hard to time it just right. After sunset, the High Roller is illuminated by 2,000 LED lights.

You exit the ride into the gift shop, where you can check out your green-screen photos and select one of four backdrops. If you want to take a photo home, it's $25 for one print and $30 for two.

THE PARK Not to be outdone, MGM Resorts International has created an entertainment district in the canyon of open space between the Park MGM and New York–New York resorts. Christened **The Park,** this version encloses a compact 8-acre tranquil oasis slightly off-Strip and includes colorful xeriscapes and lush desert gardens with misters, patio seating, alcoves, and a 100-foot dual water wall. All foliage and the resident 200 trees are native to Nevada. Whimsical statuesque tulip-shaped sculptures provide daytime sun shelters and imaginative patterned LED light shows after dark. At the west end, the graceful 40-foot steel mesh figure *Bliss Dance,* introduced at Northern Nevada's 2010 Burning Man Festival in Black Rock Desert, celebrates the liberated human spirit as The Park's spectacular centerpiece. The leafy serpentine green space winds along the north side of New York–New York and leads to the state-of-the-art **T-Mobile Arena** fronted by Toshiba Plaza. Bordering the promenade are five casual restaurants and taverns: **Beerhaus, Bruxie Waffles, California Pizza Kitchen, Sake Rok,** and **Shake Shack,** all with indoor-outdoor seating. Artists, musicians, dancers, jugglers, and other performers entertain along the pathways. The Park is accessible 24/7. The two bookend hotels have restructured their Strip-front facades with new-to-the-Strip dining sites on both arboreal plazas, and each has added cobblestone walks leading into The Park. The innovative restaurants in residence at New York–New York include **Tom's Urban** and an expanded **Nine Fine Irishmen** pub. Interspersed are **Swatch, Superidiotic** for offbeat items, and **I Love NYNY** souvenirs. The focal point is a bilevel **Hershey's Chocolate World,** with exterior sculptures of branded candies. Inside are models of the Statue of Liberty and Empire State Building fashioned from melted candy bars, a gluttony-inducing pastry counter, and a mini-kitchen where chocoholics can cook up personalized sweets. On the north side of Park Avenue (formerly Rue de Monte Carlo) at Park MGM, dining spots include **Primrose** for French cuisine, **Bavette's Steakhouse, Double Barrel Roadhouse, Eataly,** and **Roy Choi,** the first Korean restaurant on the Strip. There's also a Starbucks.

Strip Roller Coasters

There are currently three roller coasters on the Strip. After careful sampling, we have decided that, although shorter, the **Canyon Blaster** and **El Loco** at Adventuredome offer better rides than the more visually appealing **Big Apple Coaster** at New York–New York. The Canyon Blaster still provides a tight (if no longer oh-so-smooth) ride two decades after its construction, and El Loco redefines the concept of air-time with a truly twisted track design—thank goodness for the in-seat speakers blasting cheesy pop music to drown out your screams!

The Big Apple Coaster at New York–New York, on the other hand, goes along in fits and starts, all of which are jerky and rough. Despite having been upgraded over the years with new trains and magnetic brakes by Premiere Rides, it remains one of the most painful rides defunct track manufacturer Togo ever created. It does, however, provide a great view of the Strip as it zips in and out of the various New York–New York buildings. As if the ride weren't already abusive enough, New York–New York has added an ill-advised virtual-reality option to their coaster. The 3-D graphics, which depict you pursuing alien invaders from an Area 51–like laboratory to Strip landmarks such as the Bellagio fountains, are sharp enough and well synchronized to the vehicle's movement. But the added weight on your head makes your neck's impact against the uncomfortable shoulder restraints even more aggravating, and being unable to see the actual track eliminates your body's ability to brace against the turns. You'll pay an extra $5 per ride (on top of the standard $15 ticket) for the VR version, which is restricted to guests age 13 and older; all coaster riders must be at least 54 inches tall. If you insist on braving it, don't wait for the cashier at the arcade's entrance; go straight through the rear of the arcade to the coaster's ticketing queue.

 El Loco at Adventuredome is the *Unofficial* team's favorite of the Vegas Strip coasters.

Virtual Reality (VR) on the Strip

VR is making its introduction on the Strip. **VR Adventures** (☎ 702-734-0642, caesars.com/linq/promenade) on the LINQ Promenade offers a number of short VR programs, including dangling from a zip line atop Caesars Palace, flying over the Strip like Superman, House of Horrors, and Fly n' Shoot. Most of the graphics are sharp, but we also encountered a couple of blurry ones. Plus, at $20 for a single adventure, it's a bit expensive for a 5-minute experience. The cost goes down to about $15 per experience if you bundle two, three, or all four adventures.

The Void (thevoid.com/locations/lasvegas), a leading virtual reality company with outlets in Anaheim and Orlando, opened its first Las Vegas location in 2018 at St. Mark's Square within The Venetian's Grand Canal Shoppes. Their initial offering, **Star Wars: Secrets of the Empire,** was created in collaboration with ILMxLAB. This 30-minute, high-tech adventure turns you and three friends into spies for the Rebellion, tasked by Rogue One's Captain Cassian with breaking into an Imperial base disguised as Stormtroopers and retrieving a top-secret artifact. The 3-D headsets you wear are a bit awkward (especially if you wear prescription eyeglasses), but the visuals are sharp, tracking your head and hand movements with no nauseating lag. Physical effects like heat and wind, and tactile feedback from your vibrating vest, all greatly enhance the immersion; you can even reach out and touch a friendly droid. The VR portion of the attraction lasts under 15 minutes, and replay value is limited, but even at $33–$37 per player this is a must-do for hardcore gamers and *Star Wars* geeks. Operating hours are Sunday–Thursday 10 a.m.–11 p.m. and Friday and Saturday 10 a.m.–midnight; book your time slot in advance to avoid a wait.

The **Level Up** gaming lounge at MGM Grand (☎ 702-891-7871, mgmgrand.com/en/nightlife/level-up.html) boasts bowling lanes, pool tables, esports consoles, retro arcade games, and slot machines disguised as retro arcade games, but its headlining attraction is **Zero Latency Virtual Reality.** For $50 per person, up to eight participants can spend a half hour running around a warehouselike arena, zapping virtual space aliens or shotgunning zombies in the head. Players suit up with a 3-D headset, which is attached to a backpack-mounted computer, and a large plastic gun. Zero Latency's VR technology isn't quite as immersive as their rival The Void, but the intense action of their Singularity and Outbreak Origins scenarios should satisfy competitive First Person Shooter fans and laser tag enthusiasts. Be warned that the gravity-defying Engineerium game, with its M.C. Escher–esque directional distortions, may leave you crawling on the floor if you suffer from vertigo or balance issues.

DOWNTOWN ATTRACTIONS

DOWNTOWN LAS VEGAS IS TIED TOGETHER under the canopy of the **Fremont Street Experience** (☎ 702-678-5777, vegasexperience .com), a high-tech, overhead sound-and-light show. The 12.5-million-light canopy extends from Main Street to Las Vegas Boulevard, covering the five-block pedestrian concourse where most Downtown casinos are situated. Canopy shows occur on the hour, with the first show at 8 p.m. and the last show at midnight (subject to seasonal change). The canopy show is free, as are nightly concerts on the **3rd Street Stage,** located outdoors between Four Queens and The D, and the **Main Street Stage,** situated in front of the Golden Gate between First and Main Streets. Beer cans and glass containers are prohibited outdoors at the Fremont Street Experience. Across Las Vegas Boulevard beyond the canopied pedestrian plaza is the **Fremont East District,** a burgeoning nightlife and dining venue.

The **Slotzilla** high-tech attraction at Fremont Street offers the intrepid and newly brave the thrill of flying under the 12.5 million LEDs of the Fremont Street Experience. Riders are strapped into a harness, take a flying leap, and whiz down a steel wire while controlling the momentum by tilting their bodies at various angles. There are two experience levels with four zip lines each. The lower zip launch is 75 feet above the pedestrian mall and extends 850 feet with riders in a seated position. The higher zoom launch begins as the reels spin on the 115-foot-high platform of world's largest slot machine; for this steeper run riders are horizontal and finish a third of a mile away. This hard-to-miss longer jaunt begins between Casino Center Boulevard and Third Street, soars over the traffic on Third, scoots through the LED canopy, and ends 4 blocks to the west in front of the Golden Gate Hotel. Speeds can reach 35 mph, and flyers can and do race. Open daily, 1 p.m.–midnight (or later). Cost for the lower ride is $20–$25, and the higher ride is $40–$45.

Entertainment aside, Fremont Street's most renowned attraction is the flashing neon marquees of the Downtown casinos, the reason Fremont Street is called "Glitter Gulch." Augmenting the neon of the casinos are vintage Las Vegas neon signs dating back to the 1940s. The **Neon Museum,** located at 770 Las Vegas Blvd. N., is a visually opulent 2.27-acre outdoor collection of more than 150 vintage neon signs celebrating Las Vegas's small-town, bright-lights era. Signs are stacked along pathways winding through a maze of metal sculpture, huge panels of light bulbs, and yards of glass tubing. Among huge classic structures are

Sassy Sally's facade of lights, Debbie Reynolds's autograph, the Barbary Coast's lavish *B*, and the graceful green and yellow flowering plant designating the Yucca Motel. Each recalls the era when hotels and motels outdid each other with extravagant signage. The glory days of the now-departed Dunes, Moulin Rouge, Stardust, Sahara, and Desert Inn are also remembered by their signature marquees, which are prominently exhibited. Even the museum's name is spelled in capital letters from the famous hotels. The visitor center is vintage as well; the former lobby of the La Concha Motel, a midcentury-modern structure, was transported from its previous location next to the Riviera Hotel.

The guide's commentary about these treasures is intertwined with the colorful history of Las Vegas. Tours of the boneyard last 55 minutes and are conducted daily, every half hour, from 10 a.m. until 5 p.m. After dusk, evening tours held between 7 and 8:30 p.m. show off the museum's 11 fully-restored neon signs, with the remainder of the collection illuminated by spotlights. Cost of the tour is $19 for general admission; $15 for seniors, students, active military and veterans, and Nevada residents; and free for children age 6 and younger. Night tours cost $28 for general admission and $24 for the above-mentioned groups. Each night (except Tuesdays) the Neon Museum transforms its boneyard into a virtual wonderland with *Brilliant!*, a magical multimedia presentation by noted digital artist Craig Winslow that rivals the most sophisticated projection-mapping shows from Disney. Dozens of high-definition video projectors bring the derelict signs back to life, simulating their original neon glory and casting vintage Vegas film footage across their faces. The entire 25-minute experience is tied together with a smartly selected soundtrack of Sin City's favorite musicians, from Elvis and Elton to The Killers and Johnny Cash. No recording is permitted during the performance, but you're allowed to take pictures during the brief encore afterwards. Admission is $23 for adults, $15 for children ages 7–17, and free for kids under 7; discounts are available for students, seniors, and military. Shows start every hour on the half hour 8:30–11:30 p.m., and often sell out, so book in advance. Be sure to wear closed-toe shoes to avoid stepping on metal, glass, and other detritus of disintegrating signs, though the gravel pathways are ADA compliant for wheelchair access. All tours can be booked online, and those taking the daytime tour during warmer weather are advised to book for early in the day and wear a hat. For reservations or more information, call ☎ 702- 387-NEON (6366) or visit neonmuseum.org.

The **National Museum of Organized Crime and Law Enforcement,** or **The Mob Museum** (☎ 702-229-2734, themobmuseum.org), commemorates the extensive nationwide history of the La Cosa Nostra and its influence on Las Vegas. The interactive exhibits on three floors provide diverse viewpoints about the impact of organized crime and the feds who worked to crush the gangs. The museum is in the city's former federal courthouse (at 300 Stewart Ave.), the only Las Vegas building listed in the National Register of Historic Places. It houses the courtroom where the Kefauver Hearings on Organized Crime were conducted in 1950. Among the exhibits are the barber's chair where Albert Anastasia was shot and the bullet-strewn garage wall from Chicago's 1929 St. Valentine's Day Massacre. Near the end, you'll find a machine gun simulator and a rotating display of props from crime films and TV shows, such as Walter White's hazmat suit from *Breaking Bad*. The museum's exhibits are all well produced but very text-heavy, with lots of poorly lit small print. Crowd flow can also feel quite congested on busy days. Admission is $27–$42 with discounts for seniors, locals, and groups.

The Mob Museum also hosts a couple of optional exhibits that require an extra-cost admission with an assigned time. The **Crime Lab Experience** ($33.95 including general admission) lets guests spend 25 minutes as a CSI, exploring hands-on exhibits on DNA matching, fingerprint analysis, ballistics, and other forms of forensics. The room's highlight is a digital autopsy table that lets you play Operation with a photo-realistic virtual corpse. However, several of the stations are either confusing or too simplistic, and the talky intro videos are poorly paced, leaving guests feeling rushed to complete all their tasks in time. Much better is the **Use of Force Experience** ($38.95 including general admission, or $41.95 with both experiences), which replicates training methods used by real police officers. Participants are geared up with an authentic Sig Sauer pistol—which has been adapted for laser target practice with CO_2 cartridges that provide a realistic kick—and sent into simulated situations with suspects, first video projected and then in person. The goal is to *not* shoot anyone if you can help it, with a strong emphasis on deescalation, and the brief but intense 15-minute exercise will give you a better appreciation of what law enforcement officers experience. Lastly, **The Underground** speakeasy and on-site moonshine distillery mix up craft cocktails inspired by the Prohibition Era (hopefully without the bathtub gin-induced blindness).

With the advent of legal recreational marijuana, you just knew this was coming. Located in Neonopolis, a ne'er-do-well shopping-and-entertainment complex at the corner of Fremont and Las Vegas Boulevard, is the **Cannabition Cannabis Museum** (cannabition.com), featuring exhibits on cannabis history, education, and culture. Highlights are a 360-degree theater and (we're not making this up) a 22-foot-tall bong. Admission starts at $24.20; must be 21 or older to enter.

One mile south of the Freemont Street Experience, you'll find the **Las Vegas Arts District,** an 18-square-block area that's flourishing with funky restaurants, art galleries, and antiques stores. Many shops in the district are closed on Sunday and Monday; the free monthly First Friday event is an ideal time to stop by. Start at the **Arts Factory** (107 E. Charleston Blvd., ☎ 702-383-3133, theartsfactory.com), home to an ever-changing array of artists' studios selling everything from steampunk jewelry to creepy Disney dolls and Catholic kitsch. **Art Square** next door has more galleries, along with a small theater and a lovely outdoor lounge/bar. It's also the home to nonprofit **Burlesque Hall of Fame** (1027 S. Main St., Suite

110, ☎ 888-661-6465, burlesquehall.com), which packs an impressive amount of history into a tiny space. A comprehensive time line charting the evolution of striptease from the 1800s to today's punk-influenced neoburlesque runs along the walls, illustrated by artifacts such as antique G-strings and feathers from Sally Rand's fan. One corner holds a rotating display of recent costume acquisitions. There are some images of vintage skin on display, but nothing offensive or salacious. A careful examination of everything will take about 30 minutes. Admission is $15 and $12 for locals, students, and military. The exhibit is open Tuesday–Saturday, 10 a.m.–6 p.m.

Next, cross Charleston Boulevard for some delicious meat pies from the **Cornish Pasty Co.** (10 E. Charleston Blvd., ☎ 702-862-4538, cornishpastyco.com) and continue south on Main Street to explore the many hip independent boutiques, such as **Retro Vegas** (midcentury modern furniture and casino cast-offs), **Vintage Vegas** (old toys and movie memorabilia), and **Buffalo Exchange** (trendy used clothing). The arts district continues nearly all the way down to the Stratosphere, but the walk is deceptively long; don't be shy about calling an Uber if your feet and wallet wear out before the end. Another option for getting around is the **Downtown Loop,** which connects the Arts District, Premium Outlets North, the Mob Museum, Pawn Plaza, and other downtown areas via two free shuttles that operate nine hours a day.

Just east of Las Vegas Boulevard on Freemont Street you'll run into **Downtown Container Park** (707 Fremont St., downtowncontainerpark .com), home to a massive metal praying mantis sculpture that spews fire at night, and an elaborate tree house playground that's packed with kids by day. Also at Container Park is the 55-seat **Dome Planetarium.** It runs six high-definition programs, including three rock shows (Led Zeppelin, Pink Floyd's *The Wall,* and U2), shows centering on exploring the universe and on dinosaurs, and an interactive video game called Earth Defender. Projection plays on a 360-degree screen inside the dome with 14 million pixels projected from 36,000 lights. Shows run 8–50 minutes and cost $9– $30. For showtimes and other information see thedomelv .com or call ☎ 702-637-4244.

Based on the popular AMC television series, **Fear the Walking Dead: Survival** (☎ 844-947-8342, vegasexperience.com/fear-walking-dead -survival-attraction-las-vegas) casts Freemont Street tourists as refugees from a zombie apocalypse, seeking refuge from the flesh-eaters inside a supposedly secure military installation. The 20-minute multidimensional attraction combines a gruesomely detailed haunted house–style maze with aggressively interactive live actors, high-tech special effects, and simple escape room puzzles. The grand finale is a 3-D video game created by Triotech (trio-tech.com), where you sit on shaking seats and shoot laser guns at computer-generated ghouls; it's a good example of the genre, but the virtual violence feels anticlimactic following the visceral earlier experiences. Tickets cost $24 ($15 for kids under 13; 40-inch minimum height required) and come with an assigned entry time, but expect things to run behind schedule on busy weekends.

About a mile north of Downtown, just off Las Vegas Boulevard, is **Veterans Memorial Park,** at 555 East Washington Avenue. Featuring 18 larger-than-life statues from the Revolutionary War to the War on Terror, the 2-acre park is open to the public without charge.

OTHER AREA ATTRACTIONS
Bus Tours

Privately owned **Big Bus Tours** (☎ 702-685-6578; bigbustours.com) operates distinctive red double-deckers that run day and night up the Strip and around Downtown. The daytime tours run daily from 10 a.m. to just past 7 p.m. and are hop on/hop off, so you are free to exit and reboard at any scheduled stop. Buses circulate on two loops: The Red route goes up and down the Strip, intersecting with the Blue Downtown route at Circus Circus, where you can transfer between the two. The Red route reaches as far south as the iconic Welcome to Las Vegas Sign, while the Blue circuit includes sights like the Frank Gehry–designed Lou Ruvo Center for Brain Health and Downtown's burgeoning Arts District.

Nighttime tours depart from Circus Circus at 7 p.m. and The Excalibur at 7:30 p.m.; they run from the southern Strip to the Freemont Street Experience. You can't get off and on the nighttime tour at will, but you do get an hour to explore Downtown before the returning bus departs from the Golden Nugget. Day or night, the tour guides are all extremely knowledgeable about local lore, and each gives their own spin on the narration; make sure you pick a seat near a working speaker. Daytime tours cost $47 per day for adults, $38 for kids ages 5–15; book online to get a second consecutive day of touring free. Night tours start at $41 for adults, $27 for kids. If you are riding solo and getting off at two or more stops, the daytime bus is cheaper transportation than a cab and a lot more entertaining.

Quirky Tours

Among many guided tours of various ilk available in Las Vegas are the **Vegas Mob Tour** and **Haunted Vegas Ghost Hunt.** The Mob Tour traces organized crime's history in Las Vegas and visits the sites of various murders, suicides, and celebrity deaths. The tour operates from the Tuscany and includes a pizza dinner. Cost is $106 for approximately 2½ hours of mob madness. The Haunted Vegas Ghost Hunt features haunted casinos, Elvis hauntings, and the antics of Bugsy Siegel's ghost, among other imponderables. This tour also originates at the Tuscany and lasts about 2½ hours. Cost is $89.95 plus tax. For tickets and information call ☎ 866-218-4935 or visit vegasmobtour.com and haunted vegastours.com. The minimum age is 13 for Haunted Vegas and 16 for the Vegas Mob Tour. Anyone under 18 must be accompanied by an adult. The tours, in addition to being great fun, serve up large doses of little-known Vegas history and are quite substantive. Look for discount coupons in *What's On* and other Las Vegas visitor magazines.

The host of the Travel Channel series *Ghost Adventures* has assembled his paranormal artifacts inside a purportedly possessed historic downtown mansion, and spook-seeking guests are now invited—if they dare—inside **Zak Bagans's The Haunted Museum** (600 E. Charleston Blvd., ☎ 702-444-0744, thehauntedmuseum.com). Each of the Winchester-esque house's 30-plus rooms have been meticulously themed after the macabre objects inside, which range from real-life relics that inspired fright films (including the Dybbuk Box from *The Possession* and cellar staircase from *Demon House)* to ghoulish celebrity murder memorabilia, such as Charles Manson's dentures and candlesticks from the yacht where Natalie Wood died. Knowledgeable goth-garbed guides lead groups of 12 through 90-minute tours, which isn't nearly long enough to fully examine everything on display, while managing to keep a straight face despite any skeptics. P. T. Barnum would have appreciated some of the cheesier carnie elements—little people popping out of the walls delivering Cockney monologues and a brief funhouse filled with creepy clowns—but the exhibit of Dr. Kevorkian's suicide van (complete with dummy corpse) demonstrates poor taste. A few missteps aside, The Haunted Museum is well done and worth a visit. Tickets are $44; you must be 16 or older and sign a waiver to enter, and those under 18 are barred from certain "heavy" rooms, where even some guides refuse to go. Tours are Monday and Wednesday–Saturday 1–9 p.m. and Sunday noon–8 p.m.

Water Parks

Las Vegas has two water parks. Both are open seasonally, beginning in March and running through late September to mid-October. The former Splash Canyon water park is now **Wet 'n' Wild** (☎ 702-979-1600, wetnwildlasvegas.com), a family-friendly water park located 11 miles from the South Strip at 7055 S. Fort Apache Road. The 41-acre park is a full-service hydro-adventure with sandy beaches, the 17,000-square-foot Red Rock Bay wave pond, the 1,000-foot Colorado Cooler lazy river, slides of various degrees and angles, a mat racer, the requisite altitudinal thrill experiences, and a lengthy, convoluted tube ride. Splash Island houses RainFortress, a four-story aquatic playground with a 500-gallon bucket that cascades water on all beneath and nearby. There's also a stage with a DJ spinning tunes. Private cabanas, free inner tubes, lounge chairs, lockers, and showers are available. Several refreshment stands are positioned throughout the complex. No coolers allowed. Admission is priced according to height: $39.99 for everyone 42 inches and taller, $29.99 for juniors under 42 inches, and free for children under age 2. Parking is $8. Wet 'n' Wild is open daily 10 a.m.–6 p.m. or later.

An endless summer awaits at the 1960s surf-themed, 23-acre water park **Cowabunga Bay** (cowabungabay.com). The park salutes the many US beaches, from Atlantic City's Boardwalk to California's Surf Cities and across the Pacific to Hawaii's aloha sands. The park's focal point is Wild Surf, where four-rider rubber rafts are hurled from a height of 55 feet into huge waves thrusting them to and fro. You'll also find the six-story Cowabunga Splash, housing a net climb and a maze of tunnels, bridges, slides, platforms, and playful water devices; Surf-A-Rama, a 33,000-square-foot wave pool; and 25 more attractions, including body slides, two bucket dumps, a tube slide, kids' cove, and a vertical inner tube ride. Two restaurants and VIP cabanas with table service are also on site. Coolers are allowed in picnic areas outside the park. Located at Galleria Drive and Gibson Road in suburban Henderson, the park is a 25-minute drive from the South Strip. Admission is priced according to height: $40 for everyone 48 inches and taller; $30 for juniors under 48 inches.

Thrills on Wheels

For $159 to more than $3,100, you can fly a foot off the ground at the **Richard Petty Driving Experience** (☎ 702-643-4343, drivepetty.com). Here you can get behind the wheel of a 600-horsepower NASCAR Winston Cup–style stock car. The Driving Experience is located at Las Vegas Motor Speedway, 15 minutes north of the Strip.

Also at Las Vegas Motor Speedway is **Dream Racing** (☎ 702-599-5199, dreamracing.com), where you can drive a track-ready Ferrari 430 GT around a 1.1-mile track with nine low-, medium-, and high-speed corners. Cost is $500 for five laps plus 13 minutes of training in a 3-D simulator. For $99–$250 you can ride two laps as a passenger with a professional driver. Race suit and helmet are included, as is round-trip transportation from Crystals. Check the website for discounts.

EXR Exotics Racing (☎ 702-802-5662, exoticsracing.com) operates on a private 1.2-mile track at the Las Vegas Motor Speedway. Here you can drive or ride in a huge selection of exotic cars, including Ferrari, Lamborghini, Porsche, Mercedes, Corvette, Aston Martin, and Audi R8, among many others. You can also choose from among six driving school programs. Cost to drive a Ferrari F430 F1 ranges from $299 for 5 laps to $899 for 20 laps. Same prices apply to driving a Corvette for an equal number of laps.

SPEEDVEGAS has transformed 100 acres of South Las Vegas Boulevard into a race-modified, elite sports car experience with a welcome center, event center, and a driving course featuring 2,200 feet of straightway, more than 60 feet of elevation change, and 12 banked turns. SPEEDVEGAS is located 10 minutes south of the famous welcome to las vegas sign. For more information see speedvegas.com.

Only a half mile west of the Strip is **Dig This Heavy Equipment Playground** (3012 S. Rancho Drive, ☎ 702-222-4344, digthisvegas.com), where you can play with real bulldozers and excavators. Following an orientation and a breathalyzer test—hey, it's Vegas—your personal instructor takes you out on the lot to move some dirt. Communicating with you over a headset, he actually teaches you to operate the earth-moving equipment (squishing the highway cones is considered bad form). Cabs are air-conditioned, so you'll be comfortable on hot days.

If you want to admire some speed machines without getting behind the wheel, the **Shelby Heritage Center** (6405 Ensworth St., ☎ 702-942-7325, shelby.com) opens its showroom museum and gift shop to the public 7 days a week, with free guided tours Monday–Friday at 10:30 a.m. and 1:30 p.m., and Saturday at 10:30 a.m. only. The tour is advertised as 60–90 minutes, but ours (conducted by a 50-year veteran of Ford Motors) lasted nearly 2 hours, covering Carroll Shelby's complete career from championship driver to pioneering entrepreneur who went toe to toe with Enzo Ferrari and Lee Iacocca. The dozens of vehicles on display include the original CSX2000 #1, the first Shelby car preserved in survivor condition with shredded upholstery, and a rare Series 1, one of only 249 ever produced. Tours conclude with a walk through Shelby American's headquarters garage. The cars are gorgeous, but unless you're a hardcore gearhead the tour will feel like overkill before the first hour is up.

Go-Karts and Buggies

Do you feel the need for scaled-down speed? Vegas boasts a number of midget racetracks, where kids and adults alike can live out their Le Mans fantasies in souped-up go-karts.

Pole Position Raceway (4175 S. Arville St., ☎ 702-227-7223, pole positionraceway.com/lasvegas) houses a single snaking road-style track inside an air-conditioned warehouse, along with a small arcade and a snack bar serving alcohol (for after the race only, of course). Adults run a 10-minute, 12-lap race at speeds up to 45 mph; kids at least 6 years old and 4 feet tall can race at up to 25 mph. Group parties and free shuttles from the Strip are available, but you'll need an annual membership ($55 and up) or "temporary license" ($5.99 per week) before you can drive; after that, individual races cost $25.50 for adults ($22 for kids), including rental of mandatory full-face protective helmets.

If you can handle the heat, **Las Vegas Mini Grand Prix** (1401 N. Rainbow Blvd., ☎ 702-500-1794, lvmgp.com) has four fun outdoor courses, including one reserved for little racers (38–54 inches), and another restricted to ages 16 and up that requires a real driver's license. The signature "Adult Grand Prix" course features vehicles that could hit an astonishing 80 mph with their automatic transmission engines, if not for all the hairpin turns. You'll also find a small arcade with redemption games; a food counter serving inexpensive sandwiches and pizza pies; and a few kiddie rides, such as a fun slide and Dragon mini-coaster. Each go-kart race requires an $8 ticket, or you can get a 1-hour wristband valid on all rides for $23.

If you're really looking to get off the beaten path, and are willing to get a little—ok, a lot—dusty, **Sunbuggy Fun Rentals** (6925 Speedway Blvd., ☎ 866-728-4443, sunbuggy.com/lasvegas) will let you careen over sand dunes in custom-built buggies that seat up to six. Driving instructions, safety helmets, and a trained guide are included in all packages, which start at $199 for a 30-minute "chase" through the desert; "insanely scary" nighttime trips are available for an extra charge. Round-trip transportation is offered, with the entire experience taking about 4 hours door-to-door from a Strip hotel. If you call to book, specials are often available with savings of up to $40.

If You're Feeling Jumpy

Las Vegas has three mega-trampoline attractions, none located close to the Strip. **FlipNOut Xtreme** (☎ 702-579-9999, flipnoutextreme.com) has two locations: 4245 S. Grand Canyon Drive in Summerlin and 1235 Warm Springs Road in Henderson. The Summerlin branch has 14 trampoline and airbag attractions, plus a game arcade. Trampoline dodgeball and basketball dunk hoops are favorites. There's also laser tag, a laser maze, and climbing walls. In the 6-and-under area, parents can bounce with their children. The Henderson facility is more modest but has all the basics along with a few unique offerings, including a three-story Fun Factory climbing maze for 12-and-unders and a jousting pit. Waivers, available online, are required, and reservations are recommended. Grip socks are not required, but those without must jump barefoot.

    Gravady (7350 Prairie Falcon Road, ☎ 702-843-0395, gravady .com) is comparable in size to FlipNOut and offers a similar array of attractions, although foam pits rather than airbags are the rule. Standouts include a trapeze attraction, a Ninja Obstacle Course, angled wall trampolines, and a ball hanging over the main tramp area luring jumpers to reach it (not easy). As at FlipNOut, you must jump barefoot if you don't have gripper socks. Waivers and reservations are available online.

Skydiving

Do you dream of free-fall but fear boarding a plane, much less leaping out of one? **Vegas Indoor Skydiving** (200 Convention Center Drive, ☎ 702-731-4768, vegasindoorskydiving.com) will give you a taste of the sport on solid ground, with the help of a gargantuan vertical wind tunnel and some supremely silly-looking parachute suits. After watching a short safety briefing, you'll sign your life away and suit up in the provided safety equipment before stepping atop an enormous industrial fan. For about 3 minutes, you'll flail a few feet off the ground in a gale-force wind, with a friendly employee to fling you into the well-padded walls when your flight is over. The whole experience lasts less than an hour and is exhilarating but exhausting; you'll need multiple visits to get the hang of controlling your midair contortions. It's almost as much fun just to watch others wobble in the wind using the free observation windows. A single flight costs $75, and a second on the same day is $50; photo and video services cost $20–$50. There's no age limit, but for safety reasons there are strict weight minimums (40 pounds) and maximums (170–245 pounds, depending on gender and height).

    Real skydiving is offered by **Las Vegas Outdoor Adventures** (☎ 702-602-6333, vegasoutdooradventures.com), an adventure outfitter that offers everything from zip lines to sniper training.

Gaming

Ever since you were a young boy (or girl) you've played the silver ball, but you ain't seen nothing like the **Pinball Hall of Fame** (1610 E. Tropicana Ave., ☎ 702-597-2627, pinballmuseum.org). Whether you're an old-school Bally table king or part of the post-Pong generation, you're sure to find a coin-operated time machine to transport you back to your youth inside this 10,000-square-foot all-ages arcade founded by Tim Arnold and operated by members of the Las Vegas Pinball Collectors Club. Housed in an unpretentious utilitarian warehouse, the Pinball Hall of Fame contains one of the world's largest pinball collections, all of which are available to play (as long as the staff can keep their flippers flipping), and many with informative hand-written histories. Machines range from the 1940s through the present and include rare unreleased prototypes (a two-of-a-kind multilevel Pinball Circus), current pop-culture tie-ins *(Star Trek, Transformers, The Dark Knight)*, and even a digital table that can emulate dozens of different models. Games cost 25¢–75¢ for five balls, so bring cash for the quarter-changers; no tokens needed here.

Haven't had enough gaming? **GameWorks** (6587 Las Vegas Blvd. S., Ste. 171, ☎ 702-978-4263, gameworks.com) is a 7,000-square-foot games arcade at Town Square that features a small bowling alley, a T.G.I. Fridays–esque restaurant, and a full liquor bar. Games include a handful of pinball machines and retro coin-ops, several of which were broken, and some cutting-edge models (such as Star Wars Battle Pod). Also at GameWorks is Dark Ride XD, a 3-D, motion simulator dark ride where you use "light guns" to pop mummies, aliens, pirates, and zombies. Think Buzz Lightyear at the Disney parks or Men in Black at Universal, but in a ride vehicle that doesn't actually go anywhere. Cost is $7. GameWorks also added an esports LAN gaming zone for competitions. All machines require game cards, not quarters, which start at $5 for 20 credits; most games cost 2–10 credits per play.

To play many of the same machines for less money, head to the **Fun Dungeon** beneath Excalibur's gaming floor instead. Though the decor is dated, Excalibur has its fair share of late-model games, along with cheesy carnival contests that are more generous with their prize tickets than GameWorks or Circus Circus.

Esports

Esports (electronic sports, competitive video gaming) competitions are held at the **Millennial Esports Arena** Downtown at Neonopolis, the **Downtown Grand**, the esports LAN gaming zone at **GameWorks,** and at the **Luxor, MGM Grand,** and **Rio.** A calendar of scheduled events can be found at esportsinlasvegas.com/event-calendar.

Escape Rooms

If arcades aren't immersive enough for you, you can step inside a puzzle-solving mystery adventure at any one of a number of escape rooms that have sprung up around town. In all, a small team is locked in a room and asked to ransack its contents, searching for clues and tasks that will unlock the door to freedom before time elapses (don't worry, losers aren't imprisoned, only embarrassed). Different escape rooms offer various themes to frame their games, which cost about $35 per person. We tried out **Lockdown** (3271 S. Highland Drive, ☎ 702-998-8723, lockdownrooms.com), which offers a Hostage Rescue scenario suitable for 2–6 novice players, in which we had an hour to hack into a computer before our kidnapped friend was kaput. Lockdown's set dressings were minimally themed but effective, and the puzzles largely fair despite some sticky locks. If you try it or a similar escape room, remember to search every object carefully, divide tasks among your team, and save your hints for when they're really needed; the rush you get from cracking the case in time rivals any digital victory.

Escapology (2797 S. Maryland Pkwy., ☎ 702-359-0805, escapology.com/en/las-vegas-nv) is a large upscale facility offering eight escape experiences, ranging from Antidote (rogue scientist develops a deadly virus for bio warfare) to Cuban Crisis (CIA agent infiltrates Fidel Castro's palace during the Cuban missile crisis). What sets Escapology apart are the detailed and elaborate plot scenarios—it's not just about escaping. All games are designed for 2–6 players and last an hour, plus a pregame briefing. Though up to six players can be accommodated, Escapology doesn't pair your party with other players. Each game is $30–$35 per person. Hours are daily, 10 a.m.–midnight.

Of all the escape rooms we've sampled, **The Official SAW Escape Room** (2121 Industrial Road, ☎ 702-323-6483, sawescaperoom.com) is easily the most theatrical . . . and most terrifying. Players arrive at a seemingly semi-abandoned meat-packing plant in an industrial neighborhood, where the first of several well-cast actors checks you in for your tour of the facility. Following an introductory video, groups of 10 are handed flashlights and notepads before being dispatched into the dismal corridors. The sightseeing quickly goes south when the doors lock and Jigsaw (voiced by series star Tobin Bell) taunts you over the loudspeaker, challenging you to solve his perverse puzzles before the clock counts down. During your hour-long ordeal, Jigsaw's games lead you through an extensive series of exquisitely icky environments, culminating in the iconic bathroom from the original film. There, you'll find a performer chained to the wall with a hacksaw that he'll use to self-amputate if you fail—talk about pressure! The tasks are similar to other escape rooms, but gathering the necessary clues will require crawling through an offal-strewn tunnel, climbing into a crematorium, and reaching into a gory grinder. You don't need to know trivia about the *Saw* movies to succeed, but you will need to carefully communicate and cooperate with your fellow victims (er, players), which is difficult when many of you are shrieking in fear. Tickets are $50 on Wednesday, Thursday, and Sunday; $60 on Friday and Saturday. Operating hours are Wednesday and Thursday, 5–11 p.m., Friday 5 p.m.–midnight, Saturday 4 p.m.–midnight, and Sunday 4–11 p.m. There's no age limit, but a parent must be present to sign the required waiver for anyone under 18, and kids under 16 must be accompanied by an adult.

Guns

Gun stores and firing ranges often come in the same package in Las Vegas, and it's debatable whether these establishments are retailers, attractions, or both. Want to fire a machine gun? There are a number of venues where anyone over 18 can blast away without a firearms license or any previous experience (God bless America!). All operate essentially the same way: you'll select a package (ranging from around $100 to $1,000 and up), including weapons rental, ammunition, paper targets, and safety equipment; then you'll receive basic handling instructions before stepping into the shooting range. Firearm brands typically include Uzi, Thompson, and Madsen; massive mini-guns, sniper rifles, and even cannons may be available.

Las Vegas's oldest established indoor shooting establishment is **The Gun Store** (2900 E. Tropicana Ave., ☎ 702-454-1110, thegunstorelas vegas.com), founded by self-defense advocate Bob "Fired Up" Irwin, who furnished firearms for films like *Fear and Loathing in Las Vegas*. The staff focuses on customer service in a family-friendly environment, with accompanied minors as young as 5 permitted to shoot on a case-by-case basis.

Battlefield Vegas (2771 Industrial Road, ☎ 702-566-1000, battle fieldvegas.com), located just behind Circus Circus, has a parking lot full of decommissioned military vehicles to take photos with, including a Sherman tank and Vietnam-era helicopter. Call at least two hours ahead to reserve your shooting time, and they'll send a Humvee to pick you up at no extra charge.

The largest indoor facility in town is **The Range 702** (5999 Dean Martin Drive, ☎ 702-485-3232, therange702.com), which features a café serving breakfast and lunch and free carry concealed weapons (CCW) classes for Nevada and Florida residents.

For an upscale clublike experience, **MGV: Machine Gun Vegas** (3501 Aldebaran Ave., ☎ 800-75-shoot, machinegunsvegas.com) ditches the drab warehouse look for hardwood floors and exposed brick. Their charming majority-female staff can arrange bachelor or bachelorette party packages, offering adventures with exotic dancers or exotic cars after your shoot-em-up experience.

Zombie-themed warfare simulations have sprung up across the country, and **Adventure Combat Ops** (4375 S. Valley View Blvd., Ste. G, ☎ 855-219-4479, adventurecombatops.com) is the best of its kind we've experienced so far. The 100-minute adventure begins with an explosive introduction to the premise, as we learn that terrorists have unleashed an undead plague in our backyard. During your 45-minute briefing and boot camp, team leaders demonstrate proper use of the realistic-looking Airsoft assault rifles (they fire foam bullets that shouldn't seriously wound but do sting) and teach tactics for clearing bad guys from buildings. Those skills are put to the test once you enter the 33,000-square-foot arena, which re-creates an entire neighborhood, complete with a dozen full-size houses and derelict vehicles. At your instructor's command, your squadmates storm through town, kicking down doors and ransacking furniture in search of intelligence documents, while wasting walkers who lurk in closets and refrigerators. The final showdown, during which wave after wave bear down on your team, is like living through an episode of *The Walking Dead*. Prices start at $199 for a basic package, which includes the complete experience with a gun and safety equipment, but discounts are available if you book online, where a starter package is $120 (be sure to upgrade it with an additional clip of ammo). While the experience is intense, kids as young as 6 have participated along with their parents, though the suggested minimum age is 16. Hours are Thursday–Sunday, 9 a.m.–10 p.m., with sessions starting at 10 a.m., 1 p.m., 4 p.m., and 7 p.m.; book online or call ahead to confirm availability.

If Airsoft isn't quite masochistic enough for you, Vegas's burgeoning "gun district" offers a couple of even more extreme options. Like a Chuck E. Cheese for adults with anger management issues, **Top Shot** (3084 S. Highland Drive, Ste. C, ☎ 702-478-8550, topshotlasvegas .com) offers a suite of video simulators and a 1,200-square-foot maze-like "shoot house" similar to those used for police and military training. Players can choose between wearing high-voltage vests that deliver an electrical shock when struck by a laser gun (the feeling is similar to being poked in the stomach with a sharp stick from the inside), or even more painful "man-marker" wax bullets fired from real Glock or AR-15 weapons. Packages start at $85 and cover required equipment, including full face masks and padded Michelin Man suits, plus the aid of a range safety officer. Annual memberships, which cost $100, include free admission and weapon rental with discounts on à la carte ammo.

Next door, **Las Vegas Gun Fights** (3068 S. Highland Drive, ☎ 702-486-7338, lvgunfights.com) ups the agony ante with even more powerful Simunition ammo, capable of breaking skin and noses. After training in a mock Middle Eastern village, contestants enter a barrel-strewn indoor arena for full-contact force-on-force gunfights; think of it as UFC with live firearms. 9mm pistol combat packages start at $100; you can upgrade and add an AR-15 rifle for $40. If you've always wanted to shoot your buddies point-blank in the brain, this is the place, and there's a hookah lounge attached for the ultimate *Hangover*-style bad-idea bachelor party. Consider simply spectating, as the National Gunfight League competitors—many of whom are ex-military or bounty hunters, like the facility's founder—go mano a mano, if you want to avoid having to explain your fresh flesh wounds back home.

Playing with Sharp Objects

For something decidedly different, try **Axe Monkeys** (3525 E. Post Road, Ste. 110, ☎ 866-293-6665, axemonkeys.com). Here you'll find 23 indoor axe-throwing lanes, where you can heave a 1.5-pound axe at a pine bull's-eye target. Gratefully, the throwing lanes are separated by a chain-link fence. Pricing is by the hour, and you can choose 1 hour ($25 adult/$20 child) or 2 hours ($40 adult/$25 child). As someone who has thrown axes, the activity takes a toll on your throwing arm, so a 1-hour session is more than plenty for most. Also available, at a higher price, are knives, ninja stars, and steel-throwing cards, though mastering these is more difficult than learning to throw an axe. Stumps and live chickens can be had by special arrangement (not). Anyone over 7 years old can throw. Participants must wear closed-toe shoes.

Museums and More

If you have children, try the **Discovery Children's Museum,** at 360 Promenade Place, next to the Smith Center for the Performing Arts (☎ 702-382-5437, discoverykidslv.org), for a rewarding afternoon of exploration and enjoyable education. The three-story facility is one of the best of its kind, rivaling Philadelphia's Franklin Institute, and we were impressed by how immaculately maintained all the hands-on exhibits are. Highlights include a room full of interactive water sculptures (ponchos provided); a kid-size pirate ship and castle to clamber on; an "Eco City," complete with hospital, bank, grocery, and airport, where kids can earn pretend paychecks; a ghost town where pint-size detectives can crack a murder mystery, similar to MGM's CSI attraction; and a multilevel climbing structure running straight up the center of the building. There's a small gift shop stocked with educational toys and snack rooms with vending machines, but no hot food. Admission is $14.50 for visitors age 1 and up, $12.50 for locals. Summer hours (Memorial Day–Labor Day) are Monday–Saturday, 10 a.m.–5 p.m. and Sunday, noon–5 p.m. The rest of the year hours are Tuesday–Friday, 9 a.m.–4p.m.; Saturday, 10 a.m.– 5p.m.; and Sunday, noon–5 p.m. Plan on a minimum of an hour just to sample all three floors, 2-plus hours to fully explore, or half a day if you want to participate in the many free daily workshops.

You can also check out the **Las Vegas Natural History Museum** (☎ 702-384-3466, lvnhm.org), about a mile away at 900 Las Vegas Blvd. N., near Heritage Park. Filled with old-fashioned static displays of stuffed animals both native to Nevada and exotic—including giraffes and giant crocodiles—the museum's Smithsonian-style dioramas are either beautiful or creepy, depending on your taste for taxidermy. The basement boasts a more modern exhibit of stiffly moving dinosaurs (no threat to Disneyland's animatronics) and a colorful play area stocked with live bugs and lizards. For longtime Vegas visitors, the highlight is the Treasures of Egypt gallery, which holds a replica of King Tut's tomb that was originally housed at the Luxor. Admission costs a reasonable $12 for adults; $10 for seniors, military, and students; and $6 for children ages 3–11. The museum is open daily, 9 a.m.–4 p.m., and you should be able to see it all in 60–75 minutes.

Located inside the floundering Boulevard Mall, **SeaQuest Interactive Aquarium** (3528 S. Maryland Pkwy., ☎ 702-906-1901, visitseaquest .com/vegas) is a family-friendly fish exhibit similar to the Merlin Sea Life attractions found around the world. Different rooms are devoted to various ecosystems, such as a Caribbean cove, Californian coast, or

Amazonian rainforest. The decorative theming is mostly made up of flat painted murals and simple faux rockwork, and can't compete with the detailed scenery in Mandalay Bay's Shark Reef (see pages 424–425), but SeaQuest has the edge in allowing visitors to feed and touch many of its denizens. Admission is only $14.95 for adults and $9.95 for children ages 2–11, but you'll want to purchase a handful of $2.50 tokens for buying baby shrimp or sardines to feed the stingrays and sharks. For $39.95 (admission included) you can even climb into a tank and snorkel alongside the ray-stocked reef. In addition to its ichthyic inhabitants, the aquarium also has a parakeet enclosure that you can enter at select times to hand-feed the feisty feathered flock. Open Monday–Thursday, 11 a.m.–8 p.m.; Friday, 11 a.m.–9 p.m.; Saturday, 10 a.m.–9 p.m.; and Sunday, 11 a.m.–7 p.m. Adults should plan to visit for 45 minutes, while kids could easily explore for an hour or more.

Unique to Las Vegas is the **Atomic Testing Museum** (☎ 702-794-5151, nationalatomictestingmuseum.org), which chronicles through exhibits and film the history of the Nevada Test Site, where atomic bombs were detonated only 65 miles from Las Vegas. A vital sense of place, artifacts, and good storytelling come together here to create a powerful museum experience. This museum is cerebral, instructive, and entertaining. Laden with artifacts, there is much to look at (and much to read for a full encounter). A good balance of videos and interactive stations can engage anyone with a passing interest in this seemingly and sadly ever-important topic. In one of two small theaters, the brief, overpowering experience of a nuclear test explosion is alone nearly worth the price of admission.

The museum is the first ever to feature a special exhibit, *Area 51: Myth or Reality*, about that top-secret stretch of wasteland adjacent to the Mojave Desert range where atomic tests occurred in the 1950s. This interactive adventure takes you to the most classified place in America, long considered the domain of UFOs, extraterrestrials, and ancient visitors. Eerie, suspenseful, and thought-provoking, is it what you think it is or something else?

If you are looking for some brain stimulation to escape the midway atmosphere of the casinos, you can't do better than the Atomic Testing Museum, created in association with the Smithsonian Institution. Open daily, the museum is located at 755 E. Flamingo Road. Admission is $22 adults and $16 children.

The Hollywood Cars Museum (5115 Dean Martin Drive, Ste. 905, ☎ 702-331-6400, hollywoodcarsmuseum.com) showcases a large collection of cars used in movies and on television. Many of them are quite famous, such as the DeLorean from *Back to the Future*, the Batmobile, Herbie the Love Bug, James Bond's Lotus submarine car, and the death car from *Bonnie and Clyde*. The Liberace Garage exhibit showcases the Las Vegas icon's collection of automobiles, some as eccentric as his wardrobe. In addition to the vehicles, photos and artifacts from Liberace's homes are also on display. The 30,000-square-foot museum displays in excess of 100 cars and is open daily, 10 a.m.–5 p.m.

High-quality chocolatier **Ethel M** offers a self-guided factory tour that takes you all the way from cocoa beans to finished candies. You can linger to observe the process for as long as you like. Also on factory property is a 4-acre cactus garden showcasing more than 300 species of cacti and drought-tolerant ornamentals from all over the world. The plants are labeled for identification and serve as a good grounding in desert flora that will enhance hikes or walks you might take in the Las Vegas area. The factory and garden are located in Henderson (2 Cactus Garden Drive, ☎ 702-435-2655, ethelm.com), about 20 minutes east of the Strip. Open daily, 8 a.m.–8 p.m. Both the factory tour and cactus garden are free and open to the public. Many visitors drop by en route to or from Hoover Dam.

For aficionados of the iron horses that tamed the Wild West, a visit to the **Nevada State Railroad Museum** (601 Yucca St., Boulder City; ☎ 702-486-5952; nevadasouthern.com) is in order. A 30-minute drive from the Strip, the museum is home to the Nevada Southern Railway, a historic line that dates back to the construction of the Boulder Dam in the 1930s. Today, families flock to the train on weekends for a scenic 4-mile excursion. Open-air cars give the best view of the geologically interesting geography on milder days, but the vintage Pullman coaches offer the advantage of air-conditioning. The round-trip journey takes about 35 minutes, and you can kill another hour exploring the exhibits of antique train cars, elaborate scale model railways, and other locomotive memorabilia. Train fare is $10 for adults, $5 for kids ages 4–11. Departures are at 10 a.m., 11:30 a.m., 1 p.m., and 2:30 p.m. every Saturday and Sunday; the museum exhibits are open daily (except holidays), 9 a.m.–3:30pm.

Old West Fun

Near scenic Red Rock Canyon, a side trip just outside of Las Vegas is **Bonnie Springs Old Nevada** (☎ 702-875-4191, bonniesprings.com). This rustic re-creation of an Old West town features trinket stores, a saloon, two museums, a restaurant, a petting zoo, a zombie bus (?!), and guided horse rides. The hoot that goes with this holler is the low-budget melodrama. The kicker is the real live Western hanging that takes place at noon, 2, and 4 p.m. "You can't hang me, sheriff!" "Why not?!" "Cause yer wife'll miss me!" Cost to get in—$10 adults, $7 children. Real rope, real fun.

About 30 minutes southwest of Las Vegas, in the one-horse town of Goodsprings, Nevada, is the **Pioneer Saloon** (310 W. Spring St., ☎ 702-874-9362, pioneersaloon.info). The saloon is pretty much the same as when it was built in 1913, with interior and exterior walls of stamped tin manufactured by Sears and Roebuck. Decorative accents include bullet holes from brawls dating back to 1915. The saloon became famous in 1941 when actress Carole Lombard's plane crashed not far away. Her husband, Clark Gable, sat at the bar chain-smoking for three days while awaiting word of Lombard's fate (all 22 aboard were killed). There's live rock or country music on Sunday afternoons.

Also southwest of Las Vegas is **Sandy Valley Ranch** (1411 Kingston Road, Sandy Valley, NV 80901; ☎ 702-242-0955; sandyvalleyranch .com), where you can cut a steer from the herd, round up cattle and chase them into the corral, or trail-ride in the southern foothills of the Spring Mountains, all followed by a dinner featuring big wads o' meat and a near-conflagration of a campfire. No riding experience necessary—the horses are very smart and sweet (ask for old Gonad Stomper).

NOTE There are a goodly number of Las Vegas attractions that we don't have space to cover in the *Unofficial Guide*. All of them are listed and described at vegas.com/attractions. If you provide your name and address they'll mail you a free brochure. The site is sponsored by Museums and Attractions in Nevada (MAIN) in partnership with the Nevada Commission on Tourism.

NATURAL ATTRACTIONS NEAR LAS VEGAS

IN THE MEXICAN PAVILION of Epcot at Walt Disney World, tourists rush obliviously past some of the rarest and most valuable artifacts of the Spanish Colonial period in order to take a short, uninspired boat ride. Many Las Vegas visitors, likewise, never look beyond the Strip. Like the Epcot tourists, they are missing something pretty special.

Las Vegas's geological and topographical diversity, in combination with its stellar outdoor resources, provides the best opportunities for worthwhile sightseeing. So different and varied are the flora, fauna, and geology at each distinct level of elevation that traveling from the banks of Lake Mead to the high, ponderosa pine forests of Mount Charleston encompasses (in 90 minutes) as much environmental change as driving from Mexico to Alaska.

Red Rock Canyon, the **Valley of Fire,** the **Mojave Desert,** and the **Black Canyon of the Colorado River** are world-class scenic attractions. In combination with the summits of the **Spring Mountains,** they compose one of the most dramatically diversified natural areas on the North American continent.

Springs Preserve

This 180-acre natural oasis, approximately 3 miles west of Downtown Las Vegas, is filled with museums, galleries, an interpretive trail system, botanical gardens, a re-creation of a 1905 Las Vegas street, and plenty of wildlife. The **Origen Museum** is the preserve's focal point for history, geology, and wildlife and features three galleries with more than 75 exhibits emphasizing Las Vegas's precarious dependence on water. The family-focused interactive displays are equal to those in the Franklin Institute and Smithsonian; don't miss the 8-minute introductory film narrated by Martin Sheen, flash flood simulation, and indoor-outdoor animal habitats. The property is also home to the **Nevada State Museum** (museums. nevadaculture.org/nsmlv-home; open Tuesday–Sunday, 9 a.m.–5 p.m.), which covers much of the same material from a more mature perspective, with an emphasis on the area's mining and gambling history. It's home to feathered costumes from the *Folies Bergère* and artifacts from Bugsy Siegel and Howard Hughes. Plan on at least an hour to explore the Origen Museum (more if your kids are into natural history) and 45 minutes for the Nevada State Museum. **Boomtown 1905** depicts well-known buildings, including the Lincoln Hotel, the Arizona Club, the Majestic Theatre, First State Bank, Las Vegas Mercantile, and a train depot from Downtown Las Vegas at the turn of the 20th century. There are also four original railroad cottages where railroad workers lived. One cottage has been restored to its original pre-1911 condition. The historical setting doesn't end on the street; most buildings can be explored inside as well. You can walk a quarter-mile paved road to Boomtown, or for $5 you can ride a train. **WaterWorks** is inside the Charleston Heights Pumping Station, an operational water-pumping facility, across from Boomtown 1905. The hands-on experience offers an educational behind-the-scenes look at water-resource treatment and delivery, or, in other words, the journey water takes to reach your tap. Entry is included with your general admission ticket. Open daily 9:30 a.m.–4:30 p.m. The preserve also features a 25-acre, re-created desert wetland with more than 35 species of wildlife and an 1,800-seat amphitheater. A walk around the entire property could easily eat up most of the day; if you are short on time or energy, pay the $5 fare for the 20-minute narrated train ride, or rent a bicycle for $8 an hour. If you need a bite to eat after your hike, visit **Divine Cafe** for healthy American cuisine. The preserve is open daily, 9 a.m.–5 p.m. (trails close at dusk). Admission to museums and exhibits is $19.95 adults and $10.95 children (ages 5–17). Admission to trails is free. For more information, visit springspreserve.org.

Driving Tours

If you wish to sample the natural diversity of the Las Vegas area, we recommend the following driving tours. The trips begin and end in Las Vegas and take from 2 hours to all day, depending on the number of stops and side trips. The driving tours can conveniently be combined with picnicking, hiking, horseback riding, and sightseeing. If you have the bucks, we also recommend taking one of the air/ground tours of the Grand Canyon.

1. MOUNT CHARLESTON, KYLE CANYON, LEE CANYON, AND THE TOIYABE NATIONAL FOREST 4–6 hours

If you have had more than enough desert, this is the drive for you. Head north out of Las Vegas on US 95 and turn left on NV 157. Leave the desert and head into the pine and fir forest of the Spring Mountains. Continue up Kyle Canyon to the Mount Charleston Inn (a good place for lunch) and from there to the end of the canyon. Backtracking a few miles, take NV 158 over Robbers Roost and into Lee Canyon. When you hit NV 156, turn left and proceed to the Lee Canyon Ski Area. For the return trip, simply take NV 156 out of the mountains until it intersects US 95. Turn south (right) on US 95 to return to Las Vegas. If you start feeling your oats once you get into the mountains, there are some nice short hikes (less than a mile) to

Las Vegas–Area Driving Tours

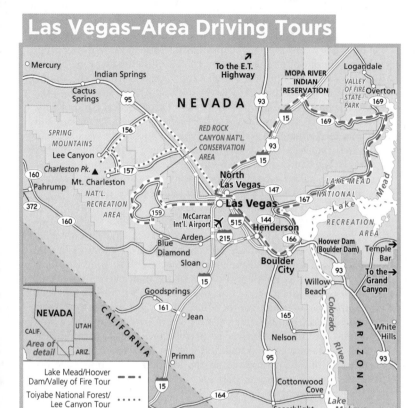

especially scenic overlooks. If you are so inclined, there is also horseback riding, and there are some great places for picnics.

2. RED ROCK CANYON SCENIC LOOP 1½–3 hours Red Rock Canyon is a stunningly beautiful desert canyonland 20 minutes from Las Vegas. A scenic loop winds among imposing, rust-red Aztec sandstone towers. There is a visitor center, as well as hiking trails and picnic areas. With very little effort you can walk to popular rock-climbing sites and watch the action. From Las Vegas, head west on Charleston Boulevard (NV 159) directly to Red Rock Canyon. The scenic loop is 13 miles (one-way), with numerous places to stop and enjoy the rugged vistas. The loop road brings you back to NV 159. Turn left and return to town via Charleston Boulevard.

3. LAKE MEAD AND THE VALLEY OF FIRE 5–8 hours This drive takes you to the Lake Mead National Recreation Area and Valley of Fire State Park. How long the drive takes depends on how many side trips you make. If you plan to visit Hoover Dam during your visit, it will be convenient to work it into this itinerary. The same is true if you wish to tour the Ethel M (as in Mars bars) Chocolate Factory and Cactus Garden.

Head south out of Las Vegas on US 95/93 (detour west on Sunset Road to visit the Chocolate Factory and Cactus Garden), continuing straight on US 93 to Boulder City. From Boulder City continue to the Hoover Dam on US 93 (if desired) or turn left on the Lakeshore Scenic Drive (NV 166) to continue the drive. Travel through the washes and canyons above the lake until you reach the Northshore Scenic Drive (NV 147 and NV 167). Turn right, continuing to the right on NV 167 when the routes split. If you wish, you can descend to the lake at Callville Bay, Echo Bay, or Overton Beach. If you are hungry, Callville Bay and Echo Bay have restaurants and lounges. Overton Beach has a snack bar, but Echo Bay has the best beach.

Near Overton Beach, turn left to NV 169 and follow signs for Valley of Fire State Park. Bear left on NV 169 away from Overton. Valley of Fire features exceptional desert canyon scenery, panoramic vistas, unusual and colorful sandstone formations, and Indian petroglyphs. The road branching uphill next to the visitor center accesses some of the most extraordinary terrain in the American Southwest. On your way to the road's terminus at the White Domes, you'll have the opportunity to explore Mouse's Tank (Petroglyph Canyon), enjoy Rainbow Vista, and hike to Fire Canyon—a playlist of the park's greatest hits. A short 2-mile scenic loop makes it easy to see some of the valley's most interesting formations. After the loop (and any other detours that interest you), continue west on NV 169 until it intersects I-15. Head south to return to Las Vegas.

Eldorado Canyon

When you've covered Las Vegas for as long as we have it's really an event to bump into something totally new and different. Actually, to be precise, we stumbled onto something *old* and different. About a 40-minute drive from the Strip via US 95 and NV 165, is Eldorado Canyon, so named by the Spanish circa 1776 when gold and silver were discovered there.

Gold was rediscovered, along with nickel and lead, in 1859, leading to the establishment of the Techatticup Mine, which operated until 1945. A place of rough-and-tumble life with little order and much violence, the town of Nelson attracted a number of deserters from both the Union and Confederate armies during the Civil War. Lawlessness was so commonplace in the mine's heyday (the nearest sheriff was a one-week ride away on horseback) that a company of infantrymen was stationed nearby to discourage the killings and disputes among the miners themselves and with American Indians.

At the bottom of the canyon was Nelson's Landing on the Colorado River, where the gold was loaded on riverboats to Yuma, Arizona, and sent downstream to California. The landing and a small village surrounding it were destroyed by a flash flood in 1974. By then, however, several dams had long since rendered the Colorado unusable for commercial purposes.

If you've ever wanted to drive from the canyon rim to the bottom of the Grand Canyon, the drive from the top of Eldorado Canyon to the Colorado River is a good facsimile. The road is good, and the vistas are glorious as you descend. At the bottom, there is a recreational area alongside the river, and the river itself, on a sunny day, is the darkest shade of blue imaginable. Be sure to top off your gas tank before leaving Las Vegas.

Eldorado Canyon is a recreational treasure trove. Mine tours, as well as guided kayak, mountain-biking, hiking, ATV, and horseback tours, are available. Outfitters for guided trips include **Awesome Adventures** (☎ 800-519-2243, awesomeadventures.com); **Adventure Las Vegas** (☎ 888-867-6259, adventurelasvegas.com); and **Desert Adventures** (☎ 702-293-5026, kayaklasvegas.com). Of course, you can also do all of this on your own using your own or rented equipment. For mine tours, try **Eldorado Canyon Mine Tours** (☎ 702-291-0026, eldorado canyonminetours.com) or **DETOURS of Nevada** (☎ 855-458-7511, detoursnv.com).

Black Canyon Adventures (☎ 800-455-3490, blackcanyonadventures.com) offers guided raft trips on the Colorado River in Black Canyon below the Hoover Dam. The Hoover Dam Postcard Tour departs from the downstream side of the dam and explores a section of the canyon with a view of the Mike O'Callaghan–Pat Tillman Memorial Bridge, winner of the 2012 Outstanding Civil Engineering Achievement (OCEA) Award, and an opportunity to photograph the dam. Cost is $33. The tour last 90 minutes with 30 minutes on the river. The Black Canyon Raft Tour begins below the dam and travels 3 hours downstream to Willow Beach on the Arizona side of the river. Cost is $114 for ages 13 and up, $81 for kids ages 5–12, and free for kids age 4 and younger; cost includes the $15 National Park Service fee, lunch, and water. Transportation from Strip hotels is available for $59 or you can meet the trip at the check-in desk located at the Lake Meade RV Village. All tours use large motorized inflatable rafts.

Pink Jeep Tours offers guided off-road experiences to Eldorado Canyon, Red Rock Canyon, and Valley of Fire in the Las Vegas area. Excursions farther afield include Death Valley, the Grand Canyon's North, South, and West Rims, and Zion National Park. Jeeps seat 10 people and are pretty plush. Guides are certified by the National Association for Interpretation. Lunch is included on most outings. For additional information and prices call ☎ 888-900-4480 or visit pinkjeeptourslasvegas.com.

Skywalk

Located 121 miles from Las Vegas over some primitive roads, Skywalk is a horseshoe-shaped observation platform projecting from the remote western edge of the Grand Canyon on the Hualapai reservation. The ends of the horseshoe are anchored to the rim of the canyon while the rounded section, the observation platform, cantilevers into space 4,000 feet above the canyon floor. Both the sides and the floor of the platform are transparent. Although the flexible Skywalk is designed to withstand 100-mile-per-hour winds and 8.0-magnitude earthquakes and to support 71 million pounds—it wobbles and vibrates a little. The sensation is a bit like walking on a cruise ship—not unpleasant at sea but disconcerting when you're hanging over the Grand Canyon. Add the fact that the walls are only about mid–chest high and Skywalk begins to seem as much a thrill ride as a spectacular viewing spot.

Speaking of the view, it's magnificent. From Skywalk you can see standing waves on the Colorado River to the left (they look like tiny ripples from this height) and Eagle Point to the right, where the configuration of the canyon looks like the outstretched wings of a bird.

To walk on Skywalk you must purchase a Legacy Gold package, which also includes a visit to the Hualapai Ranch, Guano Point, and Eagle Point, a Native American cultural performance, and an all-you-can-eat meal among other things (see grandcanyonwest.com or call ☎ 888-868-9378). The package runs $86 (including taxes and fees) for adults and $72 for children ages 4–11. A wheelchair ramp is available. There's no limit to the time you can spend on Skywalk and no maximum weight for visitors. You are not allowed to bring cameras or any personal belongings onto Skywalk. For additional information see grandcanyonskywalk.com.

Because the drive is a little more than 3 hours one-way from Las Vegas, you'll have to leave early to take advantage of all the elements of the tour package. If you want to drive over prior to your tour, you can spend the night at the Hualapai Lodge in the hardscrabble town of Peach Springs (49 miles away), the center of the Hualapai Tribe; call ☎ 928-769-2636 or visit grandcanyonwest.com for reservations.

If you don't want to drive, these companies will fly you there:

VISION HOLIDAYS ☎ 800-256-8767	
MAVERICK HELICOPTERS maverickhelicopter.com	☎ 888-261-4414
SUNDANCE HELICOPTERS sundancehelicopters.com	☎ 800-653-1881

Fares range from $250 to more than $600 round-trip, although sometimes a discount can be found on the internet.

Hoover Dam

Hoover Dam is definitely worth seeing. There is a film, a guided tour, and a theater presentation on the Colorado River drainage, as well as some static exhibits. Try to go on a Monday, Thursday, or Friday. Arrive no later than 9 a.m., when the visitor area opens, and do one of the tours first. You can choose between the guided, 30-minute **Power Plant Tour** that visits the power plant and visitor center ($15 adults, $12 children ages 4–16 and seniors) and the 1-hour **Hoover Dam Tour** that covers the dam passageways in addition to the visitor center and power plant. Admission for the Hoover Dam Tour is $30 (no children under 8 years of age allowed). Tickets for the Power Plant Tour can be purchased in advance through usbr.gov/lc/hooverdam, but you must purchase Hoover Dam Tour admissions in person on site. After 9:30 a.m. or so, long lines form for the tour, especially on Tuesday, Wednesday, Saturday, and Sunday. The dam is closed to visitors at 6 p.m. (tickets sold until 5:15 p.m.; 4:15 p.m. in winter).

Other than chauffeured transportation, there is no advantage in going to Hoover Dam on a bus tour, although there is a $10 parking fee. You will still have to wait in line for the tour of the dam and to see the other presentations. If you are the sort of person who tours quickly, you probably will have a lot of time to kill waiting for the rest of the folks to return to the bus.

With the opening of the bypass bridge, those few miles of US 93, which traverse the historic dam and pass by the visitor center, will no longer accommodate through traffic. Now the only access to the dam is from the Nevada side. It is still possible to drive across the dam for a sweeping view of Lake Mead and the lower Colorado, but the existing road terminates on the Arizona side just above the last parking lot at the top of the hill. For more information, call ☎ 702-494-2517.

HOOVER DAM BYPASS BRIDGE   The long-awaited and long-delayed $114-million Hoover Dam bypass bridge opened in 2010, saving travelers minutes to hours of driving time between Nevada and Arizona. Officially named the Mike O'Callaghan–Pat Tillman Memorial Bridge, after a former Nevada governor and an Arizona football player/US Army Ranger killed in Afghanistan, the structure features two enormous cable-less arches projecting from the sheer cliffs above the waterway to buttress the road. Intrepid visitors can walk across the one-third-mile, four-lane bypass rising 850 feet above the choppy Colorado River. A sidewalk begins on the Nevada side and stretches the length of the span. The view of the canyon, the river, and the bridge's remarkable engineering is stunning. It is the longest and highest arch concrete bridge in the Western Hemisphere. An information plaza, hiking trail, and parking area are on the Nevada side.

The Canyons of the Southwest

Las Vegas tourist magazines claim **Bryce Canyon** (400 miles round-trip; ☎ 435-834-5322) and **Zion Canyon, Utah** (350 miles round-trip; ☎ 435-772-3256), as well as the **Grand Canyon, Arizona** (☎ 928-638-7888) as local attractions. We recommend all of the canyons if you are on an extended drive through the Southwest. If your time is limited, however, you might consider taking one of the air day tours that visit the canyons from Las Vegas. Running roughly $200–$600 per passenger, the excursions follow one of two basic formats: air only or air and ground combined. Some tour companies offer discounted fares for a second person if the first person pays full fare.

Almost all canyon tours include a pass over **Lake Mead** and **Hoover Dam.** The trip involving the least commitment of time and money is a round-trip flyover of one or more of the canyons. A Grand Canyon flyover, for example, takeoff to touchdown, takes about 2 hours. While flying over any of the canyons is an exhilarating experience, air traffic restrictions concerning the Grand Canyon severely limit what air passengers can see. Flying over the other canyons is somewhat less restricted.

 If you want to get a real feel for the Grand Canyon particularly, go with one of the air/ground excursions. The Grand Canyon is much more impressive from the ground than from the air.

The air/ground trips fly over the Grand Canyon and then land. Passengers transfer to a bus that motors them along the rim of the canyon, stopping en route for lunch. Excursions may also include boat and helicopter rides. These multifaceted tours last 7–10 hours. Many flights offer multilingual translations of the tour narrative.

A number of companies offer scenic air tours out of Las Vegas via helicopter or small fixed-wing aircraft. The free tourist magazines are dominated by **Papillon Group** (☎ 702-736-7243, papillon.com), which also operates under the brand names **Grand Canyon** (grandcanyonairlines.com) and **Scenic Airlines** (scenic.com). Flip to a random flight tour advertisement, and it's probably associated with Papillon. They feature fixed-wing Vistaliner Twin Otter turbine aircraft, which hold up to 19 passengers, and EC130 helicopters with stadium seating for wraparound views. Papillon also partners with **Gray Line** (☎ 702-739-7777, graylinelasvegas.com) on motorcoach/fight combination tours and with **Las Vegas Outdoor Adventures** (☎ 702-825-1411, vegasoutdooradventures.com) for scenic flights paired with ATV, monster truck, or motorcycle rides.

Papillon's chief competitor is **Maverick** (☎ 702-405-4300, flymaverick.com), which boasts a private bluff inside the Grand Canyon where you can land for a champagne toast. Maverick also operates as **Mustang** (☎ 702-851-3290, soarmustang.com) at slightly cheaper rates from the south side of town, though their trips don't include a Strip flyover. A third outfit called **Sundance Helicopters** (☎ 702-736-0606, sundancehelicopters.com) advertises some of the lowest rates to the Grand Canyon, with flyover-only trips starting at $399, and 7 a.m. early bird landing flights for $400.

In 2017 Papillon introduced additional flightseeing tours that take advantage of a new heliport next to the Hoover Dam Lodge to get closer than ever to Lake Mead, Black Canyon, and the dam itself. Meanwhile, Maverick teamed with Four Seasons Las Vegas to offer a 3-hour "Natural Wonders Experience" that combines helicopter landings in the Valley of Fire and Grand Canyon with a gourmet lunch on a private bluff below the rim, 300 feet above the canyon floor.

All of the aircraft used will feel very small to anyone accustomed to flying on big commercial jets. Most of the planes carry 8–20 passengers. The captain often performs the duties of both flight attendant and pilot. Be aware that all aircraft have middle seats, some of which (especially on A-Star helicopters) provide poor visibility, so ask about the seating configuration when booking. Cabin conditions for the most part are spartan, and there is usually no toilet on board.

Because small aircraft sometimes get bounced around and buffeted by air currents, we recommend taking an over-the-counter motion-sickness medication if you think you might be adversely affected. The other thing you want to do for sure is to relieve your bladder *immediately* before boarding.

Save some money by reserving your flight through **GC Flight** (☎ 702-629-7776, gcflight.com) or **viator.com,** which resell seats on Scenic and Maverick for less than booking through the companies directly.

There's any number of combo, mix and match, tours to the Grand Canyon available. Albeit expensive, **Grand Canyon Helicopters** (☎ 855-326-9617, grandcanyonhelicopter.com) has paired up a helicopter tour with 4 hours of rafting on the Colorado River, including some notable rapids. This is singular in terms of river running options out of Las Vegas. There are no rapids on the Colorado downstream of Hoover Dam, and raft or boating excursions upstream of the dam operate on sections of the river with little or no current. **Hualapai River Runners** handles the boating segment of the tour with eight-person motorized rafts. Overall, the trip covers about 40 miles, with the whitewater all coming in the first 12 miles. The run is broken up with stops to hike to Travertine Cavern Falls and to have lunch. After the rafting, the tour continues with a 4,000-foot helicopter ascent out of the canyon, an aircraft switch at the Grand Canyon West airport, and the helicopter return flight back to Las Vegas. The outing takes about 12 hours, and you must be at least 8 years old to participate. Outbound flights are on EC130 choppers with good views even from the center seats. It's a different story with the A-Star helicopters used on the return, which have especially bad views from the center seats.

Grand Canyon tours are a perfect respite from the glitz and frenetic activity of the Strip. Whether you're looking for a flyby or great photo ops, it can be found with one of the tour companies we describe.

PART SIX

EXERCISE *and* RECREATION

WORKING OUT

MOST OF THE FOLKS ON OUR *UNOFFICIAL GUIDE* research team work out routinely. Some bike; some run; some lift weights or do yoga. Staying in hotels on the Strip and Downtown, they realized that working out in Las Vegas presents its own peculiar challenges.

The best time of year for outdoor exercise is October–April. The rest of the year it is extremely hot, though mornings and evenings are generally pleasant in September and May. During the scorching summer, particularly for visitors, we recommend working out indoors or, for bikers and runners, very early in the morning.

 If you do anything strenuous outside, at any time of year, drink plenty of water. Dehydration and heat exhaustion can overtake you quickly in Las Vegas's desert climate. For outdoor workouts in Las Vegas comparable to what you are used to at home, you will deplete your body's water at 2–3 times the usual rate.

WALKING

PRIMARILY FLAT, LAS VEGAS is made for walking and great people-watching. Security is very good both Downtown and on the Strip, making for a safe walking environment at practically all hours of the day and night. Downtown, everything is concentrated in such a small area that you might be inclined to venture away from the casino center. While this is no more perilous than walking in any other city, the areas surrounding Downtown are not particularly interesting or aesthetically compelling. If the Downtown casino center is not large enough to accommodate your exercise needs, you are better off commuting to the Strip and doing your walking there.

If you are walking the Strip, it is about 4 miles from Mandalay Bay on the south end to the Stratosphere on the north end. Because the topography is so flat, however, it does not look that far. We met a number of people who set out on foot along the Strip and managed to overextend themselves. Check out our Strip walking-distances map on

Las Vegas Strip Walking Map

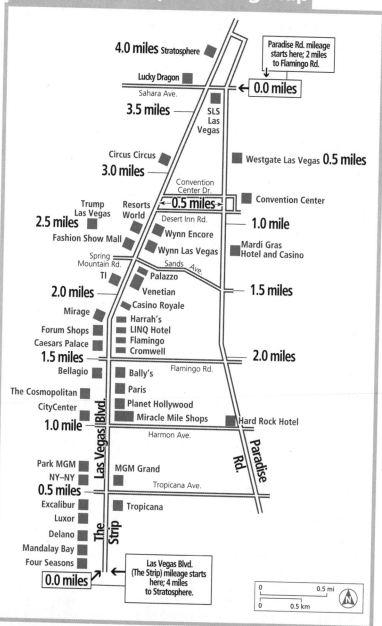

4.0 miles Stratosphere

Paradise Rd. mileage starts here; 2 miles to Flamingo Rd.

0.0 miles

Lucky Dragon

Sahara Ave.

3.5 miles SLS Las Vegas

Westgate Las Vegas **0.5 miles**

Circus Circus
3.0 miles

Convention Center Dr.

←**0.5 miles**→ Convention Center

Trump Las Vegas   Resorts World

2.5 miles Desert Inn Rd. **1.0 mile**

Fashion Show Mall   Wynn Encore

Mardi Gras Hotel and Casino

Spring Mountain Rd.   Wynn Las Vegas

Sands Ave.

TI   Palazzo

2.0 miles Venetian **1.5 miles**

Casino Royale

Mirage

Harrah's

Forum Shops   LINQ Hotel

Caesars Palace   Flamingo

1.5 miles Cromwell **2.0 miles**

Bellagio   Bally's

Flamingo Rd.

The Cosmopolitan   Paris

CityCenter   Planet Hollywood

1.0 mile Miracle Mile Shops   Hard Rock Hotel

Harmon Ave.

Park MGM

NY–NY   MGM Grand

0.5 miles Tropicana Ave.

Excalibur

Luxor   Tropicana

Delano

Mandalay Bay

Four Seasons

0.0 miles

Las Vegas Blvd. (The Strip) mileage starts here; 4 miles to Stratosphere.

Las Vegas Blvd.

The Strip

Paradise Rd.

0   0.5 mi

0   0.5 km

the previous page before you go, and bear in mind that even without hills, marching in the arid desert climate will take a lot out of you.

 When walking the Strip, carry enough money to buy refreshments en route and to take a cab or bus back to your hotel if you poop out or develop a blister.

RUNNING

ON THE STRIP, those of us who are used to running on pavement ran on the broad sidewalks of Las Vegas Boulevard South. These runs are great for people-watching but are frequently interrupted by long minutes of jogging in place at intersections, waiting for traffic lights to change.

Sidewalks Downtown are less congested than those on the Strip, and there are fewer intersections and traffic lights with which to contend. A good Downtown route is east from the Plaza Hotel on Fremont Street along the pedestrian promenade and on to El Cortez, cutting left on Sixth Street to Ogden. Follow Ogden west, turning left on Main Street to the Plaza to complete the circuit. If you want to run Downtown, particularly on Fremont Street, try to exercise before 10 a.m.

If you dislike pounding the blacktop or exercising early in the morning, a convenient option is to run on the track at the University of Nevada, Las Vegas. Located about 2 miles east of the Strip on Harmon Avenue, **UNLV** offers a regulation track and some large, grassy athletic fields. Park in the dirt lot near the tennis courts if you do not have a university parking sticker. For more information, call ☎ 702-895-4729.

If you have a car and a little time, two of the better off-road runs in the area are at **Red Rock Canyon,** out Charleston Boulevard, 35 minutes west of town. Red Rock Canyon Conservation Area, managed by the U.S. Bureau of Land Management, is Western desert and canyon scenery at its best. Spectacular geology combined with the unique desert flora and fauna make Red Rock Canyon a truly memorable place. Maps and information can be obtained at the visitor center, on-site. A 2-mile round-trip, **Moenkopi Loop,** begins and ends at the visitor center. A 3-mile circuit, **Willow Springs Trail,** begins at Willow Springs Picnic Area and circles around to Lost Creek Canyon. Both routes are moderately hilly, with pretty good footing. Moenkopi Loop is characterized by open desert and expansive vistas, while the Willow Springs Trail ventures into the canyons. The Willow Springs Trail is also distinguished by numerous Indian petroglyphs and other artifacts. Both trails, of course, are great for hiking as well as for running.

For other options farther afield from the Strip and Downtown, see the section on Multiuse Trails starting on page 476.

SWIMMING AND SUNBATHING

SWIMMING, DURING WARM-WEATHER MONTHS, is the most dependable and generally accessible form of exercise in Las Vegas. Most Strip hotels and a couple of the Downtown hotels have nice pools. Sometimes the pools are too congested for swimming laps, but usually it is possible to stake out a lane.

If the pool at your hotel is a funny shape or too crowded for a workout, there are pools more conducive to serious swimming at the **Las Vegas Athletic Club** on Flamingo Road and in the **McDermott Physical Education Complex** of UNLV.

For those who want to work on their tans in style, the **Mirage, Cosmopolitan, Tropicana, Wynn Las Vegas, Wynn Encore, M Resort, Mandalay Bay, Venetian, Palazzo, Aria, Paris, Park MGM, MGM Grand, TI, Caesars Palace, Rio, Westgate Las Vegas, Flamingo, Palms, Green Valley Ranch, Hard Rock Hotel, Bellagio, Planet Hollywood,** and **JW Marriott Las Vegas,** among others, have particularly elegant facilities.

Sunbathing in Las Vegas can be dangerous. The climate is so arid that you will not feel yourself perspiring. If there is a breeze, particularly on a pleasant fall or spring day, you may never feel hot or uncomfortable until you come out of the sun and discover you're fried.

 You can get sunburned quickly if you do not protect yourself properly. Use a broad-spectrum sunscreen with an SPF of 15 or higher, and reapply often. There is no such thing as waterproof sunscreen.

HEALTH CLUBS

IF YOU CAN GET BY WITH A LIFECYCLE, a StairMaster, or a rowing machine, the fitness rooms of most major hotels should serve your needs. Fortunately, local health clubs welcome visitors for a daily ($15–$20) or weekly ($30–$50) fee. All of the clubs described here are coed.

The **Las Vegas Athletic Clubs,** with six locations, offer racquetball, tennis, basketball, exercise equipment, and aerobics, though not all features are provided at each location. These clubs depend more on local patronage than on visitors; their facilities are commodious but not luxurious, and fees are at the lower end of the range. While reasonably convenient to the Strip, only the West Sahara club is within walking distance. For rates and additional info visit lvac.com or call:

- 5200 W. Sahara Ave. ☎ 702-364-5822
- 1725 N. Rainbow Blvd. ☎ 702-835-5822
- 2655 S. Maryland Pkwy. ☎ 702-734-5822
- 3830 E. Flamingo Rd. ☎ 702-898-5822
- 9065 S. Eastern Ave. ☎ 702-853-5822
- 9615 W. Flamingo Rd. ☎ 702-798-5822

There are four YMCA locations in Las Vegas. The closest to the Strip and Downtown is the **Bill and Lillie Heinrich YMCA** at 4141 Meadows Lane to the west (☎ 702-877-9622, lasvegasymca.org).

FREE WEIGHTS AND MACHINES

ALMOST ALL OF THE MAJOR HOTELS have a spa or fitness room with weight-lifting equipment. Some properties have a single Universal machine, while others offer a wide range of free-weight and Hoist/Cybex equipment. Hotels with above-average facilities for pumping iron are the **Westgate Las Vegas, Bellagio, Venetian, Caesars Palace, Cosmopolitan, Aria, Golden Nugget, Mirage, Paris, Wynn Las Vegas, Wynn Encore, M Resort, Mandalay Bay, Park MGM, MGM Grand, Luxor,** and **TI.**

PROFESSIONAL SPORTS

FOOTBALL The **NFL Oakland Raiders** are relocating to Las Vegas. A stadium being constructed adjacent to I-15 just west of Mandalay Bay will be ready for the 2020–2021 season. Until then, expect construction mayhem with the addition of new ramps/interchanges on I-15 to serve the stadium.

ICE HOCKEY One of the big sports stories of 2018 was the NHL expansion team the **Vegas Golden Knights** making it all the way to the Stanley Cup championship before being beaten by the Washington Capitals. The Golden Knights play home games at T-Mobile Arena, located behind New York–New York. For the 2018–19 schedule see nhl.com/golden knights/schedule, and for tickets see nhl.com/goldenknights/tickets. Tickets are expensive, and many games sell out in this newly hockey-crazed town. Golden Knights practices are held at the City National Arena in Summerlin at 1550 S. Pavilion Center Drive from 10 a.m. to 1 p.m. most days. All practices are open and free to the public on a first-come, first-serve basis until arena capacity is maxed. To find out what time the team will go on the ice, follow the Golden Knights on Twitter or call guest services at ☎ 702-902-4904.

BASKETBALL MGM Resorts bought the WNBA's San Antonio Stars and moved them to Sin City rechristened as the **Las Vegas Aces.** The Aces play their games at the Mandalay Bay Events Center. For schedule and tickets, see axs.com/WNBA/Las_Vegas_Aces. The Women's NBA regular season runs from May to August.

If you want to see the boys, Las Vegas hosts the NBA Summer League. For the first time in 2018, all 30 NBA teams participated. Games are played at the Thomas & Mack Center and at Cox Pavilion. In 2018, single game tickets started at $35. See nba.com/summerleague.

SOCCER The **Las Vegas Lights,** a United Soccer League (USL) expansion team, began play during the 2018 season. The USL Division II team was the 33rd club to join the league. During the 2018 season, the team played 16 regular season games at Cashman Field. For information, tickets, and schedule see asvegaslightsfc.com.

BASEBALL In 2019 the **Las Vegas 51s** Triple-A minor league baseball club will move to the new $150 million, 10,000-seat Las Vegas Ballpark in downtown Summerlin west of the Strip. Previously affiliated with the New York Mets, the club will seek a new major league affiliate for the 2019 season.

GOLF

PEAK SEASON FOR GOLF in Las Vegas is October through May. The other four months are considered prohibitively warm for most golfers, but greens fees are reduced substantially at most courses during summer. In most cases, you can get the best rates through individual course websites, where all sorts of internet specials can be found daily. Alternatively, several sites compile last-minute deals (see below). Most courses also have reduced rates for locals, and many offer discounts for guests staying at partner hotels or discounted stay-and-play packages combining lodging and greens fees. These discounts are also online, so make sure you check the course's website before booking.

Also, almost all Las Vegas–area courses offer discounted twilight rates, which, depending on time of year, start as early as noon. In general, morning tee times are more desirable and difficult to arrange than afternoons. Call the pro shop at least one day before you wish to play. Same-day phone calls are discouraged. In summer most courses and driving ranges stay open until at least 7:30 p.m.

Another way to save big is with companies that offer last-minute unsold tee times from dozens of courses in Las Vegas, plus more in Laughlin and Mesquite, at discounts of 40%–80%. Most define "last-minute" as 24–72 hours in advance. These sites often include many of the area's best courses. Check out **golfnow.com/lasvegas, teeoff.com, lvteetimes.com,** and **golf18network.com.** Vegas-based **VIPGolfServices. com** offers custom multiday packages (2 or more days) with increasing discounts for combining more courses.

In winter and early spring, temperatures drop rapidly near sundown, so always bring a sweater or jacket. It can also be very windy. Las Vegas has an elevation of 2,000 feet and is considered high desert. Take this into account when making club selections.

IMPORTANT NOTES Several top Las Vegas courses are private clubs that do not allow outside access, and thus are not listed. Additionally, during its boom years, Las Vegas created a unique sort of "almost private" golf course affiliated with a particular casino hotel. With the permanent closing of Wynn Golf Club in December 2017 and the sale of Cascata in 2018, the sole surviving example of this is **Shadow Creek Country Club,** built specifically for the highest of high rollers and now owned by MGM Resorts International. The course is open to overnight guests of all its many hotels, but on a very limited basis, as it still targets high roller comp play and offers only a handful of public tee times each day (Monday through Thursday only)—and always at a cost of $500 per person.

Despite the number of golf courses in the Las Vegas area, for serious golf travel fans there are only two choices that could accurately be called golf resorts—and that is a bit of a stretch. **Lake Las Vegas,** about half an hour from the Strip, was once one of the top self-contained golf resorts in the nation. However, it has seesawed as an economic victim of over-leveraging, at one point losing both of its resort courses and the Ritz-Carlton and Loews hotels. The shuttered flagship layout, Reflection Bay, reopened at the end of 2014. With the exception of elite Shadow Creek, this is arguably the very best course in town. More good news is that the hotels reopened, with Hilton in the former Ritz property and Westin taking over the Loews. The new owners of Lake Las Vegas brought back original architect Jack Nicklaus to renovate his Signature Course, and today Reflection Bay is better than ever and ranked #4 in all of Nevada by *Golfweek*. Unfortunately, its onetime sibling, the Tom Weiskopf–designed Falls course, is permanently closed. In **Summerlin,** about 25 minutes from the Strip, the JW Marriott is surrounded by six courses within 10 minutes and is about 20 minutes from the trio at the Paiute Golf Club. The resort is partnered with the adjacent top-tier TPC Las Vegas, offering attractive stay-and-play packages year-round. Both of these resorts have lavish spas, pools, activities, multiple restaurants, bars, and casinos.

With the closing of Wynn Golf Club, there are no urban golf resorts left on the Strip. That leaves **Bali Hai** as the only real course located directly on the Strip. The Schmidt/Curley–designed course is highlighted by 7 acres of water features, a spectacular island green, and more than 4,000 trees, including 2,500 stands of towering palms and 100,000 tropical plants and flowers. Amazing views of the Strip can be found from fairways and tee boxes throughout the course. The course has long been rumored to be on its last legs, and most recently is being touted as a possible future site of parking lots for the new Raiders NFL stadium under construction nearby.

Recent additions to the Las Vegas golf scene are decidedly offbeat. First is the **Las Vegas Golf Center** (lasvegasgolfcenters.com), formerly the TaylorMade Golf Experience, along Las Vegas Boulevard just south of Mandalay Bay. The 42-acre campus includes a 9-hole, par-3 course with holes playing 110–185 yards and a bilevel, 113-bay driving range, both fully lighted for night play. There is also a full on-site learning academy, the Eric Meeks School of Golf; an extensive custom club-fitting program with high-tech swing analyzers (free with club purchase); a retail center; putting and short game practice areas; and a bar and grill.

The latest newcomer is **Topgolf Las Vegas** from Topgolf International, a European company that has been frantically building high-tech golf-entertainment centers. Guests rent a driving range bay and use special microprocessor balls to play a variety of computer-controlled games, with goals like distance or accuracy. The facilities also offer instruction, along with full bar and food service. The concept has been wildly popular, with more than 40 locations worldwide . . . and more on the way. Topgolf Las Vegas is the US flagship and nation's largest, with a four-level range featuring 102 bays and spanning 8 acres. The one-of-a-kind facility has quickly proven popular and is part of the MGM Grand but has its own entrance on Koval Lane one block east of the Strip. For more on Topgolf Las Vegas, see pages 425–426 in Part Five.

GOLF COURSE RATINGS	
QUALITY RATING	**VALUE RATING**
★★★ Championship, challenging	**1** A good bargain
★★ Playable, suitable for all caliber golfers	**2** A fair price
★ Preferred by beginners and casual golfers	**3** Overpriced

Angel Park Golf Club

ESTABLISHED 1989 | STATUS MUNICIPAL | QUALITY ★★ | VALUE ★★

100 S. Rampart Blvd., Las Vegas, NV 89145; ☎ 888-446-5358; angelpark.com

TEES

PALM COURSE
- Professional: 6,500 yards, par 70, USGA 70.3, slope 124
- Championship: 5,857 yards, par 70, USGA 67.1, slope 115
- Forward: 4,578 yards, par 70, USGA 66.8, slope 110

MOUNTAIN COURSE
- Professional: 6,722 yards, par 71, USGA 71.1, slope 130
- Championship: 6,223 yards, par 71, USGA 68.8, slope 125
- Forward: 5,150 yards, par 71, USGA 69.1, slope 114

FEES Nonresidents: $47–$135; residents: $30–$66

FACILITIES Pro shop, night-lit driving range, 12-hole par-3 course and 9-hole putting course, putting green, restaurant, snack bar, bar, tennis courts, golf club and shoe rentals.

COMMENTS Angel Park, a good, functional golf complex, is one of the most successful public golf facilities in the United States. Its courses are well designed—by Arnold Palmer, no less—and the sophisticated 18-hole putting course is a popular attraction even for nongolfers. Its Cloud Nine short course is unique and great for golfers needing a quick fix, with reproductions of 12 famous par-3 holes from around the world, 9 of which are lit for night play. There is also a lighted natural-grass putting course—think fancy mini-golf. Both courses are crowded year-round, as the facility is close to the Strip and popular with locals.

Bali Hai

ESTABLISHED 2000 | STATUS PUBLIC | QUALITY ★★ | VALUE ★★

5160 S. Las Vegas Blvd., Las Vegas, NV 89119; ☎ 888-427-6678; balihaigolfclub.com

TEES
- Black: 7,002 yards, par 71, USGA 73.0, slope 130
- Gold: 6,601 yards, par 72, USGA 70.2, slope 125
- Silver: 6,156 yards, par 72, USGA 68.6, slope 113
- Bronze: 5,511 yards, par 72, USGA 71.5, slope 122

FEES $79–$349, depending on time of day and year; see website for details. Club rentals, $55–$100. Bali Hai's website offers a low-rate guarantee and up-to-date deals for same- and next-day bookings.

FACILITIES Pro shop, driving range, putting green, snack bar, restaurant, full locker facilities, caddies, fore-caddies, club and shoe rentals.

COMMENTS In real estate, location is everything, and the only reason Bali Hai commands these outrageous greens fees is its location on the Strip next to Mandalay Bay. It is the only course located so close to the major casinos. Designed in a tropical theme, Bali Hai features water everywhere, with an island green, endless tropical flora, and vast expanses of black "coral" and white sand. Bali Hai is undeniably beautiful, but that does not make it a great course. Better golf can be had for less, even with cab fares.

Bear's Best

ESTABLISHED 2002 | STATUS PUBLIC | QUALITY ★★★ | VALUE ★★

11111 W. Flamingo Rd., Las Vegas, NV 89135; ☎ 702-804-8500; clubcorp.com

TEES

- Gold: 7,194 yards, par 72, USGA 74.0, slope 147
- Green: 6,628 yards, par 72, USGA 71.3, slope 130
- White: 6,043 yards, par 72, USGA 68.3, slope 122
- Orange: 5,043 yards, par 72, USGA 68.7, slope 116

FEES $59–$279, depending on time of day; see website for details. Club rentals, $65.

FACILITIES Pro shop, driving range, putting green, restaurant, full locker facilities, golf academy, caddies, fore-caddies, club and shoe rentals.

COMMENTS One of only two Bear's Best courses (the other is in Atlanta), this is a tribute by Jack Nicklaus, aka the Golden Bear, to himself. Here Nicklaus has re-created holes from his favorite original designs, but unlike most tribute or replica courses, including Vegas's Royal Links, the holes were specifically chosen to fit the desert setting. As a result, this is one of the best of these gimmicky layouts in the world. Fans have the opportunity to play holes from Nicklaus's most acclaimed public courses, such as Cabo del Sol, Palmilla, and Castle Pines, along with very private ones from Desert Mountain, Desert Highlands, and PGA West. Since opening it has been ranked among the city's best courses. The facility is now home to the Paul Wilson Golf School.

Black Mountain Golf and Country Club

ESTABLISHED 1959 | STATUS SEMIPRIVATE | QUALITY ★ | VALUE ★★

500 Greenway Road, Henderson, NV 89015; ☎ 702-565-7933; golfblackmountain.com

TEES

- Championship: 6,579 yards, par 72, USGA 70.6–71.1, slope 124–129
- Men's: 6,148–6,279 yards, par 72, USGA 69.0–69.6, slope 121–128
- Ladies': 5,148–5,319 yards, par 72, USGA 69.4–70.2, slope 111–114

FEES Nonresidents: high season, $89 (carts included on weekends only); low season, $69. Residents: $9–$70. Club rentals $20–$45.

FACILITIES Pro shop, clubhouse, driving range, putting green, restaurant, club rentals, snack bar, bar.

COMMENTS Black Mountain is a conventional 18-hole course set amid the Henderson hills, 20 minutes from the Strip. Many who prefer walking to riding play here, as it's one of the few area courses that doesn't require electric carts during the week. Many bunkers and unimproved areas off fairways make for tough recovery shots. A good course for beginning and intermediate golfers and juniors—and a good value year-round. The course is uniquely semiprivate, fully owned by members but wide-open and welcoming to visitors.

Cascata

ESTABLISHED 2000 | STATUS PUBLIC | QUALITY ★★★ | VALUE ★★★

1 Cascata Drive, Boulder City, NV 89142; ☎ 702-294-2005; cascatagolf.com

TEES

- Black: 7,137 yards, par 72, USGA 74.6, slope 143
- Blue: 6,664 yards, par 72, USGA 71.7, slope 138

- Gold: 6,206 yards, par 72, USGA 69.9, slope 135
- Red: 5,591 yards, par 72, USGA 67.2, slope 117

FEES $195–$425. Fees do not include transportation or caddy (caddy required, fee $25, plus recommended tip of $25 per person).

FACILITIES Pro shop, driving range, putting green, restaurant, full locker facilities, caddies.

COMMENTS After the runaway success of Shadow Creek, another casino group built the even more expensive Cascata, said to have the highest golf course construction price tag ever, for its high rollers. Recently sold by Caesars Entertainment, it is now independent but remains a truly unique design in golf. Acclaimed designer Rees Jones blasted the course out of a rocky mountain. The holes are built in a series of narrow, parallel finger canyons radiating from the summit and running up and down the rocky slopes. Sitting in the canyons, the lush green fairways are completely isolated from one another by sloped canyon walls. The par-3s are especially dramatic, often backed by amphitheater cliffs and waterfalls. Because its name is Italian for "waterfall," Jones built one 40 stories high that pours through the center of the marble Italian palazzo–style clubhouse.

Coyote Springs Golf Club

ESTABLISHED 2008 | STATUS SEMIPRIVATE | QUALITY ★★★ | VALUE ★★

3100 NV 168, Coyote Springs, NV 89037; ☎ 702-422-1400; coyotesprings.com

TEES

- Black: 7,471 yards, par 72, USGA 75.8, slope 141
- Blue: 6,807 yards, par 72, USGA 72, slope 137
- White: 6,215 yards, par 72, USGA 69.3, slope 132
- Red: 5,288 yards, par 72, USGA 70.5, slope 127

FEES $60–$149.

FACILITIES Pro shop, driving range, putting green, snack bar, restaurant, full locker facilities.

COMMENTS Developed by the PGA of America, the course opened in May 2008 to rave reviews—named "Best New U.S. Public Course" in 2009 by *Links* and in the top 10 new courses by *Golf Magazine* and *Golf Digest*. A Jack Nicklaus Signature course, Coyote Springs is reminiscent of Reflection Bay, with elaborate rock-lined water features—11 lakes in all—but has more dramatic fairways and pronounced undulations, and the desert hazards are sandier and more landscaped, less wild, than many area courses. Nicklaus is famed for his dramatic waterfront finishes, and this course is no exception, with the last four holes curving around lakes. Prices are in line with the more expensive Vegas-area courses, but the quality is better than most. However, it's not as good a value as the equally far-flung courses of Primm and Mesquite, Nevada. In an interesting homage to the setting, each hole is named for Vegas slang, such as On Tilt and Shooter. In summer, free replay is offered daily.

Desert Pines Golf Club

ESTABLISHED 1997 | STATUS PUBLIC | QUALITY ★ | VALUE ★★

3415 E. Bonanza Road, Las Vegas, NV 89101; ☎ 702-388-4400; desertpinesgolfclub.com

TEES
- Championship: 6,810 yards, par 71, USGA 70.6, slope 125
- Men's: 6,494 yards, par 71, USGA 67.9, slope 118
- Ladies': 5,873 yards, par 71, USGA 69.4, slope 116

FEES Peak Season: $169 Sunday–Thursday, $200 Friday–Sunday ($99 twilight). Rates vary widely by time, even in peak season.

FACILITIES Pro shop, driving range, putting green, snack bar, restaurant.

COMMENTS Desert Pines is a 6,810-yard course on Bonanza Road between Mojave and Pecos Roads. Inspired by the Pinehurst courses in North Carolina, its fairways and greens are flanked by trees, some already as tall as 40 feet. Instead of rough, original developer Bill Walters laid down 45,000 bales of red-pine needles imported from South Carolina, making it hard to lose a ball here. Its low off-season rates make it one of the best hot-weather choices in the region. The course recently renovated its fairways and putting surfaces and is in its best shape in years. Desert Pines offers golfboards, a motorized skateboard-style alternative to golf carts.

Highland Falls Golf Club

ESTABLISHED 1992 | STATUS SEMIPRIVATE | QUALITY ★★★ | VALUE ★★

10201 Sun City Blvd., Las Vegas, NV 89134; ☎ 702-254-7010; golfsummerlin.com

TEES
- Championship: 6,512 yards, par 72, USGA 70.1, slope 119
- Men's: 6,017 yards, par 72, USGA 68.1, slope 118
- Gold: 5,579 yards, par 72, USGA 71.4, slope 122
- Ladies': 5,099 yards, par 72, USGA 68.4, slope 112

FEES Nonresidents: $30–$99; residents: $21–$60.

FACILITIES Pro shop, driving range, putting green, restaurant, luncheon area, patio for outside dining, bar.

COMMENTS This course is a testing layout designed by Hall of Famer Billy Casper's company, Casper-Nash Associates. The unique design sits in the mountains at over 3,000 feet, and the cooler weather allows it to use superior quality bentgrass greens, unusual in this climate, and Bermuda fairways to combine the best of both worlds. It has more undulations than most desert courses, with several demanding holes. No one broke par for the first six months after opening. The course now offers specials to its Twitter and e-club followers.

Las Vegas Golf Club

ESTABLISHED 1938 | STATUS PUBLIC | QUALITY ★ | VALUE ★★

4300 W. Washington Ave., Las Vegas, NV 89107; ☎ 702-646-3003; lasvegasgc.com

TEES
- Championship: 6,290 yards, par 72, USGA 69.8, slope 121
- Men's: 5,917 yards, par 72, USGA 68.2, slope 116
- Ladies': 5,260 yards, par 72, USGA 69.9, slope 113

FEES $39–$75.

FACILITIES Pro shop, night-lit driving range, putting green, restaurant, snack bar, bar, and beverage-cart girls who patrol the course.

COMMENTS The past several years have seen $5 million in renovations and improvements pumped into the first and oldest golf course in Las Vegas, laid out by the legendary William Bell in 1938, including a new clubhouse. It has remained a popular public course and a site of many local amateur tournaments. A good choice for recreational golfers, with fairly wide-open fairways and little trouble, so play should move briskly.

Las Vegas National

ESTABLISHED 1961 | STATUS PUBLIC (privately owned) **| QUALITY ★★ | VALUE ★★**

1911 E. Desert Inn Road, Las Vegas NV 89169; ☎ 866-695-1961 or 702-734-1796 (tee-time service and other reservations); lasvegasnational.com

TEES

- Championship: 6,773 yards, par 72, USGA 73.5, slope 137
- Men's: 6,260 yards, par 71, USGA 71.6, slope 133
- Ladies': 5,640 yards, par 72, USGA 68.8, slope 130

FEES Weekdays, $59–$139; weekends, $79–$139; twilight, $35–$89. Club rentals, $59.

FACILITIES Pro shop, night-lit driving range, putting green, restaurant, bar.

COMMENTS Lower rates, almost always less than $99 year-round, make this one of the best and most convenient buys in town. A championship course that has at one time cohosted the Tournament of Champions, the Sahara Invitational, and the Ladies' Sahara Classic. Tiger Woods is a past champion here (he shot 70 to win his very first PGA Tour event). The course is convenient to the Strip and offers an excellent variety of holes, with good bunkering and elevation changes uncharacteristic of a desert course. Better for intermediate and advanced golfers. Take in the local history with a post-round cocktail in the Rat Pack Bar & Grill, home to the Las Vegas Golf Hall of Fame exhibit. The club recently added both the skateboard-style motorized golfboards and fat-tire golf scooters.

Las Vegas Paiute Resort

ESTABLISHED 1995 | STATUS PUBLIC | QUALITY ★★ (Snow/Sun) **★★★** (Wolf) **VALUE ★★** (Snow/Sun/Wolf)

10325 Nu-Wav Kaiv Blvd., Las Vegas, NV 89124 (US 95 between Kyle Canyon and Lee Canyon turn-off to Mount Charleston); ☎ 702-658-1400 or 800-711-2833; lvpaiutegolf.com

TEES

SNOW MOUNTAIN

- Tournament: 7,146 yards, par 72, USGA 73.3, slope 125
- Championship: 6,645 yards, par 72, USGA 71.2, slope 120
- Regular: 6,035 yards, par 72, USGA 68.6, slope 112
- Forward: 5,341 yards, par 72, USGA 70.4, slope 117

SUN MOUNTAIN

- Tournament: 7,112 yards, par 72, USGA 73.3, slope 130
- Championship: 6,631 yards, par 72, USGA 70.9, slope 124
- Regular: 6,074 yards, par 72, USGA 68.8, slope 116
- Forward: 5,465 yards, par 72, USGA 71.0, slope 123

WOLF

- Tournament: 7,604 yards, par 72, USGA 76.3, slope 149
- Black: 7,009 yards, par 72, USGA 73.5, slope 134

- Yellow: 6,483 yards, par 72, USGA 71.4, slope 130
- White: 5,910 yards, par 72, USGA 76.5, slope 125
- Red: 5,130 yards, par 72, USGA 68.5, slope 116

FEES Prices are $69–$199 and depend on day of week and time of day. There is always a $10–$20 surcharge to play the Wolf course. They offer a wide array of discounts for multiday play, for military, plus internet specials.

FACILITIES Pro shop, driving range, 2 putting greens, restaurant, snack bar, bar with gaming.

COMMENTS Paiute is the region's only 54-hole resort golf complex, and all three courses are Pete Dye designs. The original two layouts, Snow and Sun Mountain, are comfortable desert courses, beauty without brawn, and have remained among the public favorites in the region since opening. Not so for Wolf, which is one of, if not the most, difficult courses in Las Vegas. From the tips it is 500 yards longer than any course most golfers have played, and strewn with hazards of the wet and dry variety. Still, it is as well conditioned and thought out as its tamer siblings and has a near re-creation of Dye's famous island hole par-3 he pioneered at the TPC Sawgrass. Despite its stiff challenge, it has become the most demanded course here and is accordingly priced slightly higher. The Paiute Resort offers heavily discounted same-day replays and full-day Golfapalooza packages, which include lunch, 50% off rentals, and two same-day rounds on different courses from just $159.

Legacy Golf Club

ESTABLISHED 1989 | STATUS PUBLIC (*PRIVATELY OWNED*) **| QUALITY ★★ | VALUE ★★**

130 Par Excellence Drive, Henderson, NV 89074; ☎ 888-629-3930; thelegacygc.com

TEES
- Championship: 7,233 yards, par 72, USGA 74.5, slope 137
- Men's: 6,744 yards, par 72, USGA 71.5, slope 128
- Ladies': 5,340 yards, par 72, USGA 71.5, slope 128
- Resort: 6,211 yards, par 72, USGA 69.3, slope 119

FEES Weekdays, $119; weekends and holidays, $129. All greens fees include mandatory carts. Club rentals, $68 ($40 twilight).

FACILITIES Clubhouse, pro shop, driving range, chipping facility, putting green, restaurant, snack bar, bar.

COMMENTS A long course by Arthur Hills, the Legacy is a mixture of rolling fairways and target golf. It is also one of the most photographed courses in Las Vegas because its tees are shaped like playing card suits. Championship tees require a long carry on the tee-ball to clear desert mounding. One big plus for visiting golfers without rental cars is that the Legacy offers a free golf shuttle with pick-up from most major casinos.

Painted Desert

ESTABLISHED 1987 | STATUS PUBLIC | QUALITY ★★ | VALUE ★★

5555 Painted Mirage Road, Las Vegas, NV 89149; ☎ 702-645-2570; painteddesertgc.com

TEES
- Championship: 6,781 yards, par 72, USGA 71.8, slope 129

- Men's: 6,269 yards, par 72, USGA 69.9, slope 125
- Ladies': 5,647 yards, par 72, USGA 72.2, slope 126

FEES $40–$125; club rentals, $45 (includes 2 sleeves of golf balls).

FACILITIES Pro shop, driving range, putting green, restaurant, bar.

COMMENTS This target course designed by renowned architect Jay Morrish, Tom Weiskopf's partner, features lush fairway landing pads and well-manicured greens, but make certain you're on target. The rough is pure waste-area. The course formerly hosted the Nevada Open.

Reflection Bay Golf Club

ESTABLISHED 1998 | STATUS RESORT, PUBLIC | QUALITY ★★★ | VALUE ★★

75 Monte Lago Blvd., Henderson, NV 89011; ☎ 702-740-4653; reflectionbaygolf.com

TEES

- Gold: 7,261 yards, par 72, USGA 74.8, slope 138
- Black: 6,862 yards, par 72, USGA 73.2, slope 135
- White: 6,391 yards, par 72, USGA 70.3, slope 128
- Silver: 5,891 yards, par 72, USGA 68.1, slope 124
- Bronze: 5,166 yards, par 72, USGA 70, slope 127

FEES $69–$219. Lodging and golf packages available.

FACILITIES Pro shop, driving range, putting green, snack bar, restaurant, full locker facilities.

COMMENTS Expensive but worth it. With sweeping views of 320-acre Lake Las Vegas, the reopened Reflection Bay is a Signature Design by Jack Nicklaus that boasts five dramatic waterfront holes, including peninsulas, and the inland desert and mountain holes are just as good. Named to virtually every "best course" list by *Golf* and *Golf Digest*, the course, which long hosted the Wendy's 3-Tour Championship, is a stunner, second only to Shadow Creek as tops in greater Las Vegas. The course is both beautiful and challenging, with numerous forced carries over canyons and water and substantial elevation changes, plus high-quality bentgrass greens.

The Revere at Anthem

ESTABLISHED 1999 | STATUS PUBLIC | QUALITY ★★ | VALUE ★★

2600 Hampton Road, Henderson, NV 89052; ☎ 702-259-4653 or 877-273-8373; reveregolf.com

TEES

LEXINGTON

- Black: 7,143 yards, par 72, USGA 73.5, slope 138
- Gold: 6,590 yards, par 72, USGA 70.8, slope 131
- Silver (Ladies'): 5,941 yards, par 72, USGA 73.3, slope 127
- Bronze (Ladies'): 5,216 yards, par 72, USGA 69.9, slope 118

CONCORD

- Black: 7,034 yards, par 72, USGA 72.8, slope 126
- Gold: 6,546 yards, par 72, USGA 69.8, slope 121
- Silver: 6,094 yards, par 72, USGA 67.6, slope 119
- Bronze (Ladies'): 5,171 yards, par 72, USGA 69.7, slope 118

FEES $60–$199; club rentals, $65.

FACILITIES Fully stocked clubhouse and snack bar, golf shop, restaurant.

COMMENTS Both courses were designed by Billy Casper and Greg Nash, and the club is consistently rated among the city's top 10. About 20 minutes from the Strip in the southeast Las Vegas Valley, Revere is built in a natural canyon, with a feel that is secluded and intimate. Lexington is the longer and more challenging layout, with numerous risk-reward opportunities, while the slightly shorter Concord features wider fairways and larger greens. Much of the year, 36-hole specials are offered for playing both courses in the same day.

Rio Secco Golf Club

ESTABLISHED 1997 | STATUS RESORT, PUBLIC | QUALITY ★★ | VALUE ★★★

2851 Grand Hills Drive, Henderson, NV 89052; ☎ 888-867-3226 or 702-777-2400; riosecco.net

TEES
- Championship: 7,313 yards, par 72, USGA 75.0, slope 153
- Blue: 6,927 yards, par 72, USGA 73.0, slope 149
- Middle: 6,375 yards, par 72, USGA 70.7, slope 136
- Forward: 5,758 yards, par 72, USGA 70.7, slope 127

FEES $89–$279; rates vary—visit their website for the most current information. Club rentals, $65–$75 (includes 2 sleeves of balls).

FACILITIES Pro shop, driving range, putting green, snack bar, restaurant, full locker facilities, Butch Harmon Golf School.

COMMENTS The best and closest of Las Vegas's pure desert-style courses, Rio Secco is set amid 240 acres of dramatic canyons just 12 minutes from the Strip. Variety, beauty, and strategic design highlighted by 88 bunkers make this a challenging but beautiful course. However, its perimeter is heavily lined with homes, negating some of the desert feel. Rio Secco is also golf-school headquarters for celebrity instructor Butch Harmon, whose former pupil, Tiger Woods, holds the course record with a stunning 63. Like sister course Cascata, it was designed by "U.S. Open Doctor" Rees Jones, who returned in 2017 and did a major refurbishment, and was recently sold by Caesars to independent operator Vici Golf.

Royal Links

ESTABLISHED 1999 | STATUS PUBLIC | QUALITY ★★ | VALUE ★★★

5995 E. Vegas Valley Road, Las Vegas, NV 89142; ☎ 888-427-6678; royallinksgolfclub.com

TEES
- Royal: 7,029 yards, par 72, USGA 73.7, slope 135
- Gold: 6,602 yards, par 72, USGA 71.2, slope 131
- Ruby: 5,864 yards, par 72, USGA 68.4, slope 125
- Emerald: 5,142 yards, par 72, USGA 69.8, slope 115

FEES $52–$230; club rentals (includes golf shoes), $75, lower in summer.

FACILITIES Pro shop, driving range, putting green, restaurant, English pub, full locker facilities, fore-caddies.

COMMENTS Royal Links sets out to emulate 18 holes from British Open venues in England and Scotland. In many ways the course succeeds, with excellent representations of links bunkering, exposure to fierce winds, and authentic rough and gorse. But nearly every course represented is on the ocean, something that cannot be replicated in the desert, and the re-creations are far from exact. As a result, the course is more fun the less you know about the real thing. Once very expensive among Vegas courses, the layout is now middle-of-the-pack and worth playing, especially as a novelty if you've never been to the British courses. Royal Links has stay-and-play packages with a number of top resorts, such as Aria, and after being sold by longtime operator Walters Golf, it has recently made an effort to go more upscale, offering both traditional carrying caddies and forecaddies.

Shadow Creek Golf Club

ESTABLISHED 1990 | STATUS RESORT | QUALITY ★★ | VALUE ★★★

3 Shadow Creek Dr., Las Vegas, NV 89030; ☎ 866-260-0069; shadowcreek.com

TEES
- Championship: 7,560 yards, par 72, USGA 71.0, slope 115
- Regular: 7,102 yards, par 72, USGA 68.9, slope 113

FEES Monday–Thursday $500, includes caddy and limo transportation; must be a guest of an MGM Resorts International hotel to play, but weekends it's invited guests only.

FACILITIES Pro shop, driving range, putting green, restaurant, full locker facilities, caddies.

COMMENTS Shadow Creek is widely rated as not just the best course in Las Vegas, but among the best in the country. It is ranked 66th in the nation, including privates, by *Golf Magazine,* and in the top 20 among public courses, deservedly. Shadow Creek is better considered barely near public, with the nation's highest greens fees, and those allowed only Monday through Thursday, with weekends reserved for VIPs and high-rolling gamblers. Nonetheless, when the required lodging and dining are thrown in, Shadow Creek falls in the same price range as Pebble Beach and Pinehurst Number Two and offers a far more luxurious experience than either. The course is always empty and meticulously maintained, the caddies are excellent, and the layout is both gorgeous and fun to play. An engineering marvel that transported a classic, heavily wooded Carolina-style parkland layout to the desert, it is rumored to be one of the most expensive courses ever built, having cost about $38 million in the 1980s. The finishing three holes are as memorable and dramatic a close as you will find in the golf world.

Siena Golf Club

ESTABLISHED 2000 | STATUS SEMIPRIVATE | QUALITY ★★ | VALUE ★★★

10575 Siena Monte Ave., Las Vegas, NV 89135; ☎ 888-689-6469 or ☎ 702-341-9200; sienagolfclub.com

TEES
- Gold: 6,843 yards, par 72, USGA 71.7, slope 131
- Black: 6,538 yards, par 72, USGA 70.4, slope 129
- Blue: 6,146 yards, par 72, USGA 68.6, slope 125
- White: 5,639 yards, par 72, USGA 66.4, slope 114
- Green: 4,978 yards, par 72, USGA 68.0, slope 112

FEES $40–$189; rates are seasonal—visit their website for the most current information; special twilight rates available.

FACILITIES Pro shop, driving range, putting green, snack bar, restaurant, full locker facilities.

COMMENTS A sleeper course in the Summerlin residential community, Siena welcomes outside play and is one of the region's best buys. The bargain replay option is a good deal, and other special promotions are occasionally offered. The course showcases extensive rock outcroppings and water features, including cascading waterfalls around the 18th green. All four par-3s are unique and notable, including sunken treasure, a gorgeous island green. Well-separated tees offer the right challenge for every player.

TPC Las Vegas

ESTABLISHED 1996 | STATUS PUBLIC | QUALITY ★★★ | VALUE ★★★

9851 Canyon Run Drive, Las Vegas, NV 89144; ☎ 702-256-2500; tpc.com

TEES
- TPC: 7,081 yards, par 71, USGA 73.4, slope 136
- Blue: 6,769 yards, par 71, USGA 71.0, slope 128
- White: 6,047 yards, par 71, USGA 68.0, slope 127
- Red: 4,963 yards, par 71, USGA 67.8, slope 117

FEES $44–$325; rates are seasonal—visit their website for the most current information. Club rentals, $60–$80.

FACILITIES Pro shop, driving range, putting green, snack bar, restaurant, full locker facilities.

COMMENTS Long known as TPC Canyons, this course by any name is one of the few public offerings among the Tournament Players Clubs, or the TPC network, so-called "stadium courses," designed specifically to host and showcase tournaments and owned by the PGA Tour. Designed by Bobby Weed and Ray Floyd, it has hosted the Las Vegas Invitational and the Michelob Championship. This is a tough desert course, with plenty of opportunities to lose balls in the dry wash and cacti, but is well designed and appealing to the better player. The facilities are first-rate, but they should be at this price. The course has packages with the adjacent JW Marriott Summerlin and several Strip resorts.

OUTDOOR RECREATION

LAS VEGAS AND THE SURROUNDING AREA offer a host of outdoor and adventure activities. The following section provides information on the activities available.

Warning: Cell phone signal strength in Clark County and greater Las Vegas is spotty to put it charitably. This applies doubly in desert/wilderness areas. If you plan to hike, bike, climb, ski, or boat during your stay you will not always be able to use your cell phone. This makes it imperative that someone knows where you are going and when you expect to return.

MULTIUSE TRAIL RESOURCES

THERE ARE SEVERAL DELIGHTFUL multipurpose recreation trails in the greater Las Vegas area that accommodate road bikers, mountain bikers, walkers, hikers, runners, and birders. Unique is the **Clark County**

Wetlands Park and Nature Preserve, an east–west linear park with miles of both paved and unpaved trails, including a 13-mile loop trail. The wetlands, which stand in stark contrast to the surrounding desert, are the product of the Las Vegas wash, a 12-mile channel that feeds runoff from a number of tributaries into Lake Mead. The creeks create a long oasis with ponds and small islands, grasses and other wetland flora, as well as a diverse assortment of wildlife. Adjoining the parking areas is a large and well-conceived nature center highlighting the geology and history of the wash and showcasing the wetlands birds, reptiles, and mammals. Dozens of unpaved trails intersect the paved trails, making any number of loop hikes possible. Though the trails are marked, it's easy to get turned around or even lost, but there are numerous landmarks to regain your bearing. The terrain is pancake flat, and there is even a little shade, especially in the morning or late afternoon. The park is located east of Las Vegas off East Tropicana and Wetlands Park Lane. For directions to other trailheads, visit clarkcountynv.gov/parks. Trail maps are available free at the nature center.

The Wetlands Park connects to the 34-mile paved **River Mountain Loop Trail.** The loop circumnavigates the River Mountains passing to the east of Henderson, north of Boulder, through the Lake Mead Recreation Area on the eastern side, and on around in the north to hook up with the Wetlands Park trails. There are numerous access points, and near Boulder, a couple of out-and-back canyon trails. The elevation of the trail varies by 1,500 feet from its highest to lowest points. The mountains provide shade on the west side in the morning and on the east side in the afternoon. Similar to Wetlands Park trails, the River Mountain Loop is open to all nonmotorized recreational use. For more, see rivermountainstrail.org.

Finally, consider the **Historic Railroad Tunnel Trail,** which runs for 3.7 miles from the Alan Bible Visitor Center in the Lake Mead National Recreation Area to the Hoover Dam parking garage. The trail passes through five 300-foot tunnels, exiting the dark to great panoramic views of Lake Mead, Boulder Basin, and Fortification Hill. The tunnels were created in 1931 to transport materials and large equipment to the Boulder Dam construction site. Superb for both hiking and biking, the trail was designated as a National Historic Trail in 2015.

To reach the Lake Mead National Recreation Area Alan Bible Visitor Center trailhead, from Las Vegas take Interstate 215 to I-515 south. Follow I-515 south for 5.8 miles to US 93 toward Boulder City. After 9.6 miles, take a left onto NV 166. Look for the Lake Mead Visitor Center sign. The trailhead is just over 0.3 mile ahead on the right. To park at the Hoover Dam, from Boulder City take US 93 for about 5 miles to the turnoff to NV 172/Hoover Dam Access Road. Follow it for about 2 miles to the dam.

For the multiuse trails mentioned above, both mountain bikes and road bikes can be rented at **River Mountain Bike Shop** (2310 East Lake Mead Parkway, Henderson; ☎ 702-564-3058; rivermountains bikeshop.com).

BICYCLING

ASK ANY CYCLIST IN LAS VEGAS about the on- and off-road riding nearby and you'll probably hear two kinds of comments. First, why pedaling in the desert is such a treat: excellent surface conditions; the option of pancake-flat or hilly riding; starkly beautiful scenery any time of year, and cactus blossoms in March and April; the possibility of spying raptors or jack rabbits or wild burros as you pedal; the unbelievably colorful limestone and sandstone formations.

Unfortunately, newcomers to desert and high-elevation biking often recall only these comments and not the "Be sure to carry . . ." warnings, which fellow riders usually provide after getting you all revved up. So read the following and remember that bikers are subject to those same conditions—heat and aridity—that make the desert so breathtaking.

Biking Essentials

1. TIME OF DAY Desert biking in late spring, summer, and early fall is best done early or late in the day. Know your seasons, listen to weather reports, and don't overestimate your speed and ability.

2. CLOTHING Ever see someone perched on a camel? What was he wearing? Right, it wasn't a tank top and Lycra shorts. The point is protection—from the sun during the day, from the cold in the morning and evening. And if you don't use a helmet (and you should), wear a hat.

3. SUNSCREEN In the desert, even well-tanned riders need this stuff.

4. SUNGLASSES The glare will blind you without them.

5. WATER The first time we rode in the desert, we carried as much water as we would have used on a ride of comparable distance in the eastern United States. Big mistake. Our need for water was at least twice what it normally would be in New York or Atlanta. We were thirsty the entire trip and might have gotten into serious trouble had we not cut our ride short.

You already know that you will need extra water, but how much? Well, a human working hard in 90°F temperature requires 10 quarts of fluid replenishment every day. Ten *quarts*. That's two and a half gallons—12 large water bottles, or 16 small ones. And with water weighing in at 8 pounds per gallon, a one-day supply comes to a whopping 20 pounds.

 Pack along two or three bottles even for the shortest rides. For longer rides, we carry a large Camelbak water carrier along with two bottles of water on the bike frame and a third stuffed inside the mesh of the Camelbak.

In the desert, the heat is dry, and you do not notice much perspiration because your sweat evaporates as quickly as it surfaces. Combine the dry heat with a little wind, and you can become extremely dehydrated before realizing it. Folks from the East (like us) tend to regard sweating as a barometer of our level of exertion (if you are not sweating much, in other words, you must not be exercising very hard). In the desert, it doesn't work that way. You may never notice that you are sweating. In the desert you need to stay ahead of dehydration by drinking more frequently and more regularly and by consuming much more than the same amount of exercise would warrant in other climates. Desert days literally suck the water right out of you, even during the cooler times of the year.

6. ELECTROLYTES Electrolytes are minerals found in your blood, sweat, and urine. The ones you'll hear about most often are sodium, magnesium, and potassium because they affect your fluid balance. Bikers (and hikers and others who exercise hard outdoors) sweat. Sodium is the primary electrolyte lost in sweat. Your kidneys can do a better job of retaining the fluid your body requires when you have enough sodium. If you fail to replace that sodium, you'll lose more fluid when you sweat and pee, dehydrating you, even if you've been consuming water.

When I played football in high school, they issued salt tablets to keep our sodium levels up. Now, we have sodium-replacing sports drinks that also replenish minerals such as magnesium and potassium. Sodium, however, is still the big enchilada, and what you need to monitor. Some sports drinks are high in carbohydrates. These are different from hydration sports drinks designed to replace the fluid and salts lost during exercise. Nutrition and exercise are complicated, and it's easy to get lost in the weeds. A good guide to understanding sports drinks can be found at cyclingweekly.com/news/the-complete-guide-to-sports-drinks-31549. The takeaway here is that water alone is not enough. You can swallow half of Lake Meade, but if you're not replacing sodium you can do yourself some serious damage.

7. TOOLS Each rider has a personal "absolute minimum list," which usually includes most of the following:

• tire levers	• spoke wrench
• chain rivet tool	• Allen wrenches (3, 4, 5, and 6 mm)
• spare tube and patch kit	• 6-inch crescent (adjustable-end) wrench
• spare chain link	• small flat-blade screwdriver
• air pump or CO2 cartridges	

8. FIRST AID KIT This, too, is a personal matter, usually including those items a rider has needed due to past mishaps. So, with the desert in mind, add a pair of tweezers (for close encounters of the cactus kind).

Road Biking

Road biking on the Strip, Downtown, or in any of Las Vegas's high-traffic areas is suicidal. Each year an astoundingly high number of bikers are injured or killed playing Russian roulette with Las Vegas motorists. If you want to bike, either confine yourself to sleepy subdivisions or get way out of town on a road with wide shoulders and little traffic.

There are a number of superb rides within a 30- to 40-minute drive from Downtown or the Strip. The best is the **Red Rock Canyon Scenic Loop ride,** due west of town, which carves a 15.4-mile circuit through the canyon's massive, russet-colored, sandstone cliffs. The route is arduous, with a 1,000-foot elevation gain in the first 6 miles, followed by 8 miles of downhill and flats with one more steep hill. One-way traffic on the scenic loop applies to cyclists and motorists alike. Although there is a fair amount of traffic on weekends, the road is wide and the speed limit is a conservative 35 miles per hour. If you park your car at the Red Rock Canyon Visitor Center, take careful note of when the area closes. If you are delayed on your ride and get back late, your car might be trapped behind locked gates.

A second ride in the same area follows NV 159 from the town of Blue Diamond to the entrance of Red Rock Canyon Scenic Loop Drive and back again, approximately 15.5 miles. From Blue Diamond the highway traverses undulating hills, with a net elevation gain of 193 feet on the outbound leg. In general, the ride offers gentle, long grades alternating with relatively flat stretches. Cliff walls and desert flora provide stunning vistas throughout. Traffic on NV 159 is a little heavy on weekends, but the road is plenty wide, with a good surface and wide shoulders. In the village of Blue Diamond there is a bike shop and a small store.

Another good out-and-back begins at Overton Beach on Lake Mead, northeast of Las Vegas, and ascends 867 feet in 8 miles to the visitor center at the Valley of Fire State Park. (You can, of course, begin your round-trip at the visitor center, but we always prefer to tackle the uphill leg first.) Geology in the park is spectacular, with the same red sandstone found in the cliffs and formations of the Grand Canyon. There are no shoulders, but traffic is light and the road surface is good. Since the route runs pretty much east–west, we like to schedule our ride in the afternoon so that we will have the setting sun at our back as we coast down to the lake on the return leg. Another good option is an early-morning ride with the sun at your back as you ascend and high in the sky as you return. Easy, flat riding can be enjoyed at Clark County Wetlands Park, and more challenging, hillier riding on the River Mountain Loop Trail, both described on page 477.

Dressing for a bike ride in the canyons and high country around Las Vegas is a challenge. In early December, when we rode the Red Rock loop, it was about 62°F in town and about 10°F cooler in the canyon. We started out in Lycra bike shorts and polypro long-sleeve windbreakers. By the time we completed the 6-mile uphill, we were about to die of heat prostration. On the long, fast downhill, we froze. Our recommendation is to layer on cooler days so that you can add or shuck clothing as conditions warrant. On warm days, try to bike early in the morning or late in the afternoon and wear light clothing. Always wear a helmet and always, always carry lots of water.

Except for the bike shop in Blue Diamond, there is no place on any of these routes to get help with a broken bike. You should bring extra tubes and a pump or CO_2 cartridges and know how to fix flats and make other necessary repairs. Water is available at Blue Diamond and at the Red Rock and Valley of Fire visitor centers, but almost no place else. Always replenish when you have the opportunity.

If you have a car, there are plenty of places to rent bikes, including four shops on the west side of town close to the rides described above. The shop in Blue Diamond also rents. For any of the five, just park, rent, and go. If you want to ride farther afield, some stores rent bike racks for your car. For a list of the shops, Google "bike rentals Las Vegas."

Mountain Biking

Las Vegas, most unexpectedly, has become a mountain-biking destination. Southwest of Las Vegas on NV 160 is Cottonwood Valley, with more than 200 miles of singletrack and doubletrack for all skill levels. There are five named loop trails, two named out-and-backs, and miles of unnamed trails and unpaved roads. Trail surface is mostly packed sand (good traction) with loose rock and a little soft sand. Trails on the north side of NV 160 are mellower in general, though there's some advanced riding below the east face of Wilson Cliffs. If it's your first time in the area, start with the figure-eight Mustang Trail. Almost all singletrack on good surface, this trail over rolling high desert offers moderate climbs, gradual descents, and great views of the Red Rock cliffs and valleys. A number of trails branch off Mustang if you want to lengthen your ride or opt for more advanced terrain.

On the south side of NV 160, the rides require more climbing. The showcase trail is the Dead Horse Loop, 14 miles of intermediate to advanced singletrack. Site of NORBA races, the route climbs to an overlook, with a stunning view of Las Vegas in the distance, and then drops off the mountain in a blue-cruiser known locally as the 3-mile smile. Out-and-backs and additional loops connecting to Dead Horse serve up more technical climbs and descents.

There are two ways to reach Cottonwood Valley. The fastest is to go south on I-15, exit onto NV 160, and head west 16 miles to the Mustang Trailhead parking lot (on the right) or 17 miles to the Cottonwood Valley Trailhead on the left. You can also go west out of town on Charleston Boulevard, which becomes NV 159. Take NV 159 until it intersects NV 160 south of Blue Diamond. Turn right on NV 160 for 5–6 miles to the parking lots.

 Try riding Cottonwood Valley first. If Cottonwood doesn't offer enough challenge, try Bootleg Canyon.

Southeast of Las Vegas near Boulder City, Hoover Dam, and Lake Mead is Bootleg Canyon, primarily an advanced-skill-level mountain-bike park, though it does offer something for all skill levels on its 36 miles of trails. While mostly known for its full-body-armor downhills and jumps, the park also serves up some technical cross-country, great views of Boulder City, and, on the backside, Lake Mead. Though hard to get really lost, the layout, with lots of crisscrossing trails, is confusing to many bikers riding there for the first time. A lot, if not most, of the riding is hard core, as are the riders who hang here. Surface is packed dirt or sand and a lot of rock, much of it loose. Trails, carved into the side of the hill, are frequently off-camber. To get there from Las Vegas, take NV 93 to Boulder City. Turn left at the light onto Buchanan Boulevard, and then left onto Canyon Road. Continue beyond where the pavement gives way to dirt to the Bootleg Canyon parking lot situated between two hills. Usually there are freebie maps of the park in a box at the parking lot, but if possible, team up with locals who know the area and terrain. Mellow, unpaved trails can be found at the Clark County Wetlands Park, described on page 477. The Historic Railroad Tunnel Trail, also on page 477, is an easy low-gradient pedal.

If you're not used to riding in the high desert, you won't believe how much water you consume. We recommend a full Camelbak plus as many water bottles as you can carry on the frame. Wind, almost always howling out of the west, is a factor at both biking destinations, so much so that trails are generally laid out on a north–south axis with as little east–west as possible. Even so, tackling a tough climb into a headwind will probably be part of your Nevada biking baptism. Finally, almost all of the riding is exposed. If you want shade, bring an umbrella—seriously.

Other area rides include the Bristlecone Pine Trail in Lee Canyon on Mount Charleston, about an hour northwest of Las Vegas. Though just under 6 miles in length, this loop trail is at altitude (above 7,500 feet) with a 700-foot rise and fall in elevation. Take US 95 north and then follow NV 157 for 17 miles up into the mountains until you see a dirt road where you can turn off and park.

Bicycles are available for rent at **Escape Adventures** (10575 Discovery Drive, ☎ 702-596-2953, escapeadventures.com). Helmets, bike racks, water bottles, Cottonwood Valley trail maps, and other gear are likewise available for rent or for sale. Escape also offers guided mountain-bike tours daily, with trails chosen based on the skill level of the group. If you book a tour, Escape will pick you up at your hotel or one close by.

Another option is to rent a bike from **McGhie's Bike Outpost** (☎ 702-875-4820, mcghies.com) in the little desert town of Blue Diamond. Blue Diamond is off NV 159 about 3 miles north of the intersection with NV 160. Located on the east end of Cottonwood Valley, you can actually get on the trail outside the back door of the shop. That said, you have to bike quite a way uphill and west to access the popular loop trails.

In addition to the foregoing, many mountain bikers ride the paved scenic loop at Red Rock Canyon (described under "Road Biking," pages 479–480). Visit redrockcanyonlv.org for more information.

HIKING AND BACKPACKING

HIKING OR BACKPACKING IN THE DESERT can be a very enjoyable experience. It can also be a hazardous adventure if you travel unprepared. Lake Mead ranger Debbie Savage suggests the following:

The best months for hiking are the cooler months of November through March. Hiking is not recommended in the summer, when temperatures reach 120°F in the shade. Never hike alone and always tell someone where you are going and when you plan to return. Carry plenty of water (at least a half-gallon per person) and drink often.

Know your limits. Hiking the canyons and washes in the desert often means traveling over rough, steep terrain with frequent elevation changes. Try to pick a route that best suits your abilities. Distances in the desert are often deceiving. Be sure to check the weather forecast before departure. Sudden storms can cause flash flooding. Seek higher ground if thunderstorms threaten.

Essential equipment includes sturdy walking shoes and proper clothing. Long pants are suggested for protection from rocks and cacti. A hat, sunscreen, and sunglasses are also recommended. Carry a small daypack to hold items such as a first aid kit, lunch, water, a light jacket, and a flashlight.

Canyons and washes often contain an impressive diversity of plant life, most easily observed during the spring wildflower season. Desert springs are located in some of the canyons and support a unique community of plants and animals. They are often the only source of water for many miles around. Take care not to contaminate them with trash or other human wastes. Along similar lines, understand that desert soils are often very fragile and take a long time to recover if disturbed. These surfaces are recognizable by their comparatively darker appearance and should be avoided whenever possible.

Poisonous animals such as snakes, spiders, and scorpions are most active after dark and are not often seen during daylight hours by hikers. Speckled rattlesnakes are common but are not aggressive. Scorpion stings are no more harmful than a bee sting, unless you are allergic. Black widow spiders are shy and secretive and are most often found around man-made structures. Watch where you place your hands and feet, and don't disturb obvious hiding places.

The Las Vegas area offers quite a diversity of hiking options. Trips that include a choice of canyons, lakes, desert, mountains, or ponderosa pine forest can be found within an hour's drive of Las Vegas. There are two great guidebooks to hiking the Las Vegas–southern Nevada area: *Hiking Las Vegas: The All-in-One Guide to Exploring Red Rock Canyon, Mt. Charleston, and Lake Mead,* by Branch Whitney (Huntington Press, 392 pages, $18.71) and *Afoot and Afield Las Vegas and Southern Nevada: A Comprehensive Hiking Guide,* by Brian Beffort (Wilderness Press, 312 pages, $18.95). You really can't go wrong with either guide. A comprehensive Las Vegas hiking and birding website is birdandhike.com.

Red Rock Canyon National Conservation Area Only 40 minutes from Las Vegas, Red Rock Canyon contains some of the most rugged rock formations in the West and offers loop as well as out-and-back trails of varying lengths (see map on page 485). The short Moenkopi Loop originates at the visitor center, and it takes about 90 minutes to walk over undulating terrain in a broad desert valley. Other popular short hikes include out-and-backs to Lost Creek (0.3 mile, one-way), Icebox Canyon (1.3 miles, one-way), and Pine Creek Canyon (1.5 miles, one-way), leading to the ruins of a historic homestead near a running creek surrounded by large ponderosa pine trees. Our favorite trail, and certainly one of the most scenic, is the out-and-back Calico Tanks Trail (2.5 miles, round-trip), which winds up through a narrow canyon to a *tinaja*—a circular canyon, or "tank," that forms a natural lake. The hike is a stunner, even in hot dry months when there's little or no water in the tank, and ends at the top of the canyon with a knockout view of Las Vegas on the distant valley floor. However, the trek does involve a lot of boulder scrambling, and the trail is not consistently well marked.

Altogether there are 19 trails: 4 rated easy, 5 rated easy to moderate, 9 rated moderate, and 1 classified as difficult. Distances range from 0.75 mile to 6 miles. We should emphasize that Red Rock trail ratings are astonishingly understated. Many of the trails rated "moderate" would be rated "difficult" by hikers not used to a steady diet of boulders. Most trails are poorly marked and require a great deal of boulder scrambling. Often a trail dead-ends at a boulder canyon. You intuit that the trail picks up again beyond the boulders, but there's not a hint regarding which boulders to climb to get you there. Hiking poles are great on the trail but just get in the way when you're bouldering. Hiking time for the easier trails is 1–2½ hours, and up to 4½ hours for the more difficult ones. Hiking guidebooks for the area generally use the recreation area's ratings, so be sure to read all of the detail relating to the hike you're contemplating. Most of the easy and easy-to-moderate trails are pretty level. Elevation gain for moderate and difficult trails is 300–1,700 feet. Maps and hiking information are available free when you pay your entrance fee and for sale in the visitor center. For more information about Red Rock trails, see planetware.com/nevada/top-rated-hikes-in-red-rock-canyon-national-conservation-area-us-nv-35.htm. If you'd like to spend a few days here and camp, Red Rock offers a campground (see profile below). For more information, call ☎ 702-515-5350 or check out desertusa.com/redrock.

Red Rock Canyon Campground

RV ★★★   TENT ★★   BEAUTY ★★★   SITE PRIVACY ★   SPACIOUSNESS ★★½
QUIET ★★★½   SECURITY ★★   CLEANLINESS ★★★   INSECT CONTROL ★★★

Red Rock Canyon National Conservation Area, 3293 Moenkopi Road, Las Vegas, NV 89124; ☎ 702-515-5350; redrockcanyonlv.org/redrockcanyon/camping-at-red-rock-canyon

FACILITIES Acres 60. **Number of RV sites** 5. **Number of tent-only sites** 71. **Number of multipurpose sites** 52. **Site to acreage ratio** 1:0.8. **Hookups** None. **Each site** Table, fire pit. **Dump station** No. **Laundry** No. **Restrooms and showers** Restrooms, no showers. **Fuel** No. **Propane** No. **Internal roads**

Red Rock Canyon

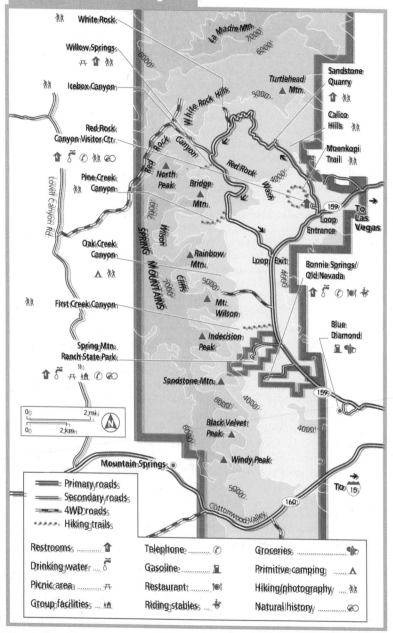

White Rock

Willow Springs

Icebox Canyon

Red Rock
Canyon Visitor Ctr.

Pine Creek
Canyon

Oak Creek
Canyon

First Creek Canyon

Spring Mtn.
Ranch State Park

La Madre Mtn.
7000'
6000'

White Rock Hills

Turtlehead
▲ Mtn.

Sandstone
Quarry

5000'

Calico
Hills

Red Rock Canyon

Moenkopi
Trail

Red Rock
Wash

4000'

North
▲ Peak

Bridge
▲ Mtn.

Bell Rock Canyon

Lovell Canyon Rd.

Wilson

SPRING MOUNTAINS

159

Loop
Entrance

To
Las
Vegas

Loop Exit

4000'

Bonnie Springs/
Old Nevada

Rainbow
▲ Mtn.

Cliffs

7000'

5000'

▲ Mt.
Wilson

▲ Indecision
Peak

Blue
Diamond

Sandstone Mtn. ▲

6000' 4000'

159

Black Velvet
Peak ▲

6000'

4000'

0   2 mi
0   2 km

N

▲ Windy Peak

Mountain Springs ◉

5000'

To
15

Cottonwood Valley

160

Primary roads

Secondary roads

4WD roads

Hiking trails

Restrooms .... ⬆

Drinking water ..... ⬆

Picnic area .... ⛽

Group facilities ... ⛺

Telephone .... ✆

Gasoline .... ⛽

Restaurant .... 🍴

Riding stables ... 🐎

Groceries .... 🛒

Primitive camping .... ▲

Hiking/photography ... 🚶

Natural history .... ∞

Dirt. **RV service** No. **Market** No. **Restaurant** No. **General store** No. **Vending** No. **Swimming** No. **Playground** No. **Nearby attractions** Red Rock Canyon National Conservation Area.

KEY INFORMATION Operated by Bureau of Land Management. **Open** September–May. **Site assignment** First come, first served. **Registration** At ranger station. **Fee** $20 per day per site. **Parking** Maximum 2 vehicles per site.

RESTRICTIONS Pets On leash only. **Fires** Allowed; sites have fire pits; firewood is available for purchase from campground hosts September 1–May 31. **Alcoholic beverages** Not allowed. **Vehicle maximum length** 16 feet.

TO GET THERE From Las Vegas, drive west on Charleston Boulevard/NV 159 for 6 miles. Just 2 miles before the Red Rock Canyon scenic drive, turn left on Moenkopi Road. Pass the fire station on the right, the group campground on the left, then drive down the hill to the campground.

DESCRIPTION It's the desert, and nothing but. Set in a low hollow just below the Calico Hills, Red Rock Canyon Campground offers the bare minimum: a place to pitch your tent. The campground's compact main loop is bisected by two spoke roads, with sites feathering off at regular angles. Pit toilets are set at the corners. There's no foliage to screen your site from neighbors, who are not that far off in any case. A small RV loop and a similar-size walk-in tent-only loop dangle off to the south, near the campground host. Seven large group sites are set out near the entrance. The low setting makes views of the hills problematic, but it's extremely serene and quiet—and even with the lights of the Strip a few miles away, the clear night sky makes for great stargazing.

VALLEY OF FIRE STATE PARK Located an hour northeast of Las Vegas, Valley of Fire surpasses even Red Rock Canyon for exotic landscapes, geological variety, and sheer beauty. The *Las Vegas Advisor* compares hiking the Valley of Fire with being "beamed" onto another planet. We were reminded of the rock houses and fantasy formations of the World Heritage site in Cappadocia, Turkey. If Valley of Fire were more tolerable in the hot months, we're convinced it would be a national park. If you only have one day to hike, make Valley of Fire State Park your destination.

Where the better hikes in Red Rock National Recreation Area require difficult boulder scrambling, the hiking in Valley of Fire is accessible to most everyone (though there's significant elevation gain and loss on some trails). Arguably, the park's highlights are clustered along the White Domes Road. Branching off uphill from the visitor center, the road will take you to Mouse's Tank (Petroglyph Canyon), the Rainbow Vista (primarily a photo point), the peppermint formations of the Fire Wave, and the mammoth White Domes sandstone formations at the road's terminus. There is a parking lot and trailhead at each feature. Best of all, the hikes are short, ranging from 30–80 minutes, so you have plenty of time to do all of them in a one-day visit. The remainder of the park's highlights are arrayed along the Valley of Fire Road and the Scenic Loop Road. The park fee is $12 ($10 for locals). For more information, call ☎ 702-397-2088 or visit parks.nv.gov/parks/valley-of-fire-state-park.

LAKE MEAD NATIONAL RECREATION AREA An hour southeast of Las Vegas, Lake Mead NRA offers a variety of hiking experiences, although there are few designated trails. Included within the NRA are Lakes Mead and Mohave, and part of the Mojave Desert. Ranger-led hikes are offered February–April. Outings cover 6–8 miles and are moderate to strenuous in difficulty. If you prefer to explore on your own, detailed maps and instructions to the most popular areas are available at the visitor centers. An admission fee of $20 per vehicle ($10 on foot or bike) is good for seven days. For information, call ☎ 702-293-8990 or visit nps.gov/lame.

HUMBOLDT-TOIYABE NATIONAL FOREST High in the mountains 40 minutes northwest of Las Vegas, Humboldt-Toiyabe National Forest provides a totally different outdoor experience. The air is cool, and the trails run among stately forests of ponderosa pine, quaking aspen, white fir, and mountain mahogany. Hikes range in distance from 0.1 mile to 21 miles, and in difficulty from easy to very difficult. Most popular are the Cathedral Rock Trail (2 miles round-trip), which climbs 900 feet to a stark summit overlooking Kyle Canyon, and Bristlecone, a 5-mile loop that traverses the ridges above the Lee Canyon Ski Area. Though the distances of these loops are not great, the terrain is exceedingly rugged, and the hikes are not recommended for one-day outings unless you begin very early in the morning and are used to strenuous exercise at high elevations. For more information, call ☎ 775-331-6444.

ROCK CLIMBING AND BOULDERING

THE RED ROCK CANYON NATIONAL CONSERVATION AREA is one of the top rock-climbing resources in the United States. With more than 1,000 routes, abundant holds, and approaches ranging from roadside to remote wilderness, the area rivals Yosemite in scope and variety for climbers. Offering amazing diversity for every skill level amid desert canyon scenery second to none, the area is less than a 40-minute drive from Las Vegas.

Though there is some granite and limestone, almost all of the climbing is done on sandstone. Overall, the rock is pretty solid, although there are some places where the sandstone gets a little crumbly, especially after a rain. Bolting is allowed but discouraged (local climbers have been systematically replacing bolts on some of the older routes with more modern bolts that blend with the rock). There are some great spots for bouldering, some of the best top-roping in the United States, a lifetime supply of big walls, and even some bivouac routes. Climbs range in difficulty from nonbelayed scrambles to 5.13 big-wall overhangs. You can climb year-round at Red Rock. Wind can be a problem, as can most of the other conditions that make a desert environment challenging. Having enough water can be a logistical nightmare on a long climb.

The Red Rocks of Southern Nevada by Joanne Urioste describes a number of the older routes. Newer route descriptions can be obtained from **Desert Rock Sports** in Las Vegas (☎ 702-254-1143, desertrocksportslv.com). Desert Rock Sports can also help you find camping and showers and tell you where the loose rock is. Offering climbing-shoe rentals, the store is at 8221 West Charleston, conveniently on the way to the canyon from Las Vegas. The **Red Rock Climbing Center** (☎ 702-254-5604, redrockclimbingcenter.com) is next to Desert Rock Sports and offers excellent indoor climbing and showers (but no towels). Guides and/or instruction are available from Desert Rock Sports.

RIVER RUNNING

THE BLACK CANYON OF THE COLORADO RIVER can be run year-round below Hoover Dam. The most popular trip is from the tailwaters of the dam to Willow Beach. In this 9.5-mile section, canyon walls rise almost vertically from the water's edge, with scenery and wildlife very similar to that of the Colorado River in the Grand Canyon above Lake Mead. There are numerous warm springs and waterfalls on feeder streams, presenting the opportunity for good side-trip hikes. Small beaches provide good rest and lunch sites. Bighorn sheep roam the bluffs, and wild burros can often be seen up the canyons. The water in the river, about 53°F year-round, is drawn from the bottom of Lake Mead and released downstream through the Hoover Dam hydroelectric generators.

Under normal conditions, the Black Canyon is a nice flatwater float trip with a steady current to help you along. There are places along the river, such as Ringbolt Rapids and the Chute, that are named for falls and rapids long since covered up and flattened out by the voluminous discharge of water from the dam. There is nothing remaining on the run in the way of paddling challenges beyond a few swells and ripples. The Black Canyon is suitable for canoes, kayaks, and rafts. Motorized craft cannot be launched below the dam but can come upstream to the dam from Willow Beach or from other marinas farther downstream. The downstream paddle takes about 6 hours, including side trips and lunch, for a canoe or kayak, and about 3½ hours for a commercial motorized raft.

There are several ways you can get into serious trouble. The put-in below the dam is rocky and slippery. More than a few boaters have accidentally launched their boat before they climbed aboard, while others have managed to arrive in the river ahead of their boat. Once you're under way, it's important to keep your group close together. With the water temperature at 53°F, you want to pluck people out of the river posthaste in the event of a capsize. When you go ashore to explore, pull your boat way up out of the water and tie it to something sturdy. If at the dam they happen to crank up an extra generator or two while you're off hiking in a side canyon, it's possible for the river to rise several feet, sweeping any unsecured boats and equipment downstream.

 If the weather service predicts headwinds in excess of 12 miles an hour, cancel your paddling trip, even if it means losing your permit fee.

For the most part, the 9.5-mile run from the dam to Willow Beach does not require any prior paddling experience. On most days, you could practically float to the takeout, with breaks for lunch and exploring, in 5 hours. The exception, and it's a big one, is when headwinds blow up the canyon from the west. Though headwinds of less than 10 miles an hour won't affect the paddling situation much, winds of 11 miles an hour or higher require more experience and advanced boat-handling skills. When the wind is high, it can blow you upstream, making forward progress grueling or impossible, and can whip up crosscurrents as well as waves up to 3 feet high. Chances of capsizing grow exponentially with wind speed, and rescue efforts become correspondingly more difficult.

Private parties must obtain a launch permit from **Black Canyon/ Willow Beach River Adventures** (☎ 800-455-3490, blackcanyon adventures.com); **Desert River Outfitters** (☎ 928-763-3033, desert riveroutfitters.com); or **Boulder City River Riders** (☎ 702-293-1190, bouldercityriverriders.com). The permits are sold as part of a launch/ shuttle package and are not available except from licensed outfitters. The outfitter of your choice, along with dam security officers, will take you into the dam's secure area to put in below the dam.

Only 30 boats are allowed to launch from below the dam each day, so weekends sell out well in advance. On weekdays, it's sometimes possible to get a permit on short notice. Permits can be obtained on a first-come, first-serve basis six months in advance. The permits and fees apply to a specific date and are nonrefundable, though if there's space available, the permitting authority will try to assign you an alternate date in the event of bad weather, high winds, or other mitigating circumstances.

The best time to run the Canyon is in the fall through December. The spring is prettiest, with new green foliage seen on the beaches and in the side canyons. The spring, along with January and February, tend to be the windiest times of year, however. Summers are hot, and the canyons tend to hold the heat. The water, however, provides some natural cooling. Canoeists and kayakers can make the run in one day or alternatively camp overnight in the canyon en route. Commercial raft trips are one-day/half-day affairs.

If you don't have your own equipment, you can rent one- and two-person kayaks (including shuttle and permit) from Boulder City River Riders and Desert River Outfitters referenced above. The kayaks are open-cockpit and usually rented without spray skirts. This essentially means that 53°F water drips off the paddle into your lap every time you take a paddle stroke. If spray skirts are available, we recommend you use them. In addition to providing equipment, the outfitters also transport you and your boat to the river. At the end of the run, they pick you up at Willow Beach and drive you back to your car. If you have your own boat, the same shuttle service is available for $60 per person.

Boulder City River Riders also offers guided one- and two-person kayak tours from the bottom of Hoover Dam to Willow Beach. Trips include lunch, transportation to and from the river, and paddling instruction if necessary. Trip cost is $280 with a minimum group size of 2 and is offered year-round except Thanksgiving and Christmas.

In addition to granting launch permits, Black Canyon/Willow Beach River Adventures also operates guided, motorized raft trips, with guest transportation provided from the Strip and Downtown. No permit is required for these trips. The raft outing is unlike most commercial river trips. First, the rafts are huge, accommodating more than two dozen guests. Second, the trip is entirely passive—no paddling required. The rafts motor up from Willow Beach in the morning and pick up their passengers at the put-in below the dam. From there, it's a scenic, narrated 3-hour-or-so float back to Willow Beach, where guests are loaded up and transported back to their cars or delivered to their Las Vegas hotel. The trips run $99 for adults and $66 for children ages 5–12. For transportation from your Las Vegas hotel, add $59.

There is little protection from the sun in the Black Canyon, and temperatures can surpass 110°F in the warmer months. Long-sleeve shirts, long pants, tennis shoes, and a hat are recommended minimum attire year-round. Be sure to take sunscreen and lots of drinking water.

Whitewater Rafting

The Colorado River through the Grand Canyon is one of the most famous whitewater rafting/paddling runs in the world. Once the river empties into the lake pool of Lake Mead there are no more rapids. Now, however, a combination helicopter tour of the canyon and whitewater rafting is available from **Grand Canyon Helicopters.** For additional information, see page 459.

SNOW SKIING

LEE CANYON IS a 1-hour drive from Las Vegas. Situated in a granite canyon in the Spring Mountain range, the resort provides one quad, one triple, one double chairlift, and a surface lift servicing 30 runs. Though the mountain is small and the runs short by Western standards, the skiing is solid intermediate. Of the 30 named runs, 14 are blue, 15 are black (mostly short), and there is one short green. There is also a terrain park. Base elevation of 8,510 feet notwithstanding, snow conditions are usually dependable only during January, though snow-making covers 43% of the lifts. Because of its southerly location and the proximity of the hot, arid desert, there is a lot of thawing and refreezing in Lee Canyon, and hence, frequently icy skiing conditions. If the snow is good, a day at Lee Canyon is a great outing. If the mountain is icy, do something else.

Snowmaking equipment allows the resort to operate from Thanksgiving to Easter. There is no lodging on site and only a modest restaurant and bar. Parking is quite a hike from the base facility. From Las Vegas, take US 95 north approximately 30 miles to NV 156, Lee Canyon. Follow NV 156 for 17 miles to where it dead-ends at the resort.

Skis can be rented at the ski area. For information on lift tickets or snow conditions, call the ski-area office at ☎ 702-385-2754 or see leecanyonlv.com. For summer events, check the resort's website.

HORSEBACK RIDING

THE CLOSEST HORSEBACK-RIDING OUTFITTERS are in the Red Rock Canyon area half an hour west of Las Vegas. Riding is allowed on only a couple of trails in the Red Rock National Conservation Area, but there's a lot of riding to be found just outside the Conservation Area. **Bonnie Springs** (☎ 702-875-4191, bonniesprings.com) and **Cowboy Trail Rides** (☎ 702-387-2457, cowboytrailrides.com) are both located within a 4- to 10-minute drive from Red Rock Canyon.

FISHING

THE LAKE MEAD NATIONAL RECREATION AREA offers some of the best fishing in the United States. Lake Mead is the largest lake, with Lake Mohave, downstream on the Colorado River, offering the most diverse fishery. Largemouth bass, striped bass, channel catfish, crappie, and bluegill are found in both lakes. Rainbow and cutthroat trout are present only in Lake Mohave. Remote and beautiful in its upmost reaches, Lake Mohave is farther from Las Vegas but provides truly exceptional fishing. Bass and trout often run 3 pounds, and some trout weigh 10 pounds or more. Willow Beach, near where the Colorado River enters the pool waters of Lake Mohave, is where many of the larger trout are taken.

Lake Mead, broader, more open, and much closer to Las Vegas, has become famous for its stripers, with an occasional catch weighing in at over 40 pounds. Bass fishing is consistently good throughout Lake Mead. The Overton Arm (accessed from Echo Bay or Overton Beach) offers the best panfish and catfish action.

Because Lakes Mead and Mohave form the Arizona–Nevada state line, fishing license regulations are a little strange. If you are bank fishing, all you need is a license from the state you are in. If you fish from a boat, however, you need a fishing license from one state and a special-use stamp from the other. All required stamps and licenses can be obtained from marinas and local bait and tackle shops in either state.

Nonresidents have the option of purchasing 1- to 10-day fishing permits in lieu of a license. Permits are $18 for one day (with a $7 charge per additional consecutive days) and $69 for annual, and apply to the entire state of Nevada. In addition to the permit, a special-use stamp costing $3 is required for those fishing from a boat. Plus, a $10 trout stamp is necessary to take trout if you buy the annual permit; the trout stamp is included in the price of the daily permit. In addition, a $10 stamp is available for fishing with two rods. Youngsters age 12 years and under in the company of a properly licensed, permitted, and stamped adult can fish without any sort of documentation.

Seventeen-foot aluminum fishing boats (that seat five) can be rented on both lakes by the hour (about $40 with a 2-hour minimum), by the half-day (4–5 hours for about $50), or by the day (about $215). Bass boats, houseboats, and pontoon craft are also available. Rods and reels rent for about $5 for 4 hours or less and about $12 a day.

LAKE MEAD BAIT AND TACKLE, BOAT RENTAL, FUEL, AND SUPPLIES
CALLVILLE BAY RESORT ☎ 800-255-5561; callvillebay.com
COTTONWOOD COVE RESORT ☎ 800-255-5561; cottonwoodcoveresort.com
KATHERINE LANDING ☎ 928-754-3245; katherinelanding.com
TEMPLE BAR RESORT (AZ) ☎ 928-767-3211; templebarlakemead.com

PLEASURE BOATING, SAILING, WATER-SKIING, AND JET SKIING

LAKE MEAD AND LAKE MOHAVE are both excellent sites for pleasure boating, water-skiing, and other activities. Both lakes are so large that it is easy to find a secluded spot. Rock formations on the lakes are spectacular, and boaters can visit scenic canyons and coves that are inaccessible to those traveling by car. Boats, for example, can travel into the narrow, steep-walled gorge of Iceberg Canyon in Lake Mead or upstream into the Black Canyon from Lake Mohave.

First-timers, particularly on Lake Mead, frequently underestimate its vast size. It is not difficult to get lost on the open waters of Lake Mead or to get caught in bad weather. Winds can be severe on the lake, and waves of 6 feet sometimes arise during storms. In general, there is no shade on the lakes, and the steep rock formations along the shore do not make hospitable emergency landing sites. When you boat on either lake, take plenty of water, dress properly, be equipped, and be sure to tell someone where you are going and when you expect to return.

Most of the resorts listed under "Fishing" rent various types of pleasure craft and water-skiing equipment, and the Callville Bay Resort also rents personal watercraft. In addition, at Callville Bay on Lake Mead and Cottonwood Cove on Lake Mohave, luxury houseboats are available for rental. For rates and other information concerning houseboats, call ☎ 800-255-5561 or visit callvillebay.com or cottonwoodcoveresort.com.

SPA 101

GETTING THE INSIDE TRACK ON SPA KNOW-HOW

LET'S FACE IT. Most people spend more time and money on preventive maintenance for their cars than on themselves. After all, changing the oil and checking tire pressure go a long way in extending the life of a car, let alone ensuring a smoother ride along the way. Believe it or not, this analogy fits for why we should participate in spa experiences. Call it preventative or maintenance medicine of your chassis, and a whole lot more.

SPA LINGO

ACUPRESSURE AND ACUPUNCTURE Acupressure, or fingertip massage, is said to free the body's energy channels, or "meridians," for a relaxing and energizing treatment. Acupuncture uses ultrafine needles for more specific and chronic ailments.

AROMATHERAPY A full-body massage using scented essential oils and light, smoothing movements. Different oils are used for different therapeutic benefits.

AYURVEDA The ancient system of traditional Indian medicine and science that incorporates nutrition, herbal medicine, aromatherapy, massage, and meditation.

BODY SCRUB A light massage and exfoliation that stimulates blood circulation and prepares the skin for mineralization and moisturizing.

BODY WRAP Strips of cloth, steeped in a variety of aromatic herbs and/or sea enzymes, are wrapped around the body, which is then covered with blankets or towels to prevent the moist heat from escaping. Body wrap is a relaxing treatment to soothe soreness and soften skin.

HOT-STONE MASSAGE This type of massage—also known as La Stone Therapy—uses smooth, dark, heated stones to relieve stiffness and soreness and to restore energy.

HYDROTHERAPY This relaxing therapy includes underwater jet massage, showers, jet sprays, and mineral baths.

MASSAGE THERAPY Massaging skin, muscles, and joints relieves muscle spasms and tension, and improves flexibility and circulation. Various types of massage range from gentle aromatherapy to a sports massage directed at specific muscles used in athletic activities to deep-tissue Swedish massage, which kneads and separates muscle groups while stretching connective tissue to help realign the body.

MINERAL WATERS Originating from natural springs and wells, these waters contain high concentrations of rare or biologically active elements that are claimed to improve circulation, detoxify the body, and ease ailments such as rheumatism and arthritis.

REFLEXOLOGY A Chinese-based massage of the feet and hands that includes pressure points to areas said to correspond with organs and tissues throughout the body. Treats a wide range of ailments.

SALT GLOW A mixture of salt, oils, and water is used to scrub the body to remove dead skin, clean pores, and stimulate circulation.

SHIATSU A Japanese massage therapy during which practitioners apply rhythmic finger pressure at specific points on the body in order to relieve pain, and release and balance blocked energy.

THAI MASSAGE In this form of massage a therapist manipulates the body using passive, yogalike stretching and applies gentle pressure with his or her hands and feet along "energy lines" in the body.

THALASSOTHERAPY A full-body exfoliation and detoxification treatment that uses nutrient-rich marine elements along with other skin-conditioning agents.

VICHY SHOWER MASSAGE This relaxing massage is performed under sprinklers to improve the body's circulation; water is heated to body temperature.

GETTING DOWN TO SPA BASICS

A GOOD SPA is defined by the purity of experience it provides and how it makes you feel the moment you enter it. A spa needs to engage and soothe all five senses and provide an ambience that removes you from the outside world. Often you can't put into words the nurturing wave of care that envelops you, yet the feeling is instant and palpable.

Five things to watch for in a spa:

- The hair salon should be well separated from the spa—the noise of dryers and smell of perm solution fly in the face of serenity and jasmine-scented air.
- The gym should be considered a part of the spa in name only; sharing locker space with treadmill enthusiasts isn't conducive to the spa ethos.
- Retail sales should be physically a part of the reception and transaction area rather than any transition zone.
- There should be RMTs (registered massage therapists) on staff, in addition to body-care workers.
- Skin-care products should be eco-friendly and free from animal testing.

SPA NEOPHYTE: THE NAKED TRUTH

ALL SPAS CATER TO THE FIRST-TIME VISITOR—and ease anxiety about those nagging questions regarding nudity and massage. Don't worry. Treatments are usually explained to you prior to the start of any session, and therapists use professional draping techniques to ensure privacy. For example, when you're having a full-body massage and are asked to turn over, your therapist will raise the covering sheet so high that no one gets a boo at your privates, and the sheet will be settled over your body only when the therapist notes that your feet are facing in the right direction. Always let the spa know if you have a preference for either a male or female therapist.

Most people strip to the buff for full-body massages and wraps, but if modesty is a concern, disrobe to your level of comfort, keep your undies on, or ask the spa if they have disposable panties. If you and your teen are venturing into a side-by-side massage, spas usually ask that your child wear a swimsuit so that they (and you) have a sense of comfort about being touched. If you are having any form of body treatment or men's facial, don't shave for at least 4 hours before your service. And let the spa know in advance of any special conditions such as pregnancy, high blood pressure, heart ailments, or any condition where certain heat therapies, massage, or skin care might not be appropriate. If waxing services are on your agenda, a presteam or sauna is not recommended, and, please, don't eat a full meal just before any spa visit.

Lastly, remove your contact lenses before heading into a eucalyptus steam; its astringent qualities may cause your eyes to sting.

During your treatment, your therapist will take their lead from you and be as silent or as talkative as you wish. Some will talk you through the process, especially during a facial, so that you know what sensations to expect as the therapist cleanses, tones, steams, and applies a mask. The choice is always yours.

THE "SHOULDS" TO NOTE

THERAPISTS SHOULD ALWAYS check in on your comfort with and preference for lighting (too bright?), music (too loud or not loud enough?), warmth (we love spas with heated bed pads), and pressure of massage touch.

On the latter, know that an RMT is highly skilled at finding those stubborn knots, and kneading their release might cause minor discomfort; that's why you warm up muscles in a steam or sauna first. Still, RMTs are not there to hurt you. Breathe, moan, exhale dramatically—these are all great ways to help your therapist help you relieve tension.

Don't think you have to buy into product sales pitches. Estheticians are well versed to share the benefits of the products they use, and experienced practitioners should share comparisons between these and others you might know. Conversation should be informational only.

THE "SHOULD NOTS" TO NOTE

YOUR THERAPIST SHOULD NOT leave the room without informing you. During your treatment, therapists should not move around the room in search of products, water, and equipment. Everything should have been preset for easy access. For full-body work, they should have warmed their hands before contact, "tuned" into your space by noting the rhythm of your breathing, and never should they lose contact with you for more than a split second. An unexpected touch, however gentle, can awaken the senses very abruptly. At the conclusion of your session, therapists shouldn't flick on the lights or slap you on the backside and say "Go, bucko, go." Bedside manner is everything.

SPA BELLS AND WHISTLES

UNLESS YOU'RE VISITING A SMALL DAY SPA where space limits facilities, here are some complimentary amenities you can expect.

- Same-sex changing rooms with personal lockers, spa sandals, robes, and towels.
- Some spas will have either same-sex (swimsuit-optional) steam rooms, saunas, and mineral pools, or will provide direct access to similar coed facilities (swimsuit mandatory).
- A grooming bar with hairstyling products, moisturizers, and sundry items.
- Easy or direct access to either a same-sex or coed relaxation area for pre- and posttreatment "integration" time. This is an opportunity to snooze, bask in your newly acquired mellow mood, and read. Popular magazines and inspirational texts are usually on hand.

- The relaxation area should also provide healthy grazing foods like nuts and fresh fruit as well as tea infusions and other refreshments. Don't expect coffee.
- When you have a body scrub, it is customary for the spa staff to offer you the loofah brush or mitten to take home.
- When you receive a manicure or pedicure, some spas provide mini-bottles of polish for touch-ups, as well as the emery board used during the treatment.
- When you enjoy a facial, ask for free samples (see A Word about Retail below) of the products used or recommended. That way you'll always have a travel-size supply at hand for that overnight getaway.
- Spas that are really on the ball will offer value-added services to every treatment, at no additional cost. Examples include a hand, foot, or scalp massage with every facial and a paraffin-wax treatment with every manicure. The idea is to engage as many of the five senses as possible with every treatment.

TO TIP OR NOT TO TIP?

GRATUITIES ARE USUALLY left to a guest's discretion and are similar to that given for hair-salon services, that is, 15%–20% of the price of the service provided. At all-inclusive resorts, verify the spa's tipping policy upon arrival. Unlike a hair salon where you sometimes have to track down your stylist and slip a little gratitude into their pocket, spas operate with gratuity envelopes, which are administered by the reception staff. Tips can also be charged to your debit or credit card.

BE THERE OR BE SQUARE

TREATMENTS ARE BLOCKED BY TIME, and synchronized with Swiss efficiency so that rooms can be quickly flipped. As a courtesy, arrive early (especially if you want to take advantage of a spa's amenities) and leave your treatment room promptly. You can take all the "zone-out" time you wish in the relaxation lounge. Be aware that if you arrive late, your treatment will still end at the appointed time since there's another client scheduled right behind you. Be sure to check the spa's cancellation policy when you make your reservation; no-shows are generally charged at least 50% of the full treatment fee. Remember to silence your cell phone before entering the spa.

A WORD ABOUT RETAIL

SPA-INDUSTRY EXPERTS CLAIM that retail sales should make up some 30% of a spa's revenues, but most spas generate about half that figure, largely because, inexplicably, they haven't caught up with the very world they have created in terms of maximizing retail opportunities. Consequently, there's pressure on staff to sell, and estheticians especially walk a fine line of wanting to be genuinely helpful and needing to meet commission quotas. There is absolutely no obligation to buy, however nicely the product is presented (often in a basket at the end of your treatment alongside a customized treatment regimen for you to take home).

However, if you like a product and feel its results, then why not buy it? Ask for travel samples as well. After all, you have just spent good money for an excellent treatment, and manufacturer's samples cost the

LAS VEGAS HEALTH SPAS

SPAS OPEN TO THE PUBLIC

- **Aria** The Spa at Aria ☎ 702-590-9600
- **Bellagio** Spa Bellagio ☎ 702-693-7472
- **Caesars Palace** Qua Baths and Spa ☎ 866-782-0655
- **The Cosmopolitan** Sahra Spa & Hammam ☎ 702-698-7000
- **El Cortez** Happy Feet Spa ☎ 702-885-6612
- **Excalibur** The Spa at Excalibur ☎ 702-597-7772
- **Flamingo** The Spa at Flamingo ☎ 702-733-3535
- **Four Seasons** The Spa at Four Seasons ☎ 702-632-5302
- **Golden Nugget** The Spa at Golden Nugget ☎ 702-386-8186
- **Green Valley Ranch Resort and Spa** The Spa at Green Valley Ranch
  ☎ 702-617-7570
- **Hard Rock Hotel** Reliquary Spa & Salon ☎ 702-693-5520
- **Harrah's** The Spa at Harrah's ☎ 702-369-5126
- **Luxor** Nurture Spa ☎ 702-730-5720
- **MGM Grand** MGM Grand Spa ☎ 702-891-3077
- **Mirage** The Spa at the Mirage ☎ 702-791-7472
- **New York–New York** The Spa at New York–New York ☎ 702-740-6955
- **Paris Las Vegas** Spa by Mandara ☎ 702-946-4366
- **Planet Hollywood** Mandara Spa ☎ 702-785-5772
- **Red Rock Resort** The Spa at Red Rock (Mon.-Fri.) ☎ 702-797-7878
- **Rio** Rio Spa ☎ 702-777-7779
- **SLS** Ciel Spa ☎ 702-761-7757
- **TI** Oleksandra Spa & Salon ☎ 702-894-7472
- **Trump International Hotel** The Spa at Trump ☎ 702-476-8000
- **The Venetian** Canyon Ranch SpaClub ☎ 702-414-3600
- **Westgate Las Vegas** The Spa at Westgate ☎ 702-732-5648
- **Westin Lake Las Vegas** Spa Moulay ☎ 702-567-6049 (Thurs.-Mon.)
- **Wynn Encore** The Spa at Wynn Encore ☎ 702-770-8000 (Sun.-Thurs.)

SPAS FOR HOTEL GUESTS ONLY

- **Mandalay Bay** Spa Mandalay ☎ 702-632-7220
- **Wynn Las Vegas** Spa at Wynn Las Vegas ☎ 702-770-8000

spa nothing but goodwill. Lastly, if the product you like is widely available, it might be less expensive at home, or even cheaper on eBay.

UNOFFICIAL OVERVIEW OF SIN CITY SPAS

IN A CITY THAT REINVENTS ITSELF at least every decade, it comes as no surprise that its spas do the same. With more than 45 luxury resort spas, Las Vegas spas have transformed themselves from being simply sidekicks that offer guests beauty amenities to lucrative mind-body-soul profit centers of Disneyesque proportions.

In the competition to entertain an increasingly aware spa crowd, destinations are constantly trying to out-spa one another in design, therapies, products, and promises. Like everything in Las Vegas, most spas present larger-than-life experiences within vast expanses of square footage with lots of service add-ons such as steam rooms and saunas, thus turning a simple pedicure into an all-day retreat.

Surprisingly, in spite of the spa scene's meteoric growth, the overall quality and professionalism of practitioners are high. The desire to be a part of "the next big idea" sees therapists move from one spa to the next. Consequently, many of them not only maintain a hyper, Red-Bull enthusiasm (sometimes counterintuitive to the spa experience) but also a diverse knowledge of different products and competitive brands. If products are your thing, then therapists are a resource worth plumbing.

Our advice is to take full advantage of a spa's facilities. Get a day pass so you can pop back in later for a relaxing steam—the moisture will feel delicious after tripsing around in the desert heat. Ask the spa if they'll spring for a pass for your partner; it only costs them laundry pennies to extend this privilege. Be aware, though, that their answer may depend on whether your service is a multisensory package or just a quick polish change. If you're a hotel guest, however, negotiate a pass for the hotel's on-site spa regardless.

Las Vegas's keep-up-with-the-Joneses climate means that spas are constantly catching, or creating, the newest wave. In recent years, **Caesars Palace, Mandalay Bay, Bellagio,** and **The Venetian** have all undergone multimillion-dollar expansions for an updated look and service standard, while the **Wynn** and **Trump** hotels have countered the city's penchant for splashy with more intimate spa surroundings. Meanwhile, traditionalists like the **Four Seasons** hotel have stayed the course with pricey, elegant refinement.

The spa scene in Las Vegas can be large-scale, confusing, and generic, but the individual Strip spas are opulent, accessible, diverse, and pay-through-the-nose fun. For *Unofficial* purposes, we're staying on the Strip (with one exception) with what we consider the spas that best epitomize Las Vegas's sizzle and audacity.

Bathhouse ★ ★ ★ ★
Delano 3950 Las Vegas Blvd. S.; ☎ 877-632-9636; delanolasvegas.com

---

Customer service ★★★★. **Facilities** ★★★★. **Amenities** ★★★★. **Sales pressure** Low. **Price range** $45–$310, spa services; $45–$310, nail and refinement services. **Spa amenities** Complimentary with spa services for hotel guests; complimentary for non-hotel guests with spa services over $60; spa pass $30 per day for hotel guests only.

SUMMARY AND COMMENTS The Bathhouse pioneered communal spa-ing on the Strip. With its stylish fixtures and brightly colored furniture, it retains a quasi-nightclub atmosphere, only rock and rhythm is replaced with sounds of trickling water. This is in-your-face, modern-bat-cave relaxation with soaring, monolithic black-slate walls and floors inset with a narrow, softly lit soaking pool. With only 12 treatment rooms, this spa is small by Las Vegas standards, but because every room has a private shower, they feel like mini-suites. A hybrid massage of hot stones, aromatherapy, and Swedish techniques is excellent. Add an express facial with an oxygen spray for a youthful glow.

RECOMMEND The Bathhouse Sampler combines a customized Scents-of-You bath, a Swedish massage, a refresher facial, and classic pedicure.

LOVE The contrasting exotica (no, not erotica) environment of Mandalay Spa. Its traditional Zen environment is a sigh of relief to the Bathhouse.

THE ULTIMATE It may be an illusion, but the Mocha Java Sculpting Wrap really does seem to dissolve some of those cellulite dimples, at least for a while.

DISLIKE A private cabana is nice, but Mandalay would do well to have a spa-only area on the beach to keep moods mellow.

TIP Organize a spa treatment for every day of your stay to enjoy free daily access to the spa and fitness amenities.

Canyon Ranch SpaClub   ★ ★ ★ ½

The Venetian/Palazzo 3355 Las Vegas Blvd. S.;
☎ 702-414-3600; canyonranch.com/las-vegas

Customer service ★★. Facilities ★★★★★. Amenities ★★★★★. Sales pressure Medium. **Price range** $175–$385, spa services; $49–$385, nail and refinement services. **Spa and fitness center amenities** Free with the purchase of any service over $50; $60 per day without spa services; SpaClub Day Passport includes access to fitness center.

SUMMARY AND COMMENTS Covering a staggering 134,000 square feet of treatment areas, this is the mother of all spas, complete with a separate gym. This is a top-notch spa that exemplifies the venerable and much-heralded Canyon Ranch ethos of promoting lifestyle wellness. The rather aloof front desk staff doesn't always convey the care you'll receive once you're in the spa's inner sanctum. Canyon Ranch is often described as an upmarket (read: celebrity) spa, and because there are no easy-to-buy packages, spa-ing here can add up to a chunk of change when stringing together different services. If money's tight, buy a SpaClub Day Passport that lets you into the fitness center and all its classes and wellness presentations, as well as enjoy the spa's extensive amenities that are nothing short of fabulous. Coed environments (bring your swimsuit) include a salt grotto and a multisensory wave room that simulates the look and feel of breaking waves under a domed canopy.

RECOMMEND Rasul Ceremony. Slather your skin, or your partner's, with purifying mud and relax for 50 minutes in a gently warmed, tiled chair in a private, ornately tiled steam chamber.

LOVE Canyon Ranch's skin-care products—Pro-NAD—which deliver time-released vitamin-B complex, as well as Goji juice, one of nature's most powerful antioxidants derived from the wolfberry.

THE ULTIMATE Canyon Ranch has the most "shared-experience" spa space on the Strip, so share this spa with your honey.

DISLIKE Services such as a jet-lag-relief scalp massage that come as add-on expenses rather than easy-to-incorporate value-added inclusions.

TIP Pretreatment, mix your oils, scrubs, and body butters at the spa's Living Essentials boutique.

Qua Baths and Spa ★★★★½

Caesars Palace 3570 Las Vegas Blvd. S.; ☎ 866-782-0655; caesarspalace.com

---

Customer service ★★★★. Facilities ★★★★★. Amenities ★★★★★. Sales pressure Medium. **Price range** $165–$325, with specialty treatments up to $1,200; $75–$150, nail and refinement services. **Spa amenities** Complimentary with all spa treatments; spa passes run $25–$65, depending on when you go and if you're a resort guest.

SUMMARY AND COMMENTS Qua Baths and Spa is top-class branding and Las Vegas showmanship—a 21st-century Roman-inspired pleasure that has set the standard for "gathering-space" spas. The Roman baths consist of three distinct pools of varying temperatures: the Tepidarium, a warm mineral-enriched bath; the hotter Caldarium; and the much cooler Frigidarium. You can also languish in the coed, circular Laconium sauna, where the climate is kept at a constant 140°F and 35% humidity—the optimum conditions for relaxation. The Laconium is also quite the hot spot for get-togethers. The Arctic room is a real treat. The floor and benches are heated even though the room temperature is a crisp 55°F—cold enough to have snow fall from the ceiling and melt on your hot skin. Qua's menu of services runs the gamut from wet rooms with Vichy showers to a crystal-body-art room where a body scrub and massage are combined with a style of Swarovski body art.

RECOMMEND Chakra Balancing Treatment—a combination of energy and massage that balances your energy centers.

LOVE The in-house tea sommelier who pairs various teas with spa treatments. The dream-interpretation coach runs a close second.

THE ULTIMATE The personal hydrotherapy tub with its changing pulsating rhythms and colored lights.

DISLIKE Shopaholics might think this is a real bonus, but Qua has retail down to an art; a plethora of spa stuff bombards you coming and going.

TIP Remember your swimsuit.

Sahra Spa & Hammam ★★★½

The Cosmopolitan of Las Vegas 3708 Las Vegas Blvd. S.; ☎ 702-698-7000; cosmopolitanlasvegas.com

---

Customer service ★★★★. Facilities ★★★★. Amenities ★★★. Sales pressure Low. **Price range** $105–$435 spa services; $65–$165 for most nail and salon services. **Spa amenities** Complimentary with treatment of $95 and up; spa and fitness center pass $45–$75 a day without treatment.

SUMMARY AND COMMENTS Sahra Spa & Hammam provides a serene oasis amid the natural grandeur of the desert. Breathtaking sculptural walls mirror poetic canyons. Veining of silver throughout the facility reflects the naturally occurring metallic element of the region. Soothing artesian wells quench the mind, body, and soul. At the heart of Sahra's 45,000-square-foot sanctuary is the stone hammam, a ritual space that pays modern homage to a sensual, centuries-old practice of purification. Steady heat provides detoxification and renewal, conducted amid the heated stone slab and separate alcoves for steam and cool-water plunge pools. Sahra Spa & Hammam features a full menu of services to achieve total relaxation and balance. Separate men's and women's lounges include steam rooms, saunas, vitality pools with experiential monsoon rain showers, cold mist rooms, and wet lounges with meditation loungers. The Bridge Lounge is a comfortable coed area where couples can meet between treatments. Sahra also boasts a full-service salon and a state-of-the-art fitness center. Unique to the center is the boxing ring, where guests can take one-on-one classes for the ultimate workout. The fitness center also boasts two tennis courts, a rare find in today's Las Vegas resorts.

RECOMMEND Take in the view of the magnificent Bellagio fountains while working out in the fitness center. Schedule a one-on-one training prior to the spa treatment for the ultimate wellness experience.

LOVE The Space Between is a virtual transport, surrounded by towering sculptural sandstone walls. The traditional Turkish hammam is one of two in the city.

THE ULTIMATE The well-appointed Sahra Suite offers exclusive pampering with closest friends. Arrive via the private VIP elevator to a relaxing and comfortably plush living and entertaining area. The suite is complete with a wet bar, flat-panel television, semiprivate treatment area, side-by-side whirlpool tubs, steam room, shower, and changing and vanity area.

DISLIKE The waiting areas, while intimate, fall a bit short in offering and showcasing all the nutritious edibles that you would expect in a resort spa. Furthermore, the drinks are lost behind a solid refrigerator door.

TIP Try the cool mist shower for an invigorating experience after a hot soak in the warm vitality pool. The spa's rugged and masculine atmosphere makes it a great option for men.

The Spa at Aria ★★★★

Aria 3730 Las Vegas Blvd. S.; ☎ 702-590-9600; arialasvegas.com

Customer service ★★★★. Facilities ★★★★. Amenities ★★★★. Sales pressure Low. **Price range** $105–$580 spa services; $15–$200 nail and refinement services. **Spa amenities** Complimentary with treatment; spa pass is $50 for hotel guests and $100 for nonguests per day without treatment.

SUMMARY AND COMMENTS The Spa at Aria synchronizes beauty and progressive luxury with a conscious respect and preservation of nature's elements. Natural stone, wood, and metal mingle like a melodic dance inside the 80,000-square-foot, bilevel total wellness sanctuary. Inspired by the East, from the freestanding petrified wood from Thailand that greets salon customers to Japanese water gardens adorned with sacred Aji stones, the spa is distinctively warm and tranquil. The Spa at Aria features a full complement of services to promote peace and harmony, with such offerings as Ashiatsu, couples' massage, Thai massage, hydrotherapy, and Vichy. The Japanese Ganbanyoku stone-bed relaxation area provides guests with heated black mineral stone beds that emit negative ions, helping to improve circulation and increase metabolism. Two steps away is the Shio Salt Room lined entirely with illuminated amber-colored salt blocks, providing dewy, marine-rich salt-infused air. The Spa at Aria also boasts a full-service salon, which includes one barber station for gents. An advanced fitness center showcases top-of-the-line equipment, a semiprivate stretch area, one-on-one training sessions, and movement classes. The Spa at Aria is a complete wellness center that elevates guests to a meditative state for introspection, relaxation, and inspiration.

RECOMMEND The Thai Poultice Massage, a signature service, is based on a century-old healing practice that soothes away tension with a set of warm poultices infused with lemongrass, ginger, and prai extract.

LOVE The Spa is loaded with coed spaces, such as the fitness center, the Ganbanyoku heated-stone beds, Shio Salt Room, an outdoor balcony, a therapy pool, and a fire lounge.

THE ULTIMATE A "spa within a spa" private suite comes complete with a personal spa attendant and amenities such as a three-person hydrotherapy tub, relaxation area, and flat-panel television.

DISLIKE The spa offers far too many "add-on" services, when in fact some of them should be included in their signature offerings.

TIP Don't forget your swimsuit to experience the outdoor infinity-edge therapy pool. Take in the view and experience the social vibe.

The Spa at Bellagio ★★★

Bellagio 3600 Las Vegas Blvd. S.; ☎ 702-693-7472; bellagio.com

Customer service ★★★★. Facilities ★★★. Amenities ★★★. Sales pressure Low. **Price range** $170–$365, spa services; $40–$180, nail and refinement services. **Spa amenities** Spa pass is $50 for hotel guests and $100 for non-guests per day.

SUMMARY AND COMMENTS While the bright and airy entrance of this 56-room classic spa bespeaks "spa," the rest of the decor misses the mark. Because it doesn't have the techno-wizardry of some of its competitors, it would have done well to employ some of Dale Chihuly's glass art that has made the Bellagio lobby such a landmark; instead, the long corridors are nondescript and dimly lit, so the water wall and illuminated aqua-colored glass features lose their impact. But overall, this is a classy spa with an exceptionally high standard of treatments, especially in skin care. Attention to detail and value-added extras make every treatment here a five-sensory affair.

RECOMMEND Bellagio's signature Watsu Massage, an aquatic experience in which you float, cradled in the arms of a therapist who combines gentle Shiatsu stretches with movements in, out, under, and over the 94°F warm water.

LOVE Hot Toe Bliss, a warm-stone tootsies massage (with elements of reflexology) that truly works wonders after walking the Strip.

THE ULTIMATE Ultimate HydraFacial. Unlike its competitors, Bellagio includes all five specialty-treatment steps in the service, including a crystal-free microdermabrasion. It's pricey but it works.

DISLIKE Decor doesn't reflect the elegance of the Bellagio name.

TIP This place has a great range of product samples.

The Spa at Trump ★★★★

Trump International Hotel 2000 Fashion Show Drive; ☎ 702-476-8000; trumplasvegashotel.com

Customer service ★★★★★. Facilities ★★★★. Amenities ★★★. Sales pressure Low. **Price range** $60–$315, spa services; $45–$125, nail and refinement services. **Spa amenities** Complimentary with any spa service over $85; $20 hotel guests; pass includes access to fitness center.

SUMMARY AND COMMENTS With only nine treatment rooms, this refreshingly small spa emanates a modern elegance with quiet finesse. Spa treatments embrace the philosophy described in the best-selling *The Secret*—each blends your personal intention with oils and lotions that are mixed to embody balance, healing, revitalization, calm, and purity. Rooms are named for the healing intentions of various gemstones, as are many oils. Choose Ruby to fire enthusiasm and detoxify the body, blood, and lymph systems. Opt for Emerald to overcome misfortunes, or go for rebalancing Diamond.

RECOMMEND Royal Lulur Ritual involves a body scrub, bath, and moisturizing massage with jasmine- and frangipani-infused products.

LOVE The Morning After Eye Cure, a 30-minute makeover for tired eyes.

THE ULTIMATE The Organic Radiance Ritual for $250.

DISLIKE Twenty-percent service charge that's automatically charged to your bill, even though it's a discretionary gratuity.

TIP Spa-goers have direct access to the hotel's sun deck and outdoor pool. Have your personal spa attaché organize lunch in a shaded cabana.

The Spas at Wynn ★★★½

3131 Las Vegas Blvd. S.; ☎ 702-770-8000; wynnlasvegas.com

Customer service ★★★★. Facilities ★★★★. Amenities ★★★★. Sales pressure Medium. **Price range** $100–$810, spa services; $35–$600, nail and refinement services. **Spa amenities** Complimentary with treatment of $75 and above; spa and fitness center pass $75 per day without treatment/$30 for hotel guest; $30 for fitness class.

SUMMARY AND COMMENTS Wynn is all about over-the-top indulgence, so the spas at Wynn and Encore radiate lavish elegance that appeals to the heavy-wallet brigade and honeymooners. The full spa experience is as much about anticipation as it is delivery, and on this, in both spas, Wynn scores top marks. Encore's spa, however, raises the bar even higher with an opulent Zen-inspired lush tropical environment. The staff is excellent. Not only have they been drilled in customer service, but also spa practitioners are knowledgeable, professional, and top of their form. Wynn has a good number of male estheticians, so be sure to specify if you have a gender preference. In terms of services, the menus may appear different in treatment descriptions between the two spas, but, in reality, a number of therapies are quite similar. If you have the time, enjoy a treatment in both. If not, go for Encore. It has an atmosphere of tranquil glitz, which is an oxymoron only possible in a place like Las Vegas.

RECOMMEND The signature Good Luck Ritual Massage is based on the five elements of feng shui: health, wealth, prosperity, happiness, and harmony. It's a yummy head-to-toe event.

LOVE A massage in a private poolside cabana, or even in-room.

THE ULTIMATE A couple's stone massage in one of the four oversized couples suites—the nicest on the Strip.

DISLIKE Like most casino resorts, getting to anywhere is a marathon through a maze of slot machines (in Encore especially); directional signs need improvement.

TIP Spa is exclusive to hotel guests Friday and Saturday.

INDEX

2019 UNOFFICIAL GUIDE READER SURVEY

If you'd like to express your opinion in writing about Las Vegas or this guidebook, complete the following survey and mail it to:

Unofficial Guide Reader Survey
2204 1st Ave. S., Suite 102
Birmingham, AL 35233

Inclusive dates of your visit: _____

Members of your party:	Person 1	Person 2	Person 3	Person 4	Person 5	Person 6
Gender:	M F	M F	M F	M F	M F	M F
Age:	_____	_____	_____	_____	_____	_____

How many times have you been to Las Vegas? _____

LODGING On your most recent trip, where did you stay?

Concerning your accommodations On a scale of 100 as best and 0 as worst, how would you rate:

- The quality of your room? _____
- The quietness of your room _____
- Shuttle service to the airport?_____
- The value of your room?_____
- Check-in/check-out efficiency? _____
- Swimming pool facilities? _____

CAR RENTALS Did you rent a car? If so, from what company? _____

Concerning your rental car, on a scale of 100 being best and 0 worst, how would you rate:

Pickup-processing efficiency? _____   Cleanliness of the car? _____

Return-processing efficiency? _____   Airport-shuttle efficiency? _____

Condition of the car? _____

DINING Concerning your dining experiences, estimate your meals in restaurants per day?
_____

Approximately how much did your party spend on meals per day? _____
Favorite restaurants in Las Vegas: _____
_____

Did you buy this guide before leaving? _____   While on your trip?_____

How did you hear about this guide? (check all that apply)

❑ Radio or TV   ❑ Library   ❑ Internet   ❑ Newspaper or magazine

❑ Bookstore salesperson   ❑ Chose it on my own   ❑ Loaned or recommended by a friend

What other guidebooks did you use on this trip?
Please rate them on a scale of 100 as best and 0 as worst. _____
_____
_____
_____

Using the same scale, how would you rate the Unofficial Guide(s)? _____

Are Unofficial Guides readily available at bookstores in your area? _____

Which other Unofficial Guides have you used? _____
_____
_____

If you like, on a separate sheet include comments about your Las Vegas trip or the Unofficial Guides(s).